Letters Home
80 Years Later

Dana Adams Schmidt
1915–1994

Elizabeth Schmidt Crahan

nprnt press

All letters and newspaper articles by Dana Adams Schmidt are facsimile transcriptions. The New York Times articles are © 1944, 1945, 1946 The New York Times Company. All rights reserved. Used under licence.

Copyright © 2022 Charles Acker
All rights reserved

No part of this book may be reproduced in any form or by any electronic or mechanical means, including information storage and retrieval systems, without written permission, except for brief passages quoted in a book review.

First printing: July 2022

Published by
nprnt press
www.nprntpress.com
ISBN 978-1-9992812-2-9

Table of Contents

Foreword vii
Introduction 1
Early Years 7
1938 23
1939 39
WORLD WAR 57
1940 75
1941 103
1942 135
1943 165
1944 227
1945 319
1946 411
1947 671
1948 749
Epilogue 819
Appendix 827
About the Author 875

ELIZABETH SCHMIDT CRAHAN

Dana Jr., Dana, and King Hussein of Jordan

Foreword

Dana Adams Schmidt was my uncle. This account of his life as a news correspondent throughout pre– and post–World War II is the great achievement of my mother, his sister, Elizabeth Schmidt Crahan, undertaken in the last years of her life. Her move from Los Angeles to the Mendocino Coast in 2000 involved the discovery of the letters he had written home, as she explains in the book. As a medical librarian, her skills to read critically and find special significance in written words, plus the fact that she lived through the events of the war and beyond, especially as seen through her brother's eyes, equipped her for this project.

In 1960, when I was 10 years old, it was arranged that I visit my Uncle and his family in Washington, D.C., with the hopes I might become better acquainted with his only son, my cousin, Dana Junior, who was 8 years old at the time and suffering the beginnings of his life affected by schizophrenia. During the visit, Uncle Dana took us on tours of the monuments and museums. One morning, he asked if we would like to meet a real king. It wasn't until many years later, as we looked through the letters, articles and images for this book, that I realized the "king" I had met was King Hussein of Jordan. I had been given a ceremonial curved dagger and a keffiyeh that were resigned to the bottom of a toy chest for years. Had I been more aware, I would have cherished the gifts, and most importantly, the experience of meeting a key figure of modern history.

By 2012, my mother was 99 years old and had reached the limit of her ability to finish the book. Upon her passing in 2014, at nearly 101 years old, my siblings and I committed to seeing the book finished and published. Now, eight years later, we are honoring our commitment.

FOREWORD

This book takes the reader through key events in the war, starting in Berlin in 1938 with perhaps Dana's most significant post. His perfect command of the German language gave him an advantage in understanding the issues of the time and place. From Kristallnacht to Nuremberg, you will find a unique perspective from Dana's own words.

Charles Acker
June 2022

<u>NOTE</u>

Dana Schmidt's letters have been copied here just as they were written. This means typographical and spelling errors have not been corrected. The actual letters were intended for personal communication and not publication. The intent is to present the reader with the "Letters Home" as realistically as possible.

Dana at age 23, soon after his arrival in Berlin, on a walk in the Tiergarten

Introduction

"Do you want us to pack up those cartons of old papers in the basement?" asked one of the men loading the moving van to take me to Mendocino [California, USA]. The dusty cartons had been put in the basement when my mother died, and I had never examined them. On opening a few, I found a treasure—my brother's papers.

My brother, Dana Adams Schmidt, was a foreign correspondent during World War II in Europe and North Africa, first with the *United Press,* beginning in Germany, and after 1944, with the *New York Times* in the Middle East, North Africa and Europe again. In the boxes, I found letters to and from college friends, early documents on the building of the state of Israel and the history of the Palestinians, hundreds of clippings with Dana's by-line and what turned out to be about a thousand letters to our mother and the family. There were even proofs of books he had written.

I decided that as soon as possible, I would try to pull all of this material together and write an account of his

Dana, our mother, and me (Elizabeth), ca. 1920

life. I am Dana's only sibling, and our parents died many years ago. Because his widow, Tania, is not very well, and his son is ill, it is up to me to make this record of his life. A friend recently said of Dana, "he was a giant of journalism." I hope to do justice to his outstanding record and the contribution he made to our understanding of Europe and the Middle East. I hope to reflect his adventuresome spirit, his kindness and fairness, and the impartiality for which he was known.

When our parents named my brother Dana Adams Schmidt, Mother hoped he would follow in the footsteps of the Dana or Adams families, whose roots reach back to early New England. Many were writers or publishers.

Embarking on a voyage across the Atlantic in the 17th century to evade religious persecution or just to seek a better life on the unknown American continent took idealistic, adventuresome men and women. Many of them passed on characteristics or perhaps genes that produced generations of outstanding citizens.

The Danas settled in Plymouth around 1640 and became well-known leaders of the community. Through the years, they produced prominent statesmen, scientists, jurists, writers, journalists, ministers and poets. One commenter said of the Danas, "They are aristocrats with a common fiber."

Richard Henry Dana is the author of the well-known classic, *Two Years Before the Mast,* 1840. His father was a poet who co-founded the literary journal, *North American Review.* Our great grandfather, George Adams, married Elizabeth B. Dana in 1852. George Adams was a student at Western Reserve in Hudson, Ohio, and later opened a bookstore in Warren, Ohio.

Our mother, Margaret, was proud of being an Adams. She liked to recount that our ancestor, John Adams, who arrived at Plymouth on the ship *Fortune* in 1621, was the first Adams on American soil. Henry Adams, the forefather of two presidents, arrived a few years later. John Adams became a member of the Council that incorporated Plymouth in 1633, the first example of self-government by the Pilgrim Fathers. His descendants were vigorous pioneers, hunters, farmers, schoolteachers and ministers; some were soldiers. Asael Adams fought with George Washington at Valley Forge during that dreadful cold winter.

The story Dana and I liked best was about Asael Adams carrying the mail on horseback between Cleveland and Pittsburgh, a distance of about 135 miles. He would leave Cleveland on Monday at two p.m. and arrive at Pittsburgh on Thursday at six p.m. Dense woods skirted both sides of the bad roads. Wolves, bears, and other wild animals roamed through the great forests. He made the trip once a week in 1812 and 1813. When he encountered streams where the bridge had washed out, he put the mail on his shoulders and swam across with his horse. Sometimes he had two horses. He would ride on one and lead the other loaded with goods and provisions.

Interesting to me is Comfort Avery Adams, who was born in 1816. He compiled a genealogy of the Adams family, from which much of this information is taken. In 1855, together with G.W. Hapgood, he purchased the *Western Reserve Chronicle*. They published this paper until 1865. Comfort Adams served as editor. George Hapgood was the husband of Adaline Adams. His father was an eminent printer and taught his son the trade.

Members of the Adams family founded a paper company that survived for several generations and became the Cleveland Akron Bag Company, then finally the Chase Bag Company. Our grandparents, George Dana and Grace Field Adams, often traveled to the Orient and, especially, to India, to buy jute for burlap bags. As a young girl, our mother accompanied them on these trips and acquired a love of travel.

Our father, Edward Schmidt[1], was born in Hanover, Germany. When Dana was in Germany, he went to see the house Father lived in as a boy. Father was a scholarly sort of man, an expert on European history, as Dana relates in his autobiographical chapter (page 7). Father's family, too, did its share of traveling. His grandfather came to America in the early 1800s to hunt buffalo. A sea lion's tusk, engraved with the words "South China Sea," bears testimony to his further travels.

No account of Dana's forebears, and their influence on his life, would be complete without including the Field family. The Adams and Field families were joined when Mary Elizabeth Schofield married Alfred Stone Field and

---

[1] Edward Schmidt, December 10, 1886–March 25, 1943.

their daughter, Grace Field (our mother's mother), married George Dana Adams (our mother's father).

I remember Great Grandmother Field (Mary Elizabeth Field) very well. She traveled often to California during the cold Cleveland winters. In her nineties, she took a cruise around the world, traveling by herself. She loved the theatre, and we children heard about the plays she attended, though we were too young to be included. A memento I have of our great grandmother is a watch chain she wove from her hair to give to her fiancé, Alfred Stone Field.

The first Field to come to America was Zechariah in 1629. He was the grandson of John Field, who introduced the heliocentric theory of Copernicus to England. Several generations later, his descendant, David Dudley Field, born in 1781 in East Guilford (now Madison, Connecticut), became a distinguished minister at a time when the local Congregational minister was the most important person in every New England community. He found time to write books on local history that remain useful today. He served as his Yale class historian and published his memoirs. Visitors would come to his house for theological discussions over wine and brandy. Cyrus Field was the seventh of Reverend Field's eight sons.

Cyrus was less studious than some of his older brothers who attended Williams College. His father decided to allow him to go into business. He started work for a New York department store as an office boy, and by the age of twenty, he became a partner in a paper manufacturing company. At forty, Cyrus retired as a wealthy man. But his greatest achievement lay ahead of him.

Cyrus had the vision to see what an advantage it would be to business and to families if instantaneous communication could be established between America and Europe. He imagined that a telegraph cable could be laid across the Atlantic. To many people, it seemed like an impossible idea. Cyrus discussed it with engineers and ship owners and finally adopted a plan and raised funds from wealthy businessmen to finance the project. It turned out to be more difficult than anyone imagined. There were disheartening setbacks. Time and again the cable broke. Through it all, Cyrus never gave up. More than once he was financially ruined but still, he persisted. Success came in 1866. For this achievement, he was awarded a Congressional medal. [2]

These are some of the people who have gone before us. Many of their characteristics and their interests seem to have come together in Dana: his love of travel and adventure, his ability to write, his love of newspapers, his fairness and his ability to see all sides of a situation.

Our parents met aboard a ship crossing from Europe to the United States in 1912. Mother was returning to Cleveland after a year at the Sorbonne in Paris, and Father was traveling to America to start a new life. Mother had a ticket on the maiden voyage of the Titanic, but at the last minute, decided to delay her trip. She changed to the ship my father had chosen. A year later, they were married in Cleveland.

---

[2]   Gordon, John Steele. *A Thread Across The Ocean*, New York: Walker & Company, 2002.

Early Years

A few years before my brother died, I suggested to him that he write an autobiography. In the first chapter of the proposed autobiography, Dana described his early childhood and the flavor of life at Eagle Cliff so vividly that I am quoting him in full:

I was born at Bay Village, now part of Cleveland, Ohio, on September 6, 1915. In my childhood, until I was six years old, we spent the summers at Eagle Cliff on the shores of Lake Erie. In the winter we lived in various rented houses or apartments in the city or at Shaker Heights. I remember our house at the lake well. Here we had happy summers with Mother, Father and my sister, Elizabeth. Mother was always in the lead, partly because Father went to work in the city every day, I believe at the Cleveland Akron Bag Company. The house at Eagle Cliff was roomy, with a large living room and fireplace and dining room facing the lake. We had a playroom off the living room where once I decided to build a small fire next to the chimney. This was a very serious event and talked about for many years. The house had screened porches on three sides. A large cement area at the back gave access to the garage from the adjoining street and was a great place for riding tricycles and playing with wagons. The rainwater collected here drained into a capacious cistern in the basement. This water was used for everything except drinking water, which came from a well and had to be pumped up.

Between our house and the neighboring cottage on the west was a thickly wooded area. The cottage was the summer home of the Stones. Alice Stone was a dear old lady who was very good to us children and remained a friend for many years. On the far side of the house Mother planted a vegetable garden—I suppose a "victory" garden. Elizabeth and I were assigned chores, which we thoroughly disliked, such as weeding the garden. From time to time, children lived in the house east of us. I remember especially a little boy with whom I played. He had a big slide, and we had a sandbox and swing hung from the branches of a tall tree. Once, one of the great trees was felled in a storm. The lightning and thunder in these summer storms was memorable. On the lawn we sometimes played croquet.

Beyond the lawn was a fence to keep people back from the dangerous steep cliff. Once one of our pet rabbits fell over the cliff and was drowned in the lake. I can still remember his stiff body. On the Fourth of July, relatives and friends came for a picnic and then at night, fireworks.

Across the road there was a thick forest. A narrow wooden path led through the woods to the railway and a shack to shelter anyone waiting for the train. We often walked along the tracks to pick wild strawberries and mushrooms and I remember the wildflowers.

Mother ruled the family then as she did for her entire life. Grandma visited from time to time and I remember her reading from the Bible. She was a Christian Scientist. Mother read us stories of all kinds from books and magazines.

My birthday in September was the occasion for a festive children's party with games such as pin-the-tail on the donkey and London Bridge. Elizabeth could never understand why my birthday came first, because she was two years older than I, but her birthday was in October.

When we went back to Cleveland in the winter, life was more serious than at the lake. I attended some sort of pre-school in Cleveland and probably Christian Science Sunday School due to my grandmother's influence. This reminds me that later when we lived in Europe, Mother wrote articles for the Christian Science Monitor *and other American newspapers. Much later, I was on the staff of the* Monitor *in Washington for a few years.*

Our father was a tall, strong man, but gentle and rather scholarly. He knew a great deal about European history and the intricate relationships of the royal families. As a boy he traveled extensively. We still have pictures which he took of the Egyptian pyramids. Mostly he worked in my grandfather's company.

Grandpa was a dynamic and successful businessman, dictatorial and feared by most of the men in his company. From time to time, Mother drove Elizabeth and me down to Grandpa's club for lunch. Here we had delicious ice cream with lots of chocolate sauce, in spite of Mother's objections. Grandpa was all smiles and laughter on these occasions, but I sensed even then that this was a man of authority. He was, nevertheless, the source of many presents for us—often animal or bird books that have survived until this day. Sometimes we visited him at the factory, where I remember the smell of burlap and the glass-enclosed offices and huge service elevators.

My grandparents were divorced, so we never saw them together and we children were admonished not to mention them to each other. Grandma lived in a splendid house in a nice section of Cleveland near Wade Park and the Art Museum. One winter when I was five, Elizabeth and I lived with Grandma while Mother went to Europe to be with our father. At that time he was in some sort of exporting business. Grandma's neighbors across the back lot wall were two families with children—the Mathers and the Morleys. Each family had elaborate trapeze and swing sets and there were lots of girls about my age.

Grandma had a beautiful formal garden which you reached by walking through a winding and somewhat mysterious tree and vine covered walk. The flowers in the formal garden with its clipped hedges looked like a European parterre. The flowers seemed to me extraordinary and I feel I have never since seen such flowers.

Grandma was a beautiful woman, a Christian Scientist, as I have said before. When she lived in Montreux, Switzerland, and Elizabeth and I were at schools nearby, she arranged for us to go to Christian Science Sunday School. I went to Chillon College and Elizabeth to Châtelard, both English schools.

When I was six, we moved to Vienna. This was the end of a chapter in our lives and the beginning of another—for Father a new kind of work for the Chase Bag Company and for Mother social satisfaction (she always liked visiting Europe) and for Elizabeth and me, Austrian schools. Eventually, living in Europe led to work that took me on a roller coaster through Europe and the Middle East—perhaps to new vision.

A significant comment here is that "Mother ruled the family then as she did for her entire life." Her rule certainly had a profound effect on Dana, as it did on the whole family, even on the next generation. To understand her influence, you need to know something about Mother. She was well educated, having attended Pelham Manor, an academically oriented girls' school in New York. She studied for several years at Western Reserve University in Cleveland and finally spent a year at the Sorbonne in Paris. One summer, while Dana

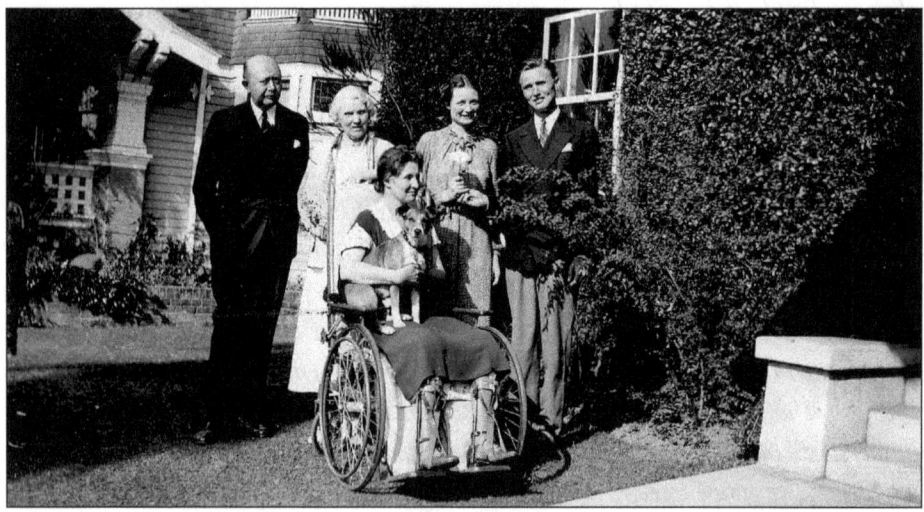

Father, Grandmother Adams, me (Elizabeth), Dana, Mother and Torrey Pines, 1937

and I were at camp, Mother took a course at Columbia's Graduate School of Journalism, which she thoroughly enjoyed and often mentioned. No doubt she would have loved to be a full-time journalist. She did write news articles for American papers while we lived abroad and children's stories for magazines such as *St. Nicholas*. But this was not enough to satisfy her. She transferred her life's ambition to her son.

Mother recognized Dana's talent for writing quite early and made sure that he had the education and the background he would need to be a journalist. Although she loved him dearly, she rarely made him feel that he was successful. She was often critical of his work and urged him to achieve more. Of course, she thought that her criticisms were helpful and didn't understand their destructive impact. These negative comments, especially concerning his wife, pushed him away from her emotionally in later years. She had an overriding ambition for his success and, through it, unconsciously, she hoped to satisfy her own longing.

Mother expected, really insisted, that Dana write her a letter every week when he was away from home. Since Mother kept his letters, we have a wonderful record of his life from preparatory schools through his years abroad as a foreign correspondent. The demand for letters didn't distress Dana too much, as he liked to write and, in return, he received responses from Mother with news of the family and friends that he cared about.

Dana mentions that Mother always loved living in Europe, and he absorbed her love of travel. This was, I believe, a factor in his becoming a foreign correspondent.

When Dana was six and I eight, we moved to Vienna and never spent another summer at Eagle Cliff. I have heard that the house burned to the ground, probably during one of the electric storms so frequent in that part of the country.

In Vienna, we lived in an apartment which we sub-leased from the von Sarnheim family. This was soon after World War One, and many wealthy and noble families were impoverished, partly by the rampant inflation. The von Sarnheims retired to their country estate and rented their apartment in Vienna, reserving a couple of rooms in case they needed to return to the city. They left us their excellent cook and hard-working maid.

The apartment was spacious with high ceilings—much higher than we were accustomed to in the United States. There was a formal "salon," which was used only on special occasions, and a large living room, which also served as a dining room. A grand piano, on which we had lessons, stood in one corner, and at a huge desk opposite the piano, Mother wrote every morning. Dana and I shared a large room with a play table in the center. There were no closets. Instead, we each had a wardrobe. High double doors between our room and that of our parents provided a doorway for a swing. At lunch, there were almost always guests. We children were included at lunch but never at dinner, which we ate with our governess in our room.

The apartment was in the center of Vienna, two or three blocks from the Opera House and overlooked the Karlsplatz. [3] The many political parties assembled here for demonstrations, usually on holidays. Often there was fighting and sometimes shooting. Dana and I didn't understand the seriousness of these events and liked to watch from our apartment windows, high above the square. Of course, our governess did not approve and tried to keep us away.

We walked to school with our governess and were told not to speak English on the street, as this would single us out as Americans who were hated in post-World War One Vienna. We soon learned German and liked to practice with each other at night after we were put to bed.

One winter, Dana had a very bad cold and cough. It was decided that he needed to get out of the city and breathe some mountain air. So we were sent to Garmisch-Partenkirchen in Bavaria. This is where Dana's life-long love of skiing began. We also enjoyed going on the bobsled run with one of the instructors. Altogether we had a wonderful time. I remember walking back to the hotel and passing many fountains with clear cold spring water. Our governess didn't like us to drink the cold water when we were hot from climbing and skiing. In those days, there were few ski lifts, so we did a lot of climbing. After two years in Vienna, we returned to Cleveland for a year. Then my father's work with the Chase Bag Company took us to Hamburg, Germany. Mother was happy to return to Europe. We went to German schools here as in Vienna. We enjoyed going out in rowboats on the Alster [4] and loved the fireworks on this lake on weekends. A great many English people lived in Hamburg at that time, and the English-American Club had a clubhouse on the lake. We also took horseback riding lessons and sometimes even performed in a quadrille at special events.

Since we were beginning to forget English, it was decided we should go to English schools. First, Dana was sent to Chillon College at Villeneuve in Switzerland on the Lake of Geneva. I missed him very much. After this, we were never under the same roof for very long. Soon, I was sent to a boarding

---

[3]   A large square near the center of Vienna, dominated by a handsome Baroque church, the Karlskirche. Many large apartment houses front onto this square.
[4]   Alster Lake dominates the heart of Hamburg and gives the city its special image.

The Alster, a lake at the center of Hamburg, that provided much pleasure for us as children, boating in the summer, skating in the winter, and fireworks over the water on special occasions

school for girls, Châtelard, at Chamby in the hills above Montreux, also on the Lake of Geneva.

From Chillon College, Dana wrote, *In addition to skiing and rowing on the lake, I discovered that one thing I could do well and earn plaudits* [from] *was writing essays.*

Dana loved Chillon, but after two years, Mother sent him back to the United States to Western Reserve Academy at Hudson, Ohio, for his junior and senior years of high school. Although Dana wrote in his draft autobiography that he regretted leaving Chillon, he soon began to like Western Reserve.

What made it especially agreeable for me, he wrote, *was the* Reserve Record, *the weekly newspaper which was supervised by LaRue Piercy.* [5] *Writing*

---

[5] Mr. Piercy followed Dana's career and often sent clippings of Dana's work on to Mother.

for the Record was one of the things that gave me the idea that I might become a newspaperman. Mr. Piercy cultivated all kinds of contributions from straight news to poetry. He became my favorite master, and after school, I went to see him at his house. I kept in touch with him for many years. Reserve *also got me to playing soccer. I liked it but really never excelled, probably because I was too slight. If you weren't playing soccer or basketball, you were expected to go for a run. That built up my endurance, I do believe.*

After Western Reserve, Dana went to Pomona College in Claremont, California. During his freshman year, he won a Bank of America scholarship for $1500 for an essay titled *The World Thirty Years From Now*.[6] Dana joined the fraternity Kappa Theta Epsilon, whose home was a big room under a building containing classrooms.

I enjoyed the company of fraternity brothers, he wrote, *and it provided a place to relax and a place to learn to feel and talk like an American after living years abroad.*

A.P. Giannini, founder of the Bank of America, presents Dana with the fifteen hundred dollar scholarship for his essay, The World Thirty Years From Now. (See Appendix for essay)

His best friend was George Martin [7], *who had a better understanding of American politics than I,* Dana said. They remained friends until Dana died in

---

[6] See Appendix.
[7] George Martin, a long-time friend of Dana's beginning with their student days at Pomona College. They remained friends until Dana died in 1994. A precocious student, George entered Pomona at the age of 15 or 16. George's fine deep voice brought him broadcasting jobs. I remember one with *KNX* and another more unusual one for the *Times*, reporting traffic conditions around Los Angeles from a helicopter. Much later, he retired to

1994. At Pomona, Dana enjoyed skiing on Mount Baldy and also writing for the school paper, the *Pomona College Daily Student Life*. With several friends, he initiated a column called "Beyond our Gates," which summarized foreign news. This was an addition to the paper for which Dana received many letters of approval and appreciation. He graduated in 1937, but not with honors, to Mother's great disappointment. Apparently, he neglected his French classes because he knew French well and preferred to spend his time skiing on Mount Baldy and writing for the student newspaper. Mother was quite bitter about Dana's not receiving honors, and I remember that she complained endlessly. His professors, on the other hand, recommended that he enter Columbia's Graduate School of Journalism because of the quality of his writing and work on *Student Life*.

Our parents agreed, and Dana enrolled at Columbia. In order to get from California to New York, he found a job on a Union Oil Company tanker, the *S.S. Cathwood*, boarded it in San Pedro and worked his way as a wiper through the Panama Canal to Baltimore.

On August 2, 1937, aboard the tanker off Panama, in a letter to Mother, he wrote:

It has been hot—steaming hot—sea water up to nearly 90 degrees off lower Mexico—engine room up to 117. But tonight it is cool, with a brisk breeze blowing from the lush green shores of Panama. At this very moment, in fact it is blowing quite a gale through the porthole and a fine shower of rain with it, so I'll move inland before rust catches up with me after all.

. . . there are many fine fellows, interesting characters, etc. aboard. Alex, the middle-aged Russian who sleeps in the bunk below me, spent all Sunday evening telling me about his escape from Russia at the end of the War. Tish, who sleeps opposite me has been telling about the navy, and how much money he made in the oil fields, but he won't tell, so far, why he left the oil fields in a hurry.

---

the Napa Valley, where he developed a news program that he broadcast to Australia. During the War, he wanted and would have been well suited to being a journalist in Europe, but it never worked out.

Another fireman, whose wife is Finnish, has been telling me about the Finnish community in Washington where he used to live.

My activities have centered around painting the machine shop. First "soojy," or "soogey," which means washing bulkheads, ship side, ceiling etc. with a strong soap solution, then chip off rusty spots, then daub with "red lead," then paint with DuPont glossy white. Occasionally I help one of the engineers, as today, when I helped the "second" fit some pipes in the bilge. I was so greasy when I came out that I had to wipe off my whole body with kerosene (no one except the engineers wears shirts anymore) and then take a shower to wipe off the kerosene. Tomorrow I'll be on deck all day. The "first" said not to go below at all. I'll merely have to oil something now and again.

Just before writing this I indulged in my second or third laundry, at this time cleansing dungarees. The approved process appears to be as follows; grate about one half cake of dark brown soap into a pail, fill with water, insert into end of steam pipe until water approaches boil. Pail plus clothes are left standing anywhere between one and four days, depending on the humor of the sailor, except for occasional cleansing pokes. Then the slime is poured off and anything which seems to merit such attention is subjected to scrubbing with one of the stiffest brushes in existence next to a cow curry. Finally clothes are hung on the rails of the "fidley," which is the upper part of the boiler rooms. No one knows why it's called the fidley, but then why not.

When the *Cathwood* reached Baltimore, Dana took a train to New York and registered at Columbia. Following the first weeks of class on October 11, he wrote:

Over the weekend I typed up my notes to date—42 typewritten pages of them already. In addition there is the daily report on the ten most important news events, with comments, a semi-weekly report on some prominent newspaper, 1000 words due weekly in the seminar on political writing, assorted required and reading tests for our spare time, and outside reading.

From Thursday to Friday we were given the assignment of getting a news story on a store—any store. I decided to kill two birds with one stone and looked up the only manufacturer of skis located in New York City, a little firm of recently immigrated Germans on the East Side. The story worked out rather well and Miss Carrell thinks I can work it over into a feature saleable to the magazine Cue.

My clothes are in good shape. . . . I have established connections with a Chinese laundry which does good work somewhat more cheaply than our much advertised "Student Laundry Agency," which gets 15 cents per shirt.

Dana found outside jobs to supplement the fund from the Bank of America contest and a $150 faculty scholarship he received at the end of the first semester. He tutored students in various subjects, including German and English. Occasionally, he wrote letters for a dentist. One day, he received a request through the School's office to teach skiing to the four Sulzberger children, a boy and three girls aged 11 to about 19. This was a particularly welcome job. Aside from the opportunities to ski, he hoped to meet the children's father, Arthur Hays Sulzberger, publisher of the *New York Times*. Soon he did meet him. *I was very much taken by his friendly personality,* he wrote. *At our first meeting, he generously offered to give a talk to the school.* Dana lost no time in relaying this offer to Dean Ackerman, who invited Mr. Sulzberger to address Columbia's commencement ceremonies that year. Unfortunately, Mr. Sulzberger was scheduled for a European trip that spring and had to decline.

One of the most important assignments during this year at Columbia was for Mr. Pitkin's class. Each student was to select an area of the United States and make a detailed survey of existing newspapers and the possible need for papers or magazines. They were to study the population, government, resources, colleges, manufacturing, business, tourism, etc.—in other words, make a thorough survey that might be suitable to present to someone considering publishing a paper in the area. Dana had selected Las Vegas and the newly built Boulder Dam and surrounding area. He had hoped someday to own or be editor of a small-town newspaper, and this project suited him perfectly. He had a good friend in Las Vegas from Pomona College days—Pete Woodruff. Mr. Pitkin himself was interested in the idea and even offered to help find financing. One of Dana's classmates, Harvey Mathews, whose family had connections with U.S. Steel, was also interested and offered to help with financing. Dana was fascinated with Boulder Dam and what it would do for the area. *The Dam newspaper and magazine seem like an opportunity to create something real, to let down roots and be part of a real community. To take part in the building of a promising section of the country,* Dana wrote in a letter to Mother.

At the end of the second semester at Columbia, Dana was awarded a Pulitzer Traveling Fellowship. Of course, he was thrilled with the honor, but he quickly realized that if he accepted, it would mean giving up his cherished plans for the Nevada paper that he had been studying and promoting during most of the school year. Now, it was close to reality with Pete Woodruff, Mr. Pitkin and Harvey Mathews, all enthusiastic about the idea and ready to go ahead.

Accepting the fellowship meant spending a year traveling in Europe. By then, the opportunity for the Nevada paper might be gone. It was a hard decision:

Of course if I take the fellowship it might lead into foreign correspondence, but I know right well that I'm not a good reporter. I'm a feature writer, and maybe I can write fiction, and I'm not a bad editor—I know a good story and I can tell other people what to write. I know something about printing, and I know a good deal about the Boulder Dam region. I've spent more time on the [Nevada] survey than on any single thing this year.

If I take the fellowship it will mean spending one more year being a "promising young man" with nothing real to show except the confidence of some people in what I am going to do. However, if I were to turn down the fellowship, I'd be the first person in history to do so.

Eventually, after much debating and consultation with Mr. Pitkin and other faculty members, as well as his parents and grandfather, he accepted the fellowship.

Dana and me (Elizabeth)

ELIZABETH SCHMIDT CRAHAN

>Hotel Coburg
>Berlin, Germany
>September 19, 1938

Dear Mother:

    Just see where I've got to! It happened this way. Day after I wrote my last letter I saw Mr. Pinkley and was introduced to Webb Miller and several other U.P. men. They all said extra help was urgently needed in Berlin--and I can bear them out on that now. Next morning Pinkley phoned and wanted to know how soon I could leave for Berlin.

    Friday morning I left, arriving here Saturday noon. Incidentally, I stopped off at Brussels to phone Mrs. Karuso, who wasn't in, and managed to lose my train, thus causing myself some hours delay and four separate transfers all over Belgium and Germany as it seemed.

    Here I was immediately set to learning the intricacies of relaying messages from all central European capitals to London and Amsterdam, running the teletype, translating articles, and reading the file of dispatches for the past two weeks (to get me properly informed and initiate me into the language of cabless). Today I translated a "mail," i.e. slow story on German warnings against Hollywood films, which are now to be regarded as cariers of Communist virus following Dies committee investigations. With me I have three articles in German on commercial, foreign and domestic political conditions in Poland, likewise "mail."

    There is a good chance that as soon as I have mastered the office routine here I will be sent to some point of interest to the southeast. But I am not yet officially an employe of U.P., although Pinkley thought he could make me one in about two weeks. Consequently I still have the privilege of using tourist marks.

    This is a wonderful, magnificent situation. There is probably no spot on earth more important right now than Berlin. And U.P. probably is getting the best information of any press service in the world--been beating A.P. all along, and of course, as Americans, no interference with what is said.

    There is no time for anything but United Press for me now. I worked Sunday although didn't have to, merely taking about two hours for a walk through the Tier Garten and environs. Everyone looking immensely vigorous (the beer does it no doubt) and prosperous too in that part of town. Of course there is tremendous tension--everyone talking politics, by contrast with England--and convinced Hitler will have his way. Uniforms everywhere--the train was jammed with soldiers. In Berlin Hitler youth swarm everywhere in their very handsome uniforms.

    Write to me care American Express in Berlin now, as that will always reach me. Anything already sent to London will be forwarded.

    I got your last letter in London, and very glad to have it. That was a grand idea to add to my bank account as a birthday present. I don't

Dana's September 19, 1938 letter to his mother, page one of two think I'll get very rich over here. No one has even mentioned how much I'll be paid, if as, and when. But what experience!!

With best love to all,

Dana

Dana's September 19, 1938 letter to his mother, page two of two

1938

Dana had an amazing ability to maintain friendships throughout his life and this, no doubt, contributed to his success as a journalist. He had decided that if he took the Pulitzer fellowship and went to Europe, he would look up old friends. On August 25, 1938, he sailed from San Pedro, California on a Black Diamond freighter, the *Black Tern*, to Antwerp and made his way to London, then back across the Channel to Brussels, expressly to see friends from Vienna days—the Kurusus.

Saburo Kurusu[8] was Japanese Ambassador to Austria when we lived in Vienna as children. He had married an American woman, Alice, and they had two children about Dana's and my ages, Jay and Norman, with whom we often played.

On phoning, he found that Mr. Kurusu, now Ambassador to Belgium, was in London but would be back the next day. Mrs. Kurusu welcomed Dana warmly. She said she would have insisted that he stay at the Embassy, but the only guest room was occupied. She invited him for dinner that night

The *Black Tern*. Dana sailed August 25, 1938 from New York to Antwerp, Holland, where he began his journalism career.

---

[8]   See Appendix.

and, as it developed, for lunch and dinner during the following two days of his visit. She also took him on a sightseeing trip through the Bois, the large public park which surrounds most of Brussels, and she showed him the spot where King Leopold fell from a cliff and was killed. He learned that their daughter, Jay, was traveling in Germany, and their son, Norman, was in Japan studying engineering.

April 12, Dana wrote:

We talked a good deal of politics at the Embassy, from the Japanese point of view, and I got considerable advice from Mrs. Kurusu on journalism. She is a woman of extraordinary mental brilliance—one of those people who really does see both sides of every question. Nevertheless I got a strong feeling of softness, lethargy, about her, quite the opposite from Mr. Kurusu.

On the last evening a young Jewish fellow came to dinner and we spent a good deal of the evening talking about the Jewish problem and race prejudice, extraordinary in a gathering of a Jew, a German-American, a Japanese and the American woman to whom he is married, and surely a thing possible only where the finest intelligence prevails.

Back in London, Dana went to the *United Press* office with a letter of introduction to Mr. Clem Randau, Vice president of *United Press*.[9] Mr. Randau suggested that Dana talk with Virgil Pinkley, Editor and General Manager, *United Press* London. Pinkley was glad to see a fellow Californian, and they talked awhile about San Bernardino, Pinkley's hometown, and Southern California. He had just returned from a holiday and was swamped with work—so they didn't talk about Dana's chief interest, working for *United Press*. Pinkley asked him to come back on Wednesday "for a real talk," as he put it.

---

[9] The letter was from Harry B. Averill, publisher of the *Mount Vernon Daily Herald*, father of Dana's friend, Betty Averill, student at Scripps College.

It developed that the Berlin office was shorthanded, and Pinkley asked Dana to go to Berlin immediately. During his job interview in Berlin, Dana told Mr. Oechsner, head of the bureau, of his love of skiing and got his word that he would be given time off "for the mountains."

Dana standing in front of his apartment house at Oliverplatz, where he lived in Berlin

September 9:

Here I was immediately set to learning the intricacies of relaying messages from all central European capitals to London and Amsterdam, running the teletype, translating articles, and reading the file of dispatches for the past two weeks (to get me properly informed and initiate me into the language of cablese). . . . There is a good chance that as soon as I have mastered the office routine here I will be sent to some point of interest in the southeast. But I am not yet officially an employee of United Press, *although Pinkley thought he could make me one in about two weeks.*

At 23, Dana was highly enthusiastic about his first job in Europe.

There is probably no spot on earth more important right now than Berlin. And UP *probably is getting the best information of any press service in the world, been beating* A.P. *all along. There is no time for anything but* United Press *for me now. I worked Sunday, although I didn't have to, merely taking about two hours for a walk through the Tiergarten and environs. Everyone looked immensely vigorous (the beer does it no doubt) and prosperous too in that part of town. Of course there is tremendous tension—everyone talking politics, by contrast with England—and convinced Hitler will have his way. In Berlin, Hitler youth swarm everywhere in their very handsome uniforms.*

I had graduated from the University of Southern California with a degree in architecture and married an architect.
Dana wrote me:

Berlin is having an orgy of building. The center of town is all torn up for Hitler's beautification plans (temporarily halted because most workers are shipped to the western front to work on new fortifications). Sunday I was excused from the usual twelve hour stretch and went out to Tempelhof airdrome, where what amounts to a whole town is going up.

You can tell our job-hunting friends that there is no such thing in Deutschland now. In every department there is acute labor shortage. The papers carry pages of "Men wanted" ads. The old anti-female workers has been forgotten in the scramble, too. Incidentally these want ads are about the only thing worth reading in the press here, unless you are bent on finding out what the Propaganda Ministry has to say. There are lots of very amusing things about America; of course they're no more one-sided and naive than the stuff Americans print about Germany. . . . Last night's speech [by Hitler] *was an obvious demonstration of the Germans' spontaneous* Begeisterung [wild enthusiasm] *for the regime, but rather shocking to anyone who believes in individual judgment and restraint.* "Führer befehle, wir folgen." [Führer (leader) orders—we follow.] "Treue um Treue." [German paratrooper motto: "Loyalty begets loyalty."]

In my first assignment I became the "Jewish specialist." I fell heir to this task presumably because I was the "junior" member of the staff, and because no one else was eager to come closely to grips with this depressing and frightening subject. One bleak day in the winter of 1938-1939, I went to the Juedische Gemeinderate [Jewish Community Council]. *Here I discovered a number of gentle, intelligent, delightful, but miserable people who had been obliged by the Nazis to organize their own people to most effectively carry out the German Government's orders. As an American, and neutral, I was able to maintain these contacts with impunity.*

In *Armageddon in the Middle East*[10], he wrote further of the plight of the Jews in Germany. *From these people I heard in the most objective and restrained terms, which hid their personal agony, many things. I heard of their frustrated attempts to emigrate. Endlessly they pored over prospects in North or South America, Africa, Australia, Western Europe and finally Palestine.*

---

[10] Schmidt, Dana A., *Armageddon in the Middle East*, New York, The John Day Company, 1974.

Dana had scarcely been in Berlin for a month when the *United Press* asked him to accompany the German army as it occupied the Sudetenland. On October 1, 1938, he set out for Dresden and joined journalists from other papers who had been invited to observe the invasion.

On October 12, 1938, after returning from the five-day tour with the Sudeten invasion, he wrote:

Today I find your letter at the American Express Office expressing some worry for my safety. But you see I am hale and healthy and very much delighted with my work. I've been in a lot of places where there has been shooting, but I haven't heard a shot yet.

Journalists who accompanied the Nazi invasion of Sudetenland; photo by Dana A. Schmidt

Children arranging flowers on the road for Hilter's visit to the Sudeten Territory. No throwing of flowers was allowed because Hilter had been scratched by a bouquet thrown in another town. Photo by Dana A. Schmidt

The nearest to actual conflict I've come was on my last day in ex-Czechoslovakia, at Aussig where we found a crowd of people on the bridge across the Elbe staring at a revolting pool of blood, a foul bit of human brain and a bullet hole in one of the girders. We thereupon hurried to the hospital to talk to three seriously wounded survivors of a scrap between retiring Czech police and officers and Sudeten Freicorps men. The Germans made the affair out as a horrible murder on the part of the Czechs, even after they heard the first hand story. My story made it clear that this was just another "incident" in which both sides shared the blame. It appears that the Sudeten shot first, but that a Czech menaced him with a machine gun first.

Perhaps you have seen some of my stories—they went out under my name and may have been so printed. Most of the time I wrote in the first person which is rather an unusual privilege for one who hasn't been at work a month

Hilter saluting the troops at Jagerndorf, Sudetenland; photo by Dana A. Schmidt

yet.... *Of course I won't know how or where the stories have been used for two or three weeks when the* N.Y. World Telegram *arrives.*

Among the stories were accounts of German entry into the second zone, again at Tetschen-Bodenbach; entry fourth zone from Ziegenhals to Herrmannstadt and other towns; visit of Hitler and his speech at Jaegendorf; entry of Germans and Hitler's speech at Reichenberg in fifth zone; further in a march into fifth zone with incident at Aussig and two short features: one on a Catholic priest at Bruex thanking God publicly for delivery from Czech concentration camp and another on German army trucks put at the disposal of Czechs to hasten their retreat.

In this letter, Dana wrote that he believed the occupation of the Sudetenland could be justified on several counts. The Munich Agreement of

Hitler addressing the crowd in Jägerndorf, Sutendenland, 1938;
photo by Dana A. Schmidt

September 29 had allocated the Sudetenland to Germany. [11] At the Versailles Treaty, President Wilson had proclaimed the concept of self-determination, which provided that people had the right to determine the government under which they wished to live. The area of Sudetenland had a large German-speaking population:

Sudeten man greeting German soldiers; photo by Dana A. Schmidt

That the Sudetens who have joined the Reich are Germanic and wanted to join can be doubted by no one who was there and talked to scores and scores during past weeks. Had they been intelligently and decently treated by the Czechs and had there not been organized propaganda from the Reich, on the other hand, they might very likely have been content where they were. But instead of giving them equal rights the Czechs tried to make over the Sudetens into Czechs . . . saddled them with all-Czech officials in police, post office, railway etc. services, deprived them of German schools, and encouraged Czech migration into Sudeten territory. In addition to all that, there was great unemployment (in part because Sudeten textiles, coal, porcelain, etc. were excluded by tariffs from Germany) while Germany was enjoying relative prosperity. So why shouldn't the Sudetens want to join the Reich? In addition there is the point that they were formerly a part of Austria, now amalgamated. [12]

---

[11] Munich Treaty on September 29, 1938. Chamberlain, Daladier, Mussolini and Hitler met. By disclaiming further expansionist plans, Hitler won approval to occupy the Sudentenland. Chamberlain returned to England and announced that he had "secured peace for our time."

[12] The Anschluss occurred on March 12-13, 1938.

The moral arguments are all on the side of the Germans in this matter, whatever the Anglo-American press may say. Of course the forceful methods Hitler used to gain his end are to say the least, morally questionable. The German press at the same time has been waging the most fiendish atrocity campaign against the Czechs you can imagine. . . .

The matter of food rationing was on everyone's mind in Germany. Adequate food was understood to be vital to sustaining morale and the war effort itself. Dana wrote a detailed account of rationing published November 2 in many papers, including the *New York Post*.

FOOD NEWS IN THE REICH RIVALS WAR REPORTS FROM HOME

. . . It was the lack of food, Nazis say, which cost Germany the victory in 1918. Now the propaganda leaders have proclaimed war on "the inner front," a drive to prevent the fatal collapse of morale such as occurred twenty-one years ago.

The German Government ordered food rationing even before hostilities started, and Nazis say a system has been perfected under which the populace can go on eating indefinitely at the present rate with the prospects of dietary improvement as Poland is exploited and supplies roll in from Russia and the Balkans.

Nazis say, "Germany cannot be starved out."

When Dana returned to Berlin from the Sudetenland, he found that Hotel Coburg had sold all its rooms, including his. He moved to Hotel Continental but began to feel tired of hotel life. He thought he might find a German family with whom he could live and improve his facility with the language at the same time.

He consulted the Amerika Institute, and they gave him a dozen or so numbers to call, but none of the families seemed appropriate. Fred Oechsner heard that an English economist whom he knew, Robert Crozier Long, had died leaving his "very blue-blooded Russian wife and Americanized daughter Tania, a divorcee, without overly much cash." Mr. Long had been correspondent and expert for the *New York Times* and the *London Economist*. Oechsner suggested Dana talk to Mrs. Long, and he found that she would be pleased to spare a few rooms in her spacious apartment.

Here I am, he wrote, *with a very nice front room, breakfast, bath and dinner upon request.* He felt like part of the family. On his first Sunday morning, Ed Beattie,[13] "ace" correspondent of the *United Press*, had been invited for breakfast. Dana soon found that through the Longs, he was in touch with the social life of the local journalistic world, and he clearly enjoyed this interesting and congenial family.

The apartment is filled with the best of books. All the German papers come daily, also the London Times *and other English papers, and the* New York Times *once a week. In addition the Longs are enthusiastic skiers.*

Many of Dana's letters include generous thanks and appreciation to Steinie[14] for cookies and fudge and even dates and oranges she and Mother sent him. On October 24, soon after he became part of the Longs' household, he wrote:

This morning there was general celebration in the household here because there were eggs! A great deal of the time eggs are not to be had at any price, and most of the rest of the time the housewife must first make a large purchase of something plentiful like cabbage and is then slipped a couple of eggs. The same goes for oranges which are thus surreptitiously handed out in exchange for a large purchase of meager German apples. The same goes for almonds, better meat cuts, American cereals, onions and most anything imported. All such horse-trading is of course strictly "verboten" [forbidden]. As for butter, I can't remember the number of grams allotted to each family, but Mrs. Long assures me it is smaller than at this time last year.

---

[13] See Appendix.
[14] Steinie, our mother's long-time nurse and companion was loved by all of us. She took care of Mother from 1930, when Mother's back was broken in an automobile accident and she became a paraplegic, until her death in 1978.

Tomorrow I must register with the police so that we can get an extra butter allotment. Already they [the Longs] have gone to considerable trouble to ensure my having eggs for breakfast. Many people here live chiefly on cabbage and potatoes, and are compensated with uniforms and brass bands. Incidentally the uniforms contain about 25 per cent wood . . . . The bread, it must be admitted, has improved somewhat since I arrived, as result of an unusually good harvest. . . .

. . . . and on October 30, Dana wrote Mother:

As far as this week's work is concerned I can only think of Jews, of course I mean the expulsion of Poles from Germany, most of whom are Jews. Two of our men have been arrested during the past two days, Hottelet and Kidd, both at the border covering the expulsions. Surely there is no Pole, let alone a Jew, who will not be a mortal enemy of this country from now on. And of course the effect on the newspapermen arrested is not likely to be endearing, although it does provide them with a good story. Hottelet seems to have fallen into the hands of a singularly arrogant, stupid, and inhuman bunch of officials.

The value of human life has fallen pretty low when it is possible to . . . root out a whole segment of the population of a country and push them across the border. I begin to appreciate what the Bill of Rights means. People talk about our "liberty," as "liberty to starve" which is regrettably true; but it also means liberty to live and go where you please, without reporting to the authorities every time you turn around, without the danger of being kicked around like a sack of potatoes.

All this does not mean that my eyes are not open to the genuine accomplishments of the regime. Social welfare services for those who fall in line are unequalled I am sure. The youth organizations are splendid at least for the physical development of boys and girls. Classical music is cultivated, as is the theater, with enthusiasm. The network of Autobahns *is fantastically good. Everyone works. One begins to feel enthusiastic, and then one meets a painter who no longer paints, by official decree, because his style did not meet*

> **Shop Wrecked by Germans**
>
> NAZI VANDALS ARE SHOWN standing by a Berlin Jewish shop which they wrecked and looted. Thousands of Jewish shops and homes in Germany have been destroyed by nazis allegedly aroused by the fatal shooting in Paris of a German embassy secretary by a Polish Jew.—Acme Radiophoto.

This was Crystal Night.

with the approval of the totalitarians. There is so much stark tragedy involved in making a whole nation keep step.

On November 10, he was awakened by Tania Long, who reported widespread violent demonstrations. Dana hurried to the downtown area, and as he described later in his book *Armageddon in the Middle East*:

. . . I arrived just after the storm troopers had, under cover of darkness, smashed the windows of hundreds of Jewish shops, systematically, from one end of

the city to the other—but with a special fury in the fashionable Kurfuerstendamm. The windows of Jewish shops were broken, their doors and pavements smeared with such inscriptions in paint or tar as, "Out with the Jews" "Jewish swine," "Germans don't buy from Jews." The Nazis were lashing themselves into a racist trance, during which they would commit one of the most incredible crimes in history—the murder of six million Jews. I was no longer in Germany when this crime was being committed, but I saw how it started. [15]

The ostensible provocation for the Kristallnacht pogrom was the fatal shooting of a young German diplomat—Ernst von Rath by a Polish Jew named Hershel Grynszpan.

Still, life went on in Berlin in spite of the nightmarish "Crystal Night."

On November 21, Dana wrote:

Imagine who bobbed up in Berlin: James Parker Wilson, erstwhile business manager of Student Life *[at Pomona College]. I had heard he was connected to the diplomatic service in the Balkans and recently dropped him a note at Bucharest. Then Saturday night the Oechsners gave a cocktail party where I met the agricultural attache of the Embassy, Mr. Steer. To my delight I discovered in him a fellow Pomonan, and he imparted the amazing information that he had yet another Pomona product in his office, to wit J.P. Wilson.*

Dana's social life improved greatly with Wilson's arrival. In time for Christmas, he finally got the news he had been waiting for. He was made a permanent employee of the *United Press* with a salary of $25.00 a week. *It's not so much,* he wrote, *but it means I belong to the organization, which is the main thing.* He knew that eventually, there would be raises.

About this time, Tania Long came back from a trip to London with the news that she had a job with the *Herald Tribune*. This added to the general camaraderie at the Longs.

---

[15] See Appendix for news report Friday, November 18, 1938: *'Hostile World' Warned at German's Bier—Nazis Hurl Sharp Warning To World.*

After Hitler had taken over the Sudetenland and then in March had appropriated all of Czechoslovakia, he began agitating for the return of Danzig and a corridor across Poland to connect East Prussia to Germany.

Duchi d'Aosta, the hotel at Sestriere, Italian Alps,
where Dana had a happy skiing holiday, 1939

1939

Dana found release from the seriousness of the events he was reporting through trips to indulge in his life-long avocation.

I have had three days of most delightful skiing, he wrote in early January. *Poor Jimmy Wilson got a real baptism of icicles and blizzard and generally of the skiers' primitive existence. We hiked two hours from Bad Flinsberg to the Langhammer Baude near Gross Iser (all in the Iser Gebirge) where we found the parents and two sisters of Percy Knauth of the* Herald Tribune. *Since this Baude, like all the others, was filled up for the holiday season we consented to sleep on straw sacks on the floor of the Cafe Stube. Unfortunately people came to drink cafe early in the morning and we had to rustle our sore bones out of the straw.*

Jimmy negotiated a very long (for him) tour the second day and appears to have completely recovered. The third day he had to return to Berlin while the girls and I made a tour to the top of the Tafelfichte on the Sudeten side of the mountain where we indulged in some of the best Wiener Schnitzel I've met so far. Of course these mountains are practically sea-level compared to California.

I feel hundreds of percent better after the three days in the mountains, (even if I didn't get a decent wash during that time.) In the two days since I got back I've got more done than in the week before I left. It's remarkable how one can bog down if something doesn't come along to break up the monotony and give one a new perspective.

Dana was writing at the office and interrupted this letter:

Time out, while I relay an unintelligible tale from Prague which requires complete rewriting as well as translating, while I take in a press release over the phone from the Deutsche Bank, translate a DNB [16] *Meldung [report] on Hitler and Beck, drink some of Mister Kidd's* Apfelsaft [apple juice], *compose a box about three ovens which are drying out the plaster in the new chancellery, take Moscow on the phone, translate a* DNB *comment on the Niekisch trial and generally carry on with the typical activities of the Berlin bureau. ...*

It's now pretty close to closing time for me and I'm tired due to my early rising this morning. . . . I'm getting drowsier by the minute—got to bed at two thirty last night.

In his next letter, he enquired about a gift he had sent home because:

I have been told about a marzipan gift which arrived in England in hundreds of very neatly sliced pieces: the customs men apparently expected to find something like diamonds, dope or radium.

On February 15, Dana received a cable telling him that our grandfather, George Dana Adams, had died. Dana had enjoyed his grandfather's approval and interest in his career.

I don't think I am silly when I say quite simply, Grandpa was a great man. I admired him more and more during the last few years when I was beginning to be old enough to respect that terrific energy and perseverance. It is not simple to explain . . . just what it was that I admired about him. It was a kind of fire and fighting spirit.

Lately when I have started on work of my own, I have repeatedly caught myself thinking, or perhaps hoping that I was acting the way he might. I remember when I was in Cleveland, how he would be at work ahead of the entire office in the morning to get the routine out of the way and be ready for new and important things, and how much pride he took in knowing more about the business than anyone else.

---

[16]   Deutsche Nachberichten, the German propaganda agency.

Grandpa was an American, the type of business man who has made modern America great in the same way that the pioneer made America great a hundred years ago. I know how much his death must mean to you who knew him so much better than I did. It was a great pleasure and stimulus to me to know through his letters to you that he had confidence in me.

Mother, you should write something about Grandpa. [17] *You probably know more about him than anyone else and it would be a sort of honor to him.*

February 27:

Jimmy and I are talking skiing again—or is it still. I must pull myself together and broach the subject again. After all, I have pretty good claims on a bit of a ski-holiday: that extra month [when he wasn't on the payroll] *and the fact that Oechsner promised me time for the mountains at the very start. I suppose I'll have to ask for a salary raise, too, since there is obviously no chance of getting anything you don't make a kick for.*

We originally talked about Switzerland, but that is far and expensive. Probably we'll go somewhere in Germany, although I'd like to persuade Jimmy to make a foray into the easternmost tip of Czechoslovakia, and have a look at the Carpatho-Ukrainians while skiing over the Carpathians. It is very undeveloped country, and the Czechoslovakian travel bureau couldn't tell me much about it, except that the mountains are very high and that there are inns to be found.

Dana had decided long ago that he would like to meet relatives on our father's side of the family while he was in Berlin. On February 27, he wrote, *I had Sunday off and used it to call on Herr und Frau Sandrock.* Dana didn't know much about the Sandrocks, except that we were distant cousins and that Herr Sandrock was a painter. A large, mysterious, dark painting of a harbor scene that he had painted hung over a couch in Mother's house on Windsor Boulevard in Los Angeles.

---

[17] To the best of my knowledge, my mother never did.

They [the Sandrocks] *were mighty surprised to see me, as you can imagine. They are a very charming old couple indeed. He apparently has weathered the changes of recent years excellently and is managing some sort of war-veterans art exhibition at the moment. He promised to send me an invitation to its opening. . . . They had to keep an appointment about an hour after I arrived and my short visit was devoted largely to telling about the family. So I didn't hear very much about them. They are anxious that I call on relatives in Hanover and a family which runs some sort of "Bad"* [resort]

Hitler's retreat at Berchtesgaden; photo by Dana A. Schmidt

near Berchtesgaden. Incidentally, Mr. Sandrock seems to have quite a family resemblance to Father.

In early March, Dana went to Hanover and found Father's childhood home:

. . . lovely, one of the most charming, picturesque places I have seen. During the evening I walked to Am Schiffgraben 44, the house in which Father lived as

a child. You have probably seen it, a single-gabled house with a jutting first story. It is now occupied by a Dr. Med. R. Feldmann, Fachartzt fuer Hals, Nase und Ohrenleiden [specialist for ear, nose and throat complaints]. *In fact the whole neighborhood, at least, the houses on both sides are occupied by doctors.*

Early in the morning I took a taxi out to Misburg, where the first person I approached readily told me where Ernst Kreis lived, with the additional information that it is the oldest "Hof" [court] *in the village.* [Our grandmother on my father's side was Maria Johann Kreis.

Childhood home of Dana's father, Edward Schmidt

Ernst Kreis and his wife Klara were our aunt and uncle.] *Ernst Kreis, a big, outdoorish-looking, middle-aged man welcomed me with some amazement and produced Tante Klara who produced tea and a daughter. I don't mean to be facetious. They were exceedingly hospitable and chagrined that I had to catch an early train back to Berlin. I gladly promised that I would visit them again and stay a few days in the spring or summer. Ernst Kreis and I took a long walk around his property which has unfortunately been marred in recent years by the dust from enormous nearby cement plants and fumes from an oil-refinery. He has rented out most of his land, running only a sort of kitchen garden himself now. Before I left they insisted on giving me a photograph of Father in an Austrian officer's uniform* [18] *which they were sure we didn't have.*

Later that week, Dana and Jimmy Wilson were at the home of German acquaintances of Jimmy's.

Among the guests was a young chap in flying cadet's uniform. I happened to mention to him that I had lived in Hamburg. He said he too had lived in Hamburg. In fact he'd been to Heinrich Hertz Realgymnasium! He is 23 years old, and we figured out we must have been at Heinrich Hertz at the same time! We could remember some boys and teachers we both knew! What an extraordinarily small world it is.

Hitler's invasion of Czechoslovakia interrupted Dana's nostalgic journey. He was concerned with covering each new development first and accurately and seemed to thrill with being on the scene of important events. No effort was too great if a story was in the offing.

I was up all last night checking the movements of Hacha, Chevalkovsky, [19] *Ribbentrop and others in and out of the Chancellery, the Foreign Office and the Adlon Hotel,* he wrote on March 15. *Almost all the foreign correspondents of English-speaking newspapers camped out in the Adlon lobby until four seventeen a.m. when Hacha and Chevalkovsky came back from the Chancellery. After that they* [the correspondents] *thinned out until only the* Reuters *man, Clifford, and I were left. We were waiting for some sort of communique or the possibility that the representative of the official Czech news agency who accompanied Hacha would come down and tell us something. Finally even* Reuters *left and I sat with a slightly daffy representative of a bank until 6:00 a.m. At that time my daffy friend turned on his portable radio and—my*

---

[18] Before becoming an American citizen, our father had become an Austrian citizen because he was not in sympathy with the German government.
[19] Hacha was the Czech president who replaced Benes on his resignation. Chevalkovsky was the Czech Minister of Foreign Affairs.

god—out dribbled the official communique on the conference. It was a break. After that I was in the office until about eight, and I was back in the office again at three-thirty this afternoon. So I'm getting sort of worn down.

At the all night meeting it became clear that the occupation of Sudetenland was just a step for Hitler in taking over all of Czechoslovakia, indeed his army was already in Prague. At this night's meeting Hitler obtained protectorates over Bohemia and Moravia. Previously Tiso had declared the independence of Slovakia.

After the intensity of the negotiations over Hitler's usurpation of Czechoslovakia, Dana was fortunate to be able to take a short break.

Since last I wrote I have climbed numerous mountains and had a couple of days of magnificent skiing and acquired a remarkable heavy coat of tan, he wrote on the 14th.

After I finished my note to you last week I barely managed to catch my train. I was underway all night and most of the next day. At Langen [near Frankfort] a bus met the would-be skiers and carried us as far as the road was open, where horse drawn sleds picked us up for the last two hours' ride. I had no idea I was getting into such remote parts.

But the hotel at Lech [Austrian Alps] gave no evidence of remoteness at all, with ballroom and bar and band, and, best of all whipped cream (verboten in Berlin). It was a tremendous thrill for me—after wanting to get away for skiing so long, especially at a real Alpine resort at that. I was out before the sun reached the huge open slopes the next morning.

It wasn't long before I got to know some people, among them some friends of the Kurusus in Brussels. Their names were Alice and Elizabeth van Wassenhove. It seems they have been going to Lech every winter for years, although they almost missed this time because their families were so nervous about entering the very maw of what looked like a prospective enemy.

No one would think such a thing as war was possible at such a skiing resort, with every possible nationality playing together in friendliest fashion. No one asks who or what you are. I met a young fellow at lunch at Zuers and *went on a tour with him half the afternoon; I didn't find out he was a German officer and he that I was a member of the "*hetzende Auslandspresse*" [the hated foreign press] until tea or beer-time.*

*Drinking "*Fünf-uhr Tee*" [five o'clock tea] at Lech I got talking to a young fellow not much older than I am who is manager of a "Lebkuchen" [gingerbread] factory at Nuremberg. His father owns the factory. This chap takes a couple of months vacation every spring because his business is seasonal. (He'd better not let Goering's Four-Year Planners hear about it—they'll make him drain swamps or something during the off season.) I went on a long tour across the Kattlochjoch with the Lebkuchen boy and couple from Stuttgart, through the best skiing country I have ever seen.*

On Friday evening Jimmy Wilson turned up and I moved to the very ritzy Zuerserhof in Zuers to join him. At that the Zuerserhof was only 12 marks a day with full pension [meals included]. It is the sort of place one imagines to exist at St. Moritz, with starch-shirted lackeys in every doorway, marble floors and indirect lighting. Very nouveau riche, but very amusing for the single day I was there. I called the office after the fifth day as per agreement and was told to pack up and come home right away.

So I'm back, although the excitement has quieted down again.

Now we are waiting for Hitler's birthday when all the big and little shots of Central Europe will be in town conspiring in hotel lobbies, and making rumors flow thick and fast.

Berlin is being spruced up most elaborately, with infinitely bad taste. Tall white pylons capped by golden eagles have been set up at intervals of about twenty-five yards in four columns down Unter den Linden. [20] *They're so thick they're a regular woods. The extension of Unter den Linden, which is the so called Ost-West Achse, six or eight lanes wide, is similarly over-decorated.*

---

[20]   Literally "Under the Lime Trees." This is the famous boulevard in Berlin lined with Linden (sometimes called lime) trees. Linden trees are thick and grow about twenty-two feet tall. The boulevard dates from 1647 when King Frederick Wilhelm developed it as a bridle path extending from the palace to the Tiergarten (Animal Garden), his hunting park. It now ends at the Brandenburg Gate, symbol of Berlin. The Unter den Linden developed as a central mall with streets for traffic on either side.

When they get the bunting and flaming torches and bands and mobs all thrown in on top, it will be quite a madhouse. [21]

Although Dana loved skiing, traveling in Europe also exerted a strong pull. On May 1, he wrote:

Well, I've got a story that's worth getting off to Los Angeles by the first plane. Oechsner today wanted to know when we wanted our vacations. And he and I decided that I should take mine in June, politics permitting, and that I should spend it rambling amiably from Unipress *bureau to* Unipress *bureau by airplane. Tentatively we talked about going via Budapest, Rome, London, and back to Berlin. I don't know whether I'll want to make more stops or not.*
Since I'm a member of the "Verein Auslaendischer Pressevertreter" [Association of Foreign Press] *now I'll be able to use the airways at the same cost as for second class railway fare. It will be a whale of a lot of fun and exceedingly instructive, besides bringing me to the attention of the* United Press *at large. Admittedly costs would be not inconsiderable, although I could swing it, but Oechsner mentioned vaguely the possibility of U.P. helping out on expenses. Incidentally, Beattie* [who preceded Dana in the Berlin Office and was one of UP's best reporters] *made a similar swing through Europe a number of years ago.*

On June 4, just before he started on his much anticipated working vacation, Dana wrote:

Twelve hours from now I'll be in the air on my way to Warsaw and points beyond. And I won't be back till the 23rd or 24th! I hope to keep up a running fire of missives along the way.
Today I was honored in exceptional fashion by being invited to Fred Oechsner's as sole lunch guest. We talked over the men and bureaus I'll be

---

[21]   Hitler was not noted for artistic discrimination. His regime labeled some of the great masterpieces of modern art "degenerate art."

visiting and he and Dorothy [Oechsner's wife] *made out a list of things in each town they thought I would enjoy seeing. I shan't carry a letter of introduction but simply walk in in true* UP *fashion. Of course I have already a telephone acquaintance with Besterman in Warsaw, Best in Vienna, and Kaldor in Budapest. And I've written to Mr. Roberts at Chillon and trust he'll have the guest room prepared when I arrive. In Paris I know Kecksemeti and Depury—who has been transferred away from Berlin again—and in London of course there is Beattie and Hinckly and my friends Grahame and Sydney Smith.*

It is going to be a wonderful holiday—almost over when you get this. I am so pleased that you did not say at all that airplanes had their risks, or anything about it. After all, it's really an unavoidable part of my work.

On June 11, one week into his tour of Europe, he wrote from Rome:

I've dashed over a good deal of the map. It has so far been exceedingly successful, both from the busman's holiday and the pleasure point of view. Of course, my sightseeing has been slight and my impressions superficial. But then I don't like intensive sightseeing anyway. Besterman in Warsaw, Kaldor in Budapest, and Best in Vienna, have been most cordial hosts from whom I learned much about their countries. Incidentally they all poured out their experiences with UP *which were equally instructive.*

Here in Rome I haven't yet seen much of anybody except a young fellow named Atkinson who appears to have gone to Pomona for a year while I was there and who remembers me although I can't place him at all. Atkinson seized me, and together with his voluptuous Roman girl friend, we toured some of the sights in a buggy last night. I expect I'll have lunch with the head of the bureau, Stewart Brown, tomorrow.

Imagine my surprise when I appeared at the UP *office here, I found Earl Johnson (our news manager from New York, who also visited Berlin) in the office. He had that day flown from London and sailed for the U.S. this morning from Genoa. He was no less surprised than I and said to Stewart Brown, "This is the fellow I was describing to you." So God knows what may be brewing for me. Brown is quitting in a few weeks to become Public Relations director of the* American Red Cross, *and it is possible I may be considered to replenish the manpower of the office.*

Tomorrow morning Atkinson is coming at nine to take me to the Vatican State. Today I spent visiting on foot some of the places we passed last night— the Piazza Venezzia with Mussolini's residence, the Capitoline Hill, and the various emperors' fora [Latin, plural of forum] *along the route to the Colosseum. The Colosseum is stupendous. Unbelievable to think it was built about twenty centuries ago, yet most of it is still there, and almost as gargantuan as the twentieth century "wonders" we gasp at. This afternoon I was at the Mussolini Forum—a magnificent marble shrine to Sport, but so expensive (10 lire) by Italian standards that it was almost empty.*

Everywhere, as in Germany to a lesser extent, is the effort to connect Fascist Italy with glorious ancient Rome. That is probably one motive for Mussolini's digging out and restoring all available relics and lighting the old wonders dramatically at night. In the midst of the most numerous aggregation of ruins, near the Colosseum are five billboards showing the rise of Rome from one city to an empire including England and most of Germany, and finally showing the modern Italian empire with Libya and Ethiopia.

But I must tell you about Warsaw, Budapest and Vienna.

Poverty stricken peasants and Jews, a touch of the past, and something which I suppose is modern Poland—an extraordinary combination.

You may have seen slums in New York, but they are model residences compared with the Old City and the Ghetto of Warsaw. Tiny holes on the ground floor of ancient and picturesque buildings serve as shops, the shopkeeper as often as not sitting on the floor with his goods piled around him; old men carrying enormous loads on their backs or pulling carts quite big enough for two horses; deformed and wretched, ragged people everywhere.

All that goes for the Ghetto too, where a large percentage of the Jews wear ringlets over both ears, black smocks and great beards. Where so many people are pressed together one cannot help notice among the mass of bestial, spiritless faces dulled by poverty, some strikingly sensitive, even beautiful ones. I am thinking of a rabbi, quite young, apparently, who stared for a long time at my uncalled for presence curiously with great, glowing black eyes.

Besterman (Warsaw UP man) who is Jewish, tells me that the Jews of the professional class who have risen out of the Polish Ghettoes, most often try to throw off everything Jewish, and have their children baptized. So many do so in fact, that the last figures for persons of Jewish religion in Poland showed a two percent decline, although there is a high birth rate in the Ghettoes. But I'm afraid their baptizing is in vain, for anti-Semitism is growing stronger by the day, although temporarily checked by the common fear of Germany. If there is a rapprochement with Germany we may lose our Jewish Besterman, as we are soon going to lose Jewish Kaldor in Budapest. Some parts of Warsaw are very beautiful, some modern. But the predominant impression is one of shoddiness and squalor.

The flight to Budapest was beautiful, as we crossed a few hundred meters above the snow-covered Tatra Mountains. At Cracow a typical Polish impression—gleaming new airport—with a one-hole, no flush, no-paper privy for sanitation.

At Budapest I found Kaldor preparing for a vacation, but he gave us supper in his little house on a hill overlooking the city. He is skirting Germany via Gdynia as do even many Aryans, on his way to Copenhagen. Since he was not named to the Hungarian Press Chamber he may soon have to give up his work.

Incidentally, these two are our only Jewish correspondents now. Until quite recently, Beattie has told me, there were very few good newspapermen available in Eastern and Southeastern Europe who were not Jews.

Szalai, Kaldor's substitute, took me to Budapest's famous Arizona vjetchub and a gypsy-music Hungarian restaurant, while I alone investigated Die Burg, where lives Horthy[22] *and St. Margaret's Island. My chatty guide at the Burg threw in a lecture on Hungarian National Socialism, which he conceived of as largely Socialistic in nature, intended to break up the feudal estates and generally redistribute property! I think it most likely that out and out Nazis will triumph in Hungary in the next few years.*

---

[22]   Nicholas Horthy de Nagybanya (1868-1957). See Appendix.

Best in Vienna was being philosophical about a letter he had just received from London reducing him from a staff to a string correspondent. Now, he will be paid by the message—ten shillings apiece.

In the morning I went to the Karlsplatz, Nibelungengasse #1, where we lived as children. It looked about as I remembered it, but since no one there could remember me, it seemed somewhat purposeless. I suppose this makes me an egotist.

In the afternoon Best and I sat in the office and gossiped politics and UP except for a few hours when we tried unsuccessfully to get a photograph of Schuschnigg's [23] *son in a Hitler uniform.*

Best is a man who moralizes painfully (which I hate) about journalism. He is very friendly with the local Nazis, although no Nazi himself. Still, he is so intent on being fair that he is accused of being a Nazi. Even the German newspaperman with whom we had a beer in the evening said: "Na, du wirst doch noch den Deutschen Adler bekommen." [You may yet receive the German Eagle.]

Unfortunately it was cloudy most of the way across the Alps. I stopped over for four hours in Venice—only long enough to take a long walk and a motor-boat ride across the bay from the airport, and to see that Venice, along with Budapest, is one of the most gorgeous places I've seen. The masses here are wretched by comparison with those of Germany (even if they can get butter and fruit) and so much poorer than northeastern and eastern United States that there is no comparison. Of course I don't know the South or the Dust Bowl farms.

I seem to be hitting the most expensive hotels—but they are the ones Oechsner suggested. He said I might as well "go the whole hog"—so I am.

A young fellow from the Berlin propaganda ministry just came over to say hello, and I must go to the bar so we can explain to each other why we are both here.

---

[23] Kurt von Schuschnigg (1897-1977) was the chancellor of Austria (1934-38) who resisted the Anschluss. I'm sure the son disliked Hitler as much as his father.

A week later, on June 23, Dana wrote from the Goodwood Hotel in Hyde Park:

I have almost finished the last and best part of my vacation—London. I haven't found any place in Europe where I feel quite so happy.

Of course, apart from London's natural charm, my sentiments are due to being able to be with old, even if half forgotten, friends, and be in a country which speaks my language . . . and where I can buy at their best all the goods which can't properly be had in Germany or elsewhere.

Sydney Smith stays at this little hotel—a most old-fashioned place with gas heaters into which one must drop coins—not that they are needed, despite the semi-total absence of sun.

I have spent two evenings with Stewart Lyon, a lad who was my roommate for more than a year [at Chillon College]. *He meant to go into the army as his family has for four or five generations! But was stricken by almost total blindness after two years at Woodwind. Now he gets along with some extraordinary looking goggles and a secretary and has turned to politics. He appears, although I never knew it before, to belong to a wealthy landed family, and is thus able to indulge in expensive English politics—organizing clubs, hiring speakers and giving speeches himself. He is a most brilliant fellow and may go far—studied history at Oxford and is capable of beating most any political arguments.*

Lyon and I saw Confessions of a Nazi Spy *last night—I don't expect to see it in Berlin. It is indeed tendentious, exaggerated—unfair, but is nonetheless a remarkable job. You should see it. I don't know enough about affairs in America to say whether Nazi espionage is really as highly developed and whether it is connected with the Bund, but I rather doubt it.*

A chap named Lang—another ex-roommate, who is working very hard for the Territorials, came around to Lyon's with me after I called on him at his Club—one of the well-known big Tory-filled London clubs. It's strange how little most of these boys change in fundamentals.

Do you remember Topping? I must have mentioned him often at Chillon. Yet another roommate—my first. He now works for the BBC *third man in the electrical recording department and very important, as he made sure to impress upon Sydney and me. He has grown up into an icy-mannered, formal, perfect gentleman with cane and gloves, but a few beers revealed that he was really quite the same as ever.*

I may see both Topping and Lyon again as both think they might take a trip to Germany. Lyon goes there every year to keep himself up to date. I really shouldn't be a bit surprised to see him an M.P. one day soon.

Another thing I like about London is our own office. All our top men are here and they are all very decent, especially Flory [UP executive] *who figuratively patted me on the back, apologized for the delay in my living allowance, pointed out that while the pay is small in the lower ranks, the* UP *pays well for her top men and that he thought I had an excellent future, that Earl Johnson had brought back a complimentary report on me. All very soft soap, but I prefer to believe it.*

I have been buying things—lots of things. A new blue-grey business and semi-formal suit, a Harris tweed, dark red-brown sports coat to go with flannels; new shoes, 4 ties, and a HAT.

Sydney insisted that nothing but a black Homburg would do, a la Anthony Cohn—and I don't look bad in it. Most hats look ridiculous on me. I'll send you a picture. Also, of course, I've filled up on Gillette razor blades, English tobacco, American cigarettes and toothpaste—all horribly expensive or unobtainable in Berlin.

My purchases, entertainment, hotel here will take about $100, while I spent $300 on the rest of the trip and 300 of my remaining registered Marks on airplane tickets. It leaves me with a little more than $500 on deposit with the UP *and some 300 registered Marks in Berlin. Of course I can't get registered Marks any more and will also soon have to begin having part of my salary sent to Berlin. Then I shall see what can be done with Black Marks— illegal exchange up to about 9 Marks to the dollar! Probably half of Berlin newspapermen get them. Isn't it grand to be able to write about such things and know no one is going to tamper with your letter. Even in France you can't be quite sure—we recently had cables regarding the submarine, Phoenix, held up in Paris* [by the censors]. *England is the only major free country left in Europe.*

Tonight at 5:15 I leave for Amsterdam where I will spend the night and then spend Saturday really systematically informing myself about the technical transmission arrangements there. Flory volunteered to pay hotel and other expenses there; then sent a message ahead to Buurman. I will be the only person in Berlin with firsthand knowledge of the set up in Amsterdam.

Flory recently spent some two weeks in Amsterdam making arrangements for setting up our chief bureau there in time of war. That is very secret, so don't repeat it. There is a good chance that Holland would remain neutral while bombs were dropping on London and censorship was slapped down.

Actually there is very little that I have hesitated to put in my letters from Berlin and they are only rarely opened. Of course you have gathered that I have become our Jew specialist—in fact I have a phone call in to Reichburo right now to a Jew who used to be a good source in Berlin.

There is no risk to me in such work, but considerable for the Jew who would be arrested immediately if caught giving information to a foreign newspaperman. Of course even regular Germans must be very careful. A London Times tipster was executed a few years ago. Jews are an unpleasant topic to work on, but it's a vital topic, provides one with a lot of credit and good-natured kidding. I go straight to the heads of the Jewish organizations at their offices or homes. I also have a private tipster—a very unpleasant Polish Jew who requires payment only in an occasional beer or dinner. Once I gave him 5 Marks. He has given me perhaps a half dozen good stories. There is a woman high up in the "Reichsvertretung der Juden in Deutschland" [Bureau representing Jews in Germany] who is one of the most admirable, intellectual and charming persons I have met in Berlin.

I think this is long enough. Perhaps I'll sing further praise of London some other time.

On August 14, back in Berlin:

The lights in Europe's chancelleries burned late last night. The tension was very great. This was a meeting of Ciano[24] *and von Ribbentrop. The details were not announced immediately.*

---

[24] Count Galeazzo Ciano, Mussolini's son-in-law and Foreign Minister.

WORLD WAR

1939

When you read your history book twenty years from now you will be able to imagine that this has been a lively evening. . . . We are keeping a full staff at the office all night. Even DNB is operating all night . . . Dana wrote on September 1.

This, of course, is the night Germany published the rejected proposals to Poland, and Germany and Russia ratified their non-aggression pact.
And it was the day Germany invaded Poland, the official beginning of World War Two, September 1, 1939.

All communications were cut off to England. . . . Fred requested that we all bring a change of clothing and a toothbrush down to the office in a bag so that we can go out to a nearby hotel for a few hours of sleep if necessary.
About all I can add is something you and every other halfway intelligent person knows—that the ordinary German doesn't in the least want war . . . but unfortunately this show isn't being run by average anybodies.

Four days later, he wrote:

For the past four days I, as well as most of the rest of the staff, have been living at the Bristol Hotel, so as to be close to the office in case an urgent story requiring man-power should break during the night. And of course you understand it is sometimes a little awkward getting about town in the early morning hours. Berlin is most thoroughly blacked-out every night.

For several days our only connection, in addition to cable, with the outside world was via Amsterdam. Now that has gone too and we must send everything by direct cable to New York.

Last night George Kidd got through from Danzig by phone for the first time since August 31 and gave us a magnificent account of the capture of the city. . . . Now his problem is how to get out of the place.

Tonight [September 5th] *we had the first report of British planes bombing German territory—Cuxhaven and Bremerhaven. . . . The personal life of all of us has come to more or less of a standstill. We staffers just circulate between the hotel and the office.*

For the ordinary Berliner life has thus far gone on very much as always, except for the elimination of night life, and the limitation of restaurant menus to a relatively few items. The food at the Bristol is still pretty darned good, though, especially when Unipress *pays.*

On September 13, Dana opened his letter with the startling announcement: "*It is four a.m. here, but the radio announces eleven p.m. at the Rainbow Room in New York City.*"

I am doing the overnight trick manning the UP *office from midnight to eight a.m. because Eric Kaiser decided to get sick. . . . I fully understand why Eric tends to fold up every now and again. He's been on the night trick most of the time for the past year. The procedure is something like this. You come on at midnight, read the day's file, get the morning papers at about one thirty, and try to send out any worthwhile items or comment from them before two thirty, when Holland Radio closes down in Amsterdam. In addition it may be necessary to write an "overnighter" which is a piece which can be held in New York and Buenos Aires for the first afternoon papers of the following day. Then you trot out the wretched folding bed and retire at a strategic point between three telephones and the* Hellschreiber [teletype]. *The radio buzzes in the next room and the teletype may start to clatter any time at the other end of the office. As you are beginning to doze off, the Hellschreiber begins to grunt and squeal, making unsuccessful efforts to print. With a little help it produces the startling information that the next message will be sent at six a.m. Then, most likely* DNB *will phone with a bloodcurdling tale about atrocities in Poland, six sheets of which may be fetched by a messenger. Presently you are almost asleep again when the* Hellschreiber *groans and repeats its startling six a.m. warning in French. Of course one mustn't take any of that too seriously, as it is likely to change its mind and grind out a little piece from Montevideo just to fool you. Along about this time someone bursts in from the Continental department with a service message from Santiago de Chile frantically querying about some ridiculous message report by Havas. So you wake up the Herr von Dienst at the Propaganda Ministry, only to discover "ihm ist nichts bekannt." [He knows nothing about it.] This is duly recorded for the benefit of South Americans and you retire once more. Formerly there was the additional menace of phone calls from London, but that has been effectively eliminated.*

And Bucharest, Sofia, Warsaw, and the Baltic States no longer bother us. Budapest and Belgrade, however, remain a potential danger.

At six a.m. the radio begins to boom "The March of the Germans in Poland" (most popular tune in Germany), the Hellschreiber *bursts into an unremitting whine, the* Reinmachefrau *[cleaning lady] enters with mops and brooms, the* Zwoelfuhr Blatt *[the twelve o'clock paper] arrives, and most likely, the telephone rings and the Oberkommando asks for Mr. Oechsner. I inform them that he, oddly, has not yet come to the office, but that I am his* Stellvertreter *[representative] and would be glad to record the latest military communique.*

After a while you get time to put the bed away. Willke arrives for the early morning shift and you trot home for some SLEEP. The net result of all this trouble is usually nil as far as news is concerned—but then there are exceptions. The communique may be hot, or, as a few nights ago, there may be an air raid alarm during the night.

The night of the recent alarm I managed to get Amsterdam on the teletype, put through a flash to New York and went down to the air raid protection cellar. Nothing happened, as you may have seen in the papers. Some British planes dropped leaflets over some North German towns. . . . I don't think we are likely to have much in the way of raids over Berlin. It's too far away, and the Saarland is much more vulnerable.

After the invasion of Poland, the Longs moved to Copenhagen, and Tania had most of the furniture stored. Dana asked his friends, Jimmy Wilson and Paul Pearson of the U.S. Embassy, to share the apartment. They rented furniture and were quite pleased with the results. On September 22, Dana wrote:

Jimmy and I will take care of the lights, gas and the maid and contribute a proportionate share toward food. An excellent arrangement for me since I will be getting in on Danish butter and eggs, American coffee, Scotch whiskey, French Vermouth, soap, chocolate, and similar items not so easily obtained on this side of the Great International Divide.

He added, *"There's about as much enthusiasm for this war over here as there is for the measles."*

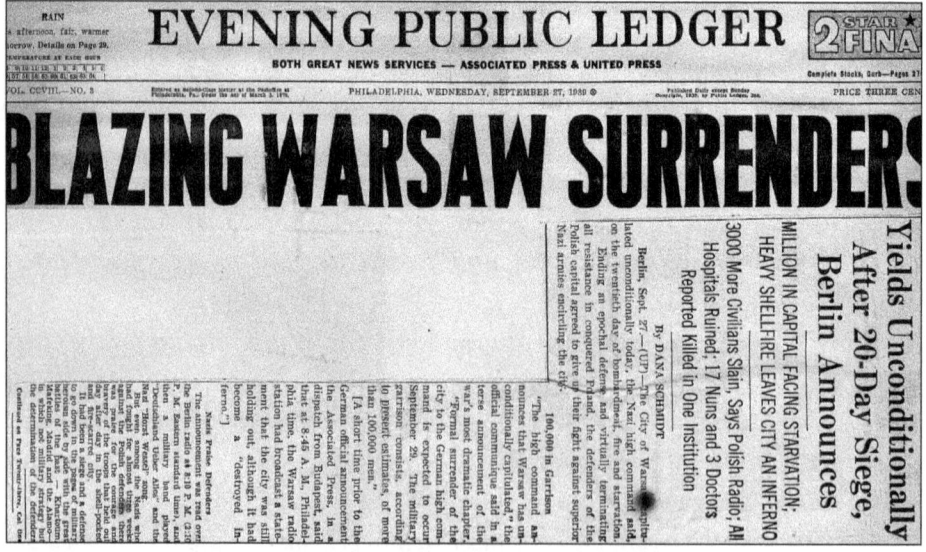

Dana's article on Warsaw surrender, September 17, 1939

On September 27, Dana wrote in a dispatch that received bold headlines:

BLAZING WARSAW SURRENDERS

**Yields Unconditionally
After 20-Day Siege,
Berlin Announces**

**MILLION IN CAPITAL FACING STARVATION;
HEAVY SHELLFIRE LEAVES CITY AN INFERNO**

**3000 More Civilians Slain, Says Polish Radio; All
Hospitals Ruined; 17 Nuns and 3 Doctors
Reported Killed in One Institution**

By DANA SCHMIDT
Berlin, Sept. 27.—(UP)—The City of Warsaw capitulated unconditionally today, the Nazi high command said, on the twentieth day of bombardment, fire and starvation.

Ending an epochal defense and virtually terminating all resistance in conquered Poland, the defenders of the Polish capital agreed to give up their fight against superior Nazi armies encircling the city.

100,000 in Garrison
"The high command announces that Warsaw has unconditionally capitulated," the official communique said in a terse announcement of the war's most dramatic chapter.

"Formal surrender of the city to the German high command is expected to occur September 29. The military garrison consists, according to present estimates, of more than 100,000 men."

[A short time prior to the German official announcement the Associated Press, in a dispatch from Budapest, said that at 8:45 A.M., Philadelphia time, the Warsaw radio station had broadcast a statement that the city was still holding out, although it had become a "destroyed inferno."]

Nazis Praise Defenders

The announcement was read over the Berlin radio at 8:10 P.M. (2:10 P.M. Eastern standard time), and then a military band played "Deutschland Ueber Alles" and the Nazi "Horst Wessel" song.

But even among the Nazis who had fought for almost three weeks against the Polish defenders there was praise for the courage and bravery of the troops that held out day after day in the shell-pocked and fire-scarred city.

It had been a siege and a defense to go down in the pages of military heroism side by side with the great battles of the past—Khartoum, Mafeking, Madrid and the Alamo—in which not military strategy but the determination of the defenders had been the outstanding factor—win or lose.

. . . For the defense of Warsaw had been far more than the ability of some 100,000 soldiers to barricade themselves in the suburbs or to turn every home into a fort. There had been perhaps million persons hurled suddenly into the wild chaos of open warfare at its worst.

Civilians, many of them refugees from other cities in the west, had battled with the soldiers, dug trenches, fought fires and hung on stubbornly as they saw their capital falling to pieces around them under almost continuous aerial and artillery bombardment.

Before the end they butchered horses and burrowed into the debris of churches and public buildings that their defiance of the inevitable might continue in the hope that Great Britain and France could send aid ....

A final big-scale assault to wipe out Poland's defenses was launched Tuesday. Today's regular morning communiqué of the German high command, said, in part:

"The attack yesterday brought the first line of fortresses in the North and the second line of fortresses in the South into our possession. Under the thrust of theses attacks, the Polish commander this afternoon offered the surrender of the city and the military force. The chief of the army commissioned Gen. Von Blaskowitz to conduct negotiations for the surrender."

Among newspapers that carried this story of September 27, were *The Evening News*, Buffalo, New York; *The Evening Public Ledger*, Philadelphia; *The Cleveland Press*, and *New York Post*.

In mid-October, Dana was asked to substitute for a *CBS* man in a radio broadcast. On October 18, he wrote:

I was scheduled at the studio at ten thirty p.m. At ten, no taxis to be had, pitch darkness and rain. I'd never been to that part of town on the subway before—Took the subway, with two transfers, about an hour and a half. The studios were so blacked out no one could tell they were there. Finally I ran across, or into, a soldier guarding a gate who wanted to know what the hell I wanted. He wanted to see my identification, being a foreigner didn't help any.—Couldn't seem to get the idea that I had to broadcast in a few minutes. He didn't know the way into the building: couldn't find the right door in the dark. So he finally took me around a back way under bushes over fences etc. and handed me over to another soldier who took me to the wrong entrance. Nobody could find the right one.

At last we stumbled upon the gent in charge of the news broadcasts who had just given me up for dead and phoned the Columbia *man to rush down and go on himself. We decided to put me on the air nonetheless and whipped my script through the censoring process in record time. Then the poor* Columbia *man came rushing in dripping with sweat and waving a cable from my office saying that Schmidt is too busy to broadcast. But the poor* Columbia *lad had no script and no time to get it censored if he had, so we told New York, by radio, that Schmidt wasn't too busy after all and I went ahead. There weren't any kicks, but the next day came blanket orders for UP to refuse all radio invitations.*

On November 9, Dana wrote:

Last night was a hectic one, believe me, but Unipress *kept comfortably ahead all the way, which should calm me. Nevertheless, I'm sufficiently on* edge today to be up early and in plenty of time to pound out a letter before office hours.

Dana was referring to the explosion at the Buergerbrau Keller on the night of November 8, an apparent attempt to assassinate Hitler. He had delivered his traditional speech on the anniversary of the 1923 Beer Hall Putsch. [25] This time, the bomb went off just after he left the hall.

Later in November, he wrote:

We are having quite a few guests in, especially since I am at home for both lunch and dinner. . . . We've had all sorts of odd persons here. An Arab, some people from the Quaker relief organization, fellow diplomats and newspapermen, a fellow who does English broadcasts on the German shortwave, and at least one very nice girl from the Embassy. She has invited us over to her place next Saturday for some sort of feed.

Tonight Brooke Peters, one of the junior members of the New York Times *staff is having dinner with us. . . . Really our dinners here are strange affairs, especially in their setting in the midst of wartime Germany. We toast bread during the meal in an American Toastmaster, and everybody, including the sometimes slightly surprised guests drink milk. It was the new maid's rather novel idea . . . but most people like it, and we have let it go at that.*

We don't have any wine during dinner, but before dinner we sometimes produce some French Vermouth, if the guest seems worthy of it. (This is practically extinct in Germany, as you can imagine. But Jimmy can get it.) And after dinner they sometimes get some "Dom" Benedictine, which is Jimmy's pride and joy. Later on there may be some Scotch whiskey. The whiskey belongs to me, actually left over from Jimmy's and my joint cocktail party.

Jimmy just came in with his consignment of butter and eggs from Denmark. He doesn't seem to appreciate the unique plenty we live in. He says it's a bother to carry it home.

---

[25] The 1923 Putsch was Hitler's attempt to overthrow the Weimar government of President Ebert and establish a right-wing nationalistic one in its place, even though the Nazi party was very small at that time.

On December 1, a story by Dana received bold headlines in the *Cleveland Press*:

GERMANS FROM BALTIC STATES ARE "BACK HOME"

The German minorities of Esthonia and Latvia, many of whom had lived in these Baltic States for many generations, now have all been "brought home" to Germany's reconquered territories in Poland.

To make room for the repatriated Germans, the Poles and Jews were moved eastward to the vicinity of Lublin. Thus the first move actually has been made in the gigantic reshuffling of the peoples of Eastern Europe proclaimed by Adolf Hitler the week after the war began.

The next major move is expected to be the resettlement of the Germans of Lithuania, probably next spring. Meantime German peasants are arriving in the former Polish Corridor from eastern sections of Poland now absorbed by Russia, and eventually Poles, Jews, Ukrainians and White Russians in Germany's part of the country will be moved to the Russian sphere of influence. Jews also are being moved from the protectorate of Bohemia and Moravia (formerly Czechoslovakia to the vicinity of Lublin.)

The resettlement of Poles and Jews has been carried out hastily. . . . Little is known of their living conditions except that tremendous overcrowding has been reported.

On the other hand, the resettlement of something like 45,000 Germans from Esthonia and Latvia has been carried out thus far with all consideration possible for the well being of the Germans considering the hasty departure.

The Nazi explanation for the withdrawal of these German "outposts" on the Baltic, in the words of one publication, is: "They are given a new task, namely, to build a bulwark of the German race which will for all time protect the German Reich against population pressure from the east."

One member of a German family, whose ancestors settled in Esthonia before the discovery of America, offered this explanation.

"The Baltic Germans played a prominent role in Czarist Russia. (Before the World War, the Baltic countries were a part of the Russian empire.) Now Soviet troops are tramping in, and our situation was intolerable, because, in the expansion of Soviet power, we risked not only our property, but our personal safety. Hitler offered to put the Reich's resources at our disposal for us to move out and settle in the eastern provinces. And so I was happy to do so.". . . .

The Baltic Germans were allowed to take along movable property except things of special historic, artistic or scientific value. Even cattle, except pedigreed stock, were brought along, and owners of important farms in Latvia brought their silver foxes to Germany. At Tallinn, however, some families found that their portraits of distinguished ancestors were classed as non-exportable state treasures.

Germany and Esthonia are still negotiating some aspects of the disposal of German property. One item under discussion is a library of 100,000 volumes, a historical collection relating every aspect of the lives of Baltic Germans from early czarist times, the property of the Esthonian Literary Association. Here are such records as those of the expeditions to Alaska and the Arctic by the noted explorer Wrangel, whose descendants are among those now being transported to Germany. Germany thinks these collections should also go to Germany. . . .

Even the undesirables go along "home" if they are German. From Latvia have come 120 jailbirds and 80 madmen, who will continue their lives in German institutions.

Dana's December 5 letter reflects his worry: the Russians had just invaded Finland.

The Finnish matter isn't a bit funny. Some Swedish contacts of mine think the Finns have a good chance of holding out all winter and think the Swedes might come to their assistance if they are convinced that the matter is not a lost cause from the start. As one Swede put it: "It would be better for the Swedes and the Finns to take the Russians on together than to have the Russians overrun one after the other."

The Germans hint that the destruction of Finland was in the German Russian deal from the start, but you can't tell me that the Germans like it. In the first place there is a great deal of popular sentiment favoring the Finns, and in the second place the Russians are gaining more and more strategic positions in the Baltic and will soon dominate the entire Scandinavian peninsula. Personally, I think Britain is going to have to fight Russia sooner or later, when the Russians get around to trying invasions of Turkey and Rumania . . . so perhaps it would be better to start right now giving the Finns open assistance. Unfortunately, that's not the way the game is being played.

A little later, in the same letter, he added: *Don't assume that I take this war lightly. Although nothing flashy is going on, most of Europe can feel an awful pressure of blockade and counter-blockade. The thing everyone is discussing at the moment is what counter-measures Germany will or can take against the Anglo-French decisions to start confiscating German exports. The Germans say their answer will be drastic, but won't say what it will be.*

A tragic report Dana mentioned in this letter came from one of his "very special sources" and stated that the Jews in Poland were being forced to wear yellow armbands and were being shot by the Nazis: *This was also printed in a German-language newspaper in Warsaw for all the world to see.* Reporters were not allowed to enter Poland at this time.

In a happier vein, he tells of being invited to supper by Virginia Lane, one of the secretaries at the American Embassy.

Virginia, born in Bakersfield, educated at U.S.C. [University of Southern California], *in addition to being most charming is fabulously learned. She came here on some sort of exchange scholarship and ended up getting a job with the Naval attache at the Embassy. She lives with two girls one of whom acts in German television programs while the other is just an ordinary actress. All three girls work at the Embassy.*

Food continues to be adequate here. I'm told supplies are much scarcer in Berlin than in most smaller cities. No one will succeed in starving Germany out, I believe. The decisive factor, however, is more likely to be raw materials. This war requires infinitely more equipment and raw materials than did the last one. The most reliable experts seriously question whether German technical advances and imports from Russia can provide the extra materials which will be required whenever the war flares into real action.

The thing people in Berlin feel most at present is the scarcity of textile goods. The new program of one hundred points per person per year is based on the five-year average of the needs of a workman. That's going to make it pretty tough for a lot of people. Jews, incidentally, are not getting the new clothes cards at all! Some sort of special arrangement is supposed to be made for them.

Driving is one thing one does not do in Germany just now. Only cars which have been given a special red triangle for their windshield may go forth at all, and these usually get some two hundred liters of gasoline per month. A taxi is supposed to refuse to carry people traveling for mere pleasure or convenience, as to theaters, or to a party. But you can get around that by giving the nearest street corner as your destination. Often taxis will take fares in one direction only, if they are almost out of gas and want to find a fare that will enable them to make some money out of the last drop on the way home. Everyone does a lot of walking now—but shoe leather is scarce too.

Dana noticed in the *DNB* that:

. . . the new Japanese Ambassador Kurusu would arrive in Berlin today. I put on my Portland overcoat and Anthony Eden hat and called at the Japanese Embassy sometime after lunch. Mrs. Kurusu was most surprised to see me, but soon got over it and left me in the care of Jay and a whiskey and soda while she went off to the hairdresser.

I must admit I feel somewhat awkward at the Kurusus because of the vast deal of bowing going on. Somehow I didn't notice it in Brussels.

Jay is a VERY pretty girl. Her Mother suggested I show her Berlin, which is easier said than done. But I shall try day after tomorrow.

The Japanese Embassy is a most un-Japanese looking place with vast and endlessly succeeding themselves rooms full of gold-rimmed mirrors and chandeliers. The garden is mouldy. Jay and I explored the place.

This was the second Christmas Dana, at twenty-four, was away from home and missed us.

Christmas is certainly already in the air here. The tennis courts around the corner from our apartment are flooded for ice-skating and all the kids for miles have forgathered. Christmas presents are arriving. . . . It will be a grand treat when the package of fruit-cake and Steinie-cookies and other articles arrives. I'm sure Jimmy will be quite delighted—and the six shirts—that is really fine.

To my dismay I find that I didn't take my skates to Europe. Well, b'gosh, with all that Xmas money [he was promised a check from home] *I'll buy some. Not hockey skates this time, but fancy ones.*

Another thing to buy is a Christmas tree. We must have a tree, that's one thing you can't take away from a German Christmas. Christmas Eve I'll be at the Oechsners, and Christmas Day I don't know where. Jimmy is thinking of going to Zurich and Paul will see his Danish fiance in Copenhagen. (He can't marry her because of the idiotic foreign service regulations, which make a man hand in his resignation along with his application to marry a foreigner.)

I broached the topic of a bit of a skiing holiday for Schmidt (quite irregular) to Fred Oechsner, and it looks as though it might be done in February, when our replacement for Eric Kaiser (recently fired) arrives.

In a front-page article of the *Herald Express*, Cleveland, on December 25, Dana described the average German family's Christmas in the first year of the war:

> . . . this Christmas was one of trying to make Yule cheer with what there was available. Few dinner tables had the traditional goose, most families having had to make the best of a small piece of pork or veal that the housewife may have been able to get after standing in line for hours at the butcher's.
>
> The housewife's troubles were eased slightly by rationing of an extra quarter-pound of butter per person. But with a weekly ration of one egg each it was bit much to do any Christmas cake baking with.
>
> Giving presents was a big headache. With clothes of all kinds rationed, there were no neckties, slippers, handkerchiefs, or silk stockings lying under Christmas trees.

About the only things Germans could give each other for Christmas were liquor and books. This created such a run on liquor that for the past week the majority of wine merchants in Berlin had notices pasted on their doors saying they were entirely out of schnapps. Toward the end of the week it was impossible to buy anything except beer or a bottle of Rhine wine.

There also was a tremendous run on gramophone records, despite the fact that all stores now demand that an old record be turned in for every new one purchased (Britain controls most of the world's shellac supplies).

Biggest demand of all was for records of Germany's number one war song, "We Are Sailing Against England." Six million records of this song have been sold since the start of the war and it now is practically unobtainable.

While 80,000,000 Germans behind the lines were trying to eke out skimpy wartime rations in the semblance of a Christmas dinner, the Nazis saw to it that Santa Claus did not miss the front line troops.

Thousands of bunkers were decorated with Christmas trees and tinsel to cheer up homesick soldiers who on Christmas Eve sat around listening to the radio, playing carols on accordions and opening packages from home.

Every German family sent special "fieldpost packets" to every soldier, sailor or airman it knew. Even soldiers without families or girlfriends were not neglected. According to the Nazi press, tens of thousands of packages have been sent by Hitler maidens, as well as private individuals in response to an appeal to the public to "adopt" lonely soldiers.

In his December 29 letter, Dana reported on his Christmas:

It was grand to talk to you all. It was such a bad line I'm afraid we couldn't tell each other very much, but I could at least hear everybody's voices, rising out of the fog and fading away again—sounds as though it went by radio. I put the call in at 11:15 p.m. on the twenty-fifth, thinking to get you all just after Christmas dinner, if the call came through about midnight. It didn't come until 3:30 a.m. Some sort of listener-in in Berlin insisted on knowing my name before the connection went through. Everybody sounded just like they always did, Mother, Father, Grandma, Elizabeth. I'd like to have spoken to everybody at the Christmas gathering, but that would hardly do. We talked about six minutes, but I expect to be charged only for three because of the "schlechte Verstaendigung" [bad communications]. That's customary on bad connections. . . . Sometimes on the calls to Moscow the line is so bad we give it up as a bad job, and we are not charged at all.

Mother asked me when I was coming home, and I said, "Next spring, I hope," I suppose that, in view of the war, was a burst of unjustified enthusiasm. I told Fred about your question the next day, and he said, "That's what all families want to know. You'd better tell them, not for a long time." As usual, it's no good planning too far in advance. It all depends on the war news. To go home in the middle of it seems, in a way, like running out on something I ought to see through, not to mention letting down my organization. On the other hand, if things continue as dull as they are at present in Berlin, I shouldn't feel any compunction about going home for a while.

I saw Jimmy off to Geneva several days before Christmas. It was the most gosh-awful human jam trying to get on that train I have seen in my life, including even the New York subways—people heaving and shoving and pushing and clawing like cattle in the half-light of the blacked-out station. The train full, and then fuller, and finally packed with a couple of hundred more people. I saw one man lifted in through a window at the last moment. There was no getting in the doors, with corridors and platforms sardine-tight with humanity. Scores, maybe hundreds of people must have been left behind because they were physically unable to get on that train.

The Oechsners' Christmas Eve party was very nice. I presented them with several bars of chocolate (from Switzerland) and got a fancy calendar in return. The dinner was remarkable, especially considering the times—must have cost an awful lot of time, finagling and trouble. There were perhaps fifty people, three turkeys, French wine, cocktails, dancing, radio-phonograph music.

On Christmas day I had a little gathering about a Christmas tree of my own. Yes, I bought an enormous if not overly beautiful tree for 1.50 Marks, decorated it with the Longs' Xmas tree trimmings. My guests were bachelors and bachelorettes: Joe Grigg[26]*, Russel Hill (*Herald Tribune*). Virginia Lane, and her German apartment mate, Analies Schneider.*

I made a cocktail consisting of our last French Vermouth and a good deal of gin, and lit the Christmas tree and we opened our presents which Santa Claus had left under the tree. The presents were of an exclusively musical nature, including sirens, whistles, a bugle. Virginia who seems to be talented in almost all respects, immediately played tattoos and reveilles and such on her bugle. Altogether I believe we awakened several dead. Our dinner was very good, I think. Fraulein Turk (our aged maid) had baked a most commendable cake for the occasion.

About 4:30 we gathered up some of my diplomatic milk, and some eggs, and repaired to Virginia's and Analies' flat to make an eggnog and admire their tree and presents. Somehow or other I stayed there until after 11, when I had to repair to the office for the overnight trick.

Last night I had dinner at a Chinese restaurant with some German shortwave people I have met recently and some Germans who have had to return from China.

The family, and especially Mother, was very proud of Dana's work with the *United Press* and his achievements as a writer. Most of his letters were addressed to Mother, but it was understood that she would share them with the whole family. When a week passed with no letter, she would become despondent and could speak of nothing else, which made life difficult for everyone around her. Mother subscribed to clipping services, and she and Steinie put those in scrapbooks, along with occasional pictures Dana sent.

She wrote to Dana every week, but unfortunately, Dana did not keep her letters. She followed the news assiduously; for instance, she did not think of going to bed before the eleven o'clock radio news. She was constantly reading magazines and books, followed the writings of other correspondents, and knew their names and affiliations.

---

[26]   Joe Griggs was on the staff of the *United Press.*

United Press of America
December 29, 1938

Dear Mother and Father:

Well, after telephoning home, I suppose I don't really need to write a letter. But then, it may be a year or so until I do so again, so here goes on the typewriter. Mr. Kirk, being a millionaire telephones his family once a week. Think what he saves in postage.

It was grand to talk to you all. It was such a bad line I'm afraid we couldn't tell each other very much, but I could at least hear everybody's voices, rising out of the fog and fading away again. Sounds as though it went by radio.

We have a "genehmigte Nummer" for calls abroad so there was no difficulty about putting in the call. That I did at 11:15 p.m. on the twentyfifth, thinking to get you all just after Christmas dinner, if the call came through about midnight. It didn't come until 3:30, however. Some sort of listener-in in Berlin insisted on knowing my name before the connection went through. I hope he learned a lot from our talk.

Everybody sounded just like they always did, Mother, Father, Grandma, Elizabeth. I'd like to have spoken to everybody at the Christmas gathering, but that would hardly do. We talked about six minutes, but I expect to be charged only for three, because of the "schlechte Verstaendigung." That's customary on bad connections. Sometimes on calls to Moscow the line is so bad we give it up as a bad job, and we are not charged at all.

We are quite a clan, aren't we, especially when we all get together at a Christmas party and talk on a transatlantic phone. Mother asked me when I was coming home, and I said "Next spring, I hope." I suppose that, in view of the war, that was a burst of unjustified enthusiasm. I told Fred about your question the next day, and he said " That's what all families want to know. You'd better tell them, not for a long time." As usual, it's no good planning too far in advance. It all depends on the war now. To go home in the middle of it seems, in a way, like running out on something I ought to see through, not to mention letting down my organization. On the other hand, if things continue as dull as they are at present in Berlin I shouldn't feel any compunctions about going home for a while. Well, we'll just keep it in mind this way—that I'll come home the first time an opportunity shows itself.

Starting in chronologically on the holidays....I saw Jimmy off to Geneva several days before Christmas. It was the

Dana's letter December 29, 1938; page one

Dana returning from a ski run, 1940

1940

In March 1940, Dana finally got the promised week of skiing in the mountains. Although in the previous year he had gone to Lech in the Austrian Alps, this year he decided to go to Sestrière in the Italian Alps, which he notes is at 2,035 meters. He made reservations at the Duchi d'Aosta Hotel. On the way to Sestrière, he stopped in Milan, where he was able to do some shopping: a trench coat for summer, a dark blue suit, grey flannels—all better quality than available in Berlin. From Sestrière, he wrote:

This is a mighty welcome holiday for me and I feel a lot better for it already. The skiing is only fair, snow rather wet blown off all the high places, but it is nonetheless a diversion. Food splendid, piles of oranges, creamy milk, five course dinners. . . .

A holiday alone isn't all it might be, but I've met a very nice young English couple with whom I exchanged low downs on our respective battlefronts. He's here for health—has to stay above 2,000 meters for two months.

Two bright Italian girls, who speak both English and French proved good skiers, but left today. They're apparently of the high-class professional variety (of which the place is full). They pretend they're sisters and married, but my theory is that some good rich friend in Turin treats them to a holiday now and then. They were fetched in a fancy car with chauffeur from Turin.

Saturday, my fifth and last day, I hope to make a tour to the highest peak hereabouts, something over 3,000 meters, with a guide. But right now the "Boulera," a violent cold wind is shaking this fantastic tower mercilessly and the tour prospects are poor.

Finally there's not much I can tell you that I didn't write from Germany. (You know my political slant and how I feel about the war. Tragic as its continuance is, it will be even more tragic if the Nazis win it.) Talking to this Englishman (very well informed, of a shipping family) I feel considerably encouraged about the prospects.

(I try to keep the corrupt Nazis and Germans separate, difficult as it is, when all that is non-Nazi is necessarily mute. And then there are the numerous unhappy souls who hate the regime's cruelties and perversions of patriotism, of religion, art, literature, not to mention journalism and all the rest of it, but who nevertheless feel they must support their country, Nazis or no Nazis. It's tough for them, but there just isn't any answer.)

Shortly after Dana returned from skiing at Sestrière, on April 17, he wrote:

Tomorrow, or the day after, I am to fly to Stockholm to help out the staff which is groaning from overwork and under-sleeping. [This was only a week after the invasion of Norway by the Nazis, and the volume of news of the war was overwhelming.] *We had the devil of a time getting exit visas from Germany. After weeks of waiting we got the American Embassy to intervene . . . and that turned the trick.*

The German invasion of Denmark and Norway had cut Sweden off from the rest of the world. While food and other supplies seemed to be plentiful in Stockholm, Dana wrote of the concern about finding alternative trade routes for bringing supplies to Sweden.

In an article published in the *Pittsburgh Press* and other papers on April 30, 1940, Dana discussed this problem:

. . . . Mines and naval battles block the normal route to the North Sea and the fighting in Narvik and the Trondheim areas block the main overland routes to Norway.

For the time being Sweden must dig into existing large stocks of imported raw materials, the most important of which are oil, rubber, fodder, southern fruits and British and French luxury goods.

It is understood that only one ship, which carried British coal, has reached Stockholm since April 9.

Even air communications have ceased, although it is expected that airmail and passenger service with Great Britain and France will be resumed this week via Moscow and Sofia.

In addition to the present Swedish-German trade talks, similar trade negotiations with Russia are expected to be held with a view towards using the White Sea Canal for sea transports and obtaining Russian oil.

Another possible alternative supply route is through the Finnish Arctic port of Petsamo.

It is understood that Sweden has on hand about a six-month oil supply which would be used up far sooner in event of a national emergency.

Drastic limitations on the use of gasoline for private cars will be put into effect about the middle of May, it is said.

Coffee purchases have been limited to 250 grams monthly per person. Prices of oranges, grapes and other foods and imported luxury goods have risen rapidly. The price of one kind of silk stockings rose from six to nine kroner within a week.

King Gustav V was the first subscriber yesterday to Sweden's defense loan, buying 250,000 crowns worth of defense bonds. The Crown Prince bought 50,000 crowns worth and the royal family was reported to have made purchases totaling 500,000 crowns.

At current exchange rates, the King's purchase was the equivalent of $59,375 and the Crown Prince $11,875 and the entire royal family $118,750.

On May 4, he wrote:

Now I am trying to arrange to go to Norway on the German side while others do the other side. As usual I must wait upon the decision of the Berlin authorities . . . .

After Berlin rations, the superfluity here seems unbelievable. After you have rather your fill of Smorgasbord, they bring on cheese, then when you are stuffed to the gills, the main course begins.

> *My only regret in leaving Berlin for an indefinite period is that I cannot sail my new boat.* [27]
>
> *Stockholm is an expensive place, and this hotel is the most expensive place in it. I am glad I am on an expense account. And I hope to stay for a while to come. I have written my flat-mates in Berlin to try to take in a new boarder during my absence.*
>
> *Sunday one of the men on the continental UP staff here has asked us all to his home for dinner, so I'll see a real Scandinavian household. The Grand is hardly typical – "Us" is Ralph Forte, once of the Rome Bureau and lately of Finland, Peter Rhodes who just got a brilliant story out of being in Narvik and coming out on skis, a highly adventurous circumstance at the right time. He has just got permission from* United Press *to sell his story to* Colliers.

Although many Norwegians were Quislings, that is they supported the Nazis, there were also some brave men who resisted. Dana wrote a story about two such groups, published on May 8 in the *News, New York,* and presumably in others. In *New York,* the heading was:

LONE BAND OF NORSE MAKES STAND IN HILLS

Three hundred Norwegians who refused to surrender to the German army tonight were reported making a "fight-unto-death" stand against Nazi forces in the evacuated Trondheim coastal region in west central Norway.

Using guerrilla tactics, the small force of Norwegians was said to be operating in the mountainous sections southeast of Trondheim in the Guldal Valley between Singsaas and Holtalen.

Norwegian guerilla bands also were reported active in the heavily wooded mountains around the German-held Norwegian capital of Oslo as well as in the northern Oester Valley.

---

[27] Shortly before leaving Berlin, he had bought a sixteen-foot sailboat he named the JUNK. In the months to come, Dana had many adventures aboard. Although Berlin has a surprising network of waterways, he probably sailed on the River Spree, the largest flowing through the city.

Lone Band of Norse Makes Stand in Hills

By DANA SCHMIDT.

Stockholm, May 8 (U.P.).—Three hundred Norwegians who refused to surrender to the German army tonight were reported making a "fight-unto-death" stand against Nazi forces in the evacuated Trondheim coastal region in west central Norway.

Using guerrilla tactics, the small force of Norsemen was said to be operating in the mountainous sections southeast of Trondheim in the Guldal Valley between Singsaas and Holtalen.

Norwegian guerrilla bands also were reported active in the heavily wooded mountains around the German-held Norwegian capital of Oslo as well as in the northern Oester Valley.

The Germans, meanwhile, were said to have left Grong and Formofoss, east of Namsos. The towns are now unoccupied. The Nazi forces were reported hurrying northward toward Narvik to aid the besieged German garrison of about 3,500 there under a severe Allied bombardment.

It was understood here that the German forces still were south of Mo, which is about 125 miles from the Norwegian iron ore port.

Norwegians denied today that the Germans had reached either Mosjoen or Mo, or had entered Nordland Province.

"In fact," the semi-official Swedish news agency quoted Norwegian officers as saying, "no German soldier has yet passed the district boundary line which runs through the Nam Valley south of Lake Majavatn."

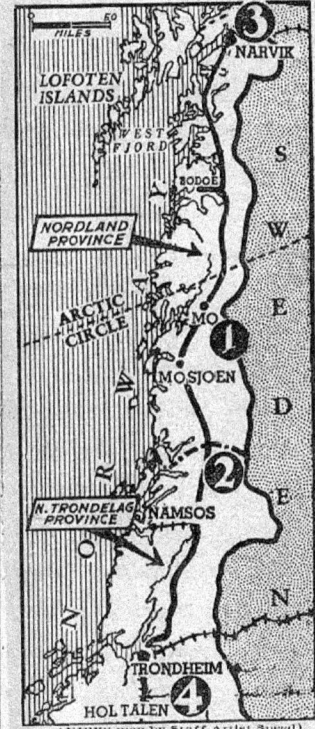

Nazis claim to have thrust northward almost to Mo (1), but Norwegians say Germans haven't passed boundary (2) of North Trondelag Province. Germans yesterday bombed British at Narvik (3), reporting damage to ships and communications on land at the contested port.

The Swedish Government announced a new series of mines had been laid in territorial waters of the Archipelago off Stockholm from a point approximately 50 miles north to 50 miles south of the capital to facilitate its neutrality guard, the Associated Press reported. The mines will not affect the use of the harbor.

Dana's article May 8, 1940

The Germans, meanwhile, were said to have left Grong and Formofoss, east of Namsos. The towns are now unoccupied. The Nazi forces were reported hurrying northward toward Narvik to aid the besieged German garrison of about 3,500 there under a severe Allied bombardment.

It was understood here that the German forces were still south of Mo, which is about 125 miles from the Norwegian iron ore port.

Norwegians denied today that the Germans had reached either Mosjoen or Mo, or had entered Nordland Province.

On May 10, 1940, German forces—violating the neutrality of the Netherlands, Belgium, and Luxembourg, invaded France through the Ardennes Forest and drove a wedge between the French forces, leading to the evacuation of three hundred and thirty eight thousand British and French at Dunkirk.

May 11:
One busy splendid week in Stockholm and now I must go back to the seething continent. Just got instructions from Flory in London. Somehow I hoped developments would warrant my staying here, as I am fed up with my old post, though it will doubtless yield ample by-lines. Wonder if I got much of anything under the Stockholm dateline . . . we really came too late.

(Reporting at my old post is really psychologically deadening. In the first place there is the constant feeling of conflict with your surroundings . . . how far can I go without getting into trouble . . . how much of what I think can I say. There is the maddening vicariousness of our work. Rarely can we report an event first hand. Most of the time it's rewriting stuff that you hate, and stuff that is either official, tautologous, involved, stuffy or overwritten and gross.)

Sometimes you can make something meaty out of it that is fairly good reading in the press at home, but I must say for a steady diet I'd rather deal with things and live in surroundings with which I sympathize.

He continued with a description of the hotel scene in Stockholm:

. . . overrun with newspapermen, diplomats and spies and Englishmen who can't get home. Italians who can't go home through Germany but must go through Tallinn, Moscow and Bucharest, because of something they've written.

Persons of uncertain occupation who are however always well-posted on events and anxious to discuss them . . . and report what they hear to some legation. Volunteers of the Finnish war who are not allowed to proceed to Norway, and don't know what to do—volunteers from Norway who will sell their experiences for fifty dollars—the divorced seventh wife of a Swedish baron—an American oil salesman, drunk and surrounded by blondes, who is trying to sell the Swedish government some oil, if a way can be found to get it here—Germans, English, French, Italians, Americans all drinking cocktails together, sometimes, although more often split according to political affiliations—and constant bicker about strategy, and mutual brain-picking. I think I will write a story about the place—if I can avoid being libelous.

Tonight Stockholm will be blacked out, just like the warring countries' cities. It is expected to be permanent. Whether there is special significance in the measure or not, no one knows, although it's rather odd it should go into effect Sunday night when no one can buy black paper, etc.

We have very little to do here at present . . . . Last night I saw a recent American movie for the first time in ages—Suwannee River I think it was called . . . very sentimental, but very good entertainment. About half of the pictures shown here seem to be American. The effect, the spread of the English language, and popularization of things American can be imagined. Here the girls make up like Americans, smoke American cigarettes if they can afford it, drink American-type cocktails, eat ice-cream. One thing they don't do a la Americaine, though, is eating. There isn't room on the ordinary American dining-room table let alone soda fountain, to hold the snacks they serve up here.

After Norway was occupied, Dana returned to Berlin from Stockholm. Hitler's armies now turned to the Netherlands and then Belgium. On May 22, Dana wrote of relaying a story from Fred Oechsner, who was with the German Army in Belgium. Fred was phoning from Aachen. Dana wrote, *When an air raid was in progress, we could distinctly hear the clickety-click of anti-aircraft guns and bombs over the telephone.* This was almost the end of the Belgian resistance—the Belgian armies capitulated on May 26.

Dana had a chance to enjoy his boat one more time before he left Berlin:

On Memorial Day, Virginia, Kit Vinson (probationary vice consul) and I went sailing in the Boat. We sailed merrily and swiftly downwind after struggling to put up the sails for an hour or so, when it began to rain. So we started back, only to find that the wind had died, and what there was, was coming the wrong way. We tacked back and forth over every foot of the river for miles and got soaked and frozen and sang everything from Onward Christian Soldiers *to* It Ain't Gonna Rain No More.

Strangely enough no one suffered any ill effects. Ain't civilization grand when you get back from that sort of thing?

Dana on his boat the JUNK

By June 4, the French and the British, who had come to their aid with 252,000 men, were forced to withdraw from Dunkirk, abandoning most of their equipment. Later, Dana was to see this devastation from the air. He described the process of relaying Fred Oechsner's story:

Last night four staffers including myself were here 'till all hours. It's amazing how many people can work over one story, moving it along fast. First there's Oechsner himself phoning it, and one of us taking it in on the dictaphone, passing out records of each bulletin to someone else, who takes it off the record and hands out bulletin by bulletin to yet another person who punches a tape of it. The tape runs through the telex and registers in Zurich under the supervision of still another person. In Zurich an automatic reperforating machine makes a new tape which is used to send the bulletins on to the Press Wireless office in Bern, whence it finally gets off to America. The net result is that our desk in New York is probably shooting out Oechsner's first bulletins to the far corners while Oechsner is still phoning the last ones through to us. The point of the whole rush, of course, is that Lochner of the Associated Press *is trying to do the same thing through his own Berlin Bureau, and whoever gets to the newspapers in America first gets printed.*

We also use direct cable and phone via Rome at various times of day and [for] certain types of material.

I know the radio increasingly often beats all the papers, but radio will not replace newspapers for the (to me) simple reason that you can't take a radio story, put it in your pocket and carry it away for later reading. A newspaper story is there waiting for you whenever you are good and ready to read it.

On June 16, Dana wrote:

It looks as if the war in France is over. . . . But I do not think the war is over by a long shot . . . and a lot of shooting. England is going to be one tough nut to crack, and licking the Dominions, or trying to, is one of the likeliest ways in which the U.S.A. is going to get drawn in.

It is distinctly "Hochsommer" [mid-summer] *here, swimming and tennis and sunbathing. Very peaceful, too, with war like a bad dream we read about in the newspapers. Food has improved lately; lots more vegetables and fresh fruit. We are still getting butter and eggs from what used to be Denmark.*

Fred's stories from Paris, also those of Glenn Stadler, have been bell-ringers, and we have thus far been pushing them across ahead of Associated. *Good play in the West?* [He was wondering how many of these stories had appeared in California.] *Last night,* he continued, *I signed the flash announcing the French had asked cessation of hostilities and followed up with a very powerful night lead. Did it show in L.A?* [28]

One night last week I was at the office 'till 7:35 a.m. (theoretically I'm off at midnight) and another night 'till about 4:00 a.m., mostly because of Fred's stories coming in late and things like the overrunning of the Baltic States (by the Russians) and various German stories breaking just at midnight. New York has phoned twice direct, at the crack of dawn when nobody is likely to have anything new, asking about separate peace possibilities. Their hunch was right, however. . . . .

Had a very good game of tennis with Russell Hill whom I think you mentioned in a letter—helps Bill Shirer for Columbia *and writes for the* Herald Tribune.

The German army soon reached Paris, and on June 22, France surrendered. Germany divided France into two sections, with a German-controlled section in the north and the Vichy government in the southeast.

The fall of France enabled Germany to develop submarine bases on the coast of Brittany, furthering the German submarine menace in the Atlantic and endangering the vital shipping lanes.

Dana described Hitler's reaction to France's surrender in an article that was widely published:

---

[28] The only stories from the fall of France in my mother's scrapbooks of Dana's writing were a story about Hitler's joy at the fall of France and several stories on the failure of the Maginot Line, supposedly impregnable, as part of the reason for the rapid collapse.

HITLER LETS DOWN HIS HAIR IN VICTORY LAUGH

BERLIN, June 26—Adolf Hitler shook with laughter, snapped his fingers and all but broke into a dance step when word was brought to him that crushed France was pleading for peace, a newsreel of "the happiest moment of the Fuehrer's life" revealed tonight.

The official Nazi newsreel photographer caught Hitler in the historic moment just outside his headquarters on the Western front, as he wrote a message to Premier Mussolini to meet him in Munich to decide the conditions of the French armistice.

The Generals surrounding the Fuehrer, including Field Marshall Hermann Goering, were so excited that one of them dropped the pen with which Hitler had just signed the message to Il Duce.

The newsreel, entitled "The Happiest Moment of the Fuehrer's Life," was given a preview before foreign correspondents in Berlin and shows Hitler in an unaccustomed jovial mood.

His first reaction to the news of France's capitulation, after only six weeks of blitzkrieg, was to snap his booted heels together, roll his head back and grin.

Then he burst into a round, full laugh and thrust his arms straight out at the sides of his body, snapping his fingers.

This gave way to a lapse of all his usual restraint when he lifted one knee and stomped his heel down into the dust in what looked like the first steps of a solo victory dance.

On July 7, Dana wrote:

Last time I had a day off (a rather irregular occurrence) Virginia, Carl Maas, and a girlfriend of his went sailing with me. We had just gotten under way successfully, the sails were filling beautifully, when Virginia gave the alarm that the boat was rapidly filling with water. Sure enough, we had a large leak, and had to put back to port and console ourselves with swimming off the dock and off a "borrowed" tub. Presently it began to rain (as it usually does) and we all came home rather like drowned rats. This Sunday I have let

Carl go out in the boat with his friends alone. There is no use its rotting in the sunshine just because I have to work.

Dana had long understood the value of pictures to illustrate his stories and had taken many himself, as when he went with the German army to Sudetenland. So when *ACME News Pictures* asked him to take on the task of looking after their interests in Berlin on a temporary basis, he was eager to try it.

July 7:

It involves, deciding what pictures are to be sent by wireless, how much we are to pay for them, etc. It has taken a good deal of time so far. A week later he wrote: *The picture business is still keeping me pretty busy, although gradually I'm getting sources lined up. This morning I was at the UFA offices [ACME], arranging for them to send over pictures which they consider newsworthy.*
I don't suppose there is a great deal of interest in German films in the States, but occasionally there is something like "Feuertaufe," [Baptism by Fire] depicting the Blitzkrieg in Poland, a propaganda film which is really sensational. And it is possible we might use some typical propaganda shots, if they are amusing. The UFA people wanted to give me a slew of girls with pretty legs, but I told them we had a great many in America.
A week later, he wrote:
It has finally been decided, after I've been at it a month, that ACME shall pay me 75 Marks a week for my efforts on their behalf. Thus, my regular salary including living allowances, plus this spare-time job gives me an income of almost $80.00 a week.
And the 17th:
.... We had a tragedy the last time we were out in the boat—Virginia and I and Joe Grigg. As we were nipping along at a fine clip there was a sudden crack and the top end of the sail came crashing down. The wire that attaches the gaff (or something) to the mast had pulled out. But we managed to limp into port despite our broken wing and spent the balance of the day sun bathing (until it rained).

As a matter of fact we almost always have tragedies on my boat. But it is a very good sport, if we survive, and the boat is magnificent considering the price I paid for it.

July 24:

We have been very limited in our activities the past month as we are operating under strict official warnings that any sort of speculation, even the ordinary "think piece"—"well informed Berlin political quarters, diplomatic circles," and all that—will be rewarded by the immediate out chucking of the persons involved. One of the better Swiss newspapermen was given twenty-four hours to leave a few days ago.

The number of newspapermen who are not mere pawns in the hand of the Propaganda Ministry can be counted on about one and a half hands now. In the first place there is our office. There is constant tension between us and the authorities. If Fred weren't such a smart and exceedingly careful and conservative newspaperman, and if UP weren't so important, we would have been out long ago. In practice about what happens, is that, while we bow to official desires as to what shall not be sent, we also decline to send their propaganda, except in very obvious quotation marks. And then we manage to sneak in most of what we really think by judicious quoting from newspapers, by the arrangement and emphasis of our stories, by prodding authorized quarters (the Propaganda Ministry, whom, I hope, nobody believes) into denying, or stating that nothing is known about things which we are pretty sure are true.

If you see a hot and righteous "categorical" denial from Berlin, you can be fairly sure of a spark of truth in that which is denied—the truer the story, the better the denial. Ralph Barnes got thrown out for his story that Hitler was angry because of the Russian occupation of the Baltic countries. The Swiss got thrown out for mentioning that high Nazis were annoyed because of the Russian occupation of North Bukowina, which hadn't been agreed upon. Both stories undoubtedly true.

Had anyone mentioned that German troops were concentrated on the Russian border at the time of the occupation of North Bukowina he would probably have been drawn and quartered. But it is true, and generally known here. Of course there are exceptions to this. I don't blame the Germans for getting heated about some of the silly stories that are put out in London. Definitely it is very hard to differentiate between tall tales and truth.

POOR CONCRETE, NAZI TRAINING
SPELLED DOOM OF MAGINOT LINE

STRASBOURG, Wednesday, July 31—How France's Maginot Line, once believed to be the mightiest fortification in the world, collapsed in a few weeks is one of the stories that remains to be told about this strangest of wars.

With a party of four newspapermen from Berlin, I participated in the first civilians' visit to the Line under guidance of Nazi officials since the end of the war in France. The following is what I saw and what I was told by soldiers from both sides during the conducted tour.

The concrete with which the bunkers were constructed was excellent for sidewalks, but not for resisting a blitzkrieg. A German engineer told me that the French concrete was made of coarse gravel and a thin mixture of cement adequate only for non-military purposes.

Further the front and side walls of the French bunkers are appropriately ten feet thick, but the flat rear wall is only a little more than four feet thick. As a result, as soon as the Germans broke one link in the chain of forts, they were able to take the rest of the Line from the weakly defended rear.

How the German high command determined what was the weakest point in the line was explained to us by our guides. The weakest fire came from Kaiserstuhl Mountain north of the village of Breisach.

Swiftly and secretly the Germans studded the forests and hills around Breisach with guns. At 10 o'clock on the morning of June 15, German guns suddenly began blasting with concentrated fire. Anti-tank shells ripped holes as big as a man's hand in steel turrets from all angles before the French could recover from their surprise. Exactly twenty minutes later, the first-line bunkers were silent, their guns destroyed, the bunkers heaps of loose gray gravel.

The most important factor of all is the intangible one of the psychological training of troops, the German said. French psychology was the psychology of defense. The basis of defense was the bunker. Come hell or high water, the French stayed in their bunkers.

The Germans were educated to movement and attack and considered their forts only temporary accessories to be resorted to only when under heaviest fire and in order to give their own artillery time to work up an effective counter-fire under which they could go over to attack.

It was a contest between old tested warfare and a new and revolutionary warfare. The Maginot Line was a symbol of the one which lost.

At the beginning of August, Dana and several other correspondents were invited by the German air force on a tour to see the Stuka bases along the English Channel on the German side. In an article that was published in many newspapers, he wrote:

With swift Messerschmitt fighters all round us, I flew up the English Channel coast to within 20 minutes flying distance of London today [August 4] and visited the "jumping-off" points of Germany's aerial offensive against the British Isles.

Eight Messerschmitts-09 fighters escorted our big Junkers-52 transport plane aboard which we visited Germany's bases for "Stuka" dive-bombers and pursuit planes which are staging daily attacks against shipping and British objectives . . . .

The tour was arranged by Field Marshal General Albert Kesselring of the German high command.

So close were we to Britain—in our big Swastika-marked plane—that we could have seen the English coast had it not been for a heavy fog.

The eight Messerschmitts constantly flew around us, in and out of the clouds, searching for British planes.

We circled low over La Panne and over Dunkerque, where the wreckage of a hundred or more British freighters, destroyers and other small craft jutted out of the water and the burned out remains of the city lay below us like a skeleton—ghostly reminders of the British retreat from Flanders and flight by sea from Dunkerque.

Thousands of wrecked automobiles and tanks of the defeated British expeditionary force still choked the roads around Dunkerque and were strewn all along the beach there.

We saw thin lanes through the fields where German tanks had swept westward to the coast, criss-crossing here and there, where battles had occurred.

The "Stuka" dive-bomber base where we landed cannot be identified here, but it is "somewhere near Bruges," inland from Dunkerque and Boulogne.

Immediately upon our arrival orders were given for a mock attack on the air base and three "Stukas" went up and exhibited their screaming dives.

The "Stukas", loaded with unfused bombs, climbed for 15 minutes to a height of 16,400 feet. While the deputy commander of the group of 30 planes at the base was telling of his dive-bombing experiences, the "Stukas" appeared as specks in the sun.

The leader dipped and plummeted toward us at a 70-degree angle. The others rolled over behind him. The sound rose from a distant whine to a terrifying shriek mixed with the undertone of the roaring motors.

Later an officer told me that two small propellers mounted on the landing gear just above the wheels were "heul" [Howling like

DESCRIBES TOUR OVER CHANNEL

German Planes Range Close To Isles

Editor's Note—The following dispatch by United Press Correspondent Dana Schmidt describes a flight up the English channel coast in a German Junkers plane—through the heart of the battle area of the intensified British-German war in the air.

By DANA SCHMIDT

GHENT, Belgium, Aug. 4.—(UP)—(Delayed) with Swift Messerschmitt fighters all around us, I flew up the English channel coast to within 20 minutes flying distance of London today and visited the "jumping off" points of Germany's aerial offensive against the British Isles.

Eight Messerschmitt-109 fighters escorted our big Junkers-52 transport plane abroad which a group of foreign correspondents visited Germany's bases for "Stuka" bombers and pursuit planes which are staging daily attacks against shipping and British objectives.

The tour was arranged by Field Marshal Gen. Albert Kesselring of the German high command.

So close were we to Britain—in our big Swastika-marked plane—that we could have seen the English coast had it not been for a heavy fog.

The eight Messerschmitts constantly zoomed around us, in and out of the clouds, searching for British planes.

We circled low over La Panne and over Dunkerque where the wreckage of a hundred or more British freighters, destroyers and other small craft jutted out of the water and the burned-out remains of the city lay below us like a skeleton—ghostly reminders of the British retreat from Flanders and flight by sea from Dunkerque.

Thousands of wrecked automobiles and tanks of the defeated British expeditionary force still choked the roads around Dunkerque and were strewn all along the beach there.

We saw thin lanes through the fields where German tanks had swept westward to the coast, criss-crossing here and there where battles had occurred.

The "Stuka" dive-bomber base where we landed cannot be identified here but it is "somewhere near Bruges," a small town inland from Dunkerque and Boulogne.

Dana's article August 4, 1940

sirens] shriek propellers. But he refused to say how they worked, even whether they were attached to sirens.

The officer said that some Polish prisoners still flee to the ditches in panic when they hear the "Stukas". It often throws into panic the people within a radius of six miles, he said.

Kesselring said, "Germany's air fleet is ready for the offensive against Great Britain and—when the word is given—will attack with the unpredictability of lightning . . . . Only the time for the attack must yet be decided," the field marshal said . . . . The captain of a "Stuka" dive-bomber added: the "grand attack" on the British Isles will be "simply frightful and annihilating."

On August 16, on his return from Ghent and the Stuka dive-bomber demonstrations, he wrote:

Yesterday I sent [ACME] *an excellent shipment consisting of pictures taken on my recent trip to France and Belgium, a series on training U-boat men, and the first selections from the German "War Newsreel" which anyone can obtain.*

THROUGH BERLIN STREETS
By DANA SCHMIDT

BERLIN, Germany—(UP)—British bombers stole Berlin's sleep for the third time in four nights Wednesday night and if all the residents were as troubled as I was it may be said that the raiders attained their chief objective.

The now familiar rising and falling wail of the warning that the bombers' hour had arrived caught me leaving the United Press office after listening to a British news broadcast.

From the opened, darkened windows of the office Jack Fleischer and I watched. At first there was nothing to see or hear except hustling crowds, laughing and running down Unter den Linden in an effort to get home.

Then the first big flashes of anti-aircraft guns lit up the western horizon. They were too far away for the sound of their firing to be heard.

As the planes drew nearer the firing became a faint rumble and then a slow, methodical booming. Usually there were three or four in succession, mixed with the quick, impatient bang of the antiaircraft artillery. Unter Den Linden then fell into dead silence.

Searchlights fingered the clouds and drew strange patterns in the pitch-black night, fanning back and forth but failing to catch British planes in their beams.

As planes grew nearer we could see the reddish burst of antiaircraft shells. They looked like vast fireflies.

Then we heard distinctly the hum of an airplane. It must have been British because German pursuit planes do not go up at night when antiaircraft batteries are in action.

Through Berlin Streets

By DANA SCHMIDT

Berlin, Germany - (U.P.) - British bombers stole Berlin's sleep for the third time in four nights Wednesday night and if all residents were as troubled as I was it may be said that the raiders attained their chief objective.

The now familiar rising and falling wail of warning that the bombers' hour had arrived caught me leaving the United Press office after listening to a British news broadcast.

From the open, darkened windows of the office Jack Fleischer and I watched. At first there was nothing to see or hear except hustling crowds, laughing and running down Unter Den Linden in an effort to get home.

Then the first big flashes of antiaircraft guns lit up the western horizon. They were too far away for the sound of their firing to be heard.

As the planes drew nearer the firing became a faint rumble and then a slow, methodical booming. Usually there were three or four in succession, mixed with the quick, impatient bang of light antiaircraft artillery. Unter Den Linden then fell into a dead silence.

Searchlights fingered the clouds and drew strange patterns in the pitch black night, fanning back and forth but failing to catch British planes in their beams.

As planes drew nearer we could see the reddish bursts of antiaircraft shells. They looked like vast fireflies.

Then we heard distinctly the hum of an airplane. It must have been British because German pursuit planes do not go up at night when antiaircraft batteries are in action.

The firing was so close that our office building shook and we heard mixed with the bombs several heavy crunches. These last must have been the high explosive bombs which killed several persons in Kottbusserstrasse in southeast Berlin.

I was told that two British flares hung from their parachutes for almost 10 minutes in the eastern sky and that afterward the glow of several attics ignited by incendiary bombs could be seen.

After that there was an ebb in the firing and I slept a bit on a couch. When I awakened the building again vibrated with antiaircraft fire, probably as a new wave of bombers soared over the city. After almost three hours of steady howling the sirens signaled the end of the raid.

Dana's article August 29, 1940

The firing was so close that our office building shook and we heard mixed with the bombs several heavy crunches. These last must have been the high explosive bombs which killed several persons in Kottbusserstrasse in southwest Berlin.

I was told that two British flares hung from their parachutes for almost ten minutes in the eastern sky and that afterward the glow of several attics ignited by the incendiary bombs could be seen.

After that there was an ebb in the firing and I slept on the couch.

When I awakened the building again vibrated with the antiaircraft fire, probably as a new wave of bombers soared over the city. After almost three hours of steady howling the sirens signaled the end of the raid.

RAF RAIDERS MADE "INVISIBLE" BY VARNISH
WE CAN'T SEE 'EM, BERLIN WAILS
By DANA SCHMIDT

BERLIN—(UP)—A secret type of varnish which makes British bombers invisible under the glare of searchlights has made it impossible for German antiaircraft gunners to turn their fire on enemy raiders attacking Berlin, air force officials said today.

The British bombers, such as those which attacked the capital for nearly three hours early Thursday, were said to have been "completely invisible" when the full glare of searchlights was turned upon them.

As result, it was asserted, the "Germany antiaircraft guns protecting the capital were able to shoot only at the shadows which the raiders threw against the clouds."

The varnish, a thick black substance, was said to be painted on the underside of the wings of the British bombers and is a secret which the British alone possess.

After one British bomber was brought down recently the new-type varnish was discovered and German experts began making tests, the air force sources asserted.

The side of the wing painted with the varnish was held in the ray of an automobile headlight and "immediately became invisible."

These same quarters said the British raiders had used shrewd tactics in their attacks on Berlin, such as flying at varying heights from 6,000 to 15,000 feet above the city. Their frequent variation of altitude, it was said, altered the tone of their motors and made difficult the work of the German sound-detecting apparatus.

The British planes were believed to have come over the city in several waves, with each wave apparently remaining 10 or 15 minutes over Berlin and then returning home, to be followed by another wave.

Berlin headquarters also said the British hits on the German capital were remarkable feats of navigation and suggested that veteran commercial air pilots probably carried out the attacks.

❖ ❖ ❖

(In London the suggestion of a "secret varnish" was termed a German excuse for the failure of Berlin searchlight crews to spot the British planes.)

RAF Raiders Made 'Invisible' by Varnish

We Can't See 'Em, Berlin Wails

By DANA SCHMIDT

BERLIN—(U.P.)—A secret type of varnish which makes British bombers invisible under the glare of searchlights has made it impossible for German anti-aircraft gunners to turn their fire on enemy raiders attacking Berlin, air force officials said today.

The British bombers, such as those which attacked the capital for nearly three hours early Thursday, were said to have been "completely invisible" when the full glare of searchlights was turned upon them.

As result, it was asserted, the "German anti-aircraft guns protecting the capital were able to shoot only at the shadows which the raiders threw against the clouds."

The varnish, a thick black substance, was said to be painted on the underside of the wings of the British bombers and is a secret which the British alone possess.

After one British bomber was brought down recently the new-type varnish was discovered and German experts began making tests, the air force sources asserted.

The side of the wing painted with the varnish was held in the ray of an automobile headlight and "immediately became invisible."

◊ ◊ ◊

These same quarters said the British raiders had used shrewd tactics in their attacks on Berlin, such as flying at varying heights from 6,000 to 15,000 feet above the city. Their frequent variation of altitude, it was said, altered the tone of their motors and made difficult the work of the German sound-detecting apparatus.

The British planes were believed to have come over the city in several waves, with each wave apparently remaining 10 or 15 minutes over Berlin and then returning home, to be followed by another wave.

Berlin headquarters also said the British hits on the German capital were remarkable feats of navigation and suggested that veteran commercial air pilots probably carried out the attacks.

◊ ◊ ◊

(In London the suggestion of a "secret varnish" was termed a German excuse for the failure of Berlin searchlight crews to spot the British planes.)

Dana's article August 30, 1940

On September 25, Dana noted that *ACME's* Paris man—Graffia:

... finally succeeded in getting to Berlin and we have been going the rounds of the various important political contacts and picture sources together. I have been exceedingly interested to learn something about this picture business from an expert.

October 7:

Graffia has taken over most of my ACME work now, I having efficiently and energetically got him accredited and started and done myself out of a nice job. I really enjoyed it while it lasted. I don't mind a bit having to work all hours of day plus night if it's the right kind of work. About all that's left now is for me to write a monumental report to the bosses in New York and Buenos Aires giving them the lowdown on what I've found out about the picture situation in "the new capital of Europe."

Later, he noted:

Got a letter from Picture Editor Derman in New York thanking me and congratulating me on the good job I'd done for him. Well, that was nice, even if it was the first personal communication I'd had from him.

Graffia was planning a trip to Rome for *ACME* and Dana hoped to accompany him using the week-long holiday which he had accrued. When Graffia's trip was cancelled, Dana decided to go to Rome alone.

October 27:

Somehow I hoped for sunshine in Italy, but the opposite is the case. My airplane flew to Zurich through snow flurries and through dense clouds to Venice. At Venice we learned the plane would fly no further because of bad weather, so I was stranded for eight hours 'till I could catch the sleeper to

Rome. Unfortunately it was drizzly and dismal in Venice and I spent most of the time trying to get my letter of credit cashed.

I've just been out eating an enormous T-bone steak with the Packards[29] *.... I think I'm going to like this place. As we were going out to lunch a little while ago, Packard suddenly began shouting and, lo and behold, there was the Duce inspecting a new square, which had been created by tearing down some old buildings. I was "very lucky" as I was told to see him on my first day in town.*

A week later:

I was having a look at Frascati [an historic town] *in the Alban hills above Rome when the word suddenly came telling me to start collecting visas for a trip to Sofia immediately.* [That was just after the Italian invasion of Greece started.] *Much to my surprise everything was lined up in a day and the Orient Express got me here in no time.*

November 6, from Sofia:

This is the great day when Roosevelt has been reelected and the American Minister—ex Gov. Earl—is giving a cocktail party this evening in celebration.

I sent a rather good story out of here last night, but I imagine it had tough sledding with the election going full blast. It concerned the territory Bulgaria may get after the war if she fights for the Axis.

Sofia is a fascinating place, quite different from anything I've seen before. I'm told it's a dull place, but things seem pretty perky just now. Henry Gorrell was here when I arrived, but has now gone on to Saloniki [Thessaloniki, Greece]. *He is a fine fellow, except that he left his girl behind and I have to look out for her, more or less, 'till he comes back.*

---

[29] The Packards were heads of the *United Press* office in Rome.

I am now going to go to the Turkish ministry, and this evening the Bulgarian press chief is going to stop here to take me to the Minister's celebration. Just at the moment I am the only American newspaperman in town, although there are a number of Bulgarians representing American concerns. They have all gone on to Greece or Turkey, although some will come back. The English correspondents have also disappeared.

November 13:

My hotel room [Hotel Bulgaria] *faces out over the gardens of King Boris' palace, but there hasn't been any sign of life there yet.*

Last night I met the president of the American College at the British Press attache's home and on Saturday I'm going there to visit one of the teachers, who happens to be our former Munich correspondent. The number of American schools and colleges in this part of the world is quite astounding. They have a high reputation and have made Americans very well liked.

People here spend a great deal of their time sitting around in cafes drinking Turkish coffee, or "Cafe Americaine," which is just ordinary coffee, or "Viennese coffee," which appears to be something else again. They also drink a lot of a rather sticky and quite cheap cognac. I can't say that I enjoy Turkish coffee much. It seems too sweet. The best coffee I know of is still that obtainable at the Griddle Restaurant on Broadway opposite Columbia University.

Everyone has been exceedingly nice to me here. I've been out to dinner and lunch at a number of American, English and Bulgarian homes. People are much more considerate of a newspaperman here than they would be in Berlin. Of course as one man put it, in a little place like this, which hardly has been the center of international interest in recent years, we are very glad of any sort of new tea in the pot.

If I should stay here all winter and things should quiet down, I may be able to write some of those articles based on my last two years which I never had time for in Berlin.

ELIZABETH SCHMIDT CRAHAN

December 17, Hotel Londra, Istanbul:

In case my previous letters have not arrived, which is probable, since I have discovered there is no airmail from here, I will explain that I was sent to Istanbul to replace our previous correspondent, who was asked to leave as a result of some misunderstandings with the Turkish press authorities.

The first thing I did here, after watching my predecessor depart midst much gaiety, was to go to Ankara to get a press card. Everyone was very cordial, and I do not foresee any trouble. Ankara is an extraordinary place which reminds me of Boulder City [Colorado] . . . built by and for the government in the midst of a semi-desert. Most of it is in modernistic pre-Nazi German style, but there is an old town built on the sides of a steep hill under an old Roman fortress. Its streets are narrow, cobble-stoned and unsanitary, and lined with the real thing in Turkish bazaars. Old men and small boys stagger up and down carrying enormous loads of goods of all kinds, coal, and . . . water. Everywhere water is sold at a fraction of a cent per glass. Another part of the town consists of corrugated iron huts reminiscent of a "Hoover-town," where the workmen attracted by the new capital live. Peasants come into the town in the slack farming seasons wearing the most ragged rags on earth; after they have earned some money on a construction job, or at some other heavy labor, they buy a fine new suit and depart to the village. I imagine that well over half the population is illiterate.

Istanbul, alias Constantinople, is of course much more extraordinary than Ankara, but I haven't yet had time to see much of it. There are some good restaurants, and one good hotel, at which I am not staying. However, this will do until I find a flat with a telephone, which is a problem. One thing shocking to me to see are the half-naked beggars, women and children, in the streets in this horrible weather.

At Ankara I met a lot of very nice people, including the former London Times *Berlin correspondent, and here I am gradually getting to know people too. I have a young Turkish newspaperman to read the newspapers and act as tipster here and a Turkish girl who is the daughter of the chief of the official agency to keep an eye on things in Ankara, so I'm pretty well protected. It's amazing how I've improved my French here and in Sofia, where everyone speaks it and most of the news comes out in it. German is rarely heard here, as you can imagine.*

The former Havas [30] *bureau chief in Berlin is also here, representing the Free French Agency. I had lunch with him yesterday.*

I will mail this letter to Sofia for remailing by airmail. None of your letters have reached me since I left Berlin on the 24th of October. I am not worrying though, as I know you would cable if anything very noteworthy or disastrous were to happen. If ever you really can't get in touch with me, you can send a wire to Virgil Pinkley at Zurich, or to Joe Alex Moore, the head cable editor, in New York [often referred to by Dana as Jalex].

December 21:

Quite the most pleasant correspondents I have met are Agronsky, [31] *the* NBC *man at Ankara, and Fowle of* Time, CBS *and an English paper. Agronsky is a rather tough-looking Jewish man, the one who flew over Brindisi in a British bomber a while back. He is extraordinarily hardworking . . . and gets a large salary from* NBC. *It seems silly, and is a thing radio people will probably get away from, but a radio job doesn't carry the same prestige as a newspaper job here.*

Although it was a long time since the election, Dana commented on it again in this letter to his Grandmother:

Sorry you were disappointed about the election. Almost all Americans abroad were pleased, with astonishing unanimity. I don't know a newspaperman in Berlin who is not a supporter of Roosevelt. That is because we are chiefly interested in the issues of foreign policy and because his defeat would have been

---

[30] A French news service.
[31] Martin Agronsky (1915-1999) was a well-known journalist and television moderator for *Face the Nation* from 1965-1969. Later, he hosted a program called *At Issues* and a news program called *Agronsky and Company*.

Dana with fellow reporters outside a public building in Ankara, Turkey

interpreted as a weakness and a sign of disunity. Inside America one can have little idea what prestige the name Roosevelt carries to most foreigners. Also, the fact that persons of a certain political slant were so anxious to be rid of him would have made Roosevelt's defeat seem like a German victory.

Shortly before Christmas, the American consul took Dana to see the magnificent and unforgettable Hagia Sophia and to meet a young architect named Robert Van Nice, who was studying the building. [32]

. . . so I was introduced to the place by an expert. Until about 1929 it was used as a mosque, but now it is exclusively a museum and the remarkable Byzantine frescoes and mosaics are being divested of Islamic paint by an

---

[32]   See Appendix.

American expert named Thomas Whittemore. The place has been shaken by earthquakes and altered and rebuilt so often that there is not a symmetrical arch, or two alike, in the entire building. They seem to have been squeezed like putty through the centuries and have assumed extraordinary shapes.

Waiting for Hitler's arrival at the Turnverein [Gymnastics Club], 1941
Photo by Dana A. Schmidt

1941

Dana spent most of 1941 in Istanbul and Ankara, but in late November, he was transferred to Cairo. This turbulent year of the war provided Dana with much work and many stories. Turkey was in a precarious position as guardian of the Dardanelles and the Bosphorus, gates to the Mediterranean, the Black Sea and the Caucasus. On the south, Syria provided access to the oil of Iraq and Iran, coveted by Germany and Britain. On the north, the Nazis in Rumania, and the threat of German attack through Bulgaria, added to the insecurity of the Turks. The Soviet Union, on the southeastern border of Turkey, not yet firmly on the side of the Allies, was considered a possible aggressor. War seemed to be coming ever closer to Turkey.

Dana produced a wealth of dispatches covering this complicated war zone, which were published in an array of papers that subscribed to the *United Press Service*.

Despite the demands of his work, Dana managed to write his weekly letters to Mother and the family, avoiding mention of dangers but instead concentrating on the social world of diplomacy, vital to his work. He also wrote about everyday life, lost dogs, and trips to the bazaars and beaches. Neither the British, American nor Turkish censors would allow references to geographical entities and sensitive material.

Soon after the New Year began, he found an apartment complete with a maid and was able to move from the Hotel Londra. He said he had things in fairly smooth working order, and on January 10, wrote home:

Tomorrow I am having a really rather large "drop in for a drink" party from six p.m. in the evening on. The idea is to christen, baptize, house-warm and generally break in the apartment. But don't think I am being extravagant. The party is the sort of thing any new correspondent has to do, and the flat is most modest.

He was indebted to the many people who had welcomed him to Istanbul and entertained him.

Today, I had a talk with the foreign minister, Saracoglu, who is here over the Kourban Bayram holiday, when good Moslems sacrifice a sheep to bring them good fortune. Saracoglu was very friendly and very interesting, but unfortunately the talk was not supposed to be an interview, but merely for my information. It is funny how easily such meetings are arranged sometimes. I had feared that it would be difficult; but when I sent in my card to Saracoglu's secretary at the Park Hotel, he came right out and five minutes later ushered me into the great presence. Saracoglu seemed rather a professorial sort of man, I think he would get on well with Doctor Story at Pomona, for instance. He doesn't look very Turkish, probably Greek ancestry.

Day before yesterday my Turkish assistant and I went to the bazaar and I bought some brass silver-plated candle sticks for the dining room table, a little pestle and mortar which can be used as a bell on the table, and a standard for a lamp consisting of a thing that was used to hold a big candle in a mosque. I think they are all quite attractive. Relative to other things here they were cheap enough, but considering the rate of exchange, I paid plenty. Anyway, I think they would be nice to have anywhere.

The other night I had the head of the local British Information Office [BIO] to dinner here, and next week I'm having the American Consul and BIO's assistant. Today the Bulgarian Press attache is coming to lunch. And the American Naval attache has been here many times. So, I'm getting full value out of my place.

One of my friends from Sofia, Derrick Patmore, of the News-Chronicle, *has been transferred here. It is nice to have people around with whom you can exchange news, without feeling that you are consorting with the enemy.*

Actually, my enemies, the Hancocks, of A.P., are about the nicest people in town.

In January, Dana's *UP* dispatches reported that the British under General Archibald Wavell achieved a decisive victory over the Italians in Libya. This aroused fears among the Nazis that Wavell would bring his forces to Greece, where the Axis had already established a foothold. Indeed the British and Americans did soon come to Greece.

In his February 2 letter home, he wrote:

Last night the American Consul, Fred Latimer, and Mr. and Mrs. Parker of the British Information Office came to dinner. My maid did beautifully; the table looked nice with its candle sticks and for the first time I had the little living room lighted with the lamp made out of the old mosque candlestick. I am getting to be an old woman with my household affairs.

Next Sunday I am invited to the American Girls' College for dinner and am supposed to "interview" a Turkish editor for the benefit of the girls and their guests. It would appear that the editor involved says he can't make a speech, so they thought up this stunt. Fortunately, I have got the A.P. man, Hancock, to come along and help, so it may not be too bad.

The other day when I was seeing off Donovan at the American Embassy, I suddenly ran across Stevens, the Christian Science Monitor *correspondent I knew in Stockholm. The* Monitor *has, after months*

Dana interviewing Sir John Thompson, diplomat, 1941

of prodding, allowed him to go home to see his family. The condition was that he take the "journalistically most interesting route" through Turkey and the near east to Cairo and by airplane across Africa and up to Lisbon. I wouldn't mind that sort of thing a bit.

It still takes all my concentration to remember my address and write it down correctly. The trouble really is that up to quite recently there were no street numbers and often no names . . . one merely lived in a certain section of town in a house of a certain name. My street's name means "Foreign office palace," because the Foreign Minister had his residence hereabouts once upon a time, but the name of my apartment "Giermati" is much more important.

Dana's address at his flat in Istanbul was:
Hariciye konagi 7-9,
Giermati apt 5,
Ayaspasa, Istanbul
Often Dana's letters began with a complaint about the mail.

Many letters to this country [from the U.S.] are three months en route. The problem appears to be that for some obscure political reasons mail to us is routed via Rumania instead of through Sofia, Bulgaria and comes down on a boat about once a week; also there is no airmail out of this country until the letter gets to Belgrade, because the Turks don't use the Lufthansa which comes down all the way to Sofia. What happens to airmail letters coming this way I don't know. Outgoing airmail letters have to be presented at the post office in person.

Beginning in February 1941, Turkey and her relationship with Bulgaria were the source of many of Dana's news reports and much nervousness in Turkey. The Turkish non-aggression pact with Bulgaria seemed to ease the situation, but later Turkey repudiated the pact because Bulgaria had permitted German forces to cross Bulgarian territory to attack Greece through Thrace.

A story that provided comfort to the Turks concerned saboteurs in Bulgaria and Rumania. Dana reported that they were said to have produced the greatest sabotage campaign ever seen in southeastern Europe. The saboteurs dynamited at least two German oil trains, blew up bridges and cut through telegraph lines. When sixty French prisoners from a concentration camp were ordered to repair damage to a big oil pipeline done by saboteurs, they created new leaks themselves.

Later in February, Dana wrote an important report, printed in a number of papers, concerning a meeting of British Foreign Minister Anthony Eden with Turkey's Minister Sükrü Saracoglu, at which they reached an agreement bolstering their alliance against Germany's invasion of the Balkan countries.

Other February dispatches detailed Germany's overtures to Turkey in an attempt to win the right to bring German troops across Turkey to access the oil-rich countries of Iran and Iraq. But as Dana put it: *Turkey refused all blandishments. Turkey will remain faithful to her alliances.* Among the German offers were gifts of some of the Aegean islands the Germans had taken from Greece.

In March, Dana wrote about American power beginning to materialize in the Balkans following the passage of the Lend-Lease Act on March 4, which gave Roosevelt the authority to direct

Nazis Pitch Woo to Turks
BY DANA ADAMS SCHMIDT
ANKARA, March 20 — (UP) — German diplomats are hurriedly tightening their grip on the Balkans, brushing aside the ancient hatreds and intrigues of those countries in an attempt to line them up for her spring offensive against Russia, it was reported tonight.

Reports from Sofia said Bulgaria's cabinet had capitulated to German pressure and agreed to declare war on Russia before the German spring drive, and that the Bulgarian minister here, Kiro Kiroff, will go to Sofia soon to report on the Turkish attitude toward this development.

Franz von Papen, German ambassador to Turkey, has gone home, presumably to report on the general Balkan situation, and the United States, taking a hand in the diplomatic play to keep Turkey out of the Axis camp, reportedly has started a substantial flow of armaments to Turkey under the lend-lease agreement.

Frank Kaufman, special assistant to United States Ambassador Laurence A. Steinhardt in connection with lend-lease matters, arrived in Turkey today from the United States, and coincidentally it was said that some American armaments for Turkey already had arrived in the Middle East and that more were on the seas.

(The Stockholm newspaper Demokraten said in a dispatch from its Berlin correspondent that Germany had proposed that Turkey join the war on the Axis side, with the reward of Syria and a protectorate over Iran and Mosul in event of an Axis victory. The Turkish ambassador to Berlin, he said, was en route to Ankara with the proposal.

(The Stockholm paper also asserted that Papen's trip to Germany was to discuss this proposal and it added that the German press has revived its interest in Gibraltar.)

Dana's article March 20, 1941

material aid to countries furthering the war effort in Europe, the Middle East and Asia.

In Istanbul, the threat of invasion was so great that the government ordered the evacuation of civilians to the interior of Turkey. The government provided transportation for all who were willing to leave. Istanbul had a population of 880,000 at that time.

Dana's stories concerning the bombing and apparent attempted assassination of the British Minister to Bulgaria, George Rendel, were published in many papers. Rendel and his entourage arrived at the Pera Palas Hotel in Istanbul. Bombs that had been hidden surreptitiously in their luggage exploded shortly after their arrival, killing six people and doing serious damage to the hotel. It may have been an attempt by the Nazis to obtain important papers, which the Minister was thought to have with him.

In mid-March, the confrontation between the Germans and British in Greece was a major concern.

Dana wrote under the headlines:

NAZIS 150,000 MEN AHEAD IN BIG RACE
By DANA ADAMS SCHMIDT

Another great battle between British and German troops—10 months after Dunkirk and the collapse of France—appeared in the making last night (March 18) as reports from Greece told of British troops arriving there in a steady stream. Some 200,000 British troops were said to have arrived in Greece already, with more arriving daily.

From Bulgaria, meanwhile came reports that the Germans were still pouring into the country on Greece's frontier and now totaled 350,000 men. . . . Despite reports that the Germans in Bulgaria are so distributed that they could attack either Turkey or Greece, Turkey as yet has not allowed the British to establish bases on land or air forces on her own territory.

The British are staying in very close touch with the Turks, nevertheless, maintaining permanent liaison officers in Ankara and making ready men and material in Iraq, from where they could be rushed to Turkey on short notice.

In late March, Dana reported that Turkey and Russia had signed a joint restatement of friendship and non-aggression intentions, removing the fear that Russia might attack Turkey from the rear (in the Caucasus) while she was fighting the Germans on another front. The Russian / Turkish declaration implied that there was some increase in a rapprochement between Russia and Britain.

Meanwhile, in his letter home on March 23, Dana wrote:

Last Sunday I took a beautiful walk out on the Bosphorus. I went with Gedye, of the New York Times, *the local Free Frenchman, and several others, out past Bebek, where Roberts College is located, to the old fortifications which the Turks stormed in the mid-fifteenth century. We ducked under an arch and found we could walk right into the old fortifications and walls. A post office and a lot of ramshackle slum houses have been built inside. What may have been a moat or a well is now a pea green stagnant pool. We climbed right through this remarkable place, up the hill, and then came down around Roberts College to a magnificent fish dinner. We were going to have fresh lobster out of the Bosphorus, but discovered in time that nothing had been caught in that vicinity for months and all the lobster were being brought out from the Istanbul market. Having seen the Istanbul marketplace, I prefer to stick to whatever is fresh.*

In his letter at the end of March, Dana made some observations about people living abroad at that time. Certainly, by now, he was a little lonely for true companionship.

Everyone out here seems just a trifle abnormal to me. One reason for that is that almost all the English speaking people are refugees from somewhere; and another reason is that foreigners living in the Balkans always seem to become a little abnormal; the war and the nervousness it causes don't help either. The foreigners in Balkan countries live on a social island, detached from the real life of the country, detached from the standards, restraints and reality of their own homes. I think it's a lousy way to live. I wouldn't mind if I never saw the inside of another hotel, bar, nightclub or embassy again. I would like to go for a climb on Mount Baldy [near Pomona College] and sleep in the Ski Hut and feel that I am a human being again. All the diplomats have to do is chase each other's tails, and the newspapermen chase around after them.

Everybody is trying to find out something from everybody else. It is difficult to get an invitation to a real Turkish home; and once one is there, there is no real companionship; I am just a spy trying to find out how they live; and they are uneasy and self-conscious, half afraid that I am contemptuous. That was true in Germany and it is more true in a country which is semi-oriental, such as Turkey. A person who really does "live in" and becomes a part of his environment, has "gone native" and is regarded with contempt by the foreigners he has deserted. This is the more true here because most Anglo-Saxon foreigners consider themselves superior to their foreign environment. Only in England, I believe, would an American gain in social status by "going native" and then only under some circumstances.

(Being a foreign correspondent means living on the fringes of the life of the country he is "observing," for an observer is never accepted by the subjects of his attention. It is "interesting" in an intellectual sort of way, and it may occasionally involve some pleasure. But it is not a very satisfactory sort of life. It is too limited, too introverted, too nervous and too artificial.)

Another thing that affects the foreigners here—lack of women. Most of the American and English women have been sent to places which are supposed to be safer.

The war is getting pretty close now. There's a chance that I'll move up to Ankara before we are ordered to do so.

In the meantime, life went on in Istanbul:

Tomorrow night Claire Hollingsworth and I have organized a party which will wind up in the gypsy section of Istanbul. Some sort of entertainment, dancing and singing, is said to be available there—just inside the ancient walls of Constantinople. First there will be an informal beer and sausage supper at Claire's apartment. Gedye, Tuggle, the Naval Attache, Mrs. St. John, wife of the A.P. correspondent now in Belgrade, will be along.

During the week before the [German] attack on Yugoslavia, I got in a tremendous amount of tennis. Played almost every morning with my Turkish assistant and got quite sunburned. Unfortunately, my racket, along with most of my clothes, is still in Berlin, so I had to buy a new one.

Realizing that he was soon to leave Istanbul, he wrote:

Sometimes in the drab streets of this town one suddenly comes upon a view of the Bosphorus, or the Golden Horn, with ships and mosques that is shockingly beautiful. Today the Bosphorus was unbelievably deep blue. We were looking out at it from Cedric Salter's flat when the Soviet boat came in, shining and white with music blaring, presumably to show how happy everybody is on a Soviet boat. Unfortunately, I am told, they make the beds only once on every voyage of this boat. It was built in Scandinavia with all sorts of gorgeous gymnasiums, playrooms and nurseries, etc. But the Russians closed up all these places of frivolity.

I have, incidentally, been greatly helped by exchanging news with Martin Agronsky the NBC man in Ankara. He is very good, but a frightful prima donna, and consequently difficult to get on with. He just cannot bear the thought, refuses to recognize that he might be wrong, or that somebody might have a story he missed.

On April 30, Dana wrote:

I've managed to play a good deal of tennis and get quite brown, in spite of the critical times. Also, an American courier, one Jimmy Scott, asked me to have dinner with him. For an hour we talked of sundry things, and finally worked around to Hamburg. He had spent a number of years there, as some sort of U.S. Trade Commissioner and lo and behold, he knew you [Mother] and

Father. He knew the Bells, the Willgresses, the Heinleins, Landis's, Schroeders, Sommers, and many others. He also knew the Kurusus and maintains that he had dinner at our apartment on Hartungstrasse.

Dana must have been pleased to meet someone who remembered his family and knew many of his old friends.
In May:

Things are relatively quiet just now, and I have received reinforcements to boot. One Ben Ames, formerly manager of our Athens bureau has been sent here to help me, in case we have events similar to those in Greece . . . . We get on very well and his presence will give me a chance to get up to Ankara more often and perhaps see some of the rest of the country and perhaps take a day off now and then. He (Ames) came out of Athens with a convoy and then flew from Cairo to Adana via Cypress.

To answer your question about reporters at United Press—*some of our really good men are Fred Oechsner, Joseph Grigg, Cliff Day, and Pat Conger.*

Our best spot-reporter, in my opinion, is Ed Beattie, whose by-lines you probably see often. A very swell fellow—I knew him well of course at my old post [Berlin].

Yesterday I went swimming at a beach called Floria with Henderson of the British Press Office, Jouve, the Free Frenchman, their wives, George Tabori, the Hungarian who works with me and a pair of girls from the Taxim Casino, also Hungarian. Floria . . . can't compare with our humblest California beaches. However, sunshine and air and water are about the same all over.

For reasons that are all too clear, the lousy proprietor of my finally deloused apartment has decided that hot water two days a week is plenty during the summer. If I had known that he was going to try to make money that way I never would have moved in here. But, it is too much trouble to move when any day might be my day of departure to Ankara. So many people have left Istanbul for points which are considered safer that there are many fine apartments to be had <u>cheap</u>.

.... and at the end of May:

My reinforcement, Ben Ames, hasn't been much use yet as he has been ill with bronchitis most of the time and doesn't leave his room much.

My Turkish stringer in Ankara, Nermin Menemencioglu, threatens to get married shortly. I thought the danger was imminent and went to Ankara partly to see about a new correspondent but found that the war had slowed things up. She is to marry a British flying officer now in Cairo (greatest gesture of Anglo-Turkish friendship since the alliance was signed, she says). So I didn't hand over the wedding present I had brought along and the other night I gave it to another couple, this one Turkish-American. My present was a silver snuff box, gold plated, with a stone, the name of which I have forgotten, on the top. It may have belonged to a Sultan and could be used for cigarettes. Cost about seven dollars. By the way, I've got the best man in the bazaar looking for the right kind of after dinner coffee cups for Elizabeth. [33] *I also bought some Persian prints and two Byzantine coins—altogether a terrific splurge (in the bazaar).*

Dana regretted leaving this post. On June 6, he wrote:

It is very nice here in Istanbul just now, and it's a great shame to go off to Ankara which is hot and dusty.

Last Sunday I went out to Prinkipo with a young English professor from Roberts College and spent some three hours vigorously walking right around the island.

I haven't had time for much swimming but have been out to restaurants along the Bosphorus for dining frequently. Some of the big places in town have open air restaurants too, which are very pleasant in the evening.

---

[33] He did find some and sent them to me, but unfortunately, they were broken when they arrived. Dana made several additional attempts to give me Turkish cups, but they all failed.

> *There is one reason why I am not entirely sorry to go to Ankara. . . . There are still bugs in my apartment. They appear to be ineradicable.*

June was an eventful month in the war. Dana wrote extensively on the British and Free French invasion of Syria, where the Vichy French and Germany had seized power on June 1, 1940. Syria would be a convenient stepping stone on Germany's path to the oil fields of Iraq and Iran. The Germans maintained a shuttle plane service between the Dodecanese Islands and Syria "to transport war material and soldiers disguised as civilians." [34] At the end of the first week of hostilities, it was evident that the Allies would prevail, to the great relief of the "jubilant" Turks, as Dana said, who were concerned with the German-backed Syrians on their long border.

A widely distributed dispatch of June 7 received bold headlines in the Washington D.C. *Times Herald*:

FREE FRENCH AND BRITISH ENTER SYRIA
NAZIS ALSO REPORTED FLYING OVER TURKEY TO THE
FRENCH MANDATE

Swarms of airplanes presumably German, are flying into Syria in the direction of the great airport of Aleppo reports from Alexandretta said tonight.

The roar of planes flying over the southern tip of Turkey constantly fills the air . . . and two German planes have made forced landings near Alexandretta . . . about 15 miles from the Syrian border at the closest point and about 60 miles west of Aleppo, one of the four large airports built by the French in the mandated area.

There was ample evidence the Germans were organizing Syrian airdromes [airports]. . . .

Although the conflict appeared to be raging with increasing intensity ever nearer Turkish shores . . . government circles (in Ankara) appeared calmer than at any time since the start of German infiltration in Syria.

---

[34]   See Appendix.

This calmness, it was said, was based on rumors reaching official quarters that German troop concentrations in the south Balkans were being decreased.

The rumors were interpreted as meaning that Germany was withdrawing troops, possibly for an invasion attempt against Britain or to strengthen forces facing Russia.

There was growing belief in informed Turkish quarters that Germany does not intend to make Syria a stage in a great campaign against the Suez Canal, but rather a diversion for British forces in the Middle East.

In his June 13 letter home, Dana wrote:

I have just come down from Ankara after a three day visit and am going back up there tonight. It seems that now the chief interest is to the south [in Syria]. Ankara is the better news center.[35] *I am moving my household, including the maid and her husband to Ankara and am moving them into Martin Agronsky's flat. I am replacing his flat-mate, Jimmy Holburn of the* London Times *who has been transferred to Palestine.*

The place is quite nice . . . and was formerly the home of the ex-Minister of Justice, Fethi Okyar.

We have been out playing baseball again—Americans vs. British Embassy, he wrote on July 7. *And this time the Americans only managed to win by one run. I find these Sunday baseball sessions fun although I really never played before. As for that other great American pastime poker, I think I'll let it go for a while. It's too expensive.*

We have been doing a good deal of entertaining at our flat. Tonight the new Counselor at the British Embassy is coming to dinner and tomorrow night we are having the British air attache over.

Bob Law, the Liberty *writer who was captured in Syria, and I went into a tennis tournament here the other day, but came out with great rapidity, with a score of 6-0, 6-0* [they lost]. *The courts here are lovely, however, a real pleasure to play on.*

---

[35] The Free French and British troops re-occupied Syria, beginning June 8, 1941.

My maid and her husband from Istanbul, have come up here to take care of the flat, as I mentioned previously. We found that Martin's former servant had got his room simply crawling with bugs. We had to get a new bed and have the room cleaned with alcohol and whitewashed.

I have applied for a visa to Moscow but don't have much hopes of getting there before the Germans do. It would probably be an Experience with a capital E if one could get in. Practically everyone here is trying to go.

On July 10, Dana was the first to report the terms of the British / Vichy Armistice before either London or Vichy newspapers published them. Important among the provisions was that British authorities demanded Vichy forces in Syria hand over all warships in Syrian waters and all other war equipment.

Meanwhile, in a letter home on July 13, Dana wrote:

We have had a number of fairly good stories here lately, including the terms of the armistice in Syria, which we had about four days before they were published in London or Vichy.

I wish that Ben Ames could take over the whole show for me for a while so that I could take a holiday. I really feel that I am due one. Not that we lead a bad life here in Ankara. Last night Alma deLucy, the wife of the A.P. correspondent here, got up a picnic at the dam, or "barrage" behind which Ankara's water supply is accumulated. There is a very pretty park out there, and the flowing water makes it seem cool. It reminds me of Boulder Dam on a miniature scale.

Night before last we were invited to dinner, Martin and I, at the home of one of the secretaries of the British Embassy. They had a buffet supper on the roof from where we watched a remarkable display of heat lightning. Then we went below to play THE game 'till three in the morning. THE game has addled the brains of many of the diplomats and correspondents here; it is simply a form of charades, but when taken in large doses I find that it disturbs the mental equilibrium. Some people have been playing it nightly down at the Ankara Palace.

We seem to have defeated the bugs in our house at last. But now we are confronted with mosquito and fly problems. Screens are unknown in this part of the world. We have hung up strips of gluey paper, but find that the flies get rather unsightly . . . . Every night the insects come and feast on our exposed heads, hands and feet. Sometimes it isn't even funny; there is a type of insect called the sandfly which sometimes imparts a very unpleasant "sandfly fever."

Otherwise we are very comfortable in this flat. Our cook produces remarkable American nut-bread and doughnuts. She is going to try some brownies, using your recipe. We have people in to lunch and dinner a good deal.

July 24:

Dana playing tennis

Not much in a news way at the moment and I've had time for tennis almost daily. It gets blistering hot, but one can stand it for an hour. I am beginning to understand why some people hate Ankara like the pest. It is the monotony . . . a small crowd of people you see again and again, only two decent restaurants, few amusements; in other words, small town, no variety. Reporting consists almost exclusively of "embassy touring," calling on one diplomat after another. As it happens, this procedure yields a good deal of news around here, but it does get tiresome, especially for the men who have been doing real frontline reporting.

We have all been wondering what will happen to us if, or perhaps I should say when, we come into the war. It looks as though most of us would be used for some sort of intelligence work, probably right in the region where we are now located.

We are still crowing about our Syrian armistice terms story, which beat Cairo by a week. Some people from Cairo tell us that the newspaper boys there were gnashing their teeth.

I am now sending my letters by my special secret route which I believe is quite good. Hope you're getting them. [36]

August 1:

Well, we've got a new dog. Our Great Dane was taken away to Istanbul by its owner. This is a cross between a bloodhound, a pointer, a setter, and a spaniel. Not exactly a prize specimen, but he was so devoted and grateful and sad-looking right from the start that we haven't had the heart to send him away. We've had all our friends in town looking out for dogs for us for a month, and now it is suddenly raining dogs. Tonight a setter puppy is to arrive and tomorrow morning some other kind of puppy is rumored to be coming to our house. Maybe we will start a menagerie. Dogs are hard to get in this country because the Turks don't like them, for religious reasons. [37] *Pure-bred dogs are almost impossible to find.*

Our pup's name, so we were told, is Jimmy. He doesn't answer to it but we are teaching him, we hope. He is as scrawny as the dogs in Esquire *cartoons of Tennessee mountaineers, but we'll fix that too. We had him out to the vet's the other day and ascertained that he has no serious ailments and isn't much more than two and a half years old. But we think he has worms and plan to send him to the vet for a course of treatments. When he came he seemed so lacking in energy that it was all he could do to get back up on his feet once he was lying down.*

---

[36] Mail from Europe was always undependable during the War. Occasionally, Dana found someone who was returning to the States to carry it, or a friend in the diplomatic service, who would add it to the diplomatic pouch.
[37] See Appendix.

We are still entertaining a good deal. The other night we had a buffet supper for some twelve people from the British Embassy. Before dinner we had drinks at one of their homes. It seems to me that they are an unusually nice crowd. Perhaps our being all together in such a small town helps.

I was really shocked when I heard Betty Averill had been married. Although I hadn't been quite conscious of it, she was the only girl left in America in whom I was in any way interested. In fact I was furious when I heard she was married already. Curiously enough, early in June I got the idea to write her several letters, but I suppose they arrived after the marriage. There is no doubt she is first rate in every respect and quite the best girl I knew at college. I should be pleased to hear that the marriage had not taken place, or that something had happened to the groom.

During his college years, Dana was very fond of Betty Averill, a student at nearby Scripps College. They often went skiing together. They kept up regular correspondence throughout Dana's college years and travels. Betty's father, Harry B. Averill, was a writer and the publisher of the *Mount Vernon Daily Herald* in the Pacific Northwest. When Dana went to Europe on the Pulitzer traveling fellowship, Mr. Averill gave him the letter of introduction to the head of *United Press* in London which helped Dana obtain his job.

Dana's letters home were filled with stories of his beloved dogs and his domestic and social life. Of course, he covered the political events, often in great detail, in his newspaper articles.

ANKARA, Aug. 7 (UP)—A purported German peace plan, offering the liberation of Nazi-held Western Europe and respect for the entire British empire, circulated today among diplomats who heard that the offer would be launched if and when Germany's armies strike across Russia to the Urals.

There was no confirmation that the so-called peace plan actually came from Berlin, but it was disclosed that two unidentified officials of the German foreign office had arrived in Turkey by special plane to confer with German Ambassador Baron Franz von Papen.

Von Papen was reported seeking to establish contact with the British ambassador here, Sir Hughe Knatenbull-Huggessen, to persuade Britain to disassociate herself from the Russian-German war. The Germans were represented as anxious to persuade the British that the time had come to abandon a "useless" struggle between the two great "Aryan" powers.

A special German plane arrived at Istanbul airport Tuesday night with two men and three women who immediately rushed to von Papen's summer embassy residence. German officials refused to divulge the names of the individuals but said they were officials of the foreign office in Berlin.

Under the reported peace plan Germany would cease hostilities on all fronts for a time after obtaining her objectives in Russia and rely upon public opinion in the United States to force Britain to halt the war on these seven conditions.

1. A 25-year German occupation of Russia as far as the Ural mountains, meaning the occupation of Moscow, Kiev and other large centers, and a semiautonomous Ukraine under the direction of Dr. Alfred Rosenburg, the chief administrator of German-occupied Russia.
2. A semi-autonomous Poland generally consisting of an extension of the present German occupied Polish territory to include those parts of Eastern Poland seized by Russia in 1939.
3. British and United States recognition of Germany's right to freedom of action in eastern Europe whereby the Czechs would be given a restricted autonomy, but not reunion with the Slovaks and only Rumania, Hungary and Bulgaria would be regarded as permanently under German "protection" as they are now.
4. Parts of the territories of Jugoslavia and Greece would be given varying degrees of restricted autonomy.
5. Germany would evacuate Norway, Denmark, Holland, Belgium and France, retaining only Alsace-Lorraine which is former German territory.
6. Italy would regain Ethiopia and restore the situation existing after her 1936 conquest, would retain Libya and obtain Tunisia from France.

7. The territories of the British empire would in no way be affected by the settlement.

Some diplomatic observers in Ankara said they were convinced the Germans, having encountered heavy troubles in Russia, are now seriously worried in view of the growing British-United States power, even if they ultimately defeat the Russians.

Later in August, he wrote to Mother:

Yesterday was one of the most enjoyable days I have spent up here. We went to a Turkish village for the day. One of the men at the radio station knew the headman of the village and arranged for us to eat lunch in his vineyard and to be shown around.

We drove more than an hour over remarkably unkempt roads and absolutely barren hills to the village—a couple of hundred mud huts. Not a single building of stone or timber, since neither of these substances are to be found for some distance around. The only trees are in the valleys where they are carefully irrigated.

It is harvest time and the wheat is being threshed from dawn to dusk, in exactly the same way it was done here five hundred years ago. The wheat is spread out in a circle on the ground. The peasant, or one of his sons and daughters down to the age of five, stands on a wooden "sled" which has sharp stones fitted into its bottom and drives his horses, pulling the sled, round and round over the wheat. The horse's hoofs and the sled, over a period of more than a month, shred the wheat to a point where it can be tossed into the air to let the wind blow away the chaff.

Almost all of the farm implements in the village were made out of wood. They had some Russian tractors, but they fell apart. Four Russian tractor seats were, in fact, the seating accommodations on the "porch" where we had lunch. They say the German tractors are not much better in the stony Anatolian soil and that American tractors, which will stand up to all tests, are unobtainable now. The village carpenter follows the men around in the fields and sits near them during the threshing to repair their wooden tools as fast as they break.

We gathered that the most notable improvement in the village since it had last been visited by foreigners, about a year ago, was that the head man had acquired a pair of earphones for his radio.

These peasants are poorer and more primitive than any of the Balkan peasants. It should interest Mr. H. [Hitler] that most of them hereabout are blond, especially in youth, and many are blue-eyed. The children get such burns on their faces from the unvarying summer sun that their cheeks look like burned paper. I am told that racially they are a Celtic type. Of course the Turks are very much mixed. Other sections are dark and even Mongolian in appearance.

Late in the day we drove to a lake set in totally barren hills for a swim. The water is almost stagnant and slightly saline. In any event the water was delightfully soft and warm.

Unfortunately, although this excursion was most interesting, Dana, Martin Agronsky and the man accompanying them were all three quite ill with intestinal problems the next day. The following week, he wrote:

Last night we had Mr. Kelly, Counselor of our Embassy and the doctor who looked after us, to dinner. The doctor was one of the most famous doctors in Germany before Hitler. We are doing our best to cover something of the Iranian War from here, but it's difficult since there are no communications with that country at present. We had a man on his way to Teheran, but he got there too late. Unfortunately the A.P. got their man there. The situation was reversed, however, in the case of Syria.

September 9:

I am waiting for the communique about the end of the Turkish-German trade negotiations. I hate times like this. Everything is so loosely organized here that one never knows where the information will come from first, the agency, the foreign affairs office, the German delegation, a tipster, or goodness knows what.

We are having a spell of most splendid weather here. Cold at night and brilliant sunshine during the days. Down in Istanbul it is already quite rainy and nasty. We hope to play tennis here until the end of November.

Did I tell you about Jimmy's fight at the tennis courts? I was sitting peacefully holding Jimmy on his leash when a large Airedale belonging to the manager of the courts leapt upon Jimmy without warning. Being what he is Jimmy fled as best he could, actually breaking the leash, while Martin broke his tennis racket clean in half on the head of the Airedale. As far as I can make out we are still more or less persona non grata at the courts, although we are not actually chased off when we appear.

Another unfortunate aspect of our dog-life is that local chicken-owners have acquired a most annoying habit of claiming that our dog has slaughtered any number of their fowl.

It is all my fault because, not knowing the real value of a chicken, I once gave a woman two and a half pounds for a chicken which Shakey had killed [another dog who had since been run over and killed]. *This so pleased the proprietors of chickens that they would like our dogs to kill as many chickens as possible and, in fact, claim that Jimmy does so, although the poor dog never takes the slightest notice of chickens.*

September 10:

It was fine to receive your birthday cable. I had honestly forgotten all about it being my birthday 'till I got the cable about noon. At first I couldn't imagine what it was all about. I didn't do anything about it being my birthday, except feel rather shocked to be 27. [Later, he realized he was only 26.] *I still feel about college sophomore age and could slip back into that life without hesitation. Three years ago on my birthday I landed in Antwerp.*

Speaking of Martin Agronsky: He guessed the time of the outbreak of the Iranian campaign[38] *so closely that the Mid Eastern General Staff sent a telegram to the British Embassy asking where he was getting his information. But the British know his value, and the Germans genuinely hate and fear him. The German Embassy protests continually about his stuff at the foreign office, and there is danger he will be put off the air. Anything like straight news is so rare a thing in this part of the world that he has a huge listening public all over the Middle East; comments have even come in from India and Sweden. I suppose the point is that he is really talented and temperamental, completely egotistical, but fundamentally sensitive and can produce genuine charm when he wants to.*

September 16:

I hope to begin broadcasting my news to New York the way the New York Times *does . . . . If the office okays my plans and reception is satisfactory, I'll be on the air from 20.05 GMT*[39] *'till 20.15 GMT every night on nine four six five (9465) kilocycles. I'm afraid it is most unlikely that you will be able to hear me at that hour on the Pacific Coast. It's unlikely that even New York will be able to get me at that hour as a matter of fact, and I may have to try a later hour. But London and Zurich will be able to pick me up I believe, which in itself should be a saving in time and money.*

The mail nips through pretty regularly now. A few days ago your letter of August 18, and yesterday Elizabeth's of August 21 [arrived]. *I think I have a pretty good family when it comes to letter writing. Practically no one else around here gets any letters. Most people seem to feel so remote that they just give up letters altogether. And the Embassy people, who use the diplomatic pouch, have to wait two or three months for their letters.*

This noon we are having to lunch a Paramount *photographer who has just returned from Egypt, and this evening we are having a Turkish editor and his Finnish wife and a secretary from the British Embassy.*

---

[38] See ibid ftn. 37.
[39] Greenwich Mean Time.

Another major story Dana covered this year was the invasion of Iran by the British and Soviets (August 25, 1941). The Turks expressed strong disapproval of the invasion, but Dana reported the backing of Britain and Russia by the United States.

September 28:

My efforts to sell UP [to Turkish papers] have led to all kinds of complications. The leading Jewish daily at Istanbul suddenly came out with a nasty little editorial suggesting that the UP was just another transoceanic agency, disseminating German propaganda in the guise of an American organization. I have written him a friendly and explicit letter, which I hope will be published, and complained to the Press Chief. That ought to stop that.

October 21:

I've been seriously considering going down to Istanbul for a few days, perhaps after the President [Inönü] makes his speech on November 1. On the 29th of this month there will be a terrific ball at the Ankara Palace; or rather the ball comes after a great state reception for which all the diplomats get dressed up in their gold braid and top hats, etc. The Press Dept. just phoned asking me whether I would like to come. I should be delighted, certainly, but I won't go in a rented pair of tails. I'll write down to a fellow I know in Istanbul whose tails just fit me.

Through our dog Jimmy I got acquainted with a daughter of the Secretary-General to the President, and the other day Martin and I were invited up to lunch with the Secretary-General's two daughters. They really are very nice people. They live in, shall we say, comfortable circumstances. Their house is between the presidential residence and the Prime Minister's house, and has attached to it a tennis court and a small swimming pool, not to mention vineyards, chickens, an aviary, etc., etc. Furthermore, the family is one of perhaps half a dozen in town who are privileged to drive a car for pleasure; for most people gasoline rationing is stricter than in Germany.

The sisters have asked us to go to the opera tomorrow, which, I think, is all to the good. (Yes, there is an opera here . . . a sort of experimental affair operated by the school of music I gather. I don't think the Turks take naturally to opera.)

Tonight we are having dinner at the Czech Minister's house. He is in a curious situation—no longer officially recognized by the Turkish government, although still received at the foreign office, and recognized by his Russian, American and British colleagues.

Problems with the mail continued. On October 30, he wrote:

Two of your letters came through the other day, and very welcome they were. They were dated September 9 and September 2. One was "Opened by Egyptian Censorship" and was stamped "To be forwarded by air from Singapore" although you had written ATLANTIC CLIPPER LISBON on the envelope. The other one had been opened by a British censor, but one can't see where. I wonder whether there is not some new policy of sending letters from the Pacific coast by the Pacific route, no matter how they are marked.

You ask about our famous dog. He is not much of a hunting dog and is of mixed and somewhat uncertain ancestry. He looks like a combination setter, pointer and blood hound, or possibly just like Pluto, Walt Disney's Pluto.

On November 14 (from a letter to his grandmother, Grace Field Adams, in Los Angeles):

In another twenty days I'll have been in Turkey for one year. I ought to be taking out my first papers soon, but figure I'll be moved somewhere before I really get to be a hundred per cent Turkish.

We all get pretty tired of the monotonous life here in this remote little capital, but I must say I've been relatively fortunate.

I share one of the finest flats in town with Martin Agronsky of the NBC and two dogs. You have heard about one of our dogs, Jimmy, and the little fellow who was run over, but now I'm going to tell you about the latest arrival, MUTTO.

It was a dark and stormy night and I came home very late from Ankara's only edible restaurant to take Jimmy out for a walk. On the doorstep we saw a small brown animal. Jimmy sniffed disdainfully and we went for our walk. Returning we found the brown object still there and looking very sad. Jimmy sniffed some more, and I sat down to consider. With Jimmy's help I coaxed the little fellow out into the light. It was a mutt. Hello MUTTO said I. Jimmy had apparently decided he liked Mutto, so we invited him in. We gave Mutto a bath, some much needed instruction on how to live in a house, a bone and a ball, and now Mutto lives at our house.

Mutto claims to be an Anatolian sheep dog, although some have suggested that his mother had an affair with a rug. That's because he is so fuzzy. It has also been suggested that a sheep and a cat figure among his ancestors, because his fur is so soft and his whiskers so long (two and a half inches).

Jimmy sometimes expresses doubt about the wisdom of having taken him in, because when Mutto is not chasing his own tail he is chasing Jimmy's, which Jimmy considers undignified.

We have a good cook and do quite a lot of entertaining. Tonight, unfortunately, Martin merrily invited seven people without knowing that I already have a date at the Ankara Palace Hotel. Our regular cook is in Istanbul having a baby, but the substitute has turned out better than she was.

In his November 23 letter home, he spoke of leaving Turkey:

This is my Christmas letter, although it doesn't look much like Christmas around here just now and will probably look even less like Christmas where I am going. Tomorrow night I am leaving for Cairo, I hope. My office has instructed me to get going down there as soon as possible, to help keep the situation in Libya under control.

Ben Ames is causing some trouble and may delay me 'till Wednesday or even altogether, as he threatens to leave Turkey and leave us without coverage if he can't get his wife up here from India. But if everything goes well, I'll move south along with Richard Dimbleby of the BBC, *George Mathews of the* London Herald *and maybe my old friend Preston Grover of the* A.P. *The*

British and the Egyptians have promised me visas tomorrow morning, but there may be slips.

I am considering taking Mutto with me. It depends on how much trouble there is about health certificates, etc.

We have had little work here lately, beyond commenting on the wars in Russia and Libya in terms that would probably not get by the respective censorships of those countries. But there has been a good deal of social activity. Thanksgiving there was a turkey buffet luncheon, with American coffee and cigarettes and everything. The whole American colony, totaling perhaps thirty people, was there and ate itself into a stupor. By evening we had digested enough to go to a supper at our military attache's, eat more turkey, and play poker until two in the morning. Poker is really good fun when you get on to it, and when the stakes are kept sufficiently low that no one really gets hurt. I had a tremendous run of luck the first part of the evening, but ended up almost even.

A Turkish girl I met in Istanbul a long time ago turned up here the other day. We have been dancing several times and she has been to dinner. She studied law of all things, in Geneva and at Oxford, and is considered one of the most beautiful and best chaperoned girls in Turkey. She wanted me to celebrate Christmas at her house in Istanbul, but I don't suppose I'll be around.

I hope Father got down south for Christmas and that you are all together. [He represented the Chase Bag Company on the West Coast out of Portland, Oregon.] *Love to you all and a Merry, Merry Christmas, Dana*

In a December 1 letter to Mother and the family:

Safely arrived in Cairo and not quite sure yet where I'll be going from here. We have three men in Libya and can't send any more until some of them come back. Then I may go, or I may be attached to the fleet....

The trip here took just three days, about as fast as it can be done without an airplane. I wish I could do it again, much more slowly, stopping off here and there. The drive from Beirut south along the coast is as beautiful as anything in California, and the climate happened to be perfect and California-ish during my trip.

I was tremendously impressed by the Australian troops all along the way . . . so unlike any I've seen in the past few years, friendly and full of life and intelligence. . . .

The Arabs are a great relief after having Turks about for a whole year. These people are always smiling, laughing and moving. The Turks were stolid, mirthless creatures. But the people here are even poorer than the Turks, and Cairo isn't by any means the cleanest city in the world. Flies buzz everywhere even at this season. The natives don't pay the slightest attention to them. Trachoma [bacterial eye disease which, untreated, can lead to blindness] *is the most prevalent disease; often you see flies crawling about unmolested on some child's pus-filled eyes.*

I stopped only for lunch in Beirut and saw nothing, but the countryside was lovely, with curious conical mud houses of the Syrian peasants and great waterwheels, lifting water for irrigation along the roadsides.

I traveled south from Ankara on the Taurus Express accompanied by Dimbleby of the BBC *and Mathews of the* London Daily Herald *and a ministry of information official. Dimbleby had arranged for a military car to meet us at Tripoli, so we drove together as far as Beirut. There the others turned off to go to Iran, and I drove to Haifa. South of Beirut you could still see evidence of fighting, with wrecked cars in the ditches and shell-holes about. The road leads through the biggest olive grove in the world (say the Syrians) and a huge banana grove through which the Australians fought their way when they occupied Beirut. We also passed a great rock, where Napoleon the Third had left his name carved, along with sundry other military figures who have marched up and down the coastal road through the ages.*

It was dark when I reached Haifa, but I could tell that it was the most modern, well-built, well-kept town I'd seen since I left the U.S.A. I was told that the Jews have done an even better job at Tel Aviv. I had to have an exit visa to get out of Palestine next morning, so I went round to police headquarters, despite the fact that it had closed some hours earlier. Everything was blacked out and dead, but an Arab doorman led me through the dark corridors to the room where an English police officer watches over a telephone all night. He was having a beer, was delighted to have an American newspaperman to talk to, sent out for some beer for me, and fixed me up in no time. Where else in the world could you expect service like that? Incidentally he wasn't much older than I am.

The ride south from Haifa was the most strenuous part of the whole journey . . . from seven thirty in the morning 'till twelve thirty the next morning in a crowded day coach. There was a very pleasant Highlander Captain and an English oil technician, and the day went quickly. At every stop Arabs in the white nightgown-like robes swarmed around the train to sell cigarettes and candy to the soldiers and little boys and girls rushed about with the hand outstretched yelping for "bakshish," or a tip. They don't consider it begging, apparently, just the custom of the country. Even at this time of year it got quite uncomfortably hot as we crossed the desert to Suez and sand filtered through the train and into our clothes and lungs. The Australians in the compartment said that's just like it is in the Western Desert.

Suez turned out to be a narrow, unimportant-looking canal as we saw it in the gathering darkness from our ancient ferry.

I was pretty well washed up when I got to Cairo. Unfortunately the leading hotel, the Continental, turned out to be of 1890 vintage with draughty rooms, bad service and lukewarm water.

Here for the moment I'm covering the embassies, editing the copy from the front and covering the press conferences part of the time. It isn't very heavy work, although the local boys seem to think they are being worked to a frazzle. Yesterday afternoon I went to the races and won three pounds, to my great surprise. Today I've spent most of my time trying unsuccessfully to track down some German prisoners.

Everywhere I go here I run into people I have met in Turkey or in the Balkans. They all seem to have gravitated down here. It is pleasant to find people you know in a town as big as this.

My faithfully preserved list of family dates, reminds me again, that December 10 is Father's birthday. This is probably getting to California *considerably after that, but, nonetheless, here's HAPPY BIRTHDAY TO FATHER and many happy returns of the day! I hope that you will be able to come south more often this winter so you will not be apart so much of the time.*

December 8:

You can imagine that these have been fairly lively days for me. To my great sorrow I have not been able to get out to the desert; we already have too many accredited correspondents and I just couldn't edge my way in.

New York has come through with a message saying that I should be "ready to return to Ankara quickly" when the horde of correspondents who are converging on Cairo (rather late) begin to trickle in. A man named Yindrich and MacMillan, both accredited, and Kay, who was formerly in Belgrade, should be arriving any day. I'm going to try to spend Christmas and New Year's at Cedars of Lebanon, where the skiing is said to be great. It would be a nice holiday and one which I am beginning to think that I have earned. I've been signing a good many stories out of here, but don't suppose they've had much play, considering the show in the Pacific.

[Japan attacked Pearl Harbor on December 7, 1941.]

Pinkley is still here. I've had some very long and useful talks with him. Next time he is in California he will really come to see you. He is a very fine fellow, an extraordinarily hard and conscientious worker. Even out in the desert he was sending back service messages to be fired all over the world, concerning our service in Europe and the British Empire, which is his main concern. When he got back, he had a terrific fever and had to spend most of the next three days in bed.

I've not got about much in Cairo yet, except at night, as there has been a fair amount of work. The bureau manager, Collins, a very new recruit to the UP, is rather resentful of my activity. So was Gorrell, who thought I was trying to beat him out of his job in the desert and created a scene at the hotel in Haifa. In the end the doctors told Gorrell his health was too bad for him to go to the desert, and neither of us went.

I'm helping them handle the incoming service here . . . and a big bunch of cables has just come in . . . .

Dana didn't write articles about the stunning attack at Pearl Harbor, probably because he was assigned to the European theater and writing about Pearl Harbor might be seen as intruding on other correspondents. He did sometimes mention in letters home that the war in the Pacific was so important that the papers were neglecting Europe.

December 21, Cairo:

I am leaving tomorrow morning at the crack of dawn for Beirut. I'm to have a holiday, believe it or not, with the blessings of all the powers that be.

Christmas I expect to be at Cedars of Lebanon, in the good old snowy mountains. What a holiday this is going to be. Am I going to be lazy! I am really very tired—particularly at the moment but also, just generally. I've been handling the incoming service, just because I'm the sort of dope who goes around doing other people's work. It meant being on duty every morning early, and then covering the usual round of news during the day and going out in the evening, all of which was too much of a good thing. But it was instructive, to be sure.

The other day a fellow named Stephen Barber, Unipress employee, and I went out to have a look at the pyramids. I differ from most people; I was not disappointed. The pyramids are all right. They are just as big as I expected them to be and a lot more rocky. Huge rocks, at that, but all coming to bits. We went inside with a guide who was a total loss, and crept about passages by candlelight at the risk of our lives 'till we got to large rectangular rooms where the kings and the queens sarcophaguses were located. . . .

The Sphinx I admit, was rather smaller than I anticipated, and not as sphinx-like. I think its mysterious smile has been overdone, but its profile is most unimpressive—quite Nubian in spite of the lacking nose. I was told by unreliable sources that members of Napoleon's army fired a cannon at the Sphinx and bunged it right on the nose.

Enclosed is a picture of Schmidt, Sphinx, Barber, pyramid, camel and Arab. I made my camel gallop, more or less, causing no end of alarm to the Arab, who thought I was going to gallop all the way to Cairo. So did I, as a matter of fact. I like my camel's saucy expression. Barber's looks as though it were about to spit. Actually it was busy at the other end.

I must end this literary effort as I feel very near a state of collapse. Haven't been so tired for ages.

Love to everybody,
Dana

Dana at the Pyramids, soon after his transfer to Cairo, December 1941

Istanbul, Turkey

1942

Once again, Dana got his wish for a skiing holiday on January 7. At the Hotel Mon Repos, Cedars of Lebanon, he wrote home:

> *I've had two weeks of glorious skiing up here and haven't managed to write any letters during that time. Except for three days of blizzard we've had sunshine every day and I have acquired the deepest possible shade of angry red as complexion. Perhaps you saw the story I managed to get out of the holiday. Now I must get back to Ankara by the 14th unless I can persuade Ben Ames to stay a little longer. He is going home at last . . . . I'd like to go to Jerusalem and even Baghdad if possible. But if I only get this skiing holiday, I'll be quite satisfied. I've rarely felt better. The sun and the snow here are very much like Southern California's. Almost every day I go off on an all-day trip.*
>
> *Christmas and New Year's were rather dull because the road was blocked and the hotel didn't go to much trouble for so few people. I met the ex-Vice Captain of the British Olympic Ski Team who is teaching Australians to ski.*
>
> *A few minutes ago I got your New Year's telegram saying that you got the Cairo letter. It was phoned up to me from Tripoli* [Lebanon].

Dana was disappointed to be sent back to Ankara. While he was in Cairo, he had hoped to go out on the desert in Libya, where the action was. But as he explained, the number of correspondents permitted in the war zone was limited.

As a journalist, Dana acknowledged the New Year by looking back at the past year and forward to some possibilities for the futures of Turkey and the Balkans.

IS TURKEY'S STRADDLING ENDED?

January 16—Turkey enters 1942 with its little capital on the Anatolian plateau seething with international intrigue. This intrigue might develop into genuine peace proposals, but it is equally, if not more, likely that Turkey, like its Balkan neighbors, will be extinguished as a free nation or that it will be in a battleground.

President İnönü made overtures toward the first alternative when he told the Turkish National Assembly on its first winter session Nov. 1 that he hoped Turkey would "become the source of peace," but at the same time he recognized that the war probably will embrace ever-wider circles during the next year.

A comparison between the President's speech this year and the one he made on the same occasion last year shows how Turkey's foreign policy has altered as war closed around its frontiers. In 1940 he indicated that Turkey was a "non-belligerent" and that its policy was based on her alliance with Great Britain. In his most recent speech he described Turkey as a neutral and referred only to its determination to observe its engagements. He also mentioned Turkey's unalterable friendship with Germany.

Shifts with Battle

Germany's invasion of the Balkans is responsible for the shift. Only Britain's growing strength in the Middle East and Germany's difficulties in Russia prevented it from going further. Britain's successes in Libya further stabilized Turkey's position.

Because of Turkey's small stature among the warring powers, it is inevitable that it should reflect the play of force beyond its frontiers. Turkish statesmen, however, probably are telling the truth when they say their country would resist any invader despite its strength.

On the whole the Germans have the edge in the diplomatic tussle which has gone on here all year.

Anthony Eden came to Turkey in February to get Turkey to promise to declare war against Germany if Germany invaded the Balkans. His visit, as later events have shown, was almost a total failure. Turkey hedged, arguing it was all in favor of united Balkan resistance, but putting it up to Yugoslavia and Bulgaria. Bulgaria, of course, already was secretly committed to Germany, and Yugoslavia decided too late to defy the Nazis. So no joint defense plan was worked out.

When the Germans occupied Bulgaria and attacked Yugoslavia and Greece, Turkey did nothing. Again, as later events have shown, that was probably very fortunate for Britain. Had Turkey thrown its slight military weight into the scales, chances are that the Nazis would have overrun Turkey in addition to Greece and might now be in Cairo.

Reassured by Hitler

Just as Eden finished his visit, Hitler sent president İnönü a personal letter by special plane, assuring him that Germany had no intention of attacking Turkey. It now appears likely that the strategic idea behind Germany's entire Balkan campaign was the protection of her right flank for the coming attack on Russia, and that Hitler decided that he had gone far enough for this purpose.

Meanwhile, shortly after Eden departed, a joint Turkish-Russian communiqué was issued, reaffirming the existing non-aggression pact and declaring that either country would look on with comprehension should the other be attacked. Few persons knew it at the time, but this communiqué actually was suggested by the British ambassador in Moscow, Sir Stafford Cripps, who had flown to Ankara for Eden's visit. It was the first evidence that Britain's relations with the Kremlin were improving and that all was not well with the Russo-German tie-up.

Arriving back in Ankara, Dana found two British officers occupying his flat.

January 18:

Although unexpected, this has turned out to be very satisfactory. [It] *makes it that much cheaper, and they're good company. If and when Martin should come back, they agree to clear out within a week. But Martin's mighty far away now, I reckon. Don't know for sure though whether he ever got to Singapore....*

The trip up from Beirut wasn't exactly a pleasure cruise. The Taurus Express was still recovering from the super cold wave that had us snowed in at the Cedars. There had been a bad accident on the line between Adana and Ankara; they hadn't been able to overhaul the rolling stock, and our train consequently had no diner, no water, and most of the time no heat. But the Polish Ambassador, his wife, a Standard Oil man, an English diplomat and I lived quite merrily on sandwiches bought at Aleppo, bad Syrian beer, good Palestinian chocolate, oranges and honest to goodness American ketchup, which I bought in Beirut.

I bought two bottles of maple syrup, a bottle of French cognac, a can of Heinz baked beans, a flask of Scotch whiskey and assorted American toothpastes, cold-creams, etc. all in Beirut—also six pairs of American silk stockings and a bottle of perfume! Things American are mighty rare and worth their weight in gold around here.

I don't think you're going to see much of mine in the papers for several months. There's too much going on elsewhere. In March, April or May something may begin to develop here though. If we get through the summer without being attacked—I feel that we won't be—but that's a pretty risky prediction.

Jimmy, the famous hound dog, survived Martin's and my absence very well and is getting to be a better looking dog all the time. But poor little Mutto, who was really my favorite, has disappeared. The dopey servant who was in charge of the house said he ran away, but I learned from the proprietor's son, that the proprietor, finding him digging up the garden, took him away and put him in charge of a foreman on a construction job. I haven't located him yet.

After a short trip to Istanbul, Dana wrote on February 3:

It snowed a good deal of the time while I was in Istanbul, stopping most transportation. Taxi prices automatically about trebled, since only a few have chains. Snow causes no end of trouble here, particularly holding up trains.

Don't think I'll be going down to Istanbul again for a while, unless I do so unofficially and entirely at my own expense. Just got a cable informing me that the "basic shift" in news interest [to the Pacific] necessitated my cutting expenses "bone-ward" eliminating all unnecessary travel, tipsters, stringers, etc., etc. Of course I had realized that, but am hoping interest in the Far East will slacken in a few months.

Well, I got in some more skiing on Sunday—right outside Ankara and quite good. We have a lot of mountains about here, but most seasons the fall is too thin to make for good skiing.

The train that brought me back from Istanbul was ten hours late due to a freight train going off the rails ahead of us, and we went through Eskishekir in daylight. That's where just about all the world's Meerschaum comes from. I hopped out and bought a fair Meerschaum pipe (which I am smoking at this moment) and have arranged with a young English flying instructor who goes there to buy me a really fine one—beautifully carved and with Barbarossa beard about six inches high.

When there was little news in Ankara, Dana wrote they sometimes picked up stories from people who were traveling through Turkey from the Far East, Russia, Africa, Germany, or the Balkan countries. He called this sort of second-hand reporting "dreamings-up."

On February 9, he wrote:

Cy Sulzberger[40] will be here shortly from Moscow (he just got married in Beirut), so the volume of dreamings-up is likely to increase....
All this week, or rather last week, my precious dog Jimmy has been lost. But just now some one called up to say they had found him and were bringing him back. By the time I'm finished [with this letter] I should be able to tell you whether it is really Jimmy or not.
The way it happened: I went to the Anatolian Agency and left Jimmy outside because there is a dog who lives inside. Ordinarily Jimmy, who is very fond of his happy home, would have waited quietly. But, when I came out, he was gone. I spent the rest of the afternoon and evening wearing out shoe-leather and running up taxi bills trying to find him, to no avail. I put an

---

[40] Cyrus Sulzberger (1912-1993) was the nephew of Arthur Hayes Sulzberger, then publisher of the *New York Times*. During this period, Cyrus was the *NYT* Balkan Bureau manager.

ad in the paper and notified the police, Jimmy's and my friends. Still no dog. If this isn't my dog that's coming I'm going to offer a fifty lira reward. This is actually the fifth day he's been gone. [It wasn't Jimmy.]

A few days later:

Well, I haven't got my dog back and have inserted an advertisement in the local paper offering fifty Turkish lira for his return. If that doesn't do it nothing will.

What happened this afternoon was most disillusioning. A man came around to the door saying that he had the dog, apparently expecting me to hand out some money. I said that was splendid, called a taxi and told him to lead on.

He took me to a very disreputable part of the old city and went into an ancient house where the dog was presumably being kept. Presently he emerged and said he would have to go somewhere else to get the key. I waited an hour and he never came back. Quite obviously he had no idea where the dog was but was keen to collect the reward.

February 16:

Here's the final chapter about the dog. . . . A sergeant of the Turkish Army appeared one morning to say he thought he had Jimmy. We got a taxi and went out to a cavalry camp where half a dozen dogs were crowded into a filthy pen, and Jimmy [was] *one of them. He gave me to understand that one of the dogs there was supposed to have been Jimmy's mother and that Jimmy had been stolen from him a year ago. An interpreter finally made it clear that the sergeant considered that he was now really selling Jimmy to me for fifty liras and wanted ten liras more for keeping him for eight days. I succumbed to that. Then he wanted me to pay for his taxi back home, which seemed a bit thick . . . . Fortunately just then an English officer friend of mine appeared on the scene and blasted the sergeant out of sight with excellent Turkish invective. I suppose Jimmy will be kidnapped and held for ransom every other week now.*

Yesterday, I had a splendid day of skiing at Atash, about forty kilometers out from Ankara. Went on a bus full of ski enthusiasts and I came back in the Belgian minister's car. A fellow named Peck and I climbed the highest peak in the vicinity, about six hours of steady up and down work. Got one of those good old fashioned California sunburns for my trouble, too.

On February 25, Dana reported the story of the bombing of Franz von Papen, the Nazi ambassador to Turkey, in a widely distributed dispatch. In part, he wrote:

Von Papen was walking in the avenue (Atatürk Boulevard) with his wife. He had reached a point opposite the Italian embassy when a well-dressed man approached.

Then von Papen and his wife were thrown to the ground by an explosion. Both were knocked out by the blast. They lay there for several minutes until a police car approached.

The bomb had exploded 55 feet from von Papen. The man who had been approaching had been blown to pieces.

A foreign office motorcycle dispatch rider, returning from the home of President Ismet Inönü, helped von Papen and his wife, both covered with blood of the bomb victim, into the Italian embassy.

Identification of the bomber was difficult because torn fragments of his body were strewn for 10 yards around, along with bits of clothing. [Later he was identified as Omer Tokat, a Yugoslavian law student who went to Istanbul two years ago and arrived in Ankara several days before the explosion.]

Neither von Papen nor his wife was seriously injured, although later it developed that von Papen had been deafened in one ear.

In news reports, Dana wrote that although the authorities held six Russians under arrest in connection with the bombing, Soviet Ambassador Sergei Vinograf, in a conference with Foreign Minister Sükrü Saracoglu, was said to have emphasized that the Soviet government disassociated itself entirely from the suspects in the bombing. In a March 2 *UP* dispatch, Dana wrote:

Russian authorities were perhaps not directly involved, but two of the accused men worked at the Russian embassy. The sentiments of the four accused men, the two Russians and two Turks who were put on trial, were naturally against the Germans. The Turks felt threatened by German troops that had been assembled on the Bulgarian-Turkey front and by German requests to allow troops to cross Turkey to reach the oil deposits in the Caucasus. The Russians feared and hated the Nazi troops that were invading Russia and the two students who were born in Yugoslavia were obviously distressed with the German occupation.

Meanwhile, in Dana's March 3 letter home, he wrote:

Martin Agronsky's uncle, Gershon, is here and I have been running about the place with him. He is the editor and publisher of the Palestine Post, *the only tolerable English language newspaper published in the Middle East. In fact his paper is excellent. Martin, I have learned fairly definitely, is in Australia.*

In Dana's *UP* dispatch of March 7, he wrote of the Nazi planned invasion of Iraq:

IRAQ, BRITISH OIL LAND, SEEN NAZI GOAL, VIA TURKEY

Reports of an impending German attack across Turkey to Iraq and Britain's rich Mosul oil fields, attributed to the boasts of German army officers, were brought to Ankara today by travelers. German officers in Nazi occupied Romania were said to be talking freely of "the coming invasion of Iraq" through Turkey or, perhaps with Russian aid, from the Tiflis area between the Black Sea and the Caspian.

The Foreign Minister of Iraq, Gen. Nuri Es-Said, arrived in Cairo Thursday, presumably to confer with British Foreign Secretary Anthony Eden on the German menace to the Iraq oil fields which are vital to Britain's war effort. Iraq is under British protection.

With the Turkish government said to be opposing German pressure, it was revealed that all members of the Turkish Cabinet today turned down an invitation of the German Ambassador Franz von Papen to attend a showing of the German war film, "Victory in the West."

"We are not amused by this film," said one prominent Turk.

Only two Turkish newspapermen attended.

May Stay on Defensive

Opinion hardened, meanwhile, that Turkey, instead of aiding Greece, would remain on the defensive unless attacked.

Turkey already has between 300,000 and 500,000 troops along the western frontier in Thrace, facing German troops occupying virtually the entire length of the Bulgarian-Turkish boundary.

In the event of a German attack on Turkey, however, it was believed that co-operative measures worked out here by Eden and Turkish leaders would become effective immediately.

These measures, it was said, would provide for the establishment of British airbases, at least, in Turkey.

Meanwhile, back on the canine front:

I'll have to write one more time about my dogs for they are both back in the house with me just now, Dana wrote on March 9. *This month I told the landlord I would not pay the rent until he brought back the Anatolian sheepdog he had dognapped. Mutto was back in two hours.*

The wind has changed to the south, from Syria and the desert, and it is suddenly strangely warm and heavy. I like the change, he wrote on March 31.

Tonight the Soviets are showing a film to which all the allied diplomats and many of the newspapermen have been invited. I must leave early as I am having six people for dinner including the International Red Cross *representative, the British Consul from Trebizond, a transient* Time, Life, Fortune *correspondent named Preston and a secretary from the British Embassy. Last night I also gave a dinner party, including the Counselor of the British Embassy, and our new assistant air attache, the new lend lease* administration representative, and the Greek millionairess to whom my flatmate, Guy Sitwell, is going to get married. Did I ever tell you that he was a cousin of the well-known Edith Sitwell? So you see I have been keeping myself socially well occupied, and helping along the news gathering job.

Incidentally, all UP stories from Turkey are filed by me now, including those datelined Istanbul. When you write that you have seen a signed story of mine, could you make a point of adding what the story was about as I like to check on which stories have gone across well. We are still operating under strict "downhold"[41] orders here, but I think interest is returning to this corner of the world gradually.

Still no news about Martin Agronsky, other than your mentioning you heard him from Java. If you have heard him lately please let me know. There is a rumor which I think I mentioned before that he was captured by the Japanese.

And from April 6:

Day after tomorrow the bombing trial will start up again. The first day, last week, was hectic, but I got my stuff away hours ahead of any of my Anglo-American competition. I arranged to use a dentist's office next to the courthouse as office and had my people inside slip out of the courtroom from time to time [bringing] news up to my office from where I rushed it off to the telegraph office in a waiting taxi. Two hundred spectators including British Minister James Morgan were present at the opening session of the trial.

April 15:

I haven't learned much Turkish and constantly intend to start lessons. Arabic would be useful, too, south of Turkey, but English and French, especially French, get you through most places.

---

[41] A downhold cable in the newspaper world meant that the editor was asking the reporter to reduce the number and length of dispatches because public interest was elsewhere or for economy's sake.

May 14:

This week I am planning to have myself vaccinated, inoculated, etc. in preparation for the summer and any of the places I might be moving to in months to come. I once started to have myself inoculated against typhoid and smallpox last summer but never got the business finished. People who come out from America have some dozen different inoculations, but people out here get very slack about it all.

Not only was entertaining a relief from the seriousness of war, it was an important way in which correspondents could find out what was happening in the diplomatic world.

June 2:

This household is in the process of reorganizing itself after the whirlwind shock of a cocktail party of ninety-two people followed by a buffet supper and dancing to the victrola. Practically all the notables in town were present . . . . Frank [Frank Kaufman, was one of Dana's flat mates] *had the original thought of having the three of us dress up like waiters, with tuxedo trousers, white jacket, napkin over arm and pad and pencil for orders. Frank operated a special bar dispensing his own special mint juleps (ingredients a la turque), I ran the cocktail bar, and Bob circulated about with sandwiches. Other touches which helped amuse the crowd were a map of the U.S.A. with arrows pointing to San Francisco, Los Angeles and Baltimore, our respective home towns, also an arrow on the map of the world pointing to Ankara, as Jimmy's* [the dog's] *home town, and cuttings from American magazine advertisements indicating the places where cocktails, mint juleps, beer and tea could be obtained. Frank used the window of his bedroom as his bar, passing out the drinks to the clients congregating in vast number on the balcony.*

The climax of the evening occurred after the most distinguished guests, including the Steinhardts [American Ambassador and his wife] *had left. Our military attache produced his own favorite phonograph record and went into an exotic dance involving a summersault and a cartwheel, thereby causing indescribable excitement and pleasure to Jimmy, who pranced wildly about barking and in all respects doing the music justice. When the music ended Jimmy could not bear the letdown. He stopped in the middle of the floor, squatted, and, for all to see, began to leak. Not a little leak, but a two and a half minute leak which flowed larger and larger over the floor while the assembled guests rocked with merriment. At any other time of the day or night such a performance would have disgraced Jimmy beyond measure, but at that particular moment it proved a fitting conclusion not only to the dance but to the party.*

Beginning in May, Dana had asked for a transfer to Moscow or Cairo or the Middle East. He particularly "wanted to do some real reporting" from a front. In almost every letter, he mentions his frustration and disappointment when no transfer came through. He noted that, in Ankara and Istanbul, he often had to relay news from the Balkans or the mid-East, when all he wanted was to be nearer the action.

In a letter to me, he wrote:

The essential of this place is of course to appraise military events going on around it and to write "inside" stuff about the Balkans and Germany. That means you must know and maintain contact with a lot of diplomats and Turkish political people and get in touch with as many people as possible traveling north and south.

June 11:

Harry Flory [UP executive] has replied (by cable) from New York to my insistence on a transfer by promising to "utmost give you chance in fall if Turkey continues quiet summer long." Furthermore, as I think I mentioned earlier, he is arranging to have me accredited to the American Forces. That would give me the rank of Captain when I get my transfer to a country where our forces are operating. I especially suggested that I would be keen on a transfer to Moscow and still think that might be swung, although New York seems to think there are all sorts of difficulties.

In the same letter, he was able to say:

My Turkish lessons still take place every morning. Gradually I am catching on, but it is slow work. The language is totally different in construction and sound from anything I have experienced. It is a poor language, incidentally, with a limited vocabulary, few shades of meaning and the awkwardness entailed by putting the verb at the end of the sentence.

Dana reported the first real war news from Ankara in a dispatch that made headlines on June 12. The bombing of the Romanian oil fields was an early demonstration of the value of American power to the war effort.

U.S. BOMBS RUMANIAN OIL FIELDS; 7 PLANES ARE DOWN IN TURKEY

American pilots have "successfully" bombed the big Rumanian oil fields, it was reliably reported tonight after a number of big four-motored United States bombers were forced down on Turkish soil in route back to their unidentified base.

Four American planes of the Liberator type, (which carry four tons of bombs each and have a range of 3,000 miles), were forced down—one with a German Messerschmitt on its tail, and three others were reported to have landed in Turkey due to lack of fuel. At least 28 fliers were interned.

"We accomplished our mission in the Black Sea," the pilots were quoted. Other sources said that the bombers had attacked the German-held Rumanian oil fields, presumably including the Ploesti oil fields and refineries about 100 miles north of Bucharest.

A United States long-range bombing attack on the Rumanian oil fields would be designed to help crack Rumanian morale and to aid the Russians by interfering with the Axis plans for a Ukrainian offensive this summer. Hitler recently has been reported massing submarines and small naval units in

Rumanian and Bulgarian ports on the Black Sea in preparation for his projected drive toward the Caucasus oil fields.

Three American planes that landed at Ankara were viewed today by large crowds. A fourth plane landed near Arisiye and three were reported to have landed in southern Turkey. How many may have continued across Turkey to their bases was not indicated.

Turkish anti-aircraft fired on the American planes when they violated Turkish neutrality, and at least one that was hit landed in Turkish territorial waters. Two of seven in the crew were injured. The planes, which have a high ceiling, probably came down into range, however, due to lack of fuel.

Reliable reports said that the bomb bays of all the planes were empty.

The fliers were housed in a fashionable villa at Recioren on the outskirts of Ankara. . . .

A high Turkish source said: "We will give our unexpected guests, the American aviators, the best possible living quarters and care."

The 21 fliers, who landed in the three ships at the Ankara airdrome proper, met a universally friendly Turkish population. They lunched at a public restaurant in the railway station here and all were in high spirits. The planes are the largest ever seen here and they drew hundreds of gaping spectators to the airdrome.

Dana received many cables of congratulations on his reporting. From Harry Flory: "You led papers twice within a week."

Dana took great pride in being the first to report the news—especially to beat his main competition, the *Associated Press*.

I was well ahead on the Prime Minister's[42] *death and now I'm waiting for a phone call which will tell me who will be in the new cabinet.* [He wrote on July 8.] *Phone call to Zurich, Switzerland, just came through, and I'm*

---

[42]   Refik Saydam, who had been Prime Minister since 1939, died on September 7, 1942. No doubt his death was quickly announced in Turkey, so Dana would have been aware of it.

afraid I've given my honorable opposition a slight beating on the appointment of Sukru Saracoglu as new Prime Minister. One can never depend on the phone connection materializing. But when it does it beats the cables by about twenty hours.

Why Dana received the announcement of President Inönü's appointment of Sukru Saracoglu by telephone from Switzerland, Dana did not explain. It was not surprising that Inönü chose Saracoglu, who had already held important ministerial positions in the government and was known as a capable diplomat. Dana said that he reminded him of one of his favorite professors at Pomona.

Dana's "dreamings-up" article was published in the *Washington Post* under the headlines:

LAME, BLIND WAR VICTIMS HAUNT BERLIN

ISTANBUL, July 19—Travelers arriving from Berlin said today the German capital is a city of armless, eyeless war wounded, of watery beer and four cigarettes a day, and of plentiful money but little to buy.

These responsible spokesmen emphasized, however, that despite the deterioration of living conditions, the Germans likely would be able to carry on indefinitely—some said two or three or even more years—without cracking if their army suffered no impressive defeat.

Crowded With Refugees

Berlin is crowded with refugees from Cologne, Essen, Luebeck, Rostock, and the Ruhr, hardest hit by the British bombers, the travelers said. In general, hotels are booked up months ahead with two and three persons to a room.

They said the Germans were prone to observe uneasily that Berlin had not been bombed for ten months, and must be in line for one of the next 1000-bomber raids from Britain. Prominent squares have been camouflaged with nets covered with branches.

The informants said the number of war wounded seen on the streets of Berlin had increased greatly. Many of them were said to be suffering still from frostbite incurred on the Russian front last winter.

Hotels Become Hospitals

Hotels throughout the Sudetenland of former Czechoslovakia were reported requisitioned and filled with wounded and convalescent troops. Similar requisitioning was carried out in the Hungarian resort areas and the Slovakian mountains, it was said. Instances were cited of Hungarian and Bulgarian patients being moved out of hospitals in Budapest and Sofia to make room for the German wounded.

Much of the casual conversation in Berlin revolves around post-war conditions as the Germans mull over the prospects for cashing in on the victories of their armies.

Eggs and meat were reported definitely scarcer than last summer, since all available supplies are sent to the front, leaving Berlin on a diet centering on cabbage and potatoes. Frying potatoes is verboten, however, for lack of fats. For some inexplicable reason radishes are plentiful, and appear on the breakfast, lunch, and dinner menus.

The travelers said queues form at restaurants long before mealtime, since late comers are likely to find the places sold out. The tiny coffee ration, distributed for some time after the last stocks from France and the Low Countries were taken, has been discontinued. Real coffee and chocolate were more powerful trading mediums than money, buying everything on the black market.

Many Germans regard as the worst hardship of all the deterioration of German beer to a watery nondescript fluid. Often only non-alcoholic beer is available, while stronger liquors and even wine are not to be had since all available goes directly to the front. Berlin night clubs serve synthetic colored syrups with water when all else fails. Officers who get their liquor rations bring cognac flasks.

Dana wrote home on August 5:

Today I have had Saracoglu's speech on my hands. I have filed it complete with lead, interpretation and all frills, but am still waiting here on the off chance that I can get through by telephone. It is almost impossible now, but worth trying. In a few minutes I will listen to the BBC to see whether they have already picked up the speech by radio, the louses. . . . Well I couldn't get the BBC. *Some days nothing works.*

A group of Turkish newspapermen are going off to England tomorrow and I have to meet them at the station early. They may go on to America later, he writes on August 20.

The Turkish newspapermen did go on to America and California. Dana was anxious to have them meet our mother and so made those arrangements.

As I have noted, Dana had a remarkable ability to make friends and remember them. As he moved to various cities in Europe and the Middle East, he often mentioned going to see old friends as the first order of business. He writes in the same letter:

Mackintosh, my friend and A.P. correspondent in Istanbul is arriving on the train in the morning. He is one of the people I will want to remember after I leave this country. Every place I have been, I have made one or two friends that stuck. Apparently, he had received preliminary orders for a transfer to Moscow, for September 3:

To my great disappointment I received a telegram the other day saying "connection transfer hitch arisen. Please hold everything until advised." The only hitch I can think of is that Handler did not want to leave Moscow and kicked up a shindy about it. That was indicated by the telegram I got from his senior, Shapiro, saying that he would be delighted to help me get my visa as soon as he received "final instructions" and that meanwhile, informatively, "Handler reluctant leave Moscow." I sent him a nice buttery telegram explaining that of course, I didn't want to interfere with Handler's work, but that it had been a long-standing ambition of mine to work in Moscow, especially after seeing his fine work in the incoming UP *service here, which is quite true. It seems very difficult to make a move to one's own advantage without pushing someone else out of the way. ...*

Frank [one of his flat-mates] *and I were both delighted to read about your telephone conversation with Mr. Kaufman. Frank's father* [Mr. Kaufman] *also* wrote him about it. Referring to your letter he remarked, "If Dana writes as well as his mother, [43] he must be a very good correspondent."

At the end of one of Dana's letters, he added a scrawled note to Mother:

You say you recognize my stories by the style sometimes. Do I have a style? Sometimes I feel that my agency training has made me terribly wooden—writing too close to the old 5 W's formula, which can certainly bear variation.

September 12:

The last few weeks I have been thinking about very little except the possibility of getting a transfer out of here. I have had quite enough of Turkey and am very anxious to get to a war zone.

On September 16, Dana commented on a group of pictures he sent from Ankara:

You should not be over-impressed by the seeming modernity reflected in the photos. The town is really only just begun. It has no sewage system. The whole modern part of town, built on the flat, is one great sump which grows more dangerous to health every year. There are plans to install a sewage system, but there is great difficulty about getting the material. The old town was, wisely, built on a hill from which all noxious things drained off conveniently. This year, furthermore, there is a lot of malaria about, because the Turks have not been able to get the stuff to spray trees and swamps. The water, fortunately, is good. But the same cannot be said of water in Istanbul. Turkey's modernity is still very much on the surface. It is interesting to note that two and a half million Turkish pounds were spent to build a big artificial lake and a park in the center of town while general health has been endangered by lack of sanitation.

---

[43] See Appendix.

Still no definite word on my transfer, though I expect something to materialize very soon. The last word was that Jalex, [44] *who is running the foreign desk in London, cabled (..................) [deleted by censor]* [45] *I think I told you about that in my last letter. Anyway, I waited eight days and then cabled again in the strongest, or perhaps more exactly, the most appealing terms, repeating how much the (...............) [Moscow] assignment meant to me and asking what the confusion was all about. There should be an answer in the next few days.*

Mr. Willkie [Wendell] *has come and gone. The ensuing calm seems something of a vacuum. I don't think I did very brilliantly on covering Willkie. The best excuse is that I am stale on my work here.*

September 19:

Another week of waiting for a decision on when and where I am to move. If Moscow should definitely fail me, I am going to suggest a temporary assignment to Tehran in order to get myself accredited and get a news bureau organized. The other alternative is Cairo, but there it is very difficult, apparently, for me to be accredited. I had a letter from Leon Kay, who is in charge there, the other day, explaining that the UP has a full quota of accredited correspondents in Egypt and is not allowed to have any more until one of those there now is removed and hands in his accreditation.

There have been a number of additions to the journalistic corps here lately, the latest being Brewer of the Chicago Tribune. *I have known him off and on ever since he came through here after the occupation of Yugoslavia. Some time next week he is going to move in and share our apartment and I*

---

[44] Jalex was the cable name for a member of the *U.P.* executive staff in New York, Joe Alex Morris, Foreign News Editor. Because each word counts in the cost of cables, names are abbreviated, and when possible, words are omitted or combined to keep the cost down. Jalex was trying to arrange a transfer for Dana.

[45] This was Moscow. Starting in this period, many of Dana's letters were censored, indicating he was now reporting from strategically important areas of the war. The German censors, and American too, blacked out or actually cut out with a razor blade all geographic references, making it difficult, sometimes, to know from where Dana was writing.

may eventually give him my place in the apartment, if he stays on and I get my transfer.

Some months before, Dana had made an important purchase in the Istanbul bazaar, a beautiful antique dagger[46] encrusted with jewels. He had sent it home with a friend named Taylor.

September 24:

I could have sold it here for a thousand Turkish pounds this year. There are two ways of appraising it, I was told—either on the basis of the intrinsic value of the metal and the stones or on the basis of its value as a curiosity. The latter value should be considerably the higher. Put it in a safe deposit box if you think advisable, but if you like, keep it around the house where it can be seen. It is, after all, quite a show piece.

I am now in the midst of getting my various injections, preparatory to moving. My left arm is quite sore. The UP *correspondent in Beirut sent me up a bottle of Typhus vaccine which should be taken by people going to Russia.*

Interest in news from Turkey seems to have lapsed again, as I have orders to desist from my weekly "situationers" and from my biweekly mail contributions to the Special Service Bureau, *which passed them on to* News Week. *I will be awfully pleased if I can get away from here in the next few weeks.*

October 4:

In answer to my last plaintive telegram about my transfer, Jalex wired as follows from London on the 26th of last month: "I am trying upfix with Kay where Schmidt use ablest[47] mid east." (................................) he appreciated the spirit referred to in my cable. I pointed to the fact that I had

---

[46]   The dagger has long since disappeared.
[47]   "Ablest" implies that Dana was the most qualified for the work in Cairo. Dana was most pleased.

been working for UP for just four years and I was asking for nothing except the transfer to Moscow.

Tonight I have been invited to dinner by the new Chinese Minister, Chan Shan Yo. I do not really know him yet, but I was well acquainted with his predecessor, Dr. Chang, who was transferred to Chile.

Mackintosh, my assistant in Istanbul, was supposed to fly up here yesterday but the plane did not leave because of bad weather. So, he took the train in the evening, but the train did not leave because the tracks were washed out somewhere along the line. Now I dare say he won't come for a week.

October 21:

I have almost completed a week in Istanbul . . . while UP carried out a series of experimental Morse news broadcasts. And a very pleasant and interesting week it has been.

Here I have renewed many old news contacts and acquaintances. I feel a new man down here after the dullness of Ankara. If now I could get that transfer life would seem magnificent. I have been patient and placed implicit confidence in their promises to move me. Now when I get back to Ankara I am going to give my bosses a real blast. After the Republic Day festivities on the thirtieth when Inonu makes a speech there will probably not be another important spot news story in Turkey till spring. There will be no reason for my continued presence.

Yesterday and today I have had to devote several hours to having a movie made of myself, and eight or ten other British and American correspondents. The Paramount Newsreel man, Bret Harte, is making a feature about the newspapermen here. I appear in the pose of one violently correcting copy and later making a speech all about bread, the Balkans and Hitler. Much fun, as Bill Shirer would say in his diary.[48] My hands also appear, tapping vigorously at a strange typewriter.

---

[48] Shirer, William L., *Berlin Diary: The Journal of a Foreign Correspondent*, 1934-1941.

Sunday I lunched with Bob Parker, his staff and Dr. Scott and others from Roberts College, at Parker's magnificent villa. He lives there with all his five colleagues, a Packard, a windmill, and a frog-pond. It won't be so funny this winter however, considering that they haven't been able to get any coal to heat the score of rooms.

On this return trip to Istanbul, Dana again spoke of its beauty:

Istanbul is really a very lovely city with a powerful and individual character. The fact that it is down at heel and has been systematically neglected while Turkey built Ankara has if anything heightened its charm . . . . At the moment there is a light undercurrent of excitement, not because of the war, which people have grown accustomed to, but because of the steadily rising prices and the distinct threat of inflation. It is far more noticeable here than in Ankara where the government manages to keep prices pretty well controlled. In the few nightclubs here the few really wealthy Turks and the foreigners can be seen spending hordes of money every night, as though it would be worthless tomorrow. And that it may be, if matters continue along present lines.

My friend Derek Patmore of the London News Chronicle *is an acquaintance of Halide Edib*[49] *and has promised to try to introduce me, but it is quite difficult. She never accepts invitations, lives on the other side of the Bosphorus and has no telephone. She doesn't really like visitors any more, it seems, as she is spending all her time working on a history of English literature in Turkish.*

I have spent a fair amount of time with Sam Brewer of the Chicago Tribune *here. He has been ordered to India and has refused to go. He was there a few months ago and says that the restrictions on the press are so great that it is not worth being there. Nonetheless, I wish we could switch jobs. . . .*

The first mention that I can find in Dana's letters of the malaria he contracted in late August came in his November 17 letter, when he says he

---

[49] Halidé Edib (1882-1964). Author and one of Turkey's leading feminists.

has recuperated. In spite of his illness, he filed dispatches regularly and wrote letters home. A little of Christian Science from his grandmother seems to have rubbed off on him.

Well, here I am back at my desk and feeling fine. This jaundice [as he calls it, avoiding the word "malaria"] *is very unpleasant while it is going, but when it is finished one gets well again very fast.*

The weather has turned crisp and wintry here which very much agrees with me. Cold, ice and snow seem to have a peculiar fascination for me. If I get a holiday before my transfer to the mid-east, I've made tentative plans to go skiing with our American military attache, Colonel Jadwin, at Cedars of Lebanon, where I was last year. But there's no telling how things will work out.

A young fellow named Wadsworth came up the other day to be a clerk in the military attache's office and we are putting him up at our flat until he can find something. He doesn't speak a word other than English, as is the case with most of the young fellows being sent out. Our national neglect of foreign languages is a terrible weakness when we start working abroad.

J.A. Macintosh, who is the United Press *local correspondent in Istanbul, in addition to representing* Arab News Agency *and* Britanova, *tells me that his mother is now in Bermuda, Princess Hotel, where she is running all the canteens. Mac thought you might like to get in touch with her and said he would write a similar suggestion himself to his mother (although I gather he never does write.) Mac has become one of my best friends in Turkey. Sometimes I stay at his house when I go to Istanbul, and sometimes he stays here at our flat. He is full of nonsense and fun and I suspect from what he says that his mother is quite as good a sport as he.*

While I was ill I read Ingersoll's excellent Action on all Fronts, *about his trip around the world and especially in Moscow.* [50] *The name of Schmidt rates a mention in connection with dinner eaten at Agronsky's and my flat. And is, incidentally, one of the few names connected with Turkey which he managed to spell correctly. But altogether the book is a brilliant job of reporting. The*

---

[50] Ingersoll, Ralph, *Action On All Fronts: A Personal Account Of The War*, 1942.

argumentative chapters at the end are a bit too argumentative to make good reading, although I thoroughly agreed with him on most points.

In Dana's *UP* "dreamings-up" dispatch carried in many papers on November 18, he wrote:

BALKANS INCREASING RESISTANCE TO GERMAN RULE AS TIDE IS REVERSED
By DANA ADAMS SCHMIDT, United Press

ANKARA—Sabotage and resistance of all forms to German domination have increased throughout the Balkans as a result of the United States landing in Africa and the British sweep through Libya, reliable neutral diplomatic sources said today.

Diplomats newly arrived from the Balkans said that in Hungary families were playing the Star Spangled Banner and the Marseillaise in their homes and that last Sunday the American and French anthems were even played in some churches in the guise of church hymns.

In Rumania, Germans in civilian clothes were reported to be speaking French instead of German in public, as they had done on past occasions when things had gone wrong for the Axis.

From Greece came the report that olive oil workers had named the lower half of their presses Alexander, for the British Middle East commander, the other half Eisenhower, and the olives Rommel.

The dominant pro-Allied elements in Turkey were jubilant over African developments and both officials and private citizens showed new confidence in the Allies, especially in the ability of the United States to take the initiative.

In just a few hours my friend Bob Parker, head of the Office of War Information in Turkey, is heading for the United States, and he has volunteered to take this letter and a few things from Santa Claus! He is certain to reach the U.S.A. just about the right time, Dana wrote on November 27.

Father and Kenneth[51] *are out of luck, I'm afraid, because Santa Claus missed the boat, or the plane; the Brownies, or whoever does that kind of thing, had not finished initialing their handkerchiefs of Bursa silk*[52] *in time for sending, but they will be* [sent] *at earliest opportunity.*

Elizabeth too, will have to wait 'till Santa Claus makes his second round, as her coffee cups have not yet arrived from Istanbul and goodness only knows how they can be sent anyway; but they'll keep in cold storage.

Enclosed in their Christmas stockings however, Mother will find a strip of Turkish brocade with flowers on it and another which is identifiable by the large spot; Grandma will find one with boats and another with coffee pots. They are all supposed to be sixty to a hundred years old. The big pieces were used as towels in the old days and the smaller ones simply for decorative purposes, the sort of thing a girl was supposed to present her husband to show that she was very industrious.

For Steinie, Santa (the Turkish one) has sent about seven yards of finest Turkish [Bursa] *silk. Knowing Steinie, I'm sure she will find something nice to make out of it.*

Finally, news of me, which you will have received by cable already. I am scheduled to leave for Syria December 7 and will stay there several weeks to a month after which I [will] *get a new assignment. It was a long battle to get out of here, and it took a bout with malaria and jaundice to do it, but there it is at last! I'm feeling fine now.* He adds in the margin: *I'll probably get a little skiing* [in Syria].

November 28:

This is, probably, my last week in Ankara. I may postpone my departure a week if I see a chance of clearing up certain business matters [probably related to selling the Turkish press the services of *United Press*].

---

[51] See Appendix.
[52] Bursa silk is manufactured in the city of Bursa in northwestern Turkey, just south of Istanbul, located on the westernmost extension of the famous Silk Road. The silkworm is cultivated throughout the territory; there are more than fifty silk mills in the town.

Several special requests for stories have come in to bother me: a thousand words on conditions in Germany and a sketch of the Bulgarian prime minister. I'm trying to collect my wits to write a long-projected magazine article, too.

Now just imagine . . . I have just received five letters from you and one from Grandma which are all about a year old. They were addressed to me in Cairo and have only just been forwarded! There is one of Oct. 14, 1941, enclosing a recipe for Chocolate Devil's food cake which I will pass on to our present cook, Agathe, and then take with me to greener fields; one of Nov. 11 with a clipping of Elizabeth's Telesis exhibition[53]*; one of Nov. 4, and one of October 20. Grandma's letter of Oct. 14 enclosed a review of Ida Treat's book* The Anchored Heart[54] *which sounds most fascinating. Incidentally, I never received the copy of Ida's book.*

I am feeling very fit now, but shall be glad to have a few weeks off when I tear myself away from here. Most of all I shall regret leaving my dog Jimmy and our pleasant flat. But it would not be right to take Jimmy when my future movements are so uncertain. I would like to send for him if I settle down elsewhere, but that would break Agathe's [Dana's cook] heart.

When I leave I am abandoning all my old clothes, taking with me only the few good things. The shortage here is such that I can get a good price from an old clothes dealer and it is about time I invested in some new things. I will try to do so in Jerusalem. The stuff I got in Cairo last year turned out to be of very poor quality and poorly tailored. I won't try any cut-rate Indian tailors again.

Tonight Kaufman and Brown and I are dining at the Ankara Palace where, it is reported, a variety show is to be seen. Hasn't been anything like that around here in more than a year. Unfortunately the artists are pretty uniformly enemy subjects—Rumanians and Hungarians.

Turkish journalists were traveling around the United States, and Dana had asked his mother to welcome them with a dinner in Los Angeles. She

---

[53] See Appendix.
[54] The book concerns a wonderful old stone house that Ida Treat bought at Bréhat, an island on the coast of Brittany. Dana and I spent summers there as teenagers with Ida and Mother and a delightful French family. See Appendix.

went to a lot of trouble to arrange a dinner party with interesting guests. The newspapermen accepted but unfortunately miscalculated the distance from Boulder Dam, which they visited, to Los Angeles and missed the party.

It is such a shame that you did not manage to meet with the Turkish journalists when they came through L.A., Dana wrote on December 8. *Shukru Esmer came back with Mr. Steinhardt and I went around to see him yesterday. He apologized profoundly for not being able to have dinner with you and explained that he had had no idea that the trip to Boulder Dam was so far and that he would not be able to get back in time for dinner. It seems that he had to put in a long distance telephone call from Las Vegas to L.A. in order to find someone who knew your telephone number and could tell you he couldn't come. Nonetheless I am distinctly disappointed in him and the other editors and think they should have tried a little harder to see you. I have had Esmer and his wife to dinner several times and have also been invited to their house. It was perfectly grand of you to plan such a fine dinner with interesting people for them. Some of them complained that they did not meet enough people of their own intellectual class during the trip. . . . Well, if they didn't take advantage of invitations, such as yours, it was their own fault.*

Emin Yalman, who wrote you a letter from the East, has also returned but did not bring the presents you sent with him. He had to leave them in Egypt because his baggage was over weight, but they will be sent up on one of the next planes. I am delighted at the prospect of getting the [typewriter] *ribbons and toothbrushes; these are little things which cause plenty of annoyances when they are absent.*

Well, about my transfer. It looks as though December 19 would be the date of my departure. I would like to get to Beirut in time for Christmas. But I have several items of business I must clear here before leaving, and I have to know about when Eleanor Packard will arrive before I go.

Eleanor Packard was half the team of Reynolds and Eleanor Packard, responsible to *UP* for coverage from the front, Italy and North Africa. She had been transferred to Ankara, and until she arrived, Dana could not leave. On

December 24, Dana was able to report on an accord that would be welcomed by the Allies:

FORTHCOMING TURK-RUSS ACCORD
DIPLOMATIC VICTORY FOR ALLIES

ANKARA, Dec. 12—A Forthcoming Turko-Russian diplomatic accord, containing United States pledges to Turkey, will constitute a supreme accomplishment for the United Nations diplomacy in its efforts to overcome mutual suspicions between the two neighboring powers, it was believed today.

The accord probably will be announced next week, and it is reported that the United States will promise to serve as intermediary in case future misunderstandings arise between Turkey and Russia, confirm its respect of Turkey's territorial integrity and help Turkey in the event of invasion.

Turkey has been particularly apprehensive that a victorious Russia might occupy the Balkans after the war, obtaining a foothold from which she might threaten or actually take over the Dardenelles and the Bosphorus straits, fulfilling a centuries-old Russian dream of a free outlet to a warm water port and depriving Turkey of her position as an important power.

The term United Nations was coined by President Roosevelt in January 1942, when he met with representatives of 26 nations who pledged their governments to continue the fight against the Axis powers. The term was loosely used during the War to refer to the Allies. It was not until an international meeting in San Francisco on June 26, 1945, that the term became the official name of the organization of some 50 nations that we know today as the United Nations.

ARMY OF FRENCH OFFERED TO HITLER
LAVAL ALSO PLEDGES WAR EQUIPMENT

ANKARA, Dec. 24—Pierre Laval has agreed to send four divisions of French "volunteers" to aid Adolf Hitler in Russia, well informed sources said today.

The same neutral sources also said Laval will turn over to the Germans the physical equipment of the French army and navy.

Both moves would be subject to the approval of Marshall Henri Pétain, it was said.

Laval, bringing France into even closer collaboration with the Axis, has conferred with Hitler and Italian Foreign Minister Galeazzo Ciano.

Under the agreement, it was said, Germany after taking over the equipment of the French army and what is left of the French navy will repay France for its losses after the war.

Other provisions of the Laval-Hitler agreement, it was said, were:

1—Anti-aircraft guns all over France will be manned by units of the French army under German command in an attempt to inflict heavier damage on Anglo-American raiders against occupied Europe.

2—German technicians will direct the work in French munition factories and will have charge of French food distribution.

3—French labor laws will be changed to permit longer working hours for women.

4—France will send 300,000 specialists to work in German Factories.

5—There will be a campaign to place all persons opposing Franco-German collaboration into concentration camps.

Dana had hoped to be in Beirut for Christmas, but in his dispatch of December 24, still datelined Ankara, he was, instead, detailing this disheartening news of Pierre Laval, prime minister of Vichy France under Phillipe Pétain, working ever more closely with Germany and Italy. Convinced the Axis would ultimately prevail, Laval had veered far afield from his politics of the early 1900s when he was compared to Clarence Darrow for his championing of the French laboring class.

Yet, by the end of the following year, Dana's stories bore unmistakable signs that the tide of the war was about to turn.

Dana's apartment building in Ankara, Turkey

1943

January 3:

Still at the old address, [307 Atatürk Blvd, Ankara] *but not for much longer now I think.*

My latest notion is to take Jimmy with me when I go. I could park him with Gershon Agronsky at Jerusalem for a while if necessary. After all, half of him belongs to Gershon's nephew, Martin.

Goodness, imagine forgetting to mention the real news of the week. The other day I got a cable from New York saying that Washington has approved my credentials as a war correspondent. It took them a long time, but that doesn't matter. Now I'm all set to go anywhere the UP wants to assign me!

Yesterday an enormous package of magazines arrived at the Embassy for me—Esquire, Story, Saturday Review of Literature, American Mercury—*and a little envelope with the words "Dean Mary."*[55] *I appreciate it immensely. These magazines are very rare around here. We get a good many copies of* Life, Time, *and the* Readers Digest. *Dean Mary will get a letter from me shortly.*

This week, he wrote on January 12, *I have been up to my ears in preparation for departure. All that has been made more difficult by the fact that almost every meal has been a social engagement. The night I leave, Friday, there will be a big cocktail party for me at our house given by my roommates.*

I have decided to take Jimmy with me and have obtained the most elaborate certificate testifying to his good health. I fancy that I will park him with Gershon Agronsky at Jerusalem if he shows any desire at all to have him.

---

[55]　Dean Mary was Mary Sinclair Crawford, Dean of Women at the University of Southern California, a good friend of the family.

The office has been swell these last few days, telling me to stay on holiday until I feel completely and entirely "recuperated." I have actually been feeling very well for more than a month but the leave will do me good just the same. During the first week I will take an "Atabrine cure"[56] *which will take care of any possibility of the malaria recurring. I simply take a couple of Atabrine pills three times a day.*

A fellow named Leonard Kirschen is taking over the UP *for me here. He is a British subject of Rumanian origin and also works for the* London Daily Telegraph *and the* Exchange Telegraph, *a small British agency.*

I finally really and truly nailed down the Anatolian Agency as an honest to goodness customer of the UP with a real contract. The director of the Agency signed up about six hours before he left on a month's tour of India and China.

I am going to have to make this short this week. Among other things I'm trying to get an interview with Prime Minister Saracoglu before I leave.

January 23, Beirut:

Here we are, Jimmy and I, out of Turkey at last. We came the hard way, via Mersin, Iskenderun and Aleppo, instead of taking the Taurus Express which goes straight from Ankara to Tripoli.

I traveled with Frank Kaufman and a fellow named Jackson down to Mersin, where we looked over the port, and then by special private Diesel coach across to Iskenderun, where we looked over more docks and warehouses. From there they returned to Ankara and I took a taxi to the Syrian frontier, whence another taxi to Aleppo. [The censor removed the next line.]

The two Turkish ports are important enough to be interesting under any circumstance, but as towns they are about as dreary as possible. To make it drearier it rained all the time and we had wet feet for the better part of a week. Fortunately we were put up at the UKCC rest-house at Mersin, for

---

[56] A synthetic quinine substitute, synthesized from coal tar and widely used in World War II as therapy for malaria.

Britishers ordinarily, and at the British consulate at Iskenderun, after one stinking, literally, night at a pesthouse called Ankara Palas.

Aleppo was interesting for its huge covered bazaar and its thoroughly civilized hotel. And now, finally, I'm in Beirut, a delightful town with a fine seafront and snowcapped mountains inland. The sun has reappeared and it is pleasant and warm, a good place to spend that long-desired holiday before my new assignment. It doesn't look as though I'll have much idleness, however, as there seem to be all sorts of stories lying around. I'll be lucky if I get away for a little skiing.

Jimmy has behaved beautifully throughout, sleeping quietly on the floor in the wagon-lits [sleeping-cars] *and displaying his most charming manners to doubtful hotel keepers. It is not exactly cheap having him along, as it constantly involves extra tips, and the hotels charge a stiff price for his meals. I had thought of taking him to Jerusalem and leaving him with Agronsky,*

Jimmy, star of many stories

but now I think I'll take him to Cairo. I should think I'll be here another ten days and will then go on to Cairo. My latest telegrams indicate that I might then be assigned to the fleet. In any event I'll be in an American uniform.

There are a lot of people here whom I used to know in Ankara, most of them members of the French Embassy who have joined the Fighting French. I am having dinner with one tonight and lunch with another on Monday.

Did you see or get clippings on my interview with Saracoglu the day I left Ankara?[57] *It was a terrific scramble, arranging for, getting, writing, and getting censored, while I was trying to hand my office over to Leonard Kirschen, pack and go to a couple of parties all at the same time. I also went to all sorts of trouble to get the proper medical papers and certificates for Jimmy, but at the frontier the guards wouldn't even look at them. Jimmy was most insulted.*

This "recuperation leave" of mine has been so long delayed, I really don't need it at all anymore. I'm in as fine health as I have ever been.

Shortly after Dana visited the Adana region of Turkey with the ports of Mersin and Iskenderun on his way to Cairo, Prime Minister Winston Churchill visited Adana and the ports to confer with Turkish political and military leaders.

In a dispatch from Beirut on February 3, which was featured in the *Daily News*, Los Angeles, the *Pittsburgh Press* and many other papers, he wrote:

MATA HARI OF ADANA

Prime Minister Winston Churchill invaded the German espionage center for the whole Middle East when he went to Adana to confer with Turkish political and military leaders.

As a result he must have given spry 60 years old Fräulein Paula Koch, German espionage chief with headquarters at Adana, the busiest days in her life trying to pry out the secrets of the momentous conferences.

Fräulein Koch has been referred to as the Mata Hari of World War II and although this appellation appears extravagant, she certainly has been most active in Adana and the nearby ports of Mersin and Iskenderun, through which pass all Anglo-American supply shipments to Turkey.

---

[57] I found no clippings of this interview in Mother's collection.

Every 10 days or so she visits Iskenderun and sorts over reports from agents. They include the German Vice-Consul Hans Ulrich von Schweinitz, the dapper Italian consul Ignazui San Felice; numerous waiters who listen to table conversations and pump British sailors; Vichy Frenchmen who have taken refuge in the frontier town of Antioch, and finally, shadowy agents who slip across the border into Syria.

At similar intervals, she visits Mersin. Her activities of late however have been checkmated considerably by the newly-arrived American consul Hedley Cook; the shipping counselor, Hal Noble, and the British Consul General.

Turkish secret service agents also have taken effective measures toward limiting movements across the Syrian-Turkish frontier and otherwise hampering Axis agents.

February 6, Jerusalem:

I am writing this in a hurry, while I wait for our local correspondent to come and take me on a drive to the Dead Sea. I'm on my way to Cairo but have made a detour via Jerusalem to see Martin's uncle, Gershon Agronsky.

There are so many things I have seen in the past week . . . . I went up to the Cedars to ski for four days, but unfortunately it snowed all the time except the day I left. Had to leave on skis, carrying suitcase strapped on my back because the snow was too deep for porters—covered only seven miles first day. Next day got porters and covered twenty miles on skis and foot to a point where the snow ended and we were met by a military car. A British officer who had to get back on the job made the trip with me. What a business it was. It reminded me of the fantastic ski trip Dick Decou and several other friends and I tried to make in the High Sierra between Christmas and New Year's about six years ago.

Took me a full day to drive from Beirut to Jerusalem because the taxi drivers would squabble for hours over the cost of transporting my circus . . . two large suitcases, a pair of skis and a large dog. I got to Jerusalem in a state of physical, mental and moral exhaustion but recovered in the warm glow of Agronsky's hospitality. I spent most of yesterday with his assistant, who drove me out to Bethlehem to see the church of the Nativity. The church is interesting, to be sure, because of its historic associations. But it is not beautiful, and there is something a little sordid about the way different sects control particular alcoves of the place.

Two days later, he wrote:

A few hours ago, I arrived in Cairo after sitting up all night from Jerusalem. Am waiting for Leon Kay, our local bureau manager, to come and get me started in quest of my uniform and other equipment. It is still very much in doubt just what I am to do and where. Jimmy and I are staying at Kay's flat.

Before I left Jerusalem, I took a trip out to one of the cooperative settlements, which are primitively communistic . . . the sort of thing the Russians did twenty years ago. I went to the old city and visited the Mosque of Omar and the Wailing Wall. Neither are particularly impressive as far as their physical presence is concerned. . . . They become fascinating when you realize the past and present political significance, the conflict, ideals and hatreds which they represent.

The whole of Jerusalem and its surroundings is packed with points of historic, and also current interest. It is all on a small scale, not grandiose like our California surroundings, but close-packed with importance. Our Jerusalem correspondent drove me down to the Dead Sea and to Jericho. I would have gone swimming in the Dead Sea, but there was not time. It was very warm, much warmer than Jerusalem. Jimmy actually had sense enough to sniff but not to lick the water. You put your hand in it and it stays sticky with salt and chemicals for hours if you do not wash with fresh water.

There is almost nothing to see at Jericho unless you have time to investigate the excavations. We walked across Allenby Bridge to Transjordan. The town is a pleasant Arab village, a summer resort for wealthy Arabs.

But of course the most interesting thing about my trip was what I picked up on political discussions...which is too much and complicated to write about now. The whole trip has been thoroughly worthwhile from a personal and from a news point of view.

HEADQUARTERS
UNITED STATES ARMY FORCES
IN THE MIDDLE EAST

Cairo, Egypt.
February 11, 1943

AGREEMENT

In connection with authority granted by the War Department to me, the undersigned, to accompany U.S. Army Forces in the Middle East for the purpose of securing news or story material, still pictures or to engage in radio broadcasting, I subscribe to the following conditions:

1. That, as a civilian accredited to the Army of the United States within or without the territorial limits of the United States, I am subject to the Articles of War and all regulations for the Government of the Army issued pursuant to law.

2. That, I will govern my movements and actions in accordance with the instructions of the War Department and the commanding officer of the Army unit to which I am accredited, which includes the submitting for the purpose of censorship all statements, written material, and all photography intended for publication or release either while with the Army or after my return, if the interviews, written matter, or photography are based on my observations made during the period or pertain to the places visited under this authority. I further agree that I will submit for purposes of censorship all such material even though written after my return, if the interview, written material, or statements are based on my observations made during the period or pertain to the places visited under this authority. This includes all lectures, public talks, "off the record" speeches, and all photography intended for publication or releases, either while with the armed forces or after my return, if they are based upon my observations during this period or pertain to the places visited.

3. That, I waive all claims against the United States for losses, damages, or injuries which may be suffered as a result of this authority.

4. That, this authority is for the period February 11, 1943 to February 10, 1944 and subject to revocation at any time.

5. That, at the termination of my assignment, I shall surrender my credentials without delay to the Public Relations Branch, United States Army Forces in the Middle East.

Signed: Dana Adams Schmidt

Representing: United Press Associates
(Company, syndicate, or agency)

Witnessing officer: H W Campbell
1st Lt., A.G.D.
Asst. P.R.O.
(grade and organization)

Dana's agreement with the US Army in the Middle East February 11, 1943

I left a number of things in Ankara with C.D. Jackson. He promised to take them to the States with him. They include some black coffee cups which may be the very things Elizabeth really wanted. Anyway, they are hers.

February 17, [location removed by censor]:

Well, at last I am in uniform, even if only in the bastard capacity of war correspondent. That means that I am "subject to military law and entitled to be treated as an officer." I am a civilian as far as my newspaper work and the orders as to what I do and where I do it are concerned, but if I were captured I would be treated like any other prisoner of war. Of course a war correspondent carries no arms and is technically a non-combatant.

For the time being the UP *has side-tracked me down here, but soon I hope to have a more active assignment.*

My post-malaria leave didn't last very long. I found that I was feeling fine and cut the time to a week. When I read that Churchill had gone to Adana, I felt that I must get back on the job again. At the time I wrote a little feature about the so-called "Matahari of Adana" which you may have seen.

Dana in uniform. 1943; photo by J. Weinberg

The dog Jimmy is being taken care of by an [deleted by censor, but probably Egyptian boy] *who works out (................ .....) His folks have a house with a garden which should be fine for Jimmy—better than he had in Turkey.*

No letters from you for a long time, but doubtless they will all be forwarded and will catch up to me in a bunch.

Your birthday and Father's have gone by without my even writing a letter, I fear, with all the excitement of my leaving Turkey.

Life in town here (.......) [Cairo?] *is a great improvement on (........... ...)* [Ankara?] *All the amenities such as American cigarettes, toilet articles, movies, clothes, etc. are plentiful and cheap by comparison with Turkey. You can buy anything here with a minimum of restrictions and rationing. In fact, the only place I've struck where there was as serious rationing was (...............)* [Palestine?] *copying England; they call it "austerity." Some difficulty was encountered in putting it across, however, as there is no such word in Hebrew. As for the (........)* [Jews?] *they don't pay much attention anyway.*

In future I think you will get my mail more regularly than when I had to use the open civilian mails.

All my love to Grandma and Eliza and Ken, Father and Steinie. Jimmy sends fraternal sniffs to Torrey Pines.

Love,
Dana

Dana's War Correspondent credentials

Mother had received a request for information about Dana from the Columbia School of Journalism. On February 26, Dana was happy to be able to say:

You can now tell them that I am a war correspondent accredited both to the American and British forces in the Middle East. I am also now accredited to the British Navy.

So far it hasn't done me much good as far as writing stories is concerned. It's been mostly a matter of getting acquainted and getting my bearings. For the time being I have to stay in town but hope to get out to where things are happening soon.

It is very pleasant here just now, rather like California at its best. But I am told that it won't last long. It is quite indefinite how long I will stay here or where I might go from here, but, just in case it should work out that way, I am looking for an apartment that would serve as headquarters for me. When I am not in town Jimmy stays with Sam Souki who has a fine house and garden. In fact he has taken to Sam in a big way and doesn't seem to mind his master's absence a bit.

My American uniform has just come back from the tailor and I expect to wear it to go out dancing tonight. . . . I must consult one of the old hands concerning details such as shoes, socks, tie, and shirt. It all makes me feel a little self conscious, considering that I am as thoroughly unmilitary a gent as ever banged a typewriter. Education will come in time, doubtless.

March 3, Cairo:

I am now fairly well settled here and am getting to work on a few "enterprisers," which appear to be my chief concern for the moment and about all that can be done from here now. This is a much bigger puddle and quite a different one from (............) [Ankara?]. It takes some time to get organized . . . line up friends and news sources and find out just where you stand. But it is experience which you agreed with me that I needed after having the relatively small puddle (........ . .) [Turkey?] to myself so long.

March 3, 1943

Dear Mother:

I am now fairly well settled here and am getting to work on a few "enterprisers," which appears to be my chief concern for the moment and about all that can be done from here now. This is a much bigger puddle and quite a different one from _____ . It takes some time to get organized...line up friends and news sources and find out just where you stand. But it is experience which you agreed with me that I needed after having the relatively small puddle o _____ to myself so long.

Just after my arrival I cabled a 4,500 word magazine article about _____ to our special service department. Thusfar, I regret to say, they have not sold it, and I xx may be left holding the bag with my cable expenses, more than 700 dollars. I have told them that I will pay these and any other expenses involved in placing the article, so you may get a bill of sizable proportions to be paid out of my account before long.

Leon Kay, to whom this bureau belongs, is away on a trip so that I am covering press conferences. But they produce very little news, _____ is the spot just now.

A great many of my old friends from _____ , and also from the _____ are down here. In fact Turkey is now more or less deserted by the press, excepting visiting firemen who go up for a few weeks at a time. I wonder whether you have see many stories from there since I left, apart from the one big one about Churchill's visit.

The office here has an expense account system which is much more favorable than the one I was operating under in So ?I do not think it will be necessary for me to have the office hold part of my salary, as I cabled I was going to have them do. We get fifty dollars a week flat for expenses here, and it is possible to live on that most of the time. I am greatly relieved to be rid of the complications of financing myself which I had in _____ . Occasionally I will probably cable for some money, but most of the time you can count on saving the salary you get for me from U.P. Whenever you think advisable, invest. Preferably in things which are likely to be active after the warx and which pay dividends.

One nice thing about being here is that there are a few good-looking girls. In spite of their alleged emancipation, one rarely saw much of _____ , and most of the British and American ones had been sent elsewhere. Here there are quite a few American girls, including xxxxx nurses, some English, a lot of Greek and Jewish. Some of the _____ are quite attractive, too.

It is taking xx a great deal of patience to get used to British, or perhaps I should say Eastern, hours. Practically nothing can be done between 1 and 5 in the afternoon. Offices are then open from 5 till 8. Actually, the American army's offices have insisted on keeping American hours, casing no little confusion.

All my love,

Dana Adams Schmidt
War Correspondent
APO 616
care postmaster N. Y., N. Y.

Dana's censored letter March 3, 1943

Just after my arrival I cabled a 4,500 word magazine article about (.......) to our special service department. Thus far, I regret to say, they have not sold it, and I may be left holding the bag with my cable expenses, more than 700 dollars. I have told them that I will pay these and any other expenses involved in placing the article, so you may get a bill of sizable proportions to be paid out of my account before long.

Leon Kay, to whom this bureau belongs, is away on a trip so that I am covering press conferences. But they produce very little news. (......... . . .) [Tunis?] is the spot just now.

A great many of my old friends from (..........) [Turkey?] and also from the (............ . . .) are down here. In fact Turkey is now more or less deserted by the press, excepting visiting firemen who go up for a few weeks at a time. I wonder whether you have seen many stories from there since I left, apart from the one big one about Churchill's visit.

The office here has an expense account system which is much more favorable than the one I was operating under in (......... . . . .) [Turkey?]. So I do not think it will be necessary for me to have the office hold part of my salary, as I cabled I was going to have them do.

Meanwhile, one of Dana's articles appeared in the *New York Times*:

UNESCORTED LIBERATORS CARRY WAR
TO FAR AXIS MEDITERRANEAN BASES
U.S. BUILT CRAFT IN MIDDLE EAST COMMAND
HAVE LONG-RANGE BOMBING MONOPOLY—
RECORD IN ENEMY PLANES DOWNED IS 104

CAIRO, Egypt, March 7 (UP)—American made Consolidated Liberator bombers, whose sting has proved so fatal to the enemy that fighter escorts are unnecessary, tonight were revealed to be doing virtually all the long-range strategic bombing from the Middle East of Axis Central Mediterranean communication lines.

Disclosing that the Consolidateds are the work horses of the eastern end of the Allied aerial pincers, Colonel Hugo P. Bush, chief of the United States

Dana's War Correspondent badge with raised brass letters on cloth—one for each shoulder

Ninth Air Force's Heavy Bomber Command, said that Naples is the toughest and best-defended target the Americans have hit thus far. In nine day and night raids since December 4, which marked the first United States attack on continental Italy, the big B24s have dropped 600,000 pounds of explosives on the shipping and installations in Naples Harbor.

Colonel Bush, who is 43 years old and comes from New Providence, Pa., rejected the view that the American-style "pin-point" bombing could be done only in daylight. He explained that under bright moonlight, night operations were equally effective.

Long missions, averaging ten hours each, are the forte of the Liberators in the Middle East, he said. At no time have they been supported by fighter escorts. The concentrated fire of their heavy machine guns, as the ships fly in tight formation, is said to have proved so effective that many Messerschmitts wheel away without attacking.

In the seven months ending in February, all Ninth Air Force units under Major Gen. Lewis H. Brereton—but not including a Royal Air Force squadron under his command—have shot down 104 enemy planes and probably destroyed or damaged another 200. The American losses total 66 planes of all types plus several interned in Turkey.

Colonel Bush stressed that this was far below the 10 percent which all air forces regard as the maximum loss permissible for economic operations.

In addition the Ninth Air Force sank 51 ships, probably sent 30 more to the bottom, and damaged an additional 20.

In about 600 missions and about 6,000 sorties, almost 9,000,000 pounds were dropped. The biggest weight on any one target, 850,000 pounds, fell on Benghazi Harbor; Tripoli was second with 700,000 pounds, and Naples was third with 600,000.

Dana had great confidence in Mother to make good investments. She kept informed about business developments, belonged to an investment club, and had trusted advisors.

We get fifty dollars a week flat for expenses here, and it is possible to live on that most of the time. . . . Occasionally I will probably cable for some money, but most of the time you can count on saving the salary you get for me from UP. *Whenever you think advisable, invest. Preferably in things which are likely to be active after the war and which pay dividends.*

One nice thing about being here is that there are a few good-looking girls. In spite of their alleged emancipation, one rarely saw much of (..........) [Turkish girls?] *and most of the British and American ones had been sent elsewhere. Here there are quite a few American girls, including nurses, some English, a lot of Greek and Jewish. Some of the (..........)* [Egyptian girls?] *are quite attractive, too.*

It is taking a great deal of patience to get used to British, or perhaps I should say Eastern, hours. Practically nothing can be done between 1 and 5 in the afternoon. Offices are then open from 5 till 8. Actually, the American Army's offices have insisted on keeping American hours, causing no little confusion.

March 9, Cairo:

During the past week and more I've been handling most of the small trickle of news from here as Leon Kay is away on a trip. After a long pause, you've probably seen my by-line around again.

Jimmy is still on holiday in the country. He is staying at the house of a fellow named Quigley[58] *who edits an army newspaper.*

Quigley, to my great surprise, has turned out to be an old acquaintance from Pomona. We were never especially close, but we know a lot of people in common. He told me a shocking story about Barlow Bowen having been killed at the Claremont Inn. [In Claremont, California, just outside of Pomona College.] *Is that true?*[59]

There is nothing very striking to tell you about my life here. I eat well and drink more than I did in Turkey. There is nothing one cannot have for sufficient money. I can easily understand why the place has such a bad reputation and why it has generally been supposed to have such a demoralizing influence on people.

Last night I saw Frank Kaufman and C.D. Jackson, both on their way through to the States. Aren't they lucky? But both will be back in these parts shortly. I have, incidentally, inspired by their trip and other things, just composed a letter to the New York office suggesting that a little home leave for me might be a noble thing after four and a half years.

You should see my new camel's hair coat. I bought the camel's hair in Beirut and have just had it made up. Very warm and rather striking. Other new things of mine you might like to know about, besides the American officer's uniform I mentioned last week, are a British battle dress, which is the most practical clothing I've ever had and my usual garment, and a pair of desert shoes, with crepe soles and rough felt-like material tops. I also have

---

[58] The Egyptian lad, Sam Souki, who had been taking care of Jimmy, lived at Quigley's house as caretaker.
[59] Yes, it was true that Barlow Bowen, a Pomona College friend of Dana's was killed. To my knowledge, the circumstances were not publicly revealed, nor do I know what happened.

all the paraphernalia on hand to camp in the desert or elsewhere as soon as the UP *lets me go.*

The other day I finished reading Hemingway's For Whom the Bell Tolls. [60] *Have you read that? It is excellent, I thought. Also been reading the sections about the Arab world in Gunther's* Inside Asia. [61] *Knowing little about it, I thought it a very competent summary. Everyone affects to despise Gunther's* Inside Books. *It's a stock professional pose among newspapermen.*

I am anxiously waiting to hear whether George[62] *gets anywhere with his application for a job over here. I know very well that he could handle it nicely.*

Our father died on March 23, 1943, of a heart attack in his doctor's office in Portland, Oregon. Dana received the news in a telegram from Mother.

March 25:

Mother, I know you must feel very lonely now, even though Father was away so much. If only I could be with you, or just telephone, it would help, perhaps.

Now you must depend on me for everything I can possibly do. And you must keep well, and cheerful, now until I come home, which will not be too much longer. I depend on you, Mother, hearing from you, knowing that you are there, more than you know.

I only wish I had written to Father more often in the last few years. It is so easy to be thoughtless and forget and let the time slip by. Perhaps I did not know Father as well as I might have, although we got to know each other pretty well on several of the long automobile trips we made together. I know that he loved you very much and that you were the most important thing in his life.

---

[60] Hemingway, Ernest, 1940. Hemingway took his title from a quotation from John Donne: "Any man's death diminishes me, because I am involved in mankind, and therefore never send to know for whom the bell tolls; it tolls for thee."
[61] Gunther, John, *Inside Asia,* New York, Harper Brothers, 1939. The "Inside" books were very popular in their day. They sold 3,500,000 copies over a period of thirty years.
[62] George Martin—see footnote #7.

It is my responsibility now to look after you to the extent that I can. I don't know exactly where we stand financially, but you must tell me. [Money was hardly ever discussed in the family.] *From now on you must regard the money that is paid me by* United Press *as being as much yours as mine, to use for extraordinary or current expenses as it may be needed. It constitutes my entire salary, including a small percentage which is technically earmarked as a "living allowance," and which might be cut off at some future date. In addition I am getting fifty dollars a week locally which is vaguely identified as for "expenses." As this is not enough for me to live on most of the time, I will probably ask the* UP *to hold a part of my regular salary soon so that it can be paid to me regularly instead of my cabling you constantly.*

You can depend on me to work hard and decently. I don't know how far that will get me, but it's about all I lay claim to.

Sad as I am with you it makes me happy to think that you have near you our faithful Steinie, and Grandma, Elizabeth and Ken.

On March 24, he wrote in a letter to me:

It is so very nice to have letters from you, and I already owe you several at that. It is only sad that it is Father we must write about. I am sorry that I did not keep in closer touch with him the last few years.

Now what a shame the coffee cups were broken, mostly. I thought that sending them by hand they would be all right. No matter. I have some more, the original lot I bought for you Eliza, but never managed to send. These cups are in silver holders and much more fragile than the ones broken. I shall have to find a very, very safe hand if I dare send them at all. [Unfortunately I never received them.]

I gather you are both working very hard. It is a good thing to be faced by specific problems, as you are in architecture[63] *and such likes, to know exactly what you are up against, how many feet and inches.... I, on the contrary,*

---

[63]   I was working for Douglas Aircraft, making illustrations for job booklets. My husband, Kenneth, ran the drafting room for the Navy in Long Beach.

never know until the last minute, if then, just what I must do and how. Your job is concrete, mine is abstract and volatile—if you follow. However, not knowing much about anything else, I guess I'll have to stick to reporting.

All right Elizabeth, you wear the silver belt, and when I get me a wife, if and when, we'll make it a wedding present from us to her. I was particularly charmed by that belt, it is so flexible and graceful—much lighter than most Turkish work. [64]

I had written Dana about Judy, a cat that we acquired:

Jimmy has expressed considerable interest in this peculiar cat of yours. He has made it his life work to exterminate cats, so far as possible, and is not at all sure that he approves. But I have told him that in America all animals have equal rights, and if he doesn't make his peace with Judy he will never get his naturalization papers.

In his April 1 letter to Mother from Cairo, he wrote:

Since my last letter I have been to Alexandria for a few days holiday after a full month on duty. There is not a great deal of hot news, but a steady dribble of small stuff that keeps me busy, especially when I try to do a few "enterprisers" in addition. I like Alexandria. It is relatively clean and airy, and the Navy has seen to it that there is plenty of entertainment.

I trust your scrapbook is growing again. Not everything from (.........) [Cairo?] *is mine, of course, and all my stories are not necessarily signed, so I would suggest that you keep stuff of mine that is signed separate from (..........)* [Cairo?] *datelines. My dispatches just lately have included an interview with the Greek Premier, with Whitney Strait about air transport, with a*

---

[64]   I remember wearing the belt but don't know what happened to it. Perhaps Dana did get it back. As I remember it, the belt was made of silver mesh with a handsome silver buckle. I wore it with a black dress.

Colonel Rush about American long range bombing, mail stories about a great American depot somewhere in (............) about the Middle East Supply Center, about the adventures of a Danish sea captain who was interned in Russia, and about the political situation in Syria and Lebanon[not available]. *I have also had a couple of pieces about Turkey's political and strategic situation, and masses of routine articles about the RAF.*

Tomorrow I am going to spend the day on a trip to a Greek refugee camp which is being visited by the (................ ...). All this is of course not exactly what I wanted; I wanted to get to the battle—but it is more interesting than Turkey and I simply haven't been able to get away from here because we already have our quota of men at the front. Also, UP seems to think I am needed here.

Yes, we can send V-mail [65] *I just haven't got around to it yet. Next letter maybe.*

Martin Agronsky has completely disappeared from my ken. His uncle and I sent him a cable from Jerusalem, but no answer.

I wouldn't want to do any boasting about my Turkish, about which you inquire. I know a few words and phrases. That is all. What I did learn in Turkey was fluent French, because French is the current language of culture and of all foreigners there.

As regards to my money, I haven't yet decided whether I can manage to live on my expense money which is paid to me locally, or whether I'll have to dip into my salary. It gives me a lot of satisfaction to think that you are looking after my affairs and that they are in good shape. And you must remember that my savings account is really a joint savings account. You must not go short of things or slight yourself in order to economize while I am making a pretty good salary and actually stowing a good deal away.

---

[65] Letters to and from members of the military, their families and friends were written on specially designed letter sheets. These were put on microfilm, and the films were sent overseas, thus saving much-needed shipping space. At local centers, the letters were printed and sent to the addressee.

April 12, Cairo:

Today I received a most impressive quantity of V-mail letters from you, Elizabeth, Kenneth and Grandma. It was thoughtful for the whole family to write me about Father.

My trip "forward" to the Air Force has been postponed, to my considerable annoyance. But for the moment I have had to bow to the necessity of keeping us covered here. I'm surprised you have seen nothing at all of mine, although I realize that we are pretty much off the map just now. I think the clipping bureau will be coming along with something presently; I had a cable of commendation on my interview with the Greek Premier and another on my coverage of a (. . . .) [air]*raid by American Liberators on Messina and San Giovanni harbors.*

Tonight I am having a little dinner party, the first, as it happens, since I arrived, with a Turkish man who edits a magazine in Turkish, his sister, and an English couple I met at the (. . . . .) [ski resort, the Cedars] *more than a year ago. I try to keep in close touch with the Turks here.*

It was nice of C.D. Jackson to take the things along for me. I wrote him the other day thanking him and asking him for Frank Kaufman to get in touch with you if possible. I think a lot of C.D.—one of the best people I've met in a long time. In a few moments I must leave to go out to the airdrome and see what Archbishop Spellman has on his mind—probably a lot more than he will tell about. It is grand to think you will get this so soon, after the terrific delays we have been accustomed to. [66]

April 21:

I put this letter off a day or so hoping there would be one from you to answer and hoping to be able to tell you that at last I am off in the direction of (. . . . .) [the Front?]. *The latter hope at least has been fulfilled and*

---

[66]   See Appendix.

I am leaving in the morning to join the U.S. fighter group in (............) [Tunisia?] for a few weeks or more.

Everything has remained quite calm here of late and I fear you have seen little of my by-lines. UP doesn't want anything from my present dateline as long as the fighting is hot elsewhere and squawks every time we try to spread ourselves a bit.

Since last I wrote I've had two more all too expensive dinner parties at my hotel—trying to pay back some of accumulated social obligations. It is surprising how many there are. I sigh for my apartment in Ankara, where entertaining was convenient and relatively inexpensive.

Hal Peters, about whom I have written from time to time . . . turned up here today on his way to Tehran to represent the OWI [Office of War Information]. He said that Fred Oechsner has also left the UP and gone to work for something called, I think, the Office of Facts and Figures. I am indeed sorry to see him out of the UP. He was one of our few really outstanding men. Jack Fleischer who was in Fred's office is now in Stockholm, according to Hal. By the time this war is over the newspaper world is going to look a good deal different from what it was; it's my hunch that a lot of the fellows who have gone to work for the government will never get back into proper newspaper jobs again. Most people don't realize how easily they can be replaced.

It is now almost eleven p.m. and before I leave at seven-thirty in the morning I've to finish this, do an expense account, and write a couple of little stories. The past hour and a half I have been packing my bed-roll and suitcase under the benevolent guidance of a veteran. There is a lot more than one might think to taking the right things, leaving behind the rest, and fitting it all neatly together. One must not, it seems, forget toilet paper, matches, soap, eating utensils, plenty of typing paper, spare ribbons, whiskey, cigarettes, flashlight and goodness knows what else. Good thing I don't have to tote a gun too.

April 23:

My first letter to you from the "forward area" and may it be the first of many, because I like it up here.

. . . . Cairo was an improvement on Turkey, but now for the first time I feel that I am doing the sort of job I really want to do. The last few days I spent with an American unit and tomorrow I'll be going out to visit another one. I'm supposed to stick entirely to the Air Force, as we already have a man with the Army. Tomorrow will decide whether I'll go up in one of the bombers just yet or not.

I got here via detours and delays, since my first transport plane broke down, fortunately at a desert airdrome. I went on in another transport plane which was carrying, believe it or not, a load of toilet seats. Then I hitched a ride with some South Africans who were delivering a bomber; I rode under the gun turret from which I could see nothing except the feet of the man who was, I believe, the navigator. Unfortunately the South Africans went to the wrong airdrome, but we soon arranged for another lift, this time in a (...............) bomber; I got the same seat though.

South Africans finally put me up that night, still a lap from my destination. I shared a tent with a couple of engineering students—first rate people. Now I am parked in a tent in a pleasant olive grove. If it weren't for the fighting not many miles away and the planes passing constantly overhead, it would be a fine place for a picnic. There is also the slight inconvenience of absence of running water. I'm beginning to smell slightly and must investigate the possibilities of taking a bath out of my steel helmet. Of course it seems paradise to the fellows who have been through the desert. The fields are ablaze with poppies, white and yellow daisies, and all sorts of little blue and violet flowers I cannot identify.

Incidentally, I keep running into people from Los Angeles or Southern California around here, but none so far that I know. Bob Landry of LIFE *magazine whom I met here turns out to be an old Los Angeleno. I liked him. He is thirty, divorced, makes a lot of money, is easy-going, competent, husky, unaffected. He was with Slim Aarons of* Yank. *Landry and I agreed that the Agencies have probably missed a good bet by not spending a little or a lot of money to give the American public a lot of special wartime service—home town news about the men in the field for instance. Perhaps financial problems make it impossible. But it would have largely obviated necessity for a lot that outfits like OWI are doing.*

I'm writing this by the light of an oil lamp which reflects much more light into the great out of doors than it should. By my side is my American army cot and six English blankets to keep me warm. I wish they were American too; American ones are lighter and warmer, and it gets very cold at night. Mosquitoes and flies aren't bad where I am tonight, but they are maddening some places. I have a fine American mosquito net, with separate head-piece—again the best. Most, though not all, the American stuff is excellent. Our fellows eat infinitely better than anyone else, as might be expected. During the last few days I've had peanut butter, American coffee, canned corn, ice cream, cream of wheat, pancakes and goodness knows what else for the first time in months or years. The British love to be invited to an American mess, although they are wary of some things, like canned corn. But even plain English army food is sufficiently new for me to enjoy it. Corned beef is excellent when not repeated too often, and I didn't really mind lunch of hard biscuits, butter, and tea the other day. I'm willing to guess I put on weight.

It is very quiet tonight except for the shrill throbbing hum of many distant crickets. They are crickets, I suppose. One night we could hear the artillery barrage rumbling in the distance, but tonight it is quiet. The man who is sharing my tent, or whose tent I am sharing, is Paul Bews (..................) of the Daily Mail *of London. He is in his middle fifties but looks and acts much younger. He fought in the last war. He went to bed some time ago and has just put out his light, indicating I suppose that he would like me to stop typing. He shuns bombing raids and the like with the remark that he did his flying and fighting in the last war.*

Another man up here is Fred Bayliss of Paramount News *who has been up on twenty-one bombing raids and has made practice jumps with parachute troops to get his pictures.*

It is only 9:30 in the evening, but out here it seems very late. Life begins again at daybreak. The Tommies attached to the Public Relations unit have to get out and do set-up exercises, but correspondents may snooze as long as they like. Within limits they are free to do anything or go anywhere they like. Public relations will usually find transportation. Correspondents are welcome almost everywhere. Far more (. . . . .) [trust or confidence?] *is placed in them than would be the case in (. . . . .)* [Cairo?]. *Most officers go on the assumption that they can tell a correspondent anything and depend on his discretion.*

Most irksome thing about life in the field is the importance and complication of routine personal activities to which one never gives a thought in town. Water must be fetched and heated. Something must be found to put it in. Beds must be folded and unfolded and blankets rolled and arranged and everything packed up neatly over and over again. Shaving is a ritual instead of an almost unconscious function of a few minutes. One of the advantages is that food appears and is quickly consumed—none of this hanging around waiting for bad-tempered waiters to bring the next course.

The article below, mentioned in Dana's June 6 letter, warranted a note of praise from Jalex.

MORALE OF NAZI PILOTS SHAKEN
ALLIED SUPERIORITY IN AIR WOULD
MAKE TUNISIA EVACUATION A SLAUGHTER
By DANA ADAMS SCHMIDT

TRIPOLI, April 27 (UP)—Brig. Gen. Aubrey C. Strickland told United Press today that Allied air superiority is so great in Tunisia that the Axis will be lucky to have many planes capable of operating when the final squeeze in the coffin begins.

Strickland, who commands United States Warhawk and medium bomber groups with the western desert air striking forces, said that if the enemy decides to evacuate Tunisia, the slaughter "will be the most terrific thing you have ever imagined."

He said there were definite signs that the morale of the remaining German air crews is shaken. They now often evade combat and at other times are so vulnerable they are shot down like ducks.

Recent Allied destruction of air transport both incoming and outgoing from Tunisia, is likely to force the Germans to confine air transport attempts to night operations. German fighters, it was reported, now rarely rise to intercept allied planes except to get in the air to avoid being destroyed on the ground.

In the past five weeks, Allied air forces operating in half-circle around the Axis-held northeastern corner of Tunisia have destroyed about 500 German aircraft.

Of the 500, American crews have accounted for about 100. One American outfit, since the first of March has destroyed 81 enemy planes with five probables and 37 damaged, with a loss of only 11 men. Since the group began operating at El Alamein, their score is 146 destroyed, 17 probables, and 77 damaged.

This is going to be a short one, Dana wrote May 4, *as I have a truck waiting to take me to another air group . . . .*

It has been grand and quite a novel experience after all these years to be associating with so many Americans, and eating American food. The American flyers eat excellently, as one might expect. Even the RAF eats better than the British army. I had a steak the other night which was part of regular rations.

I am writing in a pleasant olive grove where a cool breeze wafts among the poppies(. . . . .) [in Tunisia?] *It is very nice, and makes it difficult to realize that (. . . . .) in the air and on the ground fighting is going on. Almost all the time, if you listen, you can (. . . . .)* [hear the bombing?] *in the distance.*

The driver is now getting extremely impatient and I must close.

Love to all,

Dana

U. S. PILOTS SAY P-40S OUTFLY NAZI PLANES
By DANA ADAMS SCHMIDT
United Press Correspondent

With the U.S. 57th Fighter Group in Tunisia, May 6—United States fighter pilots co-operating with the British Eighth Army said today although German Messerschmitt 109s are speedier and enjoy a higher ceiling, American P-40 Warhawks can out-maneuver the enemy at lower altitudes and with their superior fire power they average about four victories for every American plane lost.

The 57th group is credited with shooting down 150 Axis craft over the western desert and Tunisia since El Alamein.

Dana with the crew of the "Pink Lady, Earthquake Squadron," in Tunisia, 1943

"Even though we can't climb with the Messerschmitts, or dive with them, or keep up with them, we can fight with them," members of the Black Scorpion and Fighting Cock squadrons explained.

"We can't go after them, though. They can break off and go home anytime they like, but we have to hang on. One place where we beat the 109 is on the inside turns at low altitudes. An experienced German pilot never will try to turn with us, but lots of Germans now seem inexperienced."

In addition the American unit, which on April 18 shot down 77 Axis planes from a German aerial convoy noted that it enjoys numerical superiority.

"Besides" it was added, "the P-40s have excellent fire power with their six machine guns. They are sturdy enough to get home even when riddled with bullets. That makes them good for fighter bombing and strafing, but, we need a top cover for which the Spitfires are best."

May 11:

As you may have seen by my clippings, I went up with the American medium bombers on an important raid, or mission as they call it. I won't describe it at length here, as you should be able to read about it in print. Anyway, the idea of flying in one of those things doesn't scare me as much now as it did before, and I'm hoping to go up with the South Africans today!

A few days ago we found time to look around the holy city of (............ . . . .)[Kairouan, Tunisia?] a city of a hundred mosques.[67] It is the most attractive Arab town I've seen. All white houses and arcades, surprisingly (relatively) clean, and colorful, with flags draped about the bazaars, native rugs for sale, and fancy native costumes. These Arabs are much more advanced, economically and educationally than the average.

One of the boys at the American bomber group I visited had heard me quoted on the American radio the night before I arrived, telling all about the American fighter planes, so I had a good reception. And I ran into George

---

[67] The fourth holiest city of Islam (after Mecca, Medina and Jerusalem). Famous for the Sidi Oqba, the great mosque of Kairouan.

Dana speculating on lunch at a bazaar in Tunisia, 1943

Palmer (...............) correspondent, the other day, and received from him a clipping of one of my stories which appeared in the New York Times *March 7 . . . about our Liberator bombers.*

Somehow I seem to have specialized in air news down here.

Wonder how my Jimmy dog is getting along in Cairo. He would like it where I am now, but I don't think he'd make a very good airplane passenger. . . .

May 18, from somewhere on the Tunisian front [This is one of the few letters that wasn't censored]:

Well I've been having quite a few little adventures these last few days, flying about in bombers and getting lifts in Generals' private planes. With any luck you should have read some of it in the newspapers. I'll be mighty interested to hear how the clippings look.

It is amusing to think that it was from Reynolds and Peebe Packard's office in Rome that I began my peregrinations which have finally got me here. Now Peebe has taken over my Turkish job and I find Reynolds Packard here. He, incidentally, went up in a Fortress over Messina, I believe, about the same day I went up in a Mitchell. His trip probably made better headlines—bigger plane, bigger target.

Ed Beattie, whom I haven't seen since Berlin, left this place the day before I arrived. It's too bad I missed him. There is all sorts of fresh new Unipress talent around here . . . a fellow named Chris Cunningham, Phil Ault, Coe, Ned Russell, George Palmer, in addition to Pinkley, Richard MacMillan, and Packard. A most formidable gathering of the clan.

Covering my bit of the Tunisian campaign has been a considerable strain and I am distinctly tired physically. But at the same time it's done me a lot of good. I haven't been so happy with a job in a long time. Being out of doors all the time I'm sunburned and exceedingly healthy. Maybe flying is in some way akin to skiing, even if you're only a passenger.

No date, Cairo:

Here I am back from my travels and a wonderful deluge of mail awaiting me. Five from Mother, two from Elizabeth, one from Grandma, and one from the N.Y. office and one from C.D. Jackson saying he delivered the coffee cups . . . too bad they were broken. Elizabeth can tell the insurance people they cost about (............) each or about $5.55 each at the diplomatic rate of exchange. Anyway, I've got some others which are nicer for Eliza. I'm afraid that after my recent splurge of activity I'm back in a backwater. The Head office directed me to hurry back because Kay has been ill. There really isn't much of anything to be done and everyone is profoundly bored. I have and doubtless will produce a good deal of mail copy during these dull periods but it doesn't seem to get much play. Perhaps if you wrote to Joe Alex Morris, Foreign News

Editor, United Press Association, *220 East 42nd Street, N.Y.C., he could arrange to put you on the mailing list of the* United Press Red Letter [68], *in which most such mail stuff appears. It is mailed out, particularly to small backwoods clients. He'll probably try to sell you a subscription!*

I had a letter from him answering my request for home leave saying that of course you've been away from the U.S. for a long time and it is always helpful to get back here and renew your acquaintance with America. Right now, however, it seems that you are in the best possible position to do what you've been working toward for so long, the war front. Travel is extremely difficult at present and I know that you would not want to be tied up here and unable to get back to the scene of action you've been longing for when the time comes. . . . All of which is quite true. But I'll keep on pressing for home leave at the earliest opportunity.

June 6, Cairo:

Tomorrow I expect to go off on a junket to Iraq for a few days. Don't think it'll be much of a story, but a bit of useful education for the time when big stories come my way again.

Your letter of May 17 reached me some days ago. It is grand to think we are so near, in point of time, considering the fantastic delays there used to be from Turkey. I do hope you get a clipping or two on my trip in the field. You must have, as one clipping came back from the New York office, with a note saying that the story had had good play around New York and elsewhere. That was the one of my interview with General Strickland. And a couple of other stories came back in our service for the Middle East.

It has turned exceedingly hot, but I really don't mind the heat. Went swimming at the famous Gezira Club in the afternoon [see poem on next page]. *Now I'm all sun-burned and thoroughly tired out with a lot more work*

---

[68] *The United Press Red Letter* contained dispatches that were not put on their daily teletype to the mainstream newspapers but were sent to small-town newspapers.

> ODE TO A GEZIRA LOVELY.
>
> They call me Venal Vera, I'm a lovely from Gezira
> The Fuehrer pays me well for what I do
> The order of the battle I obtained from last nights rattle
> On the Gold Course with a Brigadier from "Q"
> I often have to tarry in the back seat of a Gharry,
> Its part of my profession as a spy,
> And while his mind's on fornication, I'm extracting information
> From the senior G.S.O. from G.S.I.
> When I yield to the caress of the D.D.W. (S),
> I get from him the low down on the works,
> And when sleeping in the raw with a major from C 4
> I learn of Britain's bargains with the Turks
> On the point of his emission in the twenty third position
> While he quivers in erotic ecstacy
> I hear of the location of a very secret station
> From an oversexed S.O. from O.2.E.
> So the Brigadiers and Majors and the whiskey soaked old stagers
> Who enjoy themselves away from Britain's shore
> Why should they bring victory nearer when the lovelies from Gezira
> Provide them with a lovely fucking war.

Among Dana's papers was this little "Ode" about the women of the Gezira Club, which gives one aspect of life in Cairo.

to do tonight before I go in the morning. Somehow that's the way I always go off on trips, in an exhausting splurge of activity, necessary and unnecessary.

June 15:

I'm just back from my visit to the Polish Army in the Middle East. The story must have got some play as it came back here in our incoming service—and was that a hot trip. I thought I didn't mind the heat, but I was wrong. The heat was aggravated by having to travel for the better part of two days in the back of a bouncing careening truck which did everything except cartwheels . . . . Drinking tea, hot, and cold lemonade, pop, coffee, water, whiskey, gin, beer, etc. etc. proved a temporary antidote against all these evils, but always with a boomerang effect. One simply should not drink alcohol during the heat of the day in such country and one must control one's desire for iced drinks or the stomach and general constitution rapidly revolts.

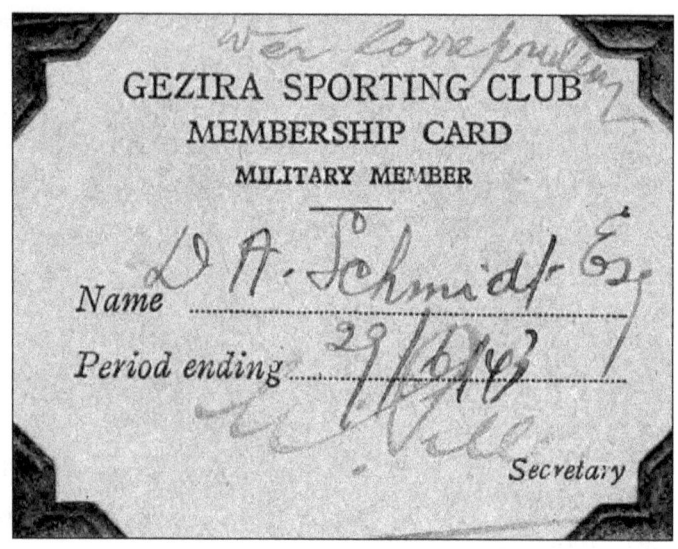

Dana's membership card for the Gezira Sporting Club in Cairo, 1943

In Baghdad I saw my old and good friend Tommy Thompson, looking taller, grimmer, thinner and more aquiline than ever, something like a cross between Punch and an American Eagle. He used to be British Counselor in Ankara. He carries a huge baton with him at all times, whether for show or protection I did not ask. He must be a terror to the Iraqis he has to deal with. I gather that the British are in pretty good control, and Tommy is the man who gives the orders and sees that they are carried out. It is a miraculous thing that a man like that should have such a soft and warm place in his heart for newspapermen. He prefers their company to that of his fellow diplomats quite evidently. He even forgives certain low characters among my Ankara colleagues who on occasion betrayed his confidence; for some perverse reason I think he prefers them.

Baghdad is a dreadful place from all points of view, the heat, the flies, the filth, the stench. Only at night it looks romantic when one sits on the terrace of the Hotel Zia, drinking the desert dream cocktails celebrated by John Gunther in his Inside Asia *and watching the lights twinkle up and down the shores of the Euphrates.*

Now it would appear that I am to join the Navy for a while. There are too many of us around here (in Cairo) and practically nothing to do. Henry Gorrell and Richard MacMillan are back, Kay has recovered from his illness, and we scarcely produce a story a day. I am not at all happy about working with Kay. He has opposed everything I wanted to do since I came and I think he has consistently worked against my interests.

Tonight I have a blind date with an American Red Cross *welfare worker—I think that's it. I am not sure whether I need any welfare work done on me, but am willing to try it.*

No letter from you this week. I still owe one to Elizabeth and Grandma. They should know that although I don't write as often as I should I am thinking of them.

June 21, Cairo:

Just got your V-mail letter telling of receiving a clipping from Tripoli. Well I hope you got a lot more than that during the period, but I'm afraid there won't be anything at all during most of June. It is distressingly quiet and it is possible that I will go to Algiers. The idea that I should go to the Navy seems to have died for the moment.

Virgil Pinkley has become New European Manager, a job last held by Webb Miller. I'm not quite sure yet how much it means, but the more it means the better I like it. He is quite a remarkable combination of the newspaperman and the businessman, but I think the balance of his talents is really in the business and administrative field—probably he works too hard.

Arthur Hays Sulzberger, the Tzar of the Times, *went through here in a brace of excitement a while back. Remember I gave his son and daughters skiing lessons at their house in White Plains when I was at Columbia? He was on his way to Moscow. Maybe I'll see him on his way back.*

I wrote a page for a magazine call Cephe, *printed half in Turkish and half in French for distribution in Turkey by British propaganda. A review of the news for the previous two weeks—supposed to net me five pounds, if the check ever comes.*

ELIZABETH SCHMIDT CRAHAN

June 29, Cairo via V-mail:

There are rumors that only V-mail will really go all the way by air, so I guess I'd better start using it again.

I have little to tell you this week as it has mostly been a matter of waiting for a hoped-for transfer to Algiers. . . . I've discovered that even the few stories we thought were in our territory are now being covered from Algiers, all most discouraging, but hardly a matter I can control.

Meanwhile I've been out to the Gezira Club [see poem on page 195] *quite regularly and getting myself a little sun-tan. Also learned to play squash, an excellent game, especially if one doesn't care to go out in the scorching sunshine. There is also a very nice swimming pool out there.*

Yesterday I got a most charming letter from Dr. Lowman. It is good of him to remember me and I will write him shortly. [69]

July 5, Cairo, via V-mail:

This week I have good news indeed. I am being transferred to Algiers. Leaving at the crack of dawn tomorrow morning. News that I was to go came early this morning, and ever since I've been on the run getting things lined up for departure. It's the same story every time—but not so bad on this occasion. How many of my letters to you in the past year have been about desires or plans to go somewhere, or arriving or leaving. Movement becomes an end in itself. And so, for that matter does all the dilly-dallying about with credentials and permits and orders. There is so much waiting and jockeying for position and politics that one almost forgets that the object is to write stories. Another bane is the tendency to become dependent on official handouts and pronunciations—very dangerous, especially so because head offices generally find they get their news quicker and cheaper that way, and to hell with quality.

---

[69] Charles Le Roy Lowman, MD, founder and head of the Orthopaedic Hospital in Los Angeles, was known for his remarkable work with paralysis resulting from polio and accidents. He took care of our mother and became a life-long friend of the family.

Yesterday there was a very fancy baseball game between correspondents and American Public Relations, a propos of July 4. In spite of my Ankara training I'm afraid I don't fit into the baseball picture very well, and I kept to the sidelines. Quentin Reynolds[70] *got some handy publicity for himself by being wheeled to his position in left field in a bath chair, the theory being that he was too drunk to walk. Mr. Kirk, the Minister, threw the first ball and General Strahm umpired. Well, I'll stick to skiing; that's my sport. Did I tell you that one of the American Public Relations Officers, Major Bill Wilber, taught me to play squash? He is going home shortly and might just possibly get out to Los Angeles and call on you. I hope he is going to bring you a lot of Turkish coffee cups, for Elizabeth.*

July 18:

It is now two weeks since I have written to you. But they were war weeks so full with frantic activity that I think I may be excused. Needless to say I haven't received any of your letters, moving around so fast. I have missed them.

My transfer from Cairo came through after unaccountable delay. The authorization seems to have been misrouted or lost for a week. Then I took off for (............) [Algiers?] just before another message arrived telling me not to go to (............) at all but to do something quite different.

All was routine as far as Tripoli. There I thought I'd gain a few hours by picking up a ride with a plane which was trying to get through to (............) that same day. They were nice boys, but I'm afraid they were just a little over-optimistic. It got dark and our radio failed when we were just ten miles out over the water. But with luck found a landing field, spent an uncomfortable night and reached (............) next morning.

I got out one story from (............) a speculative job about invasion possibilities and then moved on to my present address. I can't go into the

---

[70] Quentin Reynolds, prominent correspondent, writer and editor 1902-1965. Known for his clever quotes, such as: "The scientist split the atom, now the atom is splitting us."

details, but there was a lot of unnecessary and unfortunate confusion about my transportation and in the end I missed the first day of the invasion.

British and American ships had crossed the Mediterranean from Libya, Tunisia, and Malta. Some of the ships landed near Syracuse, on the southeastern shore of Sicily, and others on the southwestern shore. The invasion was called Operation Husky and was said to be the largest amphibious landing of the war, even larger than the Normandy landing, which didn't occur until June 6, 1944.

Unfortunately, many paratroopers were lost in the Husky landing. An unseasonable storm caused chaos in the air. Some of the pilots were inexperienced, and air navigators were handicapped by working with daytime photographs causing men to be dropped in wrong parts of Sicily. Worse, some men came down in the sea and were drowned. The ships and troops were under fire from Nazi and Italian forces. The troops battled their way across the island, a tough journey. They secured Sicily, a strategic island across from Tunisia, and controlled the sea lanes of the Mediterranean, in addition to providing a gateway to Italy and Axis-controlled Europe.

The third day of the invasion I was in Sicily. I got a little story out on that, although I was ashore only a couple of hours, and since then I've got out a few stories about the Royal Navy. Things haven't worked as well as I would like thus far, but with time our press problems should be ironed out. [Dana was assigned to both the US and the Royal Navies.]

This afternoon, waiting for transportation for my next job, is really the first time I've had to stop to think, let alone write letters. I really don't know how I'm going to send this.

This is a terribly inadequate letter considering all I have been doing and all I would have to tell if I were at home.

My love to you all,
Grandma, Elizabeth, Ken, Steinie and Torrey Pines,
Dana

August 1:

I'm writing this aboard a destroyer as you know, I trust, from my dateline (..........................)

Nothing much has come my way to make a big story with the Navy as yet, but I've been extremely busy. Things go on by night as well as by day and it's a trick to arrange a little sleep.

I'm afraid that in the rush of it all I missed writing a letter again last week so when I get the chance I plan to send you a cable to fill in the gaps. Since I've "joined the Navy," I've been out on a landing craft, on an aircraft carrier, spent four nights on patrol with the motor torpedo boats, and now I'm with a destroyer. Quite a bit for about three weeks activity. Censorship is too unpredictable to tell you all about it, but when I get home I will.

Hugh Baillie, president of all of the UP, the biggest of our big shots, has been kicking about this part of the world and I've had a number of good talks with him. I think the chances of getting a bit of leave are rosy, although I couldn't yet say when—maybe this coming winter.

This afternoon I wandered about some Sicilian countryside with two of our officers and managed to buy fifteen eggs and pick up a lot of tomatoes and lemons. All a great treat aboard. It was fascinating to walk through a little village and see that these people are really friendly and glad to see us. I don't think it is all on the surface although I suppose their main motive now is to have us get on with it and finish the war so they can go back to a normal existence.

Picking our way back to the shore I spied an American sergeant talking to a peasant and walked over to see what he was talking about. It turned out that he had quite by chance discovered some relatives of his.

These British navy people are grand fellows, especially when afloat and on an operation. It's always the same story. The only people who make difficulties, who are stuffy and grumpy and unhelpful, are back at the big bases and headquarters. Once at the "front" in whatever form, the worst stuffed shirt will give you his shirt, to make a bad pun. This is a mighty inadequate letter, but better one will be coming along. My love to you all as always, you and Eliza and Grandma Ken and Steinie, Torrey Pines too. I suppose my Jimmy back in Cairo is wondering what has become of his master.

Love,
Dana

He could write about the type of ship he was reporting from, but he could not say where they were or where they were going. The fleets visited almost all the great Italian ports and sailed back and forth to La Maddalena (a large port between Corsica and Sardinia) to bring oil and military supplies to the troops on land. The ships did their share of fighting by launching artillery and bombs on the coast of Italy.

At Messina, the ships crossed the straits, and troops landed on the mainland of Italy on September 3rd, a historic event with the Allied forces in Axis-controlled Europe. A week later, the fleet had crossed over to the west coast of Italy and landed at the ancient city of Salerno, south of Naples. [71]

August 10:

I think I'll just have to send you a couple more telegrams to fill in the gaps of my correspondence, because last week's letter hasn't gone off yet, but I could have fixed that if I weren't scurrying about on so many jobs, some of them fool's errands, some of them perhaps not.

I hope you've seen a few of my things in print, but it probably isn't as much as I should like as I've been involved in running a relay bureau of sorts for our copy from the front. That sort of work brings little glory, but it is very important in an agency.

There are so many irrelevant complications to trying to cover the war news that people begin to lose sight of the main objective—to write good stories, good as stories and good as reports on the fighting and the war effort. The real trouble is that there are too many correspondents pouring out too many words;

---

[71] See Appendix.

the authorities consequently hedge them about with restrictions in an effort to depress their numbers and productivity. I don't really understand why there are too many correspondents. In the World War there was no such complaint as far as I know. And in those days there were far more independent newspapers and agencies than there are now.

I've been to Sicily three times now, in one way or another and have been able to write a little about it. Not much, however, as I am supposed to write about the Navy only.

I've just been interrupted by the phone and asked to do a thousand word article on "Malta's preparations for the invasion—an American's impressions." I get nothing out of it except a little good will and am handicapped by the fact that I wasn't here during the period of preparation, but these are minor issues. Before I left Cairo, I produced, free for nothing, one radio broadcast, one lecture, and one full newspaper page sized article. Each took the better part of a day to prepare. This Malta thing will keep me up most of the night. Some people are very generous with other people's time and energy. I'm beginning to feel very out of touch with you and the family, having had no letters for more than a month, he wrote on August 10. *I have sent messages to Cairo and Algiers to forward everything to me here.*

I don't think any of my stuff has set the world on fire during the Sicilian show, but I've had a fairly steady flow of not-so-bad pieces. If I were assigned to the Army instead of the Navy, I'd have far better opportunities. It remains to be seen what I get during the next phase. I sent Pinkley a cable asking him not to forget, a, my desire to have a crack at covering the Army, b, my raise, c, my leave home to the U.S.A. after five years abroad.

In the end I've always got what I asked for from UP, although sometimes it's taken a lot of asking. There's a big UP meeting on in London, with Pinkley and Baillie as principals I believe, so there should be fairly swift reaction to my message.

I'm just back from Sicily for the fourth time. Of course, being with the Navy, I see only the fringes of the island. When I got back here I discovered that none of the stuff I'd sent back had yet arrived. So I re-wrote four days worth of copy into two stories.

Last night I was invited out to dinner in a destroyer by its captain. A really pleasant occasion, with the ladies in evening dress[72], the men in black trousers with black sash around the stomach and white short-sleeved shirts (me in a clean shirt too!). All the wines at their proper times, cocktails before and liqueurs after, cigars, and light conversation. It sounds ostentatious, but, in its proper place, was really very simple and natural.

I came back from Sicily in a special type of landing barge this last time and made a very uncomfortable night of it. The captain, who has to stay on the bridge, very kindly offered me his bunk. But after half an hour I found myself dripping with sweat and giddy with the heat from the engine room and galley. So in the dark I stretched out my blankets on the deck and made the best of it. In the morning I found I could have done better, as I'd been lying mostly on rivets and in a pool of oil.

A LIFE photographer named Eierman came through here a few weeks ago and took some pictures of me. The idea was that, in gratitude for the food and drink which I managed to produce for him and several other weary travelers, he would send you the pictures when he got back to the States. I hope he does. [We found no such photos in Mother's albums.]

It is very hot and just sitting here typing is enough effort to make my forearms glisten with sweat and little rivulets to run down my back. While I'm in town [Malta] *I live in a remarkable hotel. The plug in my bathtub got stuck three days ago. It's still stuck. The management views the situation with despair. Nobody can find a pair of pliers with which to move the offending plug. So I do my bathing down the hall.*

It is a slight shock to think that in few days I'll be 28 years old—a very great age. I suppose I should be thinking, "what I want for my birthday." Well, first of all, I want a round dozen of hot exclusive stories, then an airplane passage back to Los Angeles, then return to warlike scenes for the cleanup of the war and a first class appointment to one of our European bureaus. "All right?" I'll put my order in to Santa Claus too.

---

[72] I assume that the wives of various Sicilian officials and dignitaries were invited, and any wives of officers who were in Sicily would have attended dinner.

Now I must get on with the job, or I'll be fired.
Love to all, DANA

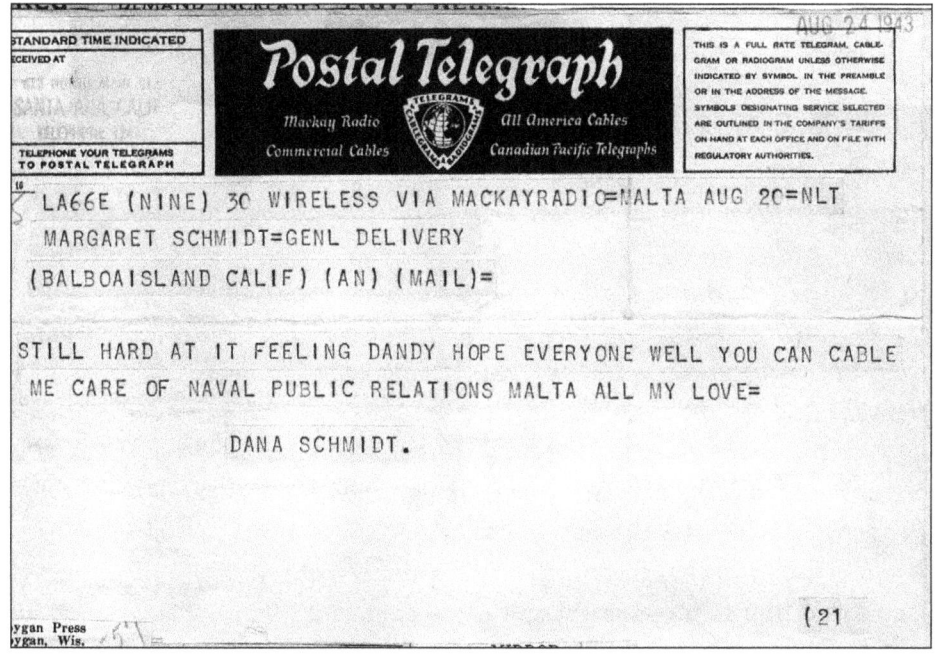

Dana's telegram from Malta August 20, 1943

August 30:

Once again I'm writing to you from Sicily, or rather from one of the harbors, where I am waiting for the next big story to break. Without any doubt at all, by the time you get this the story will be history.

There is unfortunately so little of what I have been doing and thinking that I can put into a story right now and so little I can write in a letter that would get past the censor.

I'm living in a destroyer for the moment. Not a bad place at all to be. We eat better than most people ashore. Here in Sicily we manage to add to our stores, too, by picking up lemons, tomatoes, grapes, eggs, etc. ashore. But with all that, it's not like American food. Never really realized how much better Americans eat than the British 'till I found American and British ships beside each other. When the Americans have to eat British rations there is a terrible moan, but the British are always delighted to eat American stuff.

These British naval officers are some of the best fellows I have ever known. Many of them I would like to see more of after the war. Perhaps I get along better with them than most Americans because of my years at Chillon. I often wonder what some of my old Chillon friends are doing now. I've never run into any of them, Sydney Smith, for instance, Graham, Milton, Lyon. You remember the names I think.

Before I left Malta I cabled you, but did not get an answer before I left. By the time I get back there I trust a lot of mail will have caught up with me from Cairo and Algiers. The only thing that's come through so far is a letter from the end of June from Elizabeth. I am thankful that you have kept well and cheerful and are working so hard. This winter, when the next phase of the war is over I'm going to make a really determined effort to get home. I think I've got it coming to me.

The Captain of this destroyer is a most charming man. [Dana never mentioned him to me after the war] *You would love him. Perhaps after the war he will come to Los Angeles and you will meet him. He is a four striper, a full Captain, as this is a flotilla leader, but has none of the Colonel Blimpish manner naval higher-ups sometimes develop.*

*All my love to all of you, and take care of yourselves 'till I get home,
Dana*

September 3, the day that Allied troops crossed the Straits of Messina to the mainland of Italy, was also the day when an Armistice was proposed by General Dwight D. Eisenhower on behalf of the Allies and accepted by Marshal Pietro Badoglio at Fairfield Camp, Sicily.

Marshal Badoglio, now premier and not a fascist, negotiated the armistice with the Allies. Dwight D. Eisenhower proposed the conditions of the agreement, which involved mostly the disposition of the Italian navy. It was signed in Sicily on September 3. Italy surrendered on September 8.

September 14:

It has been a happy day for me, with four letters from you, one from Grandma, not to forget the one I got from Elizabeth at Malta the other day. I also got the first installment of TIME *there. That was the first mail I've had since the beginning of the invasion of Sicily!* [July 10]

What my next job is going to be I really don't know, and likely couldn't write if I did know. Anyway, there seems to be some confusion about it. But I don't feel particularly worried one way or the other. I feel I've done pretty well with the Navy the last few weeks. Being Royal Navy you may not have seen very much of it, but it must have done fairly well in England, as the BBC *quoted my stuff repeatedly, without mentioning my name, of course. The three main ones were, the Reggio bombardment, the crossing of the Straits, and the Navy covering the landings at Salerno. I've seen a bit of the war now and handled a fairly impressive variety of stories and feel self confident enough to tell anybody to go to hell. If the* UP *doesn't do right by me, I'll just have to do that. But I think everything will be okay. It's very easy to figure up all the raw deals you've had and develop "nobody loves me persecution complex" which is usually unjustified. The newspaper world is so full of people trying to cut each other's throats and whispering about that one must not take it too much to heart.*

Apart from Grandma's splendid present and your cable, my birthday went unobserved. It happened to be one of the ship's officer's birthday too and he had invited a lot of other officers from other destroyers. So I just enjoyed myself and kept mum. I never cease to be amazed at how old I am getting. Time was when I was always the youngest of the party, no matter where. Now, in the destroyer, half the officers were younger than I.

How I sympathize with your struggling with a dictaphone. You may remember my first job with the Los Angeles News Service *involved taking stuff down from beat men on the typewriter with an earphone over one ear. Into the other ear poured the noise of typewriters, arguments, newsboys, streetcars and trucks, confusing no end. The first person to dictate to me was a female reporter in the District Attorney's office who hung up in fury after about three* minutes' struggle and then called up again to find out what the hell was going on. I never did get very good at that, although practice helped.

Then in Berlin we took down almost all the stuff relayed through the UP office from all over central Europe on a dictaphone. The rollers were often bad and the lines worse and it was usually best to take notes in pencil while the stuff was going onto the dictaphone. It was quite embarrassing to get a hot story from Bucharest or Riga and find you couldn't get a word of it off the dictaphone; especially when it took four or five hours to get your man back on the phone.

I was delighted to hear you managed to spend a month at the beach. Change is a wonderful thing. How I'd like to spend a while on one of those beaches. The only time I've been swimming this summer was once off a landing craft in Sicily. Oh yes, and once at Alexandria. I remember our lovely summer at La Jolla. Perhaps the glow of recollection is intensified by the fact that that was the famous Bank of America prize summer! No less than ten years ago. What has become of Elaine Meekins[73] at whose mother's place we (Elizabeth and I) spent a few days at Laguna? I remember that she was unusually attractive and married a naval officer like all the best girls apparently.

Malta was interesting as almost every place is if you want to be interested, but apart from that it was a good place not to spend too much time in. Food was still not over plentiful and entertainment practically nil; it's still very much in the war zone. Most of the time I was living on good British Naval rations, but that is mighty poor compared with American rations. I get used to almost anything, but that doesn't lessen my pleasure when I get back to a place like this and can eat in a first class American mess. I remember one good meal I had while with the Navy though; that was when I visited an American tanker.

I never can remember the name of the tanker in which I went down through the Panama Canal in '38 [S.S. Cathwood] nor the name of the one I crossed the Atlantic in, except that it was the Black something or other [the Black Tern]. I'll have to dig up a lot of stuff like that when I get to writing a book.

---

[73]   My friend from Wellesley College. See Appendix.

It has rained here today. A pleasant thing after the weeks of clear California-like skies we get in the summertime here. I remember it's raining once while we were in Sicily.

Winston Burdett of CBS is here and I had lunch with him. Remember, he was Martin Agronsky's great competitor in Ankara. We were bitter enemies then, he being in the opposing "pool," but it was like finding a long lost brother seeing him now. He had just been to Cairo . . . told me Ray Brock is still grinding the rumor mills of Turkey, poor fellow. Being well out of that, I feel sorry for him. He is the sort of reporter who would probably be in his element on a proper war job, but not merely covering diplomatic gossip, sez I.

More about Malta. . . . When not at sea I lived in a quaint little hotel where the toilets would flush twice a day—best place in town. I paid twelve shillings a day to buy up an extra bed and have a room and bathtub to myself. . . . [the one with the stuck plug]. When they got the plug out it broke and it took a couple more days to find a new one. After that I lived in my ship most of the time.

Of course most ships, especially destroyers are crowded and there are no cabins to spare. In my first one I slept on the couch in the wardroom or wherever I saw fit to lay my head. In the second one the first Lieutenant that would be Executive Officer in the American navy, right after the Captain, insisted on turning his bunk over to me. He insisted he always slept on deck anyway, but I never ceased to feel a little embarrassed at the attention. I got the ship mentioned by name on two different stories, again and again all day, over the BBC and the ship's company were infinitely grateful. A little recognition goes right to the heart, even of a British naval officer, even if he does profess to scorn publicity. In peace the pay-off comes in money, in war if there is any pay-off at all, it comes in recognition. Inner satisfaction at having done your bit is a great thing, but most fellows find that having other people know about it feels even better.

I feel guilty about having missed writing letters a good deal the past couple of weeks, but you will understand how difficult it is sometimes.

You should see the British tin hat which my last ship fixed up with a very special coat of arms for me. It is on the table in front of me now. It started on the bridge one day when the Signals officer asked me what the UP's motto was. Since I was unable to produce a satisfactory one, everyone started inventing a suitable one, "Sword unmightier's Pen" was the upshot, being their idea of the press cablese of "The pen is mightier than the sword," except that they modified it to "the Sword is no more mighty than the Pen," which I approved as a more modest statement of the situation.

The Signals Officer drew a rough sketch and the First Lieutenant later developed it and had a sailor who was a professional letterer before the war print it on to my tin hat. The words of the motto are draped about the feet of a fat baldheaded censor who is frantically trying to dam up a cornucopia spilling out cables. On his back rests a shield with UP painted in red on a white background surrounded by seven white stars on a blue background. Over it all flies a carrier pigeon that is variously interpreted as a pen or a spear, a little variation on the usual eagle or dove of peace theme.

I'll try to get a picture of me wearing it for you; also for UP promotional purposes. [We did not receive one.]

While we were tied up in harbor a week ago the First Lieutenant of an adjoining destroyer asked me to give a lecture to his ship's company. I couldn't very well get out of it. Needless to say what they wanted was Berlin Diary stuff which I produced quite successfully to my surprise. I was supposed to repeat the lecture for my own ship the morning I had to leave to come here.

I flew here with Paul Bewsher, the amazing little reporter with whom I shared a tent for three weeks in Tunisia while I was covering the Air Force. He has been with the Daily Mail of London for 28 years and wears a World War decoration. We flew right over the olive groves where our tent was pitched and got sentimental over the nights we pounded our typewriters by the light of an oil lamp which kept falling over and going out and the bottle of whiskey which I produced when Paul's gin ran out. Paul can't live without gin and doesn't like whiskey, but he drank it and lived and liked it in Tunisia.

Now I think I better call it a day, because I think there is a regulation about writing only one page letters. This awful paper is about finished and I hope to send you something better next time.

[It was tissue-like paper and very difficult to read.] *This letter is for Grandma and Elizabeth and Steinie for I owe so many letters I don't think I'll ever get caught up.*

All my love, Dana

**CAPITAL TAKEN
WITHOUT A SHOT**
By DANA ADAMS SCHMIDT
United Press Correspondent
AJACCIO, Corsica, Sept. 17—(Delayed) The toughest French shock troops of the North African command streamed ashore from a submarine at dawn on Sept. 13 and occupied this city without a shot.

Only thirty Germans were here, manning a coastal battery. They escaped in two motorboats just before the French spearhead force arrived.

I landed here with Moroccan troops at 1 a.m. today. We followed close behind the original invaders.

The original landing group had to dodge one U-boat torpedo and was spotted by at least three German reconnaissance planes. Because of the demonstration that greeted the arrival and could have interfered with military operations, police had shooed most of the Corsicans home early last night in order not to interfere with our arrival.

When civilians did get into the streets they asked, "When are Americans going to arrive?" "When are you going to invade France?" "Are you sending us food?"

The patriots captured an aircraft listening post and raided German communications at the southern tip of the island. The Germans, I was told, were bombing Italian troops near here. Two days ago twenty enormous brush fires were started by German planes around the town. The fires swept through the hills, burning many peasants to death.

Two Italian anti-aircraft batteries in the hills were reported still manned. One had decided after the Italian armistice to "fire on the German planes" and the other was still undecided.

The pilot who brought our destroyer to the dock said that the Germans had shot as deserters 200 Italians whom they had captured in fighting on the southern tip of the island.

A police official, whose name must remain a secret, said that on the night of the announcement of Italy's surrender, "de Gaullist members of the national front" staged a coup d'état by seizing the government buildings of the capital, which had been occupied by Vichy officials.

September 21:

Here I go starting off one more letter with, "I am about to go off on a trip," and it's one that promises some good stories. As usual, you should get my stories before you get this. I'm always glad to be getting away, always feel much better up forward than at base.

My time here has been rather dull and unproductive. [It seems to be Cairo.] *I find I don't get any sleep sharing a room with two or three fellow UP men. I find that it is not possible to send a personal telegram to you from here and so will have to rely on the mails.*

To my great surprise I ran into my old friend Tuggle whom you may remember my mentioning when I was in Istanbul. He is coming out to dinner with us tonight. C.D. Jackson and Frank Kaufman are also here. Had a drink with C.D. last night and was supposed to have dinner with them both tomorrow, but I'll be gone by then.

Autumn and the rains are coming and it is very muggy. Somebody said quite rightly the other day that there is never a breath of really "fresh" air in the Mediterranean—never crisp and sharp and invigorating. People around here like to attribute Italy's lack of war-like talents to the climate. California would be like that if it wasn't for the cool mists we get and the mountains.

October 15:

This letter is really very much overdue. But flitting about the countryside to Naples, the isle of Capri, La Maddalena and Corsica [74] *doesn't leave much time for writing letters. Or rather, it doesn't leave much opportunity for getting them sent away.*

Since I got back to my present dateline (. . . . .) [Algiers?] *I've been plunged up to the ears in the awful morass known as politics. For the moment I'm covering the North African political scene, the French, a bit of the Italians, the forthcoming Mediterranean Commission, the forthcoming meeting of the French Assembly, etc. etc. There seems to be more to it than meets the eye. Presently I hope to cover the French army again, as I have already done in Corsica during my two visits.*

Of course I'd much rather be up in Italy covering the Americans, and have told Pinkley as much. But for the moment it's no go, as Packard, our former Rome bureau manager, is wedded to the job 'till we get to Rome. I also cabled Pinkley about my getting home this winter and got an answer back saying he is "working" on the matter.

I'm looking forward to that Christmas box you write about and am so glad you at last have my correct APO address. Grandma's money-belt sounds like a good idea, but I'd probably lose it. I still have few equals at losing things. The nice thing about that is that wherever I go in the Mediterranean and the Near East I always have something to pick up that I left there once. Anyway, I can put Steinie's cookies and fruitcake in a good place where they won't get lost.

So I was featured on Battlefronts [75] *was I? I'm glad I couldn't hear it, but I'm glad to hear it happened.*

---

[74] See Appendix.
[75] *Battlefronts* was a weekly radio show. Radio reached the height of its influence during World War II, when it carried war news from the battlefronts directly to the homes of millions of listeners. Unfortunately, I never heard any of the broadcasts.

C.D. Jackson is here [Algiers] *and so is Frank Kaufman, both now working on a propaganda job. And tonight Hal Lehrman, OWI man from Istanbul, walked into the press-room. We are having dinner at a French restaurant tomorrow night, if we can find one. So far I've done all my eating at Army messes. It is extremely difficult to get anything to eat in restaurants. Food is scarce for civilians. Hard liquor is unobtainable in all its forms, except as it is rationed to the British forces. Even wine is not over-plentiful—quite a contrast from Cairo. To get a really good restaurant meal one must drive twenty or thirty miles out into the country. I haven't had time for such doings yet, but am quite happy with the American Army mess. I smile with pleasure whenever I wake up in the night and think of those hotcakes and syrup I'm going to get for breakfast, with plenty of American coffee. Now I begin to realize how badly I was eating with the British.*

I should think you must have read your fill about Naples and the other places covered by the press of late. Anyway, as you may know from the clippings, I went there by American PT boat escorting a British Admiral who wanted to be the first into the town from the seaside. That was all right, but he should have taken a chance and gone half a day earlier, because by the time we arrived all the good undamaged buildings had been requisitioned by the Army and the Navy had to take what it could.

It is amazing to me how people can be so cheerful when the city they live in and much of what they possess is in ruins. But the Neopolitans did more laughing and smiling than you will see on a New York or Los Angeles street any time. I think there is something to this psychology: If the water supply breaks down in your house and you have to get water from a spring, it is the most god awful tragic annoying nuisance that ever happened. But if the water to all of the houses in town is cut off and everybody is in the same boat and goes down to the spring together, it's not so bad. Something about misery loves company.

As it happened I left Naples after three days, before the place started blowing up from time bombs left behind by the gentle Nazis. I went back to Capri, where I'd spent the previous week going out on PT boat patrols and generally doing very little but keeping myself running in small circles.

Capri is truly all that its name conjures up. During my last three hours there I managed to go to see the blue grotto. And that lived up to its reputation too, though it was rather smaller than I imagined. When you strike the water with an oar in the grotto the water glows with a mysterious blue electric luminosity. I could only think of the color of some Chinese vases Grandma took Elizabeth and me to see in the Louvre many long years ago.

The island is covered with gardens, well-kept villas (even now) and paths winding up the hillsides overlooking still blue coves at the bottom of sheer rock cliffs. Nary a bomb has dropped nor a shot been fired in happy Capri. The rich were well stocked with food and even the poor were better off than people of the mainland. I was in Ciano's former villa and had dinner in the one that belongs to Mrs. Harrison Williams. [76] *Then we moved onto La Maddalena, the Italian Naval base at the northern end of Sardinia. That's a bleak spot, but not without its beauty too. No trees, but low shrubs climbing over miles and miles of boulders. Like Scapa Flow,* [77] *the British said. Mussolini was interned there for a while.*

I walked out to the house where Garibaldi died on the neighboring island with a man who works for the New York Sun, *McGowan, and saw his grave and statue, the house he built with his own hands, his son's boat, and the Italian guard, in spite of everything, still standing stiffly at attention—a very melancholy scene. For lack of other transportation we moved on to Bonifacio in southern Corsica in an Italian hospital ship. The Italians were at all times more than anxious to be hospitable and helpful. One could not help feeling a little sorry for them, as individuals. They kept running up to say they had an uncle in Detroit, or to show you a picture of their brother in Chicago and ask what the chances of emigration were. Everybody wants to emigrate; everybody wants to emigrate to America. Perhaps more than at any time before, America seems the promised land to the people who have suffered in this war. It is the place where they might forget and start a new chapter.*

---

[76] Widow of Harrison Williams, U.S. Senator
[77] Sea basin in Northern Scotland in the Orkney Islands.

The French Colonel at Bonifacio was very friendly over the phone (what a surprise to find a phone that worked!) and said he could get us a car as far as Sartene. Meanwhile we tried to get some food in a waterfront restaurant. The woman would produce nothing except ersatz coffee at first, but finally broke down and brought out some sour-tasting black bread, [and] *devil-smelling goats' milk cheese.*

Our car finally appeared, half filled with mangy-looking Corsicans, to my great annoyance. Everyone aboard claimed to have been a "patriot" and to have been out shooting Germans shortly before. I doubt in most cases, but there were definitely some very real patriots in the hills. I think I talked to one in a farmhouse where our driver insisted on stopping for wine. I'm in such a habit of being in a hurry that I cursed him a blue streak when he insisted on stopping. But it was worth it. The old peasant had had a real British Sten gun in the corner which had been dropped by parachute and I believe his son had really belonged to a guerilla band.

In the town of Sartene I talked to a French officer, who had organized and led some of the patriots. He was very sincere and genuine and I wrote about him at length. He fed us on "singe," the French army equivalent of bully beef.

Once up to Ajaccio, the capital, my only idea was to get on a plane and back here to get out a story. Wandering amiably about produces some pleasant stories, but I was beginning to feel somewhat off base, especially when I discovered another UP *correspondent had been sent to another part of Corsica.*

I was supposed to come back on a destroyer, since there would be no place on the planes for days, but I took a chance and went out to the airfield. Within fifteen minutes I found a plane taking off and was away. That's the way it goes. If you wait to go through official "channels" on transportation you may attain a great age without ever going anywhere.

There is lots more I might tell, I suppose, but that's about all I can do tonight.

All my very best love to all of you, Dana

October 24, Algiers:

This new job of mine, covering the French in the political situation, is exceedingly interesting and holds many possibilities for the future. The first possibility I'm working on, however, is that of getting home sometime the latter part of this winter, even if only for a short time.

The French press director here, Andre LaGuerre, who has been of the greatest help to me, is an old acquaintance of Ida Treat. It seems that she worked for him in London.

Living quarters are a problem around here. At the moment I'm in a very shabby second rate hotel where they have removed the bathtubs in order to make more rooms! There is no hot water and the elevator doesn't work. I live on the fifth floor. Soon, however, I hope to do better—possibly sharing a room with my old friend Winston Burdett of CBS, one of the fellows who was in the OTHER pool in the old Ankara press battle. I find that competition around here is not quite so bitter and vindictive as it was in the old days. Perhaps being in the army, or half way in it, has a moderating influence. Civilians are much fiercer about most things than soldiers, I find.

Last night I went to see an opera, Carmen. *I must say I am musically, most uneducated, entirely through my own fault. That sounds as though I consider myself well educated in other respects, which is an over-statement. The only thing I know anything about is politics and that is restricted to European politics. Amazing what I didn't learn at Pomona and previously . . . . If I ever have a son he is going to have a busy youth, especially reading all the books I haven't read, including the classics, in Latin AND Greek! But I'm not exactly at a disadvantage since most of my newspaper confreres are even less learned.*

I have just been talking to one of the local denizens on the subject of tennis. Having lugged all my personal belongings over here I have the wherewithal and hope to get a little exercise. I have played very little the past two years, and not at all this past summer.

November 2:

Today I have been mighty busy working on the coming meeting of the French Assembly. This political job involves a lot of rock-pile labor.

Well, Christmas has already come and gone as far as I am concerned. The lovely delicious Christmas box arrived the other day, and I finished off Steinie's cookies in short order. Some of the cake remains for future reference. And I am typing this letter on Elizabeth's new typewriter ribbon.

I haven't started on Cassidy's book [78] *yet, but it looks interesting. The package of cigarettes filled my pocket at an opportune time when I had exhausted my PX ration for some days to come, and the Dill's Best pipe tobacco provoked me into buying a new pipe at the PX, having broken all my others except for the fancy ones of Meerschaum from Turkey.*

You know I haven't had a fountain pen for a year or so, so yours was more than welcome. I generally use pencils at a great rate of overturn, stealing and losing three or four per day.

Now what am I sending you for Christmas? Nothing apparently, for all my intended gifts are still in my possession. There's a lot of fine, really nice, Malta lace, of all shapes and descriptions and two pairs of extra-fancy embroidered Moroccan evening slippers, bought on my latest trip, for distribution between you and Steinie and Elizabeth and Grandma. I don't know what's for Ken, unless he'd like a Meerschaum pipe. I've been hoping to find someone who could take these presents home for me personally, but haven't had any luck yet. I may be obliged to use the regular mail facilities, in which case you'll get my gifts around Easter.

This doesn't look as though I was using a new ribbon, but it is the fault not of the ribbon but of the typewriter, [the type face was quite faint] *including the man who types. I have recently decided that I don't like my typewriter any more. Its touch is too heavy. You have to strike it as with a sledgehammer, which slows down my progress.*

---

[78] Cassidy, Cyril Caldwell, *Air Power and Total War*, Coward-McCain, January 1, 1943

It's time now that I get to bed, to be bright and strong for General de Gaulle's speech tomorrow!

How about giving Torrey Pines an extra bone from me for Christmas. I have just had word from Cairo that Jimmy is completely recovered from his ailments. According to his guardian he was afflicted with malaria. Most strange, most strange. I didn't know dogs could get it.

All my love to you all, Dana

These are busy days and once again I'm behind schedule with my letter, he wrote on November 12. *I've been doing a good deal of running around and pounding the typewriter, in fact nothing but, so I hope the clipping bureau is coming across with a few things for you.*

Almost a hundred percent of the political stuff from the UP from here [Algiers] *is mine, especially that dealing with the French. If anyone else has had any by-lines on the French political stuff, I'd like to know about it.*

The cabinet, I should say committee, shakeup the other day was a terrible scramble. [79] *In the middle of it the usual lines of communication broke down—atmospherics—and I had to start duplicating stuff by other routes. I thought I made a terrible mess of things, but got no kickbacks.*

All my political background in Turkey is standing me in good stead now, as I'm one of the few people in the UP with any political background. Straight war reporting is something quite different.

It looks as though I was to have a little more war reporting, incidentally. I've been expecting to get started any day all week. You'll probably find out what it is before you get my letter. Anyway I won't be gone for long, as I am supposed to come back and carry on with this job.

Well, all your Christmas presents are lined up on my mantelpiece ... and waiting for me to find a suitable box in which to send them to you. In addition to the items previously mentioned there is a crocodile-leather combination handbag and market-bag. It is most handsome in my opinion. If I have not

---

[79] Dana was probably referring to the fact that de Gaulle and Giraud did not get along, and de Gaulle finally ousted him from the Committee.

been duped it comes from Dakar. Also there is a nicely worked little Moroccan leather bag.

Last night I went out to visit an A.P. photographer who was in the party on my last trip. He lives at the "Photographers' villa," a grand luxurious place well out from the center of town. Okay for photographers, but it would be too out of the way for most newsmen. Since the photographers all pool their stuff they work together and share the expense of their villa. An excellent arrangement. If I have to stay around here very long, I will try to get an apartment.

Last Sunday I managed to snitch the UP car—there actually is one, in fact two—and went out for a little drive with some friends. Since we couldn't tell how much gas was in the car and didn't know where to get any more, and didn't know just where we were going, we didn't go far. But it was fun. My first pleasure drive in many a month. Down in Alexandria I hired a car for the day on several occasions at enormous expense.

TIME and NEWS WEEK are now coming through like clockwork. It is very nice to have them.

Well, Merry Christmas once again. You never can tell how long a letter will take. And Happy New Year.

Love to all, Dana

The political storms have come roaring in from this and that side and I, standing in the middle, have suddenly found myself becalmed while the storms go by, wrote Dana on the 21st. *I'm taking advantage of that peculiar situation to get off this letter.*

The Lebanese thing is still hot, but I've written about all that can be said at the moment.

With much grunting and groaning, stuffing, wrapping, packing, tying, weighing and discussion, I got off my Xmas package to all the family some days ago. With luck you'll have it under the Xmas tree, without luck you'll have it for Easter. But just remember when the Yuletide rolls around that Santa Claus is on the way from Africa and nobody has been forgotten.

Meanwhile, in addition to all those already received, I have received another gift, presumably meant for Christmas, from an unknown donor.

The return address is W.P. Waldrop, 2637 East Florence, Huntington Park, California. I have a shrewd suspicion that Mother or Grandma were out driving and stopped in at that address to order me a box of luscious dates, figs and prunes, for that is what it was. This unexpected present turned up one wet and gloomy night when I had been working much too late. I had no idea what the box contained until I got to my room, wet and depressed. But you should have seen my spirits lift when I went to work on that feast.

Seems I said I was going to take a trip. Well, it was called off as far as I am concerned. Someone else is going. Much as I would like to have gone it was clearly impossible for me to leave the political story here with stories coming along at the rate of one or more a day. Incidentally, as usual the place that really prints my stuff in volume is South America. . . .

In a [recent] letter you mention [my] long sentences. That is a criticism very well taken. I do have a tendency to get too involved, usually because I'm trying to condense. But the stuff that appears in the newspapers is only occasionally representative of what I actually wrote. I am thoroughly disgusted with the re-write and jazz-up mill that war copy goes through. Nothing is ever hot enough, colorful enough, vivid enough for the N.Y. cable desk. So they make the battleship's shells go over my head "like an express train," which I didn't write at all. What a cliche! And it wasn't like an express train anyway.

Fortunately political copy is not tampered with so much. But in many ways the UP is getting in my hair—I haven't got the assignment I asked for, I haven't got the raise I asked for and I haven't got the home leave I asked for and justly deserve.

November 29:

My poor Jimmy has died. I am very sad. He was a lovable dog even though brainless. He didn't know how to play when Martin Agronsky and I got him, and we taught him to play 'till he was the playfullest big mutt in the world. He was so underfed, he couldn't run at first, and we fed him into a strong, handsome, lolloping mutt. The first day we saw him we thought of sending him back because he looked so worthless, but in the end I spent hundreds of dollars on finding him when he was lost and bringing him with me when I moved.

He was living with Karl Quigley's girlfriend in a house with a garden on the outskirts of Cairo. Quigley is a fellow who went to Pomona, now a liaison officer with the French. The girl fell in love with Jimmy and he was really well taken care of. She even bought him a companion, a young female with markings just like Jimmy's. . . . Recently he got through something apparently diagnosed as canine malaria. Now he has died of "canine typhus."

I've been working very hard the past month and have turned out a vast amount of copy, only a fraction of which, I fear, gets printed in the U.S. South America is the great consumer of political copy. A story on the "22 days of the French Assembly" earned me special detailed congratulations from South America, and a note from New York saying they had cut the story down to 150 words.

How is our clipping bureau and is it giving satisfaction? Harrison Salisbury with whom I discussed the subject the other day suggested that you might get more satisfaction out of subscribing to a group of the outstanding UP consuming newspapers. It might come out cheaper in the end, and you would have more chance to use your own judgment on whether a given story is mine or not, knowing more or less what my assignment is. At the moment all matters political from North Africa are mine. He suggested a selection among Chicago Daily News, N.Y. Times, N.Y. Herald Tribune, N.Y. World Telegram *(best in New York, I think)*, Detroit Free Press, Miami Herald, Pittsburgh Press, Cleveland Press, San Francisco Chronicle, *and* Montreal Star. But you can see best on the spot what is the most effective procedure.

This is my final and ultimate Xmas letter, Dana wrote on December 11. *I'll not wish any more Merry Christmases this year, although I might mention the Happy New Year just once more.*

Christmas keeps coming in by the package-load from old 1132 [Mother's address in Los Angeles] *and from Grandma too! This evening as I struggled with the vagaries of French politics . . . I was presented with a box containing a wealth of chocolate, cigarettes, Palmolive shave cream, and, best of all, delicious fruitcake and pie-sized chunks of Steinie-cookie. My mouth is full right now, as is that of the sergeant who unaccountably works at our desk of an evening.*

A few days ago came a package, from Mother, containing a grand stack of Omnibooks *and the October* Readers Digest.

I was constrained to give one Omnibook *to an* NEA [Near Eastern Affairs] *correspondent named Tom Wolf who was flying to London this morning, but am hoarding the rest for myself.*

It is too bad that we can't be together this Christmas, but it's no use glooming over it. We've all had a lot of practice in keeping in touch at long distance and being together in spirit even if not in the flesh.

Had a long talk with Harrison Salisbury, one of our outstanding New York men, before he went on to Moscow. He will be back here soon. Salisbury made me feel, whether rightly or wrongly, that my work was being appreciated at home—in the head office—and that steps would be taken to bring me to New York to get some home experience at the earliest opportunity. That may not be 'till after the war, but it might be before, if the war goes on longer than I think it will.

He told me that I will be getting a raise shortly and that I am indispensable here right now—the only available man who speaks French and has a political background. He also made me feel that I was getting in on the ground floor of a story that is growing and that should lead to an important spot in Europe after the war.

I am using a friend's typewriter because mine had the misfortune to be on a table that collapsed unexpectedly an hour or so ago. The table appears to be a wreck, but my typewriter escaped with abrasions.

Mother, your letters are an indispensable source of comfort and strength to me. Now more than ever, since I have been away so long, I look forward to them and read them with delight. I particularly like the clippings you often enclose. The one about the gal who was hit on the head with two brass candlesticks has been in the current service message file for the past two days.

I have moved to another hotel where there is heat, hot water, a bathtub, and an elevator, all of which my previous abode was lacking. It's a great step forward.

Now, all my love to you, and a Christmas kiss, and take good care of yourself 'till I do get home. If Salisbury's plans work out, when I get there it will be more than a flying visit. I'll be in the U.S. for perhaps six months.
Love to all,
Dana

December 11:

This time I'm writing on Grandma's ribbon, her Christmas one. It's a black and red job, in the true Christmas spirit, and the peculiarities of my typewriter do full justice to the color scheme. Tomorrow I'm going on a one-day flying visit to Constantine [in northern Algeria] *to hear General de Gaulle make a speech and, I hope, meet him personally. It's about time I got acquainted with the man about whose affairs I write so much.* [80] *I was talking to the sergeant who takes in copy a few minutes ago and suggested that he must be pretty well informed, reading so much stuff on the way through, censored and uncensored. "Yes," he said, "but I don't go for all this political stuff. That's your line, isn't it. Do you really like it?" I assured him that I don't, although I'm really fascinated by it all. As someone said in* News Week *I was reading over dinner, all the postwar issues are popping up prematurely in the French political struggle. At the same time I want very much to have another crack at the "battlefront." Maybe that can be arranged.*

This morning I went to the dentist, at long last, to have the cap replaced which got knocked off while I was riding in a British motor gunboat off the toe of Italy some months ago. I never mentioned that before, but now that it's being repaired. . . . Along about dawn, since nothing was happening, I slipped below from the little platform about six feet off the water which they call a bridge. The sea was quite lively and I had some difficulty remaining wedged in the long seat that runs along one side of the tiny wardroom. The minute I

---

[80] The talk was to be on the status of Moslems in Algeria. Because of problems with transportation, Dana didn't get there.

fell asleep, it seemed, something hit a terrific wallop across my face. It turned out to be a round metal plug which is supposed to fit into the portholes which had rolled off a shelf. Guess I'll claim the purple heart.

1944

Algiers:

Tomorrow I am having lunch with General de Gaulle at the Villa Oliviers. I am looking forward to it with great interest. The mere study of the man is fascinating. I think he cannot help but play a vital part in the France to come, and the sooner our State Department realizes it the better for all concerned.

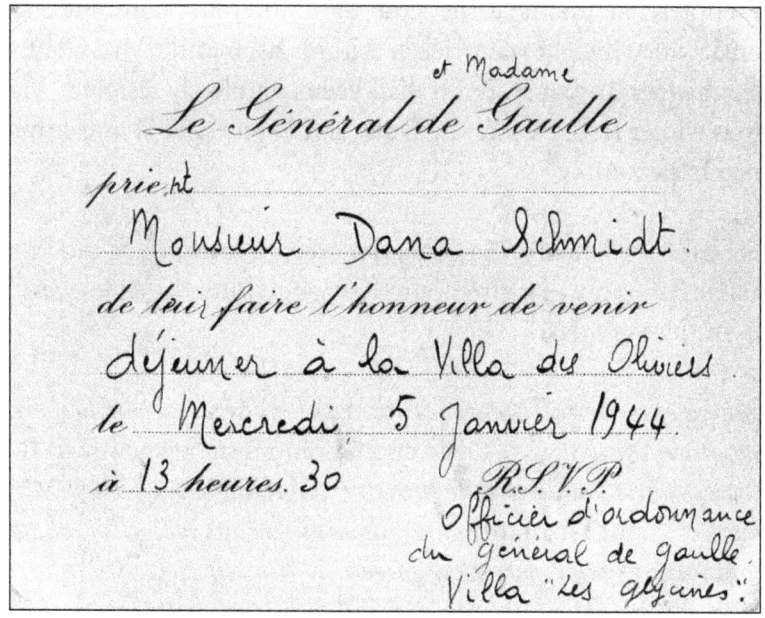

Dana's luncheon invitation from General de Gaulle

Dana didn't describe the topics discussed at the luncheon, however, they were developed at the subsequent meeting of de Gaulle and Prime Minister Churchill at Marrakesh, Morocco, which Dana covered in his dispatch of January 16:

Three questions of vital and urgent interest to the fighting French were discussed—recognition by the Allies of the complete authority over French soil of the Committee of Liberation immediately after France is freed; the participation of French forces in the liberation and the sending of arms to the French underground.

Authoritative sources said no decisions had been made on these questions by the two leaders, but that French quarters were "extremely pleased" with the meeting. They believed that recognition of de Gaulle's committee and its authority over liberated France will be granted by the Allies. Edwin C. Wilson, U.S. envoy to the committee, is going to Washington to discuss the question with President Roosevelt and Secretary of State Cordell Hull.

The conference marked the end of Churchill's convalescence from pneumonia, with which he was stricken at Tunis last month. Mrs. Churchill told de Gaulle that her husband's health had been completely restored. Marrakesh is a famous winter resort where the Duke and Duchess of Windsor frequently vacationed in peacetime.

In his letter of January 22, Dana described a meeting of the Provisional Consultative Assembly that afternoon. Known to him, the Allies were landing at Anzio on this very day:

Hundreds of tanks and thousands of troops landed on the Anzio shore against stiff German resistance.... [Anzio and Cassino form a gateway to Rome.]
We had the best session to date this afternoon [of the Assembly]. *A real riot, with shouts of "salot"* [bastard] *and "insulte"* [insult] *etc. filling the air. One of the communists came very close to getting himself ejected. Unfortunately, having just got the downhold cable, I had to be very brief.*

New York has called for a seventy-five percent reduction of political volume. Of course such orders are rarely meant literally, but it's a pretty good guide as to where popular interest is. [No doubt the war in the Pacific theater had something to do with the lack of interest in French affairs.]

Although today's session was something of a disaster, the session as a whole (finished today, thank god) has shown that the de Gaulle regime really means it when it promises to stick to democratic procedures, i.e. no de Gaulle dictatorship. The "government" has been profoundly influenced by the opinions expressed by the Assembly, although its powers are only advisory.

. . . . There are so many fascinating stories to be written about the doings of the French, political and otherwise, that I find it heartbreaking not to have a freer hand to write them. Fortunately there is a free "voicecast" available every night on which I can spread myself. But I can see by the newspapers that reach us that even that stuff is considerably cut and condensed and generally mucked up. I'm afraid we just haven't put the French story over with the American public yet. Harold Callender manages to get a lot of stuff into the New York Times, *nonetheless. . . .*

In early February, the *United Press* gave Dana a new assignment. On February 8, he wrote from somewhere on the Italian coast:

It seems as though it had been one long continuous day, merely interspersed by periods of sleep since I left Algiers to join the French Expeditionary Forces in Italy.

At last I'm getting what I wanted—a crack at reporting an army. I'd prefer working on Americans, but the French have their points. . . . I've been having the time of my life, whether the results are being appreciated by others or not. I've had my spell with the air force and flown three missions, had my spell with the navy in a fairly big way, and now I'm getting my spell with the army. Politics can wait.

It is possible that you gathered from my dispatches that I flew to Italy with General Giraud and toured the front with him. That was a very comfortable and useful way to get to Italy. Some people wait for weeks for an air passage and then take two to four days. We flitted over in four hours in the natty Lockheed which FDR presented the General. We squeezed together with Madame Catroux[81] at a little folding table for lunch as we sped over the sunny Mediterranean. Great excitement when the General's fancy American thermos bottle refused to turn off and spilled hot coffee all over his doilies marked: "Un seul but, la Victoire." [A single goal, Victory.]

Naturally I had many opportunities to talk to the General during the trip and observed many things I couldn't use in my stories. He is undoubtedly a man with high qualities of leadership and enterprise, but he is also extremely vain and largely incapable of appreciating the political side of events. He has done some astounding things by sheer calculated audacity, like escaping from Koenigstein and capturing Corsica, and he inspires considerable loyalty in his subordinates. He is very proud of his record and devoted most of his table conversation to talking about himself—his escape, his wounds, his campaigns. Doubtless a first class military leader, but whoever cut him out for a political role can only have had in mind that he would be an easily manageable puppet. When it comes to the tricky political issues of the day, the old boy is what Mr. Murphy and others call him: "Mr. Snooks."

This is the first time since I reached this chilly land that I've taken a day off. I was just too cold and tired after yesterday's trip with General Roosevelt[82] to go out this morning and have slept most of the day. Roosevelt was doing a lot of quoting from John Brown's Body,[83] including as I recall, a passage about "the dull fatigue of the last long raid."

It was really quite fantastic to go bumping over rutted, shell pocked roads, with shells dropping here and there and have Roosevelt quoting reams and reams of John Brown's Body and this at the top of his voice. I was so struck by it that I would appreciate your getting me a complete copy of the verses collected

---

[81]   Madame Catroux, wife of General Georges Catroux, was in charge of Free French volunteer women first aid workers and nurses. Lady Spears and Elaine Brault served with her.
[82]   See Appendix.
[83]   See Appendix.

under that name. He also quoted someone called "Ironquill", [84] *something called,* The Sergeant, *something about* The General, *and bits from* Siegfried's Bassoon. *I would appreciate your sending me some of this war poetry. I never gave it a thought before, but was mightily taken by the true human qualities of what Roosevelt was reciting. I like him very much. He has been truly helpful.*

Almost every day since I got here I've been to the front, often right up to the front lines. Since they are now all places which have passed by censorship, I can mention that I've been on Mount San Marino, Mount Belvedere and the hills around Mt. Abate, all integral parts of the German Gustav Line. Twice I've been up the road to Terelle as far as one can go and looked across to German positions. Yesterday afternoon we were about 2/3 of a mile from Cassino. And of course I've been all over the Rapido Valley and spent three nights there with colonels of various French outfits.

I am the first and only American accredited to the French Army in Italy specifically. There is quite a mess (mostly mess) of French correspondents for various North African newspapers, but all British and American newspapers have hitherto depended for their coverage of the French forces on their correspondents with the American-British end of the Fifth Army.

As a matter of fact the thinking (what devious origins determine our lives) that decided my coming here (rather than going to the Brazzaville conference), was the thought that we, the UP *, could probably get one more man into Rome when it falls. That of course will be a terrific story, but meanwhile I'm picking up some interesting straight war stuff.*

I find that every new enterprise (like covering this army) brings with it a rush of enterprise and energy which, at first, sublimates every aspect of the job. It is only after that first flush has faded (about now) that one discovers that it is after all extremely cold, wet, clammy, and even somewhat dangerous. One discovers that in spite of all pretty words one is very much alone and that there are very few people in the world who give a damn. That's where the test comes.

Elizabeth, I must apologize not coming through with the promised letter yet, but believe me I am delighted beyond words at the prospect of becoming

---

[84] Pseudonym for Eugene Fitch Ware.

an uncle. [85] *Grandma too, has a letter coming. Hers was the first letter I got thanking me for Xmas presents.*
All my dearest love to you all,
Dana

It must be more than three weeks since I reached this land of rain, wind, mud, and misery, Dana wrote from Italy on February 19, ... *All day yesterday and the day before I was climbing about in the snow of some rather highish mountains and couldn't help think: Thank God for my strong legs and sound wind, and the many weekends of more or less AWOL from Pomona which I spent skiing in my glorious mountains. There are not many correspondents who would have the heart and wind to go to places I've been these past few weeks.*

It is splendid to get up on a high peak and see the ranges laid out for miles around you. The mountains are still glorious, but it is no longer fun. Men are cold and hungry and insufficiently clad, but they stay on the mountains. There are dead soldiers in the gullies, in and out of the snow, and little signs marked "mines." The birds twitter as usual, but the thumping of mortar shells and the endless echo of artillery fire around Cassino are more noticeable. [The Allied bombing of Monte Cassino began on February 15 and lasted through May 18.]

. . . I've been in the general vicinity of the war, living at headquarters at the "Section Presse" of the French journalists since I arrived. The French correspondents blow in and out and spend most of their time in Naples. It's no wonder that they don't turn out much that is any use to anyone. Whenever the French command complains that the French aren't getting any publicity in the French press, the correspondents complain that they haven't enough transportation; the real reason of course is that what transportation they have is usually in Naples instead of at the front. The French have, I think, as many or more correspondents than all the rest of the Allied press put together and

---

[85] The baby was Margaret, born August 11, the first of our four children. "Margie," now Margaret Miller, is Director of the Contemporary Art Museum and Graphic Studio, as well as Professor of Art, all at the University of South Florida. She is the mother of Elizabeth Johanningmeier, an excellent dancer who has a Master's degree in Performing Arts Administration at New York University and is now working with Tricia Brown in New York.

Writer Sees Battle For Cassino at Peak

French Stand Guard in Mountain Positions They Won; Yanks Fight Way Rock by Rock

By DANA SCHMIDT
United Press War Correspondent

Mt. Belvedere, With the French Army in Italy, Feb. 4.—(UP)—From this advanced mountain position—stormed and held by French colonial troops—I watched the battle for Cassino and the final smashing of the Gustav Line near a climax yesterday.

My observation post was one of a group of round boulder-strewn heights held by the French, which are now the most advanced Allied wedge in the Gustav fortifications.

To get here I scrambled up a precarious mule track for three hours.

I could see the white blossoms of German mortar fire hanging over Cassino and the town of Cairo.

Overhead, in series of two or six or 12, what the French called "Minen" hissed over regularly to rain down on American and French positions farther back. The crash of their detonations echoed and re-eachoed through the surrounding cliffs.

I could see American infantry and tanks fighting their way rock by rock up the road to Terrelle and on to the heights above Cassino.

As we walked up the Belvedere trail, we passed handaged "walking wounded" and stretcher borne cases picking their way down. We passed a group of 20 German prisoners, carrying three of their own wounded.

Most of the attack in this climactic phase falls to the Americans. Most of the French now stand guard in the mountain positions they chewed out of the Gustav line in a week's bloody fighting.

At noon yesterday I saw nine or 10 Messerschmitts bomb Cairo and sweep up the Rosecen Valley to machine gun the mountain trails. It was the first time in eight days the Luftwaffe had appeared in this sector.

Today rain swept in from the west on a hard cold wind, making the Rapido Valley even more of a marshland, and making mountain trails dangerous mudlined toboggan runs.

turn out one hundredth as much in results, with a couple of exceptions, a pretty rum lot.

You may be interested to know that since my arrival I've been wearing both of your sleeveless sweaters pretty nearly all the time, the old red one and the new one of olive drab. In addition I am wearing two army shirts, one on top of the other, and woolen underwear. Oh, sunny Italy, where art thou now? Withal, I never felt better. Of course, as you know, I always feel fine when I'm on an active job. It is difficult to know whether any of my stuff is getting into print. A few more weeks of this and I'll probably be back in Algiers where it is easier to keep in touch.

WHITE PHOSPHORUS SHELLS burst in German-held Cassino in preliminary battering before yesterday's devastation bombing. Note remains of castle on heights, flooded area at base of town to prevent mechanized advances.—Army air force photo from Acme telephoto

On February 19, Dana also wrote me:

Dear Eliza:
For ever so long I've meant to write and tell you how delighted and proud I am at the prospect of becoming an uncle. Is it a boy or a girl, or haven't you decided? What would the little brat like to have from its uncle?
And what is he and/or she going to be named? I wouldn't be insulted if you named him Dana, but am neutral on the question if it should turn out to be her.
Here in Italy the war has become personal for me, perhaps for the first time. Certainly people lose the sense of the seriousness and tragedy of it the farther they get from the front. Even in Naples and Algiers the war begins to become somewhat abstract, something of a football game that keeps cropping up in the newspapers.
Here we live, when not off on a trip somewhere, in a fine though chilly stone building with atrocious ladies in pink dresses and billowing sashes prancing daintily on wispy clouds painted on the ceiling. There is quite a respectable library of well-bound unread books to which the curious help themselves. I should say the place was formerly inhabited by a prosperous wholesale grocery merchant who sent his daughters to school at a convent. The date 1865 is inscribed over the big fireplace (the only really good thing about these Italian houses.)
The cook, his helpers, drivers and other personnel of undefined and slight activity inhabit the room with the fireplace while the correspondents freeze in dignity in the large front room with its tile floor and broken window. Before every meal the entrance to the place is jammed with small ragged boys and girls, women carrying babies, old men who salute and say "Buon giorno!" all carrying pails and wistfully waiting, hoping for a handout from our kitchen. For all I know the grocery merchant's children are among them. These people, mostly from destroyed houses, live in half a dozen former workshops or storerooms behind our building and do our laundry. They sleep on the floor on straw, ten or fifteen in a room, and before every meal the children go out with pails to beg food wherever troops are billeted.

ELIZABETH SCHMIDT CRAHAN

I've sent this care of Mother, because I haven't got your address here

February 19, 1944

Dear Eliza:

For ever so long I've meant to write and tell you how delighted and proud I am at the prospect of becoming an uncle. Is it a boy or a girl, or haven't you decided? What would the little brat like to have from its uncle? How about a small defused bomb as a rattle?

And what is he and/or she going to be named? I wouldn't be insulted if you named him Dana, but am neutral on the question if it should turn out to be her.

I was just reading a recent Time, or maybe it was Newsweek in which it told of the tremendous population growth in California during the war and the work being done by various committees in postwar town planning. I suppose you and Ken have been involved in that. Another thing that is going to involve tremendous work after the war is replanning and reconstruction of all the devastated areas. Think of all the towns that have been bombed, and others destroyed by fighting. Between the front and Salerno there is scarcely a village which is not in ruins.

Here in Italy the war has become personal for me, perhaps for the first time. Certainly people lose the sense of the seriousness and tragedy of it the farther they get from the front. Even in Naples and Algiers it begins to become somewhat abstract, something of a football game that keeps cropping up in the newspapers.

Here we live, when not off on a trip somewhere, in a fine though chilly stone building with atrocious ladies in pink dresses and billowing sashes prancing daintily on wispy clouds painted on the ceiling. There is quite a respectable library of well-bound unread books to which the curious help themselves. I should say the place was formerly inhabited by a prosperous wholesale grocery merchant who sent his daughters to school at a convent. The date 1865 is inscribed over the big fireplace (the only really good thing about these Italian houses)

The cook, his helpers, drivers and other personnel of undefined and slight activity inhabit the room with the fireplace while the correspondents freeze in dignity in the large front room with its tile floor and broken window. Before every meal the entrance to the place is jammed with small ragged boys and girls, women carrying babies, old men who salute and say "Bon Jorno", all carrying pails and wistfully waiting, hoping for a handout from our kitchen. For all I know the grocery merchant's children are among them. These people, mostly from destroyed houses, live in half a dozen former workshops or storerooms behind our building and do our laundry. They sleep on the floor on straw, ten or fifteen in a room, and before every meal the children go out with pails to beg food wherever troops are billeted.

Please give my best wishes to Ken and congratulate him on becoming Daddy for me.

All my love, Eliza. I'm sorry I don't write more often.

Dana — *Dana Adams Schmidt, United Press war correspondent, APO 512, care Postmaster, NYC* — Dana

Please give my best wishes to Ken and congratulate him on becoming Daddy for me. All my love, Eliza. I'm sorry I don't write more often.

And a letter to Mother on February 25: *Naples has become quite a news center of late and New York sent a rush call for me to forget the French for a while and give Bob Vermillion, who has been handling the spot, a lift. No idea whether I've been getting any signers [by-lines] or not, as I'm just pinch-hitting, but my interview with Badoglio*[86] *and Sforza*[87] *should be worth something, especially for South America.*

Naples is one of the most tragic towns I have ever seen. Rarely I'm sure have a people prostituted themselves, in every sense of the word, the way the Neopolitans have—typhus, ruin, unemployment, stagnation, degradation.

ACCEPTANCE OF ITALY AS FULL ALLY PROPOSED BADOGLIO TELLS HOPE FOR PLACE AT PARLEYS AFTER WAR

By DANA ADAMS SCHMIDT

SEAT OF THE ITALIAN GOVERNMENT, Feb. 25 (UP)—Premier Gen. Pietro Badoglio expressed hope today that Italy would soon be accepted as a full ally and would be accorded diplomatic representation in allied capitals.

Italy hopes to have a seat at the peace conference after the war, Badoglio said.

Gives allies aid

In an interview with this correspondent, Badoglio pointed to the help that Italy was now giving the Allies and said that it could be increased greatly if the Italian army were given more arms and equipment.

He said that Italian air force planes were flying supplies for the Allies, that the Italian navy convoyed 14,000,000 tons of Allied shipping up to Jan. 31

---

[86]   Badoglio, Pietro (1872–1952). Following Mussolini's downfall, he formed a non-Fascist government and negotiated an armistice with the Allies (1943).
[87]   Count Carlo Sforza (1872–1952) was an Italian foreign minister.

and that the army—parts of which already are in the lines—could supply many divisions for the Allies.

Asked whether he would resign and the King abdicate after the fall of Rome, Badoglio said:

Up to the People

"The king and government have very clearly decided to respect entirely what the Italian people will decide on this question. That means also Italians who are prisoners in many parts of the world.

The present government must complete the chain which started when it declared against fascism and declared war against Germany. Abdication of the King would bring with it a most difficult interruption in the legitimacy of the representation of the Italian people and all must be consulted."

A few days later, Dana wrote an additional story reporting Badoglio's reaction to President Roosevelt's announcement of a distribution of the Italian fleet among Allied nations:

BADOGLIO HITS
SPLIT IN FLEET

NAPLES, March 5—A member of the Italian cabinet said today that Marshal Pietro Badoglio and his fellow cabinet members intended to resign unless an explanation of President Roosevelt's announcement of a division of the Italian fleet among the United States, Great Britain and Russia made the development more satisfactory.

"As the matter stands now, no self respecting government could continue to hold office," the informant said.

Italian cabinet circles said that Badoglio expected more detailed information tomorrow about the future of the Italian fleet and that he would decide then whether to resign.

According to these informants, Gen. Sir Noel Mason MacFarland, head of the Allied Control Commission, called on Badoglio yesterday at Badoglio's request.

They asserted that MacFarland was unable to give Badoglio an explanation of President Roosevelt's announcement and that he had been as surprised as was Badoglio over the Allied division plan.

The cabinet informant said that the division of the Italian fleet appeared to be particularly an "affront" to King Victor Emmanuel who was "entirely responsible" for the surrender to the Allies.

President Roosevelt's apparently arbitrary division and allocation of the Italian fleet resulted from his lack of awareness of the following agreement:

ARMISTICE WITH ITALY
EMPLOYMENT AND DISPOSITION
OF ITALIAN FLEET AND MERCHANT MARINE
(CUNNINGHAM-DE COURTEN AGREEMENT)
SEPTEMBER 23, 1943

"... The armistice having been signed between the head of the Italian Government and the Allied Commander-in-Chief under which all Italian warships and the Italian Mercantile Marine were placed unconditionally at the disposal of the United Nations, and H.M. The King of Italy and the Italian Government having since expressed the wish that the Fleet and the Italian Mercantile Marine should be employed in the Allied effort to assist in the prosecution of the war against the Axis powers, the following principles are established on which the Italian Navy and the Mercantile Marine will be disposed.

". . . all the Italian ships will continue to fly their flags. A large proportion of the Italian Navy will thus remain in active commission operating their own ships and fighting alongside the forces of the United Nations against the Axis Powers.

". . . It is the intention that the Italian Mercantile Marine should operate under the same conditions as the merchant ships of the Allied Nations. That is to say, all mercantile shipping of the United Nations is formed into a pool which is employed as may be considered necessary for the benefit of all the United Nations."

Following are other important provisions of the agreement:
"All battleships will be placed on a care and maintenance basis in ports to be designated. . . . Each ship will have on board a proportion of Italian Naval personnel to keep the ships in proper condition and the Commander-in-Chief, Mediterranean, will have the right of inspection at any time."

It is interesting that "there is no signed copy of this agreement between Sir Andrew Cunningham, Allied Naval Commander in Chief, Mediterranean, acting on behalf of the Allied Commander in Chief, and Admiral Rafaella de Courten, Italian Minister of Marine. ... Even Marshal Badoglio's adhesion was communicated verbally. It was a 'gentlemen's agreement' " and therefore may not have come to President Roosevelt's attention.

[Source: Treaties and Other International Agreements of the United States of America 1776-1949. Compiled under the direction of Charles I. Bevans LL.B. Assistant Legal Advisor Department of State. Volume 3 Multilateral 1931-1945. Department of State Publication 8484. Washington, DC: Government Printing Office, 1969.]

Meanwhile, the battle for Anzio was continuing. March 1, Dana wrote a story about the Nazis' secret weapon, which they employed on the Anzio beachhead:

RADIO-CONTROLLED TANK, FILLED WITH BIG EXPLOSIVE CHARGE, IS NAZI SECRET WEAPON

ALLIED HEADQUARTERS, Naples. (UP)—Germany has introduced a new secret weapon—a radio-controlled miniature tank—on the Anzio beachhead below Rome, it was revealed Wednesday, but lost 14 of the "explosive beetles" in the last big Nazi attack.

The tanks carrying 1,000 pounds of explosives, were designed to be directed against the chosen targets, then blown up by remote control. An official Allied announcement, however, described the tanks as "poor specimens" and said that though the wheels of the tanks went around, the tanks themselves often failed to move forward.

None of the tanks was believed to have reached the Allied lines during the big German attack more than a week ago. Most of the 14 were blown up by Allied artillery behind the German lines.

The "beetles," which have a low silhouette and a single wireless aerial, were believed to have been the secret weapon to which Adolf Hitler referred mysteriously in a recent speech.

The enemy unit entrusted with handling the "beetles" was the 309th Panzer Grenadier Regiment, formerly the crack Infantry Lehr regiment, Berlin-Spandau from the great infantry training center at Doeberitz, Germany.

The morning after the regiment's arrival at the beachhead, German troops were paraded before it prior to the big attack to be shown the weapon which the Nazi command said would pulverize the Allies.

The rest is history.

The Allied advance up the Italian peninsula was stopped at Cassino near the Anzio beachhead. The fighting at Cassino was fierce and the Allies thought that the Germans were using the monastery on top of Monte Cassino as an outlook point. On February 15, an immense attack on the mountaintop resulted in the complete destruction of the monastery, but German troops found ways of surviving in the debris.

In an article published on March 15 in many papers, Dana wrote:

NAZIS SURVIVE
CASSINO CASCADE
By DANA ADAMS SCHMIDT
United Press Correspondent

Theoretically nothing should have survived the 2,800 tons of explosives that were poured on Cassino and the mountain behind it in the heaviest and most concentrated air raid ever made on a front-line objective.

But the Germans—or at least a good many of them—did survive. They had taken refuge in deep underground shelters and deep caves dug far into the side of Mount Cassino while American bombers were overhead, then emerged fighting when Allied tanks and infantry burst into the wrecked town in the wake of the bombardment.

U.S. army engineers, struggling to clear away the rubble of blasted buildings for advancing tanks, were forced to throw down their picks and shovels repeatedly to fight off what one officer described as "suicide attacks."

The Allies fought their way into the heart of the ruins of Cassino, but sent word out that the going was tough. At nightfall, the Germans still held the monastery on top of Mount Cassino.

Not a single building remained intact in Cassino after the heavy aerial bombing and shelling. The least damaged building was a four-story hotel, the two upper stories of which were smashed.

Tens of thousands of American, British, New Zealand, Indian and French troops watched awe-struck during the bombardment. Only a few Italians, too numbed by the impact of war on their homeland to care, failed to pause in their routine to watch the death of Cassino.

An Italian peasant woman sat in the morning sunshine on the doorstep of a half-ruined house, from in front of which I witnessed the assault. Her nerves dulled to the point of indifference, she sullenly held her baby daughter in her lap and picked lice from the child's head. Not once did she look toward Cassino.

I've been getting around fairly rapidly these days, Dana wrote on March 17. *Saw the bombing of Cassino the day before yesterday, and back here [in Algiers]—in time to get off a piece about the French cabinet crisis the following night.*

. . . . In many ways I'm glad to be out of Italy, especially after a cognac-swilling midnight session with Packard and Cunningham. . . . UP internal politics are a frightening maze, but, as you know, every organization has the same trouble, especially on the upper rungs of the ladder.

On March 27, Dana reported on the meeting of the French Assembly:

Gen. Charles de Gaulle told applauding members of the French Assembly today that his French Committee "does not need to receive lessons from anyone other than the French Nation, which it must lead."

Intervening in debate on the form of provisional government to be instituted in France when the Allies open the Western Front, de Gaulle, President of the National Committee, said:

"France gave liberty to the world. She is still the champion of liberty and she does not need to worry about what is said outside her frontier."

The Assembly passed by a vote of 62 to 6 a plan to establish a Provisional Government in France after the opening of the Western Front, including a Communist amendment giving the vote to Army and Navy men.

De Gaulle's brief statement was aimed at the American and British governments, now discussing whether the French Committee shall be permitted to act as a Provisional government when France is invaded.

De Gaulle praised the Assembly for affirming the republican principles: 1) That national sovereignty may be expressed only through the votes of the people, including war prisoners; 2) That a national constituent assembly must be set up; and 3) That municipal and provincial elections must be held.

In Dana's April 1 dispatch, he indicated similar sentiments expressed by the French Committee of National Liberation [CNL]:

FRENCH SUBMIT SELF-RULE PLAN TO ALLIES
ALGIERS, April 1—The French Committee of National Liberation today announced a detailed plan for governing liberated French soil by Frenchmen instead of by an allied military government, thereby preserving what it termed French sovereignty.

Text of the plan, which the "trustee government" described as a "law," was forwarded to Washington and London two weeks ago, the committee announced, but thus far has received no reaction from the U.S. or Britain.

[*Associated Press* reported the Allies were not expected to approve the plan.]

Plans for both the initial and later periods after liberation of France, it was understood, had been submitted to the American and British governments last September with a similar lack of response.

The "law" provides for election of a constituent assembly "not later than a year after complete liberation of French territory."

A delegate representing the committee would be accredited to the Allied command in each theatre of operations on French soil, to be responsible for resumption of civilian and military administrations and renewal of economic activity.

A military delegate responsible to the committee would control liaison between the Allied command and French civilian and military administration.

Donald Coe has got away to Italy at last, Dana wrote on April 2, *and I hold the fort alone.* [Coe had been assigned to Algiers in Dana's absence in Italy.] *Frankly I am not unhappy to be alone. In working with other people I like either to be able to recognize them, or, him, as clearly my boss and superior, or as susceptible to taking orders from me. The UP, however, has a tendency to leave people to fight it out among themselves, ostensibly as equals. Result is that competition is fierce and dirty among members of the organization. Not that I meant to run down Don Coe, who is inoffensive. I was just reflecting on some of the things that went on in Italy when last I looked in.*

It has turned clear and hot here. Seems only yesterday I was freezing in jeeps in the mountainous Apennines. I'm still trying to get the picture of me in white camouflage "Goum djellaba" [88] *which I used to climb up to the front line across waist-deep snowfields on an extremely high mountain.*

We are having a cabinet crisis, or if you like, a Committee of Liberation crisis, which is getting to be somewhat of a joke. It just keeps crisising along for week after week and nothing ever happens. Gossip is unrationed and cheap

---

[88]   *Goum* is a unit of native soldiers under French officers in North Africa. *Djellaba*—a loose garment of wool or cotton, with a hood, sleeves and skirt of varying length, worn chiefly in Morocco.

and crises thrive on it. . . . We have more crises here than anything else. The French love 'em.

Beside me sits one Wareing of the London Daily Telegraph. *Firstly, he has no right to be in this pressroom, being unaccredited, secondly, he is lucky nobody drops him down a cistern, or a manhole . . . or a sewer, because nobody wants to see him very much around here. By no one I mean the French, about whom he writes the most poisonous things public decency will permit. Of course the French have it all cabled back from London, and hang it where he can see it. But he just breezes along on his flat feet and pretends he doesn't know anything about it at all and everything is just lovey-dovey. Naturally the French can't throw him out because they're so democratic and filled with love of the free press.*

The other night I went to a play called Toulon, *escorting Alice Doggett.* [89] *It was a popularized almost slapstickized epic about the sinking of the French fleet written by local talent. It was shown at the biggest theater in town, admission ten and twenty cents. The mewling and ruling of babes in arms, crackle of cellophane, peanuts, etc. and tramping of children in the aisles*

---

[89] In a March 26 letter, Dana mentions he had met a very attractive girl, Alice Doggett, from Boston.

consequently drowned out all except the more forceful passages, like people being tortured by the Gestapo or tanks going to the attack.

I'm not sure whether I ever corrected the impression left by Pinkley's letter saying that I was staying abroad at my own request. Actually what I said in my letter was that, after agitating to come home for a long time, I was now willing to stay on the job until we get to Paris, because I want to finish the story I have begun, on the understanding that after that I will get home leave at the first reasonable opportunity.

Winston Burdett, my good friend, and an extremely amusing and fairly attractive young lady whom he extracted from Egypt a little while back, want to go out of town for Easter Sunday, have lunch somewhere by the sea. Winston has to be back for a three p.m. broadcast and there's no telling whether I can make it, but it's a good idea. I'll ask Alice.

De Gaulle's rivalry with General Giraud came to a head, as Dana reported on April 5:

DE GAULLE NAMED HIGH CHIEF; GIRAUD PUT IN BACKGROUND

By DANA SCHMIDT, ALGIERS, April 5 (UP)—The reorganized French Committee for National Liberation today made General de Gaulle supreme commander of French armed forces, relegating to the background General Giraud.

De Gaulle, president of the committee, promptly broadcast to the world over Radio France that the moment Frenchmen "no longer are under German constraint, no authority is valid unless it acts in this Government's name. Traitors will be punished as they deserve."

Writes Le Trocquer

[De Gaulle addressed a letter to Andre le Trocquer, until today commissioner of war, informing him of his selection as "liaison" with the Allies "in the metropolitan territories liberated from the enemy in the interim period before the government can shoulder the entire task," the Office of War Information said in New York.]

De Gaulle's broadcast position was in sharp contrast to reports that General Eisenhower, Allied supreme commander in Western Europe, will be free to handle the situation in France as it develops.

"The war has entered the decisive stage," de Gaulle said. "The effort of all Frenchmen in the struggle must come only from one leadership."

War's General Direction

At a meeting presided over by de Gaulle, the committee voted to assume "general direction of the war," with "sole authority over the ensemble of land, naval and air forces." It then made de Gaulle "chief of the armies," conferred upon him "the wartime powers of French premiers" and implemented the new policy by "empowering de Gaulle to appoint a new general staff of national defense."

The new general staff of national defense will co-ordinate existing general staffs, thus reducing further the powers of Giraud, who hitherto performed this function as commander in chief.

A few days later, on April 10, Dana reported a reaction to Giraud's demotion:

DE GAULLE VS. GIRAUD
OUSTER OF GENERAL CALLED
SWINDLE BY COMMUNISTS
IN FRENCH GROUP
By DANA ADAMS SCHMIDT
United Press Staff Writer

ALGIERS, April 10—French Communist leaders charged tonight that their two members of the French National Committee agreed to a decree depriving General Henri Honore Giraud of his post of Commander in Chief and naming him Inspector General on the understanding that Giraud himself had agreed.

They said that they were concentrating on national unity and their men would never have agreed to the decree, which they characterized as "moral swindle," had they known it would precipitate a political row.

Giraud's Order

It was learned at Giraud's headquarters that he has written an order of the day to the armed forces, explaining his position and bidding them farewell. Giraud plans to publish the statement within a few days, it was said, unless there is a change in the situation. Giraud is said to feel that General Charles de Gaulle had no legal authority for the decree.

The chief of Giraud's private cabinet, General Paul Dewinck, told the United Press:

"It is finished. General Giraud declines to accept the post of inspector-general. He is no longer commander in chief. That is the government's decision."

De Gaullist quarters professed continued hope for some sort of agreement with Giraud, but observers believed the quarrel had gone too far for a reconciliation.

The Giraud dispute came at a time when French leaders seemed to believe that Secretary of State Cordell Hull's speech at Washington tonight would improve French American relations.

Hull's statement that he and President Roosevelt were disposed to see the French committee exercise leadership to establish law and order in France under supervision of the Allied commander-in-chief opened the way for more cordiality and less tension between Washington and Algiers, a committee spokesman said.

"The committee always believed and is now sure that there are no real differences which cannot be overcome," the spokesman said. "The same attitude is felt toward the British, with whom we already are in full agreement."

French political quarters said Hull's speech obviates the "specter" of an Allied military government ruling France and means the Allies will go into France with well-defined plans. There also will be no obstacle to the French Committee going ahead later in setting up machinery on a provisional government whether or not it is recognized as such, they added.

Press Comment

Typical French press comment on Hull's speech was published in The Republicain, which called it a concrete contribution toward the common victory and added:

"Frenchmen will be grateful without reserve whatever may be the judgment Mr. Hull has formed on the qualifications of the National Committee to act as a government, for that is a point of lesser importance.

The essential thing is that, the Committee, having been called to direct civil affairs in liberated French territory, there can no longer arise any serious discords between Frenchmen and their Allies."

De Gaulle vs. Giraud
Ouster of General Called Swindle By Communists in French Group

By DANA ADAMS SCHMIDT
United Press Staff Writer

ALGIERS, April 10—French Communist leaders charged tonight that their two members of the French National Committee agreed to a decree depriving General Henri Honore Giraud of his post of Commander in Chief and naming him Inspector General on the understanding that Giraud himself had agreed.

They said that they were concentrating on national unity and their men never would have agreed to the decree, which they characterized as "moral swindle, had they known it would precipitate a political row.

GIRAUD'S ORDER

It was learned at Giraud's headquarters that he has written an order of the day to the armed forces, explaining his position and bidding them farewell. Giraud plans to publish the statement within a few days, it was said, unless there is a change in the situation. Giraud is said to feel that General Charles de Gaulle had no legal authority for the decree.

The chief of Giraud's private cabinet, General Paul Dewinck, told the United Press:

"It is finished. General Giraud declines to accept the post of inspector-general. He is no longer commander in chief. That is the government's decision."

De Gaullist quarters professed continued hope for some sort of reement with Giraud, but observers believed the quarrel had gone too far for a reconciliation.

The Giraud dispute came at a time when French leaders seemed to believe that Secretary of State Cordell Hull's speech at Washington last night would improve French-American relations.

Hull's statement that he and President Roosevelt were disposed to see the French committee exercise leadership to establish law and order in France under supervision of the Allied commander in chief opened the way for more cordiality and less tension between Washington and Algiers, a committee spokesman said.

"The committee always believed and is now sure there are no real differences which cannot be overcome," the spokesman said. "The same attitude is felt toward the British, with whom we already are in full agreement."

French political quarters said Hull's speech obviates the "specter" of an Allied military Government ruling France and means the Allies will go into France with well-defined plans. There also will be no obstacle to the French Committee going ahead later in setting up machinery on a provisional government whether or not it is recognized as such, they added.

PRESS COMMENT

Typical French press comment on Hull's speech was published in The Republicain, which called it a concrete contribution toward the common victory and added:

"Frenchmen will be grateful without reserve what ever may be the judgment Mr. Hull has formed on the qualifications of the National Committee to act as a government, for that is a point of lesser importance.

"The essential thing is that, the Committee, having been called to direct civil affairs in liberated French territory, there can no longer arise any serious discords between Frenchmen and the Allies."

Today is Easter Sunday, Dana wrote on April 9, *and here it is nearly two thirty and I have been working all morning and haven't had any lunch. Now all the messes are closed and I have to wait for the* Red Cross *to open at three. I'd had plans to go to the races this afternoon, but what with Giraud acting up, or not acting up, I'm tied down to the old grind-stone.*

We've had a great run of fine bright weather and I wish I could get out of town for a couple of hours now and again. Since it seems to be impossible to resuscitate the various ex UP *vehicles, I've been talking about sharing in the purchase of a vehicle with one Lucas,* Daily Express of London *correspondent. He's a nice fellow, on the serious middle-aged side, who stutters.*

There is shockingly little to report on my activities this week, because it's been all work—mostly hoofing it around town trying to keep up with the crises. Having missed luncheon and dinner engagements all week, I now have made two for the same hour on Monday.

Dana had long hoped for a new typewriter. His traveling so much was very hard on the machines. He went on to say: *. . . got a nice friendly note from Harry Flory saying that my typewriter is en route, that it took three months to get all the necessary papers and that I needn't worry about income tax because my income is earned abroad.*

. . . later . . . eleven thirty p.m. and here we are still hotly in pursuit of the French Generals. Andre LaGuerre, our absolutely invaluable helpmate who heads the Direction de la Presse [Office of the Press] *has told us to stand by and he may have something in a few minutes. The* PRO [Public Relations Office], *which has to handle the copy, is busy closing down for the night and there is some doubt whether the great American public will be informed tonight or not.*

Please give my love to all, Eliza, Steinie, Grandma, Ken, Torrey-Pines and everybody,
Dana

On April 27, Dana wrote . . . *in the past few weeks I've written quite a lot about the French Resistance movements. . . . It is a most dramatic thing, though difficult perhaps for Americans to visualize.*

Dana was given detailed descriptions of activities of the "resistants," who made amazing contributions in the battle against the Vichy Government. Following is one of his dispatches:

**STORY OF FRANCE'S UNSUNG HEROES;
UNDERGROUND PATRIOTS FIGHT ON IN FACE
OF DRASTIC NAZI-VICHY LAWS
By Dana Schmidt
United Press Staff Correspondent
ALGIERS, France Fights On!**

That is the report I am able to make after having disclosed to me the record of the French underground's recent acts of resistance against the Nazis and their Vichy puppets in the enslaved homeland.

Alone, in pairs and in guerrilla armies, the French are damaging the enemy despite the threat of summary trial under Vichy law providing prison, forced labor or death for "terrorism."

Members of the French underground recently escaped told me that the Vichy government of Pierre Laval itself had announced the arrest of 5,998 "terrorists" during September. French sources here said altogether 8,000 have been arrested by the Germans and Vichy.

Since the fall of France, according to these French sources, 58,000 French patriots have paid the supreme penalty.

Here are excerpts from the unofficial record since Oct. 1 of this gallant battle against odds:

The Creusot Arms Works was put out of action for the rest of the war. In a single night the underground knocked out the power station at Chalon-sur-Saone, the transformers of the Schneider Works and high tension lines which delivered power to Germany.

A trainload of Germans en route home on leave blew up at Dimphy. Twenty-five cars loaded with German stores caught fire at Mont d'Or. Eighty meters of rails went up with a bang between Bordeaux and Sete.

At Varenne a train of tank cars rolling toward Lyon blew up so violently that a stone bridge across which the train was passing was smashed.

In a single week at Chalons-sur-Marne and Troyes, time bombs destroyed 30 locomotives in the switching gears under the very noses of German guards. Eighteen locomotives were damaged at the La Roche-Migennes Yards. In another station a locomotive suddenly tore down the tracks and crashed at 70 miles an hour into a long train of tank cars. The Germans told themselves that it was an accident.

Two men disguised as nurses walked into a hospital at Amiens, held up the staff and escaped with a Patriot hurt in a shooting with the Germans.

A Patriot rode by a German-occupied hotel at Lyon, tossed a bomb through the door and got away.

An explosive factory at Commentry and a cement plant at Isere blew up.

Eight Germans and six Patriots were killed in a pitched battle near Mont Aigouil. Fifty fighters including a British officer were captured.

Pierre Laval, it was said, recently called his security chiefs together, gave them a pep talk and sent them away with 1,500 francs apiece. But the sabotage continues.

In Dana's April 18 letter, he wrote:

A day or so ago I was running down the hall for some reason or other when a clerk from the U.S. Navy PRO office called to me that Commander Duffy, head of the Navy PRO, wanted to see me. With ready wit I retorted, "Tell him to come and see me," and the little dope went and reported my retort to his boss. To make matters worse I didn't actually get around to going to see the Commander till late that afternoon. He was icy: "Well, I'm sorry, I DID take it seriously, and I've reported it to the General." Oh my god, what have I done, thought I. We talked, and the Commander, who is really a very nice guy, gradually got over his wounded dignity, and said he'd tell the General it was all a mistake. What complications one does run into sometimes!

Did I tell you that these days I share my room with one William Schenkel of News Week, *whom I have mentioned before. He is a good roommate. We get on splendidly, do not compete and can often be mutually helpful. Idyllic.*

Last night I ran into Charov, former TASS [90] *correspondent in Ankara, to my great surprise. We had dinner together and I took him around to the principal journalistic gathering places and showed him the ropes.*

Tonight Russell Hill (of the Herald Tribune*) and I have an appointment together to see Bob Murphy (U.S. diplomatic service) at his house at 6:30. We'll get a drink out of it anyway, I guess, if not more.*

Your last letter is dated March 25 and mentions the sight I must have seen when Vesuvius erupted. But I left those sunny shores about 24 hours before it began to erupt. Funny thing is that just before I left, a French journalist told me that Vesuvius had been unusually quiet for some days and was expected to go up with a bang the next time it did anything. I thought of writing a box about it, but decided my information was too flimsy.

And on April 30, he wrote:

Here it is May Day, or the day before May Day, which is being celebrated as May Day here, and I haven't found anything better to do than to mope around the old typewriter all day.

Tonight I am dining with a lad named Michel le Troquer, son of the Commissioner, Andre le Troquer, who escaped from France earlier this month. . . . He is only 26 and a very likeable sort. [de Gaulle appointed the father, André le Troquer, President of the National Assembly. He played an important role in the international war crimes tribunals after the war.]

Some nights ago I had an extremely interesting dinner with General Jean de Lattre de Tassigny. I am tempted to tell you all about it, but suppose I shouldn't, since he asked us to consider it off the record. He is a very big name around here. [91]

I'm way behind schedule with my letter this week and two of yours, of April 15 and 24 have come in, Dana wrote on May 12. *You ask whether V-mail*

---

[90] Russian News Agency.
[91] Général de Lattre de Tassigny commanded one of the Free French divisions in the landings in southern France on August 15, 1944.

comes faster. I think it does, but not very much faster. Personally I prefer to use ordinary paper with its relative freedom.

The typewriter still hasn't put in an appearance, but should any day now. It would naturally take longer than the letter announcing its impending arrival.

You are so right about the desirability of my writing a book.

I think of it frequently, and surely will start one of these days.

I have been invited to lunch today with Andre le Troquer, the Commissioner who is supposed to head administration in liberated French territory. In fact I must leave now or I shall be even later than is permissible for a newspaperman....

Later: The le Troquer lunch was very good. Even produced a few scraps of news. Of course news from here isn't going to get much of a ride now that things have broken loose in Italy. [The Allies had finally conquered Anzio and Monte Cassino and were approaching Rome. Rome fell on June 4.]

Observing that it is Mother's Day, I have violated all my precedents and sent you a telegram. Lately it has become possible to send personal telegrams from here through the English "Eastern" cable company, although the American "Mackay" still will not accept them. If the occasion should arise, I think you could send me a telegram without difficulty addressed to "Dana Schmidt, Unipress, PRO pressroom, Allied press, Algiers."

On May 20, Dana was pleased to report:

1,000 EXCHANGED PRISONERS REACH ALGIERS ENROUTE HOME
By DANA ADAMS SCHMIDT

ALGIERS, May 20 (UP).—The Swedish exchange liner Gripsholm docked here at 2:00 p.m. today and more than 1,000 exchanged British and American prisoners of war got a taste of Coca-Cola and a look at the Allied side of the news for the first time in months.

En route to Britain and the United States via Belfast and Barcelona, the exchangees were greeted by bands playing "Stars and Stripes Forever," and "God Save the King." Red Cross workers and special service volunteers boarded the ship with beer, Coca-Cola, brandy and message blanks for telegrams home, stationery and new uniforms.

Singing and dancing aboard ship were arranged and tours of the city, movies and a tea party ashore were planned for those able to leave the ship.

Correspondents were not allowed to interview the passengers under a ruling between the British and U.S. Governments intended to keep them fresh for interrogation by Army intelligence officers.

Welcomed by Officials

The prisoners were welcomed on board by Gen. Sir Henry Maitland Wilson, Lt. Gen. Jacob L. Devers, Gen. Georges Catroux, U.S. diplomatic representative Robert D. Murphy, British minister Harold Macmillan and Sir Alfred Duff Cooper.

Special editions of army newspapers "Stars and Stripes" and the "Union Jack" were distributed.

The U.S. army newspaper carried the headlines, "Roosevelt, Dewey likely opponents," "Veteran benefits cover wide range," "Rationing eased," and "U.S. Army flyer inherits $10,000,000."

The Union Jack bore the headline, "What home will look like to you planning the new Britain."

Exchangees were told they may draw $20 during the voyage to Belfast for spending and an additional $20 after leaving that port.

This is a great day, Dana wrote on May 22, *for I have received my gorgeous new Royal typewriter from you. I wish I could write this letter of thanks on it, but there is a crack in the case and a spring is broken in the carriage, obliging me to leave it at the typewriter repair shop.*

It came through splendidly, really. The damage is very slight and should be repaired in time for my next letter. By what devious means it came I do not know. After the bill of lading came a summons to the "Civil Affairs" office, where Murphy and Macmillan have offices, and I was informed my typewriter was waiting for me on the fourth floor.

Here's some good news, maybe. Winston Burdett of CBS is leaving for Italy and asked me to pinch-hit for him over the ether while he is gone. I will be only too delighted, but permission from UP and CBS has not yet materialized. It would be good experience, not to mention the fifty dollars per broadcast, not more than three times a week.

We have just lost Donald Coe to the Blue Network and the UP is likely to be very shy of letting the radio borrow more of our men. . . .

I must come to the defense of fat men. My objections to obesity are specific, not general. Take Bill Schenkel of News Week, per example. I couldn't ask for a better friend, or a fatter one. He is, by the way, pushing off for India tomorrow morning. Doesn't want to go, but orders is orders these days.

That makes me think of my own desire to get home. I just can't do it now, Mother. We'll have to wait till this thing is over. It has been much, much too long. If I could have foreseen how year would pile on year, I would have told the UP to go stuff itself and gone home on my own long ago. But now I think we are so near the end, and the situation is so tense that it would be something like desertion to leave. As soon as the war is over will certainly be the "first reasonable opportunity," which Pinkley has promised to utilize to bring me home.

A few nights ago I was cajoled into giving another speech to another antiaircraft battery—this time on French affairs. I didn't have time to prepare it and spoke from notes and a sheaf of recent stories, but it went well. They kept asking questions for more than an hour after.

Tell Steinie that I congratulate her on her brother Victor's activities in the Sea Bees. They rate highly in this war.

And, oh yes, tell the postman that I have ascertained that his son is not around here but in Italy. I'll write to him from here if the postman hasn't had any word. [Dana often received requests to look up friends of the family in Europe.]

All my love to you all,
as always,
Dana

In early July, Dana interviewed a man who described activities of the French underground:

ESCAPED PRISONER REVEALS DETAILS OF FRENCH UNDERGROUND MOVEMENTS

By DANA ADAMS SCHMIDT

United Press Staff Correspondent

ALGIERS—(UP)—Details of the most secret of all French underground movements, the National Movement of Prisoners of War and Deportees, were revealed by the organization's leader, who escaped from a German prisoner of war camp in 1942 and left France a month ago to report to General Charles de Gaulle's headquarters.

The small, lithe, blue-eyed man, whose name cannot yet be revealed explained that the organization, which has more than 150,000 active members in Germany and France, collects military information for the Allies, sabotages the German war machine, demoralizes German guards and prepares for ultimate revolt and escape from concentration camps and German factories.

In France, he revealed, there are several maquis [92] groups composed entirely of men who have escaped from Germany. "From our headquarters there," he added, "we keep in constant touch with our representatives still imprisoned, send 'volunteers' back to work as provocateurs and maintain a constant flow of messages into and out of Germany by methods too secret to discuss."

Nazis Often Relax Guard

The German guards in the big prisoner "stalags" are now beginning to remember that they are communists, or Catholics, in addition to being Nazis. These men, he said, often relax their guard, permitting more freedom among prisoners and even help them to escape.

"Even before I fled," he said, "I knew of about 1,000 cases in which French soldiers were sent back to France as 'sick' or 'veterans of the last war' on false papers, occasionally with the complicity of the Germans."

"I wrote a pamphlet called 'The Deportees' Manual,' in which I instructed prisoners not to shun contact with the Germans, but to talk to them and

---

[92] The word maquis, from the Italian macchia, entered French through the Corsican dialect, which used it to describe the dense, scrubby landscape—possibly good to hide in. "Prendre le maquis" meant joining the Resistance and taking to the woods and hills. It meant becoming an outlaw; willing to commit sabotage; joining the underground.

undermine their morale—impress on them the conviction that the Allies will win—that they are fighting in vain."

"On one occasion," he continued, "we smuggled a powder into Germany which produced conjunctivitis—inflammation of the eyes—and hundreds of Germans used it to keep from being sent back to the front."

"Sabotage," he said, "is easy. Slowdown strikes, complaints about food and brutal guards, little deviations from the work routine, all help to slow down German production."

We are all aflutter today, Dana wrote on July 12,—*I mean the locals—as a result of Roosevelt's announcement recognizing the* CFLN *as the competent authority in liberated territory, and I must dash in and out to collect "reaction."*[93]

A week later, he wrote, *Every passing day makes it look as though I'd be home sooner than expected. Can't quite see how far it will carry us, but the attempt on Hitler's life* [on July 20] *must speed the end for sure.* [94]

Dana continued: *New York has asked for another good old "downhold" during the Democratic convention. That on top of the general "downhold" preceding the conventions must put me down somewhere below sea level. If one were to take all the service messages seriously one wouldn't file anything at all ever, unless it should be the second coming of Christ, in which case one had better hold the story up for confirmation.*

Now here is news.... The Robert M. McBride & Company of New York has asked me to write them a book. What do you think of that? Their letter was written at the suggestion of Michael Stern a NANA [North American Newspaper Alliance] *correspondent whom I mentioned a while back. Suggestion is that it should be a story of the whole fall and, perhaps,*

---

[93] Recognition of de Gaulle's government by the British, the USA, USSR, and Canada was not until October 23.

[94] For years, a group of officers had talked about saving the honor of Germany by getting rid of Adolf Hitler. Count Claus von Stauffenberg, who had been wounded in Tunisia, was the leader. Hitler's anti-Jewish pogroms and SS atrocities had turned him against Hitler (see Appendix).

resurrection, of France "including the inside story of de Gaulle's fight and temporary truce with other resistance groups, like the Communists; the story of the personal Gestapo which de Gaulle has working for him; the story of the taking of Corsica by General Giraud, and many other events which would fill out the book and with which, we understand, you are perfectly familiar." What a mixture of blarney, misinformation and what-not. Anyway, I guess I'll do it. I suppose I'll have to. I'm thinking I might start now and carry the story up to de Gaulle's entry into Paris, trying to publish as soon as possible thereafter, with the emphasis on a sort of "blueprint for France of the future."

They want 75,000 words and are "ready to offer you our regular contract, starting with royalty of 10% and rising to 15%. Also we would be prepared to offer you a generous advance, a part of which would be payable on the signing of the contract, and the remainder during the course of the writing of the manuscript."

The letter, a page and a half long, was signed by Merton S. Yewdale, Editor, and quite chatty. He says "there is no book we need more than one which tells the story of France from the time of her fall to the present day when she has reached a point where we do not know how she stands in world affairs." Furthermore, "We are very much excited about the possibility of publishing this book."

Well, Mother, it's a great challenge that Mr. Yewdale has set before me. He has thrown down the gauntlet, I believe you would say, little though he realizes it, and I will probably have to rise up from my sloth and pick it up.

My love to Eliza, Grandma and Steinie.
Dana

Dana was excited about the book proposal, but it was unrealistic. He was pleased to be asked but, thinking it over, decided not to pursue it.

I'm writing you this more or less mid-week letter, Dana wrote on July 27, in an effort to catch up to my weekly schedule, like a man who gets up an hour later each day until he finally misses a day, I have a habit of writing my letter a little later each week.

ELIZABETH SCHMIDT CRAHAN

... Had lunch today at the mess of officers of de Gaulle's military cabinet. It's the second time I've been. Many of these people are very fine and admirable, but I regret to say there is something about many others I don't like, that frightens me just a little. Something about "I know not why, I cannot tell; I do not like thee doctor Fell." Maybe I do know though; maybe it's something about the stiffness of their neck muscles and the gleam in their eyes when they mention their boss. Maybe this is all poppycock and the product of indigestion, but I recall having the same type of reaction in Berlin. I never could stomach people whose lives circulate around certain unassailable absolutes, and there is something of that in Gaullism as well as Nazism.

It may be that their constant protestations of democratic republican intentions are sincere in a great many cases. But while the principles they all propound say one thing, their actions and specific plans are quite another. I am inclined to think that the political movement which has grown around "Gaullism" will turn out to be a bigger thing than the individuals in it, and that even de Gaulle's intellectual espousal of democracy will not prevail.

I'm not yet prepared to write publicly charging fascism, or anything like that, although I have from time to time mentioned authoritarian tendencies. This movement means so much to the liberation of France that it is only fair to wait till they've had a chance to show what they will do in the homeland; that in any event is the only available course, even for Mr. Roosevelt, since they are so strong on a purely French political plain. My mind is still open. It is, for instance, conceivable that the symptoms may be misleading; that some fascist-type forms are inevitable in any country of Europe which has gone through this war, or that they may be submerged in a larger democracy.

Having heard this political disquisition, you may want some news. Can't think of a thing but politics for the moment. Went to the beach with Lauren Carroll, U.S. press attache, who is a splendid friend, but whose usefulness is limited by the fact that the U.S. Embassy activities are still limited by the old policy of non-recognition. It's not an Embassy, it's a mission.

A letter from Pete Woodruff says he has been drafted, much to his disgust. He has three daughters, but his business, in some Drive UR Self auto enterprise wasn't very essential.

Still in Algiers but expecting a transfer to Italy to cover the invasion of southern France, Dana wrote on August 1:

Still here, but hoping for a change of scene in the near future.

Elizabeth will be having her baby about the time you get this. Give her my love and congratulations. [The baby, Margaret, was born on August 11.]

The war news is so good, it begins to look almost as though it would be finished without my assistance. Could be.

UP is still spending barrels of money telling its correspondents not to spend money. I've been good and scarcely opened my mouth of late.

Callender is back and tells me he had a fine talk with you on the phone. I am so grateful to him. Lots of people promise to do these things, but mighty few do.

The heat broke a little today. What relief to have a cool breeze. I was just about wilted.

Today I had lunch at the "diplomatic restaurant," reserved for diplomats (and journalists) with Maurice Lachin who will replace me in case of my absence. He is a bright Jew who has traveled the length and breadth of Europe and of the Far East as well and is the only man available. He had a job with the London Daily Sketch, *but got fired.*

I've been reading Siegfried Sassoon's poems and find them rather somber, personal and disappointing. Also the book called History of Bigotry in the United States *which Eliza and Ken sent me for Christmas. It is full of interesting information and long words where short ones would do.*

This is the first summer I haven't played any tennis at all. War shortages can't get any worse. No tennis balls.

On August 6, Dana wrote: *This is probably my last opportunity to write you for some time.* [He couldn't say this in his letter, but he had left for the invasion of southern France.]

Just before I left my previous location [Algiers] *I got a letter from you telling of your trouble with your back. I am so very sorry. I do hope you get it entirely cleared up soon.*

ELIZABETH SCHMIDT CRAHAN

It has been a relief these past few days being quite out of touch with the office. Just imagine, I am traveling with Karl Quigley, ex-Pomona, as conducting officer. Last time, you may remember, I ran into him when he was running Stars and Stripes *in Cairo, and for a long time he looked after my dog Jimmy.*

I'm feeling very satisfied with myself because, just at the last minute, I managed to get a hair-cut and shave. It'll probably be some time till I get another hair-cut.

Elizabeth's time must have just about come now. The young lady or gentleman will be in the world by the time this reaches you.

All my love to the proud pa, ma, and offspring.

In spite of the relative heat we have been obliged to wear woolens the last few days . . . most uncomfortable, but one gets used to it, more or less. . . .

At a rough guess I'd say the next two months will decide whether I quit UP *or whether I'm going to be with them for a long time to come. It'll depend on what happens when we get to Paris and how they act about my home leave. Callender said you told him to tell me not to work too hard for* UP *I guess you're right, but I'll keep up the pressure for a bit yet.*

Dana at the Front, Southern France, 1944

UNITED PRESS
Bureau Directory

General Headquarters: 220 E. 42nd St., New York 17, N. Y.
Telephone: Murray Hill 2-0400

AUGUST 1, 1944

EUROPE, AFRICA AND ASIA

ALGIERS
    Dana Adams Schmidt   Allied Force Headquarters, A.P.O. 512, c/o Postmaster, New York City
BERNE.................Viktoriastrasse 63, Berne, Switzerland .... Berne 24779
    Aldo Forte
BOMBAY....................Times of India Bldg., Bombay, India
    K. Gopalaswami
CAIRO ....22 Sharia Kasr el Nil, Cairo, Egypt
    Walter Collins, Middle East Business Manager
CALCUTTA ....Great Eastern Hotel, Calcutta, India
    Frank Hewlett
CHUNGKING................Press Hostel, Chungking, China 2856
    Walter Rundle, Manager for China
COLOMBO.....................c/o Public Relations Officer, SEAC Headquarters, Colombo, Ceylon
    Harold Guard
ISTANBUL
    Leon Kay   Park Hotel
JERUSALEM ...................P.O. Box 456, Jerusalem, Palestine
    Eliav Simon
KUNMING ....Hotel du Commerce, Kunming, China
    Albert V. Ravenholt
LISBON....................58 Rua de Assuncao, Lisbon, Portugal .... Automatic 24160
    Adolfo V. da Rosa
LONDON ....30 Bouverie St., London E. C. 4, England .... Central 2282
    Virgil M. Pinkley, Vice President and European General Manager
    Clifford L. Day, Assistant European News Manager
MADRID ....Plaza de las Cortes 3, Madrid, Spain 18260
    Ralph Forte
MOSCOW ....Metropole Hotel, Moscow, U.S.S.R.
    Henry Shapiro
    Meyer Handler
NAPLES
    Robert Vermillion
NEW DELHI ....21 Narindar Place, Parliament St., New Delhi, India
    John R. Morris, Far Eastern Manager   c/o Press Officer, Br. Hq. USFCBI, A.P.O. 885, New York City
    Darrell G. Berrigan
ROME ....54 Via Delle Mercede
    Reynolds Packard, Manager for Italy and North Africa   c/o PRO, U.P. War Correspondent, Allied Force Advance Headquarters, A.P.O. 782, c/o Postmaster, New York City
STOCKHOLM ....Drottninggatan 10, Stockholm, Sweden
    Jack Fleischer
    Frederick Laudon
ZURICH ....Kreuzstrasse 39, Zurich, Switzerland 42632
    Ludwig Popper

Now I must investigate the problem of getting this mailed.

On August 16, Dana was finally able to write of the timing of the invasion:

**ALLIES REVEAL
INVASION SET
FOR WEEK AGO**
By DANA ADAMS SCHMIDT
ALGIERS—UP—It may now be disclosed that the Allied landings in Southern France originally had been scheduled for August 8, but were postponed for military reasons until August 14, and then until yesterday because of bad weather.

After last Tuesday's delay, official circles here displayed nervousness over the possibility that the new invasion might not take place, and Louis Jacquinot said:

"In the last week, it was difficult for me to retain any French sailor or French ship in an African port. Every seaman was feverish to participate in the landing operation, and even the crews from old ships which could hardly sail insisted their ships could sail for France."

**YANKS WINED
AND DINED
BY FRENCH**
By DANA ADAMS SCHMIDT
Representing the Combined Allied Press
ON THE ROAD FROM ST. MAXIME, Three miles inland,—(UP)—
The roads of Southern France late Wednesday were lined with French men, women and children... laughing, crying and throwing kisses to "the liberators."

"Vive La France," the cry rang down the road. "Get those Boche. It's going to be better now."

... As I moved inland with the first French troops returning to the southern part of their country, the soldiers—including several American units—were nearly flooded by the good, dry red wine offered them by the jubilant townsfolk.

LETTERS HOME: 80 YEARS LATER

"Vive La France"   MOBILE, ALA. REGISTER Cir. D. 21,433   AUG 17 1944

Yanks Wined And Dined By French

By DANA ADAMS SCHMIDT

ON THE ROAD FROM ST. MAXIME, Three miles inland, (UP)—The roads of Southern France late Wednesday were lined with Frenchmen, women and children, . . . laughing, crying and throwing kisses to "the liberators."

"Vive La France," the cry rang down the road. "Get those Boche. It's going to be better now."

The first civilian I saw in France stood by the ruins of his shell-wrecked home and shouted welcome to the invasion soldiers.

"I have lost everything, But it does not matter," he shouted. "Vive La France and drink my wine, drink!"

As I moved inland with the first French troops returning to the southern part of their country, the soldiers—including several American units—were nearly flooded by the good, dry red wine offered them by the jubilant townsfolk.

I plodded steadily ahead through the swirling dust along a roadside studded with anti-glider posts and anti-tank obstacles. As I finally reached a building not wrecked or burning from the smashing naval bombardment, about 150 silent, weary German prisoners reached the building too. Guarded by only a few American soldiers, they looked like sheep as they marched up in the darkness.

Then they settled down quietly for the night, waiting to be shipped off to prison camp in the morning.

I landed Tuesday night in an assault landing craft from a British luxury liner. Troops were streaming out from our landing ships onto a section of the beach where strips of wire netting provided a firm roadway to a tarred coastal highway across a shell-blasted five-foot-thick cement anti-tank wall.

Only once was there a sign of Germans during the entire evening. That was when a couple of German planes tried a sneak raid on the landing craft and evoked a brief round of fire from our naval anti-aircraft guns.

When the army reached St. Raphael in Southern France, the soldiers witnessed an unusual penalty for collaboration:

FRENCH TRESSES FALL TO CLIPPERS
GIRLS' HEADS SHAVED FOR NAZI COLLABORATION
By DANA ADAMS SCHMIDT
Representing the Combined American Press
ST. RAPHAEL, Southern France, August 19, (UP)—Twenty-five pretty girls had their heads shaved by the town's leading barber in front of the town hall as punishment for having been too friendly with the Germans.

While jeering townspeople and embarrassed American soldiers crowded about, the girls were plunked one by one into the chair in the center of the square.

They had been condemned to the punishment by a seven-man committee of liberation.

An old woman hit one of the girls over the head with a basket as she was made to walk through a lane of people after the hair cutting, but otherwise the crowd did not touch the girls and, unlike the Corsican precedent, none of the girls was stripped.

One well-dressed woman with large golden-brown tresses crossed her knees and tilted her head coyly as the clippers slid over her skull, but the others wept, buried their heads in their hands.

One girl fought, screamed and protested her innocence until she was taken back into the town-hall for further questioning.

This story was featured on *Battlefront Reports, UP* radio program on *NBC*, telling of the entry of US troops into Nice.

The first three nights in France, Dana wrote on September 4, *I slept on the ground and a good many other nights I've slept on wooden floors, but there have been other nights when I've slept in chateaux, sometimes in the servants' quarters sometimes in the masters' quarters. Just now I'm sleeping in the garden of a chateau. This part of France is full of chateaux, most of them inhabited by people who still think of the Marshal as the grand old man, but who are delighted to see the Allies. Confusion of thought is general. . . .*

I don't suppose I've had much printed from southern France, although my production has been voluminous. There are too many stories breaking in the northern zone. But it was certainly gratifying to read in yours and Grandmother's last letters that my story "three miles inland" was in the Times. *Wonder whether the story preceding it, about the French landing and departure was printed. So far, anyway, no complaints about over-filing.*

No decision yet about who is to run the Paris bureau or be in it. I sent a cable to Pinkley asking whether he wanted me to hie myself to Paris or continue with the French army, return to Algiers or what, but no answer. Of course return to Algiers, unless to pick up stray baggage, is no longer in question. Packard meanwhile has received a cable saying that Baillie will be in London during September and he and Pinkley will between them decide what is to be done about Paris.

Your suggestion that I should quit U.P, if I don't get the desired break in Paris sounds right to me. I can afford to. It would be a hard wrench. We shall see presently. Meanwhile I'm having the time of my life. As I've said often before I'm happiest when I'm plunged to the ears in something intense and engulfing which really absorbs all the energy I've got and then some. No one ever knows how much reserve or endurance and strength he has till he's really faced with more than he can do.

As chief for the Mediterranean, Packard is my chief here, but I, as a recognized French specialist, remain free to do as I please. He treats me with the utmost consideration, much more than he accords others, perhaps because he also would like the Paris spot. He makes a much better impression on me than ever before, I might even say I'm beginning to like him.

A fellow with whom I have really become friends during this jaunt is Gerald Norman of the London Times. *We are sharing a tent here and are going off on quite an outing tomorrow. He beat me into France by landing with the French commandos before H hour*[95]*, he knows France backwards (his mother is French) and he has been of utmost help to me.*

Can't think what's happened to Callender. He hasn't turned up here—probably got a ride to Paris.

Speaking of rides, I flew across about a third of France in a little observation plane a few days ago. A delightful experience, looking down on neat toy villages, rivers, farms, swinging in an aerial matchbox. We had to fly through a mountain pass with some nasty air currents which brought us not too many yards from the mountain sides. This worried the pilot, but did not concern me in the least till he pointed out the disadvantages of mountain passes later.

---

[95] The zero hour.

I must say Steinie's brother turned out to be a very considerate and generous boy. [96] *Congratulations to Steinie; of course one would only expect that she would have such a brother.*

So it's Christmas boxes we've come to again. Well, if you really want to give things to your son, (who should be giving things to his mother) what I need is another fountain pen and a watch. I've lost both of them. I love nice things, but I always lose them. I've still got my ring anyway. I would very much like another sweater, too, for the old ones are worn pretty much to a frazzle.

Dana was one of the first two Allied correspondents to reach Vichy. This is his September 7 dispatch:

Vichy, capital of collaborationist France, is a gloomy, nervous ward of the French Forces of the Interior tonight, with 20,000 idle Vichy officials and 60 isolated friendly and enemy diplomats with their families awaiting the arrival of the American and French armies.

> **First U. S., Briton Correspondents Arrive in Vichy; Officials Gloomily Await Allies**
>
> By DANA ADAMS SCHMIDT
>
> VICHY, France, Sept. 7 (Delayed). (U.P.)—Vichy, capital of collaborationist France, is a gloomy, nervous ward of the French Forces of the Interior tonight, with 20,000 idle Vichy officials and 60 isolated friendly and enemy diplomats with their families awaiting the arrival of the American and French armies.
>
> Driving overland with the guidance of the F. F. I., I arrived here today with Gerald Norman of the London Times to find we were the first Anglo-American correspondents to reach the city whose name had become a shameful symbol.
>
> Diplomats, the regional commissioner representing Gen. Charles de Gaulle, the police chief and F. F. I. officers and officials told us of the last days here of Marshal Henri Philippe Petain, former chief of state.
>
> They said that he sodght to surrender at the last minute to the F. F. I., but was taken prisoner by the Germans.
>
> We were told also how the F. F. I. liberated the town and the Swiss Minister, Walter Stucks, saved it from re-occupation by the Germans.
>
> We drove to Petain's headquarters. As we alighted, townspeople swarmed around us. They refused to believe at first that we had come overland through French territory freed of the Germans and they insisted we must have parachuted.
>
> Soon the people started to cheer —Vive L'Amerique and Vive L'Angleteere. They grabbed our hands and mothers held up their babies to be kissed by the first American and first Briton to reach the city; Next came the autograph fiends.
>
> At the Hotel Albert I, the head waiter brought out a bottle of the 1933 vintage of the finest red wine of the area, long secreted from Germans and Vichyites.
>
> **Road to Berlin**
>
> Russian front, 311 miles.
> North France, 336 miles.
> South France, 470 miles.
> Italian front, 556 miles.

Driving overland with the guidance of the F. F. I., I arrived here today with Gerald Norman of the London Times to find we were the first Anglo-American correspondents to reach the city whose name has become a shameful symbol.

---

[96] Mother had written to Dana about Victor's visit to Steinie in Los Angeles.

Diplomats, the regional commissioner representing Gen. Charles de Gaulle, the police chief and F. F. I. Officers and officials told us of the last days here of Marshal Henri Philippe Petain, former chief of state.

They said that he sought to surrender at the last minute to the F. F. I., but was taken prisoner by the Germans.

We were told also how the F. F. I. liberated the town and the Swiss Minister, Walter Stucks, saved it from re-occupation by the Germans.

We drove to Petain's headquarters. As we alighted, townspeople swarmed around us. They refused to believe at first that we had come overland through French territory freed of the Germans and they insisted we must have parachuted.

Soon the people started to cheer—Vive L'Amerique and Vive L'Angleterre. They grabbed our hands and mothers held up their babies to be kissed by the first American and first Briton to reach the city: Next came the autograph fiends.

At the Hotel Albert I, the headwaiter brought out a bottle of the 1933 vintage of the finest red wine of the area, long secreted from Germans and Vichyites.

On the following day, Dana filed this widely published report:

PETAIN HELD PRISONER BY GERMANS
(The following dispatch, the most authoritative and detailed of the regime in Vichy, was filed by the United Press war correspondent who was the first American reporter to reach the French wartime capital. He got in ahead of the Allied armies.)
By DANA ADAMS SCHMIDT
VICHY, France, Sept. 7—UP—Aged Marshal Henri Philippe Petain wanted to surrender to an agent of Gen. Charles de Gaulle on Aug. 21, just before the fall of Paris. He had a violent quarrel with Adolf Hitler's agent and called him a "liar." But at the last moment he gave in to a German threat to shoot 100 Frenchmen and was carried off to Germany—a prisoner.

This correspondent reached the capital of collaborationist France through the assistance of the French underground—the first American reporter here. Vichy is controlled by French Forces of the Interior—Allied armies have not yet taken over.

The regional commissioner of Gen. de Gaulle, Henri Ingrand, [a former Paris surgeon] told me the story of Petain's last days at Vichy.

Negotiated with Ingrand

After American forces broke out of the Normandy Peninsula and began their drive on Paris, Petain opened negotiations with Ingrand with the view of surrendering himself to the French patriots.

"If Petain had not been made a prisoner of the Germans on Aug. 20, I am sure he would have surrendered to me the next day," Ingrand told me. "I was still with the Maquis near Mont d'Or when Swiss Minister Walter Stucks came to me with Petain's proposals. It was a question of whether he would surrender unconditionally, be placed under arrest in his house or what.

Under Great Pressure

"I learned that on the night of Aug. 19, German Ambassador Dr. Cecil Von Renthe-Fincke called on Petain and insisted that he leave for an unnamed city in the east, where he said Pierre Laval wanted him to form a new French government.

"Petain had asked Stucks and me to be present to witness the pressure he was under.

"About 6 a.m. the next day S.S. troops forced the door of Petain's hotel and demanded to see the marshal. Told that he was asleep and could see no one, the troops broke into Petain's room and found him awake and fully dressed. He refused to leave.

"Renthe-Finck was called back and he intimated violent reprisals. Petain finally gave in."

From other sources, I heard that the Germans threatened to shoot 100 hostages if Petain did not leave with them.

Dana was returning from Vichy to the Seventh Army when he reached Le Creusot.

4-YEAR PASSIVE FIGHT IN FRENCH PLANTS TOLD
By DANA ADAMS SCHMIDT
With The American Seventh Army
In Southern France

Sept. 10,—UP—Some details of the four-year passive fight in which French factory owners, managers and workers sought to maintain production at the exact level which would keep the Germans from transferring machinery and workers to Germany were revealed to me two days ago beside the smoking ruins of the great Schneider-Creusot steel and armaments plant.

De Gaullists have criticized France's big industrialists, but the story of this great plant was told to me by Jacques Schneider, multimillionaire owner of the Creusot factories, and was backed up by others.

I was returning to the Seventh Army from Vichy when I reached Le Creusot. A few hours before, the fleeing Germans had wrecked all the key machinery and blown up the power plants.

Schneider, I found, was a member of the local committee of liberation and his workers told me that, because of his attitude during the occupation, he had the confidence of the resistance groups.

Schneider said that recent production, up to the German visitation of a few hours before, had been 2500 tons a month instead of the 20,000 of 1939.

"Wednesday we were liberated when a French Forces of the Interior company, which I had requested, entered Le Creusot," Schneider said. "But at 2 a.m. today the Germans returned from the hills in half-tracks, reoccupied the town and until 10 a.m. went around wrecking the works.

The acres of factories showed even after the German sabotage, the effect of the raids, and hundreds of homes in Le Creusot had been flattened.

Schneider explained that his problem, and that of those under him, was to slow down work for the Germans and yet maintain production at a level which would not cause the Germans to dismantle the plant.

"Apparently the Allies overestimated our production," he said, "so I smuggled the true production figures to London via Spain, and provided the underground and the French Committee of National Liberation with diagrams showing the best means of access for sabotage parties if they thought production still too high."

Schneider said that the director of his works and 60 of its leading officials were arrested and sent to Germany last February as the result of continuous rows in which the Germans had accused them of slowing production. Two thousand workmen also were deported, he said.

What a lot of things have happened since I wrote my last letter, Dana wrote on September 14. *It's been a rare day when I haven't had a story and you should have received a few clips which may make up for the shortage of letters. Yesterday I got a cable of congratulations from New York on my Vichy "beat." In fact nothing could have been more fun than that beat. Among other things we went off to Mont d'Or, which is quite a ways farther, to visit Gerald Norman's grandparents.*

It is fantastic the way vast portions of France have really liberated themselves, without our troops even coming near. All the way from Chalons-sur-Saone through the Massif Central we were in such territory.

Goodness gracious, I must be losing my news sense, for I failed to start this letter off with the main point. . . . I have been ordered to Paris. There will probably be some further days of delay while I get the necessary official authorizations, but I'll probably be driving there overland in time for my next letter. Till you hear from me, however, continue to use my 512 APO address. I'm wondering what I'll find there in the way of office politics. The telegram from Pinkley telling me to go there said I should go there "to join the staff," which might mean anything, and requested me to let him know when I would arrive so he could "let Grigg know." That means Grigg is in the Paris bureau right now—that pleases me. He is a good friend, and, furthermore, very unlikely to remain in Paris. That leaves the Paris bureau managership open . . . perhaps. We'll see.

I say I'll be driving overland because I have actually closed my grip on the vehicle I think I mentioned in my last letter. It is a French-built Ford and a very good car. Technically I suppose it isn't my property, but it's a pretty good imitation. It belongs to a physician in Dijon who left it in Grenoble. Apparently the locals in Grenoble didn't think much of the Dijon doctor for they requisitioned his car and turned it over to "les Americains"—most informal procedure. There are no papers on it at all. Nothing to say whether it was requisitioned for the American Army, for me, or what. As a result, since my knowledge of French made the deal possible, I am holding on for dear life to my Ford while PRO has obtained a Fiat.

Yesterday I got off something in the way of a scoop (shared as usual with Norman) on the junction of 3rd and 7th Armies. Gerald and I had driven up by night for a belated visit to Dijon and then decided to look for the junction. I don't think I've ever done so much driving in forty-eight hours before. We dashed from pillar to post and from division to regiment and company. In the end we struck out into the blue between the two armies and drove to Châtillon. There, by sheer blind luck, the first officers we ran into turned out to be the ones who had just returned from making the junction.

You will be interested to know that my beard has been trimmed. The barber said that it is now in the "style of the French explorers." He didn't say which explorers.

The particular occasion for the trimming was an invitation from a French officer to attend a "soiree" with champagne and lovely young things from the town in which we reside. All I can say is thank god we arrived late and left early. Surely there is not another set of girls so dull in the world. There was a phonograph which played ancient dance music too softly to hear and they didn't start serving the champagne till we'd been there for an hour. That, I suppose, is the "Junior League" of provincial France.

Incidentally, Gerald Norman has also had orders to proceed to Paris, so we will probably go together.

Now I must get busy and knock out a few human interest items I've collected—the sort of thing with names in it that we send to people's hometowns.

I've had another letter from you, from the beach, and one from Ken. I'm glad you're feeling better. The change should do you good, It was nice of Ken to write.

My special salutations to Margaret of the black hair. [Her hair soon turned blond.]

Love to you all,
Dana

P.S. I'll do my best to look up the people you mention in your letter.

September 21:

There may have been a stretch of a few days when there wasn't even a chance of your getting any clippings . . . because Gerald Norman and I took a run up to the Italian frontier which was supposed to last forty-eight hours but stretched out to nearly five days. First we got ourselves up in an Alpine valley and were stuck there for a day when a truck broke through a bridge below us. Then our lights and batteries went west; then our fuel pump went west; then the fuel line clogged. And altogether we came very near to abandoning the car and hitch-hiking back to headquarters. When we did reach headquarters it had moved, entailing another twelve hour delay.

These difficulties entailed calls at a large proportion of the garages between here and the Italian frontier. Twice we dragged garage-owners out of their homes in the middle of the night to struggle with our vehicle by candlelight. Always we found them anxious and in fact delighted to be helpful. Some would accept no money, which was hard on our supply of tobacco, sweet things *and canned goods. Almost all of them had lost their best tools and equipment which the retreating Germans had appropriated, remarking lightly, "C'est la guerre." [That is war.]*

At my present location I drove the Ford into a garage yesterday afternoon and got the "garagiste" [garage proprietor] to work on a general overhaul. When I returned this morning I found the work done, but the garagiste gone. He had been arrested by the F.F.I. on a charge of having denounced a man to the Germans some three years ago. After lunch Gerald and I are going around to see F.F.I. headquarters to find out what the score is; we are really obliged to, having promised his tearful wife that we would look into the matter.

I'm still waiting impatiently for orders which will permit me to move up to Paris in accordance with Pinkley's instructions, but the Army is slow in these matters. Meanwhile I'm enjoying every hour of work on this front.

The people of the Alps up around the Italian frontier are not very demonstrative, but their feelings are no less intense and genuine. In one town Gerald and I found every bed in the place occupied. The departing Germans had carried off the bedding from most of the hotel beds, so the accommodations were restricted. Seeing that Gerald and I were the first Britisher and American on the spot, however, the manageress of one hotel insisted on evacuating her own apartment and putting us to sleep in it. She then had wood hauled in to start the hotel's heating system and informed us we could have hot baths (my first since the landing).

It is now time for me to go next door and have lunch with the French Public Relations people. . . . They do eat well.

I trust Grandma, Eliza, little Margaret, Steinie and Torrey Pines are all well and busy.

All my love,
Dana

On September 25, Dana wrote impatiently:

My predictions about my early transfer to Paris have not yet materialized although I've moved heaven and earth, not to mention driving myself all over France, in an effort to get the thing okayed. Yesterday Norman and I took my not so trusty Ford all the way back to Lyons to see the proper people on the subject. The A.P. has resorted to writing a nasty story about the immobilization of would-be Paris correspondents, but for the moment UP policy is still to deal with Public Relations in a highly unwarranted spirit of sweetness and light.

If you are getting any of my clippings you must be surprised by the variety of date lines which I employ, now on this front, now on that, now with the French, now with the Americans, at assorted headquarters and the front. All this is made possible by FORD which whizzes over the roads of France now purring like a panther, then grunting like a pig, though sometimes lying doggo on the highway like a possum. I may have my animal kingdom somewhat mixed, but then FORD is not a normal vehicle. It has strange and unidentifiable ailments which, as often as not, are best cured by a brief rest and a smoke by the roadside. I do the smoking; FORD steams. Magic incantations sometimes help. Friend Norman now believes in ground gremlins.

The great advantage of a car of one's own is that one can pick up and move when lightning strikes, day or night. One need not consider the whims of a gee-eye [G.I.] driver who must feed regularly and sleep at night.

FORD has gorgeous red leather seats and a top which could be folded back if the sun would stay out long enough. It seats four normally, if Norman refrains from taking all his goods and chattels along, and has monstrous doors which provide access to both forward and rear accommodations. It was built in 1935 in Strassburg according to experts.

It has been raining most of the time lately and I have lost the considerable tan acquired in the early days of the invasion. Warm clothes which I unfortunately entrusted to the French PRO when I left Africa have not arrived and I've been wearing the same two shirts for more than a month. They probably smell, but I don't notice it myself, and I seem to be immune to all ills that afflict the flesh as long as I keep moving.

The lights have failed as usual and I am writing by candlelight, which isn't nearly as bad as it sounds unless I have to consult my notes. But that isn't so bad either since I find that note taking is most useful as a means of fixing *points in one's memory. To write a good story it is usually best not to get too note-bound.*

The last three days a South African named Joubert who broadcasts for the South African radio has been accompanying me on my tours. For reasons unknown to me he wears a British captain's three pips, though he functions as a war correspondent. He is quiet and intelligent and an expert in architecture. He and Norman oblige me to spend considerable time inspecting cathedrals, chateaux and hotels de villes [town halls].

Rita Hume, woman correspondent for INS, *has just left the press room to go to bed at the French* PRO *next door. Women correspondents are supposed to live at hospitals according to rules, which were obviously drawn up by ageing males, so concerned with other people's morals. She is a very pretty girl, petite and brunette, and given to singing as she works. I wonder if you ever see any of her stuff. She used to do publicity for the* American Red Cross.

You will have seen by the news, mine I hope, that General de Gaulle has unkindly predicted that the war will not be over in Europe before spring. I hope that will not delay my return home, but don't be over-optimistic. Once I get to Paris it will be much easier for me to see what my future prospects with UP *are and what I should do.*

This is the story Dana mentioned:

DE GAULLE SEES GERMAN DEFEAT ONLY IN 1945
By DANA ADAMS SCHMIDT

WITH THE FRENCH ARMY ON THE BELFORT FRONT, Sept. 24—(UP)—Warning that the hardest fighting still lies ahead inside Germany, Gen. Charles De Gaulle told French Army commanders and civilian leaders today that the end of the European war must not be expected before next spring, "contrary to hopes too hastily conceived."

"Don't let it surprise you that it will last months and months longer," he asserted during his first visit to French front line troops on this sector.

At the same time, French officers accompanying De Gaulle on his trip to a command post during a heavy rain, asserted that France would be allotted a section of Germany to be occupied after the Reich's defeat, on a basis of equality with the United States, Great Britain, and Russia.

Re-asserting France's claim to Alsace Lorraine, De Gaulle said that "those who lost Alsace Lorraine will find it again, and they will even go beyond."

"We must go farther, right into Germany, our hereditary enemy to this day," he told a cheering throng at Besancon. "Our present task consists of waging war, which is far from being finished contrary to hopes too hastily conceived. The latter phases will take place in Germany."

During his visit to the front, De Gaulle watched French artillery fire into German positions at Montbeliard, reviewed a parade of the first fully equipped FFI battalion, and conferred with a number of generals including Gen. Jean De Lattre De Tassigny, commander of French forces in southern France, and Gen. Alphonse Pierre Juin, Chief of the French General Staff.

Your letter of September 3 reached me two days ago, wrote Dana on October 1, *which is really pretty good time, considering the detours.*

I hate to be writing to you from elsewhere than Paris, but PRO is still baulking, pleading some nonsense about food shortage and overburdened communications in Paris.

I imagine you feel better after the holidays at the beach— and a bit disappointed you didn't find any clips of mine waiting for you when you got back to 1132. I do believe, however, that matters will have improved now, judging by my latest message from New York.

On September 25 McCann, one of the cable editors cabled that "Schmidt's front stuff is splendid," especially his stories on de Gaulle and the captured German soldier's letter describing the flight up the Rhone valley. [Copy of this not extant.]

Pinkley in London and Grigg in Paris are doing all they can to hasten my transfer to Paris. . . . There's nothing definite yet about who is going to be Paris bureau manager. Beattie certainly was in the running but was, at last report, a German prisoner of war. He apparently fell into a German ambush near Chaumont a few days after I was up there, to judge by the Stars and Stripes. *Gorrell has always in the past turned down bureau jobs (though he may have changed since he married) and MacMillan is a British subject . . . and quite unfit to preside over the destinies of any of his fellow men (in my opinion). So the question of Paris is still open, I believe.*

You will be glad to hear that I have written to Mme. Plaisance's housekeeper at Cannes, to the Sadouls' relations in the Basses Alpes and to Ida Treat in London. And I've got Ida Treat's friend's address in my wallet to look up when I get to Paris. As soon as I get replies or see any of these people I'll write all the details.

My birthday slipped by this year almost without my noticing it. I don't know for sure what I did that day, but I believe that I witnessed some executions at Grenoble. Now Elizabeth's [birthday] is at hand, and I have no hope of reaching her in time with congratulations. Anyway, give her all my best wishes. I'm waiting to hear from her about the dark-haired beauty Margaret.

The other day I drove up to Domremy-la-Pucelle, Joan of Arc's birthplace, and had an unfortunate encounter with a cow on the way back. The cow walked out in front of us just at the wrong moment and I jolted off it into a couple of trees. We weren't going fast enough to hurt the cow very much—but the FORD is considerably dented. It will take two days for the repairs to be made. None of the occupants incidentally, were damaged. For some reason, as the cow and trees loomed up before me the thought ran through my head: "Now I'll have to write Mother that FORD is no more." But it wasn't so bad as all that.

Bob Vermillion who has been holding down this front with me has been recalled to Rome and Pat Conger is coming here to replace him. For some reason Conger is supposed to be destined for the Berlin bureau and keeps dodging about looking for the shortest route to Berlin.

Now I must close and see about transportation to the front. It is raining again and the prospect is not too pleasant.

All my love to you all,
Dana

ELIZABETH SCHMIDT CRAHAN

Just imagine where I am, Dana wrote on October 11. *The postal censor wouldn't want me to mention it by mail. But with any luck you'll already have seen some stories of mine under that new, delightful dateline.*

This is an office typewriter and doesn't entirely submit to my desires.

(There is an unreality about walking in these streets that I haven't yet got over. It is much more beautiful than I remember from childhood visits. But if it wasn't for the early familiarity I do believe I couldn't appreciate it half so much; just as you cannot quite take in and enjoy a symphony the first time you hear it.)

It's pretty definite that Heinzen isn't going to have his old post back again. Baillie [Hugh Baillie, president of *United Press*] *was here when I arrived and was pretty well convinced that the political situation makes his return quite impossible. Nor are Gorrell or MacMillan in the running, while Beattie as POW, is out of the race. But it isn't Schmidt either. Grigg is the man. Although he's already officially appointed London bureau manager, he has closed his London apartment and was already going great guns when I arrived. He obviously intends to stay.*

But I'm not particularly upset. For one thing Grigg is supposed to move on to Berlin in due course and my chances would then be excellent. But that's not the main point. Important thing is that I'm working out something with the friend from Algiers who telephoned you long-distance during his visit to Washington. That's all I want to confide even to the mails on the subject until it's taped down.

Driving up here in my famous jalopy was quite an adventure. I was alone, with four other correspondents' luggage piled in front and back seats. I had two breakdowns and miraculous luck. There are surprisingly long uninhabited stretches along the road, in the midst of one of which I heard two sharp explosions from the entrails of my vehicle and came to a rapid halt. I set out to walk to the next village, god knows how far away, when I met a circulating ordnance repair truck. A chance in a million, and I was on my way again in ten minutes. Then at ten p.m. in the midst of a forest I felt that horrid tug at the wheel and dull rumble which indicates a flat tire. Looking around I discovered myself opposite the first farmhouse I'd seen in miles. The farmer was still up and in a helpful frame of mind and with the help of his tools and skill . . . I got going again to my destination. Once in town, everything began to go to pieces. The battery went dead, and another tire collapsed. It took most of one morning to maneuver FORD into a Ford garage where it will be hospitalized for at least a week.

It's going to be a chilly winter around here, with coal rationed at an average of a pound and a half per inhabitant per day. In fact I have already resorted to the unprecedented expedient of donning long underwear. There comes a time when one just gets too damn tired of hearing one's teeth chatter.

If there are some friends of yours or friends of friends in Paris, whom I might look up please let me know. I'm anxious to meet as many people here as possible.

Somewhere I read something about the extraordinary light of Paris. Someone said that was what made Paris a mecca for painters. There is something in it. Even today, with a grey sky, there seems to be a glow in the light which I hadn't noticed elsewhere. Or maybe the glow is purely subjective.

I must be off and about my business now.

All my love to Grandma and Eliza and little Margaret, Ken and Steinie,
Dana

October 1944 was a period of difficult decision for Dana. On October 16, he wrote:

Really I don't know what to say. I've already almost made up my mind to quit UP *but am still waiting for definite word from the* NY Times. *Callender, as you doubtless gathered from [my] previous unnecessarily cautious letter, has been trying to get me on the staff, but the deal has not yet quite gone through.*

In a handwritten note to his mother on the margin of the letter he wrote: *It's really on your advice to quit if I didn't get what I wanted in Paris that I am acting.*

It's going to be a sad wrench, but it must be done. I'm sure if you were here in Paris . . . you would advise me to go through with it. It is humiliating to be here in Paris, the star which I followed for a year from Algiers, and to have to give way to another man who doesn't know the background on most of the major stories. Grigg is a good guy, but I'll be damned if I'll play second fiddle to him in Paris. I would not, on the other hand, mind playing second fiddle to a man like Callender, who is many years my senior, worked in Paris before, and knows a hell of a lot more about politics and newspaper work than I do.

Last night de Gaulle made a speech. When Andre LaGuerre came into the Scribe Hotel restaurant with the text, Grigg and I both got up to take it. God, La Guerre has been handing me de Gaulle and every other kind of text for a solid year. But Grigg assumed the prerogative of bureau manager and said he was going to write it. From that moment I knew I would get the hell out, whether I get the job with the TIMES or not.

I have been thinking that if I quit without another job, I could go straight home as I have been planning to do so long. Still, if I can make the deal with Callender I know I will be able to get home in short order as we both expect a quiet winter.

It's been raining most of the time the last few days and I haven't seen much more of Paris than when I last wrote. Yet I am still full of delight with its beauty. What a comparison of the stodgy heaviness of Berlin, and the ill-bred display of the last Nazi building projects.

Did I tell you that I met a Miss Kerr, or something like that, an English woman who knows Ida Treat, who said she planned to come to Paris soon. She will doubtless work in Andre LaGuerre's new headquarters, which he has just obtained after a long fight with C.D. Jackson. It seems they both tried to requisition the same building, simultaneously, and C.D. won.

Did I ever tell you that I bought a watch for 600 Francs at Besancon? Thanks to Gerald Norman's way of sweeping Frenchmen off their feet in a torrent of their native language, a couple of very presentable watches were dug out of "stocks which we hid from the Germans" and sold to us at cost. I have now broken the crystal of mine and will have to wait two weeks for a new one. (That doesn't mean I would turn up my nose at any timepiece anyone may have had in mind for Christmas.)

I think that this Christmas, whether I'm here or in the U.S.A., I'm in a spot to do a heavy share of representing Santa Claus. Here I have all the perfume you might want, all kinds of silk goods, all kinds of fashionable Parisian gowns and whatnots. Will you all please fill in your orders and let me have them? Just about anything Paris was ever noted for is still to be had. Let's not have any false modesty; all except Ken among my relatives are now of the female sex, so I expect a long list of Paris requirements. (All my friends are rushing about trying to buy Chanel No 5 and Xmas night perfume. Are those the only ones Americans ever heard of?)

There was just a gentle knocking at my door, to which I opened with interest, only to be confronted by a dignified white haired gentleman who desired to shine my shoes. Since I haven't had a shine since I bought a new pair of shoes a week ago, I let him go to it—peculiar institution, at midnight.

You and Grandma both know Paris, I'll be interested in any questions about it you may have—for my personal advantage and because they might provide leads for stories. What does Dean Mary want to know?

Howard Smith, [formerly with the *United Press*] *now in uniform, is still here with his blond Danish wife. She is going to have a baby, but appeared unconsoled when I informed her that my sister had just had one. How is young Margaret, by the way?*

*I met Hal Peters, the other day; another ex-*Unipresser *now with* Blue Network. *He came through Turkey from Hungary with wife and baby while I was in Istanbul.*

I'm looking forward to the day when your letters catch up to me again.
All my love to you all, as always,
Dana

I have resigned, Dana wrote on October 21, *and asked Pinkley to let me know how long a period he wants as notice, how long he feels he needs to replace me. There are no hard feelings, no recriminations, and I made it clear that I would carry on as long as he wanted me. I haven't heard from him yet, but hope he will accept the resignation in the same good spirit in which it is tendered.*

ELIZABETH SCHMIDT CRAHAN

New York Times *will pay me one hundred dollars a week and seven and a half dollars a day living allowance. That will be quite an improvement. Harold wants me to go to work as soon as possible, but, like myself, wants no row with* UP *and wants me to carry on as long as they really think they need me.*

I'm most happy about it. I hope you are too. I think it will be a great step forward in my career. Callender is difficult to get on with, but I respect him and think things will be all right.

Last Sunday the Frenchman who handles the UP *"desk," which at present means reading all the newspapers, had an automobile accident while he was bringing his family back from Normandy, and I have been filling in since then. Reading all of this Paris press has been quite an education, but I wouldn't want to do it very long.*

A few nights ago I went out on a little expedition with one of our fellows from London to investigate the night life of Montparnasse. Pretty poor, pretty sordid and damned expensive. The whole thing makes you kind of mad when you compare it with the heroic France of the Resistants. We had to walk forty minutes to get home at three a.m. because the Metro stops running at 10:00 p.m.

They have again changed the APO *here, just when you had caught up with me again. It is now RD, SHAEF; PO 757. But it doesn't matter if you've already sent a few letters by the other one. They will reach me without delay. Unfortunately the ones that went to 512 in recent weeks have been considerably delayed. Don't forget that if anything urgent should ever arise you can always cable me through* UP *in New York, care of Mr. Flory, while I'm with* UP *and later you'll be able to do the same with* N.Y. Times. *I probably won't be able to complete the switch for a month.* UP *is likely to pretend that it is most difficult to find another French-speaking staffer.*

No word from the French people I wrote to at your request. Mail for civilians is still very slow and irregular.

Believe it or not, I've still got that beard. Montrose, an ACME *photographer who took a bunch of pictures of me and Conger and Vermillion a while back showed me some copies tonight but could not give them to me. Some are quite good. He says that if you will write to* ACME NEWS PICTURES, *220 EAST*

42nd Street, N.Y. and tell them I would like them to send you copies of the ones in which I appear and that Montrose would also appreciate it, they will probably do so. They might make a charge, I suppose. The pictures were taken at Luxeil, France.

I'm continuing on this new sheet because the other one was getting absolutely illegible. [Dana sometimes wrote on two sides of very thin transparent paper, making it hard to decipher.]

Afraid I haven't got an awful lot in the way of byline-able stories to show for my first three weeks or so in Paris. Have you seen anything? Naturally I have been somewhat distracted by the pangs of resigning, and for the last week I've had little besides newspaper pickups, while working the desk.

It has been raining pretty steadily, and I haven't been at all sorry to have a steady indoor assignment. The front must be miserable now. Thus far we are getting no hot water and no heating at all, so the prospects are chilly.

All my love, Mother, to you and all the family,
Dana

Pinkley has finally returned to London, Dana wrote on October 28, *and has received my letter of resignation, according to the service messages, but I have not yet received his letter of reply which should indicate how soon he feels* UP *Paris can dispense with my invaluable services. With Harold Callender's full approval, I'm sticking to the policy of being as nice as possible about my departure.*

Another old friend, Peter Rhodes, called in at the office this afternoon and we had a long talk about propaganda and our policy vis-a-vis Germany. He thinks our "conqueror" line is too narrow, that it doesn't provide for our finding friends in Germany at all, but isn't very hopeful about broadening it, judging by past experience in Italy. Rhodes is a fellow who worked for UP *Heinzen in Paris for three years before the war and was later at Narvik for us. I met him in Stockholm. He has been running monitoring stations and news distribution offices for psychological warfare during the war.*

Dick Hottelet turned up at the hotel the other night on his way to England to see his baby. . . . It's always fun to meet these old acquaintances, whether

they were close friends or not, but sometimes a bit of a disappointment. You just don't pick up where you left off, and there is a span of time and separate experience which it takes time to bridge.

Earlier this afternoon I went to see the Tanieres. [97] *Mr. Taniere was out for the day, but I had a nice talk with Mrs. Taniere over a couple of cognacs and her special hoard of cookies.*

She told me that her husband's mother and sisters are living in Aix-en-Provence and that the day before yesterday, for the first time in several years, she got word from them saying that all are well and safe. They had been cut off by the line of demarcation between the occupied and formerly free zones. The letter said that there had been very little damage although they were bombed for several days, but that all had suffered very much from lack of food. One of the sisters lost something like twenty kilos.

Monsieur Taniere has been living in the family's nice apartment in a high-grade new housing project all through the war, but Madame and the little girl lived in a small town near Chartres most of the time where food was easier to get. Madame Taniere's family house there was requisitioned by the Germans and converted into a blockhouse which was unfortunately somewhat battered during the liberation. Two rooms are apparently still habitable, however.

Mr. Taniere is going to telephone me and I will see the family again, at which time he will probably give me a message and more family news for Miss Riese.

During this interim period, Dana continued to write for the *United Press.* Among the articles were the following:

67,000 OF NAZIS' TOUGHEST TROOPS DIG IN AT PORTS
By DANA ADAMS SCHMIDT

PARIS, Oct. 20—(UP)—An estimated 67,000 of Germany's toughest troops were today digging in for the winter on France's "forgotten front," the port areas along the Atlantic.

---

[97] Friends of Mildred Riese, a successful and well-liked director of the Orthopaedic Hospital and a good friend of the family.

The German outfits holding the ports are largely splinters of German groups which were cracked up by the swift rush of the Allies out of Normandy.

Some 25,000 are dug in around Lorient, 30,000 around Saint Nazaire, preventing the Allies from using Nantes and the Loire river, and others holding out in the islands near Bordeaux and denying the Allies use of that port and the Gironde river.

A mixed force of Americans, Poles, Republican Spaniards, Russians, Czechs and the F. F. I. are holding the lines around these ports.

Once a week a council of war is held by the mixed nationalities with almost as many interpreters as there are units because of the diverse nature of the troops.

Fighting is sporadic. F. F. I. officers just back from behind the German lines report the Nazis sometimes use tanks to round up cattle for food while F. F. I. troops watch from nearby woods but are unable to halt the rustling because they have no weapon heavier than light rifles.

F. F. I. officers also believe the Germans receive supplies and reinforcements by air from Germany.

Ousting the Germans is expected to be a most difficult task as their commander, Lt. Gen. Wilhelm Fahrmbacher, 57, is known to be a fanatic for resistance.

FRANCE SHIFT TO DE GAULLE THOUGHT NEAR

By DANA ADAMS SCHMIDT

PARIS, Oct. 21,—(UP)—Complete Allied recognition of the provisional government of Gen. Charles de Gaulle was believed near today after the British government and Supreme Headquarters agreed to designate two thirds of France as an "interior zone," in which the de Gaulle administration will have full civilian authority.

This final step in the de facto recognition means the Allies are satisfied that the De Gaulle government can rule the rear area without danger to vital communication lines, headquarters and supply bases.

Observers believed that complete recognition, at least from the British, would follow soon.

An announcement, made after a cabinet meeting at which De Gaulle presided, said the interior zone had been defined in accordance with an agreement reached Aug. 25, by the French and British governments and the Allied Supreme Command.

The announcement did not define the zone but it was learned that it takes in all of France, including Paris, west of a line running from Boulogne to Ardennes then west of Nancy and down the Rhone Valley toward Marseilles. Boulogne, Nancy and Marseilles, however, remain in the military zone.

A French government spokesman said the shift means the government will be free to make its own decisions on questions such as admission of foreign businessmen and civilian news correspondents. Few practical changes and no slackening of the war effort were expected, he said.

That the war was continuing in full force was evident in Dana's dispatch of November 2:

DUCLOS BLAMES DE GAULLE
By DANA ADAMS SCHMIDT
PARIS, Nov. 2—Jacques Duclos, secretary of the Communist party and

France Shift to De Gaulle Thought Near

By DANA ADAMS SCHMIDT

PARIS, Oct. 21. (U.P)—Complete Allied recognition of the provisional government of Gen. Charles de Gaulle was believed near today after the British government and Supreme Headquarters agreed to designate two thirds of France as an "interior zone," in which the De Gaulle administration will have full civilian authority.

This final step in the de factor recognition means the Allies are satisfied that the De Gaulle government can rule the rear area without danger to vital communication lines, headquarters and supply bases.

Observers believed that complete recognition, at least from the British, would follow soon.

An announcement, made after a cabinet meeting at which De Gaulle presided, said the interior zone had been defined in accordance with an agreement reached Aug. 25, by the French and British governments and the Allied Supreme Command.

The announcement did not define the zone but it was learned that it takes in all of France, including Paris, west of a line running from Boulogne to Ardennes then west of Nancy and down the Rhone Valley toward Marseilles. Boulogne, Nancy and Marseilles, however, remain in the military zone.

A French government spokesman said the shift means the government will be free to make its own decisions on questions such as admission of foreign business men and civilian news correspondents. Few practical changes and no slackening of the war effort were expected, he said.

pending the arrival of Maurice Thorez, the most important Communist in France, declared today that it was the de Gaulle Government's "own fault" if there still were disorders in some parts of the country and if the patriotic militia resisted giving up its arms.

The Government, he charged, was too slow and ineffective in carrying out the purge of fifth columnists and collaborators and added that "people naturally take the law into their own hands."

In an interview at party headquarters—which once served as Joseph Darnaud's militia headquarters during the occupation—M. Duclos said:

"There are some hundred people in France who must be shot and some thousands who must be removed from their posts. By creating delays, some émigrés in the government, who have not learned what even the most conservative Frenchmen know, seek to save a few heads. They risk falling into the plight of the Belgian Government, whose émigrés also learned nothing. The Pierlot Government of course, is doomed sooner or later by prostituting itself and calling on foreign aid against the people."

Defends Militia on Arms

M. Duclos offered this defense of continued arming of the patriotic militia despite the Government's decision to enforce a pre-war law against the carrying of arms:

"It is impossible to return to a legality that led this country to defeat. If we did that de Gaulle would have to step aside and all the Senators and Deputies who betrayed the country would return to power. Now there is a new legality. Bidault [Georges Bidault, Minister of Foreign Affairs] suggested the other day that France is having a revolution by law. But it is not the law that makes revolutions but revolutions that impose their law."

"Nevertheless," he added, "the militia remained willing to compromise with the Government by storing their arms under the authority of local Mayors."

Indicating that, in spite of the Communists' numerous complaints, they intended for the time being to keep their Communist Minister in the Cabinet and avoid becoming Gen. Charles de Gaulle's open opposition. M. Duclos said his party was anxious to avoid anything that might "divide the people."

That, he said, was the reason why the party opposed the February elections and proposed to draw up a single joint list of candidates with Resistance groups if they were held. He welcomed the Socialist proposal for a discussion on unified action despite the "insincerity" of some Socialists and supporters of the Liberation Loan even though he thought that the swift confiscation of illicit profits would be more to the point.

M. Duclos admitted that the French Communist party's program was pretty conservative in the light of Marxist theory since it advocated neither the socialization of agriculture nor of industry generally.

November 5:

You can't have had much in the way of signers from me of late, I fear as we have been thrust into the background by the Pacific and the elections. Still I'm plugging away, lining up my contacts and turning up some useful dope.

Although it was almost the end of Dana's tenure with the *United Press*, Harrison Salisbury, foreign editor of the *United Press* in New York, cabled to thank him for a piece on the Consultative Assembly.

Here I am at my old spot at the [French] *front*, Dana wrote on November 28, *but for the* Times. *It's not easy to readjust one's habits to work for the* Times, *but I'm liking it. There is more time to do the job right, as I would consider it. Up to a certain point one can leave the routine to the agencies; but when something really big breaks, the* Times *expects coverage on everything as far as I can see.*

Harold Callender decided to send me down here at a moment's notice, at my suggestion, to see what kind of a political story I could get out of the liberation of Alsace. Of course as soon as I was here I fell right into the military story too. Wonder if you have seen my story on the fall of Strasbourg. [The article follows this letter.] *If only I had been around here a few days before, I could have done much better . . . by hitching myself to the French division that did the job.*

ELIZABETH SCHMIDT CRAHAN

Now Milton Bracker has turned up from Rome to spend some ten days at the front. I do not mind as it will leave me free, or rather permit me to leave the military story to him while I dig into the liberation story Callender really had in mind: what the Germans did to Germanize Alsace, what the French will do to reintegrate them, how the Alsatians feel about it, what the Germans did to build up Alsace for their war economy, how much of their industrial equipment they evacuated, to what extent they colonized Alsace, what the French will do to remove colonists and bring people who are still refugees in southern France, etc., etc. Most of these topics have already been touched on, but the whole story has not been rounded up into a whole.

Tomorrow I'm going to drive to Strasbourg and stay there for two days to get these stories: see the Bishop, the university, the new Mayor, French and American civil affairs officers, F.F.I., get samples of their schoolbooks, talk to children who've been educated as Nazis for the last four years, although they may have gone to French schools before that, etc.

There doesn't seem to be any food shortage in Alsace. It's a blessing to be in a region with enough to eat for a change.

I've got my FORD down here again, after some trouble. Had two flats on the way down from Paris and trouble with the generator. Got the Military Police to fix the last flat. There are certain definite advantages to be derived from having no tools and looking helpless. Then my gas tank started to leak. Now that's fixed, and tomorrow we'll give her another whirl.

I forgot to mention, among the inevitable FORD vicissitudes, that I was thirty kilometers from my objective, near the front. I was held up by a French army "wrecker" which was parked across the street. Having stopped, FORD would not start again, and I had to spend the night in a little French hotel. Miserable it was, nearly midnight and raining. The first hotel said it was full, and I had to trudge along in the dark to the railway station and ask for the Hotel de la Gare. There I finally got a bed in which I slept just a little too long to get breakfast when I finally made the press camp in the morning. Oh well!

Even more aggravating, however, was the loss of my lovely Royal typewriter. It was stolen out of my car while I stopped somewhere along the road from

Paris—before I stopped for the night. I am very sad about it, especially since it was a gift from you. Tomorrow in Strasbourg I may be able to liberate another one, as they say in the army. This is being written on Clinton Conger's machine. He succeeded me for the UP on this front as you may recall.

Your first Christmas packages have begun to reach me here at the press camp. A fine package of magazines came first, then a box with high-class army-style socks. They are most welcome.

Before I left Paris I sent off my Christmas presents to you and all the family. Paris being what it is, my presents are strictly feminine. There are four packages of perfume, one of which contains two small bottles. I thought each of my ladies would like one of the packages. I thought Mother would like the bottle from Paquin, the most costly, and Grandma would perhaps like the bottle from a new perfumery called "Renoir" which is set up next to the Ritz and goes in for ritzy wrapping paper, and the two smaller bottles from Houbigant, I thought Eliza and Steinie could decide which wanted which of these. But of course you may all want to make quite a different distribution, which is quite o.k. with me.

In addition there are eight handkerchiefs with hand-painted motifs inspired by the liberation of Paris. I think they are most tastefully done. The UP's *girl fashion editor*, Dudley Harmon suggested them to me as the most typically Parisian gift she had come across. One of them is for Ken who gets off rather poorly in this feminine deal. Then I'd like Dean Mary to have one, and Eloise, and Murph. Also Grandma's great friend, Mrs. Schofield, and Miss Riese and Mme. Sadoul who has been so kind in suggesting people for me to meet in France. Finally I thought Dr. Lowman might care for one.

All this isn't much in the way of Christmas presents, but I am really baffled in trying to find more suitable things.

I'll have to end this letter very soon as Conger's typewriter is falling to pieces before my eyes.

I wonder whether you got my cable saying I was sorry you had not had a letter for such a long time but that I had been writing regularly. Mackay was not sure whether or not they could take it, as private cabling is apparently technically confined to French civilians, and I had to leave Paris before I found out.

It's quite possible I'll be spending Christmas on this front. I'd rather have been home, but let's bear up. The war is really drawing to its end. And even before that there is an excellent chance of my getting home.

All my love to you all,
Dana
Dana Adams Schmidt, War Correspondent
Sixth Army Group Press headquarters
APO 23
But you'd better continue writing to my Paris APO.

Dana's first article published as a *New York Times* correspondent appeared on November 23 on page 3.

ALLIES COOPERATE TO WIN STRASBOURG
French Armor Shows Dash After Americans and French Soften Foe for Victory
By DANA ADAMS SCHMIDT
By Wireless to THE NEW YORK TIMES.

IN THE SAVERNE GAP, Nov. 23—Brig. Gen. Jacques-Philippe Leclerc's French Second Armored Division swarmed into Strasbourg from three sides and cleared the western port of the city by nightfall today after a spectacular and almost unopposed dash across the Alsatian plain from the Saverne Gap.

Rolling down from the Vosges Mountains they could see at twenty miles distance the spire and massive bulk of Strasbourg Cathedral looming above the smoke of heavy fighting in the streets of the city. The Germans, thrown off balance by the lightning advance, put up what was literally a last-ditch resistance along the vast anti-tank ditch around the city, falling back slowly through the streets toward the two road bridges and one rail bridge still intact across the Rhine to Kehl.

By liberating Strasbourg in a starring role well ahead of the main body of the United States Seventh Army, General Leclerc's division was again brilliantly demonstrating the rebirth of French armed might five days after Maj. Gen. Jean de Lattre de Tassigny's army smashed past the Belfort Gap to the Rhine. The barrier of the Vosges Mountains thus has been turned at both ends, and Germans still defending mountain ridges in between face the alternative of a fighting retreat to pontoon bridges across the Rhine or encirclement and capture.

Folding Bridges Used

Air reconnaissance reported that the Germans were using folding pontoon bridges of which four were located near Colmar. The spans are folded back against the banks in daytime to avoid aerial attack. Permanent bridges remain intact only at Karlsruhe and Strasbourg. Above Karlsruhe ten permanent and temporary bridges are believed to have been put out of commission, at least temporarily, by air attack.

Already more than three thousand prisoners have been taken in three days around the Saverne Gap, where this afternoon the writer saw Major Gen. Bruhn, commander of the German 553rd Infantry Division and Infantry Gen. Werner von Gilsa being led into the Fifteenth Army Corps headquarters for questioning. They had been taken this morning by the French, who routed them out of a hiding place in a little hotel at Birkenwald.

The American corps commander, Maj. Gen. Wade H. Haislip, told correspondents that one batch of 528 Germans had emerged from a wood that had been bypassed southeast of Sarrebourg and had given themselves up to the Seventy-ninth Division. Beaming with triumph, he said, "I take off my hat to Leclerc the way his armor negotiated this mountain terrain."

How Strasbourg Was Taken

The general picture of the Seventh Army offensive that permitted General Leclerc to enter Strasbourg is this: American infantry, including the Forty-fourth and Seventy-ninth Divisions, first smashed the main German defenses, consisting of carefully dug anti-tank ditches and wire and machine-gun posts at the foot of the north end of the high Vosges. General Leclerc's armor then passed through the American positions and forced two minor passes north and south of the heavily defended Saverne Gap—one on the road leading to Neuwiller, the other on the road leading to Wasselonne.

From these positions the French then turned and assaulted the Saverne Gap and Phalsbourg Pass from the east, while the Americans attacked from the west, thus opening two main routes for reinforcements that plunged into the plain and on to Strasbourg.

A French officer who returned to corps headquarters tonight declared:

"It was a joy to see the Alsatians lining the streets giving the V sign and amusing when I stopped to speak to some of the children to find that they didn't speak a word of French. For four years, as part of the German Reich, they have not been allowed to learn, but they will soon learn now."

But many of the towns were nearly empty since the French evacuated more than 400,000 in 1939 and the Germans deported more than 300,000 to Germany for labor and service in the German army, and many of the German sympathizers and imported colonists have fled.

Writing for the *Times* allowed Dana to write the in-depth articles he so enjoyed with the assurance, as well, that they most surely would be published.

STRASBOURG FOE PROVES ORDERLY
Allies Encounter No Sabotage
Though 40,000 From Reich
Still Remain in Town
By DANA ADAMS SCHMIDT
By Wireless to THE NEW YORK TIMES.

STRASBOURG, France, Nov. 30—Four and one half years of intensive Germanization of this capital of Alsace have made it externally purely a German town but have failed to win the Alsatians for the Reich.

A token of the German failure is that although the walls from one end of the town to the other are splashed with purple calls to join Himmler's

Volkssturm, French and American troops have encountered virtually no civilian resistance or sabotage. Two or three cases of sniping have been attributed to isolated German soldiers while the booby traps that exploded when Gauleiter Wagner's safe was opened were presumed to have been placed there by him before he escaped to Germany.

40,000 Germans in Town

Strasbourg is still swarming with about 40,000 real Germans from the Reich who, since 1940, have moved into the homes, shops and businesses of absent Alsatians or merely to take a holiday in relatively bomb-free Alsace. That makes one in four of the town's present population of 160,000 a real German; yet when I walked three miles through the center of the town last midnight American M.P.'s and the FFI were patrolling the streets in deathlike silence, with never an incident.

The senior American Civil Affairs officer in Strasbourg, Maj. Robert A. Gish, former State Youth Administrator of Cheyenne, Wyo., told me that the German civilians and even a few soldiers in civilian clothes were walking into his office daily to ask what they should do.

Major Gish said all 40,000 Germans and the most notable Alsatian collaborators would be rounded up soon as about 150 gendarmes [policemen] arrived from Paris. They will then be "screened," after which it will be up to the French regional commissioner, Charles Blondel, to find internment camps for them. Two of these are available—the Schirmeck and Stuttheim concentration camps, where the Gestapo imprisoned about 150,000 Alsatians in four and a half years.

One unsolved prisoner problem is what to do with the 3,000 Russian, Polish and Czechoslovak civilian laborers found in Strasbourg and the thirty-seven Netherlanders and one Belgian who landed in the Seventh Army territory yesterday after having chugged up the Rhine in a houseboat to escape the northern fighting zones.

Alsatians Pampered

The Germans spared no pains to make Strasbourg a loyal German city. In addition to sending in about 100,000 Germans from the Reich, they filled the schools with German teachers, painted out every word of French in public places, put up German slogans, German street names and gave Strasbourg and Alsace generally special food privileges.

A hotel proprietor said he visited Germany two months ago and found German standards far below those in Alsace. He was able to serve meat twice daily. Recently the Alsatians received a special cattle allotment. Coal also was sent from the Ruhr.

One hardship the Germans could not spare the Alsatians, however, was the lack of clothing. Because of the requirements for clothing for bombed-out refugees, adults got no clothes coupons during the past six months. It is notable that the few shops that already have reopened are well stocked. Prices are low and it is said there has been no black market.

It will undoubtedly be difficult for the Allies to maintain this standard of living. Thus far, however, the only outspoken complaint of the Strasbourgers is the rate of exchange of fifteen francs to one mark, which gives the French-American troops buying power undreamed-of in France. Under the Germans the exchange rate was twenty francs to a mark.

Temporarily the Alsatians also are discomfited by the freezing of all bank accounts.

Nevertheless, Dana did not feel completely confident in those first days at the *Times*. On December 3, he wrote to his mother:

I am simply dieing, or is it dying, he wrote on December 3, *to see your recent letters since I started writing for the* Times. *Unfortunately they are accumulating in Paris and, lest I lose them altogether, I had best let that continue till I get back.*

Right now I'm back in the French sector of the front on my way to do a few stories on southern Alsace. Pretty well any Strasbourg datelines you may have seen since the liberation are mine except for the stories Milton Brack did on the fighting around the Kehl bridge.

I still don't feel very sure of myself in writing for the Times *and fear I have been somewhat dull. There is plenty of latitude for breaking loose and really "writing," with imagination and descriptive power as I can see by*

Brack's efforts. Personally I consider things like his story about the Schirmeck concentration camp over-written.

I'm getting plenty of opportunity to exercise my German in Alsace. Speaking French and German certainly gives me an edge on most of my rivals. It is truly amazing how few speak a foreign language.

We had a press conference with General de Lattre today. I wanted to put across that I thought he was a "General pour le cinema," a showoff, without being insulting or discrediting his great qualities, but didn't quite know how to do it. I may do a magazine article on the French army which will give me an opportunity.

The censor is having a fit in the next room about a wretched French correspondent who sent his copy to Paris without getting it censored. How very important little censors think they are. This particular one is typical of the type of American who has been educated in France. A bad type, I find, even though I'm more or less in the same boat.

My car is "en panne" [out of order] as usual. The gas tank sprang a leak which I had fixed, but it is leaking again. I've picked up a couple of gas tanks from an abandoned garage in Strasbourg which may be of use. In addition the rear main spring has come to pieces in a strange way; one of the leaves of which it is composed slipped out. I had it pounded back with a sledgehammer, but that didn't help very much. I might also mention the dynamo which doesn't work and the door handle which came off.

This may reach you about Christmas time. If so, all my love to you all, and MERRY CHRISTMAS! I will probably not be able to send a Christmas cable, due to regulations, but I'll try.

Dana Adams Schmidt, War Correspondent DANA, APO 757, PRD, SHAEF

On December 10, he added:

I'm still waiting eagerly for the letter from you which will tell of seeing my first story in the Times. Your last, which I received today (forwarded from Paris) was dated November 14, the day after I started work.

The same mail brought two letters from Grandma, one of September containing a lining of most useful razor blades and the other of November. Please tell Grandma how pleased I was to have two letters from her and especially to have the addresses she enclosed. You might add that this very morning I shaved with an extremely dull razor blade and was wondering where I would get some new ones. . . .

I have been covering Seventh Army military operations (which Callender doesn't want me to do,) and now another hinting that I'd probably like to stay down here indefinitely but must not and asking for carbons of my stories so he can see "what's up." I've written him a nice letter and sent him the carbons and set next Thursday as the date for my return to Paris.

I was interested in the clipping of Mallory Brown's Harpers *article you enclosed. I think I could have written that story. He is really* Manchester Guardian *correspondent and only writes for the* Monitor *on the side. He rates as one of the people who really know the French situation. The* Monitor *frequently employs British correspondents in that way.*

When I wrote about my typewriter being stolen, I forgot a very important point that I had the excellent "four generation picture"[98] *of you all in it. I would be very happy if you would send me another copy or a new one. Tomorrow I'm going into Strasbourg for a last look around and have a glimmer of hope that Major Gish of Civil Affairs will have that liberated German typewriter he promised me. At present I'm writing on a German machine which one of the photographers "liberated." Photographers always seem to have time to "scrounge," "liberate," and generally keep themselves comfortably supplied.*

FORD spent a week waiting to be worked on in an Alsatian garage. If the job isn't done tomorrow, I don't know how I'll get him back to Paris.

All my love and Happy New Year to you and Grandma, Elizabeth, Kenneth, Steinie and all our friends. Dana

---

[98] Grace Field Adams, Great Grandmother; Margaret Adams Schmidt, Grandmother; Elizabeth Acker (now Crahan), Mother; Margaret Acker (now Miller), baby.

STRASBOURG HAILS EVICTION OF ENEMY

Army's Sound Trucks Spread News throughout the City in Two Languages

REINTEGRATION UNDER WAY

French Begin Restoring Alsace to National Sovereignty—Many Changes Seen

By DANA ADAMS SCHMIDT
By Wireless to THE NEW YORK TIMES.

STRASBOURG, France, Dec. 2—Seven Psychological Warfare Branch sound trucks circulated through Strasbourg today, spreading in French and German the glad news that the German bridgehead on the French side of the Kehl Bridge on the Rhine had been wiped out.

The people, reassured that the Germans would not be back, flocked into the streets in numbers unprecedented since Maj. Gen. Jacques Leclerc arrived eight days ago. American and French engineers, meanwhile, re-established the water supply in the downtown district, which had been dry since the Germans shelled the power plant. It is hoped to bring electricity from alternate sources within a week.

At the Hotel de Ville Mayor Charles Frey said that proclamations were ready ordering all the 40,000 German citizens remaining in town to register at the Lycée, near the cathedral. On the recommendation of the American Army, he revealed, it had been decided not to try to intern all the Germans left in town, but to oblige them to report to the police regularly. Three thousand persons already taken into custody, including the most important or most dangerous Germans and Alsatian collaborationists, will be interned.

M. Frey has just resumed his functions as Mayor after his return from Périgueux, in the Dordogne Department, where he had lived with 35,000 other Strasbourgers since the Germans entered Strasbourg in 1940. One of his assistants is Gaston Damm, a leader in the French Forces of the Interior, who is considered one of the most influential men in Alsace today. M. Damm said that he and the F.F.I. would insist on the permanent exclusion of all German citizens from the Alsace as soon as possible.

Under the periodic fire of German guns the French administration is beginning the task of reintegrating Strasbourg and Alsace into French life and blotting out the effects of four years of German annexation. The Regional Commissioner, the Prefect and the Mayor admitted that the greatest single obstacle was still the fear that the Germans might return.

Even after the battle zone has moved out of range of Strasbourg, it will be months—probably not until next spring—before the estimated 90,000 refugees will be allowed to return from southern France, according to Regional Commissioner Charles Blondel, who represents the Government in Alsace. He explained that the terrible bombing of Sept. 25 had destroyed about one-fifth of the town's housing capacity.

Looking ahead, however, M. Blondel foresaw an Alsace that would be "more French and more closely integrated with

France than ever before." The first step had been taken, he said, by the Sept. 15 decree that re-established Alsace's status exactly as it had been before the war. This includes the concordat with the Vatican under which Alsace's Catholic clergy is paid by the state.

Later steps will involve changes in French law and Alsace's local laws that will bring the two more and more together. Alsace had enjoyed a limited autonomy in such matters as social legislation since it returned to France after the first World War.

M. Blondel admitted that ravaged France might not be able for some time to assure Alsace the same standards of living that she enjoyed while being wooed by Germany, but he said that for December the German rationing system with German ration tickets would be continued. To avoid undue hardships resulting from the 15-francs-to-one-mark exchange rate, he said, bank accounts that were converted at the German rate of 20 to 2 will be allowed to reconvert at the same rate.

In the regional commissioner's and the prefect's offices I learned that three classes of Alsatian refugees were getting preferred treatment in the return to Alsace to hasten its reintegration into France—school teachers, government officials and police. The first échelon of officials is now waiting for the Allies' permission to enter military zones. An appeal has been issued throughout France for all men connected with the Alsace police in the past to report to Nancy. The French Forces of the Interior and volunteers are being organized into three "security battalions" under the military authority as has already been done in some parts of liberated France.

The Prefect, Gaston Haelleng, who was Strasbourg port director before the war, saw his task during the first months of France's return to Alsace as a moral one. "We must show the people of Alsace that Gen. Charles de Gaulle's new France issuing from the resistance thinks in the same terms that they do," he said. "The differences and the talk about autonomy before the war was largely traceable to the fact that Alsace had more progressive and democratic institutions than the rest of France.

"Our people have no more desire to be part of the German Reich than do the German-speaking Swiss, but, while Switzerland remained independent,

Alsace was torn between Germany and France for generation after generation until her people had become morally exhausted."

Dana was fascinated by Alsace following the liberation and wrote several stories about the effects on children and adults, who suddenly found that they had to learn or relearn French. One of the articles he wrote after visiting Mulhouse tells this story:

ALSACE MUDDLED AFTER LIBERATION

Difficulties Confront People Trying to Be French Again After German Occupation

By DANA ADAMS SCHMIDT
By Wireless to THE NEW YORK TIMES.
MULHOUSE, France, Dec. 9—For eighteen days, since the French First Army burst through the Belfort Gap to free Mulhouse, the people of southern Alsace have lived the mingled joy and pain of suddenly becoming French again.

After four years in a drastically German state, sealed off from France, the citizens of Mulhouse, Altkirch, Sierentz, Huningue, and St. Louis that I have visited have patched together Tricolors to hang from the "rathaus" and "gastwirtschaft" [town hall and restaurant]. They carry aged German-French phrase books in their pockets and answer their liberators haltingly or trail off into an embarrassed confusion of German and their native Alsatian dialect.

Although no trace remains of the "Reichsgrenze" [German border] there is no mistaking the line that divides the board and plaster houses of the French Vosges from the half-timbered fairy-story cottages of Alsatian villages as you wind from Belfort down into the plain along the Rhine.

People Are Confused

Here is a people torn between France and Germany so long and so frequently that at best they have developed a culture blending Gallic grace and Teutonic weightiness and, at worst, a confused cynicism. Here it is often as difficult for the native as for the visitor to distinguish the truth from pretense.

At Altkirch, a buxom innkeeper's wife, with American and Tricolor flags pinned on her breast, declaimed her joy at the liberation in broken French and gushing German. She showed us, despairingly, a picture of her son in a German soldier's uniform and then introduced her daughter, who was dressed in a flowered peasant holiday costume in preparation for a visit to wounded French soldiers.

At a billet in Sierentz a 12-year-old girl named Nicola sang alternatively Frere Jacques and O Tannenbaum to please her American guest. She did not know where New York was, but she had been taught about American gangsters. Happily munching the first peanuts she had ever seen, she imitated, with giggling roars, the "Wehrmacht news" she had heard daily at school. "London burns," she said. Then in a whispered aside she added "Bremen burns, Hamburg burns, Berlin burns."

In a German-equipped schoolhouse at near-by Uffsheim, where Nicola has been getting her education, members of the French garrison ran off for us a German propaganda film illustrating the growth of the "Gross Deutsches Reich"—but backwards.

Film Ridicules Germans

We saw—and Alsatian children will soon see—moving diagrams of Alsace, Lorraine, Czechoslovakia and Memel dropping one by one from the Reich and Reich Marshal Hermann Goering benignly withdrawing a piece of candy from a Czech child's mouth and the Wehrmacht gymnastically goosestepping back into the Reich.

Every picture on this school's walls dealt with the war, except one showing birds that, believe it or not, were birds of prey. Six shelves of brand new books dealt almost exclusively with the war and the German mess of Alsace, with only one volume of German fairy stories among them.

Particularly prominent were volumes of parading Alsatian SA men and Hitler Youth, pictures that unmistakingly revealed the faces of hundreds of Alsatians—binding evidence of their participation.

A local Alsatian present remarked regretfully: "There is no use denying that the Hitler Youth organization appealed to our children, even if they had not heard of Nazi convictions. They loved the sports, the chance of travel, the parades and to play with weapons."

He pointed to a picture of a chemistry teacher in a school at Saverne at the head of a group of SA [Société Anonyme] men and I asked what would become of him.

"Well, he won't be able to teach chemistry any more, but I doubt if anything worse will happen to him," was the reply.

It is evident that the purge of collaborationists in Alsace must be made on a plane entirely different from that of the rest of France, since the Alsatians necessarily have been drawn so deeply into German life. Where the Frenchmen in France struggled to avoid deportation as laborers the Alsatians struggled to avoid conscription as members of the German Army. Where others might bamboozle the Vichy police there was no fooling with policemen from Germany in Alsace.

Nevertheless the French Army is getting volunteers today in Alsace. There are few, since most of the able-bodied men already have been taken into the German Army. A village that would normally yield 100 men of military age now provides eight or nine, most of them members of the Wehrmacht home on leave or youngsters who have just finished sessions in pre-military training.

In the French Army they receive the same rank they had in the German Army to leave no trace of a suggestion that they might be under suspicion.

Soon after presenting this view of Alsace after the Liberation, Dana wrote another, and even more descriptive, picture from Sierentz:

THE FIRST CLASS IN FREE ALSACE GUIDES CHILD TONGUES IN FRENCH

Forty-two Little Girls in Sierentz Town Hall's School Answer to Nun's Roll-Call— She Calms Fears of Warplane

By DANA ADAMS SCHMIDT
By Wireless to THE NEW YORK TIMES.
SIERENTZ, Southern Alsace, Dec. 13—Sister Elizabeth of the Congregation of Teaching Sisters of Ribeauville stood in front of the blackboard of a classroom in the Town Hall of Sierentz this morning and recited in French, "Hail Mary, full of grace * * *"

Forty-two Alsatian girls stood at their desks, made the sign of the Cross and repeated their Ave Maria after her—the oldest in fluent French, others haltingly, while some who knew it only in German listened in embarrassment.

The first class in liberated Alsace had begun: a French nun was teaching school in Alsace again for the first time since the Nazis marched in, four and a half years ago.

As the children bustled onto the narrow benches, Sister Elizabeth called in French, "Silence!" and then translated it into the Alsatian German dialect. Translating each phrase as she went on, she said:

"This is our first class in a long time. There is much to do. All that is needed is a very good will.

"When a French soldier asks you the way, you will be able to smile and say, 'Je vous montrerai le chemin.' " [I will show you the way.]

Their French-ness Understood

For more than four years these children had sung "Deutschland, Deutschland" and the Nazi "Horst Wessel" song every morning and had been told in a thousand ways that they were German.

Sister Elizabeth did not tell them they were French. That was taken for granted.

Instead she got down to business. School would start punctually at 9 every morning. Everyone must bring paper and a sharpened pencil or a slate with two sponges, one of them damp.

The first French word Sister Elizabeth gave them was that for "Present." As she read off their names they replied with it, giggling at the unfamiliar sound.

One said her name was Paulette, although she had changed it to Paula in German school. Another said she was Claudette, although she had changed it to Christl.

They were aged 8 to 14; their hair was cut in bangs and some wore a Tricolor ribbon. Their healthy, fair faces were flushed with excitement.

A dozen parents stood in the back of the room listening seriously. In the next room another nun held class with twenty of the youngest, aged 6 to 8, both girls and boys.

There would have been a class for older boys as well, I learned from Major Jean Noutary of the French Ninth Colonial Division, but the sergeant and private, former Alsatian school teachers, whom he, as civil affairs officer, had selected to teach the boys, were wounded three days ago when the French wiped out the last German bridgehead over the Rhine in southern Alsace around the Kembs power plant at Loechle.

The major had obtained permission from the sub-prefect at Mulhouse to start this school although school teachers for Alsace, now being gathered together by the Ministry of Education, have not yet arrived.

Sister Elizabeth distributed the first schoolbooks—"Le Francais par les Choses et par les Images," by A. Lyonnet—which she had saved from bonfires the Nazis had made of French texts.

The class droned on: "Do not answer, Ja, say, Oui, ma soeur"—"This is the table. That is the wall. Here is the crucifix."

At 10 o'clock Maria Pia and Bernadette were told to open the windows.

The little girls rose on tiptoes and breathed deep. Through the windows out of the misty distance by the Rhine came the sound of guns. A truck convoy wound through the village with whining gears.

Maria Pia looked up and saw planes. As she watched her eyes widened and she put her hand over her mouth and uttered one word, Flugzeuge [airplanes]! A tremor of panic ran through the class.

The First Class in Free Alsace Guides Child Tongues in French

Forty-two Little Girls in Sierentz Town Hall's School Answer to Nun's Roll-Call—She Calms Fears of Warplane

By DANA ADAMS SCHMIDT
By Wireless to THE NEW YORK TIMES.

SIERENTZ, Southern Alsace, Dec. 13—Sister Elizabeth of the Congregation of Teaching Sisters of Ribeauville stood in front of the blackboard of a classroom in the Town Hall of Sierentz this morning and recited in French, "Hail Mary, full of grace * * *"

Forty-two Alsatian girls stood at their desks, made the sign of the Cross and repeated their Ave Maria after her—the oldest in fluent French, others haltingly, while some who knew it only in German listened in embarrassment.

The first class in liberated Alsace had begun; a French nun was teaching school in Alsace again for the first time since the Nazis marched in, four and a half years ago.

As the children bustled onto the narrow benches, Sister Elizabeth called in French, "Silence!" and then translated it into the Alsatian-German dialect. Translating each phrase as she went on, she said: "This is our first class in a long time. There is much to do. All that is needed is a very good will.

"When a French soldier asks you the way, you will be able to smile and say, 'Je vous montrerai le chemin.'"

Their French-ness Understood

For more than four years these children had sung "Deutschland, Deutschland" and the Nazi "Horst Wessel" song every morning and had been told in a thousand ways that they were German.

Sister Elizabeth did not tell them they were French. That was taken for granted.

Instead she got down to business. School would start punctually at 9 every morning. Everyone must bring paper and a sharpened pencil or a slate with two sponges, one of them damp.

The first French word Sister Elizabeth gave them was that for "Present." As she read off their names they replied with it, giggling at the unfamiliar sound.

One said her name was Paulette, although she had changed it to Paula in German school. Another said she was Claudette, although she had changed it to Christl.

They were aged 8 to 14; their hair was cut in bangs and some wore a Tricolor ribbon. Their healthy, fair faces were flushed with excitement.

A dozen parents stood in the back of the room listening seriously. In the next room another nun held class with twenty of the youngest, aged 6 to 8, both girls and boys.

There would have been a class for older boys as well, I learned from Major Jean Noutary of the French Ninth Colonel Division, but the sergeant and private, former Alsatian school teachers, whom he, as civil affairs officer, had selected to teach the boys, were wounded three days ago when the French wiped out the last German bridgehead over the Rhine in southern Alsace around the Kembs power plant at Loechle.

The major had obtained permission from the sub-prefect at Mulhouse to start this school although school teachers for Alsace, now being gathered together by the Ministry of Education, have not yet arrived.

Sister Elizabeth distributed the first schoolbooks—"Le Français par les Choses et par les Images," by A. Lyonnet—which she had saved from bonfires the Nazis had made of French texts.

The class droned on: "Do not answer, Ja, say, Oui, ma soeur"—"This is the table. That is the wall. Here is the crucifix."

At 10 o'clock Maria Pia and Bernadette were told to open the windows.

The little girls rose on tiptoes and breathed deep. Through the windows out of the misty distance by the Rhine came the sound of guns. A truck convoy wound through the village with whining gears.

Maria Pia looked up and saw planes. As she watched her eyes widened and she put her hand over her mouth and uttered one word, "Flugzuge!" A tremor of panic ran through the class.

Sister Elizabeth's voice was clear and calm: "Close the windows and sit down. We will repeat, 'This is the table. That is the wall. Here is the crucifix.'"

Sister Elizabeth's voice was clear and calm: "Close the windows and sit down. We will repeat, 'This is the table. That is the wall. Here is the crucifix.' "

Although it seemed as if the war was over at times in Strasbourg, the Germans were fighting a delaying action along the Rhine, so once more, Dana made his way to the front.

**FOE SEEKS DELAY
ON ALSACE FRONT**

**Spends Time and Men in Move
to Prevent Rhine Crossing
by Sixth Army Group**

By DANA ADAMS SCHMIDT
By Wireless to THE NEW YORK TIMES.
AT SIXTH ARMY GROUP HEADQUARTERS, in France, Dec. 14—
As winter settles in on the southern part of the European front the Germans are fighting a delaying action.

They are opposing the Seventh Army's frontal assault between Bitche and Seitz at every rock and tree. Farther south they are seeking to tie up the southern half of the sixth Army Group, Maj. Gen. Jean de Lattre de Tassigny's French First Army, by hanging on obstinately to a 600-square mile bridgehead across the Rhine around Colmar.

So long as they can hold this bridgehead the Germans may figure the French can undertake no other major move. The French, for instance, could not move north to support the Seventh Army assault or to follow it across the Rhine. General de Tassigny's command now extends from Strasbourg to the Swiss border and includes the American Thirty-sixth Infantry Division, lately known as the "Frenchmen from Texas."

Far from admitting the hopelessness of their position, the Germans are daily reinforcing this bridgehead. There, it is worth noting, they have carried out the sort of evacuation of soil that they consider German that they had not

FOE SEEKS DELAY ON ALSACE FRONT

Spends Time and Men in Move to Prevent Rhine Crossing by Sixth Army Group

By DANA ADAMS SCHMIDT
By Wireless to THE NEW YORK TIMES

AT SIXTH ARMY GROUP HEADQUARTERS, in France, Dec. 14—As winter settles in on the southern part of the European front the Germans are fighting a delaying action.

They are opposing the Seventh Army's frontal assault between Bitche and Seltz at every rock and tree. Farther south they are seeking to tie up the southern half of the Sixth Army Group, Maj. Gen. Jean de Lattre de Tassigny's French First Army, by hanging on obstinately to a 600-square mile bridgehead across the Rhine around Colmar.

So long as they can hold this bridgehead the Germans may figure the French can undertake no other major move. The French, for instance, could not move north to support the Seventh Army assault or to follow it across the Rhine. General de Tassigny's command now extends from Strasbourg to the Swiss border and includes the American Thirty-sixth Infantry Division, lately known as the "Frenchmen from Texas."

Far from admitting the hopelessness of their position, the Germans are daily reinforcing this bridgehead. There, it is worth noting, they have carried out the sort of evacuation of soil that they consider German that they had not time for at Strasbourg or Mulhouse. Two-thirds of the civilian population, or almost all of the able-bodied men and women as well as transportable industrial equipment, have been moved across the Rhine, according to civilian reports.

Weather Helps Germans

For the time being the German delaying action is helped by the Allies' difficulty in exploiting their material superiority. The Allies' air force is grounded by winter weather most of the time. Sherman tanks face not only improved models of the German Tiger tank, such as the Yak, and extremely effective German bazookas, with which one man in fifteen has been equipped, but also flooded lowlands that confine them to roads and prevent maneuver. This season is the wettest in the memory of Alsatians and has swollen the Rhine to a level exceeding the usual point in the highest spring flood.

Just what the German command hopes to do with the time gained remains a mystery. Prisoner-of-war interrogation still shows that German faith in secret weapons is the most important factor in maintaining German morale.

One inexorable problem that German ingenuity cannot hope to solve, however—one that is going to beat the enemy on this front, according to many officers — is manpower. Volksgrenadiers units of boys and old men are showing they are no substitute for able-bodied men. And the reinforcements that the German command is thrusting so boldly into the Colmar bridgehead show how few such men remain and how uneconomically the German High Command is obliged to expend them.

In addition, survivors of scores of shattered units include men who should be a guarantee of the German Army's future—officer cadets and their instructors and entire schools of noncommissioned officers—not to mention a smattering of naval and air personnel and even an occasional veterinary.

Among them are some SS troops to stiffen the morale while other SS men remain on the German side of the Rhine to shoot any man who seeks to flee back across the river.

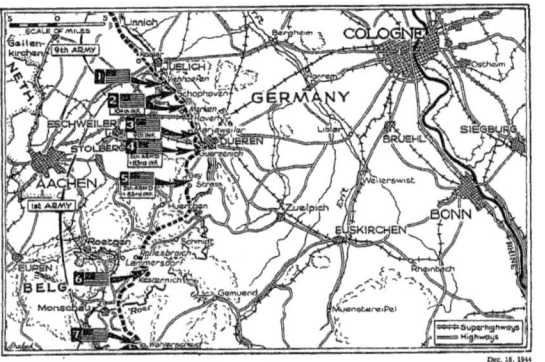

Near Juelich the Ninth Army, swinging into action again, expelled the Germans from Viehhoefen (1) and reached the Roer River, along which our troops now hold a twelve-mile front. First Army troops pushed the enemy out of Schophoven and moved to the Roer to the east of Merken (2). They also advanced to the river east of Mariaweiler (3) and near Guerzenich (4). South of Dueren our forces cleared Gey and Strass and pushed beyond (5). The right flank of the First overran Kesternich (6) and stormed to the edge of the town of Wahlerscheid (7).

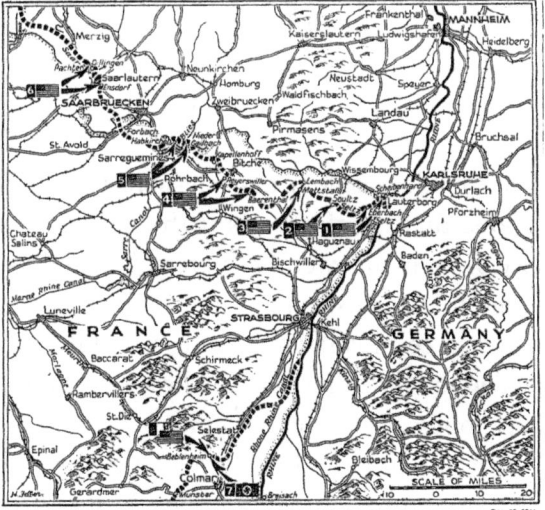

In the Karlsruhe corner the Seventh Army pressed to Scheibenhard and Eberbach (1), close to the German border. To the west units of this army went through Soultz (2) and drove from Mattstall into Lembach (3). Bitche was threatened as our troops captured Baerenthal, Reyerswiller and Kapellenhoff (4). Near Sarreguemines (5) the Americans beat off a counter-attack against our Habkirchen foothold and advanced to Nieder Gailbach. Around Saarlautern (6) they pushed through Ensdorf and eliminated resistance at the bridgehead north of Pachten. To the south the Germans sent reinforcements across the Rhine at Breisach and attacked American troops with the First French Army at Beblenheim (7), to the northwest of Colmar.

time for at Strasbourg or Mulhouse. Two-thirds of the civilian population, or almost all of the able-bodied men and women as well as transportable industrial equipment, have been moved across the Rhine, according to civilian reports.

Weather Helps Germans

For the time being the German delaying action is helped by the Allies' difficulty in exploiting their material superiority. The Allies' air force is grounded by winter weather most of the time. Sherman tanks face not only improved models of the German Tiger tank, such as the Yak, and extremely effective German bazookas, with which one man in fifteen has been equipped, but also flooded lowlands that confine them to roads and prevent maneuver. This season is the wettest in the memory of Alsatians and has swollen the Rhine to a level exceeding the usual point in the highest spring flood.

Just what the German command hopes to do with the time gained remains a mystery. Prisoner-of-war interrogation still shows that German faith in secret weapons is the most important factor in maintaining German morale.

One inexorable problem that German ingenuity cannot hope to solve, however—one that is going to beat the enemy on this front, according to many officers—is manpower. Volksgrenadiers units of boys and old men are showing they are no substitute for able-bodied men. And the reinforcements that the German command is thrusting so boldly into the Colmar bridgehead show how few such men remain and how uneconomically the German High Command is obliged to expend them.

In addition, survivors of scores of shattered units include men who should be a guarantee of the German Army's future—officer cadets and their instructors and entire schools of noncommissioned officers—not to mention a smattering of naval and air personnel and even an occasional veterinary.

Among them are some SS troops to stiffen the morale while other SS men remain on the German side of the Rhine to shoot any man who seeks to flee back across the river.

An article on the future of Alsace and Lorraine was published the following day:

ALSACE, LORRAINE FAVOR INTEGRATION

Movement for Autonomy There Said to have Been Killed by German Occupation

By DANA ADAMS SCHMIDT
By Wireless to THE NEW YORK TIMES.

PARIS, Dec. 15—France intends to integrate liberated Alsace and Lorrraine with the rest of the country more closely than ever before, according to responsible French Government officials, by the progressive narrowing of the special status of church educational and social institutions that prevailed there before the war.

In their view—borne out by my observations in Alsace during the past three weeks—the movements for an Alsatian-Lorraine autonomy are pretty well dead as the result of four and a half years of ruthless nazism and will not soon revive, unless error of too brusque Francization, committed in 1918, should be repeated.

The French Administration, therefore, is going about the task with utmost circumspection and restraint, while taking full advantage of the revulsion against Germanism among a people whose native language is Germanic dialect and whose culture is a mixture of German and French.

The French program began with the Sept. 15 decree re-establishing the status for Alsace and Lorraine exactly as before the armistice. But the German rationing systems and the German employment, medical and old-age insurance benefits, which exceed those of France, have been retained.

The vicar general of Strasbourg, Theodore Dauvier, said that many Catholics also would like to continue the system instituted by the Germans under which the state, instead of directly paying the clergyman, levied taxes among the church membership for the support of the church. He believed this system gave the church more independence.

In the educational field the shortage of teachers and the restrictions necessary in a war zone make it difficult immediately to reconstitute the old separate Catholic and Protestant school systems.

To carry out their program, the French are depending entirely on Alsatian and Lorraine officials in the lower ranks and, whenever possible, in the top positions. Several hundred officials, including all prefects and subprefects, already have reached Alsace and Lorraine or are waiting to enter the liberated territory, while half as many again are waiting for permission to enter the military zone.

Officials have been instructed to leave the purge of collaborationists strictly to the Alsatians and Lorrainers themselves, since the problem is entirely different from the rest of France. Thus members of the Nazi party who are presumed to have joined under pressure are not necessarily suspect.

The Ministry of the Interior, for the time being, is reserving its concern for the estimated 45,000 genuine Germans still in Strasbourg, only 3,000 of whom have been imprisoned. Since the remainder thus far have proved harmless they are merely being required to report to the police regularly, in accordance with recommendations of the American military authorities.

It is feared here, however, that if they should begin to receive instructions smuggled across the Rhine from Germany they would present an acute danger.

The Ministry of the Interior said that the French were unable to intern all 40,000 Germans without assistance from the American Army in providing barracks and food or transportation to some point outside Alsace, but that such assistance had not yet been forthcoming.

On December 20, Dana wrote home from Paris:

Three grand letters from you all at once, including a couple that were sent to the front for me and then back again. I'm back in Paris again after about three weeks at the front or in Alsace. You will have been able to follow me in the Times *I trust. Anyway, I understand several of my stories were mentioned in the press reviews which are received in Paris.*

Since my return I've called on Mme. Jaquier, one of the people Mme. Sadoul suggested. She is a lawyer and most interesting. In a way she looks like Elizabeth, and like Eliza is married to a man whose profession is the same as her own. I couldn't help thinking of the picture Ida [Treat] painted of Elizabeth when I saw her, particularly when she told me she was Breton. She sends her best wishes to Mme. Sadoul and Linette [her daughter].

I haven't received the letter from Mildred Riese you mention, but would certainly be delighted to have a subscription to the New Yorker. *I'm still getting* NewsWeek *and* Time *with irregular delays, I haven't had a copy of* Readers Digest *for so long I can't remember whether I have a subscription or not: if I have, you might check up to see whether they are sending it to the right* APO.

Since I spent some time at the front, where it's pretty difficult to spend money, my financial situation is solvent and I will be able to live satisfactorily on my living allowance for a while.

Since my return I've had the following stories: December 15th (in 16th paper) roundup of Alsatian autonomy as seen from Paris; 17th, meeting of military commissions of departmental committees of liberation, 19th, French Institute of Public Opinion and Socialist Radical Congress, 20th Socialist Radical Congress: and I'll be doing the socialist radicals again tomorrow.

Elizabeth's howling pride sounds like quite a circus. Wonder when I'll have one for a family of my own. Whenever I visit a family with small children in Paris I feel obligated to bring along some candy or chewing gum. That makes me very popular all round, but is hard on my sweet tooth. Not that I ever use gum. I am, incidentally, always more than delighted with any missives from home containing chocolate in any manner shape or form, particularly Steinian fudge! And while I'm begging, I've been intending to ask for a long time whether you could send me new tennis balls. It's possible to play on indoor courts here, and anyway, by the time they get here, it's likely to be warm enough to play outside.

ELIZABETH SCHMIDT CRAHAN

It is indeed a shame that I won't be with you again this Christmas. But somehow, now that I'm with the Times, *I don't feel anywhere near so far away. I know that they, being a civilized outfit, will allow me to get home soon. After all the work you have been having done on the house, and all you and Steinie appear to have done yourselves, old 1132 must be in pretty good shape and I'll be glad to see it again.*

How nice that you've been seeing Ruth Adams. I have a very pleasant recollection of her and her sister Jeanne from the days I spent vacationing in Cleveland. Or was it later? Anyway I've met them both. [Ruth and Jeanne Adams were Mother's half-sisters by our grandfather's (George Dana Adams) second marriage.]

All my love to you and the family,
Dana

The day after Christmas, Dana received some unwelcome news.

I just received your cable via Harold Callender, he wrote, *informing me that the local draft board has reclassified me I A. Harold has immediately cabled the* Times *asking them to intervene to obtain a deferment, pointing out my lengthy career as war correspondent.*

As I've said before, while the UP had me assigned in neutral Turkey, I felt ill at ease that I wasn't doing all I should as an able-bodied American. But since January '43 I've been shot at sufficiently as a war correspondent to feel that I've been doing my share . . . not that I didn't get more than a taste of the war long before we got into it. It would seem paradoxical, to say the least, for me to be drafted at this late date. I told the draft board in my original questionnaire that I felt I could be doing most for Uncle Sam by carrying on till the end of the war as a war correspondent, and I think that still holds.

You will remember that my first frontline assignment was with the RAF in Tunisia, with whom I flew two bombing missions. Later I did another mission over Sicily with an American Boston bomber outfit based on Malta. Then I was with the Royal Navy for some months and on the spot for the invasion of Sicily, the toe of Italy and Salerno. I was the only correspondent to take part in the landings at Corsica with the French, and later covered French army operations in Italy. The most interesting of all these jobs was the one with the navy, patrolling in the Straits of Messina in British motor torpedo boats, and later with American PT-boats off Naples; nor will I forget bombarding the Italian coast and being bombed by the Germans in Malta and while at anchor in a destroyer in a Sicilian port.

Since August 15 finally I've been at the front two thirds of the time, after landing in southern France on D-day, and remain accredited to the Franco-American Sixth Army Group. Just the other day I covered the break-through to Strasbourg for the Times after having covered the fighting from Marseilles and Toulon up as far as the Vosges for United Press. Right now I'm in Paris with Harold Callender covering some of the political consequences of the war, a job I've been doing between front assignments right along and for which more than six years abroad have given me some qualifications.

I wanted to send you a Christmas cable this year but found that they have been banned so as to keep communications channels free. Our Christmas was pretty sober with everyone concerned over the German counter-offensive. You have probably seen that Jack Franklin of the UP was killed at his press camp.

Your fruit cake from Saks Fifth Avenue arrived on Christmas Day! It was mighty good eating, with some still left to go. Next Christmas, surely, I'll be able to eat fruit cake at home with you.

All my love to you all,
Dana

1945

In Dana's letter from Paris on January 1, he confirmed that the *Times* had requested his draft deferment.

However, on January 15, he wrote:

James, the foreign editor of the Times, *has cabled to say that my draft board says that I am still 1A but that he is working on the matter. I am hopeful that he will be successful, but have made up my mind not to take it too hard whatever happens. It would do me no harm, in fact it might be a great background to have, to spend a period in the Army . . . though it would be something of a trial after so many years of overseas service (many at the front.)*

In the last few days, he wrote on February 17, *I have gone a long way towards clearing up my draft board troubles. The board having turned down my appeal, the general who commands Supreme Headquarters Public Relations and the General who commands the army to which I was until recently attached wrote letters confirming my status as a war correspondent. The second of the two generals went on to speak of the "irreplaceable experience' I have gained while performing 'valuable services' as a war correspondent and stated that he considered it important that I should continue, at this stage of the war, in my present capacity. I think the* Times *should be able to take care of the matter now. It goes to an appeal board with the possibility to General Hershey, Director of Selective Service.*

Dana's first story of 1945 concerned a subject that had long interested him, "the swirl of politics in France." Under the following headline, he wrote in part:

LEFT TREND MARKS PARTIES IN FRANCE

But First Elections Are Held Likely to Turn Mostly on Personality Issues

By DANA ADAMS SCHMIDT
By Wireless to THE NEW YORK TIMES.

PARIS, Jan. 1—In the swirl of French party politics since the liberation, certain currents and landmarks that may prove important in the new year can now be discerned.

It is not at all certain that the municipal and departmental elections that have been postponed until the end of April will provide the fool-proof chart of the internal political alignment for which some have hoped. Foreign observers and the French Government itself may therefore have to get along with individual judgments and guesswork for some time to come. This is partly because the local elections will turn more on personalities than on political issues and partly because the Communists are likely to impose "single tickets" drawn up by the existing local Committees of Liberation in many communities.

In the country at large the political influence of the resistance movements appears clearly to have receded in recent months and there is every prospect that it will continue to do so. In the first flush of the liberation, the resistance groups dominated the political scene and publicly pledged themselves to united political action. But it soon became evident that the unity achieved for fighting the Germans and political unity were very different things and the National Council of Resistance and other bodies have not succeeded in playing an effective independent political role.

New Life for Old Parties

What they have been able to do, however, is to reinforce, influence and rejuvenate many of the well-known old political parties, most of which are once again playing their old parts, with new gestures and zest.

The split within the Mouvement de Libération Nationale, which had united most of the non-Communist resistance groups of southern France, is typical of what is happening. A minority wants to combine with the predominantly Communist National Front, while the majority has chosen instead to work more closely with the Socialists. There are still hopes that a congress of the movement at the end of this month will iron out the question, but outsiders have already written it off as a political entity.

A similar split seems fundamental in all the groups associated with the resistance. Thus far, however, there has been great hesitation to break openly with the Communists, partly because of their vast prestige in the resistance and partly because of the pressure for unity that the Communists maintain.

Socialists Profit Most

But, as the split inevitably widens, it is the Socialist party more than any other that appears to be profiting from it by gathering around itself most of the non-Communist elements of the resistance. Having purged itself of two thirds of its pre-war members of Parliament, this party is striking out boldly, advocating "structural changes," including far-reaching nationalization and socialization, with even greater vigor than the Communists. At the same time it stands in the center of the maze of negotiations and patient dickerings aimed at "unity of action" or even fusion with a half dozen other political organizations.

The least important of these negotiations are those between the Socialists and the Communists, at which the leaders of both parties laugh privately but which they continue as a sort of polite fraud to satisfy those who believe that these two left-wing parties should practice unity of action or unite to form a great labor party.

The contacts that the Socialists are maintaining with the majority of the MLN and with a new militant Catholic group called the Mouvement Républicain Populaire, or MRP, are more significant. The MRP derives particular interest from the fact that three members of the Cabinet—Georges Bidault, Foreign Minister; Pierre-Henri Teitgen, Minister of Information, and François de Menthon, Minister of Justice—are members of the Catholic Popular Democratic party, which the MRP claims to have absorbed. It also claims René Pleven, Minister of Colonies, and René Capitant, Minister of Education, as sympathizers.

Campaigning ambitiously on a platform of "order and social transformation" inspired by M. Bidault's formula of "revolution within the law," the MRP is bidding for wider working-class support than the old Popular Democratic party ever had. Simultaneously, it is dickering with the two non-Communist resistance groups of northern France called the Organization Civile et Militaire and the Libération Nord that have formed a "labor party." By merging with them the MRP hopes to dilute its Catholic character and make itself more acceptable to the working classes.

Still Relies on Priests

This does not prevent the MRP from believing that the influence of the priests will swing the votes of many women, voting for the first time, its way. Women's registrations have proved unexpectedly heavy.

The Communists, meanwhile, put all the others in the shade with the volume of their activities. Maurice Thorez, Jacques Duclos, André Marty and other leaders roam the country from end to end, speaking and organizing, while the Communist newspaper, l'Humanité, is the best technical job and the most popular in the Paris field.

The Communists say that they are vastly more numerous than before the war in consequence of their resistance role. Others deny this with equal conviction and only the far distant national elections can settle the point. It appears certain, however, that Communist influence has been at least temporarily extended by means of what is called the strategy of union.

An example of this strategy is an organization called the Union of Women of France. It includes women of every political background but it is dominated by the Communists because they are the most active element. Similar situations exist in the National Front, in the Federation of Youth Organizations and in the Movement of Prisoners and Deportees.

The Communists are also proving adept in exploiting the hardships of French housewives and of all those too poor to buy in the black market. Troubles of all kinds are attributed to sabotage by a fifth column whose existence serves as an argument for the maintenance of armed civilian bodies run by the Communists.

Marked by Conservatism

At present, French communism is most notable for its conservatism, at least by comparison with American concepts. French communists explain that they have gone no farther than other parties in advocating socialization because the middle-class and the peasants are not ready for it and that they have supported Gen. Charles de Gaulle and restrained the activities of their quasi-military formations in the interests of unity. Others have suggested that the French-Russian pact has also been a factor in keeping the Communists in line.

It may reasonably be doubted, however, that the Communists will maintain this modesty after the war. Then they are expected to drop their present lip-service to General de Gaulle, and enter into open opposition and launch a more extremist program.

The great unknown quantity of French politics is the Radical-Socialist party, the party of the middle-class and the farmers, which dominated French politics for most of fifty years with a combination of progressive theories and conservative acts. Since the armistice, abuse has been heaped on the middle-class and the Radical-Socialists on the grounds that they accepted defeat and Marshal Henri-Philippe Pétain more readily than others, but many observers and Radical-Socialists refuse to admit that they are a conservative or right-wing party—a term of opprobrium in present-day France. But the only group that is farther to the right is keeping pretty quiet these days, for it is automatically suspected of collaborationism.

I have just had the pleasure of reading two letters from you, Dana wrote on January 7, *one from Mildred Riese and a card from Dean Mary, not to mention a note from Bob Brown, my old Ankara friend who now commands a fighter squadron. Also recently one from Mme. Plaisance and Karl Hess, my old WRA* [Western Reserve Academy] *roommate. Mail always seems to come in batches.*

The clippings you enclose are indeed interesting. Edna [a cousin] *looks a handsome girl in her flying outfit. A reference to Mildred Riese's letter reminds me that I am still shy a picture of the 'matriarchy'—Grandma, Mother, Eliza, babe* [Margaret]. *Do get me another to replace the one that was stolen with the typewriter. Why not get some taken and enlarged for me.*

This afternoon I had a ticket to the opera Boris Godunov. *Anyway I got there only in time for the last act. . . . My tardiness was caused by my finishing a story on French exports. Let me give you a schedule of the stories I've written recently, in case you want to see if they got printed:*

December 19, 29, 31, Socialist-Radicals each day; Dec. 22, parachutists scare; Dec. 23, issue of Catholic school subsidies and Mendes-France[99] *speech; Dec. 24, Christmas Eve story; Dec. 26, Assembly secret session; Dec. 27 de Gaulle's statement to Leclerc division; Dec. 29 and Dec. 30, mobilization; Jan. 1, long piece on lineup of French political parties; Jan. 3, Romain Rolland dies; Jan. 4 American business in France; Jan. 5, Paris-London train and ship*

---

[99] Pierre Mendes-France (1907–1982) French statesman. He escaped from prison in Vichy, France, went to London and joined de Gaulle and the Free French. He served as minister of economy for de Gaulle in 1945 but turned against de Gaulle. He succeeded M. Laniel as Prime Minister in 1954. His government was defeated, and he resigned in 1955. A critic of de Gaulle, he lost his seat in the Assembly in 1958 but returned in 1967 and retired in 1973 due to ill health. From: *Cambridge Biographical Dictionary,* 1990.

service; Jan 5, reconstruction; Jan. 6, Leon Henderson press conference and agreement between socialist MRP and Labor Party; Jan. 7, French exports.

We do not get copies of the paper here regularly at all. The post office won't take them for airmail and they arrive only when someone brings a personal copy. The magazines you sent, Sunday and Book Review, were avidly read by all of us even though months old. This is an odd situation, considering that the Herald Tribune actually prints here. But there it is.

I'm hitting on all twenty-nine cylinders again after a couple of days when I was feeling pretty low with a cold.

Harold has suggested I take tomorrow off. It would be my first day off since I started with the Times, even though I don't necessarily produce a story every day. I was planning to work on a magaziner on Alsace tomorrow and I guess I'll do it anyway.

Did I tell you that a young couple I met through Gerald Norman named Landolt sent me a little tricolor watch fob through the 'pneumatique' mail on Christmas day? It was a charming gesture I thought and most appreciated.

Dean Mary mentions the carpeting I have ordered for her in Algiers. I'm afraid I haven't ever had a chance to do so and don't know where I put the letter with the specifications. If you would send them to me again I'll do my best.

For some reason or other I haven't smoked more than a couple of packs of cigarettes in the last two months. I suppose I'll start again and then again maybe I won't.

I was sorry to hear Grandma has not been well and glad she is better again. All my love to you all, as always,
DANA

At the end of this letter, Dana wrote a note in pencil:

I thought the "accent on living" verses from the Atlantic Monthly you sent me were interesting. Couldn't I do something like that? I used to occasionally before I got caught up in this newspaper work.

In his January 6 letter, Dana reported that Cy Sulzberger had confirmed his six weeks vacation and that he would probably be assigned to Germany after his vacation. Cy suggested that he spend a week of his vacation in New York to get acquainted with the New York office, something Dana had already planned to do. He also suggested that in the interest of economy, Dana might return to the States by ship rather than fly.

In the same letter, he wrote:

Part of the week I was in the French zone of operation on a madly disorganized tour sponsored by the French army. We were sent down on an overnight train, sitting up six to a compartment. The train was six hours late. There was no food awaiting us. We reached Coblenz after the ceremony installing a provincial civil government was over. The party got divided and lost and some found the people they were looking for and some didn't. Then the French army put on the inevitable sumptuous banquet at which everyone ate and drank too much. A French captain ruined everyone's after dinner disposition by ordering the telephone central to accept no calls for Paris. At midnight someone decided to call a press conference. We were given four hours in which to sleep and aroused at five thirty a.m. There was no breakfast— and so on and on. I wrote only one story when I got back and didn't mention the confusion.

On the German trip my colleague from the Herald Tribune *was a young fellow named Perlman who graduated from the school of journalism at Columbia the year after I did. He was drafted and just got out of the army. The graduates of my class were the last ones to get abroad and get jobs before the war as far as I can see. All through the war I have been the youngest among the newspapermen present, with the exception of Russell Hill of the* Herald Tribune. *Only now are younger men appearing on the scene (and women too).*

In these last months before the end of the war in Europe, Dana reported on some unfortunate behavior of U.S. troops in Paris, as well as corrupt actions of French collaborationists:

12,000 TROOPS AWOL IN PARIS; THOUSANDS JOIN IN BLACK MARKET

**Commanding General of Area Scores
Lack of Discipline in Ranks
—Says Eisenhower Arrested six Officers,
Sent General Home**

By DANA ADAMS SCHMIDT
By Wireless to THE NEW YORK TIMES.
PARIS, Jan. 25—Between 12,000 and 13,000 American soldiers are AWOL as a daily average in the European theatre and a large percentage gravitate toward Paris, Brig. Gen. Pleas B. Rogers, commanding general of the Paris area, known as the Seine Section, revealed today.

This fact, he said, together with the lack of discipline it implies, explains why so many soldiers have been arrested for black market operations and other offenses in the Paris area.

General Rogers explained that, contrary to the belief of many soldiers, the current cigarette and gasoline courts martial were by no means cases of witch burning. Instead they are part of a real effort to whip the rising crime problem in which no one will be spared.

Six officers involved in the 716th Railway Battalion's black market dealings were arrested by order of Gen. Dwight D. Eisenhower, he stated. On another occasion an officer as high as a brigadier general was sent home to the United States for a similar offense.

General Rogers displayed some official statistics that showed that 743 soldiers had been arrested in the Paris area between Jan. 1 and Jan. 24, and that the trend was definitely up. Two deserters were killed, one escaped and two military policemen were wounded in a black market raid last Saturday. Of the 1,723 military personnel in the Paris guard houses today, 442 are simple AWOLs who will be returned to be dealt with by their units, while about the same number are AWOLs involved in robbery, the black market and other crimes, and will be tried in Paris.

Maj. John E. Kieffer of Buffalo, N.Y., who performs the functions of an attorney general, or trial judge advocate, in the Paris area, said today that the rising black market prices showed that the drastic police measures and stiff sentences were having the desired effect.

Following the announcement of five death sentences and others of life imprisonment or long years at hard labor, a package of American cigarettes increased from about 100 francs or $2.00 to about 175 francs, while a five-gallon can of gasoline has risen from 500 to 900 francs.

The Army opened the cigarette trials to the public as an exceptional measure to encourage wide publicity and heighten the exemplary effect in the Army, he added.

He expressed the opinion that, if the AWOL problem could be controlled, black-market operations would quickly dwindle.

"Some men come into Paris for a good time, run out of money, get scared and then discover the black market as a way to live," he said. "There is always a smart guy who lies low and uses others to bring in goods that he can sell."

"We distinguish AWOL from desertion, according to intent. If a man bought civilian clothes and obviously never intended to return to the Army, he is a deserter. Many of these have long previous crime records. Others take to AWOL like strong drink but eventually snap out of it and return."

High French police quarters, meanwhile, confessed their relative helplessness in the Army's black-market problem. Many more civilians than military personnel are arrested in each black-market raid but the French courts are so overloaded with purge cases that few have reached trial. French military tribunals thus far have dealt with only a handful of cases involving Army property and have usually handed down suspended sentences.

During this end of the war period, while the Americans were dealing with the black market and stealing by some of their troops, the illicit profiteering by French collaborationists was beginning to come to light. Many were imprisoned and their funds confiscated. Dana discusses some egregious cases:

FRENCH PROFITEER
LOSES $25,000,000

Committee on Illicit Profits
Seizes Wealth of Parisian,
36, Who Dealt with Reich

By DANA ADAMS SCHMIDT
By Wireless to THE NEW YORK TIMES.
PARIS, Feb. 1—The Paris Committee for the Confiscation of Illicit Profits, set up by Gen. Charles de Gaulle's Government in October, made its first big killing today by confiscating 1,250,000,000 francs, or $25,000,000, that André Marquer, 36 years old, had acquired largely by manufacturing clothes and blankets for the German Navy and the Luftwaffe. Of the total, 250,000,000 francs represented actual profits, while 1,000,000,000 or four times the amount of profits, represented the maximum fine that the committee might impose. The total confiscated in the Paris area to date was thereby more than tripled.

As special punishment the committee ordered full publicity on this case. There is no appeal from its decision.

Ministry of Finance officials said that hundreds of similar cases were now appearing before eighty-one committees sitting in each of France's departments as the arduous investigations of the last few months were being completed. No fewer than 15,000 cases are on the books throughout the country, nearly half of them in the Paris area. Fifty in Paris involve sums of more than the equivalent of $1,000,000.

Huge Sum Indicated

Thus if some signs point to a slowing down of the purge of collaborationists, these facts would indicate that the confiscation of fortunes made in business dealing with the Germans is only just getting into stride.

Ministry of Finance officials hesitate to estimate the total that may be confiscated throughout the country but believe it will be sufficient to be a serious contribution toward deflation. Unofficial estimates place the total at 50,000,000,000 francs at least.

André Rolland, chairman of the two committees functioning in the Department of Seine, which includes Paris, explained today that the cases fell into two categories—the black market and commerce with the Germans. The most serious ones are those combining both categories, in which businessmen resorted to the black market to serve the Germans as in the case of M. Marquer. M. Marquer, who is at present in prison awaiting trial before a purge court, used his German wife, a former cook, to make deals with the Germans. His father represented him before the committee this evening.

"Aryan" Seizures Included

The case will go to the Superior Council for Confiscation, which is empowered to confiscate the offender's entire fortune, but the matter is academic in M. Marquer's case, since his resources probably are insufficient to cover his fine.

The ordinance that originally provided for the confiscation of illicit profits last October was tightened up by Minister of Finance René Pleven on Jan. 6. He reduced the periods given to businessmen to prepare their defense from thirty to twenty days and introduced a new type of illicit profits—those made out of "Aryanization" of Jewish property. At the same time it was made clear that the committees, composed of five Ministry of Finance officials and three representatives of the departmental Committee of Liberation, had absolute power to impose fines, while the Superior Council may confiscate an entire fortune without recourse to regular tribunals.

While such a procedure might seem arbitrary to Anglo-Saxon minds, Ministry of Finance officials maintained there were precedents in French financial law for the automatic imposition of fines.

Dana found much to write about in the last months of the War. Some stories almost suggested that the War was over, particularly those on collaboration, profiteering, reviving the economy and getting the factories back to work. Stories about wounded men certainly raised hopes that the war would be over soon and there would be no more wounded men to write about.

10 PER CENT OF WOUNDED AMERICANS FLOWN STRAIGHT HOME FROM EUROPE

By DANA ADAMS SCHMIDT
By Wireless to THE NEW YORK TIMES.

PARIS, Feb. 3—One in every four wounded men is now being evacuated from the Continent by air to Britain or the United States, according to the Surgeon General's office in Paris.

One in every ten of these air evacuees is flown straight home to the United States. Of all the wounded, the men who compose this tenth are the most tragic, yet they are the most cheerful, because they are going home. By rail and ship it might take them thirty days to reach New York; by air it is only thirty hours via the Azores and Bermuda to Mitchel Field. As a rule, wounded men who may recover within a month stay in France. Those who need up to two months are sent to Britain, and those who need longer than that are sent to the United States. Of the latter, some are chosen to fly. They will not be back.

Those chosen are almost all battle casualties. They are men with amputated limbs, broken backs or nerve injuries; men whose eyesight may be saved if they can have a special operation in time, who are in urgent need of plastic surgery. Some who have suffered face wounds have their jaws wired together and travel by air because there is less chance of their being airsick than seasick.

For a healthy male to walk through the wards and gaze on such shattered bodies seemed to be at first to display an indecent curiosity. What can one say to a man who has been blinded and has lost one arm and the fingers of the other hand, or to a 19-year-old whose feet have been frozen black and shriveled?

But the patients, I discovered, do not see it that way. Their cases are tragic and, of course, they know it, but they would be the last to admit it and the first to resent such suggestions from visitors.

I encountered no lugubrious reticence about what had happened to them. One, in fact, displayed a shell splinter that had crippled him for life. A radio at the far end of the ward was softly playing dance music. A couple of Red Cross doughnuts lay on a table next to each bed.

Cheered by Thought of Home

The immediate expectation of flying home, it was explained, keeps morale in this "air holding unit" much higher that it would be in a similar "sea holding unit." At the longest the men are here for three weeks, and some are in and out again within six hours. They reach this hospital from five days to a month after they have been picked up off the battlefield.

The hospital's commanding officer, Major Frederick W. Timmerman of Morrisville, VT., said that a further morale tonic had been the recent visit of two wounded men who had returned from the United States, one with an artificial leg, the other with an artificial arm. Each new batch of patients now hears from the older residents how they demonstrated their artificial limbs with exercises.

There is a moment when morale goes far down, however, Major Timmerman remarked—when the plane is about two hours from New York. Then many are beset by fear. It is understood that they will be able to phone wherever they like. Their families do not know that they are coming.

I reached the hospital in time to hear Capt. Hugh Worsely of Chicago, air liaison officer with the air-evacuation squadron, briefing sixteen patients for the flight. Two and a half hours previously they had been shaved and washed and one and a half hours previously they had been fed.

15,000 Flown Out Since April
Captain Worsely told them that 15,000 men had been evacuated from Europe by air since April, 1944, mostly from Prestwick, Scotland; that 1,500 had gone out from France since Dec. 7, when a new route was opened. He explained the route that they would fly and what they should do in an emergency, adding that equipment such as rubber boats had never had to be used. They would not be able to smoke aboard the plane, he said, and several fumbled for their last cigarettes as German prisoners wearing Red Cross armbands stepped forward and began carrying the litters to waiting ambulances.

Some wounded men hotly resent being carried by prisoners. On one occasion, a blinded patient, hearing German voices, staggered from his bed, swinging furiously. But the hospital officers said that the Germans made exceptionally careful litter-bearers. Jealous of their jobs in warm, well fed American hospitals, they take pains to make themselves useful.

From a seat next to the ambulance driver, I could talk to four whose heads were at our backs. There were a voluble corporal from Pennsylvania who talked about the 88-mm shell that had shot off his foot; a private from El Paso, Texas, who seemed to be in pain from shoulder and chest wounds, and a private from Alabama, a non-battle casualty who said that he could not take the cold and had developed pleurisy and tuberculosis. He was much disappointed to learn that he would not be able to see either the Eiffel Tower or the Statue of Liberty from his litter in the plane. The fourth man could not speak. He was a lieutenant colonel whose head was swathed in bandages and whose jaw was wired shut.

Nurse Aboard Plane
At an airfield outside Paris, the litters were raised one by one on a hydraulic elevator to the door of a C-54 transport where Flight Nurse Marjorie Payne stood watching carefully as the litters were slung in four tiers on each side of the

plane. Miss Payne, who lives at 53 West Fifty-Seventh Street, New York, is one of thirty-five nurses attached to the air-evacuation squadron. They were picked, it was easy to see, for their good looks as well as their medical competence. Most are former air-line stewardesses. As one medical officer remarked, "A pretty nurse is an important morale factor."

As far as the Azores, Miss Payne and a flight technician who helps her to keep the patients comfortable, feed them sandwiches, hot coffee and candy and must attend to any emergency medical requirements. They must see to it that the patients use their oxygen masks. There is one beside each litter that automatically dispenses more and more oxygen as the plane rises above 8,000 feet. Occasionally, when there are many serious cases aboard, a flight surgeon accompanies the men all the way to New York.

Dana wrote a related story on reconditioning wounded soldiers, which was published the following day. He said, *"It requires a combination of good food, physiotherapy, exercise, psycho-neurology,* Red Cross *entertainment and horse sense."* There are four hospitals in Britain for prolonged treatment, but men who could be prepared for combat in 30 days were sent to the Seventh Convalescent Hospital in France. Fifty men per day were reconditioned or rehabilitated.

In thanking the family for his Christmas books in his letter of January 31, Dana wrote:

I haven't read all my books yet, but today I took time out to make the acquaintance of the author of one of them, Janet Flanner. She appears to be exceptionally nervous, with a keen mind, small, thin, almost white hair. The occasion for our meeting was a disastrous little press conference that she had the misfortune to organize. She got a French officer in to talk about his experiences with the American army. Apparently they were all unpleasant and the conference was concerned mostly with rape until Hemingway came barging in and broke up the meeting with emotional and somewhat irrelevant protests. It was the first time I had seen Hemingway and I was

NOT impressed—presumptuous, overbearing, loud, a big bruiser of a man with a slobbery mouth. . . .

My concentration is being somewhat disturbed by trying to take part in a discussion on the future of de Gaulle which is going on behind me between Archambault [a NYT reporter] and a man whose name I can't think of. I think the General is going from strength to strength and will be with us for a long time. They don't seem to be so sure. He is the only man who has given this country any moral leadership and seems to be the only one who can. Maybe he is heading towards authoritarianism of some kind, but maybe France is not fit for anything else. The phrases with which we enshroud our so-called democracy seem to apply to ravaged France and Europe generally with difficulty.

Perhaps something of our concepts of democracy can be applied to Western Europe. I mean particularly respect for the integrity of the individual. But even there the apparent necessity of various kinds of economic collectivism under government direction make it ever more difficult. As for Eastern Europe and the defeated nations, I despair. The comparisons which one can make between de Gaulle and Hitler, taking into consideration the national temperaments involved, are sometimes shocking; fortunately de Gaulle seems to lack the vicious notions which went with Hitler's system such as anti-Semitism and expansionism. I have been thinking about coining a phrase like 'benevolent fascism' for de Gaulle—but it is probably too early to use such a drastic description. He still pays homage which sounds sincere to the forms of democracy, but the substance seems lacking.

Dana was working hard—he said in his February 5 letter that he had written some sort of story every day for about three weeks. In spite of the work, he enjoyed living in Paris:

Today there is a real "Paris in spring" feel in the air. But I fear it's only a flash in the pan and we have more winter to come. What a transformation a change in the temperature can make in a town without coal—sidewalks filled up again, the panhandlers and streetwalkers back on the job and everybody seems pleased. Soon we will be moving into our chrome and plate glass office in Rue Caumartin.

Went to check up on the FORD the other day and found it still safely in the garage where I left it for some minor repairs a month or so ago—nothing like free storage. Now if I could only get some gas . . . but there isn't even enough gas for the office at present.

It is nearly three p.m., the time Frenchmen begin to drift back to their offices, so I'll see what I can find. All my love to you all,
Dana

The fate of collaborators was naturally of great concern to the loyal French.

FRANCE BARS VOTE
TO COLLABORATORS

Regional Authorities' Powers
Will Be Redefined—Leader
Calls "Resistance Dead"

By DANA ADAMS SCHMIDT
By Wireless to THE NEW YORK TIMES.
PARIS, Feb. 9—Former members of collaborationist organizations sponsored by men such as Marcel Deat and Jacques Doriot will be disqualified from voting in the municipal elections next spring even though they may not have been tried, according to an ordinance approved today by the French Cabinet.

It was unofficially estimated that 20,000 to 30,000 persons might be stricken from the lists of voters by special civil chambers which have hitherto been concerned only with inflicting the penalty of "national unworthiness" on minor collaborators.

The sixteen regional commissioners, who represent Gen. Charles de Gaulle's authority in the provinces, finished today their three-day conference with General de Gaulle and his Ministers, which was in large measure devoted to preparations for the elections. As during the two previous conferences held since the liberation of France, the growing economic problems and the suppression of outlaw remnants of the resistance groups also occupied the commissioners.

It was learned tonight that the commissioners had been told not to count on raw material imports to start idle factories before April at the earliest.

A forthcoming ordinance redefining the powers of the commissioners will facilitate their work, it is understood, by strengthening their authority on some points such as requisitions and "administrative internment" of persons considered dangerous.

It was authoritatively said that these facts show that General de Gaulle has no intention for the time being of abolishing the regional authority which was set up as a temporary expedient to coordinate the work of prefects during the liberation. Responsible officials said that it had proved an invaluable instrument of central government authority and might even be perpetuated in some form.

The regional commissioner for the Lyon area, Yves Farge, a high resistance leader, said today, "the resistance movements, as such, are dead. There is nothing left to resist." He maintained that disorders in his and in other parts of the country were steadily diminishing.

The police are rounding up irresponsible persons who managed to collect arms parachuted into France by the Allies during the occupation, he said, adding that others who thought they had the Communist party's support in continuing violence were realizing that they had been disowned.

In M. Farge's opinion, the real resistance leaders are now making their influence felt inside the traditional French political organizations, particularly the Communist party, Catholic political groups and trade unions.

"By far my greatest worries are economic," he declared. "Factories in my area will have exhausted their raw materials by the end of February. At the same time, the lack of transport has made it is so difficult to bring food into Lyon that I have planned a large-scale evacuation of children to the villages."

A surprising political development at this end of the war period was that the Socialist, rather than the Communist party proposed immediate nationalization of the banks and utilities.

In an article on February 10, Dana wrote of a M. Philip, once General de Gaulle's Minister of the Interior, who said that he believed certain steps could be taken immediately: nationalization of the transport and electrical power industries; the nationalization of reinsurance, as distinct from insurance; government control of credit, and the nationalization of France's six big banks. He thought that the following tax measures would enable France to cover 50 percent of her budget:

A tax on profits made between 1940 and 1945. These would rise almost to confiscatory levels.

A capital tax on fortunes exceeding 100,000,000 francs. These funds would be used to aid war victims.

More drastic confiscation of "illicit profits" derived from commerce with the Germans.

The calling in and exchange of bank notes to take inventory of the fortunes accumulated in cash and to stifle the black market, which is carried on mostly in cash. Check transfers would remain free . . . to avoid interference with normal commerce.

It's after midnight, Dana wrote on February 17. *Harold and Archambault have gone home leaving me alone in our little office in the Hotel Scribe. I am very late with my letter this week, but I've had a grand spate of letters from you, four of them from January 13 to February 3. Three arrived together. They all get here in the end, and I'm sure it's the same going your way. If I am late in writing any week I try to make it up the next week and have rarely missed in the last few months.*

I see by one of your clips that Mathews is scheduled to replace Daniell [Head of the London Bureau] *in London. We heard Daniell might go, but he seems to be fighting it. Having Matthews in London might improve our intra-bureau Paris London relations, and possibly improve my chances of getting to the front. I know Mathews only by reputation. He is a Columbia School of Journalism graduate, a great worker (like a lot of* Times *men I notice) and a pretty keen political observer I gather.*

In the last few days I have been quite hectically busy and fairly productive in stories which might be signed. There was an interview with Andre Philip, an interview with a Doctor Schwartz on the fate of Jews, a political piece on our policy in Germany and a piece on the Red Cross *which James, our foreign editor, requested. In the next few days I'll have a piece on UNRRA [United Nations Relief and Rehabilitation Administration]. Tonight I also did bits on a Thorez*[100] *special and on unemployment.*

Of course the signers are the stories that pay off, as far as reputation goes. But the New York desk is also keen on the short, unsignable items which may brighten up the page. For instance I may have a little box on infant mortality during the recent cold wave tomorrow (not so bright, to be sure).

I'm going to have to continue this tomorrow, as the couple next door are muttering unhappily in their bed, obviously disturbed by my tapping.

NEXT DAY.... Today yet another package arrived from home, containing delicious Steinie cookies, butternut candy, chocolate, and a new olive drab sweater and ski socks.

I certainly have an attentive family, and I wish you could all realize how much I appreciate it. I couldn't help notice the name tape, from school days, sewed into the socks. The sweater is dandy, and the cookies are going fast.

We get a regular candy ration, but I have turned into quite a candy consumer in my old age. I find that my social obligations of giving away candy and chocolate to the hungry offspring of my friends and news sources conflicts with my appetite.

In case you should still be missing my previous letters, I think I have now received all the Christmas packages, including the watch and fountain pen, both of which are now in use. I am very fond of the watch. It is handsome and really keeps time, a most important qualification when making split second calculations to get into the mess in time for breakfast. As a rule all I do with fountain pens is lose them but this one I have been keeping filled with ink

---

[100] Maurice Thorez became secretary General of the French Communist Party in 1930. He was a minister of state under de Gaulle in 1945 and deputy premier from 1946-47. See Appendix.

and have been using it for notes instead of a pencil, as an experiment. Pencil has a tendency to blur and be unclear when you come to consult your notes at the end of the day. Pen has the disadvantage of being wet, but this one seems to be fine enough to dry almost as soon as you have written.

I'd be interested to know whether they used the story on our policy in dealing with Germany politically. I just happened to notice that Johnston, who brought in his file from Seventh Army, had a similar story on the sixteenth.

Thanks for taking care of my income tax. I feel quite distinguished to be contributing to the Treasury. I seem to have accumulated a little money these last few years . . . but it wouldn't last long if I had to pay someone fifty cent an hour as a sitter. My gosh, at college we got paid forty cents an hour for hard work, and I doubt if I make such a hell of a lot more now, considering that we work seven days a week, usually from about ten A.M. till midnight, though I won't stop to figure it out.

Please tell Eliza that I am conscience stricken about not having replied to her fine letter of ever so long ago. I trust she is stuffing the baby with vitamins.

Today I had lunch at the Herter's home [friends of the Sadouls]. *They put on a very fine meal. French hosts always do and I always have the feeling I am depriving them of things they need far more than I. But M. Herter is very definitely* debrouillard. *Your French teacher will be able to tell you what that means in case it has slipped your mind* [resourceful, smart]. *Please tell Mrs. Sadoul that he* [M. Herter] *and his wife send their greetings. I haven't called on M. Sadoul yet, but will do so. He writes for the newspaper* Ce Soir. *It is a Communist afternoon paper and what he writes is, I fear, as distorted as Communist political dissertations usually are. He writes foreign affairs.*

I was interested in your suggestions for stories. They are most welcome, as are your criticisms of what I write. I did one story on schools, but it was entirely on the political side—on the question whether de Gaulle will maintain Vichy's subsidies for Catholic schools, which is going to be one of the important issues in the elections.

Harold monopolizes what you might call the 'central' story, usually political, most of the time, and I have to step fairly lively to find other topics of interest. Hence a rather wide range of topics, from the appalling fate of Jews, to hospital planes, and socialist politics.

Thanks for enclosing some of my dispatches and Harold's. We added them to our collections. I'm delighted to have them, if you have them to spare, but don't cut down on the collections of clippings you keep at 1132 [Mother's Fourth Avenue address in Los Angeles] *to send them to me.*

In a hand written postscript he added: *I got my first circular letter from the* Times *the other day with a note—"Welcome to the staff of the NYT" scrawled at the bottom by Arthur Hays Sulzberger, publisher of the* Times.

As Dana mentioned, he wrote a story about UNRRA and plans for post-war Germany. Although in February no schools had been opened, new schoolbooks had been printed in Aachen based on texts in use before 1933. The military government was training a select group of Germans as policemen. The role of UNRRA was diminishing.

UNRRA was originally scheduled to take charge of prisoners of war and deportees, but it was now decided that the military government and not UNRRA would also handle the running of camps and the evacuation of the displaced from Germany. UNRRA had been asked to provide a hundred teams of thirteen men to go into Germany, but only eight teams were now ready in France. The French government was pleased to supply an additional forty-five teams to assist UNRRA.

In this period before the end of hostilities, Dana wrote of the French people's great concern for the 2,500,000 French prisoners of war and deportees in Germany. There was fear that "in their death agony," the Nazis might "commit crimes more terrible than any before" against the many foreigners still in their hands. François de Menthon, Military Justice, feared that they would be capable of compensating their losses by killing a half-million captives.

It was also known that Allied prisoners in Germany were suffering from a desperate lack of food. The Allied Headquarters proposed to follow the plan put forward by the French Cabinet to send aid to the prisoners through Switzerland in trucks loaded with food. Other trucks could be driven to the prisoner camps near the Swiss border by International Red Cross personnel.

Dana's chances for relaxation were few, but at the beginning of March, he wrote of an excursion:

Last Sunday, Sonya, her sister and the owner of a castle all loaded into FORD and, with me at the wheel, headed for the castle at a place called Faverolles, about sixty kilometers from Paris. As for the castle, it was exquisite; just a little place of two stories built in a right angle with a broad moat around it. You sit in the shelter of an angle where the heat of the thin winter sun accumulates and look out over fields and orchards towards the village church. I was enchanted. Inside the place is very livable too, with running water and central heating. The moat is big enough to have a rowboat. Maybe I'll buy the place someday!

Following this pleasant interlude, Dana interviewed Dr. Juan Negrin, Spain's last constitutional Republican Premier.

Negrin had spent some five weeks in France organizing an anti-Franco group, from among the 130,000 Spaniards living in France. A meeting was to take place either at the Spanish Embassy in Mexico City or aboard a Spanish ship outside territorial waters. Dr. Negrin hoped to obtain the support of the Cortes, the two houses that form the Spanish legislative body, in renovating his Cabinet and forming a coalition to overthrow Franco. He hoped this anti-fascist group would also be capable of representing Spain on the international scene and at the United Nations.

The first step was to be the confirmation by the Cortes of Diego Martinez Barrio as President of the Spanish Republic. He had resigned after the fall of Madrid to General Franco. General Barrio was then to ask Dr. Negrin to form a new government. (Señor Martinez Barrio succeeded to the office of President, under provisions of the Spanish constitution, after the death of President Manuel Azana.)

If General de Gaulle continued to smile on Dr. Negrin and to be cool toward General Franco, as well as grant Spain extraterritorial rights in Paris, Dr. Negrin would probably move his government to Paris. Otherwise, his seat would be in Mexico City. While in France, Dr. Negrin had gained the support of the Communist Party and the Communist-controlled National Union.

Republican Spaniards felt these moves and the appointment of Dr. Negrin were important because the overwhelming majority of politically conscious Spaniards were thirsty for a return to the legality of the 1931 Constitution. They wanted this to be done without violence. Some remembered the bloodless collapse of the monarchy and offered that as evidence that this would be possible.

Negrin countered fears that Great Britain might back the return of a monarchy to replace Franco after the war. He said that the monarchy enjoyed no popular sympathy whatever, and was discredited and identified with Spain's decadence in the eyes of most Spaniards.

Another subject Dana wrote about in early March was food distribution to prison camps by the American Red Cross. It was becoming increasingly difficult to reach prisoners. Allied advances in the west through the Rhineland and in the east through Poland had caused the Germans to herd prisoners into central and southern Germany. These camps were receiving prisoners thirty percent beyond normal capacity and were mostly isolated from possible food supplies by railroad.

Emergency plans called for rushing food to Switzerland in Allied trucks and then trucking it to the camps by International Red Cross personnel, as previously mentioned.

In the past, the American prisoners had been the best fed since they were able to accumulate food in their camps, but since the Germans would no longer permit the accumulation of food reserves and so many prisoners of all nationalities had been herded together and moved ahead of the Allied advances, discrimination in food distribution was politically and psychologically impossible.

By March of 1945, a different kind of food crisis had developed in North Africa, Morocco, Algeria and Tunisia, the result of three years of bad harvests, each worse than its predecessor. Frosts and drought stunted the wheat and barley crops. Locusts devoured the vegetables, and hoof-and-mouth disease killed the cattle. Manpower needs of the French army cut into farm labor, and the lands which had become the symbols of plenty became dependent on imports.

In good years, the Arabs and Berbers stow away wheat in holes hollowed out in the soft rock. Now, they were down to rock bottom. Some had no more hard wheat, which they boil like rice to make couscous. In addition, there was a shortage of tea and sugar for their favorite sweet drink. These problems were added to those of the 40,000,000 hungry Frenchmen in Europe.

Programs had been developed to bridge the food gap, but shipping problems had prevented fulfillment. Meanwhile, it was feared that the famine would incite unrest and "threatening political results."

On March 12, Dana reported a better outlook for shipping. Major Gen. Frank Ross told him that the Germans had a grand strategy of destroying or occupying European ports to cut off Allied forces from their supplies, but now, the restoration of ports had opened up shipping for the Allies. Germany still held Dunkerque in the north and St. Nazaire and La Rochelle on the Atlantic coast.

The British had turned back three ports for civilian use, and the Americans had turned back most of the small ports of Brittany and Normandy, including Brest and St. Malo, which had never been used by the military. On the Mediterranean coast, the harbors of Sète and Antibes were available. Cherbourg and Le Havre were operating at greater than pre-war capacity. In spite of these restorations, it was said that it would take five or ten years to restore all French ports.

The Director of Ports, Eugene Fischer, said that no fewer than 1,220 ships of all sizes were sunk in French ports by the Germans. Some 200 had been raised. This is not considering the tragedy at Mers-el-Kébir (northwestern Algiers) in 1940 when the French fleet was destroyed by the British to prevent its falling into German hands.

In his letter of March 25, Dana gives a picture of what living in France was like at the time. It was in the form of advice for the Sadouls, who were living in the United States and thinking of coming back to France now that the war seemed to be almost over:

I should say they were foolish to try to come so soon as July. Life for civilians will still be extremely hard and expensive. The people I had lunch with today are by no means poor and they were eating meat for the first time in a month. Vegetarianism is all right when there's plenty of other food. But there hasn't been any butter or meat for more than a month in most quarters, three months in some. No coffee, no chocolate, little milk, little of anything.

Of course if you live in the country it's infinitely better; but life in France today is no picnic. Except for [American] war correspondents. We have nothing to kick about [eating in U.S. Army messes]. If I were Linette [the Sadouls daughter] I'd stick to my good job in Hollywood and forget about going to France for another year, especially considering the little boy. I'd say Europe wasn't a fit place to live in anymore except for foreigners. In parentheses, don't alarm the Sadouls too much. If one is a debrouilleur and knows how to work the black market, one need neither fear nor lack anything.

Dana also noted in this letter that Harold had ordered him a portable typewriter from London.

At this time, at the end of March, the Allies were forging deep into Germany. It seemed that the war would soon be over, and authorities in France were already considering how their cities and villages could be restored.

On March 29, Dana wrote that French authorities were hoping to have 300,000 German workers for three years for the reconstruction of ruined cities. They proposed that this could be demanded from Germany as part of reparations.

In the words of one official, "This would be a measure of the merest justice, considering that the Germans deported for labor in Germany more than half of the building trades workers of France, or between 300,000 and 350,000 men. When these men return, it would be unfair to draft them immediately into labor camps, which will be necessary for the reconstruction."

It was estimated that 1,400,000 buildings had been destroyed in the war. Plans for some 600 communities that should be rebuilt completely had already been prepared and approved. At present, since so little skilled labor was available, all that could be done was to clear away rubble and put up temporary buildings with salvaged material. Some German labor from among prisoners of war had already been put to work in clearing rubble, but it was said that trained artisans were needed.

The French, also, had plans for drawing large numbers of men from non-essential occupations and training them. Some were said to be at work already at Rouen and St. Quentin. Youth teams of volunteers aged 17 to 22 had also been organized by the Ministry of Labor. They were being taught building trades and were also receiving some basic military training.

Just before Easter, Dana wrote a piece about possible elections. Some people were eager to have municipal and cantonal elections, but the Consultative Assembly pointed out that with victory perhaps only a few days off, and 2,500,000 prisoners expected to come "streaming home," the elections should be delayed to allow these men to vote.

The Consultative Assembly was also concerned that the 565 Senators and Deputies who had voted to support Henri-Philippe Pétain in 1940 should not be eligible to hold office. The Assembly recommended that the National Council of Resistance decide which, if any, of these men were eligible. Some might have become eligible through subsequent acts of resistance.

The Assembly, Dana wrote, would be greatly changed after an election. The Center and Right would be far stronger than in the present. The greatest beneficiaries of the election would be the Radical Socialists—the party on which the resistance had heaped scorn as representing the middle classes that failed the French state, the "little men" who remained passive in the face of the Germans; they feared nationalization; they resented the claim of the Resistance to a privileged position. The second great beneficiary would be the Catholic Popular Republican Movement, the MRP. It had absorbed most of the old Christian Democrats, and like the Radical Socialists, it combined left-wing ideology with conservative acts.

At about the time that the Consultative Assembly was considering whether to postpone the elections, Dana reported the arrest of seventeen men by the French "Sûreté," similar to our F.B.I. These men had, in the last three months, tried to organize an underground revival of Jacques Doriot's *Parti Populaire Français* or PPF. It was found that they were in contact with Pierre Laval's government at Sigmaringen and in contact with German SS officers who had parachuted into France. Actually, Pierre Laval's government had moved to a location near the Swiss border.

Following these arrests, the General Direction of Studies and Research warned that a dangerous German agent, who organized the rescue of Benito Mussolini and was also prominent in the reprisals taken after the attempt on Adolf Hitler's life, was now somewhere in France. He was "Lieut. Col. Otto Skorzeny, age 37, height 6'2" and weight 220 pounds." The General Direction of Studies and Research was said to be no ministry, but responsible only to General de Gaulle. It was the successor of the organization that maintained liaison between the underground in France and General de Gaulle in London at the beginning of the war.

On April 1, Easter Sunday, Dana wrote, *I drove down to a little village called Le Bosquel (near Amiens) where the Ministry of Reconstruction is building a "village temoin"* [a model village]. *It was a little place of 240 inhabitants which was destroyed entirely except for three houses during the 1940 fighting. It was very interesting, especially since it gave me a day in the open air.*

. . . . It occurs to me that I painted a rather gloomy picture of France in my last letter. If you haven't passed it on to the Sadouls already maybe it would be better not to do so. Blood is thicker than water, they say, and if they really want to return to France they will do so whether life here is easy or hard; no use alarming them and making them feel unnecessarily bad.

As the war was drawing to an end, the Allies liberated many French military and civilian captives. In a dispatch on April 12, Dana wrote,

. . . trains are bringing 3,000 to 4,000 home daily. About 60,000 have reached their homes. More than 2,000,000 remain in Germany. One Frenchman reached his home unannounced after five years . . . too exhausted to climb five flights to his door. He asked the janitor to tell his wife he was here. When she came down he was dead of a heart attack.

French and Allied repatriation machinery is creaking ominously and official tempers on both sides of the Rhine are short. Charles Favrel, correspondent of the semi-official French Agency, speaks of bands of liberated Frenchmen living off the land, wandering along the east bank of the Rhine from bridge to bridge, trying to get across. At first they laugh and wave improvised flags at passing troops, but as they are turned back from bridge after bridge "their joy turns to bitterness."

Jean Rius, president of the Agricultural Workers Union, who was liberated by the Russians and arrived from Odessa April 1, spent ten days plodding from office to office fulfilling the formalities of "reintegration." He wore rubbers because there are no more shoes to be given out and wore a borrowed suit because there are no more suits.

The French Government has requisitioned most of the resort hotels bordering Switzerland for convalescents and is hastily improvising new sanatoriums in the Pyrenees for 250,000 Frenchmen who will return with tuberculosis.

The International Red Cross is operating several hundred trucks from Switzerland in an effort to carry food parcels and medical supplies to prisoners who are being shifted to southern Germany. The men march almost without food and attempts are made to feed them while they rest at night. Sixty-five thousand British and Slav prisoners were reported moving from the direction of Karlsruhe, many "staggering with bloody feet," in some cases the report said those who could not keep up were shot by the Germans and left by the roadside.

On April 20, Dana wrote about the trial of General Henri-Fernand Dentz. In 1940, the Vichy government under Pétain appointed General Dentz High Commissioner to Syria. At his trial, it was brought out that, in various ways, he aided the Germans. For instance, he allowed German planes to refuel in Syria on their way to Iraq. The Germans hoped to prevent the British from obtaining oil in Iraq.

While Dentz was in control of Vichy Syria, the British and Free French invaded Syria and were ultimately successful in returning Syria to the Free French. Syria was a springboard for the Allies in the Egyptian and North African campaigns. [Dana wrote about this campaign while he was in Turkey.]

At the trial, Dentz was found to be a traitor to France, and he was condemned to death.

A few days after Dentz's trial on April 25, Dana reported that a party of officials from the Ministries of Justice and War had departed, in haste, for the Swiss frontier with warrants for the arrest of Marshal Henri-Philippe Pétain.

Dana said the left-wing and Resistance circles were nervous about having Pétain in France, fearing that his presence might upset elections.

The Communists and Resistance groups were concerned that four men who had voted for Pétain were, nevertheless, running for office.

Some thought that Pétain's arrival might signal a nationwide uprising of Vichy sympathizers. Pétain's star witness would be Admiral William D. Leahy, former United States Ambassador to Vichy, who claimed, "the American knows the full story of Pétain's alleged efforts to save France." Pétain's popularity among certain people was based on his heroic command at the battle of Verdun in 1916.

Pétain's trial was postponed until July. In August, as expected, he was condemned to death as a traitor. His death sentence was later commuted to life imprisonment on the Isle of Yeu, where he died in 1957.

On April 27, Dana was pleased to report that, *I am to go to London next Sunday to work in the Bureau there for an indefinite period and presumably to have some military assignments. It all came about as the result of a squabble which has been going on for weeks between Harold and Ray Daniell on the subject of the number of accredited men in the Paris office. Daniell felt there should be more people in Europe for his German coverage and wanted us to discredit somebody. . . . It is all very complicated and technical. In the end it was decided they would send a civilian from the London office to replace me here and send me to London. The war is evolving fast and there is no telling what that may lead to. Anyway it's a great chance to get acquainted with our office there.*

All that may not be quite clear to you; and indeed it isn't clear to anybody. The point of difficulty is that we can have any number of SHAEF [101] *accredited*

---

[101] Supreme Headquarters Allied Expeditionary Force, the Allied command structure headed by General Dwight D. Eisenhower.

war correspondents in London but only a limited number on the continent. For the time being the solution is satisfactory to me.

Dana was right about the war "evolving fast." On April 12, Roosevelt died and was succeeded by Truman. On April 21, the Soviets occupied Berlin; on April 28, Mussolini was executed by Italian patriots. On April 30, Hitler committed suicide. On his deathbed, he appointed Admiral Karl Doenitz to succeed him. Doenitz immediately proclaimed that "the war against the western allies has become meaningless."

On May 3, Dana was already "up to his ears in the London Bureau" and writing a weekly letter.

As Ray Daniell remarked, it doesn't make much sense to send one of the few men we have who can speak fluent French from Paris to London and replace him with a man who doesn't speak French. But so it is, and I am not unpleased about the way it has worked out.

I haven't been able to get onto anything very important in the way of stories here yet. Monday I did a piece about Allied control commissions waiting to go to Austria and Austrian emigres. Today I visited some Russians who were taken prisoner while serving in the German army. Today I am expecting to do a piece about the redeployment of the strategic air forces and tomorrow I am to fly over the Ruhr to see what the damage our bombers did looks like.

It is a great relief not to have the world cut into two watertight compartments—politics and military—as they were in Paris—largely because of personal rivalries. Here I can do anything.

Please write me again the names and addresses of the people in London you would like me to look up as I do not have them with me.

It was icy the day I flew over to London. Snow on the last day of April, all over southern England. A fine state of affairs. I nearly froze to death. But it is warmer today with the sun out again.

Everything seems neat and prim and cheerful in this country after the disorder and hopelessness one often feels in France. The British complain that everything here is down at heel, but they haven't seen France. In Paris it was a major undertaking, especially for one's pocketbook, to eat outside an army mess: here one can eat anywhere; there are none of the horrifying lapses when there is nothing at all, no butter, no meat, etc. which there were in France. It is a matter of civic discipline no doubt, the difference between a country that lives by the black market and one that lives by the rules.

I haven't had time yet, but I will try to look up some of my old Chillon friends, though they are probably scattered to the four corners of the earth.

My first reaction, having had a very cursory and superficial look at London, is that bomb damage is not so general as I had expected. Britishers hasten to point out that many of the bombed building have been neatly cleaned up so they look like vacant lots now, and that I haven't been to quarters where whole blocks were swept away.

This sort of psychic impression is doubtless dangerous and highly unreliable but my feeling is, after seeing my first Britishers in London, looking at their faces and talking to a few of them, that this country is very much of a going concern, healthy with confidence in itself and the future. That may not seem surprising, but it impresses me because I did not at all get that impression from France. France seemed a country of endings, of things passed. England is still, with all its hoary age, a country where new beginnings are being made, a country with a future. We won't consider that one for the record, though, just a note on first arrival.

Ray Daniell turns out to be a pretty good sort of guy, though I doubt if I will ever be fond of him. He has now pushed off to the continent for a special writing assignment, leaving the acting bureau managership in the hands of E.C. Daniel, a likeable youngish fellow. Daniel was in Paris covering SHAEF *during Middleton's absence.*

There are flocks of other people, secretaries and office boys and whatnots in this office. The Times *does load itself up with a lot of overhead. There's an American named Gruson and Miss McLaughlin and two Englishmen named Vosser and Collins. Egan, a business expert is the man who is replacing me in Paris.*

Miss McLaughlin turns out to be rather more than middle ageish, kind and hardworking. She went out of her way to help me with information about how the office works and where to eat, etcetera and passed on some useful information on news sources. She is most anxious to get to France.

Well, all my love to you all. This war looks like it is about wound up, on this side of the globe anyway, DANA

Dana Adams Schmidt War Correspondent, APO 413, United Kingdom Base, Care Postmaster, New York City

RUINED RUHR AREA VIEWED FROM AIR

RAF Shows Allied Newsmen Destruction Bombs Wrought in Reich's Many 'Forges'

By DANA ADAMS SCHMIDT
By Cable to The New York Times.
LONDON, Friday, May 4—For more than five years Royal Air Force bombers have been going out over the most heavily defended area on earth, the Ruhr Basin, to destroy the industrial heart of Germany. They flew 50,000 sorties and 10,000 to 15,000 RAF men did not come back.

Today the RAF took a party of correspondents in an unarmed Dakota plane to follow the trail of bombers and view the ruin.

Now Hitler is dead and his forge is cold; smashed and idle. The industrial haze has drifted away as a shroud withdrawn from a mutilated corpse. Now the 2,000 flak guns are gone and the zigzagging trenches around them are filled with water.

The pink faces of Germans in the streets of Essen, Duisburg, Duesseldorf and Dortmund turned upward curiously today as we flew low over the rubble heaps.

54 Per Cent of Buildings Destroyed

This was that forge that made the German Army mighty, an industrial kingdom forty miles long and twenty-five miles wide with a population of

5,000,000 persons who produced as much steel and half as much coal as all of England. Now 54 per cent of all the buildings in the fourteen principle towns of the area are destroyed. At Elberfeld the destruction is as high as 94 per cent.

The destruction, almost entirely a British job, was accomplished in two phases. The first phase began March 15, 1943 with massive attacks on the Krupp works at Essen. The idea was to destroy the built-up areas mainly with the fire of incendiary bombs. Block upon block of blackened hulks in every town testify to the effectiveness of the plan. Endless rows of houses look like fantastic egg crates, with roofs and insides burned away, but outer walls and a few inner partitions left standing.

Huge Plants Mass of Ruin

In the fall of 1944, as the Allies' armies drew near, the tactical phase of the bombing began in the Ruhr Basin. Since fire would no longer spread in the devastated areas, the RAF concentrated on high explosives. Today railroad marshalling yards, factory areas, residential areas and sometimes even open countryside are pockmarked with water-filled bomb craters twinkling in the spring sunshine.

The great Krupp works, running through the center of Essen, the Rheinmetall-Borsig of Duesseldorf, Fritz Thyssen's plants at Duisburg and 100 others are masses of roofless, twisted girders, pipes and whitish gray rubble.

Patches of new red brick and tile show where the Germans vainly tried to repair the damage. Where it is new, the debris still covers the streets, and crooked paths show where the people have picked new paths through it.

German air raid shelters were so effective that human losses were low, according to best reports—not more than 150 among the Krupp workers. But one wonders where and how they will live now. This was "area bombing," the bludgeon that laid low the Ruhr. There was no glory or gloating in today's inspection of the results; only horrified sadness that so much of the world's total wealth should have been destroyed, sadness that the custodians of that wealth should have so misused it.

On May 7, the Germans surrendered unconditionally to the Western Allies and to the Soviet Union at Dwight D. Eisenhower's headquarters. The official announcement of V-E Day was made on May 8 separately by President Truman [102] in Washington, Prime Minister Churchill in London and General de Gaulle in Paris. Dana had witnessed the War from "a few drops of blood on the bridge at Sudetenland" to the "tears of joy in London"—some six years of conflict.

It took a while for all fighting to stop. Admiral General Von Friedeberg surrendered the German forces in northwestern Germany, the Netherlands and Denmark to Field Marshal Sir Bernard L. Montgomery. Although some 3,000,000 Germans had surrendered to the U.S. and Britain in 3 days, it appeared that some of the Nazis wouldn't make an overall commitment to the three: U.S., Britain and Russia. Field Marshal General Ferdinand Schoerner issued a proclamation saying that "against the Soviets, the fighting continues with fierceness and determination." Field Marshal Montgomery warned that the Allies would attack any movement of Nazi forces from the surrendered areas. But German vessels were seeking to escape from the Baltic ports, and British Coastal Command sank or damaged fifty ships and two Nazi destroyers.

From London on May 9, Dana wrote:

So it's really over. I've been writing about it for two days, but the realization of it hasn't really sunk in. After living for six years with every thought, every action conditioned by the war it scarcely seems possible that it should be ended. Of course it goes on in the Far East, but in the excitement of V-E day here few people think of it. For France and Britain the German war was THE war of course, and for me too. I wonder whether I should ask the Times *to send me to the Far East. The way I feel about it, I would be willing to go and it would have its interest, but I'm not frightfully keen about it. As far as I can see going out there would be the only way I could remain a war correspondent for many more months; how important that is for my draft status after the end of the war in Europe I really don't know. What do you think?*

---

[102]   President Roosevelt died on April 12, 1945.

Your letter of April 21 was promptly forwarded to me and I was much concerned to hear of Grandma's injury[103]. *I trust that she is much better and will write to her right away. Thank goodness Steinie is well again.*

I've just been over to the vast officers mess they call 'Willow Run' here and met Louis Gleek, a political scientist who was several years ahead of me at Pomona. He is now a foreign service officer and has been serving in Sweden and Finland. I didn't know him very well at Pomona, but we quickly got acquainted here and I expect to see him again tonight.

Tried to run down some old Chillon people in the last few days, but no luck yet. I did learn that Chillon carried on all through the war although it's down to about three boys now.

The V-E day fever here has been incredible. It is the fate of the newspaperman always to observe and analyze such things and never to enter in.

After Roosevelt's death [April 12,1945] there was a good less room for our copy in the paper and most of mine was unsigned. Since I reached London I've written a story every day. They have included, on free Austrians, on good treatment of prisoners of war of Russian origin, on my flight over the Ruhr, on War Crime situation (for the Sunday section), on redeployment of Eighth Air Force in particular, and two nights running now on V-E day delirium.

It's just possible I'll be going to Norway in the next day or so. I forgot to mention one story of mine on indications that Doenitz was ready to surrender Norway which was on the front page; like a lot of stuff done here, it was a rewrite from the oceans of stuff Reuters *pours out. The best piece I've done in some time I think was the one on the Ruhr.*

I am going to buy some civilian clothes here and have already acquired the necessary clothes coupons. Most war correspondents wear civvies while in London. For the moment, however, I'm still in uniform.

(Isn't it wonderful that the war should be over. It comes as a surprise to me every time I think of it. An odd thing about it is that many people are sorry that it's over. Not of course the men who have been doing the real fighting, but others to whom it meant a better job and greater importance than ever

---

[103]   Grandma fell while opening the front door of her apartment and fractured her hip.

LONDONERS DANCE IN PACKED STREETS

Unable to Wait, They Light Up Bonfires and Serenade King in Joyful Celebration

By DANA ADAMS SCHMIDT
By Wireless to THE NEW YORK TIMES.

LONDON, May 7—V-E Day may be tomorrow, but London could not wait. It celebrated tonight. Londoners, more entitled to cheer than most, danced and pranced in the streets and shot off flares and built great bonfires in the gaping cellars of bombed-out buildings.

Far into night fires lit the horizon as in the days of the blitz, tugboats hooted on the Thames, and Trafalgar Square, Piccadilly and a hundred other places echoed with the shouts of milling thousands. Big Ben, brilliantly illuminated once more, gleamed above a city finally rid of the air raid menace after nearly six years.

In Whitehall, where the crowds cheered Prime Minister Churchill as he solemnly drove from Downing Street after a Cabinet meeting, big yellow letters on the walls reminded Londoners of the "war against Japan."

But this was London's night. After five long years London let down and laughed as few in the grim days could have hoped she would again.

It was all strictly unofficial, for the searchlights and the speeches are for tomorrow. But that did not prevent Tommies and doughboys, Cockneys young and old and girls in and out of uniform from linking arms and sailing down Piccadilly singing "Roll Out the Barrel" and "Pistol Packin Mama."

They pranced round Piccadilly Circus and on down to Buckingham Palace, where for hours they chanted "We want the King," and fired flares and even a few pistols. The King did not appear, but they sang out "For he's a jolly good fellow," and milled on down to Trafalgar Square.

There were soldiers in every Allied uniform, with carnival hats on their heads and flags and balloons in their hands and red, white and blue rosettes in their buttonholes. They formed circles and danced round and round, singing "There'll always be an England."

Several cars were jammed in the crowd, while soldiers and girls climbed on the roofs and hooted with glee.

In Leicester Square a Royal Air Force pilot stood chanting in Arabic while laughing friends passed their hats. In Soho and Mayfair crowds tossed slates from bombed-out buildings into bonfires to hear them explode and leaped through the flames.

In Hammersmith doors were pulled off and windows wrenched from the sockets to build fires. And at Putney and Bethnal Green the officials forgot V-E Day programs and floodlighted the municipal buildings.

One old woman in the Elephant and Castle district in London's sorely tried East End had soberer thoughts as she turned away from the bonfires and rockets.

"I never want to see London's skies glow again," she said.

From Cambridge came word that the students had set fire to the town's paper-salvage dump. In Edinburgh, Scotland, crowds defied the law by building bonfires at crossroads until the Fire Department was called out.

LONDON DELIRIOUS IN V-E CARNIVAL

Hundreds of Thousands Jam Streets—Churchill, King and Queen Join Festival

By DANA ADAMS SCHMIDT
By Cable to THE NEW YORK TIMES.

LONDON, May 8—London today and tonight gave itself up to mass revelry that rivaled and perhaps surpassed that of Armistice Day after World War I.

With gay V-E Day delirium that rose to its climax at midnight—the moment of "cease fire"—hundreds of thousands squirmed and wriggled through a West End that was alive with the uniforms of half the world, with bunting and flags, rattles, police whistles, drums and fireworks.

Searchlights swept the sky, forming great V's, and lit up famous buildings and hotels, Trafalgar Square, Buckingham Palace and St. Paul's Cathedral for the first time in six years, while rockets rose from Piccadilly Circus and thousands danced and sang around bonfires in Hyde Park and in the streets.

Prime Minister Churchill was the darling of the crowd and the King its god. Fifty thousand shouted for "Good old Winnie" in Whitehall and chortled with glee when he nudged the ribs of other dignitaries to make them give the V sign on the balcony of the Ministry of Health.

Churchill Without Cigar

At twenty-five minutes past five o'clock Mr. Churchill appeared with the King on Buckinham Palace balcony. Round about in the streets leading to the Palace the crowd had risen to nearly a quarter of a million.

No, Churchill did not wave or give the V sign. He had no cigar. He just stood and gazed and at that moment a stillness crept over the crowd. Then Mr. Churchill, the man who led Britain to victory, made one deep all-embracing bow and the crowd answered him with a roar—a cry of victory. They pressed forward, laughed and whistled and many had tears in their eyes. Mr. Churchill, too, a few minutes before, as he drove into the Palace, had tears in his eyes.

King George, Queen Elizabeth and Princesses Elizabeth and Margaret Rose appeared seven times during the day and night to wave to the crowds fluctuating between 50,000 and 100,000 from a gold-and-purple-draped balcony of Buckingham Palace.

It scarcely seemed possible after last night's unofficial revelry that enthusiasm could wax ever greater today. But the endless stream of recruits from Greater London were tireless. There was nothing for them to eat and precious little to drink, since the restaurants and pubs were sold out early. Most transport ended before midnight and thousands lay down in the sultry heat of a spring night to sleep in the parks.

And tomorrow is to be another day like this, with the schools closed, shops closed, telephones unanswered, queues at subway stations, buses filled and taxis in hiding.

The taxi companies refused to let their vehicles out when the crowds began taking pleasure in upsetting them. Many West End shopkeepers took the precaution of emptying their show windows before the two-day holiday began.

The crowds were in a mood to cheer everything—every sailor who climbed a lamppost, a soldier in a top hat, a police dog with a red, white and blue dog blanket, or two American and British officers who teetered perilously in the windowsills of a Piccadilly building and tossed down coins and buckets of water.

Fleet Street contributed generously with ticker tape.

At Trafalgar Square the only unhappy creatures were the pigeons who fluttered in distress above a crowd of 100,000 looking for a place to land.

Searchlights in front of the National Gallery lit up the scene as naval officers and girls in front of the Admiralty House pranced round to the old Cockney tune "Knees Up, Mother Brown."

American soldiers who thought the British were reserved tonight felt shy and modest by contrast with the merrymaking Londoners.

Many thoughts during the day, however, turned to those who had not returned for the celebrations. While church bells rang, thousands made solemn pilgrimages to the Cenotaph in Whitehall, and to the Unknown Warrior's Tomb in Westminster Abbey. Even the aisles were jammed for the Monday service at St. Paul's which now stands in an open space left after other buildings were blitzed.

before. Many a woman in the auxiliary services doubtless has been living a more satisfying life than she could in peace. Many an officer now faces a dreary return to a job as a clerk or a cashier or what have you.

All my love to you and Grandma and Eliza, Dana

On May 17, Dana wrote from London:

As so often before, I am writing this a few moments before I leave—on this occasion for Guernsey [the island.] *When I come back, in two or three days it is possible I will leave for Norway with the Norwegian government, if Harold Callender hasn't raised too much of a squawk about my coming back by that time.*

A fine package from you containing Duranty's book[104] *on Russia, two boxes of chocolate dragees and a big chocolate bar arrived the other day and is being enjoyed. Oddly Cy Sulzberger, a later* NY Times *correspondent in Moscow, is here just now. Flew back from Moscow with Mrs. Churchill. He is a good fellow; seems to have become more balanced than in Ankara days.*

I was reflecting last night on the embarrassments of popularity, or being too much wanted. Callender wants me for his staff. London wants me for its. The Army wants me. And you want me, and I want to go home.

Just imagine, I took two whole days off! Hasn't happened for years. But they insist on people working civilized hours in London. So I went to the theater and saw Alfred Lunt and Lynn Fontaine in Love in Idleness.

It was most entertaining. A fair sort of play brilliantly acted, about what happens when a seventeen year old who has been evacuated to Canada comes home after five years and finds his mother living with a cabinet minister. All ends happily, except the cabinet minister loses his job.

I have bought myself a suit of civilian clothes, a hat, two pairs of grey flannels. The suit is a vaguely striped blue sort of business man's thing, extremely dull, but the only thing they had at Moss Bros. that would fit me, more or less.

---

[104] S.J. Taylor, *Stalin's Apologist—Walter Duranty: The New York Times Man in Moscow.*

Buying clothes here is very difficult even it you have the clothes coupons. And if you get a tailor to make some it will take at least three months, because there are so few tailors. With the flannels I am wearing the Harris tweed jacket I bought at Harrod's in '39 and some white shirts I had made in Cairo. Today, however, I have reverted to uniform for the expedition, which is organized by SHAEF.

And speaking of Channel Islands—Yesterday I phoned Ida Treat at her home at Boundary Lodge, Denham Park, near Gerrard's Cross, Bucks. I immediately recognized her voice. She was delighted and has asked me to lunch Sunday, if I'm back from Guernsey. It will be fun.

Dana said, "speaking of Channel Islands," because before the war, we had visited Ida Treat at the Isle de Bréhat, a tiny channel island off the coast of Brittany. She wrote a charming book about the house at Bréhat." [105]

Concerning the island of Guernsey, Dana wrote the following article:

**CHANNEL ISLANDS
ARE SMILING AGAIN**

Bailiff Says Germans 'Behaved Excellently'—Many Leave Offspring on Guernsey

**By DANA ADAMS SCHMIDT
By Cable to THE NEW YORK TIMES.**
ST. PETER PORT, Guernsey, May 18 (Delayed)—The people of the Channel Islands—the only part of the United Kingdom occupied by the Germans—were told by the press and radio today to bring big market baskets to the shops to collect the rations brought in by British ships.

---

[105] Ibid, page 157, footnote 55.

After five years of the German occupation they ate their fill again, and I found the Guernseyites grinning with pleasure tonight as they walked up and down the waterfront, arm and arm with the British soldiers, watching two shiploads of German prisoners pulling out for England.

After months of living on the vegetables that they produce in plenty and on the weekly Red Cross packages sent from England, today they brought cheese, rice, sugar, biscuits, tea and custard powder and received, as gifts from the King, soap, tobacco, chocolate and six ounces of flour a person.

Russians, Jews Reported Slain

Reserving their venom for the captive Russians and Jews here, the Germans apparently treated their only occupied British territory with unaccustomed mildness and the islanders reacted mildly. The mass grave of a thousand Russians and Jews reportedly exterminated on the island of Alderney was being examined today by a criminal investigation officer, a Major Cotton of Sheffield.

Unlike liberated French territory, there have been no arrests of "collaborationists" and no head shaving of women, although there are 230 offspring of German soldiers in Guernsey and more on Jersey. One woman who demanded to marry her German lover was allowed to do so on condition that she depart for Germany.

The argument that many a French collaborator has made in his defense—that he had to act as he did to survive—which the Frenchmen refused to accept, apparently has been accepted here.

The local administration, headed by Bailiff Victor G. Carey, carried on as before, and the Guernsey Parliament, called the States Assembly, was even allowed to meet. Newspapers that appeared during the occupation continue to appear now.

German Actions Praised

The Bailiff said tonight:

"The Germans behaved very excellently. They never pushed anyone off the pavement, and in the shops they stood aside for the women—when there was anything to buy."

He recalled there was one attempt by a newspaper compositor to publish a clandestine newspaper. He was deported to Germany and died in a German concentration camp. On another occasion, the Germans discovered an airplane in a garage, and it was some weeks before they calmed down.

In 1942 the Germans deported all Britishers not born in the islands—about 2,000—to Germany. Another 20,000 were evacuated to England in June 1940, just before the Germans landed. The Bailiff thought these might return within a few months, "as soon as their houses, which the Germans left in filthy condition," have been cleaned up.

And on May 20, with the title **CHANNEL ISLANDS FACE CASH INQUIRY,** [106] Dana wrote about the black market profiteering during the occupation. Mostly French manufactured goods were sold: wines, flour and coal. These were bought and probably smuggled onto the island.

Concerning the concentration camp on the Island of Alderney, it seemed unlikely that the full story would ever be told. About 1,000 Jews and Russians were apparently murdered by beatings and starvation. Two Russian prisoners who were confined in a separate camp said that at least 800 persons died. British officers were investigating the mass graves. Three thousand three hundred Germans were kept on the islands to clear the 250,000 land mines said to be buried. The men were housed on reservations in the center of each island.

Meanwhile, the islanders were returning to their normal affairs—the cultivation of tomatoes and potatoes, keeping cows, and preparing to receive tourists. Tourists were unlikely to be welcomed soon because of the food problem. From the air, the islands normally sparkle with the glass from greenhouses under which vegetables were grown before the war, mainly for the British market. Now, most of the glass was shattered by bombs or had been removed to repair broken windows.

Other things were happening in the English Channel. Ships were able to reach France with many supplies for the Allied Armies in the battle with German Armies, but gasoline was a greater problem. The British devised a system for pumping gasoline under the Channel. Dana described the development of

---

[106] See Appendix for complete article.

these pipelines in an article titled: **20 Fuel Pipelines Under Channel Fed Allied Armies Invading Reich.**

Another remarkable technical advance developed in England and which helped in winning the Battle of the Bulge at Ardennes was called Fido (Fog Investigation Disposal Operation). Dana gives Churchill credit for asking Geoffrey Lloyd, former Minister of Petroleum Warfare, who designed the pipes across the Channel, to solve the problem of the fog on the airfields that even today causes airports to be closed down. Clearing the fog made it possible for planes to take off from England to destroy the vital German supply lines in the Battle of the Bulge. Dana described this interesting solution, which involved a system of flaming petroleum jets around airfields:

**FOG OVER AIRFIELDS
OVERCOME BY "FIDO"**

**British Disclose Invention
That Permitted Fliers
to Land in
Thickest Weather**

**By DANA ADAMS SCHMIDT
By Wireless to THE NEW YORK TIMES.**

LONDON, May 31 (DELAYED)—People were always talking about the weather but nobody ever did anything about it until "Fido" was invented. Fido means "Fog Investigation Dispersal Operations," affectionately know to the Royal Air Force men as "fog, intensive dispersal of."

Geoffrey Lloyd, former Minister of Petroleum Warfare who disclosed the existence of "Pluto," or the pipelines under the Channel, last week, opened up his secret kennels today to display "Fido," which is a system of flaming petroleum jets around airfields to heat the air and disperse fog for landing aircraft.

"Fido's" greatest single claim to fame is that it permitted RAF Pathfinders to fly from England, in spite of heavy fog that blanketed their airfields during

Christmas week, to mark targets for the strategic bombing of German supply lines, which, according to a statement by Field Marshall Gen. Karl von Rundstedt, was the chief cause of the failure of the Ardennes offensive.

Used by 10,000 Airmen

Fifteen British operations airfields in England and one on the Continent were equipped with "Fido." Two thousand, five hundred Allied aircraft, with 10,000 airmen, landed on them in dense fog. Many crippled after air attacks owe their lives to "Fido."

As now used, "Fido" installations consist of a rectangle of three pipes around the landing strip—two on the ground and one above them. The pipes cover an area 2,000 yards long by 150 yards wide. Petroleum is pumped into the upper pipe and flows into the lower ones, which have tiny holes at short intervals. As a man runs along these lower pipes with a torch, a wall of flame bursts from the tiny jets with a roar like a forest fire and about as much smoke. The heat quickly causes the petroleum in the upper pipe to vaporize, after which the smoke subsides.

As the air above the field is heated, the fog is evaporated. Within ten minutes a space 1,000 yards long by 159 feet wide and 100 feet high can be clear.

In calm conditions involving ground fog, clearances of more than 500 feet high have been obtained in six minutes. In more difficult conditions, involving cloud or sea fog and high winds, it is sometimes difficult to reach as high as 100 feet.

30,000,000 Gallons Used

The petroleum burns at a rate of twenty gallons a yard of burner an hour and must raise the air temperature seven degrees Fahrenheit to get clear visibility. About 30,000,000 gallons of fuel were used up to V-E Day.

The idea is to be tried for civil aviation on the new airdrome now being built at Heath Row, Middlesex, which is expected to replace Croyden as London's principal airport. There pipes will cover an area 3,700 yards long by 200 wide. The great cost, however, is expected to limit wider application.

As in the case of "Pluto," the initiative for the fog dispersal operation came from Prime Minister Churchill, who asked Mr. Lloyd to undertake investigations on Sept. 26, 1942, at a time when the bombing offensive was getting under way and fog over the British airfields was rivaling flak over Germany as a cause of casualties.

On May 31, Dana wrote home:

I suppose that now that security regulations are off I could put a proper heading on my letters and speak more precisely about where and what I am up to. But habit is strong. [He was in London.] *I doubt if you were ever unable to figure out what I was doing. The regulations have varied and one was never quite sure where one stood. In some places exceptions were made for war correspondents (who would be able to put all sorts of things into their stories they couldn't mention in letters) and in other places we were subject to all the restrictions.*

I've just had a service message from Turner Catledge of the executive office of the Times *saying that my draft status is 2 A until October fifth of this year. That will be my thirtieth year, so, as far as I can see, the problem is solved, as I don't believe they are taking men thirty or over. Catledge gave no details so I don't know exactly how my status was finally ascertained, whether by reference back to the draft boards or by final decision of Hershey's office.*

Your work for the hospital [editing the Orthopaedic Hospital News] *certainly keeps you mighty busy. I am glad you like doing it; it is certainly in a good cause.*

Later: Well, here's news, whether one likes it or not. I am to return to Paris Friday or Saturday. It appears that the quota situation was been straightened out. You had just switched my Time *and* News Week *subscriptions. One might suppose a connection with the message from Turner Catledge but I do not think so. In any case, I shall continue to fight for the maintenance of my status as war correspondent, though this will be of decreasing importance as time goes on.*

I am writing this in our new office, on the seventh floor of the gorgeous skyscraper-like Reuters *building. While the flying bombs were flying the* Times *preferred its ground floor rooms in the massive Savoy. This is of course a much* more businesslike location. Its chief disadvantage is that you can't ring for a waiter. That will save Times staffers a lot of money.

All the Americans on the staff still live in the Savoy though there is talk of trying to get apartments. One scarcely gathers the flavor of London life in such high falutin' quarters, though they have their advantages in these days—for food, for taxis, for relatively expeditious service of all kinds. Takes them two weeks more to do laundry, however, since their own installations were destroyed during the bombing.

I am indeed happy to have had this interlude in London. It has given me a chance to show the Times that I can work satisfactorily anywhere, not just in Paris, if the interlude in Alsace had not already proved that. It has got me acquainted with a lot more Times men and given me the advantage of knowing how our London office works. And it has given me a new perspective on French affairs and the news generally, which will be useful when I get back. Last but no least, it's given me a number of new friends, such as Clifton Daniel and Sydney Gruson.

Chan Sedgwick is in the office doing a few stories on the Levant before proceeding thither. He has just had two and a half months in America, his first leave home in some five years I believe. But he has a wife in Athens. I did several stories on the Levant while I was here, mostly rewrite of Reuters from various points plus a dash of Schmidt background. About seventy percent of the volume out of here is produced in that manner. How little the reading public suspects the manifold props which a foreign correspondent must use and how rare is a truly original story.

I was interested to know about my two aunts, great aunts. Certainly count me in for their support. It does seem as though the family should be able to produce forty or fifty dollars a month without much trouble. People spend that much for dinner in Paris and never bat an eye. If you would like to increase the amount, I would be glad to make a regular contribution of whatever sum you think suitable.

It is two a.m. and we are nearly ready to begin to fold our tents. I have only done a couple of shorts tonight. Tomorrow I hope to dig up enough material for another weekender on war crimes which I am supposed to do. Am also

doing another piece on wartime engineering miracles, from a press conference. The last time it was Pluto [on the pipelines under the Channel] and made the front page. This time it's called Fido [on dispelling the fog at airports].
  All my love, Mother, to you and Grandma, Eliza and Steinie,
DANA

Dana Adams Schmidt, War Correspondent
APO 413
United Kingdom Base
Care Postmaster, NYC

P.S. I almost forgot to tell about Ida; I spent last Sunday at her house in the country at Denham, after blundering about the countryside for about two hours trying to find it.
  Ida is the same Ida I remember, full of pep and interesting talk and ideas and working on a book and various articles. Her little place, which she and her husband, when he is there, share with an English couple, is absolutely lovely. Out in the real countryside yet half an hour by train from London. We walked in the woods and talked mostly about France and French politics and what we thought of England. . . . If I were staying here longer I would love to see more of her, but she may be going to France herself, if her husband is transferred. He was not at home.
  It began to look as though we would never meet. First I went off to the Channel Islands, then Ida had to put off the date and then I was held up and could not make our tea date on time. Finally I got off the train at the wrong station and had to be taken to my destination by a kindly English bobbie with a motorbike.

June 6:

Somehow I didn't think I would be, but I am back in Paris in the same old chair writing to you on the same old typewriter I've been using the past six months.

What it stacks up to is really that H.C. raised such a continuous howl and got in everybody's hair so much that Public Relations finally winked at the quota and I was brought back. H.C. doesn't really need me here and I am, as before, in the position of having to go out and 'make' my news. What I would like to fix is a setup under which I would be free to depart on periodical sorties to Germany, while retaining my base here. It is absurd, really, to have three full time men on French politics at this time. Cy is still here and he may be able to do something about it.

We have not yet moved into the real NY Times office in the Rue Caumartin, ostensibly because the roof leaks and for various other material reasons, but actually because of inertia and H.C.'s fear of being away from the center of things. Looks like we will be cooped up in this bathroom-sized sitting room till mid July at least. It annoys me not to have a proper desk and chair, not to have adequate telephone facilities, etc., all of which we had in London. That month spoiled me. The London office is a reasonably happy family of sane people; H.C.'s office if definitely pathological. Everything about it is hyper something or other. H.C.'s self-centeredness, his exaggeration of the importance of whatever he is engaged upon, his suspiciousness. Indeed, I fear one of my values to the Times *is my ability to get on with Him in His office. . . . I came back to London exhausted in body and spirit after two weeks of it.*

Be that as it may, Paris is lovely in June, and I mean to enjoy it as best one may enjoy it under present circumstances. Come to think of it everything about Paris is hyper something and on the pathological side. London is nearer to pre-war normal life than anything I have seen in Europe. I am very fed up with things pathological and over-wrought but I fear that is going to be the <u>normal</u> state of affairs in Europe for many a year to come. Standards of what can be regarded as normal are of course variable. What may seem a normal state of affairs to a youngster growing up in a city devastated by bombs and seething with men in uniform would scarcely seem normal to his father who grew up before the last war, or between the two wars, to choose a gross example.

The day I got back I did a piece on British views on treatment of Germany, hard versus soft peace, which may or may not have got in [the paper]. *It was under London dateline. Since then I've had only short pieces on return* of Alsatians and Lorrainers to their homes, requisitioning of clothing for liberated prisoners, D-Day anniversary celebrations, the new Consultative Assembly Session. I may have a fair spate in the next few days, while Harold monopolizes the Syria crisis.

Nice of Bank of America to pay out. You have looked after my affairs extremely well. Don't forget that if any money is needed for your personal needs or for the needs of the family in any way I would be only too happy, and I mean happy, to contribute for the occasion or regularly. I would <u>like</u> to feel that the money I am earning is doing someone some good.

I may in coming months ask the office to pay part of my salary to me here since prices keep on going up, but my needs are slight, especially as long as I'm a bachelor.

I'm sorry I didn't manage to look up the Malcolms while I was in England. Now that I've broken the ice, however, the chances of my going to England again are good.

This time I have a room to myself in the Hotel Scribe, though I don't mind sharing as much as many people do. It's on the ground floor however, and rather noisy, next to an office which tends to clatter.

All my love to you, Dana

Following is the article on the D-Day celebration which Dana mentioned :

**QUIET BEACH RITES
WILL RECALL D-DAY**

**French Officials in Normandy
to Give Thanks to Allies on
Landing Anniversary**

**By DANA ADAMS SCHMIDT
By Wireless to THE NEW YORK TIMES.**
PARIS, Wednesday, June 6—One year after D-day, at thirty minutes past midnight last night, the church bells rang and the sirens shrieked in

Normandy, commemorating the landing of the liberating American, British and Allied forces.

This morning a representative of Gen. Dwight D. Eisenhower and American, British and French officers and diplomats will gather on the beach of Saint-Laurent-sur-Mer in Calvados, then move on to the beaches at Vierville at Sainte-Marie-du-Mont and at the foot of the cliffs of Arromanches, where they will gaze upon the hulks of invasion craft, still jutting from the water, and in brief memorial services will pay tribute to the men who died there.

The French Ministers for War, the Navy and for Air, André Diethelm, Louis Jacquinot and Charles Tillion, will express France's gratitude in speeches at Bayeux and Sainte-Mère-Église.

Throughout France newspapers will be authorized as an exception to appear in full-size format instead of the usual half-page size. Otherwise no special observations are planned.

A year ago Gen. Charles de Gaulle had arrived in London from Algiers after a long hesitation, just in time for the landings. He had refused to allow the use of French officers for liaison with the French civilians to take part in the first wave because no agreement on the relations of military and civil authorities had been concluded, and he feared that French sovereignty would not be respected.

During the night the British Broadcasting Corporation sent out the message, "The fox likes grapes," to the French Underground, and the French Forces of the Interior fell upon the German lines of communication with a military success that astonished the Allied Command.

The next day, when the invasion was in full swing General de Gaulle waited for five hours after General Eisenhower had broadcast to the French people, then broadcast a message saying that the Allies had undertaken "the virtual seizure of power" in France. He was gravely concerned about the French banknotes printed in America that the liberating forces carried with them.

The 4,000 ships and the 11,000 aircraft that formed the spearhead of landings swelled in succeeding months into an avalanche that not only crushed Germany but left in its wake a liberated but devastated France.

A year later Frenchmen are free but their economy is still creaking and they are worse fed and worse clothed than they were under the German occupation.

General de Gaulle's position as chief of the French Government now is unchallenged; French sovereignty is unblemished and all French money is in process of being exchanged. But General de Gaulle is still at odds with his allies.

The article concerning British views on treatment of Germany, hard versus soft peace, which he wrote on arrival back in Paris, was published with a London dateline. In part, he wrote:

While there appears to be a sort of gentleman's agreement to keep the issue off election platforms just now, it is none the less profound and growing. The Conservatives tending to take the hard and Labor the soft view.

At one extreme is Lord Vansittart and his "win the peace" movement, which begins with the premise that "all Germans are guilty" even if they share in that guilt in varying degrees, and that Adolf Hitler was the perfect expression of their spirit, aspirations, resentments, hopes and hates. At the other extreme is the National Peace Council, whose leading figures are Victor Gollanez, leftist publisher; Prof. Harold J. Laski of the University of London and Prof. Norman Bentwich of the University of Jerusalem. They take the line that the Germans are fundamentally good, that they were victimized by the Nazis and were as much sinned against by the rest of the world as sinning.

.... Gerald Bailey, director of the National Peace Council, put his views this way:

The trend away from vindictiveness concerning Germany is desirable and inevitable. The devastation of Germany, which has made the question of a menace a dead issue must be seen in Europe's terms. Europe needs German productive power to regain prosperity. The real danger to peace is in the rivalry of the great powers; it will not come from Germany unless our policy lays the foundation for a German revolution.

We must withdraw From Germany as soon as possible, encourage all democratic elements and bring Germany back into the family of nations. The process of re-education cannot be accomplished under constraint or by non-fraternization, which can only make enemies of those Germans who should be our friends.

The reports that we have suppressed anti-Nazi movements and attempted to decentralize Germany are found alarming and will merely set in motion new forces struggling for unity. It is impossible to maintain a political vacuum.

On June 11, Dana wrote proudly:

Well here's news: Your son has received the Croix de Guerre, or at least the certificate entitling him to it. I had heard some rumors about it from various French correspondents but nothing official 'till this morning when one of the PR majors rang me up and asked me to come to his office.

The certificate reads as follows: "Premiere Armee Francaise, Ordre Generale No 775, Le General d'Armee de Lattre de Tassigny, Commandant la Premiere Francaise cite a l'ordre du Corps d'Armee, S C H M I D T Dana, Correspondant de Guerre du New York Times, *pour services de guerre rendus en cooperation avec les Troupes Francaises; la presente citation comporte l'attribution de la Croix de Guerre avec l'etoile de Vermeil" signed May 28, 1945, J. de Lattre.*

A paper that goes with it states that it was issued "Apres accord des autorites Americaines" and mentions a Lt. Col. Shumaker, a Major Harrison and a Captain Stoen who were similarly honored.

I am quite childishly pleased about it. I have after all spent a fair amount of time with the French army and have at one time or another been quite seriously shot at while in the company of the French. More seriously in Italy, as a matter of fact, than in France. I don't suppose any other American correspondent has written so much about the French army—although a great deal of what I wrote for the UP *was lost in the agency shuffle. Not that I was doing it for their sake, though I came to feel affection and a certain admiration for them.*

A club of those who have been attached to French army press camps is being started in Paris and I will join.

(The big boss, Arthur Hays Sulzberger is here, waiting for his visa for Moscow. He is a very likeable man and appears to have enormous prestige. He was the only non-diplomat, non-military personality invited to de Gaulle's

dinner for Eisenhower last night, and in the course of the evening both de Gaulle and Eisenhower took pains to take him aside and talk to him. In the case of de Gaulle it was almost unprecedented. All not for publication stuff of course.)

At this dinner, de Gaulle presented Eisenhower with the Cross of Liberation. Dana wrote about this event and the honor. The headline read: **EISENHOWER GETS TOP FRENCH HONOR.** [107]

Dana continued:

Cy Sulzberger is here too and seems to have decided to set up shop here indefinitely. He is bringing his wife up from Athens. We will be quite a formidable crew. Harold is still talking about getting some more people for our staff. I think he and some of the higher ups are overstating the possible postwar importance of Paris. London is the place for the big headquarters, say I.

Haven't had any mail from you since I got back as there has been a post office snafu and everything for us, even that forwarded from London, has been forwarded to Frankfurt. Same snafu that occurred when headquarters was moving from Algiers to Naples.

But a fine big package from you containing a magnificent wealth of chocolate bars has turned up. That is grand. I guess I have a sweet tooth that I'm not likely to outgrow now.

I'm glad that the trip to Norway didn't pan out. It would have been interesting and fun but would have meant several weeks waiting around and absence from the great news centers. Furthermore it's important that I should have met Arthur Hays.

Had a delightful dinner a few nights ago in a little bistro, the kind Paris is famous for. Dudley Harmon, the UP *girl reporter and I had planned to go out to the country, but I was too late finishing my work so we had a crack at a little place called Armagnac in the Rue des Saints Peres, or something like*

---

[107] For the full text concerning this honor see Appendix.

that. We provided our own strawberries which they prepared with cognac in the absence of cream. Excellent. There was steak and fried potatoes and soup and two wines, for all of which the proprietor apologized profusely because all the good food had been eaten up. One reason why there's never enough food for the official rations in the country is that a certain fraction of the population eats too damn well.

Well, all my love till next week. Hope your letters will be coming along soon. Dana

And the following week, on June 20:

The mail is still going astray, which is most annoying, but there is nothing to be done about it. Before I forget, henceforth my correct address is as follows:
c/o Public Relations Office
Headquarters, Com Z, APO 887, US Army

That is the address for those correspondents who intend to remain in Paris, while those who move to Germany will take our old APO with them.

Believe it or not, Harold Callender broke down and went away for a week's holiday, somewhere in Normandy where there is lots of butter and eggs and sunshine. So I am having a field day writing foreign affairs, etc., not that it is easy to pick up the threads over night.

I have discovered why Harold was talking about getting two more men for the bureau. There is a plan to send Archie to South Africa, . . . to open a NYT bureau. It appears that he suggested it about a year ago and that the big boss, Arthur H., decided to let him have a shot at it. It would be a break for Archie and I'm sure he would do it very well, even though he is French and has scarcely had anything to do with South Africa before. He is quite elderly, not too keen on physical effort, but he is mighty keen and I would trust his judgment any day.

Couple of nights ago I had drinks with Carla Ogle at her apartment and mess. Nice girl. Last night I likewise had drinks and dinner with Dudley Harmon. Nice girl too.

Apart from rushing rather continuously about Paris in pursuit of information I haven't been up to much. Can you send me a pair of size eleven and a half tennis shoes? I tried to get some in England and I tried in France and I tried the Red Cross *and all has failed. Here I still have my fine new balls and a new racket and I'm not using them at all.*

I'm a little worried as to what to do with FORD. *I have not managed to arrange to get gas regularly or legitimize its somewhat informal origins and it's costing me money all the time for the garage. I have been thinking of turning it over to the nearest ordnance company but I know I would regret it as soon as I had done so.*

I trust you are all well, Grandma, the baby, Steinie and all,
Love,
Dana

On the following day, June 22, Dana continued:

I went down to mail my letter [of June 20] *and found yours of June 11 in my box, so I'll write an addendum and answer some of your questions.*

Yes, I flew over [the Channel] *in an RAF Dakota transport as it happened. It's all the same, sometimes they put you on a British plane and sometimes on an American one. Nice thing about the British one is that they give you tea and sandwiches while you're sailing over the Channel.*

Gladwin Hill is an ex A.P. man who is among the large number of A.P. men hired by Ray Daniell. He is a nice friendly fellow and evidently a good reporter. But, from my talks with him I'd say he was politically positively brainless and hence unlikely to tarry long in Europe. He is one of those fellows who lies back and issues pronunciamentoes like: "These damn Europeans, why don't they get together like we do. I think if we leave them alone, and let them put each other in concentration camps and kill each other off if they want to" etc.

This type of mentality disturbs and annoys me, but it is worth bearing in mind that it is representative of a large part of the American army. Thank God we had a Supreme Commander who was not only a soldier but a diplomat who really understood and felt the situation of the countries in which he was operating. The average American, enlisted man and officer, lives isolated from the 'natives,' surrounded by his work, his movies, funnies, Red Cross *clubs,* USO *shows and other Americana. He goes through Europe unseeing and unfeeling, except in so far as fellow soldiers are concerned, and thinks only of going home. Of course there are a million exceptions, but I'm convinced that is the gross, overall picture.*

Ida's husband has a job in an English port and circulates frequently between it and their home at Denham. I didn't meet him, but apart from being ardently Gaullist I believe he has no very violent political inclinations. I don't know in how far Ida shared her first husband's opinions, but she struck me as being merely a liberal now. We had a long talk during which I insisted that the protection of the individual, his rights, integrity and safety is a more urgent issue in Europe at the present time than social and economic injustice. The police state is the terrible menace, I said, regardless of what brand of political formulas it uses to rationalize itself. Some of the professional left wingers would say that was reactionary talk, but I don't think Ida did.

Apparently, in response to Mother's comments concerning the political views of Linette and Yvonne, Dana wrote:

I'm looking forward to seeing Linette, Topek and Yvonne Sadoul. I do NOT think the entire world is going to be socialized into Socialist Republics in two years, or 20, for that matter. I trust not, if she means that we are all going to be part of the USSR especially. I know my Communists, at least the French ones, and I've known some fancy brands of Fascists, and believe me we don't want totalitarianism, authoritarianism or any other variety of state tyranny.

(Socialism is of course a great ideal; the difficulty is that it so easily leads to vast concentrations of power in the hands of just as ruthlessly and on an infinitely larger scale than ever "trusts," the "corporations," "Wall Street," etc. All absolute solutions, socialist, or fascist, are bad. The situation becomes more complex and more vicious when, as in France, the communist party pretends to aspire to the socialist ideal, but is really merely the tool of a foreign power

and maintains itself be maneuvers of pure expediency and by bamboozling the ignorant with slogans.)

(The only political forms which can possibly lead people to health and happiness, or at least avoid large scale misery, are those based on compromise, like the compromises of everyday human life. Compromise between socialism and liberal capitalism as it has been worked out in Britain and Sweden. Enough socialism to keep economic problems in hand, enough liberal capitalism to keep the state in check. Habeas corpus, les droits de l'homme [human rights], *and NO concentration camps. The true idealism of our times, say I, is to be found somewhere around the center. NOT at extreme left or right.)*

I seem to have got rather far afield and possibly not too clear.

Anyway, it may give you an idea of the drift of my thought. For your information, D.H. [Dudley Harmon whom he had mentioned in an earlier letter] *is tall and blond and broad shouldered and comes from Boston. She is a good newspaper woman if not brilliant and attractive if not beautiful.*

"Statistics on Japan" was some dope I dug up for Markel [Lester Markel, Sunday editor of the *Times*] *for a map on Japanese dispositions. Can't think why he didn't get it in Washington.*

I guess I've already made my request for the next package—tennis shoes. I fear they may be difficult to find even in L.A. As for clips, I am pleased to see my own if you have any spares, but I don't want to take them away from your book of clippings. We are getting a rather sporadic service of Paris clippings from the New York office now. Otherwise, almost anything you see in newspapers or magazines you think would be of particular interest to me; I get so little time for reading outside of the French daily newspapers that I am delighted when something else is drawn to my attention. And so far I've enjoyed everything you've sent me. I'm getting Time, Newsweek and *the* New Yorker *and manage to dip into them with some regularity.*

I do hope you are going to take a crack at writing that book. It is so terribly hard to get started, as I well know. But I know you have a lot to say. Not only about our own life, I should say, but perhaps also a section about Grandpa's?

I just had a talk with Cy about my going to Germany. He is most anxious to stop all the quarrelling among staffers by confining them to their respective

zones of operation. And mine ain't Germany he says. But he thinks he might arrange a trip for me in a few months, when current quarrels have died down.
All my love, as ever,
Dana

In 1941, when Dana was in Ankara, he reported on the British and the Free French forces as they fought and freed Syria from the Vichy invasion. Syria, strategically situated for access to the oil of Iraq from the Mediterranean, was of great interest to the Germans. At the end of this intervention, an agreement had been made between Britain and the Free French, delegating control of Syria and Lebanon to the French. France had long had an interest in the Levant, and following World War One, Syria and Lebanon had been made French mandates.

Now, in 1945, British influences were fomenting unrest and riots against the French in Syria. France suggested a five-power conference to mediate this problem. Dana reported this development in an article published on June 23 with the heading **French Challenge Britain on Levant.** [108]

Following his interest in French politics, Dana attended the first national congress of the French Communist party—now with a strength of some 906,000 members. Maurice Thorez spoke for an incredible five hours, reviewing the last eight years of communist policy and criticizing the French industrialists and the de Gaulle government. Dana summarized and commented on the speech in his report published on June 26 and **reproduced in the Appendix.**

While problems between the French and British brewed in Syria, at the eastern end of the Mediterranean, problems were developing in Tangier at the far western end.

An ancient international city, Tangier lies at the gateway to the Mediterranean on the Atlantic shores of Morocco, within sight of Gibraltar. Its history includes the Berbers, Phoenicians, Carthaginians, Greeks, Romans, Portuguese and Spaniards. All the great powers of Europe—Britain, France, Germany, in addition to the Portuguese and Spaniards, have vied to control

---

[108]   See ftn. 104, page 358, and Appendix.

Tangier in modern times. Several international conferences attempted to solve the differences and ambitions of these states. In 1906, a conference of 13 nations took place at Algeciras (Spain). Czarist Russia and the United States participated, and Tangier became an international free port. In 1923, new problems caused another international conference to be held. Turkey surrendered rights to Tangier, and Britain, France and Spain agreed to continuing the international zone. The early importance of Tangier to European nations is shown by the gift of Tangier as dowry to Catherine Braganza of Portugal upon her marriage to Charles II in 1662. Tangier was thus transferred to the English crown, and during Charles II's reign, the port was heavily fortified. In 1684, Tangier was returned to Morocco. British trade and influence dominated until 1912, when Morocco, including Tangier, became a French protectorate. At the Tangier Convention of 1923, Tangier became an international city and port governed by a commission representing Britain, France, Spain, Portugal, Italy, Belgium, the Netherlands, Sweden and later, the United States. Tangier remained an international zone except for a period during World War II when Spain took control. In July 1945, a conference was planned to discuss the Spanish administration and a return to international status. Before the conference began, Russia asked, or demanded, to be included.

The Russians cited their interest in Tangier as early as the Algeciras Conference in 1906. The French pointed out that this was under the Czarist regime and was not valid in the present Soviet Union. Also, they noted that Russia was not a signatory to the 1923 Convention on Tangier. [109]

Dana wrote that the United States backed Russia in her demands to participate in the conference. He discussed these problems in articles published on July 2 and 4. [110]

With the problems of Tangier temporarily behind him, Dana turned to the political scene in Paris. A new French Constitution was to be written in the fall. De Gaulle was expected to insist on the election of a two-house Parliament—a Chamber of Deputies [or National Assembly] and a Senate. All left-wing and

---

[109] See Appendix: postponement of Tangier Conference, July 17.
[110] See Appendix.

resistance groups were demanding a single-chamber Assembly. Dana discussed various aspects of this problem in an article published on July 6. [111]

In his letter of July 8, Dana tells about moving to the new office of the *Times*:

We've been in the new office [in the Rue Caumartin] *a week now and are finding it more satisfactory. A change of environment like the changes in every one's state of mind. We are up high, above the surrounding houses with a view out to the copper dome of the Opera. The office is almost entirely glass enclosed, with windows that slide back and forth horizontally. Unfortunately the Germans or somebody walked off with our curtains and we haven't been able to replace them yet, so the place is a bit like a greenhouse when the sun comes streaming in. And in winter it is going to be extremely hot.*

The words The New York Times *are distributed over three floors on the exterior of the building and attract visitors. One day a couple of sergeants came in to borrow a typewriter. As far as I could see they wanted to forge a pass, but that was none of my business. Others come for a subscription to the overseas weekly which we cannot give them. We sell only at Army Post Exchanges, although I did manage exceptionally to have Bob Brown put on the mailing list. While he was in town we had cocktails with the nieces of Turkish Ambassador Numan Menemencioglu whom we knew while we were in Turkey.*

We now have two telephone operators and a dwarf office boy. The dwarf is an old member of the staff who has been working in the photo department of late. We had some pictures taken of the whole staff during the reception for Mr. Sulzberger which I will try to send to you.

Of great concern to French families at this time was the return of their men who had been taken prisoner. The American and British had sent most of their prisoners home, although some were ill and could not be transported, but many French prisoners remained in Russia. In an article published on June

---

[111]   See Appendix.

30, Dana reported a French and Russian agreement to return some 500,000 French men to France. [112]

In an effort to make life less expensive and more interesting to American troops in France, the French government cut production and transaction taxes on many items, such as perfumes and souvenirs of interest to the men. Plans were made to allow the enlisted men to see more of France than Paris, with the idea of interesting them in returning to France as visitors after the war. Dana discussed this in an article published in the *Times* on July 8.

While these constructive measures were being enacted, the Consultative Assembly had serious problems concerning Algeria to consider. Many had hoped that Algeria could be assimilated by France, but the May riots in Algiers that killed many people indicated serious opposition to French rule. Dana discusses this and the trend toward nationalism favored by some members of the elite classes in his report on the Consultative Assembly published on July 11. [113]

Aside from her interest in the political scene and great world events, Mother had questioned Dana in her last letter about "the girl" whom he had mentioned. Mother had often expressed the hope that Dana would find such a girl. He wrote on August 1:

(Your last letter lays some emphasis on "the girl." Now I don't mean at all that it might not be "the girl," but it is by no means certain. I fear I have talked more to you about it than to her. But we will see. It would make me ever so happy to be able to give away that diamond solitaire and pin.)

I've been down to Reims for a visit to the redeployment center and think I got a couple of pretty good stories out of it. Tomorrow I'm going to Compiegne to a prisoner camp where young teenage Germans are supposed to be denazified. That should be good too and I'll be interested to hear how I did on both pieces. (Cable just came in asking for more redeployment dope.)

---

[112] See Appendix.
[113] See Appendix.

You will have noticed I made the front page with a story on Laval [114] *the other day, but Archie is still handling the trials* [the Nuremberg trials]. *I am not displeased at present with my position. Harold is tied up with high diplomacy and Archie is tied down to the courtroom while I enjoy the spice that is variety. In some of my pieces in the past few weeks I've had opportunity to "write" more than ever before and I have enjoyed it.*

Let me join in another guffaw over Hank Gorrell's article. I'll forgive him though, it is tough going getting into the Post. *It is unfortunately a sort of backhanded self-glorification which rings phoney. We are all, I think, awfully fed up with phoneyness. We have so much of it in our journalism, radio and above all in advertising. That, I feel, is the real explanation of the popularity of Ernie Pyle, Mauldin, and the Sad Sack cartoon. There is no pretense about them, nothing phoney, and G.I.'s and lots of other Americans, in spite of their wise-guy veneer, like it that way.*

But I must add that of all war correspondents Hank is one of those who has seen most of the war—in a real front line sort of way. He is the guy who gave me my first and best advice about what a war correspondent should and should not do in the field. That was on the train between Alexandria and Cairo just after I came down from Turkey.

I had a brief drink with Cy Sulzberger earlier today and mentioned my two current aspirations: 1. To get home, and 2. To visit Germany. He began with a suggestion that I take a holiday in Switzerland instead of going to America, but I jumped on that hard, so he said he thought it was up to Harold. Harold is still after that apartment in which to install his wife; I got him one good lead and will keep my eyes peeled for more.

It is rather warm. I want to write a sort of "Mid Summer Night's Dream" feature about Paris. It's one of those things I've had in mind for a long time. Originally it was going to be a Paris in Spring feature. Now that I've mentioned

---

[114]   Pierre Laval. French politician known as a despicable traitor and known for his collaboration with the Vichy government under Pétain. He assisted in the deportation of Jews to Nazi death camps and sent French laborers to work in German factories; and, in every way, aided the enemy. After the liberation of France, he was tried for treason and executed at Fresnes prison. See Appendix.

it maybe I'll write it tomorrow. By the way, did you ever see a feature I did about marriage between G.I.'s and French girls? It was signed Callender, though it was mine.

All my love now to you and Grandma and Eliza and Ken and Steinie and the baby, and little Torrey Pines. There's a pet shop up on the Champs Elysees full of cute puppies panting in the heat; I felt sorry for them. Dana

On August 8, two days after the U.S. dropped the first atomic bomb on Hiroshima, Dana wrote a piece on the probable effects [of the end of the war] on American troops, with the title **Deployment Hitch seen in Quick End.**

Some troops which were scheduled for shipment to the Pacific would suddenly become eligible for returning to the United States. 318,000 men had been shipped to the United States in July en route to the Pacific either to be part of a strategic reserve or possibly, to be discharged. The large number of men sent was due to the fact that the men were so eager to return to the U.S. that they "gladly squeezed into ships beyond their usual capacity." The number to be shipped to the U.S. in August was 171,000. Even if the war in the Pacific did not end, redeployment from Europe to the United States would decline gradually until June 1946, when it was scheduled to be complete. The number of men to be sent directly to the Pacific was not disclosed, but was said not to be influenced by the gradual deployment from Europe to the United States. The shipping of troops had to be carefully planned because shipping space was needed to supply the troops already in the Pacific.

On August 14, Dana wrote his regular letter home, but he did not yet know that Emperor Hirohito had surrendered on that day, and the war was to be officially ended the following day. He wrote in this letter that:

The end of the war [in Europe and the Far East] has made news from here more or less irrelevant, although we still manage to produce quite a wad of copy each day. I've been covering the socialist congress, in case it hasn't been signed. [115]

---

[115] See Appendix.

Among important decisions was the Socialists' rejection of the plan for organic unity with the Communist party. The Secretary General Daniel Mayer explained the Socialists' rejection of the plan:

When one day there is an important change in Russian foreign policy and the French Communist party does not follow it, then we shall have a situation permitting full unity with the Communists. If we fused with the Communists, he added, "I wonder whether we would be in a position to say that the Japanese capitulation was not exclusively the result of Russian achievements, but perhaps also due to the efforts of the American, British and Chinese."

Cy's wife is grappling with the problems of living in Paris as a civilian plus bringing up a baby. She has a very efficient nurse who terrorizes her and everybody else. Yesterday she accused Marina of eating the baby's cheese. I wouldn't have thought cheese was good for babies anyway. I always heard it wasn't good for dogs.

I didn't write the medical story although I spent the better part of two days on it and quite a lot of army gasoline. I just decided that I didn't know enough of what I was talking about, a scruple I have rarely indulged in before.

I am caught between two fires, of a sort, at the moment. On the one hand I would like to continue this letter. On the other hand our pretty young telephone operator is wistfully demanding the use of my typewriter in order to type god knows what. I guess she wins, now that I'm on to the illegible second page. [Dana sometimes typed on both sides of very thin airmail paper, which made these letters incredibly hard to read.]

He signed off with his usual:
All my love to all of the family, Dana

On August 24, Dana began his letter with a lengthy explanation of its lateness:

Since Harold went away to the States, Archie has taken a few days to go to see his son in London and I have been having my hands rather more than full. Cy doesn't interfere with day to day coverage at all. So instead of clamoring for more scope as in the past, I had so much scope I didn't know what to do.

Harold has gone home for a holiday that may last a month or more. He has promised to phone you. I don't know what he will say about my vacation, but a few weeks back he assured me that I would be able to get away to the States when he got back to Paris. Since Harold left there has been a new development:

Cy Sulzberger, who is handling staff problems for the whole of Europe, told me that he was trying to arrange for me to leave on a vacation at home in October or November and wanted to know whether I would be willing to work in Germany when I came back. After some thought I told him I was not keen to work in Germany as a permanent assignment, but would like to go for a limited period. The matter is still there and depends on the result of Cy's cabled discussions with the New York office and the general progress of staff 'redeployment' in Europe. Harold doesn't know about Cy's proposal, so you'd better not mention it to him.

Archambault is scheduled to leave for South Africa in the next few months and a man whose name escapes me who was in the Paris bureau before the war is to come here to replace him.

I think these developments will please you. I think I succeeded in impressing Cy with the urgency of my getting home this year. His problem of course is that everybody on the European staff wants to go home just now.

I am so distressed about Torrey. Our poor little dog. How one does get to love a dog. I remember when I left Turkey I thought it would break my heart to leave the two dogs we had then to uncertain care; they were the one thing for which I wanted to cry when I left Ankara. I hope and pray Torrey will be all right. Certainly if anyone can pull him through it is Steinie.

And regarding the end of the war in the Pacific, he wrote:

I share your feelings of disgust at the public demonstrations over the end of the war. I'm afraid we are likely to have a new version of the jazz age that followed the end of the other war. But only in the U.S. I'd say; the only country that seems to have got temporary prosperity out of this war. Some well meaning people forget that this was a defensive war, not a crusade. We fought to keep what we had and carry on the way we were, to avoid something worse. We were not fighting for something better, at least not to start out with. It is the old thing that has won, especially in the U.S. It would be a mistake to attach exaggerated importance to the Labor victory in England I think, but at least England and the other countries that have suffered more are sober minded.

This morning I went swimming at the Racing Club. It is really a swank place in the Bois de Boulogne. The pool is delightful and the tennis courts are laid out in an informal uncrowded sort of way surrounded by gardens. We, a Reuters correspondent I knew in the Middle East, and I, went in the morning and had the place about to ourselves. We went on special chits from the Army which are rather a nuisance to get. That's why I hadn't gone before. But during what is left of the summer (if I don't take off for California) I plan to get in a little tennis out there.

No word from the Sadouls since they came through Paris. Wonder if you ever had word from Ida? I'll try to see the Tanieres again. I'm afraid I haven't been very good about that sort of thing.

With Harold gone the office car is more at my disposal and it is much easier to get around. It makes a tremendous difference in what you can get done and what it costs you in effort. I have kept poor old FORD on ice all this time, largely because I can't make up my mind what to do with him. At one point I was determined to turn FORD in but when I went out to the garage and looked at him and smelled his dear greasy red leather seats I was filled with nostalgia and paid up another month's rent to keep him. I guess what I need is a wife to make up my mind for me sometimes.

All my love to you and Steinie, Grandma and Eliza and Ken.

Although Dana had hoped to write a romantic story about mid-summer in Paris, when the opportunity came, he found Paris was not the romantic Paris he had imagined. His article published on August 26 describes a sordid picture "where underfed Parisians have been celebrating the 'heroic week' of their liberation, and well-fed American troops want to go home."

. . . But some of the Parisians are not underfed and know where to get a good meal as before the war without going to the country and where to buy candy and corned beef, etc. Some of them, sharp-eyed fellows with francs in their pockets are hanging around the Red Cross Club, where Americans back from Germany with cameras and watches and fountain pens are also hanging around nonchalantly.

Last year this time it was a heroic week. The Americans were heroic, the men of the resistance were heroic, and everybody kissed everybody. But this year nobody feels very heroic. The men of the resistance say: "We are not very sure what we wanted, but it was not this," and the only people who kiss the Americans are the peroxide blondes with thin legs and dirty bare feet in wooden-soled shoes.

Paris is not only underfed and shabby, but tired and touchy, paradoxical, psychopathic and tense: "Yes, it is a moral crisis," and the people whose business it is to worry about French-American relations worry.

. . . . The liberated no longer love their liberators, and vice versa. The Frenchmen wish the Americans would go away, which is all the Americans desire.

Not a very romantic midsummer night's dream.

On August 29, Dana wrote in a happier vein:

I was glad to get your letter saying Torrey was better. If—and it is not yet certain—I get away for that long awaited vacation in October or November, I hope to see him in good shape again.

It is now pretty certain that Lansing Warren will arrive in a week or so to join our staff. He is to replace Archambault but will make up for the absence of Callender in the meantime. I am told he is a very agreeable middle-aged sort of guy, unassuming and intelligent.

You are indeed right in describing Archie as a "wise old owl." He is as near to the tradition of the tough cynical newspaperman with the heart of gold as a Frenchman can come. Apparently Callender left him a note when he left saying he should cover the Quai d'Orsay [the French foreign office and political center] during Callender's absence, but Archie has no taste for it, as Harold doubtless knew. So I am doing that, as during previous periods of the kind.

We have had a general "downhold" request during the landings in Japan for obvious reasons so I am somewhat restricted.

A few nights ago Cy and his wife Marina had a number of friends including me in to play "The Game" the significance of which is known only to veterans of a certain period in Turkey. It is a kind of charades which was all the rage in Ankara at one time. On Sunday I am having them and a few other friends in to my room at the Scribe to consume my monthly liquor ration. (We have been getting a bottle of whiskey and a half bottle of gin per month but it is likely to be cut out soon.) Yes, I invited Dudley Harmon too, 'en priorite.' The phone just rang and a gent named Apple who is chief liaison officer between the provost Marshal and the French police accepts for himself and his wife. They are a very charming couple.

We have a new office boy named Roger, aged 15, former bellboy at the Scribe, an engaging underfed child. He learned to operate the telephone switchboard a lot quicker that I could have done.

Speaking of being underfed, did you read my story dated August 25 about "Paris in August?" It was an impressionistic sort of thing, a bit on the experimental side, and I don't know yet whether they used it. I hoped it would be printed the day de Gaulle was in New York.

There's not a very great deal to report. All my love, as always, to you all,
Dana

On the same day, Dana wrote to me directly:

Dear Elizabeth;
Goodness knows I certainly do owe you a letter, from away back. Yours written for my birthday [September 6] *came through with speed and precipitated this reply.*

I am delighted to hear that our family is going to be further enlarged. [I was pregnant with John.] *'Tis an extraordinary miracle, this business of babies, isn't it, especially when it happens in your own family. More interesting than atomic bombs, I think, even if it has been going on for quite a while.*

Had I had my wits about me I would have thought of a birthday present for little Margaret [August 11]. *Well, if I'm real lucky I might get to California in time to give you a belated present for your birthday.* [October 6] *It looks as though something like that were in the mill. What an adventure that will be, going home. My idea is that I will refuse to do anything constructive during my vacation in America. I intend to be completely passive and relax and forget about newspapers and politics and telephones and drink lots of ice cream sodas and double chocolate malted milk shakes.*

In England a doctor who was treating fellows who had suffered in German prisoner of war camps told me the thing they wanted and appreciated most, that seemed to represent the life they had lost, was ice cream. I suppose it would be hard to find a better characterization of America than "ice cream land." Not bad, don't you think?

Architecture must be breaking loose in a big way in California now that the war is over. Wonder what Ken's plans are. Everybody going back east may not be so good. I'll have to do a real good piece about the architectural styles and ideas in French reconstruction plans before I go home, just to keep the family au courant. If you want something special from Paris just speak up. (I won't promise to get it though; very hard to buy things.)

Linette told me you still speak French. I'll give you a little workout when I get home. Haven't heard from her or her mother since they came through Paris.

Well, they wouldn't be mentioning my getting the Croix de Guerre in the New York Times. A lot of people get it. They might theoretically, since I am a member of the staff, but there is a slight awkwardness about its being based mainly on the work I did as a UP *correspondent. Anyway, I showed it to the Publisher when he was here.*

Oh, my goodness, I forgot to mention in my letter to Mother that I have also been recommended for some sort of campaign ribbon. Mother asked about that in a recent letter. You can't just hang one of those things on your chest in this theater, although I suspect that certain people do at home. Anyway the campaign ribbon doesn't mean much, although I rather like my Croix

It is hot as hell in Paris just now.
All my love Eliza, to you and Margaret and Ken,
Dana
I am sorry this is such a messy letter, but I am rather tired.

In spite of the heat in Paris, Dana continued to produce a wealth of articles:

U.S. ARMY PIPELINE IN FRANCE FOR SALE revealed something probably few people knew about. In Dana's words:

The pipeline, which has been declared surplus, runs from Marseille on the Mediterranean 487 miles northward to Sarrebourg in two strings of pipe, one six-inch and the other four-inch. Its sixty-five pumping stations pumped 3,000,000 barrels of motor fuel for the American Seventh and the French First Armies at an average of 15,000 barrels daily.

Disposal of the eastern extension of the line across the Rhine to Sandhofen in Germany has not yet been decided.

In the same article, Dana reported that American soldiers were largely responsible for almost completely rehabilitating the ports of Cherbourg and Rouen, while Le Havre and Marseille had been made usable for military purposes, and Brest partly rehabilitated. Several smaller ports were cleared of wrecks and obstructions.

U. S. ARMY PIPELINE IN FRANCE FOR SALE

Rhone Valley System Is Put on Surplus List Together With 82,000 Vehicles

DANA ADAMS SCHMIDT
By Wireless to THE NEW YORK TIMES.

PARIS, Aug. 31—The Army and Navy Liquidation Commission disclosed today that 82,000 United States Army vehicles and the American Army's Rhone Valley oil and gasoline pipeline system are to be disposed of as surplus property.

The vehicles, the sale of which the War Department authorized "as they become excess" as a result of redeployment, include 25,000 jeeps, 25,000 half-ton trucks and an assortment of motorcycles, trailers, ambulances, gasoline tank trucks and other trucks.

Their sale will be a "shot in the arm" for the French and other European transportation systems, even though representing only a small fraction of the needs of their dislocated civilian economies.

The American Army in the European Theatre of Operations at present disposes of 528,382 vehicles of all kinds.

The pipeline, which has been declared surplus, runs from Marseille on the Mediterranean 487 miles northward to Sarrebourg in two strings of pipe, one six-inch and the other four-inch. Its sixty-four pumping stations pumped 3,000,000 barrels of motor fuel for the American Seventh and the French First Armies at an average of 15,-000 barrels daily.

Disposal of the eastern extension of the line across the Rhine to Sandhofen in Germany has not yet been decided.

The American Service Forces headquarters, in a review of its contributions to the rehabilitation of French railways, highways, ports, waterways and public utilities, announced today that it has put 4,500,000 man-hours of labor and $15,000,000 in soldier payrolls into such work.

Headquarters said that American soldiers were largely responsible for almost completely rehabilitating the ports of Cherbourg and Rouen while Le Havre and Marseille had been made usable for military purposes and Brest partly rehabilitated. Seven smaller ports were cleared of wrecks and obstructions.

They built or repaired 283 bridges and 242 railway bridges, 6,898 miles of double track and 1,647 miles of single track railways and 850 miles of railway yards and sidings.

They also helped to repair and maintain 3,600 miles of military highways.

Once needed for military movements, all these facilities are now being turned back to the French.

In addition, American service troops helped clear 337 miles of rivers and canals and helped with labor and equipment in putting the electrical power system back in operation.

They built or repaired 283 bridges and 242 railway bridges, 6,898 miles of double and 1,647 miles of single track railways and 850 miles of railway yards and sidings.

Once needed for military movements, all these facilities are now being turned back to the French.

In addition, American service troops helped clear 337 miles of rivers and canals and helped with labor and equipment in putting the electrical power system back in operation.

In early February, as Allied victory seemed assured, and Dana was writing about French collaborators and post-war plans for France, the big three, Roosevelt, Churchill and Stalin, were meeting at Yalta. [116]

Although it was now nearly four months since the Germans had surrendered, the terms of peace and what to do to prevent future wars was still being discussed. A meeting of five foreign ministers was called for September 10 in London, at which French Foreign Minister, Georges Bidault, was to present a plan for the amputation of the economic resources of western Germany, which he planned to put forth as a condition of a new French-British alliance. He hoped to make the plan a keystone of post-war political alignments in Western Europe. Bidault had consulted Washington and found no objections to the plan. He believed the Russians would not oppose it if the Western Powers approved. It seemed, therefore, that it was a matter to be settled between the French and British. Because the Russians had set up a skeleton German government in Russian-occupied Eastern Germany, French diplomats felt that the British would approve this plan, which had proved a stumbling block previously.

In Dana's words:

The earlier French plan had called for permanent occupation of the Rhine south of the Ruhr by French, Belgian and Netherlands troops with a bridgehead

---

[116] See Appendix.

across the river to the right bank at Coblenz, Mainz, Mannheim, Karlsruhe, Strassburg and Freiburg.

North of the Ruhr, British and Netherlands forces would occupy a belt of German territory along the Netherlands frontier . . . to the eastern extremities of the Ruhr area. The Ruhr, including the Westphalian coal fields, would be internationalized under the control of the Big Four Powers, plus the Netherlands, Belgium and Luxembourg.

The Saar area would be placed under purely "economic sovereignty."

Eventually the entire area involved might be transformed into a Rhineland state if the German inhabitants proved amenable, or into some form of protectorate.

Dana went on to say that the French felt that the military disarmament of Germany was not sufficient to ensure security for France and Western Europe, as long as the economic industrial resources of the Ruhr remained a part of the German state. They believed that because Germany had lost territories in eastern Germany, German nationalists would not rest and would attempt to use the economic resources to create the means of taking revenge or trying to regain these territories.

Concerning the objection the British might feel to bringing the Russians into the Ruhr, the French pointed out that their representative would be only one among seven other diplomats.

If this plan was not adopted, and the eventual German government were under Russian influence, the French thought that the Germans might extend their territory not merely to the Ruhr but to the frontiers of France.

The Tangier Conference, which had been postponed in July because of the Russians' request to be included, was continued in Paris in late August and an agreement was reached. Dana wrote on September 4 that the Soviet Union and Franco Spain, though diplomatically not on speaking terms, would sit together on the Tangier Control Committee along with the United States, Great Britain and France. The agreement stated that most of the burden of administration of this international zone would be provided by four nations that were among the signatories of the Treaty of Algeciras—Belgium, the Netherlands, Portugal and Sweden.

The agreement was to be submitted to the respective governments for ratification, and full details would be made within two weeks.

Meanwhile, the British and French diplomatic delegates handed to the Spanish government an Anglo-French note which called for the withdrawal of Spanish forces from Tangier within a week and for a reply within three days. The Spaniards had already expressed their willingness to withdraw their forces and although they were still to have some representation in Tangier, some uneasiness was felt in diplomatic circles that they might reject the demarche because they had not been consulted and because their position in Tangier had been diminished.

The French delegates had proposed the use of neutral administrators after Russia had asked to be invited to the conference.

Dana briefly reviewed the recent history of Tangier. Until 1940, the chief administrator was a Frenchman, with a Spanish assistant for hygiene, a Briton for finance and an Italian for the judiciary. The native gendarmerie was commanded by a Spaniard with French and Spanish officers, while the civil police were directed by a Frenchman.

Under the terms of the unratified agreement, the Spanish Consul will sit on the Control Committee with the other powers, and four Spaniards will sit in the Legislature Assembly. The Russians agreed to this in the final days of the twenty-one day conference only after having inserted a declaration expressing reservations in the strongest language regarding the Franco regime.

The new arrangements involved a sacrifice for Spain and also for France, although France had succeeded in protecting the Sultan of Morocco's nominal sovereignty and in re-establishing the prerogatives of the Sultan's representative and in maintaining the Convention of 1923 as the basis for the international status.

Anticipating the possibility that vexed Spaniards might cut off Tangier's normal source of supply, the agreement stated that the American, British, French and Russian governments would send food supplies to the zone if necessary.

Indicating that the British government would not ratify the agreements, a separate announcement from London arrived stating that there would be no international conference to change the status just agreed upon for Tangier until there was a democratic government in Spain.

It was considered necessary to include Franco Spain in the temporary accord because it was felt that the exclusion of Spain would not only inflame General Franco but would harm all Spaniards of whatever political persuasion. The Americans had argued for Spanish representation as a practical necessity because of Tangier's geographic position as an enclave within Spanish Morocco, and they also expressed the desire to protect the Spanish nation and people. After all, Tangier is within eyesight of Spanish Gibraltar.

Although Dana was stationed in Paris, he followed what was happening all over Europe, and of course, many diplomats and political émigrés came to Paris and often brought interesting information from other parts of Europe and the Middle East. He was able to interview a leader of the pro-Mikhailovitch underground from Yugoslavia, as well as anti-Communist émigrés from Poland. They told him that secret police were conducting reigns of terror in their countries, which they left in August. They declared, Dana wrote, that the Yugoslav elections scheduled for November 11 would be a farce without Allied supervision and that Deputy Premier Mikhailovitch and other non-Communists were powerless.

In this September 5 article, he reported that Dimitri Lazarevitch, former editor of the underground newspapers called *Liberty* and *Voice of Youth* said he left Yugoslavia, and on August 3 for Paris, by way of Salzburg, where the United States Army is feeding 100,000 former Yugoslav prisoners of war and political deportees who do not want to return home while Marshal Tito is in power. He said that fifty to 100 refugees from Yugoslavia were arriving at the Salzburg camp weekly to join a National Committee of the Yugoslav Kingdom, of which Stefan Traivunac is President, and he is Vice President.

According to M. Lazarevitch, the forests of Serbia were alive with fugitives from Marshal Tito's police, called the Ozna, and Gen. Mikhailovitch had again become the idol of the underground, even in Croatia. The members of the new underground call themselves Crusaders, or Krijaki in Serbian, and were particularly active in the mountains of Šumadija, where many fights between the supporters of Mikhailovitch and Marshal Tito took place during the occupation.

Mr. Lazarevitch also confirmed earlier reports of serious disturbances in Cracow on August 11, which resulted in large-scale arrests of anti-Communists by Polish troops under Russian order.

In a return to the political and military scene in Paris in early September, Dana interviewed General Harold F. Loomis, Chief of the "Rearmament Division of the United States Forces" in the European theatre. He told Dana that under Lend-Lease, the United States had invested more than $750,000,000 in rearmament of the French Army and Air Force. This was in a period from January 1943, when President Roosevelt made an agreement at Casablanca with General Giraud, up to V-E day, May 8, 1945. General Loomis pointed out that it was an investment that saved many thousands of American lives. "We might have had to send more men overseas or the war might have been longer." General Loomis went on to say that the United States was still supplying gasoline, clothing, spare parts and replacements to the French Army of some 300,000 men until July 15, when the French assumed one-third of the burden. Since August 31, he said, "we have ceased supplying food to the French Army."

The question now, he explained, was whether France would buy the considerable American stocks of arms, ammunition and equipment left on the Continent to continue her rearmament. He thought that it would depend on whether and to what extent the French Government decided it could afford to try to create a new mass army.

Reviewing the events of the war, Dana wrote that General Loomis, as chairman of the joint United States-British-French Rearmament Committee at Algiers, was in charge of carrying out the Roosevelt-Giraud agreement for arming twelve French divisions—seven infantry, four armored and one mountain division.

"It soon became evident," General Loomis recalled, that we could not raise the necessary technical personnel in Africa to service that many divisions.

Eventually, we armed eight divisions, four of which fought very brilliantly in Italy, as Dana knew well. Seven, including two armored divisions, constituted the greater part of the United States Seventh Army after it landed in southern France—a fact that is not generally realized. The eighth, Maj. Gen. Jacques-Philippe Leclerc de Hauteclocque's armored division, landed in Normandy.

Meanwhile, the French Air Force, equipped with 80 percent American and 20 percent British material, was gathered in southern France. Larger than the French Air Force of 1940, it provided most of the tactical support for the French Army. The French First Army, as it was called after its separation from our Seventh Army, often appeared less well-fed, clothed and supplied than the American forces. General Loomis explained, it was because Gen. Jean de Lattre de Tasssigny, its commander, chose to incorporate 52,000 members of the French Forces of the Interior into its ranks, thus spreading out the available supplies.

In the course of the last winter, the Allies also undertook a "liberated manpower" program to equip 172 Frenchmen as security battalions, or light infantry, to guard supply dumps and lines of communications. Actually, some 100,000 were armed with British Home Guard equipment, American 1917 rifles and other obsolescent materials.

Last autumn (1944), General Charles de Gaulle asked the United States to equip fifty French divisions. In December, President Roosevelt approved a new program to arm eight additional divisions—six infantry, one mountain and one armored with their supporting units. A large depot was set up at Lyon.

Because of general Rundstedt's Ardennes offensive and the pressure to supply American forces, General Loomis said only three divisions could be about one-third equipped under this program. The rest of the equipment for the three divisions was on the point of being delivered when V-E Day intervened. To the great disappointment of the French, that program was cut off. To complete it, they will have to buy materials.

On September 7, the Army's Troop Carrier Command invited correspondents on a trip to Germany and Greece to show how it was repatriating 6,000 Greeks stranded in Germany.

In his weekly letter, on September 10, he wrote:

Dear Mother:
I enjoyed your nice birthday telegram, for which I thank the whole family. I almost forgot my birthday this year.
I am enclosing a clipping of my piece on Paris in August. . . I hope you liked that piece, for it has earned me more reaction than any other I've done for the Times. *In particular from members of de Gaulle's party who read it in New York and didn't like it, worse luck for them. It was an experimental sort of piece, as is the one I did last night on my trip.*

[There were several "letters to the editor" on the Paris in August article. Some thought it damaged French and American relations.] [117]

Lansing Warren and wife arrived today and he will come into the office tomorrow. I'll be much interested in meeting him. All reports are favorable.
I see no harm in writing to Harold. It might be a good idea. Tell him how much you appreciate the attention he has shown me and how pleased you are that he is seeing to it that I get a much needed rest. Also how important it is that I should return, after seven years, firstly, to breathe the air of America again and refresh my American professional point of view and secondly for urgent family reasons. And that's not all hot air. It was he after all who took me into the Times *and I will not forget it.*
When I return I will presumably travel by air, unless the army alters its treatment of accredited correspondents by that time. That means it will cost me nothing as far as New York.
Mr. Sterling's [Mother's financial advisor] *latest buy sounds good.*
I don't anticipate any very considerable cash requirements in the near future, although I will want to buy some clothes and might invest in a car when I get home. It might soon be possible to ship it over here, as you suggest.

---

[117] See Appendix.

Writing about newly appointed staff to the Berlin office reminded Dana of Fred Oechsner, head of the Berlin office when Dana was there. He wrote:

He now has a very important job on Bob Murphy's staff I understand. All through the war he has been one of the big men in the OSS working on Germany. I admire him greatly; although rather brusque and lacking in cordiality, he knew how to look after his staff. I don't know whether I ever told you that once at the very beginning of the war when UP *was slow in coming across with a living allowance for me, he offered to pay my hotel bill out of his own money, but I refused. He has quite a good private income; and he needed it while working for* UP.

I understand that there is a new wave of resignations from the UP *I can't help thinking it's not a very good time, with three million G.I.s looking for jobs.*

How much you must miss Torrey Pines. I am so very sorry.

All my love to you, as always, and, as you say.

A bientot.

Dana

As the cantonal and general elections came closer, Dana was writing again about French politics. In a piece published on September 15, he wrote:

French foreign and domestic political issues are being exploited as campaign weapons, more often than not in the sense of weapons for or against Gen. Charles de Gaulle. Those groups, in particular the Communists, who are most furiously opposed to General de Gaulle's proposal for a close association of western European nations, are the same ones who on the home front have taken the lead in denouncing General de Gaulle for his allegedly "undemocratic and reactionary" election system and for refusing to receive a protesting delegation of Left Wing leaders. They are also remembering that it was a Colonel de Gaulle who wrote a book advocating a small, highly trained *"armee de metier,"* [regular army] and have taken the lead in denouncing his plans to economize by reducing the size of the army. . . .

The elections begin to assume the aspect of a plebiscite for or against General de Gaulle. The Socialist party, along with the small Catholic Popular Republican movement, appears more and more as General de Gaulle's party, with the Communist party as the principal opposition. The Radical party, traditionally moderate, has at the same time joined an uneasy alliance with the Communists, apparently in the hope of limiting the Socialists and making the best of what seems like a bad situation. The other groups of the Center and Right appear for the moment to be in eclipse.

In the light of this situation, nothing could have been more illusory than the impression of Left Wing solidarity given by the joint protest of the Communists, Socialists, Radicals, General Confederation of Labor and league for the Rights of Man against the election system.

In refusing frequent Communist offers of unity and the creation of joint election tickets, former Premier Leon Blum and Daniel Mayer of the Socialist party always have come back to the fundamental objection—the Communist party's dependence on Moscow. Red Star's blast from Moscow against General de Gaulle's "western bloc" scheme is calculated to strengthen the Socialists' hand in this respect. Careful explanations from de Gaulle quarters that the General used the term "bloc" and did not intend anything against Moscow are lost sight of in the heat of the campaign.

Radical Socialists and other left-wing groups proposed a change in the electoral system to "integral proportional representation." In an article published on September 12, Dana reported that Charles de Gaulle opposed this change. He defended the system of "proportional representation" to be used in the election as "the most equitable ever practiced in France and from this point of view not comparable with that of any other great democratic country." He agreed to increase the representation in certain densely populated areas.

He admitted that the system demanded by the Left Wingers might arithmetically provide a slightly more precise representation but argued that it would be to the disadvantage of the devastated regions which have temporarily lost many inhabitants.

On the point that the protesting groups hold most vital, he explained that he favored the distribution of votes called "remainders" that necessarily accrue in each electoral department under a system of proportional representation among the candidates in each department so that the men elected would remain representative of their home areas. The distribution of "remainders" on a national basis, to be disposed of by the Left Wingers, he pointed out, would divorce the men elected from their constituents and raise the question as to just what part of France they represented.

Instead of 598 representatives, as would be arithmetically logical, France, herself, will elect only 522, General de Gaulle said, to leave room for 64 representatives of overseas territories, not counting Indo-China.

In a piece published on September 14, Dana wrote:

While part of the French press began to show signs of irritation today at the prolongation of the dispute over the method of the October elections, the Cabinet made good Gen. Charles de Gaulle's promise to five protesting Left-wing groups by conceding sixteen additional seats in the Constitutional Assembly to the seven most populous Departments of France.

As expected, however, he made no compromise on the system of proportional representation.

The three electoral districts of Paris received a total of thirty instead of twenty-seven seats, and the three industrial suburbs got twenty-three seats, out of twenty.

Regarding the election furor, the Figaro exclaimed:

"Is this really a matter for serious quarrel on the eve of events of capital importance [to the] country?"

The *Pays* remarked that "obviously these Byzantine and endless discussions can only weary the public and reduce the prestige of the Assembly eventually elected."

"While the system is certainly not perfect," the newspaper added, "it is incontestably enormous progress over earlier ones."

Combat expressed the opinion that General de Gaulle's reply last night to the memorandum of the five left-wing groups would serve as a springboard for an anti-governmental coalition.

In confirmation of this view, Jacques Duclos of the Communist party proposed, on the basis of the left-wing unity achieved in the election dispute, to hold an inter-party mass meeting of protest and to revive the old project for joint left-wing party tickets at the elections. The political bureau of the Communist party approved of a joint campaign with the other parties against the "reactionary system."

Other signs indicated, however, that the Left-wing unity was more illusory than real. Daniel Mayer, secretary general of the Socialist party, immediately declined the proposal for joint tickets while the Socialist organ, the *Populaire*, published a front-page box entitled, "Incurable." Denouncing Georges Cogniot of the Communist *Humanite* for "systematically misrepresenting and intentionally falsifying the facts" regarding the Socialist party's position.

Communist and Socialist members of the General Confederation of Labor were at the same time reported near a split over the question whether the Confederation had exceeded its proper functions by pronouncing itself in support of the Communist views on a referendum.

The electoral system was not the only disputed subject, at this time, in France. The size of the postwar army was also a subject of controversy. Dana reported that Minister of War, Andre Diethelm, advocated a mass popular army. The Socialists and Minister of Finance René Pléven proposed a small professional army. It was settled after M. Diethelm accepted a cut of one-third in army expenditures. The cut was hard for him to accept because, as he explained, the necessity of paying for gasoline, uniforms and equipment after the end of lend-lease, and the desirability of maintaining eight divisions for the occupation of Germany and garrisons in Africa and Indo-China, made a reduction of expenditures very difficult.

Although it was only September, Dana responded to Mother's questions regarding Christmas in his September 21 letter:

It is perhaps wise to mail things, he said, *even though I will be coming home since I can carry little if I travel by air. What would I like in the way of a present you asked. Well, at thirty I'm pretty old to be given very many presents, but I feel precisely and exactly as I did when I was a sophomore at Pomona, that it to say, strictly adolescent. So I'll tell you. I'd like a gramophone. One hooked-up to a radio set if possible.*

I bought myself a recording of the "Chanson de la Liberation" the other day, although I have nothing to play it on. In an unobtrusive way it has become one of the things you hear French men whistling or humming most often. It is really a chanson de la resistance more than de la liberation and as such should be presented in a subtle, persistent, illusive manner, with humming and distant drums. Unfortunately the interpretation I had to buy presents it as a blaring victory march with full orchestra. The melody incidentally is something like "I'll take the high road and you take the low road."

I am trying to get a few other things that have appealed to me, such as "Lili Marleen," and "Wir fahren gegen England" [We're going against England] *in the original German and the Australian war song "Waltzing Matilda," which like "Lili Marleen" and all good war songs has a certain pathos about it when properly sung. I guess I'll have to look in Germany and London for those. In Paris I couldn't even buy a recording of the "March of Lorraine;" you probably know it with its comical words about the girl in her sabots.*

There are others I have taken a real fancy to in the course of 30 years, but I can't think of them. "The Swan of Tuonela," by Sibelius in one. Some Negro [Afro-American] *spirituals like "Water Boy," an obscure thing the Pomona glee club sang once. Furthermore I love almost anything Tyrolean, with yodeling. Then there are some grand things on the obscene side, like "Roll me over," etc. which is probably the thing American soldiers sing most in the streets of Paris; it is really an English song. And that delightful Cockney song called "Knees up Mother Brown" which was the most typical street song on V-E Day in London. It should be sung by little girls. Children's choirs, no matter what they sing, but especially in Christmas carols, always have an exquisite, heart-wrenching quality. Such are my musical tastes. Not very profound. I*

suppose what it stacks up to is that I like the jolly and also the mystic and the sentimental sort of thing.
  All my love again,
  Dana

With the elections behind him, Dana enjoyed an unexpected trip to Athens, arranged by the U.S. Army's Troop Carrier, who wanted to show correspondents how it was repatriating 6,000 Greeks who were stranded in Germany. On the way from Paris to Athens, they stopped in Munich and visited Adolf Hitler's Beer Hall, where he attempted to take over the Bavarian government in 1923—the Beer Hall Putsch. Following this ill-fated event, Hitler was arrested and imprisoned. While in prison, he wrote *Mein Kampf.*

At the Beer Hall, Dana talked with a Red Cross worker, Ruth Stolz, who was making a Red Cross club in the old cellar. Dana quoted her comments: "I hope I'm not here this winter. It's going to be awful. You ought to see those German children rummaging in GI garbage cans even now. And the way they follow you around, waiting for you to drop a cigarette butt." "She did not know," Dana noted, "that we were on our way to visit a country (Greece) where many thousands died of starvation under German occupation, and which is still hungry."

In Athens, the correspondents had the opportunity of climbing the Acropolis to visit the Parthenon. *I was enchanted by Athens,* he wrote in a letter to his Mother. *Its immediate charm exceeds that of any city I can think of.* Unfortunately, in Athens, Greek employees of the British and American armies and of UNRRA were on strike for a 100 percent wage increase—400 employees worked for the Air Transport Command. And so, because of a lack of personnel to handle new arrivals, the ATC had to call off the repatriation.

Back in Paris, Dana turned his attention to the trade union meeting, where representatives of 69 nations were assembled. It was hoped that a permanent world trade could be formed.

Under a September 25 dateline, Dana wrote:

The World Trade Union Conference began here today with a debate on the draft of the constitution for the World Trade Union Federation that disclosed no fundamental disagreement that would be likely to delay formation of the new organization.

Two hundred and seventy-three delegates representing more than 60,000,000 workers, met at the Palais de Chaillot, opposite the Eiffel Tower. Leon Jouhaux, secretary general of the French Confederation of Labor, opened the session from a pulpit-like speakers' platform at the top of a winding stairway that was dominated by flags of all the nations. A dove of peace was on a black velvet background.

M. Jouhaux told the delegates "the forces of labor are needed for the construction of peace and the reorganization of the world."

"There must be," he went on, "an end to the theory that a free economy is the source of all prosperity. A free economy had its uses in the period of evolution, but by its monopolies it suppressed competition and at the same time signed its own death warrant."

Americans On Committee

A rules committee, on which Albert Fitzgerald, president of the United Electrical, Radio and Machine Workers represented the CIO, was quickly approved. On the credentials committee John Green, president of the Industrial Union of Marine and Shipbuilding Workers, represented the CIO.

In the debate on the amendments to the constitution Vasili Kuznetsov, president of the Central Council of the Russian Trade Unions and the head of the Russian delegation, said the new federation must undertake "concrete and effective action." He pointed out that the organization would possess "means of pressure on Governments and employers that must be exploited to obtain the maximum profit to the working class."

He indicated that the Russians had gone a long way toward meeting the British desire to maintain the prerogatives of the existing international professional federations.

The most enthusiastic applause was aroused by Ken Hill of Jamaica, who declared: "If the major powers have known freedom so long they no longer value it, do not forget that there are colonial peoples who do not yet know the taste of freedom and would like to find out how it tastes."

S.A. Dange of India complained that the British Labor Government had done nothing to free hundreds of Indian political prisoners or help 300,000 Indians who were striking against post-war wage reductions.

Jean Brodier of the French Catholic trade union movement pointed out that Catholics insisted on separate representation in the world federation and did not intend to abandon their own international federation.

On the following day, Dana wrote that at the beginning of the meeting, Sir Walter Citrine, the British representative, announced that they would not be bludgeoned into any world trade organization by a majority vote. It developed that the British might withdraw if the new organization were not set up on a temporary basis and the machinery of International Trade Unions were not incorporated.

He [Sir Walter] took a stand clearly opposed to that of the Russian chief delegate, Vasili Kuznetsov, in rejecting a political role for the new organization. Evidently, referring to speeches yesterday by S.A. Dange of India and Ken Hill of Jamaica regarding aspirations to national independence, he said, "these are laudable objectives but are not matters for our world federation. Such questions would split it."

"An international based on rhetoric is useless," Sir Walter declared. "What we need is a practical working organization capable of serving labor interests."

To this end, he urged that the executive committee have powers to investigate the membership claims of mushrooming new unions, presumably those of Eastern Europe, and that "common sense" be used to see how the old IFTU could help.

As an argument in favor of putting the new WFTU on a temporary basis, Sit Walter pointed to the statement by J.H. Oldenvroek.

Mr. Hillman [of the CIO], who appeared to be assuming the role of mediator, replied:

"All these problems can be solved. But failure to establish a world federation now would be disastrous. Our only hope for peace and a decent living would be smashed."

He recalled that the World Trade Union Conference's request to participate in the San Francisco Conference was rejected because it was a temporary organization.

Señor Lombardo Toledano proposed that the term "initiatory period" be used instead of "temporary."

Mr. Thornton and Mr. Goodwin protested that they had spent nearly a year traveling from conference to conference and that the time had come when results must be shown because small countries could not afford to send delegates around the world indefinitely.

An additional request to the Conference was made by the Russian delegation. Dana reported this development in the following article:

RUSSIA DEMANDS LABOR SEAT IN UNO

Delegate to the Paris Congress Goes Beyond Hillman Call for Advisory Post

By DANA ADAMS SCHMIDT
By Wireless to THE NEW YORK TIMES.
PARIS, Sept. 28—Michael Tarassoff of the Russian delegation to the World Trade Union Conference proposed today, following the report by Sidney Hillman of the CIO on labor participation in postwar international conferences, that the projected World Trade Union Federation should demand a seat in the United Nations Assembly with the right to vote in the Economic and Social Council.

Mr. Tarassoff thus carried one step further Mr. Hillman's recommendation that the conference direct its executive committee to seek representation in an advisory capacity on the United Nations Economic and Social Council when such a body has been formed.

In his most notable statement to the conference, Mr. Hillman also recommended that the executive committee appoint a commission to visit Germany and make a "full examination and investigation in all zones" and take steps to have representation of the World Trade Union Federation in an advisory capacity on the Allied Control Commission in Germany.

He suggested that similar steps should be taken in Japan.

Sees Big Business Represented

"In the United States zone of occupation in Germany," Mr. Hillman declared, "I know that American Big Business is very effectively represented on all high policy-making bodies. Yet the people cannot look with confidence to these gentlemen for swift and full execution of the Potsdam program. We must recognize that there are those, and not in Germany alone, who do not want to see Germany's war potential destroyed and the roots of fascism relentlessly eradicated."

In his opinion the German workers were the only base on which a new democratic Germany could be built and that any labor movement of the world was the best equipped group to help the workers.

Mr. Hillman warned that "another and even more catastrophic war" threatens if the war-time unity of the United Nations dissolves into opposing blocs. Therefore he urged that the voice of labor "which has shown it can submerge national and ideological differences in the higher interest" should be heard "at all the councils which will be established from time to time to deal with peace and reconstruction."

While noting that the International Labor Office "quite properly" had representation as a consultant at the San Francisco Conference, he declared, "We are unanimous in the conviction that a tripartite body of this kind can neither speak for nor represent world labor in international affairs."

Indian Condemns Curbs

S.A. Dange of India, who spoke just before the close of today's session, said he "did not want to wreck the conference on political issues," but felt obliged to draw attention to the painful sight of American and British troops operating alongside the Japanese to put down "a very serious national independence movement" in many parts of the Far East.

"People who demand independence are being shot down," he said. "What is the attitude of the British, Dutch and French working classes? These are inconvenient questions, but labor must decide whether it will support the Governments responsible for such things."

Mr. Dange proposed that the executive committee set up a special colonial department to deal with the question.

September 27—In Dana's weekly letter, he wrote:

I have your letter and one from Mrs. Wieland mentioning her aunt she would like me to visit and I will do so. I'm glad to hear they are prospering; they had a hard time for many years as I recall. Mr. Wieland especially always seemed to me a lovable sort of character.

Your observations about the French are very much to the point. I like them, admire them and sympathize with them greatly, but I'm getting kind of fed up with them too. There is a sourness in the atmosphere, a sort of narrow-chested shortness of breath and pettiness. If France is to be great at all again she will have to realize on a national scale that her patrimony is gone and that she is going to have to get up early and work late to make a living. But she has not make up her mind to it. What I presume to be a Popular Front mentality of work less and consume more is still general. The gentle ease of the gracious French way of life beloved by Americans before the war will have to give way to something harder.

I'm glad that you wrote to Harold. And I'm sure he will receive the letter in the spirit in which it was intended. He cabled that he has still not begun his vacation! I think he is stalling to drag on his time in the U.S. tant mieux [so much the better]. *It will be an argument in favor of the prolongation of my own absence.*

You say Elizabeth's arm is getting well, but I didn't know there was anything wrong with it. I trust nothing serious. How nice it will be to have two babies in the family.

It has turned cold here and I am wearing your latest olive colored sleeveless sweater. The white tennis sweater will be a welcome addition.

Now, before I forget, I want you to do a little good will job for me. Please take the money required out of my funds. I would like to send a ten or eleven pound food package to Mrs. Galibert, 2, Avenue Jean Jaures, Colombes, Paris, every month for six months. I understand that Macy's in New York has a regular food parcel service and will take care of all shipping details. You might write to them if the Los Angeles shops don't provide a similar service. It should include coffee, tea, chocolate, sugar, some kinds of fats, powdered or condensed milk and other appropriate items. Mrs. Galibert is the mother of the office boy we fired; I discovered they are rather hard up.

Did I or did I not tell you that the Chicago Sun *offered me a job? Clem Randau, former business manager of the* UP, *on whom I called with a letter from Betty Averill's father in 1938, wrote me suggesting I might become their correspondent in Paris or Berlin! I replied thanking him for his kind thought but explaining that I am happy with the* Times. *The greatness of the* Times *is a thing that grows on me. I am a little embarrassed by the attitude some people from New York assume when they see one of my* Times *bylines. It is a little awful to think of people clipping and studying and analyzing what you have written.*

The job we have done in this bureau is open to some very real criticism. But we have provided the only report available to the American public on the basis of which one might form a real opinion as to what is going on in France. The Herald Tribune is good, but it has been sporadic in covering this country's affairs. The agencies are totally inadequate, much more inadequate than I realized when I was working for one.

Well, after giving myself at pat on the back by implication I guess I'll go to bed.

All my love to you all,
Dana
Dana Adams Schmidt, War Correspondent
APO B87

P.S. The army has got tough about correspondents riding home on airplanes, and I may have to take a boat. Bruce Rae, one of the big shots of the home office who has been working to get the Overseas Weekly *started in Germany, is going to have to return by boat.*

1946

Dana began the New Year with long awaited good news. On January 1, he wrote from Paris:

It looks pretty good to me and I think I'll be getting away by the middle of January. I'm particularly gratified to see that I'm now scheduled for six weeks.

Following is the text of the telegram via *Radio-France:*

SCHMIDT NEW YORK TIMES CORRESPONDENT
HOTEL SCRIBE PARIS
OKAY MAKE YOUR ARRANGEMENTS DEPART ON SIX WEEKS HOME VACATION EXCLUDING TRAVEL TIME SOONS CALLENDER RETURNS STOP TRY GET HOME BY FREE AIRTRIP IF POSSIBLE STOP FYI HOLIDAY NATURALLY ON PAY AND TRAVEL EXPENSES PAID BUT IF YOU CAN RIDE ON UNCLE SAM DO SO STOP BETTER FIGURE ON RETURNING PARIS POSTHOLIDAY UNLESS THINGS OUTWORK DIFFERENTLY WHILE YOU AWAY REGARDS SULZBERGER

Callender was supposed to have sailed on December 28, but we have had no confirmation that he actually did so.

Tonight I'm going off on a short trip to the French zone in Germany. It's a junket organized by the French government. I don't like those mass junkets but it is a good excuse to go to Germany. Lansing Warren [who had joined the staff recently] *will be left all alone but I think it will be extremely quiet. Cy will be here shortly on a trip to Spain.*

This morning I'm feeling just a little thick in the head after seeing the New Year in at the Turkish Embassy. It was a lot of fun to meet the old Ankara crowd. All the people who used to cluster around Numan Menemencioglu[118] *when he was foreign minister. I knew Numan's daughter slightly in Ankara so now I get invited to the Embassy every now and again. Our car is on the blink and in any case I wouldn't have kept the chauffeur up all night so I found myself walking home half way across Paris this morning at five.*

Among the people I met at the party was Sureja, the rather well known Turkish lawyer. She is a grand person with real charm. She was in England recently and Bevin asked to see her. In the spring she is planning to go to the United States. I believe she is a real full-blooded Turk, which is unusual among their intelligentsia. A little investigation usually uncovers a Greek grandmother, some Russian or Armenian blood. The sister of Nermin, the girl who was my string correspondent in Ankara for a time, was at the party. You remember Nermin was the daughter of Muvaffak Menemencioglu, Numan's brother and editor of the Anatolian agency. His wife was Greek, and his daughter Nermin married an Englishman. The Menemencioglus practically ruled Turkey when I was there, but they seem to be somewhat out of favor just now.

I was delighted to get answers to my Xmas cable from you and Eliza. Did Grandma get the one I sent her?

You will see by Cy's telegram that he thinks I will return to Paris after the vacation. I would be sorry if the German assignment fell through entirely, but I'm glad really that I'm not going to be sent there permanently.

I don't think I'll be coming home engaged. Maybe I'll get engaged while I'm in the States. [119]

---

[118]   See Appendix.
[119]   On numerous occasions, Mother has expressed her strong hope that Dana would find a wife. He appears to be appeasing her by mentioning various girls whom he knew.

I'm delighted with your photo of you reading the NYT *and Tuckie sunning himself. Tuckie looks a fine fellow.*
All my love now, to you all,
DANA

After Dana's trip to the French Zone of occupation, sponsored by the French government, he wrote several articles on the rehabilitation of the Saar and Rhineland and the assistance they were giving France in recovering from the war. The French, also, were trying to bring these areas closer to France. In an article published on January 3, datelined Saarbruecken, Dana wrote of these efforts by the French. In part, he wrote:

. . . responsible French civil and military authorities, who would not be quoted . . . declared that they believed the Saar also should be attached politically to France. They expressed confidence in the future of a Rhineland permanently separated from Germany and oriented toward France and Western Europe.

In spite of France's overwhelming defeat in the Saar plebiscite of 1935 and the failure of French projects for an independent Rhineland after World War I, the French authorities say they believe that the desire of the residents of the Saar and the Rhineland to escape the fate of defeated Germany provides auspicious circumstances for the realization of the French projects now.

In both areas, authorities appeared to be counting on the support of pro-French elements in the Catholic clergy, whose interests they have protected, and who are said to be fostering a new Christian Democratic party and smaller non-religious political factions. The new party's watchword is "Los von Preussen"—break away from Prussia.

The sequestration of the Saar coal mines, announced by Governor Gilbert Grandval at ceremonies today, removed German directors who hitherto operated under French control and installed an entirely French administration.

The French administrators, most of whom were in charge of the mines before 1935, already have succeeded in raising the output to 55 per cent of the pre-war level, a considerably higher percentage than that achieved by the British in the Ruhr.

While France theoretically receives 16 per cent of all German coal production, she is getting about 23 per cent of the Saar output. The rest goes to other liberated countries and Germany.

In an article dated January 6, Dana elaborated on the Saar and Rhineland:

SAAR-RHINE AREA ASSET TO FRANCE

Material Shipments Increase — Paris Is at Work Actively Toward Political Control

By DANA ADAMS SCHMIDT
By Wireless to THE NEW YORK TIMES.

PARIS, Jan. 6—Of the areas of western Germany under French occupation, France is most interested today in the Saar and in Rhineland province.

In the Saar, which holds coal reserves greater than those of all of France, the French want permanent economic and if possible political control. In the Rhine Valley, of which they now occupy the southern part, they want a buffer state against such menace as might again surge from the East.

A slowing of United States Army redeployment has lessened the need for American control of the railway center of Karlsruhe, and the French are anxious to broaden the neck of their awkwardly shaped zone in that area. They are even more anxious, however, to extend their area northward into the sections of the Rhineland now occupied by the British.

Meanwhile, the French are carrying on intensive propaganda in the Saar and the Rhineland and developing their zone economically where such development can aid the reconstruction of France.

Some light on French aims and French opposition to German centralization is cast by a brochure issued by the occupation authorities.

End of Berlin's Rule Cited

After asserting that the iron control of Prussianism which had gripped the Rhineland had now been burst asunder, the French pamphlet states:

"Denazification means deprussianization. There can be no deprussianization without the administrative and economic decentralization of Germany and unless Berlin is forever deprived of its prerogatives as the Prussian capital of Germany."

On the basis of their interpretation of history the French identify the "Germans of the West" with the Latins and the Occident.

A weak point in Paris's objectives appears to be that they could be entirely upset if a Communist Government should ensue from the next French elections. Evidence gathered by this correspondent on the tour of the French zone of Germany last week shows that these objectives are nonetheless being pressed vigorously by the authorities responsible to President de Gaulle.

A French-controlled radio station is operating at Coblenz and four others, including a shortwave station at Baden-Baden, are being repaired.

One newspaper in German, the Neue Saarbruecker Zeitung, has a circulation of 100,000; another, the Mittelrhein Kurier, has nearly 400,000. At Freiburg a literary bi-weekly, Gegenwart, has been started with former members of the staff of the old liberal Frankfurter Zeitung.

The universities of Tuebingen and Freiburg have been reopened. Out of 5,913 schools in the entire zone 4,944 have reopened, including 207 out of 228 high schools, after dismissal of nearly half of the teachers.

Under the watchful eye and indirect control of French officials, trade unions and political parties are being reorganized and local government returned to

Germans, particularly in the Saar and in Rhineland Province. About 11,000 Nazis are in concentration camps, and 45 per cent of the former German public officials have been dismissed.

In the Saar, with a population of about 700,000, there are said to have been 65,000 requests for instruction in French.

More Coal Coming From Saar

On the material side great strides have been made and the occupied zone is gradually becoming an asset to France. Most important is the Saar coal production, which has risen month by month from 11,500 tons a day last July to 20,600 tons a day in December. Of the output 23 per cent comes to France.

One of the nine blast furnaces of the Saar's steel industry was put back into service last month, and others will follow. A glass factory is producing fifteen square meters a day, of which half comes to France. The production of tiles, bricks and chinaware for France is beginning.

The occupied zone now ships 1,500 tons of paper to France monthly while 500 tons are retained for the zone. About 300,000 pairs of shoes have been produced in the Saar for the French Army and 200,000 pairs for French civilians.

In principle France must pay in foreign exchange for these supplies, but large quantities of goods have been removed unofficially from Germany and other quantities are frankly chalked up to "restitution and reparation." Under "reparations" the Rhineland alone has provided France with 3,000 head of cattle, 17,600 tons of cement, 8,500 square meters of building lumber and 1,740 tons of non-ferrous metals.

During the coming year the French-held part of the Rhineland is scheduled to send to France 225,000 cubic meters of sawn timber and 50,000 cubic meters of pulpwood and even larger quantities will be drawn from the Black Forest.

Following the trip to the French Zone, Dana attended a three-day foreign affairs debate of the Assembly in Paris. The opening discussion centered on the French government's proposed project for taking over the Ruhr and the

Rhineland to prevent Germany from building up an arsenal to be used to regain from Russia the eastern territories Germany lost during the war.

The Communist leader, Florimond Bonté, quickly gave his party's approval of the French government's plan. Daniell Mayer, speaking for the Socialists, did not address the Rhineland and Ruhr problem. Instead, he drew attention to France's future, which he said was bound up with the reconstruction of Europe as a whole. Tomorrow's Europe, he said, will be one of the principal links in the international community. It will be directed against neither the United States nor Russia. It can provide a synthesis of the American and Soviet civilizations. He continued with comments on the peace negotiations. "After the French-Soviet pact, we must have French-British and French-American pacts."

Ernest Pezel, for the Popular Republicans, declared his substantial agreement with the Socialists but emphasized the need for regional ententes as the first stage in international organization. "I do not believe that the Russian opposition to regional ententes is inspired by a desire for hegemony," he said, "but we must make it clear that federalism must be regional before it can be continental."

On January 22, Dana wrote:

This is probably the last of my epistles from Paris for some time to come. I'm due to leave for Le Havre before the weekend. I'll see that you get a cable saying when I get aboard.

Harold is back on the job and there is no need for me to delay, in spite of the crisis.

H.C. has returned in fine fettle and is much more agreeable than when he left, but quite as determined as before to monopolize the main stories.

A funny thing happened on Sunday when de Gaulle walked out. [120] *At noon we knew nothing about it and I suggested that this might be the occasion*

---

[120] De Gaulle often had battles with the left-wing members of the Assembly, but a disagreement concerning the appointment of the Premier (Prime Minister) caused him to

for me to take a real day off, and off I went. I went for a walk, revisited the remarkable exhibition of "chef d'oeuvres" at the Louvre, actually had tea, went out to dinner with some friends and to a movie, quite oblivious of the fact that the machine of the state of France was collapsing. Didn't know a thing about it till I got back to the hotel at midnight. Guess they just can't get along without me; the minute my back is turned everything goes to hell.

Next day I did a piece on popular reaction and that may be my last of any significance. There remains the magaziner for Markel, but I'm not sure it can be done just now, with everything plunged into an angry state of flux.

I thanked Harold for writing to you and he seemed pleased. He was apologetic about being away so long and making me miss Christmas at home. I met his wife and two bull terriers. She is a sculptress and very nice. Apparently a bit bewildered by the problems of life here.

With those strikes[121] *on it doesn't look as though there would be much chance of my buying much of anything at home. I'd like to get a 1946 car and bring it back with me for use in Germany. Apparently it is quite simple to get it shipped; the great problem is to buy one. I'll also want to buy a portable typewriter. Clothes too, though that is less important since I'll still be in uniform in Germany. A portable radio would also be a great boon if they are to be had.*

But buying stuff is the least of my concern. The great thing will be to be home and see my family—and to have a look at the USA.

That will be quite an adventure.

Incidentally Harold told me that Markel rather liked some of my stuff from here, in particular the much-debated "Paris in November" piece on

---

sign abruptly on January 20. The members of the Assembly insisted that the constitution of the Fourth Republic gave the Assembly the right to elect the Premier. De Gaulle insisted that the appointment of the Premier was the prerogative of the President.

[121] "In 1946, there were 4,985 strikes and the duration per worker involved reached 25.2 days—compared to 6.8 days just two years earlier. It was this spike in strike activity that prompted the Taft-Harley Act, which increased government intervention in contract disputes, and imposed new restrictions on unions 'ability to strike.' " Mario Bognanno, professor of Industrial Relations, Carlson School of Management, Minnesota.

Franco-G.I. relations. A girl who just arrived from the States mentioned it to me the other day too.

Another girl, named Sally Swing, daughter of the radioman, rang me up the other day to introduce herself as a friend of Dean Mary.[122] *She came around to the office to ask for a job. Said she didn't like her job with the* Paris Post, *an offshoot of the* NY Post. *But Harold Callender didn't give her much encouragement. Offered her a part time job doing fashions, which didn't please her very much. We haven't taken on any of the crowds of people getting out of the army who come in here day after day. Apparently Arthur Hays Sulzberger's view is that we must take care of our own people getting out of the military first, and quite rightly so. It seems that I was the last guy to get on the staff before he clamped down.*

We had a slight office "crisis" over the new franc exchange rate. Seems that our business and photo man Barriere thought people would be getting too much money if he paid our living allowances, etc. at the new rate, but HC has set that right as far as I am concerned at least. The French employees will probably not fare so well; they'll get only a partial recognition of the new rate, even though some of them had their salaries set in dollars. A little embarrassing for me, but the French staff doesn't know yet.

All my love now. I must start cleaning my personal file, desk, etc. Dreadful task.

DANA

Dana Adams Schmidt, War Correspondent
Public Relations Office
Headquarters Base Section
APO 513, US Army
P.S. That is our official new address, though the old one would still reach me if I were here. It was just changed.

The January 22 letter was, indeed, Dana's last letter home before leaving on his long-anticipated vacation. He sailed from Le Havre—the expense of a

---

[122]   Dean Mary Sinclair Crawford, Dean of Women at USC and a friend of the family.

boat trip being significantly less than flying. As planned, he spent a few days in New York visiting the staff of the *New York Times* and then flew to Los Angeles. Of course, there were no letters to Mother and family to record his vacation in Los Angeles, but I remember that it was a very busy time for him.

Mother, with her devotion to Dana, orchestrated the visit. She wanted him to meet her many friends and encouraged him to renew his friendships with Pomona friends. She planned every minute: made appointments for check-ups with doctors and dentists, and managed his social life.

In Los Angeles, at the Orthopaedic Hospital where she was a patient following her accident in 1930, Mother soon made friends among the administrative and medical staffs. She edited the hospital's news organ—the *Orthopaedic Hospital News* and served on the board of the Crippled Children's Guild. Many were interested to hear what her son, Dana, thought about the war and conditions in Europe. And so, it developed that Mother planned dinner parties and luncheons, where Dana often gave informal talks.

He was so busy that I saw little of him, but he did see our first two babies, Margaret and John, and thought they were "grand." John was born on March 3, soon after Dana's arrival in Los Angeles. Margaret was then 18 months old. Although Dana probably welcomed Mother's management during this visit, since she smoothed the way by planning his schedule, later on, he resented her controlling, especially when it became domineering.

To understand Mother, you have to remember that Dana's career in journalism represented the life she wished she had been able to pursue. She was well suited to journalism, with a broad interest in foreign affairs, an ability to write, along with a love of travel. So, to some extent, she lived her life through Dana and tried to direct him.

Dana was truly grateful to Mother for the years she followed his work and encouraged him, but her need to direct and manage became onerous, particularly after he was married.

She expected him to write to her every week, and in turn, she wrote to him every week, religiously, throughout his long years abroad. Fortunately, Mother saved his letters. Unfortunately, Dana did not save her letters or those of other members of the family.

Looking back some 60 years later, I realize that Mother had a powerful personality, along with a desire to have her family, especially her son, excel and succeed. Much of her stinging criticisms were due to an attempt to make us all perfect.

Before leaving for home on vacation, Dana had written an extraordinary number of articles, most of which were published in January. Among them was an important piece concerning war criminals. Now that the war was over, the French, who had fought bravely, suffered and resisted the occupation, understandably resented the collaborators, many of whom had profited immensely. The loyal French wanted these traitors kept from office and punished.

There were also German war criminals hiding in France. Dana wrote in an article on this subject, entitled:

**WAR CRIMINALS
HUNTED BY MACHINE**

**Card Index Files in the Central
Registry in Paris Are Used
to Find 100 a Week**

**By DANA ADAMS SCHMIDT
By Wireless to THE NEW YORK TIMES.**

PARIS, Jan. 11 (Delayed)—About 5,000 German war criminals have been located by the Central Registry of War Criminals and Security Suspects since last May and they are still being turned up at a rate of 100 a week by the convenient method of searching through card index files, Major Leon G. Turrou said today.

Major Turrou, former FBI agent and author of "Confessions of a Nazi Spy," who runs the central registry here under the general supervision of Col. George Elms of El Paso, Tex., said he was seeking 225,000 war criminals and security suspects and witnesses among the files of the 7,000,000 members of the German Army and other Germans.

The war criminals still sought by all countries number about 45,000. Most of the rest are security suspects, individuals who might be dangerous now apart from their role during the war.

Russia Seeks Most

While withholding the precise number of Germans asked for by various countries, Major Turrou said the Russian request was the largest, even though Russia had not joined the United Nations War Crimes Commission in London and contributed no information to the central registry. He deplored the absence of the Russians, pointing out that they might have contributed 7,000,000 names that would have made the system of cross indexing almost fool proof.

Codes, representing a long series of descriptive features, punched into the file cards permit machines to perform remarkable feats, such as turning up all the one-eyed army captains captured by the Western Allies or all sergeants wounded in the left arm. Thereby the search is greatly facilitated in cases of suspects whose names are not known, as is frequently the case.

Major Turrou suggested that if Elite Guard [SS] members are collectively condemned at Nuremberg to long terms of labor for devastated countries, as he anticipates, the central registry would be invaluable in segregating their professional skills.

3-Year Task Is Seen

It will take six more months to finish processing all the names and facts now at the disposal of the registry, he estimated, and another six months to finish finding the present wanted list. He believes the work may be wound up in three years.

The finding of Germans who ran a soap factory with human bodies at Danzig and the detection of several generals, hiding as privates in prisoner camps, are among the registry's accomplishments, Major Turrou said.

Out of 347 war criminals now held by the French, 175 were found by the registry.

The French Service for Detection of War Criminals said today that 103 German war criminals had been sentenced by French courts, eighty to death, nineteen to life imprisonment at hard labor and four to shorter prison terms.

Among those awaiting trial are Gauleiter Wagner of Strasbourg, Ambassador Otto Abetz, Ambassador Krug von Nidda and General von Oberg.

France is still seeking 12,215 Germans as war criminals. Complete dossiers have been established in 5,418 cases.

Before leaving Paris for his vacation, Dana presented a realistic and gloomy view of France:

FRANCE ENVELOPED IN FRUSTRATION

Despite Recovery's Progress, People Remember 1939, Rebel at New Curbs

By DANA ADAMS SCHMIDT
By Wireless to THE NEW YORK TIMES.

PARIS, Jan. 13—For France this is a winter of frustration and discouragement.

By comparison with the naked misery of Eastern Europe or with her own condition a year ago, France is not doing so badly. But Frenchmen are more inclined to make comparisons with the Cabinet's rosy promises and with their condition before the war.

In the autumn economic life showed signs of picking up. Rations were increased. There was a convalescent optimism in the air.

The winter so far has been mercifully mild. But with it has come a concentrated rush of economic crises. The Government's officials must have seen them coming, but they took the public painfully by surprise. Governmental authority and public morale appear to be disintegrating by way of reaction.

Shocked by Next Curbs

The public was irritated to learn suddenly that coal supplies were so low that electric power must be restricted again. It was shocked to learn, after enjoying the free sale of bread for two months, that bread rationing must be reimposed on a standard lower than that during the German occupation, and it was horrified when this was followed by a crisis in meat distribution that has left Paris without any fresh meat for a week, and by the news that the wine ration might have to be discontinued in a few months.

About the same time came the devaluation of the franc, which, with the steadily rising note circulation, heightened the fear of inflation despite all official assurances. Finally, the demand of public officials and other groups for increased wages raised the menace of strikes, though these to date have been confined to token demonstrations.

The most characteristic development of all was the allegation launched by the Communist Minister of Economy, François Billou that insurance companies had been insuring black marketers against police interference. No one doubted it. Was not every Frenchman obliged to live to some extent by buying or selling in the black markets operating in every corner of every town? Were not bread-ration tickets being freely bought and honored by bakers? Were not nightclubs flourishing as private clubs after having been officially closed?

Major Parties Helpless

In the face of this situation the three great parties—the Communist, the Socialists and the Popular Republicans—sharing power in a Government of national unity and at least superficially in agreement on economic policy, showed themselves to be helpless. Groping as if in a cold sweat for solutions, they were positive only in disseminating distrust of one another.

Over the week-end the Communist Minister of Production, Marcel Paul, promised to increase electric power if the public would only abide by the rules. The Socialist Minister of Supplies, Pierre Tanguy-Prigent, hoped to increase bread rations in February, but feared that heavy purchases abroad might undermine France's political independence. There was a rumor that the Cabinet had discussed bringing wine from Algeria in submarine-refuelers.

The Popular Republicans issued a statement calling on the Government to tell the public the worst. The Socialists decided to call a party congress in February. And it was rumored that the Communists might withdraw from the Government before the May elections to escape responsibility for the muddle and to seek an electoral advantage in their more accustomed role of Opposition.

Wide Agreement on Some Points

Under the circumstances, it was not surprising that the public and private comment reflected exasperation, for the present had direct forebodings for the future. On several points there was wide agreement: that President de Gaulle's prestige was suffering seriously, though no one could suggest a substitute to head a Government of national unity; that the Socialist party was showing signs of disintegration and would lose votes to the Communists on its left and the Popular Republicans on its right in May; that the decline of the Socialist party, now bridging the gulf between the Communists and the Popular Republicans, would decrease the feasibility of any Government of national unity and leave the Communists starkly facing the Popular Republicans and other Communist-fearing groups.

Such speculation led automatically to the fear that one of the two basic political combinations that divide France might ultimately seek to impose itself on the other and plunge the country into dictatorship. No one predicted violence—France seemed much too tired for such adventures for some time to come. The chances of it seemed about as remote as those of a violent conflict among the Big Three of world politics. But also no one forgot that hidden away in a thousand places throughout France are arms depots left over from the resistance. Neither Communist nor anti-Communist groups have ever turned them in.

On April 17, Dana was back in Paris following his vacation in the United States. The flight across the Atlantic was a joy ride he wrote:

. . . simpler and more uneventful than a drive downtown in Los Angeles. I leaned back for a nap over Newfoundland and when I woke up we were over Ireland. The ocean seems pretty insignificant under the circumstances. We got in to Paris at four in the morning and were taken by bus to the Grand, across the street from my old residence at the Scribe. I got a little room under the roof which is okay for the few days I am here.

Paris seems almost a second home to me now, since I know so many people, but I am eager to get to the job in Germany. Tonight am going to take Dudley out to dinner. I also wrote a note to Dorothy. Really I don't know what is going to become of the girl situation, but I don't doubt something will.

Everybody is telling me how well I look, and there is no doubt the vacation did me an awful lot of good. I think I feel stronger and more self assured. In any event it was wonderful to be home with you. I'll not allow such a long time to go by without coming home again. I saw Markel [the editor of the *New York Times* magazine] *the morning after I phoned from New York. He told me he had been 'impressed' by some of my stuff and asked me to do a piece comparing life in France and Germany when I am ready. We also talked about a possible book on postwar Germany, which he said he would be glad to help me market. I guess I can look upon him as an ally. James and Mr. Sulzberger were most cordial. When I reached Paris I phoned Cy, who suggested there were stories to be done on the British zone but left it up to Daniell.*

Middleton [Drew Middleton—prominent foreign correspondent for the *NYT*] *is in London awaiting his Russian visa and Gruson,* [Sidney Gruson]— *also a* NYT *foreign correspondent, is only temporarily in Germany. The Daniells are due to return to the US after the Nuremberg trial.*

Everything is lined up for the car. I suppose you got my telegram about the money to be sent to Park motor sale. I certainly got rid of a lot of money. My excess baggage cost fifty dollars and I had seventy left when I reached Paris.

Please give Grandma my love and tell her that after I spoke to you I tried to phone the Williams' but found they were not listed. So I took a taxi to their address, but found them out. I left a note.

Give Grandma all my love, likewise Eliza and Steinie.
Love, DANA

Apparently, responding to Mother concerning the possibility of her writing a story about dogs for *GO* magazine, Dana wrote on April 22, as usual, addressed to Mother, although usually meant for the whole family to read:

I'm glad you are keeping so busy. Yes, why not have a crack at the piece for GO, *although I'm afraid they don't pay very much. You will remember that there was a story about Dude ranches for dogs in an earlier issue of* GO, *or was it the New Yorker? It was very facetious and I suspect that they would want a facetious approach to the school story too, although it's a perfectly reasonable and serious affair. Maybe you could link it with New York which still has some signs reading "curb your dog" all over the place with some crack such as: "In California there is no need for 'curb your dog' notices. California dogs go to school and learn about such things." Or perhaps "not only does California produce better bathing beauties and fruit but also better dogs. In California dogs go to school." I guess that's not so hot. Perhaps, "California dogs may not be any bigger than other dogs, but they are better educated. That is to say they are better educated, if their masters can afford to send them to school ..."*

Well, you will be able to work something out. If GO *doesn't go for it, I should think there would be other takers who would accept a more straightforward account. Our friend at* Script *would probably be delighted if they could get it for nothing!*

My car has, I believe, reached Le Havre. I will try to phone tomorrow but cannot go to get it for about a week. I have a year's public liability and property damage insurance.

Among the letters you forwarded to me was one from one of the men who resided in my old Ankara apartment after I left. He had written to several people, at my request, to try to track down a sword-gun which I left in the apartment.

Things have been rather slow over Easter. Sundays and holidays when people are not in their offices are always annoying.

I see that the military government has announced that packages sent to US personnel overseas through the Army post office may now weigh as much as 22 pounds and be a maximum of 48 inches in length and seventy two inches in length and girth combined. If Elizabeth still wants to give me that portable radio perhaps it would fit those specifications and she could use this as a request. Apart from that I can't think of anything to ask for.

If Steinie can produce some of her splendid cookies and cakes, I would be more than delighted to have them. Furthermore, would you please buy me, out of my money, subscriptions to the New Yorker, Life Magazine *and the* Readers Digest. *I find if they aren't sent to me I never get around to buying* them at the PX and the PX is always late and doesn't have the New Yorker. If the New Yorker doesn't mind, I'd rather have the full size magazine and not the 'battle baby.' I'm counting on you to send me Harpers and Atlantic when you have finished with them, and anything else that seems pertinent to you.

Good night now. I presume that Tuckie has come home a reformed and model dog, but I doubt it. It's kind of fun to have a bit of a hellion around the house anyway.

Lots of love,
DANA

Dana's first assignment in Germany was to Frankfort on the Main. A wealth of subjects presented themselves to be explored and covered. Among them, the denazification of Germany was very important and a foremost objective of the American Military Government.

On April 1, Dana reported on the roundup of an underground Nazi organization headed by Hitler youth leaders:

**UNDERGROUND RAID
HOLDS 183 GERMANS**

**More Arrests Are Expected in
Drive to Wipe Out Resistance
— Super-Questionnaires Due**

**By DANA ADAMS SCHMIDT
By Wireless to THE NEW YORK TIMES.**
FRANKFORT ON THE MAIN, Germany, April 1—The roundup of an underground Nazi organization headed by Hitler Youth leaders, including Oberbannfuehrer Willi Heidemann, last Saturday night simmered down today to the detention of 183 Germans in the American zone. The British report on arrests still has not been made public.

This "Operation Nursery," however, stacks up as the largest and most significant affair of its kind since the beginning of the occupation when added to about a thousand individuals who have been arrested or questioned in the United States and British zones since last December.

Brig. Gen. Edwin L. Sibert, assistant chief of staff, G-2 (Intelligence), told THE NEW YORK TIMES tonight that new leads provided by the prisoners may well permit several hundred more arrests in coming weeks.

130,000 Held in Camps

At present about 88,000 Germans are being held in internment camps in the American zone, most of them not because of any overt acts of resistance, but because their rôles during the Nazi regime make them potentially dangerous. In addition, about 50,000 prisoners of war are being retained for the same reason.

Military Government officers estimate that when all the Germans in the American zone have filled out the new Fragebogen, or questionnaires, their numbers may be augmented by 30,000 more "offenders" who will serve two to ten years in labor camps as a penalty for their activities during the Nazi regime.

April 15 has been tentatively set as the date when the Germans will register for the super-questionnaires, on the basis of which boards of non- or anti-Nazi Germans will classify the entire population into five categories and mete out penalties or exoneration in accordance with the records.

Small Units Broken Up

There is no disposition on the part of Military Government officers to regard the underground Hitler Youth organization, which apparently has been crushed, as a resistance organization destined for combative action in the sense of the French Maquis.

The rare acts of violence appear, to date, to have been unorganized—an attempt by young Nazis to establish contact with one another with a view to future political activity.

For this reason, the counter-espionage corps in the last few months also has broken up several small unauthorized groups calling themselves "Edelweiss

Piraten"—the name of an organization that at one time reputedly resisted the Nazis.

Dana then tackled the subject of the enormous number of refugees and displaced persons in the American zone:

**U.S. ACTS TO CLEAR
ZONE OF REFUGEES**

**Plans to Repatriate 330,000,
Including 7,200 Poles a Day,
Under Tripartite Agreement**

By DANA ADAMS SCHMIDT
By Wireless to THE NEW YORK TIMES.
FRANKFORT ON THE MAIN, Germany, April 2—An attempt to clear the American zone of occupation of the remaining 330,000 displaced persons [123], including 180,000 Poles, now that the warm weather has returned, got under way today with an announcement of an agreement between the United States Forces in the European Theatre and the Polish and Czechoslovak Governments aiming at the repatriation of 7,200 Poles a day.

Six trains a day, each capable of transporting 1,200 persons and their personal property, such as clothing, bedding, bicycles and small tools, will be

---

[123] The large number of displaced persons in Germany after the War included refugees of various sorts. Some were members of ethnic or religious groups who were likely to be persecuted in their countries of origin. Others feared the new communist regimes in their homeland, for instance, those from Poland and Czechoslovakia; Croatians and Slovenians in Yugoslavia feared Tito's regime. Some who had collaborated with the Nazis feared reprisals or punishments if they returned to their homes in Germany. And some knew that their homes had been destroyed, so they had little incentive to go home. Some were willing to face eventual absorption into German civilian life. Some still hoped to emigrate to the United States or elsewhere.

made available in the near future. With United States military authorities, who will provide the food aboard, the trains will move through Pilsen and Prague in Czechoslovakia to reception centers at Dziedzice, fifty miles west of Kraków, and Mittelwalde, seventy-five miles south of Breslau.

Officers of the Displaced Persons Branch of the Army today doubted whether it would be possible to fill all the trains for the time being, but said they were "urging the Poles to take advantage of the opportunity to go home." At a meeting between American and Polish officers here last week, the distribution of a larger number of Warsaw newspapers and other publications in forty-three United Nations Relief and Rehabilitation Administration camps for Poles was arranged to balance the arguments against repatriation spread by sympathizers of the old London Government.

Many Poles were discouraged from returning by reports of living conditions in Poland by earlier repatriates who returned to camps during the winter. Others for the present are satisfied with the vastly improved camp conditions, have amorous interests in Germany or are willing to face eventual absorption into German civilian life. Some still hope to emigrate to the United States or elsewhere.

The UNRRA today announced the opening of five film libraries to permit the showing of at least one movie a week in all American zone camps, including the seventeen housing thirty thousand Jews. School programs are in operation in all camps and displaced persons make up 10 per cent of the enrollment in the reopened German universities at Heidelberg Erlangen and Munich.

To date, 223,000 Poles have gone home from the American zone. In the British zone, 300,000 remain, and in the French zone, 46,000.

What to do about the vast numbers of displaced persons in Germany and the possible re-emergence of Nazism were not the only concerns of the Allies. After years of dictatorship, whether the Germans would be prepared to take political responsibility when the Allies left—was another worry. Dana described what the Americans were doing about this problem:

U.S. SPEEDS RETURN OF GERMANS' RULE

Army Pushes Project to Develop More Political Responsibility Among Minister Presidents

By DANA ADAMS SCHMIDT
By Wireless to THE NEW YORK TIMES.

STUTTGART, Germany, April 5 (Delayed)—A daring United States Military Government project aimed at preparing the Germans for the assumption of political responsibility is rapidly developing here.

Under the auspices of Dr. Oscar Pollock, director of the regional governmental coordinating office, Wilhelm Hoegner, Karl Geiler and Reinhold Maier, Minister Presidents of Bavaria, Greater Hesse and Wuerttemberg-Baden, respectively, have been meeting here on the first Tuesday of every month since last October, increasing the influence and scope of their work with each meeting as they have initiated or the military government has referred to them more and larger problems.

It is not a zonal government but it is the next thing to it. Technically it is a coordinating agency, which leaves the three Laender [States] fully independent.

Starting with four committees in October the Laenderrat [Council of Minister Presidents] now has forty. They have prepared legislative action, later approved by Lieut. Gen. Lucius D. Clay, Deputy Military Governor and promulgated by the three Minister Presidents in every field of economics, including the creation of a zonal economic directorate at Munich and a transportation directorate at Frankfort on the Main.

Politically the most significant action has been the elaboration of the new denazification law, which will go into effect this month and divide 16,000,000 Germans in the United States zone into five categories, some to be penalized for Nazi activity and others to be exonerated.

There are plans for city elections this month and elections to constitutional conventions in each of the Laender in June have been worked out. One committee is busy with constitutional projects.

Three times since February the Laenderrat and its permanent officials have held meetings with Germans from the British zone. A meeting with Germans from the French zone is planned shortly and correspondence is proceeding with a view to a meeting with those from the Russian zone.

At a meeting this week British officers accompanying twenty German dignitaries made it clear that they believed the Americans were going too fast. They implied that they and the French, with centuries-long experience with the Germans, knew more than the Americans about the advisability of a rapid return of responsibility to even the most anti-Nazi Germans.

Some German officials at a "beer evening" given by Dr. Pollock in honor of the visiting Germans from the British zone, expressed concern as to whether the democratic political development of the German people was keeping pace with the development on higher levels and whether the organisms being created would prove equal to such tasks as the maintenance of denazification should the Americans withdraw.

Dr. Pollock, Professor of Political Science, on leave from the University of Michigan and author of the book "What to Do With Germany," considered such fears unjustified.

The work in the committees of the Laenderrat, in which representatives of the three Laender must reconcile their differences in a democratic manner, he regarded as the best possible political education for the Germans.

Americans connected with the project freely admit, however, that the general American desire to be done with the burden of occupation duties as soon as possible is also a basic motive for the haste. The British are considered nine months behind the Americans in the development of civil authorities and the French are even farther behind.

The Russians have established a zonal government but have worked from the top down, instead of starting with the local and state authorities and working up.

Dana expressed his feelings and interest in his new assignment in Germany:

Here I am already up to my ears and more in the job, said Dana in an April 7 letter. *It is a terrific job and the place is fairly bristling with my kind of stories, though it does take a little time to break in and get rolling.*

Hope you've already seen my name in the paper, though I haven't done anything sensational. I went down to Stuttgart for two days to see about the Laenderrat, to which we seem to be turning over authority at a remarkable clip.

The human interest stories around here abound and I think I may be able to do something about it. To start with, however, I must concentrate on the supposedly "important" political pieces I think. Cy Sulzberger suggested that one thing that wanted doing was more on what the Germans are thinking. Tomorrow I hope to get some stuff on political parties at Wiesbaden which will start me on that line.

Sidney Gruson had already left for Switzerland when I arrived but is due back next Tuesday or Wednesday. I spoke to Daniell [Ray] on the phone. He wants me to stay here for the time being while Gruson will go to Nuremberg for a while. Daniell wants me to do some pieces in the British zone. I am pleased, as this seems the right place for me to break in, in the American zone. I only hope that I'm not asked to do the Nuremberg trial, since "A," I don't know anything about it, and "B," I think it's a pretty dead story now.

I sneaked an extra day in Paris so as to have time to read the Paris file for the last two months. It wasn't really very illuminating but I feel I'm fairly well abreast of French affairs again. I also managed to go through a big pile of New York Times *I never got around to reading in L.A.*

As you can see the new typewriter is doing famously. I like it a lot.

In New York before I left I bought the following: A Brentano's America's Germany *by Bach,* Diary of a Kriegie *by Ed Beattie,* The Control of Germany and Japan *by Moulton and Marlio,* A Short History of Germany *by Steinberg, and* Germany is Our Problem *by Morgenthau. So if you send me any books, don't send me those. I would like to have any new books that come out about postwar Germany, however.*

I am installed very comfortably in the Park Hotel, one of the most comfortable places for miles. It is a big double room and bath. Gets the sun in the morning and is very agreeable. All the Public Relations offices and transmission agencies are here, like at the Scribe.

Soon after arriving in Frankfort, Dana was asked to go on a Russian government tour of the Russian Zone of occupation.

My Russian zone tour has put me a full week behind with this letter. It was thoroughly worthwhile and I will be writing quite a long series. We were rather less than free during the tour, yet we managed to gather a considerable amount of printable stuff.

An awful lot of irresponsible rumor goes on in Berlin and some quite erroneous impressions of the Russian zone are current. This is largely the Russians' own fault, because they won't adjust themselves sufficiently to western practices to give our newspapermen free access to information.

I phoned up Frankfort yesterday and learned that a number of letters from you are awaiting my return. That's fine. I find it best to keep my mail and telegrams coming to one place rather than having them forwarded because they are so likely to get lost. But remember that if you think I am away from my base and want to get in touch with me at any time you can send the telegram to Edwin L. James [Managing editor of *NYT*] *in New York and ask* him to forward it. A cable to Cyrus Sulzberger, New York Times, *London*, would perhaps be even better, as my connections with him are more personal. I was really lucky to be away on this tour at this time seeing that the job of relaying messages for Arthur Hays Sulzberger and generally playing office boy, or girl, kept Kathleen McLaughlin hopping. [Kathleen was head of the *Times* Berlin bureau.]

Kathleen has a charming little house near the press camp in Zehlendorf and is looking around for a bigger one for the time when our staff is enlarged. Almost all the correspondents live in private houses or their own here since the American sector consists mainly of villas.

When we returned from the Russian zone and drove to the Russian headquarters to drop our conducting officers, I took the opportunity to do a little sightseeing. It was a shocking experience, even though I knew what to expect. Potsdamer Platz I almost failed to recognize. The old Wertheim department store was completely gone and most of the other surrounding buildings too. The Reichs Kanzlerei has been left about as it was when the Red Army occupied it. Rubble, etc. is still strewn about as a sort of object lesson I suppose. The Brandenburger Tor is damaged and the horses on top about half smashed. The American Embassy, which moved to the Bluecher palace next to the Brandenburger Tor just before the war, is burned out. So is the French Embassy. The Adlon appears to be partly intact, although windows and doors on the street level were bricked up. Almost every building including the old *United Press* office was damaged or burned out the length of Unter den Linden. I got the driver to drive out the "East West Axis" through the Tiergarten which was almost unrecognizable because so many trees have been cut down for fuel. Then we cut across to the Kurfuerstendamm and Olivaerplatz where the Long's apartment was half sheared away by bombs. It makes it rather personal when one discovers one's former bedroom windows fire-blackened and gaping from a ruin.

Out here in Zehlendorf there is practically no damage, however, and this little house is idyllic and quiet. The Longs' old parrot walks about in the garden imitating cats and dogs, whistling, and tapping like a typewriter, etc.

All my love now to you all. I must get down to work on these Russian stories,
Dana

In the meantime, another of Dana's reports on displaced people and refugees was published:

**REFUGEES STREAM OUT OF GERMANY'S CAMPS;
SEEK THE PROMISE OF NEW LAND OR OLD HOME**

By DANA ADAMS SCHMIDT
By Wireless to THE NEW YORK TIMES.
FRANKFORT ON THE MAIN, Germany, April 10—Through Frankfort today passed 674 Jewish children on their way to Palestine, 734 Poles going back to Poland, and a few last Frenchmen, Belgians, Netherlanders, Czechs and Norwegians. Also on the way were thousands of Germans expelled from the East and a few last Italians, Hungarians, Rumanians and others.

It was springtime in Germany and they were going home—to new homes, old homes, and homes that no longer exist.

The Americans, too, whose victory made possible or necessary all this home-going, were pulling every redeployment string to get to their ships, leaving behind a dwindling army.

They passed through Frankfort's nauseous rubble, with its undiscovered dead, to spring-bright fields where now labor the discharged soldiers of the Wehrmacht instead of the captives of Europe. Victors and vanquished often were riding the same trains, singing with anticipation or silent with foreboding.

Of the Jewish children, most are survivors of concentration camps, aged 4 to 17. Eighty-four came from the Frankfort area, 102 from the British zone and 484 from Munich and the United States zone in Austria. An officer of UNRRA said that one-third of the last-named had infiltrated recently from Poland.

Laughing after months of care, they trooped off the trains into the railway station black with Germans waiting for trains twenty-four hours of the day.

Sudetens from Czechoslovakia, Swabians from Hungary, Silesians, East Prussians—all the expelled persons came out to stare from the air raid shelter.

"Juedische Kinder," they whispered, and made a lane through the crowd.

At the Jewish welfare center where the children gathered this afternoon, some danced round and round, chanting in Hebrew, from which rose shrilly over and over the word "Israel." And the Germans stared. "Deutsche kaput schlagen!" suggested a red-haired tot from Poland to her interviewer.

In new clothes, mostly contributed by Americans, they seemed happy and healthy although a few will go to tuberculosis sanitariums in Palestine.

Tonight, equipped with seven days' dry rations and considerable baggage, they traveled on under UNRRA and Jewish Agency supervision to Marseille. There, children from France, Belgium, the Netherlands and Sweden will make up the party of 850, who will be admitted to Palestine under the monthly quota of 1,500.

The Poles from the UNRRA camp at Hanau meanwhile set out on the four-day trip to Poland. They cut down boughs to decorate their boxcars, stored away baggage, tables, chairs, mattresses, rabbits and chickens.

Dana wrote a report concerning German youth that was also published in April:

YOUNG VAGABONDS
HARASS GERMANS

Gangs Roam About Country
Areas, Pilfering, Spreading
Disease and Begging

By DANA ADAMS SCHMIDT
By Wireless to THE NEW YORK TIMES.
FRANKFORT ON THE MAIN, Germany, April 12 (Delayed)—Like Russia's half-wild vagabonds after World War I, Germany's youth is on the road.

Around any Red Cross club, Army nickel bar, post exchange, mess or billet that is not protected by barbed wire, crowds of youngsters, aged 14 and up, may be seen loitering at any and all times. The girls are waiting to be picked up and the boys are waiting to run an errand to carry something, anything for a few cigarettes or a candy bar.

Others may be seen in gangs on any highway or hanging around railway stations where there are good opportunities for pilfering.

Most of this important portion of German youth, as represented in Frankfort, came with the 620,000 German refugees who have passed through the town in the past twelve months. A few are routed into one of the air-raid shelters that serve as transient hotels for the Germans, but only a few.

In a casual interrogation at a railway station several said that their parents in the French zone had sent them out on the road to shift for themselves because there was not enough to eat at home. Others from the Soviet zone sought an audience with lurid tales of the Russians, designed for American ears.

Homeless, without papers or ration cards and wary of work or confinement, they have found one way to get along—the black market. A package of twenty American cigarettes will bring in exchange food, or 50 to 80 marks, more than one probably would earn in a week's work.

These homeless youths live outside the law, finding places to sleep without registering with the police, as Germans normally must do. In the natural course of events they run into young SS men and other Nazis similarly living outside the law.

The next step is the formation of organizations, which are coming unpleasantly to the notice of the military police, such as the Edelweiss-Piraten or the Polentoeter—killers of Poles—who hold up Germans and by preference displaced persons, though they generally keep clear of Americans.

These are representative of a youth that was more regimented than any other in the world for twelve years, now wandering aimlessly, disillusioned, dissolute and without guidance. These young Germans are dirty and diseased.

A spot check of young girls in the Frankfort railway station by German police recently disclosed that 50 per cent had venereal diseases.

By the middle of April, Dana was well established in Frankfort at the Park Hotel.

This week I got your first letter which you sent to Paris. Surprisingly enough it was forwarded without a hitch and I was delighted to have it so soon after my arrival.

A cable from New York informs me that papers for my car have been airmailed to me and that the cost of shipment was $502 instead of $400. I told them to deduct the difference from my salary, so you will be getting an abbreviated check shortly. I cabled asking when and where it will be landed and will go to meet it.

Work here involves a great deal of moving around, particularly between Frankfort and Wiesbaden. Public Relations have four jeeps only and is not very happy about letting them go out for long periods. The Times *has already come through with a couple of clippings and I see I have had some signers, always encouraging. There is an infinity of stories here though I think I must be careful not to overwork the market for situationer and feature-type pieces.*

It is still bright and sunny and warm which means that the ruins are beginning to smell. Germany is flat and so are the Germans but I feel they have a fundamental vigor that will permit a comeback, for better or worse, sooner or later.

Sidney Gruson is still not back, although he wired me he would be here last Tuesday or Wednesday. I had to relay him a couple of very angry wires from Cy Sulzberger because he left for Switzerland before Cy wanted him to.

Carl Quigley who was at Pomona when I was there and whom I've run into variously in Cairo, Algiers and when he conducted the party of correspondents who landed with the French on the Riviera, is here now as correspondent for INS. *He is a likable guy all right. Percy Knauth, once with the* Times, *now with* Time, *came through with his wife on the way to Vienna. At Stuttgart I saw Dana Hodgon, formerly Consul in Berlin, now a Consul General. He and I came over on the plane with a fellow who used to be in* the Berlin Embassy. *There is a certain circle of people who work abroad who keep turning up over and over.*

Erika Mann[124] *was in the bar a few nights ago, very intense and interesting but I fear somewhat warped in her views. She is one of those people who know too much about their subject, having lived with the German problem most of her life. I wouldn't commit myself to it publicly, but I think I can be more objective about things than most correspondents, having had a bit of about everything in my life.*

You ask me about the girls. I am very uncertain in my mind—that's about all I can say about it. I find that when I commit my views to paper they begin to assume a reality, a sort of committal, that I am not really prepared to make yet. I haven't heard from Dorothy yet. I saw Dudley in Paris and am pretty sure I don't want to marry her. I wouldn't read the above to the rest of the family.

In any event the coming year is going to be a very full one in all respects. I still have that beginning of the school year feeling.

I hope you will send me copies of the pictures we took in front of the house just before I left and Elizabeth I hope will send me pictures of the babies from time to time; they are grand.

General Adler, the general manager of the Times, *came through on a publishers' tour and I have to be here again next Sunday when he comes back. Visiting executives are a nuisance.*

Give my love to Grandma and Steinie, All my love, DANA

In a hand-written postscript to this April 14 letter, he added:

Thanks for the clippings. They are particularly interesting. There is no longer need to send me my own clips, however, as I get them from the Times. *Other correspondents' pieces from Germany would always be useful.*

---

[124] Erika Mann was the eldest daughter of the novelist Thomas Mann. She had a privileged childhood, their home being a meeting place for intellectuals and artists. Becoming a writer and actress, she had lesbian affairs with prominent women—also a marriage of convenience to W.H. Auden in order to obtain British citizenship.

Although denazification and re-educating Germans were important assignments for the American Military, unfortunately, they were hindered by a lack of the important tools of U.S. publications.

U.S. PUBLICATIONS RARE IN GERMANY

Trading with the Enemy Act Makes Circulation Difficult, Hindering Re-education

By DANA ADAMS SCHMIDT
By Wireless to THE NEW YORK TIMES.

FRANKFORT ON THE MAIN, Germany, April 14—One of the most formidable obstacles at the present time to re-educating of the German people, according to leading Military Government officers in charge of education, publishing and information control, is the United States' Trading With the Enemy Act, which is hindering dissemination of American books, magazines and newspapers among the Germans.

Considering that it is the declared policy of the United Sates Government and of the Military Government not only to denazify but also to promote re-education toward democracy, it might have been expected that the occupation would be followed by a flood of selected United States publications, in English or translated. Nearly a year after V-E Day, however, there is only a trickle, and one great opportunity appears to have been lost.

At least, as one officer said, the United States cannot be accused of brusquely imposing its culture and political attitude on the German people, if that is any advantage. Now, German educators and intellectuals of all kinds have reached the point of begging for American publications, and another opportunity offers itself. But their craving cannot be satisfied. The reason, Military Government officers explained, is that the Trading With the Enemy Act still prevents American publishers from selling their products to Germans. It is not, as has been widely assumed, that the Germans are not yet considered capable of digesting the raw materials of American intellectual life, the officers said.

Efforts of various United States authorities to overcome this difficulty by acting as intermediaries in acquiring American publications and distributing them in Germany have been laudable but inadequate, in the opinion of the officers.

These efforts have included creation of American libraries by OWI men, now under State Department control, at Frankfort on the Main, Marburg, Erlangen, Stuttgart, Munich, Heidelberg and Berlin, and smaller reference libraries at half a dozen other points. The OWI has also distributed to German book shops and libraries 35,000 copies each of six important American books and has had copies of others printed in German in Switzerland. It has obtained translation rights for at least twelve American books for German publishers and is negotiating for more.

In addition, three American produced magazines, Heute, Amerikanische Rundschau and Neue Auslese, and a newspaper called Die Neue Zeitung have acquired large circulations. Some American films are being shown, but they include a high percentage of Grade B movies. No American films are yet available for schools, nor have, as far as is ascertainable, any American lecturers appeared at German institutions or elsewhere in Germany.

On the balance, the American program of denazification of German intellectual life has been effective, but it has stopped there. Re-education and promotion of democratic attitudes have had to depend mainly on German publications, which suffer and are likely to continue to suffer from a lack of paper and do not satisfy the hunger of the most positive political elements for new inspiration from America.

More than thirty German newspapers, six radio stations and about 175 publishers have now been licensed. The publishers had produced 227 books and pamphlets up to the end of February, with 250 more in type and awaiting paper.

As Dana had reported previously, German youth, who had been highly regimented during childhood and many whose families had been disrupted by the war, were now adrift, wandering about the countryside, forming gangs, stealing and generally getting into trouble. The American military was aware of the problem, and under the direction of General Joseph T. McNarney, plans were being made to assist these young people. Dana reported in an article on April 16:

**GERMANY'S YOUTH
TO RECEIVE GI AID**

**Recreational Facilities Will Be
Shared in Program Started
by General McNarney**

**By DANA ADAMS SCHMIDT
By Wireless to THE NEW YORK TIMES.**
FRANKFORT ON THE MAIN, Germany, April 16—American occupation troops will take a hand in the development of German youth activities and share requisitioned recreational and athletic facilities with young Germans, under a directive from Gen. Joseph T. McNarney, commander of United States forces in the European theatre, that is now being distributed.

Concerned over rising delinquency and vagrancy among German youth and the danger of political complications, General McNarney ordered the eleven principal tactical commands to appoint full-time liaison officers to work with the Military Government's "youth officers." One such officer is already functioning and two are eventually to be named in each of the American zone's three Laender [states].

The liaison and youth officers are to work with German youth committees, composed of school, church and similar officials, in every county on the following program, in which qualified mature American troops will take part:

First, sharing of athletic fields, gymnasiums, swimming pools, etc., which in many cases have been entirely requisitioned by the troops.

Second, turning over any used or unwanted facilities or supplies, such as balls and nets, to German youth organizations.

Third, assisting the county youth committees in setting up youth hostels, movie showings, sports competitions and handicraft programs and in promoting volunteer work in farming and repairing war damage, and meetings at which "German youth can hear about the youth of the democratic countries."

The new zonal directive permits German youth organizations for the first time to expand from a county to a state-wide basis. In Greater Hesse almost a thousand different youth groups with a membership of about one hundred thousand have been authorized by the Military Government, and the development in Wuerttemberg-Baden and Bavaria has been similar. The most numerous among the organizations are sports clubs, followed by church groups, those with cultural objectives and the Boy Scouts.

Political activities are banned and uniforms and emblems must have Military Government approval, but it is generally admitted that political parties are quietly seeking to win some of the new organizations. An application by the Social Democratic party to organize a youth section was denied in Greater Hesse.

One of Dana's reports gave a glimpse of economic and business conditions in Germany—at least in the American zone:

**AMERICAN PLANTS
IN GERMANY IN USE**

**Representatives Find Factories
Less Damaged Than Expected
After Tour in U.S. Zone**

By DANA ADAMS SCHMIDT
By Wireless to THE NEW YORK TIMES.
FRANKFORT ON THE MAIN, Germany, April 19—A total of 200 American business men have visited the United Sates zone of occupation and Berlin since last October to inspect the property of their concerns and investigate the possibilities of exports from Germany, military government sources disclosed today. About thirty are in Germany at present.

Most business men have found that their properties were less damaged than expected and have been partly responsible for the resumption of the export of such products as chemical and optical goods that will help balance the cost of necessary imports into Germany.

Hitherto, business men have enjoyed the use of most Army transportation facilities and billets free of charge because machinery to collect fees had not been set up, but they, along with newspaper correspondents, are to be put on a "pay-as-you-go" basis in the next few weeks. A vehicle with a driver will cost a minimum of $15 a day, billets about $2 and food about $1 a day.

A few business visitors have rated "very important person" treatment, having been assigned to generals' quarters, such as the Victory guesthouse near Frankfort, but most get regular officers' billets. These can rarely be compared with first-class American hotels in comfort, but are clean and heated.

No arrangements have been made yet for American businessmen to visit the British, French or Russian zones of occupation nor for the non-American business men to enter the United States zone. It is expected, however, that agreements to exchange visitors with the British and French will be worked out in the next few months. Differences regarding the removal of American-owned property from the Russian zone are expected to hold up any agreement with the Russians.

Among the American visitors have been representatives of the following companies: Chicago Pneumatic Tool, General Milk, American Overseas Airlines, Socony Vacuum, Commercial Decal, Farrand Optical, Dentists Supply of New York, Blow Knox Autoclave, General Motors, Standard Oil, Goodyear Rubber, American Cyanide, United Fruit, Texas Oil, Illinois Tool Works, Remington Rand, International Business Machines, International Telephone and Telegraph, International Harvester, Nestle-LeMur, E.R. Squibb and Bode-Voight.

Toward the end of April, Dana wrote several articles on the German elections, which were being reintroduced in the United States zone as symbols of democracy. There were four major parties. The Communists were relatively weak in the U.S. zone; they wanted to cooperate with the Soviet Union in the reconstruction of Germany, and among other aims, they wanted to keep Germany from the Ruhr, which would enable Germany to build up an arsenal and perhaps, to take back the Eastern lands which Russia took after the war. The Social Democrats, Dana said, were only mildly socialistic. There was some talk of a possible merger with the Communists. The Socialists were afraid of dictation from Moscow. The Christian Social Union, also called the Christian

Democratic Party, was in the central position with the Liberal Democrats on the right, advocating free enterprise and private property.

In an article published on April 29, Dana wrote:

The general political shift in the voting appeared to have been slightly to the Right although the Communists gained at most points by comparison with the January elections. [These were held in the rural areas to elect the Councils, who in turn, elected a Landrat, who is similar to a County Commissioner.] The elections proceeded without notable incidents except at Landsberg.

The trouble started when a rumor spread in the Jewish displaced persons camp at Diessen, thirty-six miles from Landsberg, that six Jews had been murdered by Germans armed with machine guns. A headquarters announcement, however, said that the rumor involved two Jews guarding a Jewish trade school who had disappeared.

The Jewish refugees, according to Major Thurston, marched out of their camp at 9:00 A.M. in twenty groups of twenty men and began storming election booths to avenge the rumored deaths. They set fire to one German bus and four other German vehicles, he said.

During the rioting twenty-five Jewish refugees were arrested, but a headquarters announcement said that 1,000 Jews in mass formation had prevented the arrest of three of their number by United States military police, obliging the military policemen to fire over their heads. No American soldier was injured. Two provost marshals and the military government are investigating the cause of the disorder.

Although Dana disliked the idea of reporting at the Nuremberg trials, he was, perhaps, fortunate in being assigned when Hjalmar Schacht was before the Tribunal. Schacht was an interesting man and not a rabid Nazi. According to John Weitz in *Hitler's Banker,* William Shirer called Hjalmar Schacht "the only brilliant and next to Hitler, the most interesting Nazi." Weitz also wrote that "while Schacht's genius as commissioner of currency and president of the Reichsbank saved Germany almost overnight from economic ruin and financed the world's best-equipped army and air force, he never joined the Nazi Party." In the early years before Hitler came to power, Schacht apparently thought that Hitler might be a good choice for the chancellery and good for Germany, and he supported the choice of Hitler for chancellor. Later, he realized his mistake, and after he was connected with the attempted assassination of Hitler (on July 20, 1944), he was imprisoned at Dachau. Freed by the Allies, he was re-arrested by the Americans because he had been a minister in Hitler's regime. [125]

Following is Dana's report on the Schacht trial before the Tribunal at Nuremberg:

SCHACHT ESCAPES TRAPS OF JACKSON

Banker Insists His Apparent Support of Hitler's Regime Was Purely Camouflage

By DANA ADAMS SCHMIDT
By Wireless to THE NEW YORK TIMES.
NUREMBERG, Germany, May 3—The examination of Hjalmar Schacht before the International Military Tribunal wound up inconclusively today after Schacht had spent three days on the stand—longer than any of the accused except Hermann Goering.

He was followed by the eleventh defendant, Walter Fund, Schacht's successor as president of the Reichsbank and Minister of Economy, who began his testimony with a submission of biographical details.

Up to the last Justice Robert H. Jackson, chief United States prosecutor, kept up a barrage of documents and cross-examination to prove Schacht's guilt under the first two counts of the indictment, his participation in the general Nazi conspiracy and in preparing for aggressive war.

---

[125]   Schacht, Hjalmar. *Encyclopedia Britannica*, 2007. Encyclopedia Online.

But the banker appeared to have slipped through Mr. Jackson's fingers in the opinion of most legal observers. Apart from passing references to Schacht's approval of the restrictions on Jews, no attempt was made to press the other two counts concerning war crimes and crimes against humanity.

Jackson Quotes Documents

In particular Mr. Jackson throughout sought to show that Schacht had helped to bring Adolf Hitler into power, that his struggle with Goering for the control of the four-year plan was due to personal ambition and desire for control of and more effective preparation for war and that he finally precipitated his dismissal by Hitler in January, 1939, only to dissociate himself from an anticipated financial catastrophe.

Today Mr. Jackson read an oath that Schacht, after the Anschluss, had personally administered to new Austrian employees of the Reichsbank, which forced them to swear to be faithful and obedient to Hitler. He also quoted a speech Schacht made to employees of the Austrian National Bank "exposing all the sanctimonious hypocrisy exuding from the foreign press."

The United States prosecutor charged that Schacht had taken the initiative in absorbing the Sudetenland's financial system, recounted Schacht's colonial ambitions, suggested he must have held responsibilities after January, 1939.

Says He Would Kill Hitler

Schacht's general argument was that he merely had recognized the inevitability of Hitler's accession to power, had realized that he could influence the regime only from within, had favored rearmament only to regain Germany's equality with her neighbors and then had sought to limit it and finally had resorted to sabotage and betrayal.

"I would have killed Hitler myself if I had had a chance," he said today.

Whenever his statements of Nazi ideology were thrown up to him he fell back on the argument that it had been camouflage for his real purposes in a double game.

In answer to Mr. Jackson's charges today he said the oath in Austria was a mere routine that all State officials had to take and that his Sudetenland functions were legitimate, since the western powers had handed over the Sudetenland to Germany on a "silver platter."

Human interest stories always interested Dana, and he was pleased to write about life in Germany from the point of view of army wives who had come to live in Germany:

**SOLDIER WIVES AND CHILDREN
BEGIN NEW LIFE IN GERMANY**

**First Arrivals Gasp at Bomb Wreckage but
Settle down in Comfortable Quarters**

**By DANA ADAMS SCHMIDT
By Wireless to THE NEW YORK TIMES.**
NUREMBERG, Germany, May 4—The first group of wives and children to join their soldier-husbands and fathers in the American zone of occupation in Germany were settling down in comfortable quarters this week in the midst of an adoring Army.

A high percentage of them were "Army wives" who knew already what it is to live "on post." But living as victors in a conquered land was a new experience to them all.

This week they scarcely had time to see much of Germany or the Germans beyond gasping at the wreckage left by Allied bombing in all the large towns as they drove past. Invitations were too numerous to be accepted and husbands and friends pooled their liquor rations for substantial housewarmings.

Servants' Pay Low
At Frankfort on the Main they lived in apartments within the American compound but in most of some thirty other towns throughout the zone they were scattered widely in the best houses available. Some at Wiesbaden, for example, were discovering that as many as four German families had been moved out of houses to make room for one American couple.

They were discovering that German servants were cheap at the ten mark to the dollar rate of exchange and that American women accustomed to doing their own work at home need not lift a finger in Germany. A good cook could be had for $20 a month and a maid for $10 or less, especially if there was the prospect of getting some American food.

Such worries as cropped up for the American women in the first week after the happy reunions were mostly that they were not going to find enough to do and would be bored. After one or two "brushes" with guards on the lookout for fraeuleins at Army movies the Army hastily got out an order that passports would be adequate identification for American women in civilian clothes.

Work was being rushed on shopping centers, where the women will find everything from hot water bottles to cigarettes.

Aboard ship coming over the wives got a glimpse of what "caste" distinctions may lead to overseas when generals' wives were seated at a separate table, but the problem of what clubs and messes could be attended remained to be settled.

The Army, too, had its worries, with the CID [126] men wondering whether the American women would be safe living in requisitioned homes with requisitioned furnishings, in many cases including kitchenware, in the midst of hungry and frequently resentful Germans. Transportation officers were fretting over the problem of getting the wives where they wanted to go.

Inevitably, not a few of the American women were mistaken for fraeuleins and received suggestive offers of cigarettes and chocolate and were impressed by the difference between American manners at home and abroad.

On May 6, Dana wrote in his letter home:

I'm back in Frankfort for a day and a half on my way to Stuttgart for the "Laenderrat" [Council of Ministers]. After that I'll finally get away to France to pick up my car.

A letter and an envelope full of clippings from you were waiting for me when I returned. I thoroughly enjoyed all the clippings. They are most useful. Ray Daniell's series of the "expose" variety seem only partly true to me. I think he has gone off the deep end in some of his criticism of Military Government and his belief that Nazism is still a vital force in Germany. MG is doing a

---

[126]   Criminal Investigation Department, the branch of all British Police.

better job than he gives it credit for and Nazism <u>as such</u> is, I believe, pretty dead; fascist-type tendencies may of course crop up in other forms from time to time, but the real danger in Germany as in all of Europe at this time comes from the Communists; they are the people who are endangering civil liberties. Well, I am still working out my views on Germany. Ask me again a year from now.

I spoke to Ray on the phone to Berlin last night. He says Kathleen wants to stay in Berlin, which is all right with me, and thinks I ought to make my headquarters in Munich, and cover the other two "Laender" by periodic trips to Stuttgart and Frankfort. I'm satisfied to have the run of the "zone." Anyway, I can make my headquarters where I think best when he is gone. Stuttgart is most central but lacks satisfactory communications. Munich, as Ray points out, is the center of the most important political subdivision of the American zone. Frankfort is adequately covered by the agencies; news about the American army from here is not as important as it used to be. What the agencies don't cover is the German-political type of thing.

I have had an offer to write a two thousand-word story on the army's program for German youth for the Magazine Digest *of Toronto. $250. I will accept as soon as I know I can get the material they want. The offer came via the* Times *so I guess it is all right.*

Glad to hear Tuckie is raising hell again. But they should have taught him not to steal one-quarter pound pieces of butter at the Rancho.

No, I definitely got only one picture from you, so I'll be looking forward to some more.

The Times *will pay all my operating costs for the car and Ray Daniell has promised to arrange a depreciation payment. They probably would have bought me a car in Germany anyway, but I didn't know that and I'm glad to have it my own.*

Just continue using this address at Frankfort for the time being. It is a good address and stuff can always be forwarded from here.

All my love to you all, DANA

Incidentally, you must not expect to see as many bylines from me now as I might have when working in a large capital. In compensation my stories may have more color and vitality over a period. The difference is that in a large capital a substantial amount of material is regularly and easily obtained from printed material of many kinds. In the field one must dig up one's own material from primary sources, and travel, both of which things take time.

The problem of the large number of displaced persons in the U.S. zone of occupation was still acute on May 11, when Dana wrote another piece on the subject:

There were 11,250 more persons in the United States zone of displaced persons camps on April 30 than on March 30, this source said, in spite of the fact that 16,500 persons had been repatriated and 1,350 emigrated during April.

New arrivals undoubtedly exceeded departures, he added, although the apparent figure of about 28,000 infiltrees might be exaggerated by errors in earlier counts and the recent registration of displaced persons who had been living outside the camps.

In face of the situation, G-5 (section of U.S. occupation zone) is working on a proposed directive that would declare repatriation to be at an end. This would clear the way for the Army to press for emigration of displaced persons of all kinds to potential new homes such as Latin America and France and to organize displaced persons employment more widely.

The latter hitherto has been held back by the belief that the unemployed displaced persons would be more interested in repatriation than with jobs.

The United State Military Government has asked the State Department to obtain the details of the Dominican Republic's and Brazil's recent offers before the United Nations refugee committee to take a number of displaced persons. The State Department, however, showed hesitation to interfere in what is considered United Nations business and the military government still has not received the information.

Consequently some officers are considering the possibilities of asking the countries directly involved for this information, as well as approaching other countries for the immigration information that they sought from the State Department some time ago.

With a view to employment within the zone, the UNRRA is preparing to classify all displaced persons according to occupational skills. Considerable employment opportunities will be created by the projected consolidation of many scattered depots of the continental base section into twenty or more large depots.

As a trial the Army will employ 4,000 displaced persons at one of the first such depots in Hanau, where there are large camps for Poles and Baltics. Another depot at Frankfort on the Main is to employ 2,000 more.

In the past the Army usually found the displaced persons unsatisfactory workers because they tended to report only when so inclined, an attitude partly attributable to the fact that no consumer goods can be purchased by money earned and the further fact that such money cannot be converted into foreign currency by the emigrants.

In the hopes of improving the workers' morale, G-5 also is working on a project to permit the displaced persons to exchange the money they earn for the money of the country to which they will go, although this might involve the United States Government's redeeming German money for which there is no dollar equivalent.

Army hunts for "Spongers"

The United States Army has ordered a hunt throughout its occupation zone for impostors and criminals believed sponging on United States and United Nations aid.

The Army, noting that new "displaced persons" were appearing mysteriously in free care camps, ordered that the more than 400,000 displaced persons both in and out of camps be put through a screening.

Elaborate machinery will be in operation within a few days for the project, approved by the War Department, and the result may be the forcible ouster from the camps of many so-called "displaced persons."

Army authorities also hoped the vast screening plan would reveal the perpetrators of crimes that have been attributed loosely to "displaced persons."

On May 18, Dana wrote he finally had the car he had ordered while on vacation in the United States:

Ye Lincoln Zephyr is back here with me [in Frankfort], *safe and sound, locked up in the Public Relations garage. Getting it was an interesting if somewhat hectic interlude. When I turned up in Paris, Cy immediately drafted me to help work on the Conference, although they already have a vast staff for that purpose. . . Gruson and Friedman have been brought over from London and a new fellow who, like me once upon a time, is abroad on a Pulitzer scholarship and is working for the Paris office.*

I went down to Le Havre by train, spent half a day getting the car through customs and drove back to Paris at night. She worked like a gem, all the way to Frankfort. My only trouble was one flat tire. I spent one night at Verdun on the way in a very likable hotel which provided a first class dinner. Another memorable dinner I got at a little place called Caudebec in Normandy. There's plenty of food in the provinces, however little gets to Paris. Paris incidentally seems to have picked up a lot since I left. Black market prices have come down and life for foreigners is quite tolerable, even if the Army has stopped feeding them.

Before I left I managed to get off a magaziner for Markel concerning the "little men" of Germany. Markel has an idea that too much is written about cosmic political issues and not enough about what ordinary little people do and say. Furthermore he wants such stuff written "like the New Yorker*"!*

Having to go to Nuremberg one week then to Stuttgart and to France the next has rather broken up my work around here. Now I understand a super secret trip is being organized for the next few days. Most annoying. There are a number of stories I want to handle here before I move south to Stuttgart and Munich.

It's too bad my trip to Paris didn't come just a little later. I might have seen the Williamses, but I will have other occasions to go to Paris in coming months. It is relatively easy now I have the car.

I'm glad to hear you are getting about after your bout of bronchitis. That is very bad stuff and not at all the sort of thing that is supposed to go on in

California. But I feel great confidence in Dr. Bullock. He made an excellent impression on me.

What ever became of that project to buy a beach house that cropped up just before I left? I still think it's a good idea.

I'm going to take this down and mail it before it gets any later.

All my love, as always, DANA

The "super secret trip" (for correspondents) Dana mentioned in the letter above turned out to be a raid on a multi-national smuggling ring at the point on the Danube where Germany, Czechoslovakia and Austria meet. Dana's story follows:

U.S. FORCE RAIDS DANUBE "FLEET"; RUSSIAN RIVER CONTROL DISPUTED

By DANA ADAMS SCHMIDT
By Wireless to THE NEW YORK TIMES.
VILSHOFEN, Germany, May 21—Four thousand members of the new constabulary of the United States zone, assisted by Counter-Intelligence Corps and Criminal Investigation Division agents and German river police boats, at dawn this morning seized 372 Danube River craft of a dozen nationalities. These included twelve gunboats and eighteen auxiliary craft of the Hungarian Navy that had been gathering moss for the last year tied up along a forty-five-mile stretch between Passau and Deggendorf.

Constabulary aircraft droned up and down over the formidable deployment of force, called "Operation Grab-Bag." Its officially designated purpose was to investigate and break a suspected far-flung smuggling ring and underground railroad for escaping SS [Elite Guard] men believed to be conducted by the 3,000 persons, including families, living aboard the boats.

The first check yielded five heavy machine guns in perfect working order, three radio transmitters, some gun sights, periscopes, ammunition and explosives and several holds crammed with leather, rugs, shoes, bolts of cloth, furs, candles, flour, beans, noodles, parts of motors and junk.

Some arrests were made, but no complete tally for the investigation, which will take several days, was available.

Gen. Joseph T. McNarney, commander of the United States forces in Europe, ordered the raid and directed that Hungarians, numbering several hundred, who fled to American-controlled waters after a disastrous engagement with the Russians at the end of the war, be either interned and processed for repatriation as prisoners of war or discharged as refugees.

It was the first large-scale operation for the constabulary, commanded by Maj. Gen. Ernest N. Harmon, which will become the zone's main security force when fully activated in July. The Army searched the boats for ammunition a year ago and has since raided individual craft for black market supplies, but the Hungarians, while technically prisoners of war, had freedom of movement in the area.

Among a spate of rumors about their and others' activities, which may have partly motivated today's crackdown, were reports that they were smuggling diamonds, narcotics and also arms, which in some mysterious manner were supposedly destined for Palestine; that they were running SS men to places in Austria where their tattooing was removed, and that they were somehow connected with a reported wave of nineteen murders last month in Passau, where three American Military Government officers were murdered last January.

But the most substantial fact resulting from the operation was that the United States now has direct control of the most important part of all the Danube's transport craft. The United States has continually campaigned for a revival of the paralyzed international traffic on the Danube against the opposition of the Russians, who control most of the length of the river.

Including those seized today there are in American-controlled Danube waters about 700 barges, tankers, tugboats and other craft of French, Hungarian, Rumanian, Czech, Bulgarian and other nationalities. Conflicting claims as to their ownership was offered in some quarters as one explanation for the long delay in carrying out a full-scale raid.

[Most of the boats and barges of the Danubian Shipping Company moved into the Austrian and German sections of the Danube in the closing days of the war and are now in American zones. Russia has claimed the company as a

German asset, but the United States does not agree with her interpretation of the Potsdam clause on such assets and gives every indication of retaining the boats so long as Russia continues to contend that the Danube is no longer an international waterway.]

The Hungarians were permitted to maintain their own administrative machinery, headed by a retired general, called Admiral Trunkwalter, and assisted by a man named Gerokerky, who was closely associated with Ferenc Szalasi's pro-Axis Hungarian puppet Government during the war.

Once again, Dana wrote from Frankfort:

May 24, 1946
No letter from you this week, which is only just I suppose since I am still behind schedule with mine to you. But I did get an envelope of most useful clippings. I should pay you a salary!

I'm glad to get settled down in Frankfort again for a while and to work on some of the stories I want to write. But it won't be for long since Markel has asked me to do something on the "British conception of military government" which will require a quick trip up there [to the British zone]. *Then, I must get ready to head south to Nuremberg and Munich.*

It looks as though I'd have the elections on my hands again this next Sunday as Kathleen McLaughlin has fortuitously chosen the time to make a trip to Copenhagen.

The car is proving a treasure. It is such a blessing to be able to pick up and go when you are ready, instead of having to coax transportation out of an unwilling army. Furthermore, about the day I appeared with Lincoln Zephyr the army started charging for use of its jeeps by civilians. $4.00 for the first hour! For twenty dollars I can buy enough gas and oil to keep me going for a month. After a tiring day running around Wiesbaden today, I settled behind the wheel and felt that the relaxation provided was in itself sufficient justification for all my expenditures.

Last Sunday Dick Clark of the UP, *who has become quite a friend of mine, and I went off on a little trip to call on a German abstractionist painter* named Nay [127]. *It was interesting to know that some people of that kind managed to survive the Nazi period. We will have the story for a Sunday. But more important, I bought a painting. Six hundred Marks for a watercolor purporting to represent "a man returning home," a type of universal theme of the times that appealed to him and to me. I will keep it in my room for a while and then send it to you.*

It is pretty abstract all right. It is apparently divided into two parts, one represents the outer world from which the man is coming, in red and yellow, the other represents the supernatural in the concept of home, predominantly in blue which he regards as a color representing the supernatural. In case you can't tell when you see it, the man is supposed to be reaching out towards the woman.

Ernst Nay painting: *A Man Returning Home*

---

[127]　See Appendix.

Actually this picture is considerably more pictorial and easy to understand than most. That is perhaps one reason why I chose it. There is another called "Orphans," with two very morose and abstract heads which Dick Clark wants to buy for 900 marks. I am tempted to have one of the oils at 3000.

It has been quite warm lately—mid-summerish, frequent sudden thunderstorms. There's a thrill about that kind of weather that Californians miss.

The coming month is going to be busy, with all sorts of things to be done for Markel, that youth magazine article, and the daily stuff as well.

Give my love to Grandma and Elizabeth and tell them I think of them even if I don't write, but will write one of them in days soon.

Love to Steinie too, Steinie the incomparable,

Good night, Dana

As Dana surmised, it fell to him to report the German elections. The results were summarized in the headlines:

GERMAN CITY VOTE
CLOSE IN BIG POLL
Christian Social Union Leads
for Whole U.S. Zone, With
Social Democrats Strong

COMMUNIST TALLY LAGS

Catholic Party Maintains Hold
in Bavaria but Falls Below
Its Expected Strength

By DANA ADAMS SCHMIDT
By Wireless to THE NEW YORK TIMES.
FRANKFORT ON THE MAIN, GERMANY, Monday, May 27—
Nearly complete returns from yesterday's municipal elections in the thirty-eight larger towns of the American zone showed the Christian Social Union probably

> **GERMANS CONSIDER BASIC STATE LAWS**
>
> Single or 2-Chamber Assembly and Federation or Strong Central Regime Discussed
>
> By DANA ADAMS SCHMIDT
> By Wireless to THE NEW YORK TIMES.
>
> FRANKFORT ON THE MAIN, Germany, May 30—The debate in the German press and among German party leaders on the proposed constitutions for the three Laender [States] of the United States zone is beginning to cast some light on German conceptions of the future political structure of Germany.
>
> Since the state constitutions are intended to fit into a future nation-wide constitution, the projects that are being developed by committees now for the information of the constitutional assemblies in June necessarily involve the conception of such a constitution. To that extent they will be models for it.
>
> Two main issues being debated in Greater Hesse, Bavaria and Wuerttemberg-Baden are a single chamber or a bicameral system and a unitary or federal state.
>
> How best to prevent dictatorial power from falling into the hands of one man again is also an element in most discussions. The United States and Swiss governmental structures are frequently held up as examples.
>
> **Reds for Unicameral Body**
>
> A single omnipotent chamber, such as was rejected by the French last month, thus far has found favor only among the Communists and a minority of the Social Democrats, while only the right-wingers of the Liberal Democratic party have seriously proposed re-creating the highly centralized unitary state. The questions therefore appear to be resolving themselves into "what kind of second chamber" and "what kind of federalism."
>
> The Wuerttemberg-Baden committee at Stuttgart already has made public a detailed first draft of the project, including a senate composed of twenty-four "outstanding personalities" with the right to veto measures of a Landtag, or assembly, composed of 100 elected representatives. The veto could be overridden by a two-thirds vote of the Landtag.
>
> Members of the Greater Hesse committee said it probably would recommend a second chamber composed of representatives of labor unions, employers, agriculture, churches and the like, with similar powers.
>
> While the Bavarian committee has not yet clarified this point it is showing tendencies toward a loose form of federalism and pronounced independence for the component states. It is the only committee that does not propose to insert a clause stating that any provisions conflicting with a future national constitution will become void.
>
> Bavaria's Minister President, Dr. Wilhelm Hoegner, puts emphasis on a Statenbund or federation of states, rather than a Bundestaat or federal state.
>
> **Weimar Constitution Opposed**
>
> The Weimar Constitution, under which Adolf Hitler was able to come to power, is generally considered a very imperfect model; first, because it permitted too great a centralization, and second, because it permitted the Chancellor in emergencies to suspend fundamental liberties and rule by decree without having later to obtain the approval of the Reichstag.
>
> Members of the Greater Hesse constitutional committee have suggested that on a national level such powers should be wielded only by a council composed of the President, Vice President, Chancellor, Vice Chancellor and president of a supreme court, and propose to recommend a similar council for Greater Hesse.
>
> In their emphasis on fitting the Land constitutions into the very hypothetical future national constitution the committees thus far have evaded the more realistic problem of providing machinery for the collaboration of the three states of the United States zone.

still the dominant party in the zone as a whole. The latest count gave the Christian Social Union a slight lead over the Social Democrats, who had earlier today been ahead. The Communists lagged; and any hopes that the city dwellers would swing decisively to the left seem to have been disappointed.

[Returns at 5 A.M., German time, reported by The United Press, showed: Christian Social Union, 677,984; Social Democrats, 610,697; Communists, 142,406; Liberal Democrats, 70,333; others, 86,679; invalid, 37,795.]

The Christian Social Union, which considers Bavaria its particular bailiwick, got a scare in Munich, where it won only twenty seats to the Social Democrats' seventeen, the Communists' two and one each for two smaller groups.

At Nuremberg the Social Democrats with nineteen seats topped the Christian Social Union, which got fifteen, followed by the Communists with four and others with three.

Rain Fails to Cut Balloting

The Christian Social Union, which is Catholic-supported, had won in the two earlier elections in the American zone this spring in rural and smaller communities. The Communists, while gaining yesterday over their previous showing still polled only about 10 per cent of the votes cast.

The voting was heavy, in spite of intermittent rain, exceeding 80 per cent almost everywhere. [Dana's detailed report is in the Appendix.]

With the elections over, the three Laënder (states) in the American zone focused on proposed constitutions. The basic question was whether to have a single chamber or a bicameral system. In the articles following, Dana discussed the debates and their significance for the future:

**GERMANS CONSIDER
BASIC STATE LAWS**

**Single or 2-Chamber Assembly
and Federation or Strong
Central Regime Discussed**

**By DANA ADAMS SCHMIDT
By Wireless to THE NEW YORK TIMES.**
FRANKFORT ON THE MAIN, Germany, May 30—The debate in the German press and among German party leaders on the proposed constitutions for the three Laender [States] of the United States zone is beginning to cast some light on German conceptions of the future political structure of Germany.

Since the state constitutions are intended to fit into a future nation-wide constitution, the projects that are being developed by committees now for the information of the constitutional assemblies in June necessarily involve the conception of such a constitution. To that extent they will be models for it.

Two main issues being debated in Greater Hesse, Bavaria and Wuerttemberg-Baden are a single chamber or a bicameral system and a unitary or federal state.

How best to prevent dictatorial power from falling into the hands of one man again is also an element in most discussions. The United States and Swiss governmental structures are frequently held up as examples.

Reds for Unicameral Body
A single omnipotent chamber, such as was rejected by the French last month, thus far has found favor only among the Communists and a minority

of the Social Democrats, while only the right-wingers of the Liberal Democratic party have seriously proposed re-creating the highly centralized unitary state. The questions therefore appear to be resolving themselves into "what kind of second chamber" and "what kind of federalism."

The Wuerttemberg-Baden committee at Stuttgart already has made public a detailed first draft of the project, including a senate composed of twenty-four "outstanding personalities" with the right to veto measures of a Landtag, or assembly, composed of 100 elected representatives. The veto could be overridden by a two-thirds vote of the Landtag.

Members of the Greater Hesse committee said it probably would recommend a second chamber composed of representatives of labor unions, employers, agriculture, churches and the like, with similar powers.

While the Bavarian committee has not yet clarified this point it is showing tendencies toward a loose form of federalism and pronounced independence for the component states. It is the only committee that does not propose to insert a clause stating that any provisions conflicting with a future national constitution will become void.

Bavaria's Minister President, Dr. Wilhelm Hoegner, puts emphasis on a Staatenbund or federation of states, rather than a Bundestaat, or federal state.

Weimar Constitution Opposed

The Weimar Constitution, under which Adolf Hitler was able to come to power, is generally considered a very imperfect model; first, because it permitted too great a centralization, and second, because it permitted the Chancellor in emergencies to suspend fundamental liberties and rule by decree without having later to obtain the approval of the Reichstag.

Members of the Greater Hesse constitutional committee have suggested that on a national level such powers should be wielded only by a council composed of the President, Vice President, Chancellor, Vice Chancellor and president of a supreme court, and propose to recommend a similar council for Greater Hesse.

In their emphasis on fitting the Land constitutions into the very hypothetical future national constitution, the committees thus far have evaded the more realistic problem of providing machinery for the collaboration of the three states of the United States zone.

At the end of May, Dana decided to describe what the people in Germany were thinking and feeling in the aftermath of war in defeat. Dana interviewed people on the street, in the railway station, in the parks, wherever he found anyone willing to talk. Here are some of the results of these informal interviews. They were published in the Sunday *New York Times* Magazine under the title:

LAND OF QUESTIONS WITHOUT ANSWERS

In Germany today, the people striking out with renewed energy, see only a blank future.

By DANA ADAMS SCHMIDT
FRANKFORT-ON-MAIN *(By Wireless).*
Believing that what certified Grade A anti-Nazis in high office tell the Military Government and the Military Government tells the correspondents is not necessarily what Johnny German is saying, thinking and feeling, I have been going for a few walks in search of Johnny German.

Here on the corner of the railway station square in the sunshine the soldiers stand with their fraeuleins, chewing gum. To the victor the spoils; to the vanquished, chewing gum. Up the street at an intersection of tottering ruins is the center of the black market peopled by furtive Germans, many DP's and a scattering of soldiers. There have been raids, but they always come back.

I cross the square and an elderly German steps off the curb to make way. How maddeningly obsequious he is! As though he expected a kick in the shins. If I glared at him he might doff his hat.

* * *

Inside the railway station it is dark, damp, drafty and seething. It is off limits to Americans except by courtesy of the Military Police. Here is defeated Germany in the raw. Expellees from the Sudetenland and Hungary, evacuees being sent back to the Ruhr, released prisoners with PW on their backs and unauthorized refugees from other zones. Thousands of men, women and children pressed together day and night, shuffling in line for permits, tickets and food; guarding their baggage, sleeping on the stone floor, waiting for trains.

Behind a pile of baggage heaped in the barricade across the corner, a woman is sleeping with her head propped on the stone ledge, her mouth open in a gray face. Her child sprawled on a sack of potatoes is awake, looking about with wide eyes.

There are no hotels for Germans here. But some can lie down in their clothes for a few hours in the bunks of air raid shelters. One is reserved for mothers with children, another for amputees and another for juveniles.

The women gape questioningly as we enter. What do the Americans want? Is something wrong? The floor is clean but there is a harsh animal stench as in a zoo. "The ventilators go on every two hours," says an attendant.

* * *

Two words in German to a dozing form in one of the great waiting rooms and a dozen Germans come to life. "Ach, you speak German! It is so rare." And they begin to pour out questions: "Are my papers good to stay here or do I have to go to the French zone? Would an American doctor look at my leg? It is infected. Are the French going to annex? Are the Americans going to withdraw? Is the ration going to be cut? What are the Americans going to do with us? Where can my daughter sleep?"

Questions, questions without answers. Ask about politics and they are hesitant and awkward. "We don't know much about the parties. We've had enough of politics." "Do you know what's happening in the Russian zone?"

At the door a man approaches on the sly. "Would you exchange a few Reichsmarks for Allied marks? No, wait. Here come the police. They're always watching."

* * *

It is good to be out in the sun again. The sun has been bountiful this spring, but it can never be sufficiently bountiful to dispel the sordidness of the times.

The Germans are still not badly dressed but they are wearing nothing new. There are not yet so many wooden soles as in Paris but they are increasing.

Many of the older people look hollow-cheeked and drawn. More so now, I think, than in Paris.

Yet, there is a feeling of vigor about this clanging, hurrying German life flooding through the square that is not present in Paris. These Germans may despair, commit suicide or revolt but, unlike the French, they are not capable of cultivating pessimism as a way of life. Perhaps the swarms of ever-present children account for the impression of vigor. They still look sturdier than most "liberated children." They will be the last to feel the ration cuts.

It is Saturday afternoon and the soldiers are still there with their fraeuleins. In every park they are thick, in couples and in groups on the grass. The first sugar ration for adults since V-E Day has only just been distributed, and the soldiers have plenty of PX supplies. More important, there are few young Germans left. No sugar, no men. Thirty-two per cent of the babies born in Bavaria last month were illegitimate. In the next war they say all the Americans will have to do is to send over the uniforms.

* * *

Germans, walking by, grin embarrassedly. Some undoubtedly clench fists. A hefty-looking workman steps up: "Have you a cigarette?" He is the foreman of a road repair gang.

"We patch up the roads but it is not good," he confides. "We haven't the right materials any more and my men have no strength. They don't get enough potatoes or bread. My party? Oh I'm through with all that. Now if we only had some leadership, and if we knew what the Americans want maybe we could get some material for these roads."

A 10-year old is watching a roller skating rink.

"Yes, I went to school but it only lasts three hours and there are seventy in my class. Have you a cigarette for my father? What will I do when I grow up? I'll go to America and become an American soldier."

He picks up my cap and struts up and down with it on his head.

* * *

A middle-aged man is holding forth in a loud voice: "There was a meeting for politically persecuted and they said nothing is being done for them. They lost everything and they don't get anything back. What do you know about that? I tell you if the Americans don't do something about it, in another ten of fifteen years somebody will come along with a big mouth and it will start all over again. We lost the first war and we lost the second one and look at us now! If there's another there won't be anything left at all."

* * *

On an improvised bridge across the river a young fellow is looking into the water.

"I'm studying engineering. But what's the use if you are going to de-industrialize? I wish I could emigrate. All the smart fellows at the university would emigrate if they got a chance."

I ask his companion, an older scientific student about war guilt.

"What did I have to do with it? They stuck me in the infantry for two years. I couldn't help that. We were told we must sacrifice ourselves and we did a good job. A lot of my friends were killed. Now we are told we were misled and we're lucky if we're not told we are guilty.

"I can tell you, I've had enough of their military discipline and I don't want to hear about politics. I like the easy-going way the American soldiers have. I know some nice Americans, but my cousin was beaten up by some Americans last night. Of course, they might have been DP's."

Are any of his friends still Nazis?

"Oh, yes, some of them talk big but they're just fools. They go out at night and raid farmhouses and things like that. They're crazy."

I snuff out my cigarette and give it to an urchin who is waiting for me to drop it. He puts it into a tin box and runs away.

I remember what Professor Ebbinghaus, rector of Marburg University, said the other day.

"The young people out of the Army are sensitive. They feel they have done something for their country and resent the question of guilt. They have been brought up to believe that moral issues have no meaning in political matters. But their minds are open now and they are willing to learn."

* * *

Another day I met a German girl who must be one of those who, I hear, have been doing a job of indoctrinating American soldiers.

"You must admit," she said, "Hitler did a lot a good things. Look at the autobahns. And you must admit that German soldiers behaved themselves. They didn't have anything to do with atrocities and I don't know anybody who did. And you must admit that Germans are more cultured than Americans. We know about music and Americans don't."

She denied anti-Semitism, but she said, "I don't like Corporal Blank. He's a Jew."

Her mother contributed heatedly:

"Of course I'm not guilty for what went on in the concentration camps. The people I'm sorry for are the soldiers who were wounded and don't have work and people who were bombed out. My brother lost a leg, my first husband was killed. Every family has lost someone. My mother still hasn't been dug out of the rubble. You Americans can't conceive what we've been through."

* * *

I picked up a German newspaper and read:

"In the discussion group young people spoke of their bitter needs. One heard 'we are uprooted. We want to be led. We cannot think democratically if we are shown no way into the future. We have no basis of comparison.' "

In a Military Government bulletin there was an excerpt from a composition by a girl of 12.

"All people," it read, "must promise not to fight again and then we must have a righteous dear Fuehrer who does not think himself too big and who handles his people like a father."

A 13-year-old boy, however, wrote: "My wish is that we not go back to the past but develop a new democratic Germany out of the betrayed Fatherland—so that Germany will never again be a disturber of the peace."

In another school composition which I remember, a little girl wrote that 20 per cent of the Germans are good, 10 per cent bad and 70 per cent just ordinary. "When the 20 per cent are on top," she said, "the Germans are peaceful and democratic. When the 10 per cent take over they are very bad."

* * *

Not long ago I went to see a wise old gentleman who has studied English and American literature all his life and was held down to elementary school teaching for 12 years because the Nazis found him politically unreliable.

ELIZABETH SCHMIDT CRAHAN

Except for a table and a few chairs his living room was bare, and he explained apologetically that a friendly officer had tipped him off just in time that his place was to be requisitioned so he could salvage his furniture. I thought of the editor whom the Military Government has put in charge of an important newspaper who pleaded that he could not write his article on the benefits of democracy until he had finished struggling with the Army to save his house from requisitioning.

"The little German," said the student of literature, "was shattered by the consequences of the First World War and found in Hitler leadership and personification of his aspirations and resentments. Now he is shattered again but much more so. Not to mention human losses—40 per cent of the Germans have lost all their property and another 30 per cent have lost a great deal. The scales of value true and false have collapsed and left only a sense of failure and a fear of the future. It also has left a void in the German mind.

"Therein lies the hope. Whoever fills this void first and points the way to spiritual, political and economic solutions will win the German people. You have the power to determine whether Germany finds her new leadership in authoritarianism or through democratic processes.

"If you will go beyond simple control of administration and information and bring to bear your positive cultural influences, you can point the way to political democracy. But there must be books and publications of all kinds—Germans are great readers—and men of profound and vigorous thought.

"Germans don't mind severity. They expect and respect it. But they expect clear directions. They expect positive political elements to find support, and they lose respect when they find vacillation and uncertainties of purpose.

"On the economic side I'm not so hopeful. What solutions are possible after de-industrialization? And will Americans understand that their kind of free enterprise is inapplicable in Europe, that in a country where the middle class is so thoroughly broken and so much property destroyed, some form of socialism is inevitable? Democracy won't work if we can't make a living.

"Nazism as such, as a movement, is finished. It is discredited by failure if nothing else. But the craving for authority, for certainty, is still there and will find expression in other forms of totalitarianism if Western democracy doesn't provide the answers."

* * *

So what did I find in my perambulations? I found questions but no answers, confusion and the eternal, inscrutable problems of the German mind and German economics.

A psychologist once told me that the German mind is like the deep Teutonic forest that darkens the German landscape. Occasionally it is mild, kind, friendly and promising as in a clearing, but the rest is dark, tortuous and ominous.

The American Military Government has been very busy till now chopping down this dark Teutonic forest and enlarging the clearings. It has denazified, demilitarized and is de-industrializing pretty effectively, not to mention actually sawing a lot of timber. From now on the ultimate success of the Military Government will depend on what it plants in the clearing.

In a letter on May 31, Dana expressed his warm gratitude to his mother:

I am most concerned by your last letter speaking of your illness and the necessity of your taking penicillin shots. Now do hurry and get well again. Penicillin is indeed a wonder drug and should fix you up.

(You can always count on me to write in any case but I would hate to think of losing your weekly letters. They have meant more to me all these years abroad than I can ever tell you, certainly more than I have ever said, and I am counting on going right on getting them. Knowing you are there and thinking of me and my work and hearing from you regularly is certainly what keeps me going, on the job and happy about it. It is my main encouragement and source of will power and stability.)

Since last you wrote I think you will have seen the old Schmidt by-line more frequently. I was away for a while in France, then away for the raid on the Danube, and in addition the foreign staff has been asked to "hold down" while the strikes are at their peak. I think I have had a magaziner published and today I turned out a weekender on the economic consequences of General Clay's order halting reparations shipments. Several more magaziners are in the mill, including the "Youth" one for the Digest.

With my Lincoln Zephyr at hand I've been able to get over to Wiesbaden more freely and pick up a lot of useful dope. But I have been having trouble with flat tires. The roads in Germany at present are not only pretty bad but are strewn with all kinds of debris, glass, nails and what not that gets into tires. My tires are made for civilian American use and not so resistant as army tires. I am therefore thinking seriously of having the wheels changed so I can use army tires. Of course changing tires is good exercise. In spite of my good resolutions I never seem to get any other way.

I have received the additional photos with you and Steinie and you and Grandma and Mrs. Schofield and Tuckie. Little Tuckie, does he remember all those lessons he learned at his school? You never told me about going out there for your and Steinie's lessons in dog-commanding. How in the world did you train him not to bark in the garden?

The other day I got a copy of the Pomona Alumni Bulletin which I hadn't seen for a while. Also a note from Dave Spurgeon who was in my class asking for contributions to the alumni fund. Well, they can wait till next year. When next I'm home I'll make a contribution to them.

Kathleen Mclaughlin went away to Copenhagen for a few days but is now back. I have bought her some sheets at the army clothing store which she could not get in Berlin. We have a very fine villa in Berlin I am told.

Just between you and me it must make Kathleen a little sore that Markel has been asking me to write these weekenders and magaziners. Most of them could theoretically be better written in Berlin where the seat of Military Government is located.

Did I tell you Markel wants a weekender on the British conception of military government? I must go to Stuttgart this coming week for the Laenderrat but will try to take a quick trip to the British zone after that. Perhaps I can get to Hamburg too. There is a food conference there June 1 that might bear covering.

It doesn't seem possible you have been editing the Alumni News [128] *for more than ten years. It seems just a little while ago I was talking to you about the very beginning of that job. You have certainly been faithful. Wonder how your friend Amie Davitt is making out.*

All my love now, and get well, and keep well! Dana

At the end of May, solutions were still being sought to the tremendous number of displaced persons in the camps.

**REFUGEES OVERTAX
CAMPS IN GERMANY**

**Army Maps Plan to Ship
Some Out of Country and
Put Others to Work**

**By DANA ADAMS SCHMIDT
By Wireless to THE NEW YORK TIMES.
FRANKFORT ON THE MAIN, Germany, May 31**—Faced with the fact that the number of displaced persons in the United States zone is about

---

[128] Since her days at boarding school (Pelham Manor in New York), Mother had many friends, several of whom remained friends for her entire life. Among friends in Los Angeles, a good number were connected with the Orthopaedic Hospital, where she was a patient and a very active volunteer. She served on the board of the Crippled Children's Guild and was editor of the *Alumni News*. These activities brought her in contact with the members of the administrative and medical staffs of the hospital, a number of whom were interested in foreign affairs.
Mother gave several dinner parties for Dana at this time, at which he was asked to speak formally about his experiences abroad and his views of post-war Europe. Dr. Charles LeRoy Lowman, founder of the hospital, and Dr. Harold Crowe, prominent orthopaedic surgeon and Director of the hospital, were often among the guests. And, of course, some of these friends reciprocated with more dinners and luncheons. In addition to these pleasant activities, there were the essential visits to doctors and dentists, so I saw all too little of Dana during this vacation.

REFUGEES OVERTAX CAMPS IN GERMANY

Army Maps Plan to Ship Some Out of Country and Put Others to Work

By DANA ADAMS SCHMIDT
By Wireless to The New York Times

FRANKFORT ON THE MAIN, Germany, May 31—Faced with the fact that the number of displaced persons in the United States zone is about stationary, with infiltrees approximately balancing those repatriated, officers are now seeking palliatives for an apparently insoluble problem by promoting emigration to Western Europe and overseas territories and by putting the displaced persons to work.

During the past month nearly 10,000 more refugees—most of them Polish Jews—entered the zone and only 10,00 to 12,000 persons were repatriated—most of them Poles.

The displaced persons population is somewhere around 500,000. [In a report for April Gen. Joseph T. McNarney, United States commander in the European theatre, placed the total at 532,000.]

The registration of all persons in displaced persons camps and outside now in progress is expected to establish the exact number as of May 31. A simultaneous security screening will disqualify some from receiving relief, but not more than 15,000, according to latest estimates.

May Issue Stateless Passports

To facilitate emigration to the Latin-American countries that have expressed interest it is hoped that the army soon will issue an identification paper that would serve the purpose of a Nansen—or stateless—passport for those who definitely will not return to their homeland. With the aid of the Joint Distribution Committee or an equivalent Christian organization they could leave the zone and would find it easier to obtain foreign visas.

The French Government, meanwhile, expressed the belief that some of the 18,000 holders of the genuine Nansen passports, many of them White Russians, might be allowed to settle in Morocco. And the United States State Department, it is authoritatively learned, has formally inquired about details of Brazil's and the Dominican Republic's offer to receive displaced persons.

Russian [illegible], however, seem like [illegible] destined to remain unhappy and uneasy guests in Germany for a long time. The Military Government would like to put them to work. Using a small tradition for jobs, and officers point out that it is not surprising that they are in constant conflict with German, as well as military, police over black marketing and thievery.

Will Tie Jobs to Rations

Yet there is a labor shortage in German agriculture, mining and other fields in which the Poles in particular were normally employed in large numbers long before the war.

Hitherto, Gen. Dwight D. Eisenhower's directive that no displaced person would be forced to work has stood, but now the Americans are working on a plan to put pressure on them to take jobs by tying the jobs to the ration scale. Those working, automatically will get a considerably higher calory ration than the normal ration and will have priority access to "amenity" supplies, such as candy and toilet articles, according to the plan.

Among the displaced persons of all origins it is strongly felt that the Military Government is forgetting that it is dealing with liberated slave laborers and that its perspective is blurred by its concern with displaced persons' brushes with the law.

They stoutly deny a charge, heard frequently among Military Government officers, that those remaining, apart from racial and political persecutees, include a high proportion of persons who came to Germany to work willingly and are now merely "goldbricking."

stationary, with infiltrees approximately balancing those repatriated, officers are now seeking palliatives for an apparently insolvable problem by promoting emigration to Western Europe and overseas territories and by putting the displaced persons to work.

During the past month nearly 10,000 more refugees—most of them Polish Jews—entered the zone and only 10,000 to 12,000 persons were repatriated—most of them Poles.

The displaced persons population is somewhere around 500,000. [In a report for April Gen. Joseph T. McNarney, United States commander in the European theatre, placed the total at 532,000.]

The registration of all persons in displaced persons camps and outside now in progress is expected to establish the exact number as of May 31. A simultaneous security screening will disqualify some from receiving relief, but not more than 15,000, according to latest estimates.

May Issue Stateless Passports

To facilitate emigration to the Latin-American countries that have expressed interest it is hoped that the army soon will issue an identification paper that would serve the purpose of a Nansen—or stateless—passport for those who definitely will not return to their homeland. With the aid of the Joint Distribution Committee or an equivalent Christian organization they could leave the zone and would find it easier to obtain foreign visas.

The French Government, meanwhile, expressed the belief that some of the 18,000 holders of the genuine Nansen passports, many of them White Russians, might be allowed to settle in Morocco. And the United States

Government State Department, it is authoritatively learned, has formally inquired about details of Brazil's and the Dominican Republic's offer to receive displaced persons.

Since large-scale emigration seems remote, however, and the 500,000 seem destined to remain unhappy and uneasy guests in Germany for a long time, the Military Government would like to put them to work. Only a small fraction has jobs, and officers point out that it is not surprising that they are in constant conflict with German, as well as military, police over black marketing and thievery.

Will Tie Jobs to Rations

Yet there is a labor shortage in German agriculture, mining and other fields in which the Poles in particular were normally employed in large numbers long before the war.

Hitherto, Gen. Dwight D. Eisenhower's directive that no displaced person would be forced to work has stood, but now the Americans are working on a plan to put pressure on them to take jobs by tying the jobs to the ration scale. Those working, automatically will get a considerably higher calorie ration than the normal ration and will have priority access to "amenity" supplies, such as candy and toilet articles, according to the plan.

Among the displaced persons of all origins it is strongly felt that the Military Government is forgetting that it is dealing with liberated slave laborers and that its perspective is blurred by its concern with displaced persons' brushes with the law.

They stoutly deny a charge, heard frequently among Military Government officers, that those remaining, apart from racial and political persecution, include a high proportion of persons who came to Germany to work willingly and are now merely "goldbricking."

Yet another important issue Dana covered was the denazification of Germany's Christian churches. Of course, German anti-Semitism was not uncommon, and the Nazis found converts among the clergy and their parishioners.

GERMANS TO RUN PURGE OF CHURCH

Denazification Turned Over to Ministry of Cults in Hesse After 3-Way Accord

By DANA ADAMS SCHMIDT
By Wireless to THE NEW YORK TIMES.

FRANKFORT ON THE MAIN, Germany, June 1 (Delayed)— The delicate problem of the denazification of the clergy and major church employees has been formally turned over by the military government to the German Ministry of Cults in the Land of Greater Hesse after an agreement among the Land, the military government and the Evangelical Church on the dismissal or suspension of 108 persons and the retention of 106 others, pending denazification trials, in this predominantly Evangelical or Protestant area.

The Minister of Cults will turn over all information gathered on clergymen and employees provisionally retained to the Minister of Political Liberation, who will give them priority hearings before the new German denazification tribunals. The agreement represents a major achievement in view of the church's resistance to denazification as expressed in pastoral letters circulated in April and an unsuccessful attempt by the Council of the Evangelical Church ten days ago to have Lieut. Gen. Lucius D. Clay, deputy military governor, exempt the church from the provisions of the "law for liberation from National Socialism and militarism" until Oct. 1.

All dismissals and suspensions in Greater Hesse to date have been carried out by the Evangelical Church's own denazification tribunals. Their success here is generally attributed to the growing strength of the so-called confessional element of the church, headed by Pastor Martin Niemoeller, who has taken the lead in accepting collective German guilt for the war and atrocities. Some of those removed had clear records under the technical provisions of the law but not in the eyes of their colleagues. On the other hand, many of

GERMANS TO RUN PURGE OF CHURCH

Denazification Turned Over to Ministry of Cults in Hesse After 3-Way Accord

By DANA ADAMS SCHMIDT
By Wireless to THE NEW YORK TIMES.

FRANKFORT ON THE MAIN, Germany, June 1 (Delayed)—The delicate problem of the denazification of the clergy and major church employes has been formally turned over by the military government to the German Ministry of Cults in the Land of Greater Hesse after an agreement among the Land, the military government and the Evangelical Church on the dismissal or suspension of 108 persons and the retention of 106 others, pending denazification trials, in this predominantly Evangelical or Protestant area.

The Minister of Cults will turn over all information gathered on clergymen and employes provisionally retained to the Minister of Political Liberation, who will give them priority hearings before the new German denazification tribunals. The agreement represents a major achievement in view of the church's resistance to denazification as expressed in pastoral letters circulated in April and an unsuccessful attempt by the Council of the Evangelical Church ten days ago to have Lieut. Gen. Lucius D. Clay, deputy military governor, exempt the church from the provisions of the "law for liberation from National Socialism and militarism" until Oct. 1.

All dismissals and suspensions in Greater Hesse to date have been carried out by the Evangelical Church's own denazification tribunals. Their success here is generally attributed to the growing strength of the so-called confessional element of the church, headed by Pastor Martin Niemoeller, who has taken the lead in accepting collective German guilt for the war and atrocities. Some of those removed had clear records under the technical provisions of the law but not in the eyes of their colleagues. On the other hand, many of those provisionally retained were only nominal Nazis and will be cleared by the tribunals.

Considerably greater difficulty in obtaining church cooperation in denazification, however, has been encountered in the two other Laender of the American zone, Wuerttemburg-Baden and Bavaria. But the military government, exercising the restraint dictated by American respect for the church, has at no point forced removals.

The problem is complicated by the acute shortage of clergymen, of whom 16.5 per cent are estimated to have been killed in the war. In Greater Hesse, which had 11,069 Evangelical clergymen before denazification, many are taking care of as many as three parishes.

---

those provisionally retained were only nominal Nazis and will be cleared by the tribunals.

Considerably greater difficulty in obtaining church cooperation in denazification, however, has been encountered in the two other Laender of the American zone, Wuerttemburg-Baden and Bavaria. But the Military Government, exercising the restraint dictated by American respect for the church, has at no point forced removals.

The problem is complicated by the acute shortage of clergymen, of whom 16.5 per cent are estimated to have been killed in the war. In Greater Hesse, which had 11,069 Evangelical clergymen before denazification, many are taking care of as many as three parishes.

Along with the churches, denazification of the educational system was of vital importance. The Military Government had been working on this, and Dana decided to visit a few schools in Frankfort to see the program in action.

POSITIVE TREND IN GERMAN SCHOOLS BEGUN BY AMERICAN ADMINISTRATION

Military Government's Education Officers Develop Democratic Program to Replace Nazi System They Swept Away

By DANA ADAMS SCHMIDT
By Wireless to THE NEW YORK TIMES.

FRANKFORT ON THE MAIN, Germany, June 3—Any number of men who intended to impose their will on the future have started by saying: "Give me the children." Germany gave her children to Adolf Hitler for twelve years and he spared neither expense nor effort to mold them to his pattern.

For more that one year the will of Military Government has ruled Germany. In educational matters its will has been mainly and probably necessarily negative—breaking down the old patterns, discharging more than half the teachers, sweeping away the tainted textbooks.

Now, however, a more positive era is beginning. Though handicapped by insufficient personnel and material resources, a number of enthusiastic education officers are working through the relatively democratic fraction of school officials to promote a new mentality and eventually a new school system.

Classes Simulate Elections

Today at the Falk grade school, in a working-class suburb, I listened to 13-year-olds reciting the names of the principal political parties and describing how an election should be held. A few days ago, a teacher told me, the eighth and ninth grade civics classes went through the motions of a complete municipal election. To many it must have seemed rather complicated and tiresome by comparison with their earlier experience with waving banners and roaring "Sieg Heils."

At the Goethe High School [I] heard a heated but thoroughly reasonable debate on the issue of private enterprise versus State enterprise in two top classes composed of students aged 17 to 25, many of them recently discharged soldiers who have returned to school to get their "Abetur" [Abitur] diploma. Such civics classes are being encouraged as far as the teachers are capable of giving them constructive direction.

To get at this fundamental problem of teachers, the Military Government in Greater Hesse is devoting close attention to five teachers' training institutions that will soon be turning out a new corps of teachers; for the first time in German history, almost half will be women. The principles to guide their instruction are being worked out at a series of conferences between military government education officers and German school officials.

2 Points of Agreement

One point on which agreement appears to have been reached is the precedence of personality training over subject matter. Another is the advocacy of a single universal school system to replace the traditional undemocratic system of separating those who can afford a secondary school education from the rest at about the age of 11.

Excluding the more complicated problem of the universities, some other constructive educational steps are these. The American Third Army recently ordered the evacuation of the small number of schools still occupied by troops. Almost all children are now back at school. Student councils have been elected in most high schools. Numerous adult night schools, patronized heavily by those who missed schooling during the war, have begun to operate. Civics classes have been extended to vocational schools. Enough paper has been received to print improved readers for grade schools and to begin supplying high schools with books by next autumn. The military government has approved textbooks for all high school subjects.

At two schools visited the teachers emphasized the material difficulties of the past year, which are the point of departure for any positive endeavors. Poor nourishment, they said, has caused a marked decline in concentration among students who in any case are one to two years behind in their studies as a result of wartime interruptions. There have been occasional cases of fainting among both students and teachers.

Shortage of Books

Grade schools have only one to two copies of the "emergency" texts issued by the military government for every three pupils. These cover basic subjects selected from the Weimar Republic's schoolbooks. Military-government officers agree that these are poor in content as well as printing. A grade-school principal said that most schools were not using the history book because of its military emphasis. Readers too are heavy on feats of valor and one arithmetic book, he pointed out, contains three pages of problems based on Germany's grievous losses under Versailles.

High schools have thus far received no books at all, other teachers reported, and must rely on teachers' knowledge and such approved books as can be borrowed from libraries and home collections. The average number of students per teacher in Greater Hesse, they said, is now eighty-four and it is still going up as expelled children from the Sudetenland and Hungary arrive. The teachers break up their classes into shifts but many students get only three hours' instruction daily.

In this first post-war year, the most serious problem in Germany was the lack of food, the effects of which were widespread. In an article entitled **GERMAN COLLAPSE FEARED BY BRITISH,** Dana wrote in early June:

Without adequate food there can be no substantial increase in Ruhr coal production. Inadequate coal means inadequate steel, which means inadequate manufactured goods and no prospect of enough exports to pay for food imports. Food can break the vicious circle.

In March just before normal rations were cut to 1,050 calories, coal production was approaching 200,000 tons daily and the British had worked out a "Spartan" plan to provide minimum economy for the zone. With the food cut, production dropped to 150,000 tons. That tonnage is regarded by the British as the rock-bottom minimum on which the zone can meet export commitments and keep its basic economy going—steel, transport and public services.

In a letter on June 15 from Hamburg, where Dana went to a food conference, he wrote: *The people here look very bad. This food business is telling on them.*

In the same letter, he continued:

Perhaps unwisely I tried to find out whether Fraulein Pfaff who once gave me lessons in German pronunciation, was still living. She was the only individual I could think of here I might know. At the Schroederstift I discovered her house and most of the rest had been bombed and she had evacuated to the country. The caretaker gave me the address of a brother, and there I learned that she had later moved to a place now in the Russian zone and committed suicide with her sister when the Russians came.
The caretaker at the Schroederstift and his wife looked like ancient skeletons. He said he had lost sixty-eight pounds. Anyone who can't get something extra from the country is in a very bad way, and I know from talking to British officials that things will probably get worse. It is already much worse than in the American zone.
Superficially one might not notice it. The parks are still full of young people playing football. But they don't play long, I'm told. And if you look closely at the people on the street you can see how haggard and tired they look. Herr Pfaff, [son-law of Fräulein Pfaff] *told me forty percent of his employees don't come to work, because they feel weak or are out looking for food in the country.* [129]

Dana asked Mother to send food packages, at his expense, to these people and to others, for example, the family of the woman who did his laundry.

---

[129]   The contrast between the abundant food on the tables of the Americans and the barren tables of the starving German population must have aroused jealousy and hostility towards the Americans.

The food shortage had serious effects on the economy and the ability of the British and American zones to meet war reparations that had been agreed upon at the Potsdam Conference. (The Potsdam Agreement adopted by the major victorious powers July 17 to August 2, 1945, following the German surrender of May 8, 1945—the USSR, the USA, the UK, and France. It established policy for the occupation and reconstruction of Germany, as well as reparations to be paid by Germany from the various zones of occupation.)

In an article published on June 1, Dana discussed other problems leading to low industrial output and the lack of funds for reparations. The conditions on which the Potsdam agreement for reparations was based had not been met. These included the establishment of a central German economic agency and the elimination of barriers to trade between the four zones of occupation. Labor shortage was another factor in low industrial output. The large food and raw material imports and lack of exports to balance in both the British and American zones left no surplus. Particularly, in the American zone, the necessity of food and raw material imports from the United States seemed to make further contributions to reparations unreasonable.

In his letter of June 15, Dana wrote about Hamburg:

It is extraordinary to be here again. I drove round to Hartungstrasse No. 1 and found it undamaged. [We had lived in an apartment in this building for three or four years when we were children.] *It was inhabited by Germans, but a note on the door said it had been requisitioned by the British army. Andreasbrunnen looked about the same as ever, as did the Bell's* [family friends] *apartment on Loehrsweg. But the Heinrich Hertz Realgymnasium,* [where Dana went to school] *had been hit and looked pretty badly burned out. Part of it was occupied by British military police.*

I drove down Harvestehuder Weg, and found the Anglo American tennis club which is now a club for British enlisted men. A lot of the houses on that street have been hit but I couldn't remember which belonged to our friends. [The Harvestehuder Weg borders the Alster on the west side and had many old and distinguished homes. One, I remember well, had an entrance through a greenhouse.]

On the whole the parts of Hamburg I remember are not terribly damaged. All the big hotels are functioning for the British army and the big stores like Tietz are intact. Most of the bombs fell around the harbor.

This morning I drove out to Hagenbecks—[a large, famous and progressive zoo] *which got hit badly. You will have seen my story by now if it got in. Tomorrow morning I'm going to take a tour round the harbor with a British major.*

This tour in the British zone has been pretty intensive, but the old Lincoln Zeph including the tires is holding out perfectly. No trouble at all. Tomorrow night I think I'll drive back to Herford, take a quick look at the Ruhr and then back to the American zone. I must go through Bad Kissingen to wind up that Youth story, which I'm finding rather difficult. But with that last visit I think I'll have enough good material to do the piece when I return to Frankfort.

Driving in Germany is greatly facilitated by the autobahns I find, although they are closed in many places where the Germans blew up bridges.

Just before I left Frankfort your package arrived, full of splendid things. I'm looking forward to the magazines, have stowed away the shorts, and am already well into the candy. The coffee is just the thing for the days when I miss breakfast. Let me have another can when you get around to it. If you need a request to send another box some time let this be it.

As you might expect, it has rained steadily since I got here, up to this evening when the sun came out. With double daylight saving time it stayed light until nearly midnight. Tomorrow should be fine for the ride round the harbor.

By now I trust you are quite well again and taking that rest at the beach. All the best to Steinie. All my love,
Dana

In mid-June, the CFM (Council of Foreign Ministers) was meeting in Paris. The economic problem was so great in Germany that Dana hoped that a solution to economic and ultimately political zones would be worked out which would "be mutually acceptable to all of the occupying powers." He said that "if the proposals of James F. Byrnes or Foreign Secretary Ernest

Bevin achieve a substitute for the defunct provisions on economic unity of the Potsdam Agreement, there is hope." Even then, of course, a hard struggle would be ahead to find enough industrial surplus in the western zones and enough agricultural surplus in the Russian zone for significant exchanges of commodities and products which each zone needs. Following is the text of Dana's report on the CFM:

GERMAN REGIME BIG ISSUE AT PARIS

**Americans Prepare to
Face the Problems
Of Partition**

**By DANA ADAMS SCHMIDT
By Wireless to THE NEW YORK TIMES.**
FRANKFORT ON THE MAIN, June 15—As seen from Germany, one of the most pressing tasks before the Paris Council of Foreign Ministers is that of working out a settlement of the German problem on the basis of economic and ultimately, political zones. At least the economic situation has grown so critical that time is of the essence in formulating a policy which can be mutually acceptable to all of the occupying powers.

If the proposals of Secretary James F. Byrnes or Foreign Secretary Ernest Bevin achieve a substitute for the defunct provisions on economic unity of the Potsdam Agreement, there is hope. Even then, of course, a hard struggle would be ahead to find enough industrial surplus in the western zones and enough agricultural surplus in the Russian zone for significant exchanges of commodities and products which each zone needs.

If there is renewed deadlock, however, then the policy-makers of the American and British zones, who are anything but optimistic, must draw the consequences and try to work out new and urgent solutions for a partitioned Germany.

The situation in the four zones of occupied Germany at present is briefly as follows:

The Soviet zone can live without the rest of Germany and be an asset to Russia and her eastern economy. Failure to unify Germany now cannot hurt her or her political objectives in the rest of Germany. The zone has enough industrial capacity to contribute to Russia, and has or could have a surplus of food. Coal and steel are available from parts of Silesia annexed by Poland. Plant removals as reparations have been accompanied by the stimulation of production in spheres which are useful to Russia.

Unity Made Difficult

While ostensibly the most enthusiastic advocate of joint decisions and unity in the Berlin Control Council, the Russians have made unity more difficult economically by integrating their zone economically with Eastern Europe, by failing to develop trade between the various zones, and by such moves as voting for four-power management of German imports and exports.

Politically, they made it more difficult by setting up their own zonal government and jamming through Communist-Socialist unification in a form unacceptable to the British or Americans. The Socialist Unity party, which has resulted from these maneuvers now appeals to German nationalism by damning federalism and posing as the arch advocate of unity and centralization on its own Communist or Russian terms.

The French zone, too, could exist without the rest of Germany although at considerable cost to the living standard of the inhabitants. Whether the French government would choose in the event of an international deadlock to incorporate at least the Saar Basin progressively into French economy or collaborate more closely with occupation authorities in the American and British zones remains to be seen.

French Use of Veto

The validity of French arguments for internationalization of the Ruhr and even of separation of the Rhineland from Germany is widely recognized among Americans and British in terms of western European economics and security. But French use of the veto of German economic unity to achieve these ends is thought to be defeating ultimate French objectives.

It has provided the Russians with a pretext for building up their zone as a separate entity, and has thrown additional burdens on the United States in particular in feeding the western zones, thereby reducing the resources available to the rest of the world, including France. By fostering German economic disorganization and distress, the French policy has unintentionally played into the hands of the German Communists and the Socialist Unity party.

The British zone, with its industrial concentration in the Ruhr, could make its way alone only on one condition, which would doubtless be unacceptable. If it cut off or greatly reduced coal exports to France and Eastern Europe, it could build up industry with an export capacity sufficient to pay for its food.

This could involve economic collapse in France and German competition in world export markets. Any suggestion that Britain is now building up her zone as a bulwark against Russia is, however, clearly contradicted by the fact that Britain is struggling to keep her zone barely alive, as any foreign newspaperman is perfectly free to observe.

U.S. Zone Needs Coal

The United States zone, with its excellent scenery, is no better off. It needs coal from the British and French zones and from Silesia, and at the same time it needs food from the Russian zone. As a separate entity, the only way it could manage to live would be on United States charity.

The consequences of deadlock in Paris would, therefore, logically be to hasten the integration of the Russian zone and probably the French zone into Russian and French economies, respectively. Simultaneously, it would also throw the American and British zones together in a desperate struggle for survival.

Politically, the collaboration of the American and British zones should not be too difficult. In matters such as denazification, re-education, food rationing, development of unions, political parties and civil administration, their courses have been parallel, the main difference being that the British moved more slowly than the Americans. Until SHAEF ceased to exist, the American and British Military Governments formed a single organization, and many of the most experienced officers still maintain close personal contact. Mutual distrust, existence of which among British and American officers who have arrived in Germany since V-E Day,

How they could together solve the economic problem has, however, thus far stumped everyone. In the circumstances, certainly, reparations removals would cease, the Potsdam Agreement and agreements on deindustrialization and the level of industry would have to be discarded, and coal exports restricted. The American Military Government would doubtless have to move from Berlin back to Frankfort on the Main, where headquarters formerly were situated.

Failure in Paris would mean a Germany divided and, consequently, a world divided. Most painful to Americans, perhaps, would be the consequent moral and political obligation to maintain troops in Germany indefinitely, unless Americans were prepared to abandon their zone as a sort of military vacuum while all the rest of Germany remained occupied by the Russians, British and French.

After the meeting of the Council of Foreign Ministers was over, Dana went to Bad Kissingen, where he met the Prince of Prussia, grandson of Kaiser Wilhelm II. He had an interesting outlook on governments in Europe and the relationship between Germany and the United States.

U.S. AMITY SOUGHT
BY GERMAN PRINCE

**Kaiser's Grandson Calls His
People and Americans
'Alike in So Many Ways'**

By DANA ADAMS SCHMIDT
By Wireless to THE NEW YORK TIMES.

BAD KISSINGEN, June 18 (Delayed)—Louis Ferdinand, Prince of Prussia and grandson of Kaiser Wilhelm II, said today: "If the Italian people want to be rid of the monarchy and have a republic, it is well."

Throughout Europe, he observed, "there appears to be a revolt against the old political forms. But the forms are unimportant. What matters in these times is that the integrity and dignity of the individual be preserved and that dictatorship of any kind be prevented.

"If a republic in Italy can do that," he declared, "it is good. If a monarchy can do that in other places, it is also good. There is no justification for the notion that persons of royal lineage are necessarily undemocratic or reactionary."

Hints Political Aspirations

Leaving the door open to some future political activity on his part, the Prince said: "I have not taken any part in German politics yet. I am of course, the pretender. But what becomes of me personally is unimportant. What Germany needs is politics inspired by Christian principles that uphold the individual." He denied, however, any connection with the Christian Social Union.

His Romanoff wife, Princess Kyra, and their children live in a small house next to that of Captain Merle A. Potter, chief of the Bad Kissingen military government, for whom he acts as occasional interpreter and unofficial adviser. The Prince is spending most of his time working on a book.

It will probably be called "The Red Prince," he said, and it will disclose for the first time his part in the attempt on Adolf Hitler's life, during which there was some thought that he should ascend the throne if the coup succeeded. Other chapters will tell of his four years working in a Ford factory, his adventures in Hollywood, including his affair with Lili Damita; his friendship with the late President Roosevelt, and how he opposed the Nazis and rebuffed Hitler's proposal that Hermann Goering be the godfather of his first son with the remark: "Not that murderer."

Calls Himself Refugee

Louis Ferdinand considers himself a refugee, since the East Prussian State where he lived during the war is now in Russian-annexed territory.

"I believe that there is a splendid basis for understanding between Germans and Americans," he said. "They are alike in so many ways. But Germans do not know enough about America. They know only about American materialism and not about American culture." The occupation, he believes, provided an opportunity for the thorough-going education of the Germans "if an occupation is based on the four freedoms and avoids the sort of overt propaganda that would make Germans who were made skeptical by Nazi propaganda exclaim: 'It is just more of the same.' "

He is particularly eager to introduce the American style of journalism into Germany, with objective news stories separated from editorial comment. "The straight truth is the best propaganda," he said.

June 21, 1946
Dear Mother,

Back again in Frankfort, but not for long. On Monday I hope to leave for Stuttgart and Munich. In the meantime I will have Arthur Hays Sulzberger on my hands. He is arriving tomorrow morning with a party of editors and publishers. I wish these people would stay at home. It is most tiresome to have everyone all atwitter and falling flat on their faces because god almighty is arriving from New York. Just to think, I even got out my clean uniform and got my car washed for the occasion.

I am enclosing a life insurance paper I just received from the New York office. It would appear that now that I earn more than a hundred dollars a week my life is worth $600,000, an increase of $100,000. Anyway, it doesn't cost me anything. Apparently this is the only insurance Times *employees get, as I believe I wrote after my visit in New York. But the* Times *looks after its men anyway, insurance or no, as far as I have heard.*

It was a rough trip from Iserlohn in the Ruhr to Bad Kissingen. There doesn't seem to have been any road repair work for years. But Lincoln stood up all right, except for consuming an improbable amount of oil, a condition that has now been corrected. You will have seen my piece from Essen, I imagine, and know how bad I think things are. At Bad Kissingen I picked up quite a good story it seemed to me about Prince Louis Ferdinand. It seems that he is one of Louis Lochner's[130] *old cronies.*

Here I found a splendid treasure of three letters from you awaiting me. I am so glad you have gone to the beach. It should be just the thing.

---

[130] Louis Lochner was a Pulitzer Prize winning foreign correspondent with the *Associated Press* during the war.

About this war matter. No, I still don't believe in it. The same arguments still hold good. The Russians don't want the things they are pressing for enough to go to war for them; they are not vital to her the way new raw materials and resources were vital to the Nazis once they got their war machine under way. Certainly we don't want war either. In any event tension has decreased since the Iran affair was more or less settled. As for the Major from Heidelberg . . . army officers have a way of impressing people with startling but highly unlikely information of a military or political nature. If American soldiers wander into the Russian zone without proper permission they might get shot at, certainly. Americans are not quite so trigger happy, but a Russian might get shot at under similar circumstances.

I had a letter from Mrs. Williams from Paris saying she and Anne have arrived safely and are staying at the Hotel Plaza Athenee. She urged me to call on them when I go to Paris again. I'll have to invent a good excuse, but it won't be until after the publisher has left Germany, 24 long days from now.

Yes, I have been intending to get someone to take a picture of the car and me. The right man with the right camera never seems to be around at the right time.

I turned out another weekender this week and am feeling a little weekender-happy, by which I mean groggy. As far as I'm concerned they always require a great deal of effort, although I suppose they will come easier as time goes on. I doubt it though. When things begin to become easy in the writing line, I suspect that it means the writer is lapsing into a rut and mediocrity. Unfortunately the effort detracts from my work for the daily, but I suppose that is unavoidable. This Sunday I hope to get down to that Youth thing, publisher permitting.

I am still enjoying the Hershey bars, although I give a good deal to any children I run across. Speaking of charity, yes, I quite agree, it might be a good idea to contribute something to dear Columbia. Let's make it $150, just to show we're not pikers. I must admit, however, I never hear of old Prof. Macalarney. You can send the check as from me, can't you? In case you didn't make a note of it, the appeal said checks should be made payable to Carl W. Ackerman and mailed to him at Columbia.

About the food parcels I mentioned before. Would you have Macy's or another department store send one of their eleven pound parcels to Mlle. Raymonde Pave, 297 Rue de Tolbiae, Paris XII. I'll give you the German addresses later.

My love to you all, and tell Grandma I'm not forgetting her and will write her a letter right away. Thanks for buying the baby bond and my love to Eliza.

Kathleen McLaughlin has just phoned and wants to know if I would like to go on a tour of the Russian zone on Monday. I would of course, although I hate the idea of missing the elections here. It is possible the Russians will postpone the trip.

All my love,
Dana

On June 22, Dana had an article in the *Times* that shed light on the state of industry in Germany and on the immense cost of maintaining an army of occupation:

U.S. GIVES GERMANY
FURNITURE ORDERS

12,000 Dependents' Quarters
Planned—Dutch and Danes
to Augment Army's Diet

By DANA ADAMS SCHMIDT
By Wireless to THE NEW YORK TIMES.
FRANKFORT ON THE MAIN, June 22—The United States Army has ordered considerable quantities of household furnishings from German manufacturers and smaller quantities in Sweden, Switzerland, Denmark, Belgium and Czechoslovakia for the quarters of some 12,000 dependents expected in the theatre, it was learned today.

For the occupation troops at the same time the Office of Chief Quartermaster has ordered more than 1,000,000 pounds of vegetables from the Netherlands and 4,000,000 pounds of butter and 3,000,000 pounds of cheese from Denmark, in addition to milk. It is also planning to buy fruit and vegetables in Italy.

These purchases will prove a great convenience to the dependents and the Army, since the furnishings would otherwise have to be brought from the United States while fresh foods will promote the health and well-being of the troops.

The question has been raised, however, as to how the program can be reconciled with the current desperate efforts to feed Europe, and the reconstruction of devastated areas and avoid economic collapse in Germany.

In the past the American Army has had an unparalleled world-wide reputation for supplying itself with almost all its purchases exclusively from the United States.

Orders in Germany, based on earlier estimates of 8,000 dependents, include 8,000 each of refrigerators, ranges, wardrobes, sets of chinaware for four and for eight persons, bread knives, ladles, bathroom mirrors and coffee tables as well as 32,000 each of single spring beds, single bedsteads and single mattresses, 64,000 tumblers and several score of other items.

In most instances hitherto Germans expelled from requisitioned homes have been required to leave all their household furnishings behind. New production will therefore avoid some direct hardships.

While appropriated War Department funds normally are not available to furnish dependents' quarters, a limited sum has been allocated for this year to buy from other countries items unavailable in Germany. Thus the Germans to date have succeeded in producing only eight refrigerators.

Plumbing and supplies requiring textiles, such as rugs and divans, are almost unobtainable. Glass is urgently needed for windows, and beds for the evicted and also for hospitals.

American military and civilian personnel have thus far applied for transportation for 9,540 dependents, of whom 942 have arrived. Dependents have flocked into the French zone, but the British are still postponing their own arrivals.

U. S. GIVES GERMANY FURNITURE ORDERS

12,000 Dependents' Quarters Planned—Dutch and Danes to Augment Army's Diet

By DANA ADAMS SCHMIDT
By Wireless to THE NEW YORK TIMES.

FRANKFORT ON THE MAIN, Germany, June 22 — The United States Army has ordered considerable quantities of household furnishings from German manufacturers and smaller quantities in Sweden, Switzerland, Denmark, Belgium and Czechoslovakia for the quarters of some 12,000 dependents expected in the theatre, it was learned today.

For the occupation troops at the same time the Office of Chief Quartermaster has ordered more than 1,000,000 pounds of vegetables from the Netherlands and 4,000,000 pounds of butter and 3,000,000 pounds of cheese from Denmark, in addition to milk. It is also planning to buy fruit and vegetables in Italy.

These purchases will prove a great convenience to the dependents and the Army, since the furnishings would otherwise have to be brought from the United States while fresh foods will promote the health and well-being of of the troops.

The question has been raised, however, as to how the program can be reconciled with the current desperate efforts to feed Europe, aid the reconstruction of devastated areas and avoid economic collapse in Germany.

In the past the American Army has had an unparalleled world-wide reputation for supplying itself with almost all its purchases exclusively from the United States.

Orders in Germany, based on earlier estimates of 8,000 dependents, include 8,000 each of refrigerators, ranges, wardrobes, sets of chinaware for four and for eight persons, bread knives, ladles, bathroom mirrors and coffee tables as well as 32,000 each of single spring beds, single bedsteads and single mattresses, 64,000 tumblers and several score of other items.

In most instances hitherto Germans expelled from requisitioned homes have been required to leave all their household furnishings behind. New production will therefore avoid some direct hardships.

While appropriated War Department funds normally are not available to furnish dependent's quarters, a limited sum has been allocated for this year to buy from other countries items unavailable in Germany. Thus the Germans to date have succeeded in producing only eight refrigerators.

Plumbing and supplies requiring textiles, such as rugs and divans, are almost unobtainable. Glass is urgently needed for windows, and beds for the evicted and also for hospitals.

American military and civilian personnel have thus far applied for transportation for 9,540 dependents, of whom 942 have arrived. Dependents have flocked into the French zone, but the British are still postponing their own arrivals.

Vegetables from the Netherlands began arriving at Bremen last Tuesday. They include cabbages, carrots, cucumbers, lettuce, shallots, endives, green peas and tomatoes.

James Johnson, vice president of Borden's Milk Company is in Bremen seeking a solution to the problem of the shortage of suitable milk bottles. For the time being only hospitals and children will receive Danish milk, but it is hoped that by autumn it will be available in all Army messes.

Vegetables from the Netherlands began arriving at Bremen last Tuesday. They include cabbages, carrots, cucumbers, lettuce, shallots, endives, green peas and tomatoes.

James Johnson, vice president of Borden's Milk Company is in Bremen seeking a solution to the problem of the shortage of suitable milk bottles. For the time being only hospitals and children will receive Danish milk, but it is hoped that by autumn it will be available in all Army messes.

Returning to the subject of the CFM meeting in Paris, Dana had a long piece published on June 22 reflecting again on the inter-related subjects they had to consider: the grim food shortage, the absence of an overall economic commission for the Laender, the future of the Ruhr and the Rhineland, and the eastern territories of Germany granted to, or appropriated by, Russia and Poland.

RUHR AND RHINE ACCORD
FIRST GERMAN PROBLEM

Byrnes and Bevin Must Try to Remedy
Faults of Potsdam Conference

By DANA ADAMS SCHMIDT
By Wireless to THE NEW YORK TIMES.

FRANKFORT ON THE MAIN, June 22—When the Foreign Ministers in Paris take up the German problem, the dreary and devastated area of the British zone known as the Ruhr will be uppermost in their thoughts. Here is the heart of the German problem, compared to which all others are peripheral and secondary.

Representatives of the western powers will be intent on making up for what now appears as a grave error committed at Potsdam when President Truman and Prime Minister Attlee agreed in principle to the annexation of large areas of eastern Germany by Russia and Poland, but omitted to insist on a settlement of the fate of the western German area, including the main German industrial arsenal the Ruhr and the strategically important left bank of the Rhine.

Apart from Russian obstructionism it was the ensuing French insistence on internationalization of the Ruhr and separation of the left bank of the Rhine from Germany, climaxed by the French veto of central German economic agencies, that made most of the Potsdam agreement unworkable. Proposals by Secretary Byrnes and Foreign Minister Bevin must, in final analysis, therefore be designed to meet or get around this French insistence, to find a corrective or alternative to the Potsdam agreement.

The task of finding answers, which might have been simpler while the Allies were still welded by wartime alliance at the time of the Potsdam meeting, is complicated at this late date by the wide variance of dominant motives of the Big Four powers occupying Germany—motives which are very imperfectly reflected in official statements.

Alarm of the British

During a tour of the British zone this correspondent encountered on every hand British officials who were intensely worried, in fact frightened, by the prospect of starvation and economic collapse in the zone. With the immediate motive of staving off collapse and reducing the burden of keeping the zone alive now borne by Britain, they were giving serious thought to cutting down on coal exports in order to resuscitate German economy and produce an export surplus that would make the zone more or less self-supporting.

Mr. Bevin's proposal for a loose federation of twelve German States with certain central economic organs appeared to occupation officials as an attempt to alleviate the zone's difficulties by overcoming zonal barriers while at the same time meeting some of the French demands by placing the Ruhr under international economic control. The federal idea is entirely in accord with conceptions of the American Military Government.

It is entirely possible that many Britons would like in the long run to build up their zone as a barrier to westward Russian expansion. But anyone who charges that anything of the kind is going on at present has not grasped how near the Ruhr and the entire zone are to the brink of economic disaster.

There are 107,000 unarmed German troops who are prisoners but kept in scattered organized units under German officers performing transportation and other labor duties for the British. In so far as these "Diensttruppen" salute each other and maintain military discipline and thereby keep alive the spirit of militarism, their existence seems contrary to the spirit of Potsdam. In the eyes of the British, however, they represent no menace whatever to anyone but merely are a more economical and efficient form of labor than provided by ordinary prisoners of war.

American Motives

American motives appear to be dominated by a search for means for an early withdrawal from Germany without sacrificing the occupation objectives of denazification, demilitarization and re-education. Indeed, reduction of the occupation force, abetted by redeployment hysteria, is going on apace. Whether a swift turnover of responsibility to a German civil administration is good or bad it is made unavoidable by this fact.

The Byrnes proposal for a twenty-five-year four-power pact for control of Germany would bring complete withdrawal into sight. It would imply the creation of a Central Germany Government of some kind whose authority would overcome zonal barriers and help solve the economic problems which worry the Americans almost as much as they do the British. But in substituting diplomatic guarantees for physical occupation and control, it is unlikely to satisfy the French.

The French motive is security first and last. Ostensibly and officially only against renascent German aggression, it is actually and unofficially also security against Russian expansionism and influence. Remembering their experience after the last war and noting current trends, the French are convinced that the Americans and probably the British will withdraw from Germany and they fear that Germany will then be dominated by Russia. Russian influence would then extend to the Rhine.

This, as French statesmen will admit privately, is the vital explanation of the fervor of President Bidault as chief of the intensely anti-Communist Mouvement Republicain Populaire for the detachment of the Ruhr and Rhineland from Germany. Only the popular enthusiasm for the project among Frenchmen can explain the support the French Communist party has conceded to it in contradiction to German Communists and hints from the Moscow radio.

The Russians have shown every sign of intending to maintain their grip on their zone and of extending their influence into the rest of Germany through Communist and Socialist Unity parties. They have thus far rejected the Byrnes proposal and condemned Mr. Bevin in their propaganda. If any solution to the problem of the Ruhr is found in Paris the Russians will undoubtedly demand a share in its control. And this, according to political experts in the British and American zones, would be granted only in exchange for opening up the Russian zone. [Author's note: The Russian zone is rich in agriculture and could help solve the food problem in the British and American zones.]

But if no solution is found the western zones will be obliged to make their own arrangements. The intent would not be to form a western bloc—though it might lead to such—but merely to get out of what Mr. Bevin has called an "intolerable situation."

France To Be Won Over

Without Russia the leading political representatives of the British and American zones think an agreement could be reached among the western powers on the Ruhr and many other problems whose solution has been delayed by the desire to remain loyal to Potsdam and four-power operation in Germany. In such circumstances they believe that France would fall into line and abandon insistence on political separation of the Ruhr from Germany in exchange for international economic control in which they would play the predominant part.

While Russian, and to lesser extent French, conceptions of occupation policy differ greatly from the American, there are no insurmountable points of difference with the British. The British are plagued with a somewhat milder redeployment fever and black market and fraternization problems. Having less to sell, the British soldier is preserved from many sins. On the whole the British are more aloof and dignified than the Americans in their occupation, and gain thereby the respect if not the affection of the Germans. Their relations with the Germans suffer increasingly from food shortage since the best efforts of the officials have not convinced the hungry Germans that the shortage is not deliberate and punitive or that food is not being exported to Britain.

British Want Food Pooled

The British would like to organize a food pool to give all Germans in the western zone the same rations but have found the Americans unenthusiastic since it would mean cutting rations in the American zone. A joint western food organization, short of a food pool and joint organizations controlling industry, would, however, be of unquestionable economic value.

On the political side the British, while protesting that the Americans are going too fast, are following slowly in their footsteps in turning over responsibility for civil administration, economic functions and denazification to Germans. Because of their anxiety to minimize disorganization, British denazification has been less thorough. The most significant difference is probably that whereas Americans represent no particular political philosophy beyond the general idea of democracy in their zone, the British with their socialistic Labor Government are planning more radical steps toward land reform and socialization of industry than seem likely in the American occupation zone.

With American occupation forces seeking ways of withdrawing troops from Germany, General Joseph T. McNarney indicated the possibility of such withdrawal. In an article published on June 24, Dana reported Gen. McNarney's announcement:

On July 1 the American Zone will enter an "interim" stage between full military occupation by combat troops and the police-force occupation by the constabulary that will become fully effective on July 1, 1947.

Developments during the interim stage, he said, will include the deactivation of the Third Division on August 1, the progressive removal of other combat forces from occupation duties and the consolidation of remaining military installations, in line with his recent disclosure that the occupation forces may be cut from 350,000 to 150,000, the theatre commander explained that the measures had been made essential by the reduction in the number of troops caused by redeployment.

The Third Division was organized in 1917 and had an outstanding record in both World Wars. It participated in the amphibious landings in French North Africa, Sicily, Italy and France, suffering more casualties than any other American division.

The constabulary—sometimes referred to as the "Lightning Bolt"—commanded by Maj. Gen. Ernest Harmon, will become the principal police force in the zone, operating as part of the Third Army, which is the only remaining major American field command in Europe. Its 38,000 officers and men have had more intensive training than that of any previous military conditioning program to fit them for the dual rule of soldier and special policeman. Directed from headquarters at Bamberg, it had already in operation three brigades, nine regiments and one separate squadron of school troops. These will handle border patrolling, "march and seizure" operations and zone security patrols in collaboration with the military police, the counter-intelligence corps, the Criminal Investigation Division and the German civil police.

The most mobile outfits in the United States Army, they are equipped with light tanks, armored cars and jeeps, motorcycles, horses and liaison-type aircraft. To distinguish them from other troops, they wear golden colored scarves, helmet liners with insignia and colors, Sam Browne belts, smooth surfaced combat boots and serge olive-drab blouses with matching trousers.

The Sixteenth Cavalry Group Headquarters, redesignated the Sixteenth Constabulary Squadron, will be stationed in Berlin and the Fourth Cavalry Group, renamed the Fourth Constabulary Regiment, will be in Austria.

American headquarters announced that civilian guards recruited among the United Nations displaced persons are being trained to work in collaboration with the occupation forces at the Mannheim-Kaiserthal replacement center. Five officers and twenty-five enlisted men are running the center, at which all civilians already operating as guards will be retrained and screened to eliminate undesirables. Most of those hitherto employed were Poles. Their five-week course will include the use of carbines, the control of prisoners of war and the rudiments of English as well as special classes in mechanics, carpentry, shoe repairing and mess-managing.

Following the ten-day trip for correspondents to the Russian zone, Dana wrote a series of articles illustrating communist rule—a contrast with the western zones. On July 2, he described an election in Saxony:

**SAXON PLEBISCITE
REVEALS DISSENT**

**Many Voted Against Seizure
in Russian Zone Despite One-
Sided Propaganda**

By DANA ADAMS SCHMIDT
By Wireless to THE NEW YORK TIMES.
WEIMAR, Germany, July 2 (Delayed)—In light of the tremendous and exclusive campaign for a "yes" vote that I observed in the town of Plauen yesterday during a tour of the Russian zone, the results of the plebiscite in lower Saxony constituted a demonstration of some dissent.

Not a single poster or published pronouncement for a "no" vote relieved the sea of multi-colored streamers, placards and stickers favoring "yes" that inundated this town, the third largest of the province. The results were 2,683,401, or 77 per cent, "yes" votes to 571,600, or 16.5 per cent, "no" votes on the question, as worded on the ballots, whether the voter approved the law on the handing over of enterprises belonging to war and Nazi criminals so that they become the "property of the people." In addition, 204,657, or 5.8 per cent, were invalid.

Legally the vote merely confirmed the uncompensated expropriation of some 2,100 Nazi-owned business enterprises in lower Saxony that is being carried out in the rest of the zone without benefit of plebiscite. Nineteen hundred others are being returned to their owners on the ground that they were only nominal Nazis, while the cases of about 500 are still pending because they involve the property of foreigners or of Germans in other zones. There are about 9,000 enterprises in lower Saxony.

The vote did not settle the question whether expropriated property is to be socialized or sold to politically unincriminated new private owners. Technical issues, however, were lost in the flood of propaganda involving general politics that made the real issue appear to be the approval or disapproval of the general economic and political order developing in the Russian zone.

Every other house in the center of Plauen was plastered with slogans such as: "Your 'yes' means peace and reconstruction. * * * A year ago you had no gas or light, now reconstruction is on its way. Vote 'yes.' * * * Mothers, think of your children. Vote 'yes.' * * * Youth shall live. Vote 'yes.' * * * 'Yes' means the punishment of war criminals." The Communist Mayor, Alfred Dittel, former grocer, who spent four years in concentration camps and prisons under the Nazis, said that all three authorized Russian-zone parties—Socialist Unity, Liberal Democratic and Christian Democratic Union—had held joint meetings in factories and public places in favor of a "yes" vote. The local and provincial heads of the Catholic and Protestant churches had declared themselves for "yes," he said, and nobody of any importance had opened his mouth for "no."

In an article of July 8, Dana discussed other measures taken by the Russians in their zone. These indicate some of the causes of the coming Cold War.

CAPITALISM FADING IN EAST GERMANY

Russians Using State Ownership for Political Insurance, Not for Socialization

By DANA ADAMS SCHMIDT
By Wireless to THE NEW YORK TIMES.
BERLIN, July 8—A tendency toward the substitution of public ownership or control for private enterprise was observed by American correspondents during a ten day tour of the Russian zone just completed.

The evidence of this tendency contained in key measures—land reform, the confiscation of businesses allegedly belonging to active Nazis and war criminals and the freezing of all old bank accounts—was, however, frequently ambiguous. It led me to conclude that the developments, instigated in the final analysis by the Russian occupation administration, were not intended to socialize economic life in the Russian sense. Rather they appeared primarily designed by various devices to give dominance, in the economic as in the political sphere, to elements that the Russians would consider dependable and could control. The steps in this direction during more than a year of occupation have been progressive and circumspect, taking local traditions into careful consideration.

Land reform was clearly anti-capitalistic in that it expropriated large landowners without compensation. It would have been fairly easy, at the same time, to have also collectivized the expropriated properties on the Russian model. Instead, they were divided among a large number of peasants, thereby, as the proponents of land reform maintain, strengthening the principle of private property. It incidentally gave large numbers of traditionally conservative peasants reason to be grateful to members of the Socialist Unity party, who were most active in pushing the reform.

Plebiscite Explained

The plebiscite on the confiscation of businesses belonging to active Nazis and war criminals in Lower Saxony a week ago was widely and erroneously interpreted as a vote for or against socialization. Actually it appeared to correspondents on the spot to be merely a political demonstration built around confiscations already decided on, while the issue whether individual enterprises would pass into public ownership or be turned over to new private owners remained undecided.

In Thuringia, where identical confiscations have been made by the state government without a plebiscite, the critical issue which properties shall pass into public ownership will be decided by a law now being worked out in the office of the state government's president, Dr. Rudolf Paul. In pursuance of the Allied Control Council's orders, Nazi-owned property has been similarly sequestered in other zones although doubtless not on so large a scale as in the Russian zone. In Thuringia 16 per cent of the industrial enterprises are under sequestration.

Perhaps the most drastic blow to the principle of private property in the Russian zone to date has been the blocking of all bank deposits made before May 8, 1945, the date of the German surrender. Only two minor exceptions have been made, permitting groups of individuals to draw money deposited before that date.

Unfreezing Doubted

Hans Staas, deputy president of the Thuringian government, told correspondents that he saw little prospect that the accounts would ever be unfrozen and in fact he hoped that they would not be. He argued that it was a case of bankruptcy. The Nazi government, he pointed out, printed some 75,000,000,000 marks, or $50,000,000,000 to $60,000,000,000 more than the value of the real wealth produced by Germany during the period. The national debt, at the same time, rose from 10,000,000,000 to 800,000,000,000.

The new Germany, he held, could not assume the debts of Nazi Germany by honoring accounts built up with Nazi marks or ever resume payments on the Nazi Government's bonds. The only debt that the new Germany could and would have to honor, he declared, was that of reparations for what the German Army destroyed outside Germany.

As evidence that people in the Russian zone nonetheless maintain confidence in the future of private property, he explained that, since May 8, the Thuringian State Bank has received 1,500,000,000 marks in new accounts, of which depositors may freely dispose. In addition 21,000,000,000 of obligatory insurance, 9,000,000,000 of voluntary insurance and 75,000,000 of life insurance have been taken out.

In a third article [**PARTY MERGER AIDS EAST GERMAN RULE**], following his visit to the Russian zone, Dana described the political party system that the Russians developed in their zone to reinforce and simplify control. It involved the merger of the Communist and Social Democratic parties into a Socialist Unity party, strong enough to dominate the political scene. The Communist party was too weak to accomplish this alone. The Russians feared that anti-communist tendencies might develop within their zone, as had happened in other parts of Europe.

In the presence of Russian officers, leaders of the parties in Thuringia told correspondents they all were able to develop freely, but went on to explain that they had concluded an agreement to avoid "unfair" mud-slinging, that when acrimonious differences arose between parties they were to be settled in private meetings of the leaders sometimes "with the help of a Russian officer," and that speeches at political meetings must be censored by a Russian officer before delivery.

Unity Party Has Advantage

Georg Schneider, Thuringian chairman of the Christian Democratic Union, considered that the Socialist Unity party would have the advantage in the elections because its "representatives now hold most of local government offices." He added, that his party, like the Liberal Democratic party, had acquired a 10 per cent membership of "nominal" Nazis since last November, when party memberships were thrown open to such persons throughout the zone if they had been approved by an inter-party board of review.

At the September elections, not only parties may submit candidates but also the trade unions, peasants, youth and women, all of whom, with the exception of women, are organized into single monolithic groups of the type that the United States and British Military Governments have sought to avoid.

The parties also share representation with trade union, peasant and other organizations on the advisory council which in Thuringia and most other states of the zone assist the municipal, county and state governments.

The Russians rarely interfere in the details of German administration, confining their contacts to the members of the top echelons, whom they favor with marks of respect exceeding anything observable in the Western zone and with advantages, including fine residences, automobiles and the rations ordinarily allotted only to heavy laborers.

The Russians exercise a highly effective control through the political situations described and through a fear of possible reprisals that the correspondents could feel in all conversations with German political leaders.

Although dealing with Russians on political issues in the administration of postwar Germany was a difficult experience, the Russians showed a warmer, sociable and more conciliatory aspect on the tour with the correspondents. In his article published on July 12th, he described the Russians' efforts to please and entertain:

**RUSSIANS' PARTIES
TIRE U.S. NEWSMEN**

**Group is Royally Entertained
in Soviet Zone of Germany—
Only 2 Requests Refused**

By DANA ADAMS SCHMIDT
By Wireless to THE NEW YORK TIMES.
BERLIN, July 12—American correspondents who have completed a tour of the Russian zone of occupation look back upon a strenuous tour.

For ten days in the company of the Russian hosts to the tune of imperative toasts to eternal friendship they drank beer and kirsch for breakfast and vodka and cognac by the tumblerful at other meals while consuming incalculable quantities of calories.

The Russians and Americans sang many songs, argued questions of both cosmic and immediate interest, found that they agreed on many things and enjoyed each other's company a lot. The party, which began with eight correspondents, dwindled to three by the end of the tour.

Itinerary Haphazardly Chosen
In spite of all this, more work was accomplished than on any previous tour, partly because the Russians appeared to be getting used to correspondents and did not lavish on them such "very important persons" treatment as on earlier trips.

Within the limits of a list of towns rather haphazardly agreed upon in Berlin they were free to go almost anywhere they liked and see whom they liked. But always a Russian officer had to be along, an onerous restriction, since Germans, even members of the Social Unity party, do not speak quite freely in the presence of Russian officers.

Thus the Russians compromised between complete freedom and the sort of stage-set tour in which visitors are whisked from appointment to appointment on a minute schedule.

Two requests were refused. One, for a visit to Leuna synthetic gasoline works, was rejected on the ground that they were under the direct supervision of Berlin and not of the local military administration. The other, for a visit to the Buchenwald concentration camp, was turned down on the ground, as the chief of the Thuringian military administration, General Kolissnitcho, explained, that it was being used as a tactical troop installation and was not under his command.

In any event, he add [sic] that it was not customary for foreigners to visit troop installations where "someone might think they were spies."

Concentration Camp Implied

Another explanation, which correspondents picked up in brief sidewalk conversations, was that Buchenwald is being used again as a concentration camp, for Nazis.

Beyond these places, however, there was no difficulty about visiting Buna, the Zeiss optical works and the Olympia typewriter factories, numerous German administration and party chiefs, and points of historic and cultural interest at Halle, Weimar, Jena, Erfurt and Plauen.

No hosts could have been more anxious to please than the Russians. The escorting officers were intelligent, highly educated men and charming company. But they apparently had not heard about two's being company and three's being a crowd or else they were just following orders.

"We are responsible for your safety and you must stay together and not go out alone," they said. Accordingly, two correspondents who wandered to town for an evening beer were caught by an officer, who escorted them back to their hotel by car.

When four correspondents decided they must return to Berlin early the Russians were in a quandary. "We have only one paper covering you all," they explained. "If four go to Berlin with the paper there will be none of those who are remaining. Therefore we must all go to Berlin, drop the four and come back again."

It wasted thirty-six hours, plus time for argument, for the three persons, but that is what was done. The Russian Army, perhaps more than others, has learned the lesson that no matter how much foolishness it involves it does not pay to be wrong on paper.

In an article published on July 11, Dana described an intellectual way in which the Russians sought to please and win the Germans' good will:

**RUSSIANS SPONSOR
WEIMAR ART PLANS**

**Back Fund to Rebuild Theatre
and Lend Trucks to Gather
Together Goethe Treasures**

**By DANA ADAMS SCHMIDT
By Wireless to THE NEW YORK TIMES.**
BERLIN, July 11—The Russian Military Administration at Weimar, capital of Thuringia, has gone far toward winning the loyalty of German intellectuals by assuming the role of patron of the arts and actively assisting in the reconstruction of German cultural life.

In view of the reports that the Germans deliberately destroyed Russian cultural memorials, such as the Tolstoy and Tchaikovsky museums, this appeared to be one of the most striking aspects of the Russian occupation to a group of American correspondents who spent most of a ten-day tour of the Russian zone in and around Weimar.

Maj. Gen. Kolissnitcho, chief of the Thuringian military administration, personally sponsored a special issue of postage stamps recently which raised four million marks and a drive for contributions, which raised 1,500,000 marks for the reconstruction of Weimar's National Theatre—famed as the theatre where Goethe, as its director for half a century, first produced the two parts of "Faust" and as the place where Germany's Weimar Constitution was drafted in 1919.

The present director of the theatre, 26-year-old Hans Viehweg, introduced the correspondents to some of the 350 members of the Theatre Association who were celebrating a special dispensation from the military administration granting them laborers' rations of 2,100 calories because they were assisting in the labor of reconstruction.

Enlarged Theatre Planned

Out of the tangled ruin of the bomb-blasted interior of the theatre, which is surrounded by undamaged exterior walls, Herr Viehweg said it was hoped to construct a modernized and enlarged theatre capable of seating the largest orchestra in Germany.

Plans call for completion of the reconstruction by October of next year when it will reopen with "Faust," parts one and two.

One of the first things the Russians did after they replaced Americans in Weimar more than a year ago was to supply trucks with which to gather together the contents of the Goethe Haus which had been scattered for protection in various mines, and to reopen the Museum of the man who, more than any other, made the town an attraction for generations of students.

Prof. Hans Wall, who has been in charge of the Goethe memorials since 1918, said the contents of the museum, of the Goethe-Schiller archives and of Goethe's home were all intact although Goethe's home was partly destroyed by bombing. It is to be reconstructed shortly.

Some Passages Censored

A sidelight—only one of the kind observed—was that a publication containing works on Goethe written between 1939 and 1944, which the Russians authorized for distribution to members of the association throughout the world, contained three censored passages that are clearly legible through the paper pasted over them.

One of them quotes Goethe as saying that revolutionary states can be really reorganized, not by new constitutions, but only by soldiers.

Another speaks of his fear of mechanization as a threat to art and a third, of his fear of the Russians.

Nowhere in Weimar was there any evidence that objects of artistic or cultural value had been removed to Russia nor did Germans who were interviewed know of any such removals from other parts of the zone.

In a final article on the Russian zone trip and the reports of the Paris Conference, Dana wrote the following reflecting on the future of Germany:

**RUSSIANS' ZONE FOUND
DIFFERENT FROM OTHERS**

**American Correspondents See How
Soviet Works to Strengthen Control**

By DANA ADAMS SCHMIDT
By Wireless to THE NEW YORK TIMES.
FRANKFORT ON THE MAIN, July 13—What Foreign Minister Vyacheslav M. Molotov has said in Paris about the unification of Germany and its central administrative and government agencies is not irreconcilable with the predominant American and British views, much as it may differ from the views of the French Government. But what a party of American correspondents observed in the Russian zone during a ten-day tour is much more difficult to reconcile with American and British objectives in their zones of occupation. The difference is the familiar one between diplomacy and reality.

During the delay in the German settlement until a special conference can be held sometime before the end of the year, as envisaged by Mr. Molotov, the American and British zones, if not the French, are more than likely to indulge in a measure of unification on their own, while the Russian zone continues to grow away from the rest of Germany in terms of political and economic development. So that when and if a central organization for all of Germany is eventually set up, the eastern and western parts of Germany would be difficult to amalgamate and a struggle would certainly ensue to determine whether the objectives developed in the Russian zone or those prevailing in the western zone should be applied throughout Germany.

System Not Imposed

It appeared to this correspondent in conversations with leading Russians and Germans during the tour that the Russians do not care very much whether the Germans "get religion," that is go Communist, or not. The Russians are far too astute politically and far too good as historians to try to impose their system in any wholesale and arbitrary manner on a country whose history is very different and where conditions are very different from their own.

What the Russians are interested in is control, by Soviet Russia, now in their own zone, eventually perhaps in all of Germany. It is a sort of control that goes beyond the functions of control commissions and reaches down into the economic and political structure of the country. And this they are in a fair way of achieving in their zone.

Instead of carrying through a simple socialization in agriculture and industry the Russians, always operating through the German administration, have been destroying old property rights and at the same time building up new ones whose beneficiaries have an interest in and are dependent on the preservation of the new order.

The simplest example is land reform, where large estate holders were expropriated without compensation and a large new class of small property-holding peasants substituted in their place. It was a reform long overdue in eastern Germany, in any case, and the Russians took advantage of it to create a body of peasants who can probably be depended on, in spite of their conservative traditions, to vote for the Socialist Unity party.

Nazi-owned businesses are being expropriated in the Russian zone, and the same fate appears likely to befall the largest private interests regardless of their owners political past. But only a portion are scheduled to be socialized. The remainder are to be turned over to new private owners whose future interests will be the same as those of the new peasant proprietors.

By freezing all bank accounts deposited before May 8, 1945, and letting it be known that they are likely to stay frozen, the Russians wiped out independent capital built up in the past.

It is true a business man, under the prevailing laws, can go to a bank and get credit to carry on or expand his business and can build up a new bank account of which he can freely dispose. But he can get credit and make money only in so far as it fits into the intentions of the new administration. Individuals and companies who are allowed to prosper under these circumstances are hardly likely to favor the eventual unfreezing of their competitors' accounts.

Political Control Devices

On the political side control devices are even more evident. The merger of the Communist and Social Democratic parties, unquestionably a forced one by Western standards, created a party attentive to Russian desires and sufficiently strong to dominate the political scene. Potential opposition parties—the Christian Democratic Union and the Liberal Democratic party—were not eliminated, but their ability to oppose is greatly limited by an "anti-fascist" bloc.

This, as political leaders explained to the visiting correspondents, represents their unity against Nazism and for reconstruction. It also involves a "gentlemen's agreement" not to indulge in acrimonious or mud-slinging party politics during the campaign for the September municipal elections. And it means that inter-party conflicts do not come before the public but are worked out in private committee by the heads of the parties, if necessary "with the help of a Russian officer."

All these developments are not without parallel in the western zones. The differences lie in the objectives. Whereas the Americans and the British are proceeding only against Nazi property, the Russians apparently regard all old property as the enemy. Whereas the Americans and the British consider it a part of their general respect for property rights to protect existing rights of politically uncriminated owners of land, businesses and capital against uncompensated expropriation, the Russians are building up a new propertied class.

In the Western Zones

Political parties are not quite free in the western zones either in that they must watch their step in criticizing the occupying powers. But the Americans at least, Communist allegations notwithstanding, approach the parties without ideological commitments, treat them equally, allow them equal opportunities of development and permit them to fight out their differences in public.

On the popular level there is no doubt that the Germans in the parts of the Soviet zone which were occupied by Americans for several months greatly preferred the well-groomed, carefree and generous "Amis" with their cigarettes and candy to the untidy, uncommunicative and somewhat rude Russian soldiers now in their midst. Almost no public fraternization is to be seen in the Soviet zone.

On high official levels, however, the situation is quite different. Repeatedly German officials drew comparisons between the offhand, impolite treatment they got from American officers and the consideration they now get from the Russians. The Russians exert their control almost entirely through contacts with the highest echelons of an increasingly centralized German administration on whom they lavish every mark of respect and permit to maintain luxurious residences and automobiles and ration cards in the highest category.

Interest in German Culture

Doubtless more from natural inclination than out of practical consideration Russian officers show a particular interest in German cultural life and have thereby gained the sympathy of many German intellectuals and artists. The point is that the Russians know where to spread the honey where it counts most, combining flattery with fear as an instrument of control.

Basic economic and politic rights aside, the correspondents came to the conclusion that the Germans in the parts of the Soviet zone visited are now materially better off than the Germans in the western zones. Undoubtedly in the parts now visited there are black spots as there are in the western zones. But, in spite of reparations in removals of capital equipment and from current production and heavy levies to feed the Red Army, the Germans in the Soviet zone were eating better on the average than in the West, with more consumer goods to be bought in the shops and practically no unemployment.

In large measure this is attributable to the geographical advantages of the zone in agriculture and raw materials. But it is also due to measures for stimulating peasant initiatives such as a free market for over-quota products to the deflationary effect of freezing bank accounts, which also helped to keep the black market down, and to Russian assistance in reviving industry.

If there have been many irresponsible and untrue rumors about the Russian zone it is largely the Russians' fault for making authentic information so difficult to obtain.

If instead of lifting a corner of the "iron curtain" only for periodic tours they were to remove it and allow allied correspondents to circulate freely through the zone in their own time the Russians would not have so much cause for indignation.

On returning from the Russian trip on July 15, Dana wrote:

As always after trips I came back to a wealth of letters from you. Also one from Dorothy and a check for $35.00 from the W.J. Smith Publishing Corporation for reprinting my article "Land of Questions Without Answers" in Everybody's Digest.

I'm not quite sure about the correctness of the W.J. Smith procedure in reprinting the stuff without consulting me, although I certainly don't mind. So I'm writing to Markel to ask him if it's ok before I forward you the check.

On Wednesday morning I think I'll be off to Nuremberg for a look at Hermann and company, more particularly in the interests of Markel, who wants a weekender on the status of the trials. He seems to be the man who determines my movements these days. I did a weekender on the Russian zone for him which I trust was printed. It summarized my impressions fairly completely, although I couldn't get everything in. It was a most educational experience as I already wrote from Berlin.

I'm afraid you went without a letter for quite a while. I was off touring, but you know I would have written if it had been possible.

Yesterday I went out to a DP camp at Wiesbaden to see John Tolischus, brother of the well-known NYT *correspondent who is a DP there. Poor man* has got his life considerably scrambled. He was convicted of making seditious statements in the US in the other war, returned to his native Memel, made a reputation as an anti-German, had trouble with the Germans when they took over, fled from the Russians, and is now probably going to get kicked out of the DP camp because he is not a genuine displaced person. His brother is trying to get him and family to the US, but it seems most difficult in view of his conviction. I sent a long report on him to Mr. Sulzberger who asked me to look into the matter.

No, I didn't take the car to the Russian zone. We used Army cars. The Lincoln is in good shape and I have finally got the radio working. About those food packages—I believe the nonprofit organization of which you speak is CARE. Anyway, their package sounds good. Will you have already sent, and also, to Herr Kurt Ofenloch, Ringlestrasse 44, Frankfort, and to Herr Kurt Klein, Fechenheimer Strasse 13, Frankfort. They are two deserving and rather indigent families I have run across, both with large numbers of children.

I sent the check to WRA (Western Reserve Academy) all right and got a thank you from my old history teacher and soccer coach Mr. Nickel. So they must have missed me by mistake in their list. I suppose I should make a contribution to Pomona some time.

From your letters I gather you are feeling much better. That is a relief to me. If the sea air does you good, I think you should take advantage of it. The project for a beach cottage with Nini Barry sounds splendid to me. I wish you would go ahead with it. Could I share in the expense? I would love to think I had an interest in a beach cottage, and in not such a very long time I expect to be around again where I could enjoy it.

How nice that the babies are thriving. No doubt I will have a few of my own one of these days.

The New Yorker has been coming through and is a pleasure. I hereby make a request for three back numbers of Harpers and of the Atlantic I've missed. Actually I don't have much time for reading magazines but it is nice to have them just in case.

I would also be very happy if you could send me another package with chocolate and powdered coffee and perhaps some of Steinie's cookies.

It is two a.m. now and I must go to bed. If the day were about three hours longer than it is, it would be a big help.

All my love you all,
to Grandma and Eliza and Steinie too, Dana
Added in hand writing:
Your clippings were most interesting and useful. That Taylor guy is still a phony, I see.

Although during the war, the four Allies cooperated against a common enemy, now a year after the end of the war, competition for control of all of Germany was evident between Britain and the U.S., who worked together, and the Russians in their zone. Dana described this complicated situation:

STRUGGLE IN OPEN FOR CONTROL OF ALL GERMANY

Russians Have Taken the Lead Owing
To Political and Economic Acts

By DANA ADAMS SCHMIDT
By Wireless to THE NEW YORK TIMES.
FRANKFORT ON THE MAIN, July 20—As a result of the Paris conference of Foreign Ministers, the responsibility for the failure to set up central economic agencies for all of Germany has passed to Russia, and steps toward the unification of the American and British zones have been accelerated.

Detailed instructions from Washington were expected at the end of the week, but meanwhile Anglo-American exploratory economic talks went ahead in Berlin with renewed vigor in search of common import, export, transport and food programs.

Considerable cooperation is already in effect, including the exchange of German liaison officials for food and other economic questions between the two zones. A coordinating committee of the Council of the American Zone States at Stuttgart at the end of the week also drew up a program for coordinating the administration in the two zones which will be submitted to the British zone advisory council at Hamburg.

Military Government officials said that Washington's instructions on further moves would be confined to economic and administrative realms since political unification in the west might prejudice further negotiations. The Moscow press was already charging "secret negotiations" and there was no disposition to feed the flames unnecessarily.

Foundation Already Laid

The foundations of the political unification of the American and British zones were nonetheless being laid. First, because it was inherent in economic and administrative unification, and second, because the British zone's advisory council was hard at work on plans for the reorganization of the zone into three states which would parallel the three states of the American zone and provide the machinery required for a federal political organization of the western German states under a Council of States with central economic agencies.

Whether the French zone would be drawn into this evolving western unification remained an open question, since France herself is a battleground of Communists, representing Russian influence, and other political groups more representative of Western Europe.

Between the American and Russian zones, in the past six weeks, there has been a notable increase in trade, which, regrettably, did not include food, but extended to $5,000,000 worth of Soviet-zone buna, X-ray tubes, textile machinery and alcohol, and American-zone tires, ball bearings and steel products. This, however, was purely a commercial transaction and did not involve contact on administrative or economic planning levels of the kind going on between the American and British zones.

British economic dependence on the United States—most specifically for grain to keep the British zone alive and generally as highlighted by the new loan—gives Americans the upper hand in dealing with them in Germany. But in dealing with the Russians, whose zone is not in such dire need of imports from America and is doing quite nicely by itself, American economic might cuts little ice.

There is much evidence to show that the longer Russia's Eastern Germany remains separated from the western zones through the absence of central agencies, the stronger the Russian position grows in the struggle in which the stake is all of Germany.

This would account for a distinct impression among those who have dealt with the Russians in Berlin and Paris that they desire delay in a German settlement.

Time was when the interplay of the conflicting wills of the four powers might have alone settled the future of Germany. But with the passing of months, German internal politics have grown into a factor that cannot be ignored and in which the Russians apparently think they hold a long-run advantage. No longer an inarticulate conglomeration of bewildered, beaten people, the Germans have been allowed to reorganize their political life, and German nationalism and desires for unity and reconstruction have become realities.

On these, Mr. Molotov played in his speeches at Paris, and these the Social Unity party and Communist party are exploiting in the four zones of Germany.

Competition for Favor

Competition for the favor of Germans, so often fearfully forecast even before war ended, has begun and the Russians have taken the lead.

While Lieut. Gen. Lucius D. Clay saw fit in recent days to check such tendencies by issuing a directive to American Military Government personnel to avoid excessive friendliness with Germans with whom they work, American correspondents who visited the Russian zone found top German officials glowing with satisfaction under Russian flattery and favors.

The Russians would smile to hear that American officers debated seriously whether the Minister Presidents of the three American zone states should be required to travel to Stuttgart for the Council of States meeting by train instead of by car in order to comply with gasoline conservation regulations.

To their zone in Germany, the Russians have brought a kind of democracy whose purposeful authoritarianism the Germans generally understand. It has the usual totalitarian advantage in dynamism and singleness of purpose.

Lacking scruples about individual rights, the Russians through their German officials were able by drastic and simple methods to achieve some results much desired by western powers in their zone. There is no displaced-persons problem in the Russian zone because the Russians tolerated no displaced persons. They had to leave or be absorbed into German economy. The western zones were obliged to take up the burden.

Under Russian influence short shrift was given eastern Germany's feudalistic heritage of large estates. They were expropriated and their lands divided among expelled persons from Poland and the Sudetenland and other peasants who will presumably support the Socialist Unity party if they want to keep their new property.

Expropriation Is Feared

The very much smaller problem of land reform in western Germany is giving American and British Military Government officers sleepless nights because they do not want to be responsible for expropriation of the property of innocent persons without compensation.

Expropriation of Nazi and probably other businesses has been handled with similar advantage to the Socialist Unity party. Excessive money in circulation, which plagues the western zones, was dammed up in the Russian zone by the freezing of old accounts, but persons with the right political attitude were able to get credit to stay in business and build up new accounts.

By such devices, combined with the shotgun marriage of the Social Democratic and Communist parties, the Socialist Unity party has developed into a political colossus astride the political life of the Russian zone and eager for the day when it can branch out to the other zones.

The Russians and the Socialist Unity party, meanwhile, take the credit for the advantages which geography has conferred upon the Russian zone. Fed by some of Germany's richest farming land, it is possible for zone officials to discuss increasing rations in spite of the Red Army's consumption. With an industry that can get by with little in the way of raw materials from western Germany, a high level of production and surface prosperity have been achieved in many parts which conceals the fact that most of the production is going to Russia as reparations.

From the western zones, where production is hovering around 25 per cent of capacity and fundamental improvement is not in sight, the German struggling to live on 1,100 or 1,200 calories looks across to the Russian zone and thinks he sees a light.

The German's fear of the Russians lessens with time and with what he imagines to be the hope of economic salvation. A few Germans who fled before the Red Army are reported to be returning to the Russian zone from the Ruhr. Slowly the prestige of the Russians and of the Socialist Unity party grows.

By comparison the Americans, and in a modified degree the British, have approached Germany with a high conception of democracy and of respect for the individual man, which is strange to German political tradition. It is appreciated by only a minority and lacks a specific ideological and economic content.

After denazification and demilitarization it is not clear to the Germans what we back—socialism, small-scale private enterprise, big business, or what. Except for limited British support of the Social Democrats, no political group has had official backing. No economic program has been evolved that would enable the Germans to see the direction and build up hope for the future.

German Self-Government

Instead, in the American zone, and to a lesser extent in the British, we are turning over administration, economic planning, information, even denazification and control of internment camps to the Germans. We are turning them loose and telling them to work it out for themselves, giving idealistic rationalizations of what we are obliged to do by dwindling manpower.

One of the things Molotov said at Paris must be written into any German settlement was "securing a democratic regime in Germany." He meant the Socialist Unity party kind of democracy and all that goes with it in the Russian zone.

When Messrs. Byrnes and Bevin go to work on the German settlement with Mr. Molotov they will have to decide whether the system the Russians have built up in their zone is not of such a nature that it would be irreconcilable with that prevailing in western Germany, unless it imposed itself on western Germany.

If in the end they should decide that it is impossible for us to work with Russians in Germany, it would not be difficult for the Americans and British and perhaps even the French to agree in western Germany. Then they would have to consider the German political factor, the question whether the Russians might not in the end win the Germans out from under them.

On July 22, Dana wrote in his letter home:

Much to my surprise I'm still here [in Frankfort]; *after telling you last week I was on the verge of departure. But tomorrow I'm really off, first to Stuttgart, then Munich, and next week, Nuremberg.*

My last day has been a productive one. I finally got off the Youth article. It was a real pain in the neck. Very hard to write I find. (In fact writing is such hard work I wonder why I ever took it up.)

I also got some pictures of your son [these letters were mostly written to Mother—although they were meant to be shared with the family] *standing and sitting beside and in the car, one set taken by a UP man and the other by an AP man. So we ought to get results.*

I've been so taken up the last few days working on the displaced persons series the Publisher wants and finishing that article I haven't had much time for the daily. I hope Markel gives me a rest this week.

Ted Bernstein, our cable editor who was also one of my instructors at Columbia, is coming over here in August. I'll be glad to see him. He is a very agreeable fellow and I'm sure won't be so much trouble as the Publisher.

I've taken up writing in red so as to use up the other half of my ribbon. The top half was getting a bit weak. Harold Callender, incidentally, has an affectation of always using red carbon paper, so that his stories can be distinguished in the office file, I presume.

This evening your note with the clippings of Hoffman's pieces in the British zone came in. His stuff looks very competent to me. I'm glad we have another man in Germany. Our staff looks so very undersized. But would you believe it, I didn't know he was here 'till I got the clippings. I heard a long time ago he was supposed to come and then nothing more. Apparently he went directly to the British zone without checking in at American headquarters. He was to do a series on the British zone and then return to his post in London.

Would you look over your clips and tell me whether the Times *ever used my election story from Plauen in the Soviet zone, my piece on Jews in the Soviet zone, a longish screed on Soviet treatment of private property, and on architectural reconstruction plans? I haven't seen any trace of them although a good many others were published. Our clipping service is most unreliable.*

There isn't much doing around here and I'm fed up with Frankfort anyway. It will be a good thing to have a look around other parts.

All my love to you all, Dana

It had been hoped that movies, as well as books, would help with acquainting Germans with American culture. Dana reported on the effect of some movies:

OUR MOVIES LEAVE GERMANS HOSTILE

Political and Psychological Regeneration Fails—U.S. Prestige Suffers

By DANA ADAMS SCHMIDT
By Wireless to THE NEW YORK TIMES.
FRANKFORT ON THE MAIN, Germany, July 22—The thirty-five American films shown to Germans since the end of the war have, with only a few exceptions, had no observable effect in the political and psychological re-education of the Germans and have, on the contrary, reduced American cultural prestige and probably damaged the future market for American films in Germany, according to a group of information-control offices.

Some of the most successful, if not the most educational, films, they said, have been those with military content, especially those dealing with the Pacific warfare. The two most outstanding of these, "Thirty Seconds over Tokyo" and "Destination Tokyo," have recently been withdrawn from circulation. "The Sullivans" and "So Proudly We Hail," also with war themes, continue to show, however.

One not so popular war film that has for several months aroused hostile demonstrations on almost every town of the American zone among the few Germans who go to see it, the offices reported, is "K-225," which portrays the bestial practices of U-boats. It is still being shown.

With little to spend their money on and a limited choice of entertainment, the Germans are willing to spend hours waiting in queues to get into the limited number of movies left. In addition to the thirty-five American films, only eleven politically approved German films and four foreign films have been made available, whereas the normal supply would be about 120. The German, therefore, often sees the same film several times over.

The information-control officers understood that American film distribution in Germany would be put on a commercial basis in the next few months and entertained hopes that more of the great films produced in Hollywood since their showing was cut off by the Germans would then become available. Besides those already mentioned, the American films shown to the Germans since the war are: "Here Comes Mr. Jordan," "You Were Never Lovelier," "Pride and Prejudice," "Seven Sweethearts," "Young Tom Edison," "The Gold Rush," "It Happened Tomorrow," "Shadow of a Doubt," "It Started With Eve," "I Married a Witch," "Tom, Dick and Harry," "The Human Comedy," "Across the Pacific," "Christmas in July," "All That Money Can Buy," "Remember the Day," "Appointment for Love," "Abraham Lincoln in Illinois," "Mme. Curie," "Topper Returns," "Dr. Ehrlich's Magic Bullet," "The Maltese Falcon," "Tales of Manhattan," "There's Magic in Music," "Hundred Men and a Girl," "Flesh and Fantasy," "No Time for Love," "Moontide," "Going My Way" and "The Corn Is Green."

The "Maltese Falcon" has been withdrawn and "The Corn Is Green" has not yet been distributed. The most popular, according to the officers, were "Young Tom Edison," "You Were Never Lovelier," "Seven Sweethearts," "It Started With Eve," "The Sullivans," "Mme. Curie," "Dr. Ehrlich's Magic Bullet," "A Hundred Men and A Girl," "Thirty Seconds over Tokyo," "Destination Tokyo" and "Moontide." None of these films had German sound-tracks. That is now being undertaken in Munich. The first German-speaking American films are expected to be ready in the autumn.

Dana described most clearly the tragic difficulties of the Jews living in Germany following the War in an article published on July 29:

**JEWS EMBITTERED
BY LIFE IN GERMANY**

**Incidents at Displaced
Persons' Camps Held
Symptomatic of War Reactions**

**By DANA ADAMS SCHMIDT
By Wireless to THE NEW YORK TIMES.**
MUNICH, Germany, July 29—The embitterment of Jewish displaced persons who must live in the midst of the people who destroyed most of the Jews of Europe has been heightened anew by incidents between Jews and German police and American troops outside the United Nations Relief and Rehabilitation Administration's camp for Jewish displaced persons in Foehrenwald, near Wolfratshausen, last week, and by the erroneous reports of them since then.

Isac Feldberg was shot dead and another Jew was wounded by German police on Wednesday, and six other Jews were wounded by American troops using bayonets on the following day. Because the incident is symptomatic of a series of incidents that appear destined to continue and of the tension between Jews and Germans and American troops that increases as V-E Day recedes into the past, I consulted a variety of sources in an effort to piece together an accurate chronological story. They included Edouard From, acting camp director; Sam B. Zisman, district UNRRA director; Carl Atkin, district UNRRA coordinator of Jewish affairs, and the Jewish camp-committee chairman, Gustav Lachman, as well as Army and military-government sources.

Because some sixty head of cattle had been sold or stolen for black-market purposes in as many days in the Wolfratshausen area, and there is reason to believe that displaced persons had a big part in the matter, military and German police recently kept a sharp look-out around the camp and set up a highway check point several hundred yards from its entrance. While admitting that some black-market activities were attributable to Jewish and other displaced persons, UNRRA officials maintain that it is understandable that they should seek to vary the camp fare with fresh meat such as the Germans enjoy and should entertain little respect for German property in view of their recent history.

Origin of Incident

At about 9:30 P.M. on Wednesday, while several hundred of the 5,000 camp inhabitants were taking the usual evening stroll on the road in front of the camp, two German policemen on a motorcycle caught up with a German truck containing three Jews and a German driver as it stood opposite the entrance. According to military sources, the truck had not halted at the check point.

Seeing money changing hands, the police asked what had been paid, while the strolling Jews, showing normal curiosity, gathered round. The police ordered one of the Jews from the truck into the camp and questioned the two others. The first obeyed and started for the entrance, when, according to Jewish accounts, he heard a cry for help from the others. He started back and the elder of the policemen, standing several meters from the truck, fired a carbine over his head.

This had the opposite of the effect desired, and the Jews began milling around the truck, undoubtedly cursing. The police maintain, though the Jews deny it, that the crowd tried to disarm them. It is understandable that any German at this stage in history would be frightened under the circumstances, especially since the military government's records contain reports of German police being beaten by displaced persons almost every week. Nothing apparently incites them more than the sight of an armed German.

Policeman Loses Poise

In any event, the elder policeman lost his head and cried: "We are lost!" He fired four or five shots at a level height at the milling crowd. Feldberg, who was one of the strollers, was shot through the back and another Jew was wounded. One policeman jumped on the motorcycle and the other into the truck, and they sped from the scene.

One of these policemen was allowed by German authorities to leave Wolfratshausen on the following day to visit relatives, and both have been returned to duty in another part of the country. Disciplinary action, if any, according to military sources, awaits the completion of an official investigation.

The camp's own displaced-person police herded the angry Jews back into the camp, and constabulary, MPs and infantry who had been alerted by the camp director threw a cordon around the camp. Eight Germans who had been led from the road into the camp by its police immediately after the shooting were escorted out through the military cordon at 1 A.M., and all but fifty or sixty of the military forces were withdrawn by 5:00 P.M. the next day.

Got Funeral Permission

The camp authorities had obtained permission for a truck with a hearse and sixteen mourners to leave the camp at that hour for the Jewish cemetery in Gauting, ten miles away. At the last minute someone whose identity was not established on the camp staff obtained permission from the M.P.s, but apparently not from the infantry, for other Jews to line the road leading from the camp, and several hundred Jews began to emerge. Fearing trouble, the camp chairman hurried out with his police and asked the troops to help push the crowd back into the camp.

The troops were alarmed by the sight of the Jews apparently moving toward them, and the Jews were confused and became angered as the troops and the camp police formed a cordon to push them back into the camp. Whether anyone shouted "American Gestapo" cannot be established, but worse things were probably said. The important fact is that two American soldiers, whether through carelessness or overenthusiasm, wounded six Jews in the backs and thighs with their bayonets.

In late July and early August, Dana attended the last of the 4-power Nuremberg trials. Following is one of the reports:

GESTAPO IS LINKED TO ESPIONAGE HERE

Telegram Read at Nuremberg Trial Shows Tie to Group Seized in City in 1941

By DANA ADAMS SCHMIDT
By Wireless to THE NEW YORK TIMES.

NUREMBERG, Germany, Aug. 1—In cross examining defense witnesses for the Gestapo—one of the six Nazi organizations now on trial before the international Military Tribunal—the prosecution introduced today a secret telegram from the Foreign Ministry asking on behalf of former German Foreign Minister Joachim von Ribbentrop which of the twenty persons arrested on a charge of spying in the Sperry Gyroscope plant were connected with "Sicherheits-dienst" and with the "Abwehr," both subdivisions of the Gestapo.

[The Federal Bureau of Investigation announced June 29, 1941, the seizure of twenty-nine persons, three of them women, on charges of espionage in connection with a vast spy ring that was sending information to Germany.]

The German telegram, dated July 11, 1941, was addressed to a legation counselor, Kramatz, and it ordered that a reply be made in consultation with Ambassador Dr. Hans Luther in Washington.

Gestapo Defense Broken

The document was part of the evidence by which Francis Biddle, Lieut. Comdr. Whitney Harris and Maj. Hartley Murray of the United States staff broke down the defense that the Gestapo was merely a group of ill-paid functionaries who were obliged to carry out Adolf Hitler's will and that the Sicherheits-dienst had been mainly engaged in a survey of German opinion on political and economic topics.

According to the documents introduced, Reinhard Heydrich at one point reported that "Einsatz Komandos," composed of Gestapo and Sicherheitsdienst men, had shot 31,000 Ruthenian Jews.

A message from Ernst Kaltenbrunner recommended that a French general, Mesny, be either shot in the back as though when trying to escape or gassed with carbon monoxide while being moved from Koenigstein prison. He ordered a funeral with military honors.

Complains of Few Killings

He complained furthermore that the screening of Russian prisoners was superficial because only 410 had been removed from camps to be killed.

Werner Best, former Reich plenipotentiary in Denmark and an administrative chief of the Gestapo, maintained that he heard of such things for the first time but admitted under cross-examination that he had lied in an earlier statement that he never had discussed the terror methods to be applied to the Danes with Hitler.

Another witness admitted knowledge of an order from Heinrich Himmler as early as 1937 ordering agents to beat and keep prisoners standing over long periods during interrogation.

On August 2, Dana confirmed the suggestion that the trials of military and political chiefs would end, and a project for the subsequent trial of German industrialists and other groups by the four-power tribunal would also end. In part, he wrote:

It is expected to cause some surprise, since it was the United States' enthusiasm for the four-power tribunal that put across the trials now drawing to a close in Nuremberg. The Russians were skeptical from the first and the British would have preferred brief court-martials.

Informed quarters explained, however, that while the differences of legal conceptions of the four nations could be reconciled for the purposes of this trial, the difference in economic conceptions between the Soviet Union and the Western nations might prove too much of a hurdle in a trial of industrialists.

While the Russians have been subjecting large enterprises and large fortunes in their zone to expropriation on the assumption that the owners must be "Fascist," the British, French and Americans have not made a practice of automatically considering a man to be a Nazi because he is wealthy or heads a large enterprise.

There will be subsequent trials, sponsored separately by the authorities of the various zones, however.

In the United States zone, some 20 per cent of the 70,000 internees now in camps, including some industrialists, will be moved to Dachau to await trials organized by the Office of Chief Council, which is now running the United States end of the Nuremberg trials. The remaining Germans will be turned over to German denazification tribunals.

On one of the last days of the trials, the former New York Mayor, Fiorello La Guardia, marched briskly into the Military Tribunal and sat down next to the acting American prosecutor, Thomas J. Dodd. Hermann Goering craned his neck, and several other Nazi defenders blinked recognition. [Dana continued writing in his article, **"LA GUARDIA URGENT ON U.N. RELIEF ACT,"** Aug. 3.]

For half an hour the former New York Mayor, who was once a favorite target for the Nazis' most furious anti-American and anti-Semitic propaganda, listened quietly to a one-time Elite Guard chief of Munich testify that the ordinary SS had nothing in particular to do with pograms or with concentration camp atrocities against the Jews—it disapproved of such matters.

Afterward, in an interview, Mr. La Guardia confirmed that the care by the United Nations Relief and Rehabilitation Administration of displaced persons must cease at the end of the year.

"It is simple," said UNRRA's director general. "We haven't any more money. It is a very difficult and dangerous situation, and there is nothing I can do about it."

He added that there was no ground to believe that new relief organizations to be sponsored by the United Nations will be ready to take over the job by Jan. 1.

U.N. Needs "Money" for the Job

"The International Relief Organization is supposed to take over the DP's," Mr. La Guardia remarked. "But it hasn't any money.

"The World Health Organization is supposed to take over our health work, but they won't be ready. They have asked for $370,000, which should about pay for carbon paper. That would take millions.

"Industrial rehabilitation is to be done by the International Bank for Reconstruction—which will be all right if it is just that, and not a pawnshop. How the imports needed for some countries will be handled is a most desperate question."

Mr. La Guardia assumed that the United States and British Army occupation forces would handle displaced persons until the new organizations were ready and that the armies would take over UNRRA personnel, although many of these were unfortunately quitting in anticipation of UNRRA's end. He thought the American Army had done remarkably well in working with UNRRA on the problem.

"It is an intensely human problem," he said, reflectively, "and requires much patience and understanding. These people have been kicked around for two or three or four years or more. There is no particular place they can go to. They are doing what they can to maintain their skills and keep up morale."

"At first blush they seem pretentious and demanding. But it is just the hopelessness of their situation, particularly of the children. Some of the groups will still go home. We will have to find places for the others. It is the most heartbreaking thing you have ever seen."

Says Trieste Needs "My Cops"

Mr. La Guardia reported that he received what he called an "unsatisfactory" reply from Maj. Gen. John C.H. Lee, American deputy commander of Allied Forces in the Mediterranean theatre, to his protest about the failure of the Allied Military Government in the Trieste area to protect UNRRA supplies there from wholesale pilfering.

"But I think we will be able to get together on the matter at another conference and I won't have to take it to the Combined Chiefs of Staff," he said.

"What I really need," he went on, grinning, "is some New York police. Give me twenty-five of my cops and I'll clean that thing out."

After a quick walk through the prison cells housing the Nazis, Mr. La Guardia flew to Frankfort on the Main for a conference with Gen. Joseph T. McNarney, American Commander in Europe. Later he was to fly on to Geneva for the UNRRA Council sessions opening there Monday.

He will subsequently visit Minsk and Kiev, the capitals, respectively, of White Russia and the Ukraine, and then go to Warsaw and Prague.

Meanwhile, Dana was still in Nuremberg and wrote in his letter on August 4:

It was grand to have your last two letters which were forwarded from Frankfort to me here in Nuremberg. Along with them came one from Dr. Lowman, which was most kind of him and for which I thank him through you.

I am deeply enmeshed in stories to be written, movements, things Merkel wants, what the Publisher wants and what I want to do myself. At times I am quite staggered by the problem and I am most depressed and then again when one step is successfully taken and done, I am quite exultant.

The one man I never hear from is James, (Edwin L. James, managing editor of the NYT who is after all my real boss.) On the surface it would seem fine to be left quite free to do as I please, but it leaves an awful burden of decision. Markel's constant requests give me some guidance and direction and are really a great help. Then the Publisher came along with his DP request, which required a lot of spade work, and yesterday he wired me directly, suggesting I see Rabbi Bernstein for a roundup of the Jewish problem. He also asked for more statistics for himself. I'll be off to Frankfort to see the Rabbi tomorrow and should have the DP series going later in the week

Meanwhile Markel has asked, of all things, for a piece on the translation system and mechanism employed at the trial which I will try to get before leaving for Frankfort in the morning. He also wants a piece on the Constabulary which I promised in a couple of weeks.

It is rather annoying that I should be in Stuttgart for the Laenderrat meeting on Tuesday, so I will have to rush right on from Frankfort. If I were two, or possibly three, it would be a big help.

Today, Sunday, I visited a Jewish agricultural training school at the former Streicher farm near here. There has been so much to do in connection with the trials that I really haven't gone into the Jewish matter as much as I planned here. I took Dudley Harmon along and we interviewed a woman Communist Dudley wanted to see along the way and had a fine day of it.

It is fine and hot around here and I am feeling very well. I was delighted to hear you were going to the beach again. It is just the thing for you I know and will get you in shape for the period Steinie is away. She certainly deserves a vacation and then some. I wish there was something nice I could do for her.

While I am writing a pack of correspondents are playing the piano, stomping and singing, hooting and howling in the next room. They lead a very convivial and rather communal life here. There is an organ in addition to the piano which moans most of most nights under expert and inexpert management. All the property of Herr Faber, the pencil king, who built this fabulous monument to bad taste. It is a sort of medieval castle, with turrets and towers, shocking murals, and paintings of himself in armor tilting with a pencil, etc. and the factory next door. Somebody should have got him together with the Hearsts.

How nice that you heard from Ida Treat. I'll try to see her when I get to Paris. Can't see how I'm going to swing that trip till we get more correspondents over here. No word from the Daniells.

Give my love to Eliza when she reappears from the beach. It will be nice for her kids down there, although they're so young. I look back on our summers at Eagle Cliff, which I remember quite clearly, and on the Baltic [at seaside resorts] *and at Brehat* [island on the Brittany coast, where we visited Ida Treat], *as some of the nicest periods of growing up. What is Grandma doing? I wrote her a letter not too long ago.*

All my love, Dana

The problem of finding new homes for the thousands of displaced Jewish people in Europe following the War was obviously not easily solved. It was, undoubtedly, the greatest problem faced by Rabbi Bernstein at this time, and Dana consulted him again in Frankfort following his visits to the Ukraine and Poland. Dana's article on August 5 summarized the situation:

**NEW HAVENS ASKED
FOR JEWS IN EUROPE**

**Areas in Austria, France or
Italy Proposed for Expected
100,000 Polish Emigres**

**By DANA ADAMS SCHMIDT
By Wireless to THE NEW YORK TIMES.**
FRANKFORT ON THE MAIN, Germany, Aug. 5—The possibilities of finding temporary havens in areas other than the United States zone for some of the 100,000 Jews he expects to leave Poland in the coming year was the subject of conferences held yesterday in Paris by Rabbi Phillip S. Bernstein of Rochester, N.Y., adviser on Jewish affairs to Gen. Joseph T. McNarney, United States Military Governor.

Rabbi Bernstein, following his return to Frankfort tonight, said he found a disposition among officials of the Jewish Agency in Palestine to appreciate the "generous, decent thing" the United States Army was continuing to do in giving haven to persecuted persons in the American zone, as well as the disposition to cooperate in spreading the load. Steps in this direction might include the routing of a larger number temporarily to Austria, to Italy, where Lieut. Gen. Wladyslaw Anders' Polish Second Corps vacated many camps, or to France, which might offer collective visas, especially for groups of children.

Among those consulted in Paris were Joseph Schwartz, head of the American Joint Distribution Committee; Rabbi Stephen S. Wise, president of the World Jewish Congress, and David Ben Gurion, chairman of the executive committee of the Jewish Agency.

Limitations Feared

Rabbi Bernstein expressed the opinion that the British plan for a so-called partition of Palestine would limit Jews to the land they now have, cut them off from the wastelands they would like to develop and make it extremely difficult to carry out the Anglo-American Commission's plan for the immigration of 100,000.

The morale, and consequently the orderliness, of the 92,000 Jews already in the United States zone is considered by close observers to be delicately attuned to the prospect of emigration. In addition there are some 15,000 in Austria, 20,000 in the British and French zones, 30,000 in Italy and many others in the Balkans whose desires and opportunities for leaving cannot be ascertained.

Together with the 100,000 who probably will leave Poland, this makes a total of at least 257,000 Jews anxious to emigrate. While all do not want to go to Palestine, the Anglo-American Commission's figure of 100,000 in any case seems clearly out of date.

Steps are being taken by the United Nations Relief and Rehabilitation Administration and the Army to expand existing camps and organize new ones in the United States zone, and authorities agree that there are sufficient physical possibilities of handling an influx of Jews if their stay is not prolonged. Overall arrangements, unfortunately, hang on the uncertainty caused by the probable discontinuance of the UNRRA at the end of the year.

Set-up in Poland Decried

Discussing the situation he found in Poland during a recent trip, Rabbi Bernstein declared that he regarded it as "highly unfortunate" that after all this time and after President Truman's directive reopening immigration quotas, no consular system had been set up in Poland.

"Everything I saw," he said, "pointed to the fact that the Polish Government is trying to do the right thing, first by trying to re-establish normal living conditions for Jews and passing laws against anti-Semitism, and second by placing no obstacles in the way of those who feel they must leave."

Of some 160,000 Jews now in Poland, including those recently repatriated from Russia, the Rabbi believed about 60,000 might remain. These, he said, fall into three groups, some political left wingers, those who have or hope to recover property and those who lately have been established in the formerly German territory of Lower Silesia.

"In Lower Silesia," Rabbi Bernstein disclosed, "the Polish Government has begun a remarkable experiment in providing Jews with land, housing and work."

Four factors, he hoped, would check the spread of anti-Semitism to this area where 75,000 Jews now have a feeling of relative security. These were: first, that provincialism may act as a barrier; second, both Poles and Jews are new there; third, both have a common enemy—the Germans, and fourth, there is enough land and housing for all.

The main centers of Jews in Poland, the Rabbi said, now are Lodz, with 20,000; Stettin, 18,000; Cracow, 8,000; Warsaw, 6,000, and Breslau, 15,000. Two communities have a majority of Jews—Ryschbach, with 11,000, and Bielawa, with 5,000.

Dana reported on August 6 on the resignation of Dr. James Pollack:

**AMERICAN RESIGNS
POST IN GERMANY**

**Pollock, Called Advocate of a
'Soft Peace', Devised Scheme
of Local Governments**

**By DANA ADAMS SCHMIDT
By Wireless to THE NEW YORK TIMES.**
STUTTGART, Germany, Aug. 6—Dr. James K. Pollock, director of the regional governmental coordinating office, who has played a leading role in organizing the Laenderrat, or Council of States, and the present administrative structure of the American zone, has resigned. He will be replaced by Col. Wililam W. Dawson, director of the Military Government in Wuerttemburg-Baden, Lieut. Gen. Lucius D. Clay announced today.

General Clay said that he "regretted very much" that Dr. Pollack felt it necessary to return as Professor of Political Science to the University of Michigan, from which he had been on leave, and that he had promised to return to Germany later.

Dr. Pollack has been under attack by such groups as the Society for the Prevention of World War III as an advocate of a "soft peace" who has consistently miscalculated the dangers of the German situation. There are no grounds, however, for suggestions that his withdrawal resulted from any differences with General Clay or with other Military Government officers, among whom he is generally considered one of the outstanding experts on German affairs.

Wrote Original Directive

Dr. Pollack wrote the original directive preparing the Laenderrat for Gen. Dwight D. Eisenhower and since last October he has been in charge of its steadily widening functions. There have developed the monthly conferences of the three State Minister-Presidents into the next thing to a zone government, with a permanent directorium and numerous central economic agencies. Colonel Dawson is a Professor of Law on leave from Western Reserve University. He began his new duties today.

Addressing the Laenderrat today, General Clay said that informal conversations with the British were proceeding in Berlin to solve the "difficult problem" of economic without political unification of the two zones. "We would be apprehensive," he explained, "that the political unification of the two zones might actually retard the complete unification of all zones. * * * It will be undertaken in such a way as to preserve the political structure as now established in the United States zone."

When the Americans and the British have worked out general principles, he said later, it will be up to the German authorities to merge the two zones' economic organisms. Ultimately the merger will involve an over-all Anglo-American supervisory body, point-free traffic between zones for persons sent on lawful business, an export-import program and an identical caloric ration scale in both zones. "Currency reform can, however, be worked out only on a four-power basis," he added, "since any other procedure would mean a complete break with other zones."

Youth-Amnesty Text Approved

The Laenderrat approved the text of the youth amnesty to be submitted to General Clay. Authorizing German denazification tribunals to exempt all Germans born after Jan. 1, 1919, from prosecution unless they fall in the top categories of major offenders. This amnesty, affecting about 1,000,000 Germans up to 27 years of age, was widely and erroneously reported to have gone into effect a month ago, when General Clay announced its imminence.

The Laenderrat also set up a central German economic council in the American zone with full powers to make decisions without consulting the Laenderrat on questions affecting more than one state. Composed of the three ministers of economics, it will direct the work of the zone price commissioner, the inter-zone and foreign trade commissioners and the food and agriculture commissioner. A central transport council set up at the same time will be advisory to the director general for transportation.

The Laenderrat asked the military government to allow the three Land governments to buy I.G. Farbenindustrie properties and hold them until the "financial situation has developed to a point where suitable private purchasers can be found." While this appeared on the surface to be an attempt to nationalize the properties, Laenderrat officials explained that it was designed to prevent them from falling into the hands of black-market profiteers, who may be eliminated once the currency reform has been effected.

With the imminent termination of UNRRA, some of the Jewish displaced persons who had been critical of UNRRA's management of the camps became concerned. It was also known that the Jewish displaced persons had been the most difficult to manage.

Dana wrote about these problems and the future of the displaced persons in the following article of August 7:

**UNRRA IS REVALUED
BY DISPLACED PERSONS**

**Refugees in Germany Dread
Its Termination and Interim
Control By Army**

**By DANA ADAMS SCHMIDT
By Wireless to** THE NEW YORK TIMES.
FRANKFORT ON THE MAIN, Germany, Aug. 7—When the United Nations Relief and Rehabilitation Administration's council is discussing its dissolution, it seems appropriate to evaluate the UNRRA in relation to its most difficult problem in Germany—the care of displaced Jews.

It differs from the chronic problem of Poles, Balts and others who are fairly quiescent and still going home in driblets in that it is acute. An exodus of Jews from Poland is moving into the American zone at the rate of 10,000 to 20,000 monthly, all determined to move on to Palestine or other points. The 92,000 Jews now in the zone may be more than doubled in the next year.

To almost all the Jewish leaders whom I interviewed in visits to the UNRRA's camps, the end of the UNRRA in Germany on Dec. 31 looks like a disaster. There have certainly been constant quarrels between the UNRRA and the Jews and between the UNRRA and the Army since the end of the war.

The core of the trouble has been the split between responsibility and authority. The UNRRA is responsible for the internal administration of the camps but depends for the wherewithal of operation on the Army, which wields the overall authority and bears the overall responsibility for everything that goes on in the zone.

Army's Outlook Criticized

This has meant that, while the UNRRA ran the camps, the Army's interest in displaced persons was confined to security. While Gen. Joseph T. McNarney issued admirable directives that made the zone a haven for the persecuted, on lower levels the Army's personnel saw only displaced black-marketers and trouble-makers. Resentment against Jewish and other displaced persons and against the UNRRA waxed bitterly.

The UNRRA was denounced as a neurotic and corrupt organization. But nonetheless it built up a corps of welfare workers who are a going concern, who know the job and would be capable of carrying it through the critical period of the Polish Jews' exodus.

Faced with the prospect of the UNRRA's dissolution, the most responsible Jews conclude that far too much has been said about its shortcomings and that it is after all the Jews' best friends in Germany. They feel the need for an organization that stands as a shield between them and the Army and the world.

Army Does Not Want Job

The UNRRA at present employs 2,223 persons in the American zone, of whom 31 per cent are Americans, 20 per cent Britons, 17 per cent Frenchmen, 10 per cent Belgians, 8 per cent Netherlanders and the remainder of various nationalities. It has also recruited 393 employees among displaced persons.

It is easy to say that the Army should take over this staff at the end of the year but many are not willing to work for the Army and are already leaving. Furthermore, the Army has been trying to get rid of non-military tasks, and is not equipped for and does not want this one.

In contrast, hopeful persons argue that, if full responsibility for displaced persons is thrust on the Army, at least during the interim until the new International Relief Organization takes over, the Army generally might assume a more positive interest in their problems. They would then also, in the American zone, become strictly an American responsibility. This might have a desirable effect on emigration.

Something might be done to induce Congress to revise the immigration quotas, which provide for some 25,000 Germans and only some 6,000 Polish. While a few Jews and other displaced persons can qualify for the German quota, scores of thousands of Poles are struggling for quota numbers. The President might also be induced to issue a directive correcting the regulations that limit persons eligible under the German quota to residents of the American zone.

The Jews particularly hope that, if the UNRRA must die, they will receive greater self-administration in their camps. That will be prepared soon, they trust, by official Army recognition of the Central Committee of Jews in the American zone, whose headquarters is in Munich.

It might have been better, as many believe, if the Army had handled the displaced persons directly from the first and built up its own welfare workers. Be that as it may, the switch now to the Army and later to the International Relief Organization is almost certain to produce trouble.

In a dispatch on the following day, August 8, Dana reported that the Jews were to begin to be given responsibility in running the camps. He wrote:

**REFUGEE JEWS AID
IN RUNNING CAMPS**

**Special Committee Works With
UNRRA in Providing Help
for Stateless in Germany**

By DANA ADAMS SCHMIDT
By Wireless to THE NEW YORK TIMES.

STUTTGART, Germany, Aug. 8—When the United States troops swept into Germany last summer they threw open the gates of the concentration camps and told the inmates they were free.

The liberated Jews and others, as far as their strength permitted, rushed out into the countryside, helped themselves from German houses and farms and appropriated horses, cattle and automobiles. The tactical troops on the spot smiled and said: "You're certainly entitled to it."

The Jews among these displaced persons were convinced then that very soon they would be allowed to leave Germany for new homes overseas. But as the months passed the emigration did not materialize.

The former concentration camp inmates and foreign workers roaming the countryside became a nuisance to an army concerned with order. They were herded back into the camps. And there they are today, except for those who have been repatriated and a very small number who have been able to emigrate.

Exodus of Poles Organized

Soon more Jews began to knock at the gates of the camps. They were Jews from Poland, who today comprise more than half the population of the Jewish camps.

Most, though not all, came and are still coming in organized groups by northern routes through Berlin and the British zone and by southern routes through Czechoslovakia and Austria. They believe that they will be better treated and opportunities for emigration will be better in the United States occupation zone than anywhere else.

Other groups are composed of children, most of whom have been gathered from Polish peasants who volunteered to take care of them during the days of the German executions. Often the peasants do not want to give up the children and have to be paid substantial sums.

The children arrive unannounced aboard trains or in trucks hired from Germans.

Obviously, in so far as the numerous Jewish organizations can manage it, this exodus is organized. To minimize their suffering the refugees must have help with money, food, lodging and transportation until they safely reach United Nations Relief and Rehabilitation camps.

Obviously, Palestinian Zionism exerts a powerful attraction. But the Jewish organizations did not originate the exodus. The impulse comes from persecution. If they had been welcome, most of them would have stayed in Poland.

Jews Organize Relief

In Germany, too, they are organized. Every camp has its elected committee and chairman who helps the UNRRA in running the camps. If the UNRRA disappears they are willing to do the job pretty much alone.

From the beginning the biggest concentration of Jews was around Munich. In May of last year Lieut. Abraham Klausner, a 31-year-old rabbi of New Haven, Conn., called a meeting of the camps to find a few representative Jews with whom the Army could deal.

Out of this initiative was born the Central Committee of Liberated Jews in the United States zone, which now unifies all the camp committees and works closely with a similar organization in the British zone.

Its president is Dr. Zalman Grinberg, a Swiss-trained X-ray specialist from Lithuania who barely escaped execution by the Germans in the closing days of the war. He has been to the United States and is now in Palestine.

The Lithuanian Jews, incidentally, provide the greatest part of the Jewish leadership because the German extermination program, which was always directed first at "intellectuals," apparently was less thorough in Lithuania than in Poland.

The United States Army has worked with but has never officially recognized the committee, although apart from the UNRRA and the Army it is the biggest organization dealing with displaced persons in Germany.

Own Agencies Are Established

It was allowed, however, to set up headquarters in the Deutsches Museum and later in a villa. Many Jews who still travel endlessly in search of families began writing names on the walls of the long museum corridors in the hope that such procedure might lead to a family reunion. The committee promptly began to gather the names and has since published 100,000.

It has organized an unofficial postoffice to help the Jews make contact with relatives abroad and has published a newspaper, which is still not officially authorized. A historical commission began compiling the record of ghetto struggles and partisans. The rabbinical department registered marriages and obtained kosher food.

The committee also obtained books for those whose schooling had been delayed for six years, organized athletic competitions, helped found eighty sports clubs and promoted the retraining of adults who hope to become artisans, mechanics and farmers in Palestine.

It set up a supply department for transients and refugees and established several rest homes and hospitals.

Now that the Jews in Germany are being treated as a separate nationality and a group apart from other displaced persons, the Jewish leaders feel that the time has come for the United States Army to recognize the committee officially. It is at work on a constitution, making it representative of the Jews in the zone and responsible for relief activities in camps. This, it hopes, will be satisfactory to the Army.

M'NARNEY TO CURB REFUGEES' INFLUX

Will Stop Organized Groups at Border—Fears U.S. Cost May Reach $80,000,000

By DANA ADAMS SCHMIDT
By Wireless to THE NEW YORK TIMES.
FRANKFORT ON THE MAIN, Germany, Aug. 9—The United States border patrol will not permit Jewish refugees from Poland to enter the United States zone in organized truckloads and trainloads, Gen. Joseph T. McNarney said at a press conference today.

The statement came in reply to questions about the recent halting of trainloads of Jews from the British zone and others in trucks near the Austrian frontier.

"I refer to the organized evacuation of Jews from Poland," said the United States commander in Europe. "I do not encourage large-scale movements of persons into other zones, and I do not accept them into my zone. If persecutees come across the borders individually, of course, it is a different matter, and we will accept them."

Influx of 200,000 Feared

Asked whether, considering that the movement of these Polish Jews would continue in any case, it would not be better to organize it, General McNarney replied:

"No. Let's speculate. According to Rabbi [Philip S.] Bernstein, 100,000 will come. If we send trains and food to get them, what would be the effect on the 100,000 or so who remain? And on Jews in Hungary, Rumania and Bulgaria? We could then expect another 200,000. An organized movement like that would have an effect like a rock thrown into water, spreading out and out. The United States never has adopted the policy of making the United States zone into a way station on the way to Palestine or any other place."

General McNarney disclosed, however, that he had volunteered to accept 5,000 Jews from Austria into his zone. Gen. Mark W. Clark informed him that he had reached his capacity with 27,000 and expected 4,000 to 5,000 more in a few days, General McNarney said. The movement from Austria began today.

When the United Nations Relief and Rehabilitation ceases operations in Germany, General McNarney said, the Army hopes to sign contracts with "practically all" its personnel.

He estimated that the cost to the Army of handling the UNRRA job would be $80,000,000 a year. He said that it would not be necessary to use military personnel in running the camps.

According to figures made available during the conference, 10 per cent of present inmates of UNRRA camps probably will be turned out as not entitled to displaced persons status when the current screening operations have been completed. Some will be held as war criminals.

After a visit to Stuttgart, Dana was back in Frankfort and writing his weekly letter, August 16, 1946:

Dear Mother:
I am rather late with my letter this week, so I'll make two letters of it, as I have lots of things to send along. There are the pictures of D.A. Schmidt and Lincoln Zephyr and the check from Everybody's Digest. *A note from one of Markel's assistants explaining that it was customary for the Sunday paper itself to authorize reprints of articles from foreign correspondents although in New York the correspondents are consulted. It's all right with me.*

Bernstein has come and gone. I came up from Stuttgart to meet him and went back immediately after he left. Now I'm back in Frankfort again. He was a pleasant visitor. I put him through the machinery of acquiring passes and a PX card and currency control book, introduced him to my friends, took him out to see some military government people in Wiesbaden, took him to a DP camp and for a drive in the country. All this, believe it or not, in a JEEP. This occasion would coincide with the first occasion my car has been out of action. The last spare tire burst the night before he came and I didn't manage to change over to jeep wheels and tires 'till after he left. I had cabled Bert Pierce about sending me tires a month before and cabled again suggesting sending tires by airfreight at NY Times *expense. That stirred some action from Mr. James himself who cabled that the* Times *would send the tires—by boat.*

Bernstein's mission, as he puts it, is to spy on the correspondents. He wants to get acquainted with the people whose copy he has to edit so as to have a better basis for judgment. Very sound idea. We had a long and inconclusive discussion as to why and wherefore such persons as Ray Brock and Ray Brigham were tolerated so long on the Times.

At one time Bernstein became very much intrigued by the clock in the local cathedral which appeared to be functioning in spite of the burnt-out appearance of the place. We went round to investigate and I wrote a little piece about the cathedral which may or may not have seen print.

I finally finished my Jewish DP series, topping it off with a piece on the subject for Markel. I fear there has been another riot at Wolfratshausen today.

ARMY LAW TAKEN TO SUPREME COURT

Captain in Germany Charges Military Defies Constitution and Obstructs Justice

By DANA ADAMS SCHMIDT
Special to The New York Times

FRANKFORT ON THE MAIN, Germany, Aug. 18—Capt. Earl J. Carroll, a San Francisco attorney, today addressed a letter of protest and appeal to the Chief Justice of the Supreme Court after permission had been denied him to see two men held in the Frankfort military jail, for whom he had prepared petitions for writs of habeas corpus.

He disclosed, further, that a letter, presumably from the Frankfort headquarters command, had been sent to his commanding officer requesting that he be "restrained" from the Frankfort area.

The letter to the Supreme Court was attached to petitions signed by Daniel P. Walczak, 22-year-old private first class of Detroit, and William C. McKinley, 24-year-old civilian of Bessemer, Ala., who have been held in jail for more than sixty days without legal counsel or formal charges. Walczak has been under investigation in connection with the murder of a German girl and McKinley in connection with counterfeiting and currency-control violations.

Captain Carroll cited to the Chief Justice the alleged remarks of Lieut. Col. W. F. Fratcher, Staff Judge Advocate, that if the Supreme Court granted the habeas corpus writs they would probably be "nullified," at least in the case of the soldier, who could be assigned to twenty-four-hour duty cleaning the floors in his present place of confinement.

"This type of threat by a high-ranking officer sworn to uphold the Constitution," he concluded, "is an indication of the growing attitude in this area that the military are above the law. There is but one effective answer to this challenge * * * the power of the military must be curbed to recognize the limitations that the Constitution itself places upon the exercise of that power."

The letter called attention to the "grave situation" of persons held for protracted periods without legal counsel or formal charges. Thus, it is impossible, he declared, to prepare an adequate defense in the limited time allotted to counsel only after the case has been referred to trial and after the prosecution has been prepared and key witnesses may have been removed.

"Any attorney serving with the armed forces is subject to a command policy," he wrote, "that practically precludes proper representation * * * nonetheless, such persons can obtain no other counsel in this theatre under the present circumstances."

When Captain Carroll, in accordance with arrangements made with Colonel Fratcher, tried to see Walczak and McKinley during the weekly two-hour visiting period this afternoon, the sergeant of the prison guard told him: "I've been instructed that you must have permission in writing from Colonel Summers," the headquarters commandant. He could reach neither Colonel Summers nor Colonel Fratcher.

What a nuisance! Have you been getting pretty regular checks from the Sunday paper, and how much?

Glad you've been enjoying some more beach and hope you find a suitable investment [house or lot]. *As you say, prices are fantastically high and are unlikely to stay that way forever, but you might at least locate the place we might want. As for selling the house* [family home at 1132 Fourth Ave, Los Angeles], *I should think it would depend entirely on whether you can find another place you like better. It seems a shame to leave 1132 after all the effort we have invested in it, but as you say this neighborhood may be going down hill.*

The other day a big package arrived for me full of good things to eat and food for thought too. I am enjoying it all. The Marlen chocolates are particularly good and the coffee and cocoa invaluable. I hadn't seen a marshmallow since my vacation I'm using the calling cards. I don't think I ever did acknowledge receiving the first batch of them by mail some time ago.

*All the magazines are now coming in—*New Yorker, Life *and* Readers Digest. *How bright they are by contrast with the serious dull grey European publications.*

Give my love to Grandma and Eliza and Steinie.
All my love,
Dana

P.S. Didn't the dog school teach Tuckie [family dog] *not to jump over fences?*

Dana had rarely reported on legal matters, but when he heard about two men held in the Frankfort military prison, who had not been allowed to have legal counsel, he felt that he must investigate and report this. Here is the story published on August 18:

**ARMY LAW TAKEN
TO SUPREME COURT**

**Captain in Germany Charges
Military Defies Constitution
and Obstructs Justice**

By DANA ADAMS SCHMIDT
Special to THE NEW YORK TIMES.
FRANKFORT ON THE MAIN, Germany, Aug. 18—Capt. Earl J. Carroll, a San Francisco attorney, today addressed a letter of protest and appeal to the Chief Justice of the Supreme Court after permission had been denied him to see two men held in the Frankfort military jail, for whom he had prepared petitions for writs of habeas corpus.

He disclosed, further, that a letter, presumably from the Frankfort headquarters command, had been sent to his commanding officer requesting that he be "restrained" from the Frankfort area.

The letter to the Supreme Court was attached to petitions signed by Daniel P. Walczak, 22-year-old private first class of Detroit, and William C. McKinley, 24-year-old civilian of Bessemer, Ala., who have been held in jail for more than sixty days without legal counsel or formal charges. Walczak has been under investigation in connection with the murder of a German girl and KcKinley in connection with counterfeiting and currency control violations.

Captain Carroll cited to the Chief Justice the alleged remarks of Lieut. Col. W. F. Fratcher, Staff Judge Advocate, that if the Supreme Court granted the habeas corpus writs they would probably be "nullified," at least in the case of the soldier, who could be assigned to twenty-four-hour duty cleaning the floors in his present place of confinement.

"This type of threat by a high-ranking officer sworn to uphold the Constitution," he concluded, "is an indication of the growing attitude in this area that the military are above the law. There is but one effective answer to this challenge * * * the power of the military must be curbed to recognize the limitations that the Constitution itself places upon the exercise of that power."

The letter called attention to the "grave situation" of persons held for protracted periods without legal counsel or formal charges. Thus, it is impossible, he declared, to prepare an adequate defense in the limited time allotted to counsel only after the case has been referred to trial and after the prosecution has been prepared and key witnesses may have been removed.

"Any attorney serving with the armed forces is subject to a command policy," he wrote, "that practically precludes proper representation * * * nonetheless, such persons can obtain no other counsel in this theatre under the present circumstances."

When Captain Carroll, in accordance with the arrangements made with Colonel Fratcher, tried to see Walczak and KcKinley during the weekly two-hour visiting period this afternoon, the sergeant of the prison guard told him: "I've been instructed that you must have permission in writing from Colonel Summers," the headquarters commandant. He could reach neither Colonel Summers nor Colonel Fratcher.

On August 19, with the report behind him concerning the two soldiers who were being held in jail and denied legal counsel, Dana wrote his weekly letter:

Today I got your letter of the 14th all the way from the beach. How fast it goes, and that wasn't even the fastest. It makes it seem as though one ought to be able to fly over for a weekend.

Tomorrow morning early I drive up to Fulda[131] *for the conference of Germany's Catholic bishops. Should be quite a sight. I only hope it makes quite a story.*

---

[131]   Fulda, a small town in the state of Hesse (in central Germany), is the site of a Benedictine monastery said to have been founded in 744 by a disciple of Saint Boniface. It is also the site of a Baroque Cathedral—a remodel of an earlier Dom. Fulda was made a bishopric in 1752.

I thought this was going to be a restful weekend but had the misfortune to meet a lawyer named Carroll [referring to the story already printed—see previous pages] *who convinced me that I must delve into some of the army's judicial proceedings. Believe me, they smell. So I was kept busy over the weekend and Monday too and plan if possible to get in on the end of the Lichfield trials.*

I think your idea of giving Steinie a money present is fine, not connected with any particular day or anniversary. Just a present. She can consider it as a contribution to her railroad fare if she likes. [She was going back to South Bend, Indiana for a vacation] *But lets make it $100. After all, money doesn't go very far these days. I will write Steinie a little letter to go with it and you can draw the money from my account.*

For no particular reason I have remembered the name of the Time *magazine man I couldn't identify in the pictures I sent last week. He is John Stanton, and I esteem him highly. He happened by here the other day, but our paths never seem to run parallel very long. Another man I ran into the other night was Shankey of the* AP *who was with* AP *in Berlin before the war and is still with them. We determined that* AP *has done a great deal better than* UP *in hanging on to its old timers, if our little pre-war crowd can be called old-timers. Of the old Berliner bureau* UP *has only Grigg and Beattie left; all others are happily elsewhere, but* AP *has lost only Louis Lochner who was getting superannuated anyway. He is around here again now representing the Hoover War Library, which has some connection with the Library of Congress.*

The Press Wireless *strike has been a nuisance. We have had to file on the* UP *teletype to London where we have access to the* Reuter *radio beam. You may also have noticed that some of my recent copy went by cable. That was during the first few days before the strike spread to the other companies. It is about over now fortunately.*

Yesterday. Sunday, I went to the races. The first races Frankfort has had in three years. Practically the whole town turned out and it was impossible to get near the betting windows. But a UP *man named Dees and two girls who work for* UNRRA, *one British and one Dutch, and I had fun making bets among ourselves. One horse fell on his head going over the last hurdle but was otherwise undamaged. It might have made a story, but I was too busy with the judicial system.*

Your clippings are most helpful. Don't let up on them. Dorothy sent me some too for a while but I haven't heard from her just lately.

All my love to you all, as always,

Love, Dana

P.S. Those lots [for a possible beach house] *sound awfully expensive. All the experts seem to think the upward spiral must end soon. So maybe we'd better wait until then, unless something exceptional turns up.*

P.P.S. Did my permanent driving license ever come? Remember I got a temporary one.

On August 20th, Dana drove to Fulda for the Bishops Conference. He filed several stories in which he pointed to the political influence of the conference, with some 20,000,000 Catholics in Germany. In Fulda alone, there were some 6,000 Catholics, he said. All the dioceses of Germany but one were represented. The one bishop who could not attend was from Meissen, which was in the Russian zone. He could not obtain a pass.

Concerning the topics to be discussed, Dana wrote [in his article, **GERMAN BISHOPS CONVENE IN FULDA**]:

While the sessions of the three-day conference are secret, it was learned that other discussions would concern the five points of the pastoral letter read in the western zones last Easter. They were denazification, which has been held to be slow and unjust in many cases; expulsions from Poland, Czechoslovakia and Hungary, which were called inhumane; the unjust expropriation of property in the Russian zone; the mistreatment of prisoners, particularly by the French, and the general insecurity of life and the misuse of police powers.

These points were raised in a report to the Allied Control Council after last year's conference. When the Council did not react, the Bishops, it is understood, decided to make them public in the pastoral letter. A sermon closing this conference may touch on such subjects and a new pastoral letter drafted by the Bishops will be read in Catholic churches two weeks later.

FRINGS DENOUNCES GERMAN EXPULSION

Cardinal Says Mass Removal From East Is "Madness" That Will Not Work Well

By DANA ADAMS SCHMIDT
Special to THE NEW YORK TIMES.

FULDA, Germany, Aug. 23—"It is truly madness to think that the world can be made healthy by forcing some 14,000,000 Germans from the east into a part of Germany already overcrowded," Joseph Cardinal Frings, Archbishop of Cologne, said today in an exclusive interview.

When the Allies turned over the eastern provinces of Germany to Poland they took one-third of Germany's space, he declared. Soon there will be 200 Germans to the square kilometer, compared with forty-three to the same area in the United States, he added.

Pouring expellees from Polish territory, the Sudetenland and Hungary into a deindustrialized area lacking in coal cannot turn out well, he asserted. "That is part of the Potsdam Agreement I cannot understand," he added.

Leader in Catholic Circles

Cardinal Frings presided over the Bishops' conference just ended because Michael Cardinal von Faulhaber, his senior, felt he was too old. Well clear of any compromise with the Nazis, he is regarded today as the most active leader in the Catholic Church in Germany and its most authoritative spokesman.

His is a lean quick-moving man, whose large brown eyes light up his weather-beaten face as he speaks softly, rapidly and to the point.

The Bishops' conference centered around the family, which Catholics consider the cornerstone of society, and to which most of the other questions discussed were related.

The family was endangered by the Nazis, then by the war and is now further threatened by the expulsion of Germans from eastern areas, Cardinal Frings said.

He declared that although only about one-half of the expellees had arrived in the western areas, the point had been reached where there was scarcely a German family living alone.

"Of course, they quarrel and homes are disrupted," he observed. "And to make the tragedy worse, almost all are women, children and old men, who are an added burden on an economy already short of young people.

"There must be a great emigration from Germany again, but that will be possible only if doors are opened and friends are found who can provide the cost in foreign exchange. We certainly cannot. And even that will not solve the problem."

Condemns Captives' Detention

The long detention of prisoners of war has a similar bearing on the family, in the Cardinal's opinion.

"Wives grow unfaithful as the years go by," he said, "and when the men do come back, especially from France and Russia, many are in bad condition and unfit for work. Others returning from America have been terribly demoralized by being turned over to the French or British when they thought they were going home."

He disclosed that in July he had sent the Allied Control Council in Berlin a report on the disappearance of prisoners of war returned to the Soviet zone, who apparently had been deported as laborers. The Russians rejected it on the ground that no specific facts were given, he said. He plans soon to provide examples.

Another point of special importance to the family/discussed [sic] by the conference was that of schools. "We believe that parents, and not the state, should have the right to decide whether children should attend a confessional school and what kind," Cardinal Frings declared.

Asked whether the expulsion of Germans from the East was not justified by the acts of the Germans in Poland and elsewhere he replied:

"Then it is revenge and contrary to Christian morality. Actually it is revenge, not against the guilty, but against the guiltless.

Calls Many Germans Guiltless

"Innumerable Germans are guiltless and were, like myself, incredulous when they learned of the atrocities and the numbers murdered. Those who knew did not talk or were quickly liquidated.

"One must distinguish between moral guilt and liability [Haftbarkeit]. All Germans are liable, but they are not all guilty. If we are to find a way out of the morass the German people must not be thrust aside but again drawn into the constructive work of Europe."

For these reasons, he said, he could not approve the present denazification procedure in the United States zone.

"I do not think the point of consideration by tribunals should be whether a man was a party member but solely whether he was a leader. Many fine people are being ruined. I do not think a man should suffer a whole life because he was a party member. That is not democratic.

"The suffering and poverty inflicted upon the German people bring hopelessness and are followed by radicalism, let us say communism," the Cardinal concluded. "Hopelessness is the keynote of German life today."

None the less [sic], he said, the church does not seek to take a direct part in politics, "but to educate the people to the right attitudes so as to get the right results."

Although Bishop Frings said that the Church does not take a direct part in politics, the power of the Catholic Church was evident in Germany, as Dana discussed in an article on August 24, following the conference at Fulda.

He wrote:

**CATHOLICISM ALERT
IN GERMANY TODAY**

**Opposing Communism, Its
Force Is Evident in Political
Life of the Country**

**By DANA ADAMS SCHMIDT
By Wireless to THE NEW YORK TIMES.**

FULDA, Germany, Aug. 24—The Catholic Church in Germany, as throughout Europe, is today one of the powerful forces opposing communism and by inference Russia.

As such it had the great political power that is reflected in the Christian Democratic (Christian Social) Union of Germany, the Popular Republican Movement of France and like groups in Belgium, Italy and other countries.

Any responsible member of the church hierarchy will deny, as a number did during the past week's conference of German Bishops in Fulda, that the Catholic Church is committed to any particular party.

But it remains a fact that the success of the Christian Democrats in the American zone was largely a Catholic success, and the Catholic Church has a vital stake in their success in the forthcoming elections in the Russian, British and French zones. Except in the Russian zone their prospects are good.

Themselves members of an authoritarian organization that makes wide claims upon its members, many German Catholic churchmen in the early days of the Nazi movement saw in its authoritarian leadership principle, and above all its anti-communism, a welcome development. But as Nazi excesses multiplied they realized, some sooner, some later, that here was a movement whose totalitarianism would brook no rivals and was in fact determined to destroy the church.

Part in Underground

In so far as there was a German resistance, German Catholics, like French Catholics, in due course found themselves in underground cooperation with Socialists and Communists.

In France this experience stimulated the development of a left-wing Catholicism in the form of the Popular Republican Movement, which since the war has tended to ally itself with the Socialists against the Communists.

No [sic] so in Germany. Catholics and Social Democrats (Socialists) see the Communist party and its new Russian-zone manifestation, the Socialist Unity party, as their common enemy. But an alliance, while sometimes discussed, is still far off.

On the whole the German Social Democratic leadership, including Dr. Kurt Schumacher, clings unbendingly to its Marxist lexicon and devotes much energy to assailing what it calls the "Catholic reactionaries."

Clergy Outspoken

The respect in which the Christian church is held by the Western Allies makes it almost untouchable and permits the Catholic and Protestant clergy to speak up in criticism of the occupying powers as no other group of Germans would dare. This they have done, particularly with respect to denazification policies, which they find unjust and excessively severe.

Catholic pastoral letters have also vigorously criticized the expulsion of the Germans from the east, alleged mistreatment of prisoners of war, expropriation without compensation and the insecurity of life caused by the arbitrary methods of such organizations as counter-intelligence corps.

The Communists may be exploiting German nationalism, but the Catholic Church is not far behind. The Bishops at Fulda generally evaded the question of German guilt in the War, excused German "mistakes" and commiserated with German sufferings.

If the German Catholic church lost little in the war, it learned little that is new. It may help preserve Germany from communism, but it offers little promise of yanking the Germans out of their old follow-the-Fuehrer complex or of solving their problems.

After the conference of Bishops at Fulda, Dana wrote in his weekly letter:

I always seem to be just arriving or just leaving. In any event, I've had to give up my plans to cover the end of the Nuremberg trial in order to leave for Berlin tomorrow and be on hand for a trip into the Russian zone for the elections beginning Sunday next. It should be of considerable interest.

Your letter telling me of the noises next door has come. Sounds most unfortunate all right, rather like a miniature DP camp. I take it, however, that it is the noisiness rather than the Jewishness that you find objectionable. Speaking of Jews, Markel has asked me to do a magazine article on life in a DP camp, which probably means a Jewish one. Think I can do that, although I've had just about enough of the subject for the time being.

You mention a period of some days during which you saw nothing of mine in the paper. It may well be that during that time my pieces appeared unsigned. I find that happens quite often when I file from some little known dateline; also when two pieces of mine from different datelines arrive on the same day because of bad transmission. Thus you may find my interview with the Bishop Wurm at Bad Boll and another piece on denazification from Munich which the editor threw in on the same day unsigned. Several other pieces from Stuttgart have also not been signed. Did you ever find one on the new settlement or land reform law? I never got a clipping.

There are also periods of three or four days when I just don't manage to write anything worth signing, and that is quite easy to understand. Unless you are in a capital where all kinds of information is served up to you constantly from all kinds of sources it is necessary to go out and find the news. After spending a week at, say, Fulda, it takes a few days to get reoriented and line up some stories. Same will be true after I get back from the Russian zone.

Sunday night I went to the zoo, no less, to see some fancy dances and fireworks. As for all these German affairs, practically the entire town seemed to be there. There was dancing on an island in a small lake in the light of a spotlight that cast reflections into the water and giant shadows against the trees behind. Very striking. Then the fireworks made about the biggest noise that's been heard since the war ended. Sounded just like an exploding ammunition dump.

Did I thank you for sending off the CARE packages? I know they will all be most gratefully received. The two German ones are for families who have at one time or another done my laundry. There are three children in one of the two and two in the other, all very poorly nourished. One has recently been sent to a rest home to recover from his state of malnutrition. I give them part of my rations when I can.

You will observe that I finally acquired a new ribbon.

Now, I must get busy and try to get a few things done before I leave for Berlin.

All my love, as always. Dana

P.S. If you ever get a good picture of Tuckie, do send me one.

Back in Berlin, Dana analyzed the possible outcomes of the elections. The Christian Democratic Union of Germany faced the Social Unity Party (the Communist Party). Following is his report of the first elections, published on August 30:

SAXONY REDS FACE A TEST TOMORROW

Curb-Easing on Rival Parties Intensifies Election Fight in Dresden and Leipzig

By DANA ADAMS SCHMIDT
Special to THE NEW YORK TIMES.

BERLIN, Aug. 30—The easing of limitations on the activities of the Christian Democratic Union and the Liberal Democratic party in the Province of Saxony in the Russian zone during the last week before next Sunday's municipal elections has permitted these parties to put up candidates in enough districts to cover 70 per cent of the electorate, party sources here said today.

In consequence, they pointed out that the campaign in such places as Leipzig and Dresden has waxed unexpectedly hot and the two parties who oppose the Socialist Unity party have given up the previously entertained thought of abstaining from voting there.

In other parts of the zone where elections will take place on the following two Sundays, Sept. 8 and 15, the situation, however, was considerably less equitable, these sources said, possibly because they would be less subject to worldwide scrutiny than during the first Sunday's vote.

It was estimated that in the zone as a whole the Christian Democrats and Liberal Democrats would be able to present lists of candidates in only one-quarter of the municipalities while the Socialist Unity party covered three-quarters of them. The disproportion was reported to be most striking in Mecklenburg.

In places where the Socialist Unity party is not formally represented it can count on four auxiliary groups that are permitted to draw up lists of candidates—the women, peasants, trade unions and youth associations.

In most areas the Christian Democratic Union and the Liberal Democratic party have refused to associate themselves with such allegedly nonpolitical groups, considering them another device by which the Socialist Unity party seeks to beguile the middle-class electorate into voting for Socialist Unity candidates.

Window Dressing Resorted To

A few respectable middle-class professional men are usually drafted to act as window dressing for the groups, a procedure reminiscent of the days when the French Communists succeeded in getting certain men to serve on the steering committee of the "National" front.

An original device for penetrating the middle class in the Russian zone was undoubtedly the shotgun marriage of the Communist and Social Democratic parties.

The Social Democratic leadership in the western zones has told its adherents to abstain from voting, but many will probably cast secret ballots for the Christian or Liberal Democratic parties as a protest against the forced amalgamation with the Communists. Before 1933 Saxony was a Social Democratic stronghold.

The generous means put at the disposal of their "state party" by the Russians mean that the question is only whether the Socialist Unity party's victory will be more or less overwhelming.

In the face of a combination of threats and promises used by the Unity party, votes for the two others will be more a measure of the voters' courage than of their normal political sentiments.

Socialist Unity party speakers have not hesitated to drop hints that should they not get sufficient votes rations might be cut, prisoners of war and political prisoners held indefinitely, additional plants dismantled and the occupation prolonged indefinitely. If the electorate votes as desired, they intimated that just the opposite could be expected.

It was understood from an AP report that three days before the first elections scheduled in the Russian occupation zone, the Soviet Military Government announced an increase in food rations for German coal miners there. This is still below the peak daily ration for miners in the American zone which had been set earlier this month at 4,000 calories.

On September 1, Dana's report on the first election in the Russian zone was published:

GERMAN MODERATES' VOTE STRONG IN FIRST ELECTION IN RUSSIAN ZONE

By DANA ADAMS SCHMIDT
Special to THE NEW YORK TIMES.
DRESDEN, Germany, Sept. 1—Germans of all political hues here, in Leipzig and in a half-dozen towns in between agreed today, as the first Russian-zone elections got under way, that the Socialist Unity party's victory was a foregone conclusion, though it would be nowhere near so overwhelming as the party and the Russians would like.

[Early returns showed that, while the Socialist Unity party was the strongest single organization, the combined votes of the Christian Democratic Union and the Liberal Democratic party outnumbered it in many places, a Berlin dispatch to THE TIMES said early on Monday.]

A much greater issue among the Germans was whether the municipal elections involving some 3,500,000 voters and 32,159 candidates in 2,453 communities of Saxony was fair. Socialist Unity representatives maintained that it was, while representatives of the Christian Democratic Union and the Liberal Democratic party insisted that it was not.

Foreign observers considered the election important more as an indication of political practices in the Russian zone than of genuine political sentiments there, which are distorted by several factors. The merger of the Communist and Social Democratic parties would give the Socialist Unity party a considerable bloc of strength, although many former Social Democrats undoubtedly abstain or vote for other parties. Others would be swayed to vote for or against the Socialist Unity party more by the realization that it was favored by the occupying power than by the party's platform. Finally, local rather than general political questions are naturally in the foreground in municipal elections.

American correspondents who, with Russian army escorts, visited polling places in Dresden, Leipzig and smaller towns, found them quiet, with full provision for secret marking of ballots behind curtains, and fair in all technical aspects. No incidents were observed or reported. An innovation was the separation of men's and women's polling booths in some places at the suggestion of the Socialist Unity party in order to provide an additional basis for an analysis of the results.

The argument as to fairness, however, centered round the preparations for the election. Every downtown street displayed a brilliant riot of the most varied multicolored Socialist Unity posters, stickers and streamers, calling for votes for List No. 1. Among them one could occasionally see the more sober posters of the Liberal Democrats and the Christian Democrats on Lists 2 and 3. The proportion was illustrated by reliable information that the Socialist Unity party had received 800 tons of paper for posters compared to nine tons for the two other parties combined.

Prof. Hugo Hickman, a former teacher of theology and now Christian Democratic chairman for Saxony, said that his party had presented candidates in only 600 of the 2,453 communities. Since the 600 are the largest, however, his candidates could reach 75 per cent of the electorate. The remaining 25 per cent, he explained, included 4 per cent in communities with less than 200 population, where no elections are held, 10 per cent in communities where the party has not yet formed local committees, and 11 per cent where the party's committees have not been allowed to register by the Russian military administration.

Lonnewitz, a village with 530 population, is one of many with only Socialist Unity candidates. "Those who do not like it can abstain or cast void ballots," the assistant Mayor remarked.

After the elections in the Russian zone, Dana's next focus was on Secretary Byrnes' visit. He wrote:

I am just passing through Frankfort, long enough to get a change of laundry, my uniform pressed, shoes shined, to write a weekender and a letter off to you. . . . I've spent a couple of days in Berlin and am now on my way to Stuttgart for Byrnes' visit.

As usual it is all very hectic, but with the passing of time that becomes normal, and one doesn't take it so dreadfully seriously as in the beginning.

I drove up to Berlin with Hal Foust of the Chicago Tribune *so I had to come back on the train with Bill Freese, who has just arrived to get the* NY Times *photo service organized over here. This afternoon will drive down to Stuttgart with Gosset, the second photo man, it I get everything done in time.*

It is raining and quite autumnal, which I find depressing. There is something about spring and autumn, about the change of seasons and the passing of time that is saddening.

Freese is a somewhat more than middle-aged man and apparently has quite a reputation as a photographic expert. He talks endlessly but manages to make himself entertaining about his feats and experiences with pictures. We are, it seems, the only individual newspaper with a foreign picture organization and have better studios and equipment in New York than any of the syndicates. When we liquidated Wideworld *in 1941 we kept what was best of it. All* AP *bought was the domestic organization outside New York.*

The Russian trip was moderately productive as you can judge from the paper. I picked up some ideas which I later ran down in Berlin. Kathleen took a larger house in Berlin on the assumption that the photographers would be making headquarters there, but now they think they may choose Frankfort. The new place is dark, drafty and ugly, in contrast to the charming dollhouse she had before. She still has an option on the old place in case a married couple turns up to occupy it.

My photographer friend and colleague is all ready to take off for Stuttgart and I have a lot more to do, so I will sign off with

All my love,

Dana

By now Steinie will have left on her vacation. I trust the substitute nurse is turning out all right.

From Stuttgart, Dana filed the following report on Secretary Byrnes' visit:

GERMAN RULE SEEN AS AIM OF BYRNES

U.S. Officials Say Secretary Will Urge Local Government in His Address Today

By **DANA ADAMS SCHMIDT**
Special to THE NEW YORK TIMES.
STUTTGART, Germany, Sept. 5—A clear-cut offer by United States Secretary of State James F. Byrnes to the other occupying powers to join the United States in turning over governmental responsibility to the Germans and preparing an early and final settlement of the German problem was anticipated tonight by top United States military government officers and German officials.

They jammed every billet and slept on cots and couches to be on hand for the Secretary's speech in the opera house here tomorrow.

[Mr. Byrnes arrived in Berlin early Thursday afternoon and left by train at 5:30 P.M. for Stuttgart.]

[Mr. Byrnes' speech will be broadcast over stations WOR and WABC from 6:30 to 7 A.M., Eastern daylight time, Friday, and rebroadcast in recorded form over station WEAF at 9 o'clock.]

If Mr. Byrnes' proposal should not be accepted, authoritative sources declared the United States would have to go ahead anyway with steps it considers prescribed or implied by the Potsdam Agreement within the framework of the unified United States and British zones. It must revise the level of industry upward to give the Germans enough prosperity to insure the peaceful development of the country.

Soviet Reply Awaited

The problem the United States Government faces was symbolized by the response to the invitation to Allied commanders to attend tomorrow's meeting. While Britain's highest occupation authorities were expected to be present, no reply has been received from the Russians or French.

Similarly, as announced in Berlin today, only the British joined the Americans in setting up central food, financial, transport, communications and industrial agencies, which the United States Government considers should be extended to all Germany.

British occupation authorities were expected to move swiftly in the coming months to remove the fear expressed by many United States and German officials that unification would drag down the standard of self-administration reached in the United States zone. It was understood that the British planned to set up a German council of minister-presidents of the four states in their zone, which would eventually collaborate with the Laenderrat of the United States zone in a form of provisional government. The United States also would like to have the provisional government applied to all Germany.

Burden on United States Stressed

The difficulty of bringing in the Russians and French into this plan results from divergent interpretations of the Potsdam Agreement.

By integrating their zone ever more into their own economies and dominating it economically and politically the Russians in particular have isolated Germans in that area from the rest of Germany and permitted Germany to become the scene of a tug-of-war between the East and the West, United States sources declared.

By using current production for reparations, instead of for exports with which to pay Germany's import bill, the Russians, and to a lesser extent the French, have furthermore thrust an unjustifiable burden upon the United States and Britain in supporting Germany's deficit areas. The specter of economic disintegration and inflation has risen, in spite of anything the Americans have been able to do in their zone alone.

The United States Government does not favor a vindictive peace that would break up Germany forever, officials here said, and believes Germany's frontiers should be drawn accordingly with due consideration to just claims of her neighbors for redress.

Thus while controls over all of Germany must be maintained, a special regime for the Ruhr and the Rhineland, opposed by inhabitants who wish to remain part of Germany, could not be justified, the United States officials said.

France would have to make equivalent sacrifices of reparations if she received the Saar, they said. And while commitments at Potsdam to give the Soviet Union the Koenigsberg area and Poland parts of eastern Germany must be respected, the extent of Poland's encroachment must be limited in any ultimate settlement by the necessity of creating an economically sound Germany.

The basis for United States insistence on turning over governmental responsibility to Germans was expressed by Gen. Joseph T. McNarney at a press conference in Frankfort on the Main today.

"Government agencies of the Laender and Laenderrat," he said, are doing an honest and efficient job. I can state without qualification that the German governmental machinery in the United States zone is far advanced over that existing in any other zone, that it is operating on democratic principles and that the results obtained to date give rise to optimism as to the future of Germany as a respected member of the society of nations."

The subjects of Secretary Byrnes' important talk outlining the position of the United States are indicated in these headlines and Dana's following article:

**BYRNES FOR GERMAN REGIME,
BARS FRENCH RUHR CLAIM,
DENIES ODER BORDER IS FIXED**

SELF-RULE IS ASKED

**Secretary Urges Big Four
to Let Germans Form
Central Government**

SEEKS TROOP REDUCTION

**Says U.S. Forces Will Remain
as Long as any Others—
Would give France Saar**

By DANA ADAMS SCHMIDT
Special to THE NEW YORK TIMES.
STUTTGART, Germany, Sept. 6—United States Secretary of State James F. Byrnes invited the occupying powers of all four zones of Germany today to join in the early establishment of a central provisional government that could carry out the terms of a peace settlement "whose essential terms the Allies should make clear to the German people without delay."

His statement of United States policy toward defeated Germany before 1,500 United States military government officers and troops and 150 German officials in the Stuttgart Opera House was the most comprehensive and clear cut made to date. It received special emphasis by its locale in the seat of the Laenderrat, the most important democratic German institution of the United States zone, which Mr. Byrnes held up as a model for a German national council.

BYRNES FOR GERMAN REGIME, BARS FRENCH RUHR CLAIM, DENIES ODER BORDER IS FIXED

SELF-RULE IS ASKED

Secretary Urges Big Four to Let Germans Form Central Government

SEEKS TROOP REDUCTION

Says U. S. Forces Will Remain as Long as Any Others— Would Give France Saar

The text of Secretary Byrnes' address is on Page 3.

By DANA ADAMS SCHMIDT
Special to THE NEW YORK TIMES.

STUTTGART, Germany, Sept. 6 —United States Secretary of State James F. Byrnes invited the occupying powers of all four zones of Germany today to join in the early establishment of a central provisional government that could carry out the terms of a peace settlement "whose essential terms the Allies should make clear to the German people without delay."

His statement of United States policy toward defeated Germany before 1,500 United States military government officers and troops and 150 German officials in the Stuttgart Opera House was the most comprehensive and clear cut made to date. It received special emphasis by its locale in the seat of the Laenderrat, the most important democratic German institution of the United States zone, which Mr. Byrnes held up as a model for a German national council.

Earlier Mr. Byrnes had discussed United States objectives with the German Minister-Presidents of Bavaria, Wuerttemberg-Baden and Greater Hesse in the railway car that brought him from Berlin. The car once belonged to Adolf Hitler.

Principal Objectives Cited

The principal objectives, designed to construct neither a hard nor a soft but a "lasting peace," that Mr. Byrnes outlined were:

(1) There must be a peace settlement to unify a denazified, demilitarized Germany, first with central economic agencies and later with a central government.

(2) It would assign the Koenigsberg area to the Soviet Union and parts of eastern Germany to Poland in accordance with the Potsdam commitment, although the Secretary pointed out that the present border along the Oder and the Neisse was provisional. The settlement would also give the Saar to France in return for the reduction of reparations and maintain the separation of Germany and Austria. The Ruhr and the Rhineland would remain part of Germany subject to controls applied to all of Germany.

(3) Germany would be made self-supporting by the pooling of resources and a unified export-import program and would have a standard of living approximately that of other European countries. If, however, four-power unification should prove unattainable and some powers should continue to take reparations from current production, there would be binational or trinational unification and the levels of industry set by the Allied Control Council would have to be raised.

(4) Occupation forces would be progressively reduced "so as to rely more upon a force of trained inspectors and less upon infantry," an objective that could have been realized had the United States proposal for a twenty-five to forty-year treaty on the demilitarisation of Germany been accepted.

U. S. Force to Remain

But, Mr. Byrnes added: "Security forces will probably remain in Germany for a long time. Now I want no misunderstanding. We will not shirk our duty. We are not withdrawing. As long as an occupation force is required in Germany the Army of the United States will be part of that occupation force."

"The American people want to return the government of Germany to the German people * * * to help the German people with their way back to an honorable place among

Continued on Page 8, Column 1

Earlier Mr. Byrnes had discussed United States objectives with the German Minister-Presidents of Bavaria, Wuerttemberg-Baden and Greater Hesse in the railway car that brought him from Berlin. The car once belonged to Adolf Hitler.

Principal Objectives Cited

The principle objectives, designed to construct neither a hard nor a soft but a "lasting peace," that Mr. Byrnes outlined were:

(1) There must be a peace settlement to unify a denazified, demilitarized Germany, first with central economic agencies and later with a central government.

(2) It would assign the Koenigsberg area to the Soviet Union and parts of eastern Germany to Poland in accordance with the Potsdam commitment, although the Secretary pointed out that the present border along the Oder and the Neisse was provisional. The settlement would also give the Saar to France in return for the reduction of reparations and maintain the separation of Germany and Austria. The Ruhr and the Rhineland would remain part of Germany subject to controls applied to all of Germany.

(3) Germany would be made self-supporting by the pooling of resources

and a unified export-import program and would have a standard of living approximately that of other European countries. If, however, four-power unification should prove unattainable and some powers should continue to take reparations from current production, there would be bizonal or trizonal unification and the levels of industry set by the Allied Control Council would have to be raised.

(4) Occupation forces would be progressively reduced "so as to rely more upon a force of trained inspectors and less upon infantry," an objective that could have been realized had the United States proposal for a twenty-five to forty-year treaty on the demilitarization of Germany been accepted.

U.S. Force to Remain

But, Mr. Byrnes added: "Security forces will probably remain in Germany for a long time. Now I want no misunderstanding. We will not shirk our duty. We are not withdrawing. As long as an occupation force is required in Germany the Army of the United States will be part of that occupation force."

"The American people want to return the government of Germany to the German people * * * to help the German people win their way back to an honorable place among the free and peace loving nations of the world," said Mr. Byrnes.

"More than a year has passed since hostilities ceased," he added. "The millions of German people should not be forced to live in doubt as to their fate."

A course of German developments was envisaged at Potsdam, he declared, and the United States Government now intends to follow it "to the limits of its authority."

The United States Government considers that the German people should "now be given the primary responsibility for running their own affairs," he continued. He declared that a provisional government should be set up in the form of a German national council composed of the democratically-responsible minister-presidents or other chief officials of states or provinces in each of the four zones.

This body should draw up a federal constitution insuring democracy, human rights and fundamental freedoms in the new Germany, Mr. Byrnes said. After approval in principle by the Allies it should be drafted in final form by an elected convention and then submitted to the German people for ratification.

The new Germany, he cautioned, must not "become a satellite of any power or powers or live under a dictatorship, foreign or domestic."

The United States Government will stand by the Potsdam Agreement to transfer Koenigsberg and the adjacent area to the Soviet Union. The assignment of Silesia and other eastern territories to Poland was for administrative purposes, however, he said, and while the United States will support revision in Poland's favor the extent of the area must await a final settlement.

After he approved France's claim to the Saar, Mr. Byrnes pointed out that "except as here indicated the United States will not support any encroachment on territory which is undisputedly German or any division of Germany which is not genuinely desired by the people concerned."

"So far as the United States is aware the people of the Ruhr and the Rhineland desire to remain united with the rest of Germany," he declared. "And the United States will not oppose their desire."

The agreed levels of industry may have to be raised, Mr. Byrnes explained, with obvious reference to the Soviet Union, because he said they had been based on the "assumption that the indigenous resources of Germany were to be available for distribution on an equitable basis for all Germans in Germany and that products not necessary for the use in Germany would be available for export to pay for necessary imports."

Says Reparations Hit Economy

"In fixing the level of industry no allowance was made for reparations from current production," he added. "Reparations from current production would be wholly incompatible with the levels of industry now established under the Potsdam Agreement * * *.

"Conditions which now exist in Germany make it impossible for industrial production to reach the levels which the occupying powers agreed were essential for a minimum German peacetime economy. * * * Barriers between the four zones of Germany are more difficult to surmount than those between normal independent states. * * *

"So far as many vital questions are concerned, the Control Council is neither governing Germany nor allowing Germany to govern itself."

Mr. Byrnes, therefore, proposed central German agencies for finance, transportation, communications, postal services, agriculture, industry and foreign trade.

Such agencies are now being set up for the United States and British zones.

Prof. Karl Geiler, Minister-President of Greater Hesse, hailed the "humane" attitude of the United States as exemplified by Mr. Byrnes' rejection of "harsh and vengeful measures."

Minister-Presidents Reinhold Maier of Wuerttemberg-Baden and Wilhelm Hoegner of Bavaria agreed in opposing the amputation of the Ruhr and large tracts of eastern provinces as the foundation for future peaceful realization.

On the platform behind Mr. Byrnes sat Gen. Joseph T. McNarney, his political adviser, Ambassador Robert D. Murphy, and Senators Arthur H. Vandenberg and Tom Connally, while scores of photographers' bulbs flashed and movie cameras hummed.

Following a brief chat with correspondents in the afternoon Mr. Byrnes departed by train, planning to visit the Munich export exhibition tomorrow and return to Paris Sunday.

INTER-ZONE PARLEY OF GERMANS SPED

U.S. Military Rule Authorizes Officials to Invite Those From Three Other Areas

By DANA ADAMS SCHMIDT
Special to THE NEW YORK TIMES.

STUTTGART, Germany, Sept. 7—The Secretariat of the Laenderrat, the Council of Minister-Presidents of the three States of the American zone, announced today that it had received authorization from the Military

Government to invite the Minister-Presidents or equivalent officials of States in all three other zones to a conference.

The officials invited would be the ones that Secretary of State James F. Byrnes yesterday proposed should be brought together in a national council to function as a provisional Government of all Germany. The time and place of the conference have not yet been decided, but it will probably be held in October at Bad Kissingen.

Prof. Karl Geiler, Minister-President at Greater Hesse, who has been urging this step for some time, said that he hoped that the conference would endorse the principles for the future political and economic development of Germany that were laid down by Mr. Byrnes. According to his personal knowledge almost all the Minister-Presidents in the other zones favored it entirely.

Professor Geiler disclosed that the Laenderrat had recently proposed to the Military Government a plan for a national council much like that of Mr. Byrnes. It differed however in that, failing four-power agreement, it could have been applied in two or three zones, and would in any case preserve the political control of the Council over the interzonal economic agencies now being formed.

The Germans also wished to concentrate the bizonal agencies around Kassel in the interest of efficiency, instead of scattering them throughout western Germany.

Behind these differences are several factors that gave Mr. Byrnes' statement yesterday something of a paradoxical character.

While Mr. Byrnes paid the highest tribute to the democratic and desirable character of the Laenderrat in his speech, and by his very presence in Stuttgart, the method of unification of the American and British zones announced in Berlin on the previous day would greatly reduce the Laenderrat's importance and strip it and the Governments of the American zone States of political control over economic affairs.

Method is Retrogressive

In other words, while Mr. Byrnes' ideas for the treatment of the whole of Germany were politically positive and in accordance with those evolved by

Lieut. Gen. Lucius D. Clay and men such as the former director of the regional government coordinating office, Dr. K. Pollock, the method of unification of the two zones is politically retrogressive.

In the unanimous opinion of the three American zone Minister-Presidents and of many American Military Government officials this can be corrected only by the political as well as economic unification of the American and British zones as soon as the British have developed a Laenderrat in their zone that can work with the American zone's Laenderrat.

The Minister-Presidents made this point in their talk with Mr. Byrnes yesterday.

A vital, perhaps the most important, program of the American Military government was the denazification of the German people. Dana's account in early September of the report by the three German Ministers charged with this somewhat abstract subject follows:

DENAZIFYING SLOW, GERMAN CHIEFS SAY

Only 1.35% of the Anticipated 2,000,370 Cases Acted On by Tribunals in Three States

By DANA ADAMS SCHMIDT
Special to THE NEW YORK TIMES.

STUTTGART, Germany, Sept. 10—The first zonal picture as to how denazification administered by German tribunals is working out was provided today by a report covering the first 32,042 verdicts submitted to the Laenderrat by the three Ministers of Denazification.

Pointing out that only 1.35 per cent of the 2,000,370 cases they expected to go before the tribunals in the zone had been handled to date, the Ministers differed as to how long it would take to complete the denazification.

Anton Pfeiffer of Bavaria declined to risk a guess, Gottlob Binder of Greater Hesse estimated a year and a half, while August Neuburger, the Deputy Denazification Minister of Wuerttemberg-Baden, said he thought it would be finished by next July 1.

Under the "law for liberation from national socialism and militarism" passed in March, but not in full operation until June, Germans with any sort of political past were to be divided into five categories: (1) major offenders; (2) offenders (activists, militarists and profiteers); (3) lesser offenders (probationers); (4) followers, and (5) persons exonerated.

The Verdicts Classified

The report showed the following verdicts up to the end of August:

Greater Hesse—Twenty-three in Class 1, 292 in Class 2, 1,019 in Class 3, 4,039 in Class 4 and 1,510 in Class 5.

Wuerttemberg-Baden—Five in Class 1, 79 in Class 2, 232 in Class 3, 6,500 in Class 4 and 606 in Class 5.

Bavaria—Twenty-three in Class 1, 292 in Class 2, 1,019 in Class 3, 4,639 in Class 4 and 1,510 in Class 5.

The figures indicated the more lenient procedure in Bavaria, where Herr Pfeiffer was obliged to close the tribunals for 10 days and shake up the entire system after taking over from his Communist predecessor six weeks ago. The 9,000 cases he ordered reviewed may change the Bavarian picture. Outside Bavaria, the law has worked more smoothly and only one tribunal, in Greater Hesse, has been ordered dissolved.

Thus far, sentences to labor camps ranging from six months to six years have been imposed on 140 persons in Greater Hesse, 117 in Wuerttemberg-Baden and 165 in Bavaria. In Bavaria, also, 5,593,350 marks have been collected in fines.

Of greatest concern to the Ministers were some 83,000 persons arrested by United States authorities, who now are in internment camps. Among them, they said, were both the worst Nazis and many guiltless persons against whom no charge had been brought. Herr Pfeiffer feared that great camaraderie and an anti-American neo-fascism had developed among internees of all kinds during their long confinement "under deplorable conditions."

[The problem of the internees in Germany is reminiscent of Guantanamo and Bagram today.]

Dana's letters from this period give a good picture of his life as a foreign correspondent.

ELIZABETH SCHMIDT CRAHAN

September 15, 1946

Well my birthday came and went [he was 33] *and I scarcely thought of it, what with Mr. Byrnes running around in Germany. I was down in Stuttgart for the occasion and stayed there till today. I'll be here tomorrow and then I'll move up to the British zone to cover their elections. No rest for the wicked they say.*

Callender was scheduled to come to Stuttgart but didn't after Sulzberger told him to leave it to me. He was very mad I hear. I did all right the day before the speech with my forecast but fear I fumbled the speech a bit by almost duplicating my previous day's lead and under-filing. Did they use my story and where was it placed?

The next two days I devoted entirely to turning out a Magaziner on Germany as a battleground for East-West forces. Markel however cables that I didn't give him what he wanted and I'll try again in about two weeks. It is discouraging when one has made so much effort. He also wants a weekender tomorrow and is generally driving me to distraction.

I was happy to find your letter enclosing my driver's license waiting for me here. I didn't really mean for you to send me the license but will keep it in my wallet. It might come in handy in France.

Cyrus Sulzberger cabled me that three new men are going to be sent to Germany to reinforce Kathleen and me, headed by one Delbert Clark who will be acting manager. I am very thankful for the burden on the two of us has been too great. I cabled Cy facetiously that Kathleen and I thought we would go on long, long vacations, and seriously that I would like a little vacation in Paris, seeing that I hadn't taken a full day off since April 1.

. . . A cable just came in from Markel okaying my outline for a weekender and new Magaziner. . . .

I have so much to do still tonight and tomorrow before leaving for the British zone that I must make this short. I feel as though I had been skimping my recent letters.

Glad Steinie was pleased by my present [a check] *and hope you will make out all right during her absence. I hope that money considerations are not in any way restricting the care you get. Can I count on that? Because, there is no reason for it with me accumulating most of my salary. There is nothing I would rather do than contribute to those expenses if it would be of any help.*

I was going to write to Mr. Sterling [Mother's financial advisor] *but can't find his address. Will you please send it to me.*

Recently I met Scott, the Time *magazine bureau manager who wrote a book "Behind the Urals," I think about his experiences working in a Russian factory. Could you get me that book and include it in your next box of cookies and good things? This should serve as the required request.*

All my love now, to Grandma and Steinie and Eliza and the babies too, when they come back from the beach.
DANA

September 21, 1946
Dear Mother
Your letter with the picture of Tuckie came today and reminded me that I was considerably overdue with writing. Also, a missive from Steinie aboard her train thanking me for the check. Hope she has a good time—and hope you get along all right.

By the way, I never got the birthday cable you mentioned. How did you send it? It may come limping in by mail many weeks from now. I've known that to happen before. If you have occasion to cable again Western Union is probably your best bet while I'm in Frankfort. They have an office here. It's too bad you can't use Press Wireless *for personal messages as they give the correspondents pretty conscientious services.*

I'm back, from the British zone this time, and have just got my new Magaziner off my chest. This trip wasn't productive and I was disgusted to get a clipping from this office showing some AP Hamburg election results above mine. I don't understand it since [my] figures, which the desk omitted, were more complete.

A letter from Cy, a sort of round-robin, informs me that all living allowances are being cancelled effective October 1 and that I have been granted a raise to $125 a week, also ten dollars a week for my car. I will obviously *have to begin using some of my salary. It will probably be most convenient if I have the office send me a part of it, but I will decide that later, when my present expense money, which is good for another month, runs low.*

With the stock market having recurrent fainting spells I should think Mr. Sterling might find this a suitable time to make a few new purchases, if I have accumulated enough. But that is entirely up to him.

I got a couple of grateful letters from Paris from Mlle. Pave and her family who received the ten-in-one package and in a previous one. Mlle. Pave said she had written you a thank you letter. The German packages do not appear to have arrived yet however.

Markel is still driving me nutty. His latest is a request to rewrite a piece about the Nuremberg trials written by a man named Kempner. But I haven't the text and can't find Kempner. I wish I could take a little vacation, especially from the Sunday paper. I haven't been very productive lately anyway.

With all the moving around I have done in recent weeks my room is a mess and I must get down to clearing up a maze of papers of one kind or another. Did I tell you that in a weak moment I agreed to let one of our officers and his English bride take over my big double room. I really didn't feel justified in hanging on to it since it is just the thing for them and I am here so little. I will get a small single room with bath in exchange.

I haven't entirely decided my next program, but think that after I've cleared up a few things here I will go to Bamberg for the constabulary piece Markel wants and thence to Munich. It won't be long 'till there is snow in the mountains and maybe I can get around to a little sport! Wouldn't that be nice? But I think I would like my sport in some place like Chamonix or Switzerland.

Dick Clark and I made an interesting trip to Heidelberg University on Friday and talked to a lot of students about their political attitudes. It didn't pan out too much of a story, but I'll shop around on that subject some more. The reactionary-fascist trend of student thinking has been somewhat exaggerated in my opinion. The students are simply as confused and floundering as the rest of the Germans.

A smart fellow in Wiesbaden military government named Sam Wahrhaftig invited me, a long time ago, to visit Marburg University with him and I think I'll take him up on it.

Some USFET [United States Forces European Theater] *officers have been after me to write a certain type of piece on denazification. I don't like stories that somebody "wants" written and I'm not at all sure I agree with them. Anyway it's a lead and may be worth something.*

Hope you're not having too hard time of it without Steinie. It seems incredible no full time nurse could be found in all Los Angeles. Love to Grandma and you all,
   DANA

GERMANY'S ZONES
A POLITICAL MAZE

The Varied Stages of Political Development Emphasize Divergent Policies

By DANA ADAMS SCHMIDT
Special to THE NEW YORK TIMES.

FRANKFORT ON THE MAIN, Sept. 14—The American zone, distinguished by its precocious political development, tomorrow will find itself in the position of spectator while the rest of Germany is voting. The British and French zones will be holding and the Russian zone completing the last stage of municipal elections, a step in the evolution of democratic machinery which the American zone, now working on state constitutions, went through between January and May of this year.

Into the last ten days of the three zones' electoral campaigns was dropped Secretary of State Byrnes' speech at Stuttgart. From the seat of the American zones' Laenderrat, it placed the stamp of the highest American approval on federalistic development of the American zone, called for unification of all

Germany on similar lines and provided a clear answer to demands for German unity on more centralistic lines made by Foreign Minister Molotov and the Socialist Unity party of the Russian zone.

Long before other zones even thought of elections, the Americans in January began putting the Germans, still numbed and bewildered by the Nazi collapse, to work on democratic machinery, now culminating in the writing of constitutions to be followed by a referendum and elections to legislative assemblies in December.

Christian Social Union

Throughout the zone, the Christian Social Union became dominant, overwhelmingly in conservative Catholic Bavaria and substantially in Wuerttemberg-Baden. Only in Greater Hesse with its Protestant industrial population could the Social Democrats win a slight majority.

At the same time, the Americans took the Allied Control Council's directives on denazification very literally. They fired several hundred thousands from private and public employment, herded some 80,000 into internment camps and, finally, turned the job of going over the whole population with a fine-tooth denazification comb over to the Germans.

All this permitted the American zone to wind up in September, looking upon the political growing pains of the other zones with a superior air. But it did nothing to solve economic problems. Rather they were aggravated by federalistic decentralization and removal of previous leadership in many realms.

British and French

The British and French zones, much more slowly, recently began falling in line with the federalistic American pattern. Both of these zones being composed of a multitude of historic political subdivisions, the task was difficult, especially for the French, whose bits of Wuerttemberg-Baden and Hesse Palatinate and the Saar did not fit together in any sense.

The British none the less have now set up as states the Rhineland-Westphalia area and the province of Hanover, and the French the northern half of their zone, and they are planning further elections and provisional Governments, thereby preparing the ground for an eventual political as well as economic union of German states in a federal system.

In the meantime, British colonial administrators and French officers, instead of handing responsibility to the Germans as the Americans did, ran their zones in a most direct manner. The Oberregierungs Presidents of the four regions, plus Hamburg of the British zone and the five regions of the French zone, were only figureheads, and various forms of German advisory councils remained without authority.

Saar Coal Fields

After early crises and at least one strike, the French now look after the Saar coal fields, providing wine and special rations from France for miners, but in the vineyards and orchards of the rest of the zone there are periods of genuine starvation. Although cut off from normal supplies of Bavarian potatoes, Baden vegetables and eastern German grain, the French zone must provide most of the French Army's food.

Seeing their hopes of detaching the Ruhr and Rhineland glimmering following Mr. Byrnes' speech, the French are more determined than ever to annex the Saar and unite it with the iron ore of Lorraine. They have pushed coal production to 60 per cent of the pre-war output.

In contrast to the troubled western zones, the highly centralized Russian zone has balanced food and industrial resources. The Russians are able to pursue a double aim of exploitation and control and still give the Germans a slightly better standard of living than the west.

But in spite of its dynamism and German-wide ambitions, the Socialist Unity party is disappointing its Russian sponsors in the elections. They seem to show that even the Germans in the Russian zone still think in western terms.

U.S., BRITISH ZONES EQUALIZE RATIONS

Increase Germans' Caloric Diet to 1,550 for the Winter, Exceeding Soviet Area

By DANA ADAMS SCHMIDT
Special to THE NEW YORK TIMES.

FRANKFORT ON THE MAIN, Germany, Sept. 23—The United States and British zones prepared for winter with a joint announcement today of the equalization of their food rations, which will make an increase for both to 1,550 calories a person a day. These rations, which will become effective Oct. 14, will exceed the level in the Soviet zone.

"Favorable news concerning the shipping position in the United States" permitted the decision, which had been planned for months, according to a statement from the offices of the Deputy Military Governors, Lieut. Gen. Lucius D. Clay of the United States and Lieut. Gen. Sir Brian Robertson.

From an international, and also from a strictly German, viewpoint it was the most significant specific consequence to date of the merger of the United States and British zones.

The chief beneficiaries were the 22,000,000 Germans in the British zone, whose basic ration for "normal" consumers fell to about 1,000 calories in July and August and rose to only 1,137 a month ago. The 18,000,000 Germans in the United States zone, after a dip to 1,180 calories, have been receiving 1,210 for the last month. As in all zones, however, the inhabitants of the towns received small supplements and the workers substantial supplements above the basic level.

The latest basic level reported from the Russian zone was 1,263 calories and from the French zone 1,014.

The decision to increase the ration was made in spite of the absence of a definite assurance of sufficient indigenous and imported supplies to maintain it until the next harvest, the announcement said. There was a possibility, therefore, that it would have to be cut again later.

German officials of the two zones, after recent consultations at Bad Kissingen, recommended an increase only to 1,300 calories, pointing out that despite the relatively good harvest, the United States zone could produce only about 900 and the British zone 600 calories of its ration, and that imports were uncertain.

United States and British health officials, however, have expressed the opinion that German physical resistance has been so far reduced that at least 1,500 calories would be required to avoid the danger of epidemics during the winter.

For the present, rations in the two zones will be equal only in caloric content. As soon as practicable, it is proposed to establish a common diet in various foods such as meat, fats, sugar, fish, potatoes and bread.

After writing about rationing of food and the many political factions in Germany, Dana was glad to report on a constructive but lighter subject—sports programs for the youth of Germany. Here is one of these stories:

YOUTH OF GERMANY EAGERLY JOINS U.S. SPORTS-EDUCATIONAL PROGRAM

By DANA ADAMS SCHMIDT
Special to THE NEW YORK TIMES.
BAD KISSINGEN, Germany, Sept. 24 (Delayed)—A young German who lost a leg fighting the Americans at Bastogne leaned on his crutches in the municipal park here this afternoon and wistfully watched American soldiers teaching somewhat younger Germans how to play American football, softball and volleyball and pitching horseshoes with the youngest. He was seeing part of the German youth activities program that idealistic representatives of the United States Army hope will help replace militarism and racism with democratic ideals of peaceful fair play. These Americans hope their plan will make it less likely that there will be new generations of wistful young men on crutches throughout the world.

In the five months of its existence the Twelfth Tactical Air Force's youth program here has become one of the zone's most remarkable achievements. Branching out from athletics, it has tackled fields where American ideological influence can make itself more directly felt—forums, discussion groups, a library and a band.

The program is directed by Capt. Norman F. Labarre, former music teacher in Pasadena, Calif. and Lieut. Woodruff W. Brock, who formerly worked with young people's groups in Fort Worth, Tex.

In spite of an occasional drizzle, several hundred German boys were scrambling delightedly in the park this afternoon under the patient direction of their American teachers, who are out there every afternoon and three evenings a week.

Many of the young Germans were barefooted. But a few of the most devoted have been equipped with sneakers, bats and gloves. They are members of the regular softball teams, which now frequently play teams from other towns in matches that have begun to steal the German crowd from the usual Sunday soccer games.

In a local theatre, meanwhile, the "Bad Kissingen Hepcats," 14 to 16 year olds in bright green outfits they made out of parachute silk, were rehearsing "hot beats" in preparation for an appearance before a forum in the evening.

The eight boys composing the band and the six girls who sing and dance were taken on a tour by their GI mentors during the summer vacation and played for soldiers and German audiences as far away as Nuremberg, Bamberg and Bremen. Most of them are children of expellees and refugees from the East, 10,000 of whom have been crowded into the hotels and villas of this resort town of 9,000 population before the war. A group of girls was working on curtains and murals for the community center they hope to open next week. In the center will be one room for games, another for handicrafts and a third for a library of 130 books in German and 600 in English. The young Germans are canvassing the town for more books.

Lieutenant Brock was visiting an elementary school to explain the Army's youth activities to teachers. He returned with a request from the teachers for some books and publications on American pedagogical theory.

In the evening 600 children turned out for the forum and squealed the approval of the band's version of "Don't Fence Me In," "In the Mood" and "Dinah." They cudgeled their brains over quiz questions. The winners got candy bars.

For the older and more seriously minded children there is a weekly discussion group, which is now dealing with the United States Constitution and will then take up the United Nations.

Katherine Davidson, social worker of Phoenix, Ariz. who is organizing a special discussion group for the girls, said she had found youngsters in total ignorance of what was going on in Germany and the world. Many took the attitude that it was none of their concern but soon grew interested in the discussion.

The parents of Bad Kissingen tended in the first months to view the youth program with suspicion, according to the soldiers. A few took exception to a poster depicting a United States soldier as a Pied Piper, interpreting it to mean their children would be lured away to the United States. But increasing numbers responded to invitations to attend athletic meets, forum and discussion groups and many became enthusiastic supporters.

The least of Captain Labarre's and Lieutenant Brock's problems was to arouse interest among the German youth. The soldiers soon found themselves the objects of hero worship. They had to make certain that the intense attraction of activities did not interfere with schoolwork.

There was a crisis during one afternoon when a 16-year-old drummer of a band was found to be locked up at home to do his homework. But he got out in time for the evening show.

More difficult was attracting the interest of soldiers, most of whom are volunteers. A new order authorizing the troops to devote four hours of training time weekly to the youth activities will make it easier.

The greatest and constant problem, however, remained food, for the children were made doubly hungry by sports and other activities. Their empty stomachs did not make the youngsters more receptive to democratic teachings.

Thus far youth activities officers have been authorized to supply only candy contributed by soldiers and occasional coffee, doughnuts and sandwiches.

The final days of the Nuremberg trials were approaching, and Dana wrote on September 27:

I've got to leave for Nuremberg in the morning so I'd better write this now. I hadn't expected to cover the Nuremberg verdicts but James decided at the last minute both Kathleen and I should concentrate on it.

Joe Grigg is coming up from Paris on the night train and I plan to take him and Louis Lochner along in my car. It will be a regular Berlin reunion.

Bruce Rae, the man who runs the Overseas weekly and the photo side came in by air this afternoon by American Airlines. He seemed very aged and tired when he arrived but soon perked up. He has brought over some very ambitious plans for the NY Times *publishing over here—but that is 100 percent confidential.*

As I forecast, I gave up my big double room to the Davis couple and now have a smaller but much more attractive and sunny room.

Most of the last two days I've been working for Markel, first rewriting the piece Dr. Kempner wrote on the effects of the trial on the Germans and then doing a color piece on the trials myself. It is all very well to appear in the Sunday paper, but I'll be glad to have some more people here to share the privilege. At least I think so now.

After a taste of chilly autumn we have returned to summer temperatures. It is like spring, and I feel as though I had spring fever.

The only trouble with my new room is that the man next door leaves his radio on all the time. He even goes off and forgets it. I'll have to educate him.

There isn't a great deal to tell you this week except about the job. I wonder how you are making out without Steinie.

Give my love to Grandma and Eliza,
Love,
Dana

And now, the first of Dana's articles on the trial:

NUREMBERG JUDGES IN FINAL MEETING

Put Finishing Touches on Their Case Against Germans— Security Tightened

By **DANA ADAMS SCHMIDT**
Special to THE NEW YORK TIMES.
NUREMBERG, Germany, Sept. 28—The four judges of the International Military Tribunal held their last secret meeting in the Nuremberg courthouse today to determine the fate of Hermann Wilhelm Goering and his twenty-one co-defendants and seven Nazi organizations.

They put the finishing touches on a judgment of monumental proportions, which the British President of the court Lord Justice Geofrrey [sic] Lawrence, will begin reading at 10 o'clock Monday morning.

The other judges, Francis Biddle of the United States, Donnedieu De Havres of France and Maj. Gen. Iola T. Nikitchenko of the Soviet Union, will continue reading in rotation through a review of the entire trial and legal opinions to the climax of verdicts and sentences, probably late Tuesday.

The judges and their two interpreters were in seclusion tonight and strictest security precautions at the courthouse were enforced to prevent a leakage of their decisions.

Three of Four Votes Needed

The convictions and sentences have to be imposed by affirmative votes of at least three out of the four members of the tribunal, according to the charter signed by eighteen Allied nations in London Aug. 8 last year. Since it is widely presumed that the Russians demanded death for all and the Americans and British lighter sentences for a few, the French judge may have held a position of decisive influence.

Following the judgment the defendants will pass from the jurisdiction of the tribunal to that of the Allied Control Council in Berlin, where it is unofficially reported those sentenced to death will be hanged or guillotined fifteen days later. In the interval the four-power Control Council will review the decisions and consider any appeals that are made.

The Council may reduce or alter sentences but it cannot increase their severity or reconsider the guilt or innocence of the convicted. If it uncovers fresh evidence justifying further charges it may report to a committee composed of the chief prosecutors of the four nations.

These are Justice Robert H. Jackson of the United States, Sir Hartley Shawcross of Britain, Chametier de Ribes of France and Gen. Roman Rudenko of the Soviet Union.

NUREMBERG TENSE AS VERDICTS NEAR

Security Officers Are Alert for Suicide or Escape Bids by Nazi Defendants

By DANA ADAMS SCHMIDT
Special to THE NEW YORK TIMES.

NUREMBERG, Sept. 28—With the approach of the International Military Tribunal's verdicts and sentences next Tuesday, tension rose this week in bleak and ruined Nuremberg. It rose among the tribunal and prison officials, among the correspondents and visiting dignitaries of a dozen nations, among the German defendants and their families and even among the townspeople of Nuremberg.

They were awaiting the climax of a trial that may be classed as the most remarkable in judicial history. This, by reason of the nature of the court, including American, British, Russian and French judges and prosecutors; of the defendants, including twenty-one of the highest surviving political and military chiefs of the Nazi state, plus Martin Borman in absentia, and seven principal Nazi organizations; of the charges that held the preparation for and the waging of aggressive war to be a crime, and of the length of the proceedings, stretching over ten months.

Precautions Tightened

In this last week security officers were obviously nervous. Whether they feared assassinations, escape attempts, thefts of documents, leakage of the tribunal's decisions or what, was not known, but they were taking no chances.

Secrecy became the watchword at the courthouse. All old passes were called in and new ones issued. The courthouse guards, drawn from Company K, Third Battalion of the Twenty-sixth Infantry Regiment, First Division, whose history goes back to North Africa, scrutinized the passes with care. They wanted no last-minute repetitions of the stunt executed several months ago in which a man entered and left the court house twenty-two times with a picture of a police dog on his pass.

The defendants' families, totaling some fifty persons, including their wives and children, however, remained the objects of universal curiosity. They were billeted with local families all over the town and every morning they walked, usually unrecognized, to the court house prison for a half-hour meeting with the defendants.

Goerings Draw Attention

Only buxom Emma Goering, who was an actress and who frequently appeared in public with her husband, drew attention. She and her 8-year-old daughter Edda were the guests of Goering's defense attorney, Dr. Otto Stahmer.

Frau Goering was heard to remark after seeing her husband that she realized that if the Germans had won the war they would not have shown enemy leaders such consideration. She also said:

"We have had our good days. We should not be surprised now to have bad ones."

The families could see and converse through plexiglas windows at the jail. There were emotional outbursts, but on the whole all concerned kept themselves under control. Von Schirach's children tried to put their hands through the glass on one occasion and were reproved by Edda Goering. In addition, there were five Sauckel children, several von Ribbentrop children and others who giggled and played and did not seem quite aware of what was going on.

Von Keitel's son, an officer in his thirties, was transferred from an internment camp to see his father. He told friends he had been embarrassed because his father had gone so far toward admitting his guilt.

The only defendant who, so far as known, received no visitors was Rudolf Hess, whose wife was reported to have sought a divorce. He was said to be growing more and more unbalanced, haunted by "glassy eyes" and a fear that someone would poison him.

Families Present

While in Nuremberg the families were fed at the mess used by the German court employees, a fact that soon spread among the townspeople. So many Germans gathered to stare at the families of their former rulers that military police had to post guards at the entrance. The Germans observed that the wives and children were still well dressed and apparently well enough fed.

The defendants did not look anywhere nearly so good. Although well nourished and regularly exercised, they had become haggard and their complexions yellow during the long trial. Goering seemed the most deflated of all, physically and in morale.

At the beginning he had tried to dominate the other defendants sending them notes and glances of approval and disapproval. Finally he gave it up. He even stopped writing and appeared interested only in the daily visits of his wife and daughter.

Most of the others devoted the whole time to writing appeals for mercy, justifications of their acts and memoirs. For most there was only a little time left, for a few probably a great deal more time than they would know what to do with.

WAR GUILT DECLARED

By DANA ADAMS SCHMIDT
Special to THE NEW YORK TIMES.
NUREMBERG, Germany, Sept. 30—Verdicts and sentences will be pronounced upon Hermann Wilhelm Goering and his twenty-one co-defendants by the International Military Tribunal here tomorrow.

Today, with Goering and twenty others of the accused brought before it for the first of the two days of judgment—Martin Bormann, Hitler's deputy, is missing—the Tribunal gave its basic verdict against their conspiracy of aggressive warfare as the "supreme crime."

The Tribunal declared certain groups of the Nazi regime—the Leadership Corps, the SS or Elite Guard, the SD or Security Service and the Gestapo—to be criminal. But it declined to declare the SA or Storm Troopers, the German Cabinet or the General Staff and High Command to be criminal organizations.

100,000 Words in Findings

The Tribunal's findings, argument and documentation, of which 177 pages of a total 260 pages running to 100,000 words were read during the day's sitting, was of decisive importance to the denazification procedure in the four zones of conquered Germany, to the future of Germany and to the world.

Some 400 spectators looked on and the pallid defendants squirmed under neon lights. The four-power Tribunal reviewed the history of the prosecution, the Nazis' rise to power and Germany's "criminal aggression" against twelve countries.

The president of the Tribunal, Lord Justice Sir Geoffrey Lawrence of Britain, began the reading at 10 A.M., turned it over successively to the judges and alternates representing France, the United States and Russia and wound up by reading the verdict on the organizations himself.

The declaration on criminality of the Nazi Leadership Corps, of the SS, the SD (Sicherheitsdienst) and the Gestapo fixed the criminality of their members, Lord Justice Lawrence explained. Therefore it excluded persons who did not know the criminal purposes or acts of the organizations or who were drafted into membership by the state.

It also excluded those who ceased to be members before the beginning of the war on Sept. 1, 1939.

The effect of this declaration was to establish the criminality of parts of the guilty organizations beyond possibility of argument before any court. But, furthermore, it made it clear that each case should be examined on its individual merits and that the Tribunal did not condone penalties imposed automatically upon whole categories of persons according to their memberships and ranks. It opened up hope of exoneration for some millions of Germans.

Cautious on Group Criminality

The Tribunal did not hesitate, it stated, to declare organizations to be criminal simply because the theory of "group criminality" was new or because it might be unjustly applied by some subsequent tribunals. But it must make its declarations so far as possible in such manner that innocent persons would not be punished.

In the case of the individuals of the German General Staff and High Command, Lord Justice Lawrence read in acid tones that "they have been a disgrace to the honorable profession of arms."

"Without their military guidance the aggressive ambitions of Hitler and his fellow Nazis would have been academic and sterile," he went on. "They were certainly a ruthless military caste. The contemporary German militarism flourished briefly with its recent ally, National Socialism, as well as or better than it had in the generations of the past."

Regarding the Nazis' "common plan and conspiracy" as charged in the indictments, the Tribunal declared:

"That plans were made to wage war as early as Nov. 5, 1937, and probably before that is apparent * * * but that evidence establishes with certainty the existence of many separate plans rather than a single conspiracy embracing them all.

War Guilt Declared

By DANA ADAMS SCHMIDT
Special to The New York Times.

NUREMBERG, Germany, Sept. 30 —Verdicts and sentences will be pronounced upon Hermann Wilhelm Goering and his twenty-one co-defendants by the International Military Tribunal here tomorrow.

Today, with Goering and twenty others of the accused brought before it for the first of the two days of judgment — Martin Bormann, Hitler's deputy, is missing — the Tribunal gave its basic verdict against their conspiracy of aggressive warfare as "the supreme crime."

The Tribunal declared certain groups of the Nazi regime—the Leadership Corps, the SS or Elite Guard, the SD or Security Service and the Gestapo—to be criminal. But it declined to declare the SA or Storm Troopers, the German Cabinet or the General Staff and High Command to be criminal organizations.

100,000 Words in Findings

The Tribunal's findings, argument and documentation, of which 177 pages of a total 260 pages running to 100,000 words were read during the day's sitting, was of decisive importance to the denazification procedure in the four zones of conquered Germany, to the future of Germany and to the world.

Some 400 spectators looked on and the pallid defendants squirmed under neon lights. The four-power Tribunal reviewed the history of the prosecution, the Nazis' rise to power and Germany's "criminal aggression" against twelve countries.

The president of the Tribunal, Lord Justice Sir Geoffray Lawrence of Britain, began the reading at 10 A. M., turned it over successively to the judges and alternates representing France, the United States and Russia and wound up by reading the verdict on the organizations himself.

The declaration on criminality of the Nazi Leadership Corps, of the SS, the SD (Sicherheitsdienst) and the Gestapo fixed the criminality of their members, Lord Justice Lawrence explained. Therefore it excluded persons who did not know the criminal purposes or acts of the organizations or who were drafted into membership by the state.

It also excluded those who ceased to be members before the beginning of the war on Sept. 1, 1939.

The effect of this declaration was to establish the criminality of parts of the guilty organizations beyond possibility of argument before any court. But, furthermore, it made it clear that each case should be examined on its individual merits and that the Tribunal did not condone penalties imposed automatically upon whole categories of persons according to their memberships and ranks. It opened up hope of exoneration for some millions of Germans.

Cautious on Group Criminality

The Tribunal did not hesitate, it stated, to declare organizations to be criminal simply because the theory of "group criminality" was new or because it might be unjustly applied by some subsequent tribunals. But it must make its declarations so far as possible in such manner that innocent persons would not be punished.

In the case of the individuals of

"Continued planning with aggressive war as the objective has been established beyond a doubt."

The Tribunal rejected the idea that a common plan could not exist because Hitler was a dictator. Hitler could not make aggressive war by himself, he had to have the cooperation of political and military leaders, diplomats and businessmen. When, with knowledge of his aims, they gave him that cooperation, they made themselves parties to the plan he had initiated.

The overwhelming mass of war crimes and crimes against humanity, the Tribunal traced to the Nazi conception of "total war."

Most of these crimes were the result of "cold and criminal calculation," some planned long in advance as for the plunder of occupied territories and the ill treatment of their inhabitants and for slave labor.

The Killing of 6,000,000 Jews

Concerning the frightful chapter of Jewish persecution the Tribunal noted that, after the German invasion of Russia, the SD and Gestapo were mobilized to exterminate eastern Jews. Adolf Eichman, an organizer of pogroms, estimated that these organizations killed 2,000,000 Jews and that 4,000,000 died in concentration camps such as Oswiecim.

The Tribunal found the history of the Nazi regime merged into its acts of aggression. Goering, Schacht and von Papen were significantly mentioned for their significant parts in the party's rise, culminating in accession to power and the

Reichstag fire, which the Nazis used as an excuse to suppress constitutional rights. Goering's role in building up the German air force and navy, contrary to the Versailles agreement, was set forth.

In the matter of aggressive war the Tribunal recalled that the defense had contended that, since no sovereign power had made aggressive war a crime, to impose punishment therefore was to indulge in ex post facto law.

The Tribunal held that international law was continually developing. Even though the Hague Convention did not designate breaches of its provisions as crime, acts outlawed thereunder were recognized to be crimes.

The Kellogg-Briand Pact of 1928, signed by Germany among others, made war an "illegal thing."

The further contention of the defense that heads of state were freed from responsibility by their position and that international law did not apply to individuals was rejected by the Tribunal. It held that the principle did not apply where a state had violated international law and that individuals had often been punished for violating the Hague Convention's rules of land warfare.

The defense of "superior orders," the Tribunal said, could be considered only in mitigation.

GERMANY NOT FREE, SCHACHT COMPLAINS

Von Papen Says He Has Given Up Politics—Austria Seeks Extradition for Trial

By DANA ADAMS SCHMIDT
Special to THE NEW YORK TIMES.

NUREMBERG, Germany, Oct. 1—Franz von Papen said that his political career was "absolutely ended," Hans Fritzsche asked to be tried again by a German court and Hjalmar Schacht asked for chocolate for his two children today when the three men acquitted by the International Military Tribunal appeared before 200 representatives of the world press.

Schacht got his candy bars and all reaped a harvest of cigarettes in exchange for autographs desired by some correspondents. Schacht finally had one lighted cigarette in each hand.

Asked about their political careers, Schacht, former Reichsbank president, said that he would await offers before committing himself, while Fritzsche, a former propagandist, considered the possibilities for him too remote for comment. On the subject of appearing before a German court, Schacht observed: "I prefer to await charges before making a statement. Formerly there were laws to be judged by and a free public opinion. Today there appears to be neither." He added in reply to inquiries that "formerly" meant "before the Nazis." Von Papen said that he was "too much out of contact with what was going on to judge whether it was necessary or possible to put before a German court after the International Tribunal had passed judgment."

Protest at Looting

Both von Papen and Schacht complained about the looting of their homes. Schacht declared that his wife and children had been driven from their home when the trial began and had had to walk forty miles to Berlin, while "German Communists" pillaged their house. Now, he said, his great desire is to disappear with his family to some quiet place "and never see the press again."

Von Papen and Schacht affirmed that they had most certainly expected acquittal from the beginning. Fritzsche, however, said: "The question of liberty is for me quite new and quite surprising. * * * I felt completely guiltless as regards the charges, but already during the trial I let it be known frequently that I would like to appear before a German court to make it clear before the Germans why I spoke over the German radio as I did."

GERMANY NOT FREE, SCHACHT COMPLAINS

Von Papen Says He Has Given Up Politics—Austria Seeks Extradition for Trial

By DANA ADAMS SCHMIDT
Special to THE NEW YORK TIMES.

NUREMBERG, Germany, Oct. 1—Franz von Papen said that his political career was "absolutely ended," Hans Fritzsche asked to be tried again by a German court and Hjalmar Schacht asked for chocolate for his two children today when the three men acquitted by the International Military Tribunal appeared before 200 representatives of the world press.

Schacht got his candy bars and all reaped a harvest of cigarettes

Continued on Page 20, Column 3

Col. Burton C. Andrus, security officer, read the letter that will be given to each of the acquitted men in the name of the International Military Tribunal, saying that they are free and asking the military government authorities to help them to obtain identification papers, ration cards, etc. He said that they would leave the prison as soon as transportation could be arranged. Von Papen will go to either his wife in the British zone or his daughter in the French zone. Schacht and his family will probably visit his son-in-law, who has an estate near Weilheim in the American zone, and Fritzsche will probably join his wife in Hamburg.

In a further article on trials, the *AP* reported that Wilhelm Hoegner, minister-president of Bavaria, has declared that any of the acquitted men who remained in the American zone will be placed before a German denazification board. "This certainly means several years at hard labor," he said. He called von Papen's acquittal "astounding" and branded von Papen "the real instigator of the Third Reich."

Perhaps because the jail authorities had not expected that Schacht, von Papen and Fritzsche would be acquitted, they were not freed immediately.

On October 2, Dana reported:

ACQUITTED MEN STILL IN JAIL

By DANA ADAMS SCHMIDT
Special to THE NEW YORK TIMES.
NUREMBERG, Oct. 2—Schacht, von Papen and Fritzsche, while technically free men, tonight spent their second night in the prison of Nuremberg court house since they were acquitted by the Tribunal.

Security officers explained that arrangements had not yet been completed for their transfer to complete freedom. They were allowed to receive and embrace members of their families instead of talking to them through glass, as before the verdicts.

Arrangements to transfer those with prison sentences to a four-power prison in Berlin were being made.

Hermann Goering, Baldur von Schirach and Dr. Albert Speer did not intend to appeal to the Allied Control Council for clemency, German defense lawyers said, but most of the others were busy drawing up such appeals with their counsel today. Raeder and Doenitz, it was learned, would not appeal directly, but through a third party consisting of a group of retired German admirals. [Press services said counsel appealed for those who did not file their own pleas.]

Criticism of the International Military Tribunal's judgment in Germany has centered on its "incomprehensible" decision to acquit Schacht and von Papen and its decision not to declare the SA or Storm Troopers a criminal organization.

The Tribunal's explanation that Fritzsche did not play a decisive role and that the German Cabinet and General Staff were not organizations in a true sense were more readily, though unwillingly, accepted.

The general reaction derives from the feeling that von Papen, Schacht and the Storm Troopers played leading parts in bringing Hitler to power, a fact that the Tribunal fully recognized.

Thus, Heinrich Loeblein, a leader of the Bavarian Reconstruction party, declared today he had received many telephone calls complaining that the original pillars of Nazism were set free. Such reactions, however, ignore the juridical foundation of the Tribunal's decision, which will be of some significance to the future of denazification in Germany.

This foundation is the Tribunal's somewhat indefinite but significant finding that there is a dividing line around 1937, before which the plans of Hitler and the top Nazis for aggressive war could not be clearly recognized.

Pointing out that the common plan or conspiracy as charged in the indictment covered a period of about twenty-five years from the formation of the party in 1919 to the end of the war, the Tribunal dissented:

"But the conspiracy must be clearly outlined in its criminal purposes. It must not be too far removed from the time of decision and of action. The planning, to be criminal, must not rest merely on the declaration of a party program such as are found in the twenty-five points of the Nazi party announced in 1920 or the political affirmations expressed in 'Mein Kampf' in later years. * * * That plans were made to wage war as early as Nov. 5, 1937, and probably before that is apparent."

It cited four meetings stretching over three years and beginning on that date at which Hitler progressively made clear his plans. On this basis, the Tribunal went on to rule that Schacht was opposed to aggressive war and resigned his positions as minister of economic and plenipotentiary for war economy in 1937, "when it became evident that Hitler was headed toward war. * * * It was not shown beyond reasonable doubt that he knew Hitler's aggressive plans when he aided the rearmament program in its early stages."

In the case of von Papen, it ruled that it had not been shown that he was a party to plans under which the occupation of Austria in March, 1938, was a step in the direction of further aggression.

The plight of these three men was continued in Dana's article on Oct. 3:

GERMAN POLICE FAIL TO JAIL FREED NAZIS

Clay Bars Rearrest Pending Ruling on Status—He is Said to Order Safe-Conducts

By DANA ADAMS SCHMIDT
Special to THE NEW YORK TIMES.
NUREMBERG, Germany, Oct. 3—In the hope of arresting Dr. Hjalmar Schacht, Franz von Papen and Hans Fritzsche as they left prison, German police surrounded the Nuremberg court house at 8 o'clock this morning but were called off at 1:30 P.M. by order of Lieut. Gen. Lucius A. Clay, Deputy Military Governor.

The three men, whom the International Military Tribunal ordered discharged last Tuesday morning, remained in jail, however, and tonight began their third night in prison cells that were unlocked and unwatched in token of their technical liberty.

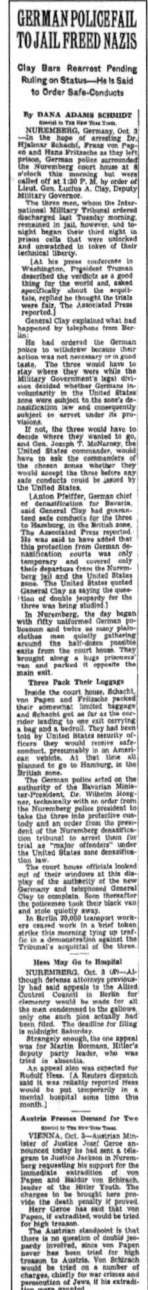

[At his press conference in Washington, President Truman described the verdicts as a good thing for the world and, asked specifically about the acquittals, replied he thought the trials were fair, the Associated Press reported.]

General Clay explained what had happened by telephone from Berlin:

He had ordered the German police to withdraw because their action was not necessary or in good taste. The three would have to stay where they were while the Military Government's legal division decided whether Germans involuntarily in the United States zone were subject to the zone's denazification law and consequently subject to arrest under its provisions.

If not, the three would have to decide where they wanted to go, and Gen. Joseph T. McNarney, the United States commander, would have to ask the commanders of the chosen zones whether they would accept the three before any safe conducts could be issued by the United States.

[Anton Pfeiffer, German chief of denazification for Bavaria, said General Clay had guaranteed safe conducts for the three to Hamburg, in the British zone, the Associated Press reported. He was said to have added that this protection from German denazification courts was only temporary and covered only their departure from the Nuremberg jail and the United States zone. The United States quoted General Clay as saying the question of double jeopardy for the three was being studied.]

In Nuremberg, the day began with fifty uniformed German policemen and twice as many plain-clothes men quietly gathering around the half-dozen possible exits from the court house. They brought along a huge prisoners' van and parked it opposite the main exit.

Three Pack Their Luggage

Inside the courthouse, Schacht, von Papen and Fritzsche packed their somewhat limited baggage and Schacht got as far as the corridor leading to one exit carrying a bag and a bedroll. They had been told by United States security officers they would receive safe-conduct, presumably in an American vehicle. At that time all planned to go to Hamburg in the British zone.

The German police acted on the authority of the Bavarian Minister-President, Dr. Wilhelm Hoegner, technically with an order from the Nuremberg police president to take the three into protective custody and an order from the president of the Nuremberg denazification tribunal to arrest them for trial as "major offenders" under the United States zone denazification law.

The court house officials looked out of their windows at this display of the authority of the new Germany and telephoned General Clay to complain. Soon thereafter the policemen took their black van and stole quietly away.

In Berlin 20,000 transport workers ceased work in a brief token strike this morning tying up traffic in a demonstration against the Tribunal's acquittal of the three.

SCHACHT HAS PLAN FOR NEW GERMANY

Former Nazi Finance 'Wizard' Cloaks Details—von Papen Still Lingers in Jail

By DANA ADAMS SCHMIDT
Special to THE NEW YORK TIMES.

NUREMBERG, GERMANY, OCT. 5—Franz von Papen stayed in jail yet another night tonight, waiting for a formal reply to his petition to enter the British zone. At the same time, Dr. Hjalmar Schacht, grudgingly, and Hans Fritsche, eagerly, gave interviews this evening in the rooms that had been assigned to them as free men in Nuremberg.

The Bavarian Military Government announced that they were "at liberty pending trial before Denazification Tribunal No. 1 in Nuremberg" and would receive police protection if they desired. German arrest warrants were

SCHACHT HAS PLAN FOR NEW GERMANY

Former Nazi Finance 'Wizard' Cloaks Details—von Papen Still Lingers in Jail

By DANA ADAMS SCHMIDT
Special to The New York Times.

NUREMBERG, Germany, Oct. 5—Franz von Papen stayed in jail yet another night tonight, waiting for a formal reply to his petition to enter the British zone. At the same time, Dr. Hjalmar Schacht, grudgingly, and Hans Fritzsche, eagerly, gave interviews this evening in the rooms that had been assigned to them as free men in Nuremberg.

The Bavarian Military Government announced that they were "at liberty pending trial before Denazification Tribunal No. 1 in Nuremberg" and would receive police protection if they desired. German arrest warrants were suspended by Military Government order after the unsuccessful attempts of the local police chief to arrest the pair last night.

While his lawyers began work to prove that the United States zone's denazification tribunals had no jurisdiction over him, Dr. Schacht, from the crowded room that he, his wife and two children occupy in the comfortable apartment of a grocery wholesaler, sent off a second request to enter the British zone.

Fritzsche, lodged in the modest quarters of his lawyer, Dr. Hein Fritz, composed a written pledge that he was at the disposal of the denazification tribunal, and he telegraphed his wife in Hamburg to join him here.

Dr. Schacht informed this correspondent that he had worked out a solution of Germany's economic problems but would disclose it only "to the men who have the power to put it into effect."

Fritzsche declared that he desired to forego politics and devote the rest of his life to "preaching the doctrine of love."

Schacht Proves 'Innocence'

In spite of their long imprisonment, Dr. Schacht, pugnacious and vitriolic, and Fritzsche, dreamily philosophical, appeared to be anything but broken men. Both were indignant over the rough treatment they had received from the local police chief, Leo Stahl, who, with revolver dangling from his belt, had appeared in their apartments to arrest them between 2 and 3 o'clock in the morning.

When asked what he had told the police chief, Dr. Schacht whipped out a copy of the international military tribunal's acquittal and read off the creditable sections. "These are my credentials," he declared. "Now, where are my crimes? I stayed in Germany and fought against the war instead of going to Switzerland."

Asked about Germany's future, Dr. Schacht explained: "Before the war Germany had to import one-fifth of her food; now she is even more crowded and must import one-third. * * * The taxpayers in America and Britain will begin to cry out at the burden of supporting Germany as a beggar people, and the German people will not starve without raising a rumpus, either," he said.

---

suspended by Military Government order after the unsuccessful attempts of the local police chief to arrest the pair last night.

While his lawyers began work to prove that the United States zone's denazification tribunals had no jurisdiction over him, Dr. Schacht, from the crowded room that he, his wife and two children occupy in the comfortable apartment of a grocery wholesaler, sent off a second request to enter the British zone.

Fritzsche, lodged in the modest quarters of his lawyer, Dr. Hein Fritz, composed a written pledge that he was at the disposal of the denazification tribunal, and he telegraphed his wife in Hamburg to join him here.

Dr. Schacht informed this correspondent that he had worked out a solution of Germany's economic problems but would disclose it only "to the men who have the power to put it into effect."

Fritzsche declared that he desired to forego politics and devote the rest of his life to "preaching the doctrine of love."

Schacht Proves 'Innocence'

In spite of their long imprisonment, Dr. Schacht, pugnacious and vitriolic, and Fritsche, dreamily philosophical, appeared to be anything but broken men. Both were indignant over the rough treatment they had received from the local police chief, Leo Stahl, who with revolver dangling from his belt, had appeared in their apartments to arrest them between 2 and 3 o'clock in the morning.

When asked what he had told the police chief, Dr. Schacht whipped out a copy of the international military tribunal's acquittal and read off the creditable sections. "These are my credentials," he declared, "Now where are my crimes? I stayed in Germany and fought against the war instead of going to Switzerland."

Asked about Germany's future, Dr. Schacht explained: "Before the war Germany had to import one-fifth of her food; now she is even more crowded and must import one-third. * * * The taxpayers in America and Britain will begin to cry out at the burden of supporting Germany as a beggar people, and the German people will not starve without raising a rumpus, either," he said.

The methods of Adam Smith's classical economics were an English invention to meet English problems and could not solve the German problem, according to Dr. Schacht. Unification with the Russian zone would help but not get at the essentials, he said. Colonial politics, commercial agreements, international banks and currency manipulation were only palliatives, he added.

Declaring that "property as such is nothing and productivity is everything," he opposed nationalization and planned economy and urged individual initiative as "the vital spark of human progress."

As for himself, he said, "I have lost all my property and must get into business somewhere."

Nuremberg
October 6, 1946
Dear Mother:
I'm writing this from the pressroom at the Nuremberg courthouse.
I think there won't be many more high spots here till the executions.
Not entirely to my pleasure I won the drawing to represent the "special" or individual newspapers at the executions. But it is not at all certain that I will attend as there are only two American seats under present regulations and they have been allotted to the Agencies and Radios. We are trying to get a third seat.
. . . There has been tremendous confusion these last days after the Tribunal's judgment because no one was prepared for acquittals. I nearly got badly scooped on the release from prison of Schacht and Fritzsche but happened to be extremely late in the courthouse pounding out a weekender and picked it up at four in the morning just in time, I trust, to make the paper, or at least late editions.

Kathleen and I made a noble effort to get part of Tuesday's judgment into that morning's paper. We had seven hours time difference on that date and the paper held open two hours extra. We worked like slaves filing urgent flashes all morning only to find that the radio transmitters were having trouble with sunspots and most of it didn't get through till far too late. The paper used UP *copy instead.* UP *had made an arrangement with* Mutual Broadcasting Company *to use some of their time for transmission by voice broadcast, and it worked.* UP *beat everybody.*

I'm glad I haven't had to spend a great deal of time covering the Nuremberg trials. Living in these enormous drafty dormitories in the castle is too depressing. Nuremberg is depressing too. It is so terribly destroyed. Social life centers around the castle and the Grand hotel, one of the few big buildings in the town that was not destroyed.

It is quite chilly, leaves are flying and one feels the advent of winter. It is going to be a very cruel one in Germany. The people generally are in poor condition, worn down by bad and insufficient food.

Delbert Clark should be here any day now. I just discovered that he was the Colonel in charge of the fifth Army press camp in Italy. I never knew him very well as I was with the French most of the time, but I do remember that he was somewhat upset because I came to Italy as a guest of General Giraud without the proper papers from Public Relations.

What did you think of Kathleen's stories from here, and what do you think of them generally? I like her very much but I feel that she is somewhat circumlocutious and labored. She is due for leave and probably won't stay very long after the reinforcements arrive. I wonder whether she will come back to Germany. She is a little grey-haired woman, very quiet but persistent, good-natured and well-liked. She has gone to endless trouble to get the house or houses fixed up for the expected arrivals in Berlin.

There isn't a great deal more to report. All work and no play certainly does make Jack a dull boy. When the reinforcements get to work there should be a bit more play for me.

All my love to you all,
Dana

A week later, on October 13, 1946, his letter was from Bamberg:

Dear Mother:
I do write to you from quite an assortment of datelines. Here I am at constabulary headquarters doing that long-delayed piece for Markel. Yesterday I was flown down to Sonthofen, at the other end of the zone, to see the constabulary school in the former Adolf Hitler Schule, and today they flew me back.

Tonight I was scheduled to depart with General Harmon in his super deluxe special train, once owned by Goering, on a tour of inspection. Somewhat to my relief it was called off at the last minute, so I have this opportunity to write a letter. Tomorrow I'll call on a Constabular squadron and then drive to Nuremberg to prepare for the finale. I don't know yet whether I'll be able to cover the hangings. If I don't I suppose I'll find something else to write about.

Old Lincoln-Zephyr has been doing the best of service, and lady luck has been favoring me in the matter of tires. I'm still awaiting the new ones sent by the office, however. While I think of it, do you think you could send me a big tin of the best car polish and some shammy cloth and soft felt cloth to go with it. They are not obtainable over here, and washing is apparently not all my sleek beauty requires.

While I flew down to Sonhofen (in an L-5, slightly bigger than a Piper Cub) I parked the car behind the house of Colonel McKinney, chief Public Relations officer. And while I was gone the Colonel's driver, entirely on his own initiative, took it into his head to wash the car and polish the metalware. I don't offhand recall anything like that happening to me before. Unless it was the time in Stuttgart when Scott, of Time *magazine, gave one of the waiters some cigarettes to dust off his Ford. The waiter went out and instead, washed, not dusted, my Lincoln, presumably because it was the most impressive vehicle in sight.*

Things military are not much to my taste, but I must grant the Constabulary that they try to be pretty smart and snappy. I suppose that where there must be an army it might as well be snappy and well-disciplined if possible. Beyond that give me civilians. Necessary though they may be uniforms are straightjackets, the outward symbol of the individuals' submission to authority, among other things. The idea of hierarchy of authority so readily accepted in the case of the military or the church easily turns into the authoritarian Fuehrerprinzip and totalitarianism when applied to political life.

The contacts I've had in recent months with bishops and high military personalities make it easier for me to understand why the French have always feared their army and the Catholic church as fountainheads of "reaction." The generals and the bishops are at one with a man like Hjalmar Schacht in despising the common man. Individual initiative and rights they all talk about. But what they have in mind is initiative and rights for a certain kind of people, what the Germans keep calling "die fuehrende Schicht."

Unfortunately the issue is confused by the existence of another kind of authoritarianism, called Communism, to which the former elements are opposed because it ostensibly at least champions the common man against the rights of the "Fuehrende Schicht."

Now I despise authoritarianism in all its forms and am also not greatly enamored of the common man. It is all very difficult.

The opposite of authoritarian leadership in which orders are passed from top to bottom by incontestable right is leadership derived from the open exchange of ideas, or public debate, by the representatives of all elements of society. That seems a fairly simple definition of democracy, but it is certainly not fully embraced by all Americans.

Only public debate, echoed and criticized by the press and all the other articulations of public opinion, can produce intelligent leadership and avoid the irresponsible or simply mistaken tangents of leadership that originate in a limited party, caste or other group which presumptuously claims a monopoly of intelligent leadership.

So my standard is intelligence, not of single men or groups, but intelligence in general, as it evolves from the free interplay of ideas.

All that is not too clear and not in very good English or perhaps the right thing for a letter. But it helps sometimes to try to straighten out one's ideas in writing, or better in a talk with Mother, and I guess this is the next best thing to talking to you.

I was only in Frankfort a day before I left for Stuttgart to cover the Laenderrat and was delighted to find a parcel full of good things from home. I have been enjoying the cookies, doubtless made by you and Steinie, the Nestles cocoa and all the other things. I have been carrying a jar of your Nescafe from the previous package with me and find it invaluable when I miss breakfast. Did I ever tell you how much I enjoyed the marshmallows in the other package? I gave some of them to some German kids and they were thrilled. They'd never seen anything like it before.

Flying down to Sonthofen was quite a pleasant experience. It was bright and clear both ways, with the friendly landscape of fully quilted fields, and patches of forest and redroofed villages clustering round their churches stretching as far as one could see across Bavaria. It is such a beautiful country; one is always shocked anew to think that so much evil could have come out of it.

I lay in bed this morning in the commandant's villa and listened to the cowbells music in the valley. The most peaceful, relaxing sound I can think of. It reminded me of Switzerland and Chillon [the English school he went to]. Sonthofen is just at the foot of the Alps. The Nazis tried to build their "Ordensburg" at Sonthoven so as to blend architecturally into the countryside. But they were attempting the impossible. The burg is a massive frowning granite fortress whose ponderous forcefulness violates the sweet and verdant valley and yet is a puny display of human arrogance beneath the magnificence of the surrounding Alps.

How I dislike arrogant and presumptuous men and things. And yet we Americans are the most arrogant and presumptuous people in the world. It is most evident abroad and is no less offensive because it is unconscious. Your ignorant GI like your ignorant General assumes it must be right and better because it is American. The psychology of the Russians is much the same. I remember a piece Francois Mauriac wrote about "the great barbarians who have overrun Europe." Callender wrote a nasty sarcastic story about it, but Mauriac wasn't entirely wrong.

I do not look upon Hitler's totalitarianism as a European thing any more than I so regard Russian totalitarianism. Not European in that they are not part of European civilization. It is probably a mistake to make such geographical generalizations, but I like to think of totalitarianism as a kind of Oriental despotism, whereas European civilization to me means the rule of reason, of moderation, of things small and exquisite, of the independent free thinking individual, of parliamentarism, of intelligence, as it still struggles for life in France and England and a few other isolated spots on the globe.

I wonder why I am waxing so philosophical tonight. I think Markel's weekenders have driven me to philosophy! The next step is obviously drink.

Delbert Clark has apparently reached Germany but is lost somewhere between Bremerhaven and Berlin. I hoped to meet him in Berlin but can't do that and cover the Constabulary and Nuremberg at the same time.

I must sleep now so as to be up bright and early for the Constabulary. They believe in the old maxim "early to bed and early to rise," etc. I only hope it is making them wise as well as healthy and wealthy.

All my love now,
Dana

P.S. I had a grand letter from Grandma. Please tell her I will write soon. Also one from Dorothy.

Following the acquittals of Hjalmar Schacht, Hans Fritzsche and Franz von Papen, Dana wrote the following, published on Oct. 5:

SCHACHT, FRITZSCHE DEPART FROM JAIL

Join Wives in Nuremberg— Ex-Banker is Rearrested by German Police, Then Freed

By DANA ADAMS SCHMIDT
Special to THE NEW YORK TIMES
NUREMBERG, Germany, Saturday, Oct. 5—Dr. Hyalmar Schacht and Hans Fritzsche, two of the three men acquitted in the war crimes trial, left the court house prison and were driven in United States Army vehicles to rooms occupied by their wives here shortly after midnight, it was learned from eyewitnesses early this morning.

Franz von Papen, the third of the Nazis to be freed, remained in prison all night at his own request, apparently still hoping for permission to enter the British zone.

Half an hour after Schacht joined his wife, he was arrested by German police as he sat drinking a cup of tea, and taken to police headquarters here, and then returned to his rooms and released on orders of a United States Army captain, an eyewitness said. The German police then posted guards around the house. Fritzsche, meanwhile, was left unmolested.

The American captain, according to an eyewitness, told Nuremberg police during a long argument that they might be able to arrest Schacht tomorrow, but that for the present he could be considered only in protective custody.

The three had recalled their lawyers to the court house last night for conferences on what to do after United States headquarters in Frankfort on the Main announced that authorities in the French zone had refused entry to all three and that officials of the British zone had declined to admit Schacht and Fritzsche.

With the possible exception of von Papen, therefore, the alternatives for the three were narrowed to applying for entry to the Soviet zone, where representatives on the tribunal had dissented from their acquittal, or giving themselves up to German authorities in the United States zone.

If they chose the latter, United States headquarters announced, "the future liability of any of the men under German laws to the people of Germany for crimes within Germany must be determined by the German courts."

Ten-Year Terms Possible

This meant that the legal division of the Office of Military Government had decided that regardless of their acquittal on international charges and their involuntary presence in the United States zone, German denazification courts had the right to try them on strictly German charges.

If convicted by such a tribunal as Category 1 "major offenders"—one of the five categories under denazification law—they would be sentenced to up to ten years in labor camps.

United States headquarters said the three men would receive safe conduct to the borders of any zone to which they could gain admittance or, subject to the approval of Gen. Joseph T. McNarney, the United States commander, to any point they might select in the American zone. German police would be notified of their arrival and "would be required to provide adequate protection against possible mob violence."

Von Papen's lawyer, Dr. Edon Kubuschok, said no formal request for admission to the British zone had yet been made on behalf of his client. Indicating that this would be done, he expressed the hope that it would be granted on the ground that von Papen had been captured in the Ruhr, in the British zone, and could claim legal residence there.

Gen. Sir Brian Robertson, deputy commander of the British zone, stated in Berlin last night that none of the three acquitted men would be admitted to the British zone. This statement was made ambiguous, however, by his addition that they could, of course, return to their legal residences. Von Papen may be able to establish that his legal residence is in the Ruhr.

Defense counsel have filed appeals with the Allied Control Council in Berlin for William Frick, Alfred Rosenberg, Hans Frank, Julius Streicher, Rudolf Hess and for the SS [Elite Guard]. Appeals for most of the others were expected to have been made by the deadline at 3:30 P.M. today.

The lawyers for Frank and Streicher appealed on their own initiative "as a professional duty" after their clients said they did not want to do so, and the same will probably be made for Hermann Goering, Albert Speer, Ernst Kaltenbrunner and Col. Gen. Alfred Jodl.

Two appeals are being prepared for Joachim von Ribbentrop by his two lawyers, who were unable to agree. Dr. Hans Stanmer, counsel for Goering, said his appeal would make no mention of mercy but would raise legal objections to the Tribunal's judgment.

The appeal on behalf of the SS caused surprise, since the judgment involved no sentence but only a declaration that it was a criminal organization. It was understood that counsel argued that many parts of the SS were no worse than the Storm Troopers, whom the Tribunal declined to declare criminal.

TWO GERMAN ZONES WILL ACT ON NAZIS

Nuremberg Verdict Serves to Unify American and British Methods of Procedure

By DANA ADAMS SCHMIDT
Special to THE NEW YORK TIMES.
STUTTGART, Oct. 12—The International Military Tribunal's judgment of twenty-one top Nazis and seven Nazi organizations at Nuremberg has quickened Allied and German efforts to unify denazification procedures at least in the American and British zones and to clear the internment camps of persons who cannot be classified as "security" threats or war criminals.

German popular reaction has concentrated almost exclusively on the acquittal of Hyalmar Schacht, Franz von Papen and Hans Fritzsche, with Communists, Social Democrats, Christian Democrats and even erstwhile Nazis joining in cries of indignation with equal vehemence.

While the tribunal held that the parts these men played in the rise of the Nazi party were not crimes, in the sense that they were not aware of Hitler's criminally aggressive intentions, articulate German public opinion has put itself on record as holding that their parts were none the less crimes against the German people.

This unanimity of German opinion has overruled the possibility that the Russian judges' dissent from the acquittals might widen the rift between East and West as far as the German people are concerned. The Germans appear agreed that the Russians were right.

Organizations Held Criminal

Of the most far-reaching effect on the Germans, however, will be the tribunal's declaration on the criminality of the organizations. It ruled that the major parts of the political leadership corps, numbering some 600,000 persons, and the SS, Gestapo and Sicherheitsdienst, numbering several hundred thousands, were criminal, but declined to so declare the storm troopers, who numbered more than a million at the outbreak of war. And from the declaration of criminality it exempted members who were forced into membership, were unaware of their organization's criminal activities or who ceased to be members before war began.

The tribunal's recommendation made the American zone law the point of departure for interzonal unification of denazification procedures. With that aim a committee of British and American zone Germans had already been appointed at a meeting in Bremen on Oct. 5 to study the matter and another meeting will be held at Bad Homburg on Oct. 23. There is a standing invitation to Russian and French zone officials to join in the deliberations, but there has been no response.

The Denazification Minister in Wuerttemberg-Baden expressed the opinion last week that the American zone law would become acceptable to the British if categories 4 and 5, consisting of nominal Nazis or followers and exonerated persons, could be dropped from the denazification mill. German officials favor a change because it would liberate them from the fruitless "paper" war concerning small fry and permit the 407 denazification tribunals now operating in the zone to concentrate on categories 1 (major offenders), 2 (offenders or active militarists and profiteers) and 3 (minor offenders or probationers).

Effects of Verdicts

In the case of Bavaria a change would mean dropping one million cases which Anton Pfeiffer, Bavarian Denazification Minister, anticipated in a report to the Laenderrat would finally fall into Categories 4 and 5 under present methods. By contrast he estimated that by the time denazification books are closed there would be 20,000 in Category 1 and 40,000 in Categories 2 and 3, with penalties ranging from fines to ten years in labor camp and total confiscation of property.

Thus far very few have drawn the heavy penalties of Categories 1 and 2 because most such cases are among the seventy to eighty thousand persons locked up by the American Army in internment camps. Camps, however, are now being turned over to German authorities and statistics of major offenders should rise rapidly, as tribunals are set up in them.

Result in American Zone

Because American zone denazification is relatively so far advanced, the effect of the International Military Tribunal's judgment and recommendations here will be limited. Gen. Lucius D. Clay has stated that in their light American automatic arrest categories are now being reviewed. But this will affect only future arrests by American forces and a small number of prisoners, estimated at around 2,000, whom the American Army will retain as dangerous security suspects or for future war crimes' trials after the internment camps are turned over to Germans.

For deciding further detention and punishment or release of internees and penalties to be imposed on other Germans, denazification tribunals already have standards set up by the zone's denazification law. No steps to modify these because of the Nuremberg rulings have yet been deemed necessary, although it may be presumed that defense counsels will make use of the precedent of the

---

U. S. Constabulary in Germany Riddled By High Turnover Rate, General Asserts

By DANA ADAMS SCHMIDT
Special to THE YORK NEW TIMES.

BAMBERG, Germany, Oct. 13— Maj. Gen. Ernest N. Harmon, commander of the United States zone constabulary, said today that redeployment would deprive him of 12,000 of his 33,000 men by the end of January. Many are to go home under the new eighteen-month limit of service.

"I am now training my second constabulary since we got started last May, and if the turnover continues at this rate, I will be starting on my third next June," he declared in an interview.

The force has had a 97.9 per cent turnover of officers and a 76.27 per cent turnover of enlisted men.

"Originally," General Harmon explained, "we set high physical and mental standards because we wanted to make the constabulary an elite organization. But except for excluding semi-literates, we have been obliged to accept about everyone we can get."

While the hard-hitting, impulsive general has nonetheless forged a highly disciplined and enthusiastic force that has won the respect of other troops, Germans and displaced persons, members of his staff asked how the constabulary could be expected to live up to its occupation mission if the United States could not supply more stable manpower.

Under such conditions, they complained, any ordinary business enterprise would go broke. "We no sooner have a man trained than he goes home," one officer said.

In September alone the constabulary lost 4,400 men, who had to be replaced by men untrained in its combination of police and military duties.

Seventy per cent of the force is composed of Regular Army men but one quarter of these are signed up for only one year. "One-year enlistments," a staff officer commented, "are a snare and a delusion."

Nuremberg tribunal's opinion that it was not possible before 1937 and in some cases not until the outbreak of the war to discern the aggressive and criminal plans of Hitler and the inner circle of Nazis.

Change in British Zone

In the British zone and possibly in others the consequences of international tribunals are expected to be more considerable.

The British have about the same number of internees in camps as the American zone but have set up no procedure for handling them or turning denazification generally over to the Germans. The British themselves, therefore, will have to review lists of internees to bring them in line with the Nuremberg rulings. Some releases are to be expected. At the same time they will probably evolve a denazification law that jibes both with the one in the American zone and with Nuremberg.

Trials of Schacht, Fritzsche and perhaps von Papen under the denazification law may in part serve the purpose which German officials of the American and British zones had in mind when they passed a resolution in Stuttgart last March 26 asking that all twenty-one Nuremberg defendants be put before German courts after the international trial. "Thereby," they declared, "one would prevent the creation of a legend that the war criminals were found guilty by an international court but not by the German people."

Following is the story Dana wrote about the Constabulary, which he mentioned that he had been asked to cover in his last letter:

U.S. CONSTABULARY IN GERMANY RIDDLED BY HIGH TURNOVER RATE, GENERAL ASSERTS

By DANA ADAMS SCHMIDT
Special to THE NEW YORK TIMES.
BAMBERG, Germany, Oct. 13—Maj. Gen. Ernest N. Harmon, commander of the United States zone constabulary, said today that redeployment would deprive him of 12,000 of his 33,000 men by the end of January. Many are to go home under the new eighteen-month limit of service.

"I am now training my second constabulary since we got started last May, and if the turnover continues at this rate, I will be starting on my third next June," he declared in an interview.

The force has had a 97.9 per cent turnover of officers and a 76.27 per cent turnover of enlisted men.

"Originally," General Harmon explained, "we set high physical and mental standards because we wanted to make the constabulary an elite organization. But except for excluding semi-literates, we have been obliged to accept about everyone we can get."

While the hard-hitting, impulsive general has nonetheless forged a highly disciplined and enthusiastic force that has won the respect of other troops, Germans and displaced persons, members of his staff asked how the constabulary could be expected to live up to its occupation mission if the United States could not supply more stable manpower.

Under such conditions, they complained, any ordinary business enterprise would go broke. "We no sooner have a man trained than he goes home," one officer said.

In September alone the constabulary lost 4,400 men, who had to be replaced by men untrained in its combination of police and military duties.

Seventy per cent of the force is composed of Regular Army men but one quarter of these are signed up for only one year. "One-year enlistments," a staff officer commented, "are a snare and a delusion."

With the Constabulary story finished, Dana returned to the grimness of Nuremberg and the implementing of the verdicts of the International

---

ARMY INVESTIGATES SUICIDE OF GOERING AS MYSTERY GROWS

No Arrests Yet Made or Due —Source of Poison, Effect of Act on Germans Puzzling

PRISON WORKERS SUSPECT

His Daily Contacts With Many of Native Staff Disclosed— Populace Chuckles at Trick

By DANA ADAMS SCHMIDT
Special to THE NEW YORK TIMES.

NUREMBERG, Germany, Oct. 16—How did Hermann Goering get the phial of potassium cyanide with which he committed suicide last night, and what effect would his thwarting of executioners representing the United States, Russia, Britain and France have on the German people? These were questions that sorely puzzled Allied officials here today.

A board of three United States officers headed by a "disinterested" Third Army officer was combing through the evidence and hoped to come to some conclusions within two days, according to Maj. Frederick Teich of the Nuremberg prison's internal security office.

He professed ignorance of the contents or what had become of three notes found in Goering's cell. It was reported one letter was addressed to Col. Burton C. Andrus, the prison security officer. Colonel Andrus said he had not seen it.

Major Teich said Goering's wife seemed "in the clear" since it was "impossible" to pass anything through the window in the visiting room through which she last saw her husband a week ago Monday. No steps had been taken against Goering's elderly lawyer, Dr. Otto Vahmer, who departed for Kiel last Friday, Major Teich said, and no arrests had been made or contemplated up to this evening.

No Action Against Guard

The major knew of no plans for any proceedings against the guard under whose eyes Goering swallowed the contents of a two-inch by half-inch glass phial, or against Colonel Andrus.

Among the numerous subjects of speculation, Major Teich mentioned as the most likely the "dozen or so" German prison workers who were in daily contact with the convicted men. They included a doctor, dentist, barber, manicurist, pedicurist, waiter and the men who

Continued on Page 2, Column 5

Tribunal. The first and most unexpected event was Goering's suicide on the night of October 15, an event that seemed impossible considering the security of the prison. Following is the first of Dana's reports on this development:

**ARMY INVESTIGATES
SUICIDE OF GOERING
AS MYSTERY GROWS**

**No Arrests Yet Made or Due
—Source of Poison, Effect of
Act on Germans Puzzling**

PRISON WORKERS SUSPECT

**His Daily Contacts With Many
of Native Staff Disclosed—
Populace Chuckles at Trick**

By DANA ADAMS SCHMIDT
Special to THE NEW YORK TIMES.
NUREMBERG, Germany, Oct. 16—How did Hermann Goering get the phial of potassium cyanide with which he committed suicide last night, and what effect would his thwarting of executioners representing the United States, Russia, Britain and France have on the German people? These were questions that sorely puzzled Allied officials here today.

A board of three United States officers headed by a "disinterested" Third Army officer was combing through the evidence and hoped to come to some conclusions within two days, according to Maj. Frederick Teich of the Nuremberg prison's internal security office.

He professed ignorance of the contents or what had become of three notes found in Goering's cell. It was reported one letter was addressed to Col. Burton C. Andrus, the prison security officer. Colonel Andrus said he had not seen it.

Major Teich said Goering's wife seemed "in the clear" since it was "impossible" to pass anything through the window in the visiting room through which she last saw her husband a week ago Monday. No steps had been taken against Goering's elderly lawyer, Dr. Otto Vahmer, who departed for Kiel last Friday, Major Teich said and no arrests had been made or contemplated up to this evening.

No Action Against Guard

The major knew of no plans for any proceedings against the guard under whose eyes Goering swallowed the contents of a two-inch by half-inch glass vial, or against Colonel Andrus.

Among the numerous subjects of speculation, Major Teich mentioned as the most likely the "dozen or so" German prison workers who were in daily contact with the convicted men. They included a doctor, dentist, barber, manicurist, pedicurist, waiter, and the men who handed around the brooms and mops with which the prisoners cleaned out their cells.

Observers also considered the possibilities that an American might be implicated, that the vial might have been secreted in Goering's long Bavarian pipe or smuggled in in the pancakes he ate at his last meal.

Major Teich gave as his personal opinion that Goering had had the vial in his possession for a long time, perhaps ever since he had been in custody. The United States officer pointed out that a similar vial had been taken from Goering at Mondorf prison in Luxembourg, where he first was held, and thought he might have received this one in the period before security arrangements were completed at Nuremberg last December by the setting up of the room with a glass partition to separate the prisoners from visitors.

Concealment a Puzzle

How Goering might have secreted the vial on his body in spite of medical examinations was anybody's guess. His refusal to take exercise ever since the day of the sentences might have been a factor, Major Teich admitted, while the inspection of his cell on the last day was "probably perfunctory."

Goering's boast to Grand Admiral Erich Raeder's lawyer, Dr. Walter Siemers, near the beginning of the trial that "they will never hang me" was recalled significantly today.

First soundings of German public opinion showed that Goering's judgment in choosing such a psychological moment for suicide, two and a half hours before his hanging was to have taken place, was having the effect he might well have desired. All other aspects of the trial and executions were completely overshadowed as thousands of Germans chuckled over the trick he had played on the occupying powers, and once more thought of him as a hero.

Weapon in Germans' Hand

Goering's dramatic gesture in death appeared to have helped these Germans to forget his crimes, the millions of deaths in the concentration camps and in the war caused by the Nazi regime, and the lessons of the ten-month trial. The event that was to have been a weapon in the hands of democracy suddenly became one in the hands of unrepentant German nationalism.

The democratically inclined Germans were as upset by the effects of the suicide as were the Allies, and hoped the public's reaction would change as the Germans gained more perspective of the event.

Since German newspapers in the United States zone appear only twice weekly, many Germans still were confused as to what happened, and rumors were rife. Some individuals interviewed in the Nuremberg streets suspected some kind of fake and refused to believe Goering or the others were dead. Why, they asked, was no German reporter admitted to the executions? Few had heard that Dr. Wilhelm Hoegner, Minister-President of Bavaria, and Dr. Jacob Leisner, prosecutor general of Nuremberg, had attended the hangings.

GUILT IS PUNISHED

No. 2 Nazi a Suicide Two Hours Before the Execution Time

OTHERS GO GRIMLY

Shout Praise of Their Country as They Mount Scaffold

By DANA ADAMS SCHMIDT
Special to THE NEW YORK TIMES.
NUREMBERG, Germany, Wednesday, Oct. 16— Ten Nazi war criminals were hanged in the prison here early today, but the eleventh, Hermann Wilhelm Goering, committed suicide by swallowing poison in his cell some two hours before he was to have gone to the gallows.

Goering, former No. 2 Nazi and chief of the Luftwaffe, took cyanide of potassium, which he somehow had succeeded in secreting, Col. Burton C. Andrus, commandant of the prison security detail, announced.

A guard saw Goering twitching on his cot at 10:45 o'clock last night and summoned aid, but Adolf Hitler's erstwhile heir-apparent could not be revived.

Colonel Adrus said glass from a capsule containing the poison was found in Goering's mouth.

Intervention Too Late

The guard did not see Goering put his hand under his blanket, and intervened the instant he saw the prisoner twitch, but it was too late.

[An envelope containing penciled notes and a small brass cartridge case that apparently had contained the poison vial were found on Goering's body, press services reported.]

Except for Goering, the executions then took place in the order of the indictment and in which the condemned men had sat in the prisoners' dock during the ten-month trial before the International Military Tribunal.

The Nazis walked to the gallows in this order:

Joachim von Ribbentrop, former Foreign Minister; Field Marshal Gen. Wilhelm Keitel, chief of the German High Command; Ernst Kaltenbrunner, head of the Gestapo; Alfred Rosenberg, Minister for Occupied Territories; Hans Frank, who led in the killing of thousands of Poles; Wilhelm Frick, former Minister of the Interior; Julius Streicher, leader of Nazi anti-Semitism; Fritz Sauckel, director of forced labor; Col. Gen. Alfred Jodl, head of the German General Staff, and Arthur Seyss-Inquart, who sold out Austria.

The condemned men were notified on two occasions of the date of the executions, authoritative sources said, but the ten who were hanged did not know the time until an hour before they began.

Repeated shouts as of the conclusion of frenzied speeches, followed by a thudding like the springing of a heavy trap door, were heard from a building at the rear of the prison courtyard between 2 and 3:15 A.M., according to the German News Agency.

The executions were the first-ever ordered by an international tribunal and established the history-making precedent that waging aggressive warfare was "the supreme crime," punishable by death.

The eleven were sentenced by the International Military Tribunal on Oct. 1, after a trial that lasted ten months. The missing Martin Bormann, Hitler's assistant, was tried in absentia and also sentenced to be hanged.

ELIZABETH SCHMIDT CRAHAN

Hermann Goering, Hitler's close confidant, destined to be his successor, was sentenced to be hanged on October 15. The attendants assigned to bring him to the court were shocked to find him dead in his bed. It was found that he had taken poison. How he had obtained the poison, nobody knew. The condemned men were closely guarded day and night. Goering is said to have left a note saying that he had the poison since he was imprisoned, but that was hard to believe since he was examined frequently in the nude by doctors, and his cell was regularly searched. Some thought that he had the poison hidden under a crown on one of his teeth; others that since he had become quite fat, he had secreted it in a fold of his skin. But none of these theories seemed viable. Sixty years passed, and the mystery was not solved.

One day in 2005, a man named Herbert Lee Stivers, a retired sheet metal worker in Hesperia near Los Angeles, went to the Los Angeles Times and claimed that he was the man who had given Goering the drug. He had been one of the guards of the men who were sentenced to be executed or hung, and he often chatted with Goering about sports and flying. (Goering was head of the Luftwaffe and knew Lindberg.) One day, the guard met a pretty girl outside the prison, and he chatted and flirted with her. She was impressed when he told her he was an honor guard and knew and talked with the prisoners. To prove it, he gave her the autograph of one of the men. One day, he gave her Goering's autograph. She was quite impressed and asked him if he could take a message to Goering. Stivers was glad to do this favor, and several messages went back and forth, secreted in the barrel of an old-fashioned fountain pen.

The girl, who called herself Mona, introduced him to two men who were anxious to meet Stivers. They, too, had messages for Goering. One day, they told Mona that Goering was quite ill but couldn't get the medicine in prison that he needed. She put a vial of the medicine in the fountain pen they used and told Stivers to tell Goering that if it helped, she could get more.

When Stivers heard that Goering had been found dead, he realized what he had done, but he was afraid to tell the authorities for fear of being prosecuted. He did tell his daughter about it much later. One day, she persuaded her father to tell his story for history's sake. It is, perhaps, a hard story to believe, but it makes more sense than other solutions that had been advanced.

Meanwhile, the eleven Nazi war criminals were cremated. Dana wrote:

**11 NAZIS CREMATED,
ASHES 'DISPERSED'**

**Allies Reveal Secret Action to
Forestall the enshrining of
War Criminals' Bodies**

GOERING INQUIRY GOES ON

**No Arrests made—His Lawyer
Under Surveillance—Earlier
Suicide Move Reported**

By DANA ADAMS SCHMIDT
Special to THE NEW YORK TIMES.
NUREMBERG, Germany, Oct. 17—The bodies of Hermann Goering and the ten Nazi war criminals who were executed yesterday morning "have been cremated and the ashes dispersed secretly," the four-power commission representing the Allied Control Council here announced this evening.

Col. Burton C. Andrus, the Nuremberg prison security officer, who read the announcement, said he was unable to elaborate on the phrase "dispersed secretly," although he met in his office this afternoon with the commission and other officers believed to be the anonymous board of three Americans investigating Goering's suicide.

The intention of the secret cremation and dispersal of ashes, it was understood, was to destroy absolutely any possibility that the location of the Nazi leaders' remains ever could become a shrine for some future brand of Nazis.

No Special Investigators

The investigating board's efforts, meanwhile, resulted in no arrests or incriminations. No special investigators appeared to aid the inquiry. Dr.

Otto Stahmer, Goering's lawyer, was reported to be under surveillance by the British at Kiel, but as far as was known neither he nor Frau Emmy Goering had been officially questioned.

A prison officer disclosed tonight that Goering apparently made an attempt to obtain a suicide weapon three months ago when he extracted a piece of celluloid from his earphones in the court room. When Goering was unable to hear the proceedings, technicians found a piece missing from the earphone, and suspicious prison guards found it in his possession. If this information is exact, it would explode the theory that Goering had the potassium cyanide phial for a long while, or before the time he tried to obtain the instrument with which he could have cut his veins.

It also was learned that Field Marshal Gen. Wilhelm Keitel on one occasion was found in possession of a piece of metal that could have served to cut his veins. A guard saw him putting the piece back into his wallet, from which it had slipped.

Nude Examinations Cited

Colonel Andrus reiterated that it was the opinion of most persons connected with the prison that the phial had been in Goering's possession for a long time, although he explained that the prisoners were subjected to nude examinations at least once a week and that their clothes and cells were searched regularly. Each prisoner, he said, had at least two suits, a good one to wear in court and one or more for cell wear. The clothes were examined each time the prisoners changed.

The men were taken to bathe twice a week in summer and once a week in winter, and on these occasions were examined by a doctor. Recently, Tuesdays had been bath days, but Colonel Andrus could not say whether Goering had a bath the day of his suicide.

The clothes of prison workers, who wore prisoner of war uniforms, also were inspected regularly, he said. They were captives who received special pay for volunteering their services and thereby prolonging their confinement, and never were allowed outside the jail.

The brass cartridge that contained Goering's phial of potassium cyanide was shown to correspondents by Maj. Frederick Teich of the prison security force, who removed it from a safe in his office. Also in the safe were bottles of drugs that Goering formerly took, and other personal effects of the war criminals.

Meanwhile, Franz von Papen spent his sixteenth "free" day in prison still waiting for a reply to his request for admission to the British zone.

Dana had some further explanation concerning Goering's death:

GOERING NOTE SAID TO EXPLAIN SUICIDE

Details of How He Got Poison Reported in One of 3 Letters — Oil Stains on Gallows Site

By DANA ADAMS SCHMIDT
Special to THE NEW YORK TIMES.
NUREMBERG, Germany, Oct. 18—Hermann Goering explained, in one of the three notes he left in an envelope, how he obtained the phial of potassium cyanide with which he committed suicide, according to a report circulating among officials in the Nuremberg court house today.

The explanation was contained in the note addressed to Col. Burton C. Andrus, the prison security officer, the report said. [The letter did not incriminate any individual and even went out of the way to exonerate various persons, said an authoritative informant quoted by The Associated Press.]

GOERING NOTE SAID TO EXPLAIN SUICIDE

Details of How He Got Poison Reported in One of 3 Letters —Oil Stains on Gallows Site

By DANA ADAMS SCHMIDT
Special to THE NEW YORK TIMES.

NUREMBERG, Germany, Oct. 18—Hermann Goering explained, in one of the three notes he left in an envelope, how he obtained the phial of potassium cyanide with which he committed suicide, according to a report circulating among officials in the Nuremberg court house today.

The explanation was contained in the note addressed to Col. Burton C. Andrus, the prison security officer, the report said. [The letter did not incriminate any individual and even went out of the way to exonerate various persons, said an authoritative informant quoted by The Associated Press.]

Goering's letter may explain why there have been no arrests, no sign that suspects are being interrogated and why no special investigators have been called in to assist the anonymous board of inquiry of three United States officers.

The two other letters, it was reported, were addressed to the German people and to Goering's wife.

The Scene Is Visited

Correspondents touring the scene of the execution this morning noted that indelible stains from the oil that dripped from the hinges of the gallows onto the floor of the prison gymnasium marked the spot where the ten chiefs of the Nazi regime were hanged eighty hours earlier.

The sharp stench of lysol used in ineffectual scrubbing hung in the air of the dim, high-vaulted hall now bare except for the exercising racks before which the scaffolds were erected, the basketball hoops at either end and two iron stoves in the corners.

Colonel Andrus and Capt. Robert Starnes, a prison officer, pointed out to correspondents the tree in the courtyard opposite the gymnasium where a mysterious flat kite with undecipherable childish scribblings landed two days before the executions.

Last August, while the prisoners were exercising in a larger courtyard, they recalled, a German paratrooper's knife was thrown from an adjoining roof where 800 SS men were making repairs. After that, guards patrolling the prison walls ordered the SS men back during the exercise periods and once fired a volley into a window casing to enforce the order. Whether the knife was intended to arm or injure the prisoners never was discovered.

The block of cells in C wing of the prison where Wilhelm Frick, Hans Frank, Dr. Alfred Rosenberg, Julius Streicher, Arthur Seyss-Inquart, Joachim von Ribbentrop, Ernst Kaltenbrunner, Col. Gen. Alfred Jodl, Field Marshal Gen. Wilhelm Keitel and Fritz Sauckel spent their last days now were occupied by the seven who escaped with prison sentences.

In another unoccupied cell, Captain Starnes showed how the guards could follow the movements of the prisoners through the porthole at all times. After the suicide of Robert Ley nearly a year ago, the guards were increased from one to every four cells to one for each prisoner. Now they have been reduced again to one for all seven remaining prisoners.

Goering's letter may explain why there have been no arrests, no sign that suspects are being interrogated and why no special investigators have been called in to assist the anonymous board of inquiry of three United States officers.

The two other letters, it was reported, were addressed to the German people and to Goering's wife.

The Scene is Visited

Correspondents touring the scene of the execution this morning noted that indelible stains from the oil that dripped from the hinges of the gallows on to the floor of the prison gymnasium marked the spot where the ten chiefs of the Nazi regime were hanged eighty hours earlier.

The sharp stench of lysol used in ineffectual scrubbing hung in the air of the dim, high-vaulted hall now bare except for the exercising racks before which the scaffolds were erected, the basketball hoops at either end and two iron stoves in the corners.

Colonel Andrus and Capt. Robert Starnes, a prison officer, pointed out to correspondents the tree in the courtyard opposite the gymnasium where a mysterious flat kite with undecipherable childish scribblings landed two days before the executions.

Last August, while the prisoners were exercising in a larger courtyard, they recalled, a German paratrooper's knife was thrown from an adjoining roof where 800 SS men were making repairs. After that, guards patrolling the prison walls ordered the SS men back during the exercise periods and once fired a volley into a window casing to enforce the order. Whether the knife was intended to arm or injure the prisoners never was discovered.

The block of cells in C wing of the prison where Wilhelm Frick, Hans Frank, Dr. Alfred Rosenberg, Julius Streicher, Arthur Seyss-Inquart, Joachim von Ribbentrop, Ernst Kaltenbrunner, Col. Gen. Alfred Jodl, Field Marshal Gen. Wilhelm Keitel and Fritz Sauckel spent their last days now were occupied by the seven who escaped with prison sentences.

In another unoccupied cell, Captain Starnes showed how the guards could follow the movements of the prisoners through the porthole at all times. After the suicide of Robert Ley nearly a year ago, the guards were increased from one to every four cells to one for each prisoner. Now they have been reduced again to one for all seven remaining prisoners.

With the trials finished, the American and British officials were able to concentrate on the government of their two zones and other zones. On October 19, Dana wrote from Nuremberg:

**TWO-ZONE AGENCIES
BEGUN IN GERMANY**

**Americans and British Speed
Up Their Plan to Make Reich
Self-Supporting Soon**

**By DANA ADAMS SCHMIDT
Special to THE NEW YORK TIMES.**
NUREMBERG, Oct. 19—The pace of the economic unification of the American and British zones was forced to a maximum this week and five bi-zonal German agencies began to take shape. At a series of meetings, Jan. 1 was set as the date when they should assume responsibility, although most officials did not believe they could be very effective before March or that beneficial economic effects would be felt before next June.

TWO-ZONE AGENCIES BEGUN IN GERMANY

Americans and British Speed Up Their Plan to Make Reich Self-Supporting Soon

By DANA ADAMS SCHMIDT
Special to THE NEW YORK TIMES.

NUREMBERG, Oct. 19—The pace of the economic unification of the American and British zones was forced to a maximum this week and five bi-zonal German agencies began to take shape. At a series of meetings, Jan. 1 was set as the date when they should assume responsibility, although most officials did not believe they could be very effective before March or that beneficial economic effects would be felt before next June.

Always harking back to their demand for a parliamentary or political super-coordinating body that would stand above the agencies, some officials complained that they were being pushed too fast, and that lack of over-all coordination on the German side might frustrate the entire project.

British Zone Represented

While the British zone was represented on agencies by British Military Government appointees, the Governments of Bavaria, Wuerttemberg-Baden and Greater Hesse sent their Ministers responsible in various fields of the agencies—general economics, food and agriculture, finance, transport, and post, telegraph and telephone. It quickly became evident that a major cause of delay would be the necessity for the British zone Germans to refer back to their British military chiefs, whereas American zone Germans could make decisions on the spot.

By all odds, the most important was the meeting of the General Economic Agency at Minden in the British zone at which General Draper set forth as the "simple but difficult basic problem" the creation of a "self-respecting, self-supporting" Germany, able to pay for its food imports in spite of the loss of rich agricultural territory.

"Exports Buy Food"

Recommending "Exports Buy Food" as the agency's slogan, he asked it to work out a three-to-five-year import-export program.

Positive assistance toward solution of this problem came a few days later with the announcement by the Reconstruction Finance Corporation Director, George E. Allen, that an agreement had been reached for expanding production in the American zone in order to reduce the cost of occupation to the American taxpayer.

In more immediate terms the Germans on the agency under the chairmanship of Rudolf Mueller, Greater Hesse Minister of Economics, saw their most urgent task in a "needles-and-pins program"—providing Germans with a minimum of consumer goods without which they could not produce efficiently.

The most active agency was transport at Bielefeld in the British zone. It decided on elimination as far as transport is concerned of the Bremen enclave and of the corridor between Bremen and the American zone, so that shipments may in future use any route desired.

The most hopeful sign of all, however, for unification, not only of American and British but of all zones, was the Allied Control Council's directive extending the principles of the American zone's denazification law to all Germany. In the light of this, it was thought that Russian and French zone Germans might be able to accept the invitation to the interzonal conference on denazification due at Bad Homburg next Wednesday.

In response to his mother's comment, Dana wrote on October 21, 1946:

Yes, of course it would be very nice if I were manager for Germany, but I do not really covet the job, unless it could be made merely titular and I had somebody else to do the managing, administration and running other people's lives is not my field. I think I should stick close to the writing line. I like to think of it as the "artist's" province as opposed to that of the practical businessman.

It looks as though I would continue pretty much what I have been doing.

Ed Murrow, who has also arrived is going up to the British zone and will also look in on the French zone, I told Clark I had been planning a trip to the French zone about this time and he told me to go ahead as Murrow won't be in the groove for a while. A third man, Raymond, is due shortly with his wife. I suspect that he will stay in Berlin and help Murrow as Kathleen is due to home leave in November. It is quite possible that she will not return but I am not sure.

Ray and Tanya Daniel are due to set up in London very shortly as European heads of the Sunday department. The plan is that suggestions and requests for Sunday pieces will be routed through Ray, and also the finished copy. I'm not too keen on that …and I'm a little dubious about how I could file directly to him in London. All our communications are with New York. However that will work itself out. It is inevitable that Clark should write a high percentage of weekenders from now on. My opportunities will be fewer, but I should be able to handle them better.

Clark was Public Relations officer for General Lee in Italy and took over the Stars and Stripes there after a big row about "freedom of speech" in the letters to the editor column. He was later offered a job as assistant to the Chief of Military Government public relations here but preferred to return to the Times. He had been running the Washington bureau administratively for eleven years before the war and was anxious to return to writing. Before that he worked for the UP for a year and a half. He didn't like it, for much the same reasons that I didn't like it, at the end at least.

One point Clark made was that with a large staff it will be possible for each correspondent to do more digging, more following up of the significant stories. He doesn't want me to compete with the agencies in covering spot developments.

In other words, whereas hitherto I felt bound to try to turn out something every day if I possibly could, now, if I want to spend three days over a story, I will feel at liberty to do so.

At the moment I am the most mobile part of the staff, since one of the two little German cars we have in Berlin has broken down and we will probably lose the other because it is a "liberated" or illegally acquired vehicle. A lot of correspondents have cars they picked up during the campaign much as I picked up my Matford.

Driving up here was quite an adventure. It was the first time I'd done so. It started with a ringing clang like a bell. I stopped and discovered gasoline flowing from a hole in my tank. So I jumped back in and headed on down the road hoping I'd find a garage or a filling station. Finally I reached an UNRRA *garage and got a pan to catch the escaping gasoline . . . . what there was left of it. The mechanic informed me that a stone had smashed a small hole in the tank and stopped it up with a piece of wood.. The wood swells and makes quite a satisfactory plug.*

Next step was to find more gas and try to reach Helmstedt before six p.m. when they close the border. Unfortunately, I ran out of gas before I could find a "petrol point" as the British call them. It was getting dark. I flagged down a Diesel truck, but that didn't help. There isn't much traffic at night. At last an American came along and volunteered to push me the rest of the way. We were only four miles from Helmstedt. He pushed about ten yards and then his car broke down. The electrical system went out completely and he couldn't get any reaction from his starter or lights.

We bemoaned our fate for a while until his wife suggested we transfer some gas from his car to mine, so I could tow him. Having no container we had to empty a wine bottle. My friend found a drainage plug on his tank and drained gas into the bottle, also up his arm and down his neck.

So I towed them into Helmstedt. It was too late to get across the border. All out arguments were in vain. It seems that there actually is some danger about driving through the Russian zone at night. There have been holdups and trouble with drunken Russian soldiers. Only full Colonels and above are allowed through at night "on their own responsibility."

We spent the night quite pleasantly at the transient billets. We were the only guests and were well enough looked after. Unfortunately just as we were turning in somebody pointed out that my car had a flat tire. My jack wouldn't work but we finally got one from the British and I put my jeep tires and wheels on, or rather, about six other people did.

To top matters off this morning the American guards at the border would not recognize my riders. I was carrying one of the new cards which allow you to travel anywhere and mine was the first one they'd seen. The private called the Sergeant and the Sergeant called the Captain and the Captain called Berlin. Berlin said to let me through.

Since I wasn't really in a tearing hurry, the whole experience was quite amusing and I met a very charming and useful couple to boot. The man I towed turned out to be a Mr. Martin, head of the decartelization branch in Military Government—the man who is supposed to take apart IG Farben and the like. He and his wife asked me to dinner on Wednesday.

You ask in what issue Magazine Digest *printed my article on Youth. I don't know whether they've published it or intend to, but they've paid me. I just got a check for $250.00 and am enclosing it in this letter. That's pretty nice, I'd say. I guess it was worth the trouble. More than Market pays, anyway. I got that Constabulary Magaziner off to him last week.*

I am so glad you are feeling fine after a month of Steinie's absence. Stay that way.

I forgot to mention that I brought up my desire for a little holiday in Paris and Clark quite agreed that I was entitled to it and should take it as soon as the new staff was functioning.

All my love to you all,
DANA
P.S. The lights have just gone out. Just like Paris last year. HO Hum. I thought I was through with all that. Yours by candlelight.

Dana continued in his next published article written in Berlin with discussion of post-war plans and recommendations in an article concerning the German banking system published on Oct. 22:

GERMAN BANK UNIT
BLOCKED BY SOVIET

Central Finance Agency,
Backed by France as Well as
U.S., Britain, Off Agenda

By DANA ADAMS SCHMIDT
Special to THE NEW YORK TIMES.
BERLIN, Oct. 22—A proposal, backed by the United States, for decentralization of the five largest German banks and the simultaneous creation

of an Allied banking board and a German central banking commission has been dropped from the agenda of the Allied Control Council, it was announced today. Russia had declined to support the plan.

The French delegate, Lieut. Gen. Joseph-Pierre Koenig, departed from precedent by agreeing to the proposal to form a central German financial agency, placing the onus of preventing fulfillment of the Potsdam agreement on central German agencies on the Russians.

The proposal, according to Theodore Ball, deputy director of the finance division, was designed to break up "the tremendous concentration of economic power over banking and business" exercised by the principal banks by decentralizing them to the Land [State] level. Each bank would be allowed to function only within the confines of its Land such as Bavaria, Hanover or Thuringia, while the central German agency, supervised by an Allied banking board, performed functions of coordination.

Banks Subject to Plan

The banks whose central boards would have been liquidated under the plan are the Kommertz und Privatbank, the Dresdner Bank Reichskreditgesellschaft, the Berliner Handelsgesellschaft and the Darmstaedter Nationalbank.

The Soviet delegate, Col. Gen. P. A. Kurochkin, contended, according to a joint communiqué, that "the desire of the other delegations to tie the question of eliminating excessive concentrations of economic power in banking with the creation of central banking machinery was an attempt to delay a decision on German monopolies, thus preserving them."

He proposed that the problem of central banking machinery be decided in conjunction with the general finance problems of Germany.

It was understood to be the Russian view that currency reform as part of the general finance problems of Germany should be linked to the creation of central banking machinery whereas American experts held that currency reform could be handled independently.

Notes Early Soviet Action

General Kurochkin noted that banking monopolies in the Soviet occupational zone were liquidated in May, 1945. He suggested that if similar measures had been taken in the other zones the reconstruction of peaceful industry would have been speeded. Except for limited withdrawals by owners of small accounts, banks in the Russian zone have been closed since that date.

Gen. Joseph T. McNarney replied for the United States that he could not agree with the Russian since it might be an indefinite time before quadripartite agreement was reached on the general financial structure of Germany.

The British delegate, Sir Brian Robertson, declared that German economy was now "in a state of paralysis" and that if it were to recover to a reasonable level there must be some adequate financial provisions.

CHARTER RATIFIED BY GERMAN STATE

Wuerttemburg-Baden First in American Zone to Adopt Liberal Constitution

BY DANA ADAMS SCHMIDT
Special to THE NEW YORK TIMES.
BERLIN, Oct. 24—The first completed state constitution in the American zone's three Laender was passed by the Constitutional Assembly of Wuerttemburg-Baden today, 88 to 1.

It had been approved by Lieut. Gen. Lucius D. Clay, deputy military governor, subject to certain reservations and minor modifications. The Bavarian and Greater Hesse Constitutional Assemblies will vote on their approved constitutions next Saturday and Tuesday. Popular referenda on the new documents and elections of legislative assemblies or Landtage will be held in Wuerttemburg-Baden on Nov. 24, in Bavaria on Dec. 1, and in Greater Hesse on Dec. 8.

Henry Parkman, chief of the civil administration, declared that a new era was opening in which the governments of the three Laender became subject only to basic occupation policies. "The Laender have set up the machinery of democracy," he said. "It remains to be seen whether they can use it in a democratic manner."

Clay Cites Limited Approval

A letter from General Clay read to the Assembly pointed out that the military government's approval was "subject to international agreements to which the United States Government is a party, to quadripartite legislation and to the powers that the military government must reserve in order to effectuate the basic policies of the occupation."

The articles of the Constitution, furthermore, permitted laws deviating from the Constitution until Jan. 1, 1949, while the denazification law is being applied; delegated transitory powers in foreign relations and economics to inter-zonal agencies and said that its provisions might be superseded by those of a future German Constitution.

The document called for a Landtag of 100 members elected for four years, who in turn will elect a Premier for four years. The Landtag also elects a Supreme Court of nine, four from nominees submitted by the Judiciary and five others. The legislative, executive and judicial branches are specifically separated. Judges are appointed for life. The Landtag may force the Premier and his government to resign by a vote of no-confidence while it itself may be dissolved by a plebiscite before its term is up.

In accordance with General Clay's request, a detailed Bill of Rights contains the same principles as those in the Constitutions of Bavaria and Greater Hesse. These include freedom of speech, assembly, the press and religion, the right of access to information and the right of judicial protection and equality before the law. "In case of imminent danger to the existence of the state," however, the Government may suspend the basic rights for one week and obtain extensions of the suspension for one month at a time by a vote of the Landtag.

Far-reaching social provisions guarantee just pay, sufficient leisure and vacations and state assistance for "the blamelessly needy." Labor's representatives receive a share in the administration and development of business enterprises. The right of employers and labor unions to organize and of unions to strike is guaranteed.

Public bodies are to regulate economic matters and "if economic policy can be better attained without the private ownership of productive resources or if the exercise of property rights conflicts with the common interests, appropriate enterprises and parts of the economy shall be transferred to public property by law."

The traditional rights of the Catholic Church in particular are preserved in that religious associations hitherto recognized as public corporations may levy taxes and the property of such associations is guaranteed. Permanent obligations of the state to make recurring payments in money or kind to churches are recognized.

GERMAN RESISTANCE THREAT HAS FAILED TO MATERIALIZE

Minor Acts of Violence Have Been Met With And They Are Expected to Continue

BY DANA ADAMS SCHMIDT
Special to THE NEW YORK TIMES.
BERLIN, Oct. 26—One of the outstanding facts of the occupation of Germany to date has been the absence of any resistance comparable to the French or Yugoslav resistance to the German occupation or even to the German resistance after World War I.

After World War I there was fighting in German provincial capitals. There were the Freikorps and the Fehme murders, the assassinations of Erzberger, Rathenau, Liebknecht and Eisner. Schlageter was hanged by the French for resistance in the Rhineland and became one of the original heroes of the Nazi movement in Germany.

After this war matters are very different. The German collapse was complete. The old regime became totally bankrupt. German life was fragmentized as regards property, business, family, politics and in every physical and moral respect. A relative security for the occupying forces has resulted from these conditions.

Werewolves Disappeared

The "Werewolf" movement got nowhere and seems now almost to be forgotten. Traces of the so-called "Edelweiss Piraten" has cropped up and are still occasionally detected among vagabond youths hanging around railway stations, but these appear to be mere evidence of adolescent bravado rather than a serious movement which might cause genuine difficulties.

In April Army officials in "Operation Nursery" closed down on a loose network of former officers and members of the Hitler Youth extending through the United States and British zones. Investigation showed that the members merely were keeping in touch with each other with a view to indefinite future action that never materialized.

There were recurring rumors throughout the summer of nests of SS men hiding out in the mountains. The constabulary followed up these reports, but found little to indicate even the nucleus of an active Nazi resurgence movement.

From time to time there were attacks on individual soldiers, but they were isolated and without wider significance. More often than not they could be traced to a quarrel over a girl or to irate husbands. Civil and military authorities found more reason to be concerned over the disorderly conduct of the soldiers themselves and of the displaced persons.

Occasionally a constabulary raid turned up small caches of arms and Nazi propaganda. In the Passau region of Bavaria posters with swastikas and quotations from Hermann Goering's Nuremberg defense appeared one night. In Stuttgart one morning an editor found a poster tacked on his door denouncing the Nuremberg trials as "not justice but murder."

Finally last Saturday night bombs were set off outside the denazification tribunal at Backnang, where Hjalmar Schacht was recently apprehended, and outside the denazification tribunal and military police station in Stuttgart, where he is now incarcerated awaiting trial.

Protest Schacht's Arrest

This was the most violent and genuinely political exhibition of resistance to date. Investigators termed it a protest against the arrest of Herr Schacht in particular and the denazification program in general. There can be no doubt that while most diehard Nazis keep in the background and carefully quiet, there also is a lunatic fringe that has been stirred up by the confusion of the Nuremberg acquittals and Goering's suicide, and that this group is capable of violence.

Yet the military government and the Army declined to become alarmed. They reported that the bombing incidents were local and without ramifications.

"The wonder of it is," declared one well informed military government officer, "that this sort of thing has not happened before. We are going to have to get used to the fact that we are an occupying power, here by force of arms, and that, like the British in Palestine or India, we will have occasional violence and casualties.

"From now on we must count on more such outbursts anytime, anywhere, sometimes directed at Germans collaborating with the occupying forces and sometimes at Americans and other allies directly."

The influx of Germans expelled from the East, the desperate overcrowding in the rubble-strewn towns and villages, the shortages of fuel and food and the simmering resentment of persons whose homes have been requisitioned or who have lost their jobs in the course of denazification all help to breed resistance.

Foreigners Not Popular

It also must be remembered that the United States and British armies, which were welcomed as liberators, genuinely or feignedly, by certain elements of the population, have steadily lost such popularity as they had. Those who hoped for the improvement of their lot as a result of the arrival of the Allies have generally been disappointed.

The affluence of the occupying troops and their indifference or violent conduct, especially in the early days, have stirred the resentment of many a German inclined to be friendly. Even some anti-Nazis, staggered by the hopelessness of their personal and general outlook, have become potential resistance recruits.

Expressions of revolt come not from those completely occupied by the struggle for existence—as has been the case of the mass of Germans until recently—but from those who are fed but not fed enough, which is the situation of a growing number of Germans.

Reprisals Opposed

The greatest mistake the Americans could make, they believe, would be to move in upon incidents such as the one in Stuttgart with a massive crackdown or reprisals. Instead, they counsel leaving these matters to German authorities, who have more to lose at the hands of a resistance movement than the Americans and who act as representatives of elements such as the Stuttgart trade unions who staged a 15-minute strike in protest against the bombings.

They recall the smothering repression with which the British met the eastern rebellion of 1916 in Ireland and its consequences as evidence of the way in which machine-gun methods can convert the gesture of a lunatic fringe into a popular opposition movement.

Acts of physical resistance in Germany now are so manifestly senseless and without prospect, however, that they are scarcely likely to become very numerous nor catch the popular imagination unless grossly mishandled. The war is over, Germany is beaten, and the Germans are universally and painfully conscious of it. Their attitude in the mass is one of groveling obsequiousness.

The real German resistance movement follows a more devious and, in the long run, a more sinister method. It consists of using legitimate political movements as a democratic cloak for the gradual revival of German nationalism and irredentism.

The Christian Democratic Union has been singled out most often for attack on this score because it is supported by many extreme Right-wingers in the western zones. However, such elements are at work in all the parties and not the least in the Communist party and the Socialist Unity party of the Russian zone.

Influence Within Parties

Little by little they expand their influence, humbly wheedle concessions from the Allies and pervert the idea of a new Germany into a new nationalism. It is difficult to distinguish them from the more genuine representatives of the parties.

It is evident that the security of the occupation and of the world cannot long remain based on the fragmentization or paralysis of German life. The only hope appears to be to create living conditions in Germany that will permit democracy to be successful and keep an upperhand over a renascent authoritarian and vengeful nationalism.

2 GERMANS REBUILD GOETHE'S HOME; SCOUR RUBBLE FOR ORIGINAL BRICKS

Stonemason and Son Painstakingly Restore Adornments Wrecked in Bombings—Weird Cycle of Swaps Necessary to Get Roof

BY DANA ADAMS SCHMIDT
Special to THE NEW YORK TIMES.
FRANKFORT ON THE MAIN, GERMANY, Oct. 30—For seventeen months a German stonemason named Hans Sommer and his 18-year-old son have been searching through the rubble of the house in which Goethe was born for the original stones and bricks and slowly putting them together again.

If he can get the necessary help and materials, Herr Sommer said today, he believes he can completely reconstruct the house and its adjoining library and museum by the 200th anniversary of Goethe's birth on Aug. 28, 1949.

Painstakingly, the mason has pieced broken sandstone blocks with iron pins and cement to recreate the doorway and window frames of the three-story Gothic façade and has begun rebuilding the walls of what was once the roccoco interior. He discovered stones with Renaissance markings that Goethe's father had covered over when he rebuilt the house and found the arch of the doorway with its brass bell, the grillwork of the lower windows and staircase and the lion's head in the courtyard.

The house where Goethe grew up and began writing had collapsed in a tangled mass or had been scattered up and down the street called Grosser Hirschgraben during three American air attacks, the last and most destructive of which was on March 22, 1944. Almost all the furniture and books were saved, however, having been moved to the country early in the war. Fifty thousand of the library's 60,000 volumes concerning the poet and his times already have been moved back and will be rearranged next week in the library, which suffered less than the rest.

An elderly Professor of Literature, Dr. Ernst Beutler, supervises the work daily and gets valuable assistance from Joseph Sturm, who guided tourists through the house for twenty-one years. Dr. Beutler is director of the Freies Deutsches Hochstift, a German cultural foundation that is financing the reconstruction at an estimated eventual cost of more than 1,500,000 marks.

The Modern Language Association in the United States and the British Goethe Society have written offering to help. Dr. Beutler is proud of a laurel wreath from the house of Shakespeare at Stratford-on-Avon which was delivered to the Goethe house three days after the war began and which he carried out during the final fire. He is even more proud, however, of the roof he succeeded in getting rebuilt for the library.

"To get wood for the roof," he recalled, "we had to supply a belt for a band saw. To get the belt we had to promise some cement in exchange. To get the cement we had to promise some wine. To get the wine we had to promise to help the wine merchant find an apartment. And we were able to find an apartment because I knew of a woman who had committed suicide because of an SS man."

At present the library roof is covered with tar paper, but Gen. Joseph-Pierre Koenig has promised to send tiles from the French zone.

October 30, 1946
Dear Mother:
I'm writing this in Frankfurt once more, after my visit to Berlin to see Clark. So far his presence hasn't made much change in my life, except that I talk to him each evening on the phone, but in the long run it should permit me to take it a little easier.

Before I left Berlin I went around to 31 Niedstrasse to see Frau Sandrock. She is indeed bedridden and looks very poorly. She repeated to me much what she had put in her card to you, about her husband having died of undernourishment. A friend was there looking after her when I called. I brought along a carton of cigarettes, which are better than money, and told her you were sending a food package. She was delighted. Her mind is bright and keen although she is physically very feeble. Next to her bed she had a pile of photographs including one of you, in plumed hat and long skirts, somewhere around the nineteen twenties. I told her of father's death, which she did not know of. She was quite moved to think that we had remembered her.

I will send up a package of "keks and sweet things" for which she expressed a desire; and I would suggest that we might send her a CARE food package about once every six weeks from now on. I would be glad to pay for them if you will handle the job of ordering.

Most of her apartment is sublet, except, for the bedroom in which she lives, but she seemed worried about money. She is trying to get hold of a collection of her husband's paintings which are stored somewhere in [the Russian zone]. I would be glad to do whatever possible to help, but I can't do much about things in the Russian zone. She has also been selling items of furniture to raise money, she said. I would be glad to help her out with some money but had no German currency when I called and am in doubt as to how to go about it without embarrassing her.

Well, the other food packages addressed to Frankfurt, arrived while I was away. My two families were profusely grateful. Will you please send each of them another CARE parcel at my expense. They are now $10. Also, please send another parcel to Mlle. Pave and her family in Paris. If you think Roger is deserving send his mother one too.

I think all this is the least one can do for people who are really pretty close to the margin at the beginning of winter.

I don't know yet when I'll be going to Paris but I will be going. Did I tell you a got a card from the Williams, from Montreux? I will of course see them in Paris.

So, Mrs. Martin's baby was finally born. I was wondering what had happened. I thought it was due a long time ago. Congratulate the two of them for me when you get a chance. Tell George I don't envy him his hours.

I am ever so glad that you are feeling fine and that Steinie is with you again. Would it be possible for me to pay for a raise for Steinie or pay for the raise you have already given her? That would take some of the burden off you.

You ask what I think of Drew Pearson and Walter Winchell's sentiments concerning Russia. As you know I have said right along that I did not believe there was going to be any war in the near future and I still believe it. There will be wars again in the world, but I think we have a pretty good chance of having a decade or so of peace, regardless of the "East-West" problems we are always talking about. It would take too long to try to build up the case, but those are my conclusions from the sum total of everything I know.

What do I want in my Christmas box? Well, I can think of one very important thing: a nail brush and a pair of good straight nail scissors, and a pocket comb. I've been trying to get these items at the PX for ages but they are always "fresh out," or perhaps they never had any. If somebody would like to give me a leather toilet case it would be welcome too; not one with all sorts of ready-made containers, but with space to hold the things I have.

You can tell Steinie I have been enjoying the brownies in my last parcel. All my love now, to you all, Dana

GERMANS SUBMIT ECONOMIC SCHEME

Bi-Zonal Board Offers Inclusive Development Program to U.S.-British Board

BY DANA ADAMS SCHMIDT
Special to THE NEW YORK TIMES.

FRANKFORT ON THE MAIN, GERMANY, Oct. 31—Comprehensive recommendations for economic recovery in the American and British zones were submitted to the joint Anglo-American military-government liaison officers by the bi-zonal German economics agency yesterday after a two-day meeting.

Tentative dates were set for the stages of the plan that would evolve from the improvement of rations in order to raise working efficiency and increase the production of coal, then of iron and other raw materials, then of machinery and finally of consumer and exportable goods. The plan also touched on reparations, foreign credits, monetary reform and price and wage revisions, according to Dr. Rudolf Mueller, Greater Hesse Minister of Economics and chairman of the bi-zonal agency.

Swift action is essential, he declared, to halt the alarming disintegration of German economic life, and the knowledge that a beginning, however modest, is being made "would be of inestimable value to the German people's morale."

He emphasized the importance of the so-called "pins-and-needles" part of the program, concerned with supplying workers with sewing materials, nails, shoe leather shoestrings and other small items related to working efficiency. A committee of coal experts headed by Prof. Erik Noelting, Economics Minister of North Rhine-Westphalia, was appointed to work with trade union officials in Duesseldorf.

American, British and German officials of the bi-zonal conference met Brig. Gen. William H. Draper, the American zone's economics chief, at the opening of the Greater Hesse export exhibition in Wiesbaden today. Like similar exhibitions in Stuttgart and Munich, it was designed to show not what is being produced but what could be produced for export if coal and raw materials were available. Seven hundred firms displayed their goods, including Opel's 1947 model truck, Henschel steam and Diesel locomotives, Adler bicycles, and leather, furs and textiles from Offenbach. There were iceboxes, radios, rubber products and a wide assortment of synthetics made from wood and coal. A large section was devoted to Leica cameras and precision instruments.

The first barges carrying American zone lumber to Britain and the Netherlands were reported to be moving down the Rhine from Karlsruhe in execution of the zone's largest export contract to date. By the end of next July Britain will have received 248,000,000 board feet of lumber valued at $16,800,000 and sufficient to build 40,000 homes. The Netherlands will receive $4,200,000 worth of lumber.

This however is precisely the kind of export that German experts seek to avoid. In order to employ her workers and make enough money to pay for imports, they say, Germany must export not raw materials but high-value finished goods such as furniture and prefabricated houses.

FRAMEWORK OF DEMOCRACY ESTABLISHED BY GERMANS

New Constitutions for States Might Serve as Pattern for Decentralized Rule

BY DANA ADAMS SCHMIDT
Special to THE NEW YORK TIMES.
FRANKFORT ON THE MAIN, GERMANY, Nov. 2—The Constitutional Assemblies of the three United States zone Laender have passed Constitutions which in varying degrees set the pattern for a decentralized, federalistic, socialistic, and democratic Germany.

Since all three are largely the products of agreement between the Social Democrats and Christian Democrats, there is little doubt that the Constitutions will be upheld when the people of Wuerttemberg-Baden, Greater Hesse and Bavaria vote successively on Nov. 24, Dec. 1 and Dec. 8.

Certain marked peculiarities of the documents were high-lighted by Lieut. Gen. Lucius D. Clay, who asked that the Greater Hesse provisions for socializing the mining, iron and steel industries and transport be subjected to a special plebiscite.

The socialism written into the Constitutions seemed to proclaim principles that are still subjects of violent debate in the United States.

Ideological Variations

This political ideology varied in industrial Hesse's mandatory socialization to conservative Bavaria's provision that "means of production that are vitally important to the community can be socialized if consideration for the general good requires it."

With similar variations in emphasis, each of the Laender called for managed economy, continued the German tradition of extensive social insurance and recognized the right to unionize and the right of workers' committees to share in the administration along with the employers.

While Bavaria mentioned the desirability of private initiative "in principle" the general line of thought was a far cry from the ideas of enterprise prevailing in the United States. In general, however, it was entirely in accordance with British Foreign Secretary Bevin's suggestion that the world's security from the ambitions of large concentrations of German capital lay in socialization or nationalization.

It was felt, too, that the Soviet Union might approve this pattern for future Germany, since the Communists voted against the constitution only in Bavaria, where they held that the protection accorded to the rights of the Catholic Church was excessive. The other two Laender, however, also maintained rights of denominational schools and the right of churches as public corporations to levy taxes and receive financial support from the State.

In each Land there will be a Legislature or Landtag directly elected for four years, which in turn elects the Prime Minister or Minister-President.

Bavaria also has a corporative Senate composed of representatives elected by various occupational groups, which can initiate legislation and delay, but not veto, acts of the Landtag. Pending the formation of corporations the Senate will be elected by the Landtag.

The bills of rights are elaborate and explicit, but can be only partly applied for some years. The exigencies of the times obliged the Laender to suspend protection from retroactive law in case of persons subject to denazification trials and to suspend the inviolability of the home and freedom to choose a place of residence and work as long as millions of expellees and refugees must be housed and employed.

The Weimar Constitution's ill-reputed Article 48, which helped Adolf Hitler to power, is mildly reflected in provisions permitting the suspension of basic rights of press, assembly and the like during periods of emergency, but the Legislatures retain the right to declare the emergency at an end.

Decentralization of Power

The centralization of power that occurred in the Weimar Republic would almost certainly not be possible under these Constitutions, although Hesse and Wuerttemberg-Baden recognize the legal precedence of a future national Constitution over their own. As these Constitutions stand German Laender would be more independent than American States.

The legislative, executive and judicial branches are declared separate in principle but it is clear that, as in the French draft, the scales are heavily weighted in favor of the legislative. Supreme Courts to decide constitutional issues are set up in each land. They are elected by Legislature, partly among professional judges and partly among non-parliamentary laymen.

Perhaps the most important thing about the Constitutions are that they signify a return to the democratic rule of law. They are democratic in letter and spirit. The proof of the pudding, however, will be in the eating.

Frankfurt,
November 3, 1946
Dear Mother:
You are ever so right about self-pity and letting oneself become rebelliously unhappy. They are only passing moods, really. And writing you about it is a form of escape, or relief. I get that way usually when I haven't been getting enough sleep. Sleep is the great regenerator of morale. I remember Fred Oechsner used to say if a man gets enough sleep and good food there is no limit to the amount of work he can do, I also remember that Grandpa used to insist on getting a lot of sleep, although that may have been because he wasn't quite well.

This past week since I returned from Berlin has been a busy one and I should have had a few bylines. I am always glad to find a period when there is no outstanding news. It gives me a chance to do some of the features I've been postponing. I've got a pack of them.

I guess I'm really going to get a week in Paris. Isn't that grand? Kathleen is probably leaving about the end of the month and I must be back before she goes. Ed Murrow will come here the middle of the month. I will spend a few days breaking him in and then take off. I want to be back for the referendums on the constitutions, too. I want to take a tour in the French zone after that.

Delbert Clark and I are getting along fine. He doesn't interfere and there's plenty of room for everybody. I'll be looking forward to clippings of his stuff and your comments on it. No, I definitely do not get the paper soon enough to be able to dispense with clippings. In fact I almost never see the paper except for the Overseas weekly which contains only Sunday stuff.

The Blue Cross Hospital Benefit Plan sounds good but I did not find the enclosure on it of which you spoke. Anyway, go ahead and sign me up for it. If I have to sign something perhaps you can send to the Times for it.

Tomorrow I am driving down to Stuttgart for the monthly Laenderrat meeting. I've also noticed that the pieces from there don't get much attention, perhaps because they usually have a strictly German angle. But it is important to go there just to gather background. John Scott of Time and I are two of the most faithful customers. I regret the departure of Dr. Pollock who was always informative and intelligent.

The other day I wrote Mr. Starling, as you suggested. Give my love to Grandma and Eliza and the babes. Steinie I am confident will get you straightened out, All my love, Dana

No, Mother, I don't know the story of the Hamburg days, although I suspected some of it. I do want to know though. Will you write it for me, or shall we let it wait till I come home again in the spring?

CLAY SCORES LAXITY ON DENAZIFICATION

In Angry Speech, He Warns German Leaders to Put Teeth Into Purge Within 60 Days

BY DANA ADAMS SCHMIDT
Special to THE NEW YORK TIMES.
STUTTGART, GERMANY, Nov. 5—Lieut. Gen. Lucius D. Clay, Deputy United States Military Governor, today gave the three Minister-Presidents of the American zone sixty days to show "real and rapid improvement" in the severity of the German denazification tribunals.

Failing such improvement, he said, the Military Government will take back the job of denazification "regardless of its effect on the German economy and regardless of the additional time it may take."

It was the most stinging rebuke General Clay ever had administered to German officials, to whom the United States Military Government had progressively transferred more responsibility than had any other Military Government.

Shortly thereafter, Dr. Wilhelm Hoegner, Minister-President of Land Bavaria, told correspondents:

"Either the Military Government has faith in us, or that faith is lacking and the Minister-Presidents will resign, and then the Military Government may look for better men than we." Dr. Reinhold Maier and Dr. Karl Geiler, Minister-Presidents of Wuerttemberg-Baden and Greater Hesse, dejectedly nodded assent. They had gathered here for the first anniversary of the Laenderrat expecting pleasant speeches of congratulation on the year's work.

Because he was "sorely disappointed" with the results of self-denazification by the Germans, General Clay said he was issuing an order today that "no one who has been removed from the Office of Military Government and subsequently tried by a tribunal can be returned to office without the approval of the Military Government."

Exonerations Pointed Out

Statistics he had examined personally, he disclosed, showed 575 cases had been classified as Class 1 or major offenders by public prosecutors. Of these, he said, 375 were classified by German denazification tribunals as "followers" in Class 4 and 49 were exonerated.

[In evident anger, General Clay told 200 top German officials that they had failed in their first task as a democracy by shirking the application of punishment to thousands of Nazis who helped Adolf Hitler plunge civilization into the Second World War, The United Press reported. "It appears that the denazification law has been used to return as many persons as possible to their former vocations, rather than to punish the guilty," General Clay declared.]

General Clay explained that the law that turned denazification over to the Germans in the United States zone seven months ago "was designed to serve as the basis for the return of self-government to the German people * * *. But we have yet to find the political will and determination to punish those who deserve to be punished."

He added that he realized one reason the record looked bad was that "the tribunals have given priority to cases in which there was little evidence of guilt, perhaps knowing that this apparent lenient action would be popular in Nazi circles. This is not the path of courage."

At a press conference, General Clay observed that he sympathized with the Germans' motives in taking up easy cases first where it was intended to get the much-needed borderline persons back to work in the German economy.

Even under present procedures, General Clay estimated that 40,000 to 50,000 Germans would be sentenced to terms in labor camps by the tribunals.

Contradicting other recent Military Government estimates that there now were 40,000 in internment camps, General Clay set the figure at 70,000, of whom the United States Army would retain several thousand for war crimes trials, turning over the others to the Germans for trial.

The three Minister-Presidents declared they were surprised at the sharpness of General Clay's reproach, coming at the end of a year of close cooperation.

All three affirmed their conviction that the German people had the will to punish those who would be punished and could do the job, in spite of some admitted abuses. They said the problem consisted of five points:

(1) Most of the major Nazis still were in internment camps, where trials were only beginning.

(2) The Americans waited too long before putting the denazification law into effect and "in the meantime many things have been forgotten."

(3) Not the lack of good-will but mechanical difficulties had hindered the effectiveness of the purge. There was an acute shortage of qualified judges and material requisites for organizations that had to start from scratch.

(4) Figures cited by General Clay appeared to apply to special group cases and not to the general run.

(5) The American concept of what constituted a Nazi from the beginning had been broader and more formalistic than the German.

GERMAN MINISTERS, HIT BY CLAY, QUIT

2 of 3 Denazification Chiefs Act on Criticism—Press Law Proclaims Freedom

BY DANA ADAMS SCHMIDT
Special to THE NEW YORK TIMES.
STUTTGART, GERMANY, NOV. 6—Two of the three German Ministers of Denazification in the American zone offered their resignations today.

This action resulted from the threat yesterday of Lieut. Gen. Lucius D. Clay, Deputy United States Military Governor, to put the Military Government back into the denazification business if German tribunals did not, within the next sixty days, mend their ways and cease whitewashing Nazis.

The Ministers were Anton Pfeiffer of Bavaria and Gottlob Kamm of Wuerttemberg-Baden, who submitted their resignations to the Minister Presidents of their states at Cabinet meetings today. Dr. Gottlieb Binder, Minister of Denazification for Greater Hesse, who will not meet his Cabinet until tomorrow stated, however, that he did not intend to offer to resign and would remain in office unless dismissed.

The resignations were the first ones of importance that have resulted directly from Military Government criticism and represented the most serious rift to date between the American occupation authority and the new German Land Governments it has created.

It appeared more than likely, none the less, that the resignations would be refused by Minister Presidents Wilhelm Hoegner of Bavaria and Reinhold Maier of Wuerttemberg-Baden after they have conferred with the directors of the Military Government of their states tomorrow.

Reaction Termed Healthy

A colonel for Wuerttemberg-Baden said tonight that he did not favor the resignations, although he would leave the decision up to the Germans.

General Clay's adviser on denazification, Dr. Walter Dorn, who arrived here today for a conference with the three Ministers, found that they had departed. He observed philosophically that it was certainly not General Clay's intention to provoke resignations, but that the reaction was "probably healthy."

Dr. Binder, questioned by telephone at Wiesbaden, said he had come to the same conclusion after rereading General Clay's speech.

Dr. Kamm's letter of resignation read:

"In consequence of declarations made yesterday by General Clay, I am obliged to inform you that, effective immediately, my position as Minister for Political Liberation is placed at your disposal."

Beyond that he and Herr Pfeiffer declined to make a statement.

The two Ministers evidently considered General Clay's sharp rebuke as an expression of lack of confidence in themselves.

Herr Pfeiffer took over Bavarian denazification three months ago from a Communist predecessor who had allowed the tribunals to deteriorate into administrative confusion. His painstaking efforts toward reviewing early decisions and reorganizing the tribunals have won him recognition from the Military Government.

Herr Kamm, a one-legged survivor of a Nazi concentration camp, is generally regarded as the most vigorous of the three Ministers and outpaced the others in the speed if not the soundness of the tribunals' operation.

Press Laws Adopted

Freedom of the press in principle was proclaimed, along with a number of limitations on its freedom in practice, in a press law and a press licensing law passed by the Laenderrat yesterday.

The laws were intended, according to Laenderrat officials, for the transition between control by the American Information Control Division and a really free press. Assuming approval by the military government, they are due to be replaced by March 31, 1947, by press regulations worked out by elected legislatures in Bavaria, Wuerttemberg-Baden and Greater Hesse.

Press councils, whose composition is to be determined by each Land government, receive power under the law to suppress newspapers for repeated violations. The police are authorized to seize a particular issue without a court order "if it tends to disturb the peace and the court order cannot be obtained in time, or if it tends to corrupt morale in the sense of the penal code."

Imprisonment up to two years or a fine are prescribed for violations.

Newspapers are placed under an obligation to print the replies of persons whom they had subjected to criticism. Necessary qualifications of editors-in-chief include that they must be 21 years of age and in full possession of civic rights. Licensed publishers must be "in sound economic circumstances," must offer "positive cooperation in the democratic reconstruction of Germany" and must not be subject to prosecution under the denazification law.

U.S. ZONE OPENED TO BUSINESS MEN

McNarney Invites Americans and Others With Dollars to Buy German Exports

BY DANA ADAMS SCHMIDT
Special to THE NEW YORK TIMES.
FRANKFORT ON THE MAIN, GERMANY, Nov. 7—Gen. Joseph T. McNarney today invited American business men interested in German exports and business men of other nationalities who can pay in dollars to visit the American zone.

A sharp upturn in American buyer interest in exportable German goods that has recently been observed, he said, offered some promise of building up dollar balances in Germany to offset the cost of the occupation to the American taxpayer. The Reconstruction Finance Corporation, through the United States Commercial Corporation, he reported, has set up a $9,000,000 fund with which to help German industry obtain raw materials and prime the pump of German exports. He anticipated that the total value of German exports during the fiscal year ending next June 30 would reach $20,000,000 out of a target total of $25,000,000 set by the military government.

By comparison, General McNarney pointed out that the Army would probably spend $200,000,000 for the occupation of Germany, including imports of food for Germans and the support of displaced persons. Since Congress allocated only $95,000,000 of the $230,000,000 requested for this purpose, he presumed that it would have to make a deficiency appropriation.

Thirty-five Buyers Already There

He said that thirty-five American buyers had thus far visited Germany in addition to hundreds of representatives of owners of industrial property in Germany who have helped to get factories back into production. Because of the limitations of suitable facilities, the total number in Germany at any one time has hitherto been limited to 100. Other Army sources understood that the limit would soon be raised to 160. For buyers' information, German authorities have gone to great trouble to set up export exhibitions in Munich, Stuttgart and Wiesbaden, showing both what is actually available and what will be when raw materials are obtained. In addition, samples have been sent to the showrooms of the United States Commercial Corporation in New York. Among the latest were some samples of wine. Hops, cameras, toys and chinaware have already been exported to the United States. The Military Government's economics officials are waiting for the first protest from American manufacturers.

In arranging purchases business men must work through Military Government channels, since Germans are still positively forbidden to engage directly in foreign trade. Contracts must be made between the American enterprise and the Military Government. Restrictions on German business correspondence with foreign countries were, however, recently eased to permit the communication of information about German products as long as no commercial agreement was involved.

Procedure Explained

In a prepared statement, General McNarney explained the procedure for American buyers desiring to visit Germany. They should consult the Department of Commerce or the commercial attaché of an American Embassy or Legation and offer "some assurance that they represent firms whose purchasing power is sufficient to make their proposed visit to Germany worth-while."

An application will then be sent for them to the military-permit secretary, Joint Chiefs of Staff in Washington, or the military-permit offices in Europe, and forwarded to the combined travel board in Berlin. The trade and commerce branch of the economics division of the American Military Government in Berlin will in turn decide whether the commodities desired are available for export. Direct approaches to military-government officers are discouraged.

In Germany, business men will get the same accommodations as transient Military Government and Army personnel. Housing, food and transport are sufficient, although abnormal conditions make inconvenience and discomfort unavoidable.

A booklet of instruction called "The Business Man's Guide to Germany" will soon be available at Embassies, Legations and military-government offices.

GERMAN BOARDS FACE TEST ON NAZIS

**Lag in Denazification
Must End or Job Will
Revert to Military**

BY DANA ADAMS SCHMIDT
Special to THE NEW YORK TIMES.
FRANKFORT ON THE MAIN, GERMANY, Nov. 9—The question that Lieut. Gen. Lucius D. Clay, United States Deputy Military Governor,

raised in his speech castigating lenient German denazification procedure at Stuttgart this week, was whether the German people have the will themselves to punish the Nazis.

The American zone denazification law, with its German tribunals, is based on the assumption that they have. The Russians, French and British have not yet accepted this assumption which the Americans made seven months ago, although the British appear to be on the verge of doing so.

Possibly it is a fundamental error. But the thought that Germany should be purged of Nazism, not by the force of the victors but by the will of the German people, is the very foundation of the American efforts to foster a sound new German democracy.

If in the next sixty days denazification does not show a "real and rapid improvement," General Clay said the Military Government would take it out of the hands of the Germans and administer denazification itself.

Clay Disappointed

The record gave General Clay ample reason to be, as he said, "sorely disappointed." He cited 575 cases classified as Class I, or major offenders, by public prosecutors. Of these the tribunals, after trials, classified 355 as followers in Class 4 and forty-nine as meriting exoneration in Class 5.

The figures for September showed that out of 8,182 cases which the special branch of the Military Government had previously placed in the "mandatory non-employment group, the German tribunals imposed employment sanctions on only 1,884, or 23 per cent.

The German defense in the case of General Clay's figures is that while the denazification law rigidly requires persons who held certain ranks and offices to be prosecuted as offenders in Classes 1 and 2, rank and office is by no means a sure guide to guilt.

Some Nazis 'Whatwashed'

In not a few instances there have been deliberate attempts to whitewash Nazis. The most abuses, however, stem from the German's deeply ingrained respect for his social "betters." Dignified, long-respected local business or professional men get off with a fine while the tribunals compensate by sentencing minor party underlings to labor camps.

While Secretary of State Byrnes' pledge that the Americans would remain in Germany as long as any other occupying power had a wholesome effect, fear plays its part in the leniency of decisions.

Up to a certain point and to an extent far exceeding anything the Germans ever encountered in the countries they occupied, the German people are willing to "collaborate," whether out of democratic conviction or expediency. When it comes actually to punishing Nazis, however, all but a minority bridle. They lack conviction or are afraid of the consequences they might suffer.

By his severe speech General Clay hoped to mobilize the minority for service in the tremendous job of putting 2,500,000 Germans affected by the law through the denazification mill, and to jolt the rest into a realization that denazification is a "must."

The consternation caused in German Government circles and the offers of resignations indicate that it had the desired effect.

Even before the speech there were signs of improvement. Wuerttemberg-Baden's figures for October show that 28 per cent of the cases were placed in Classes 1, 2 and 3. At Hanau there have been spontaneous protests against lenient decisions.

Even the bombing of the denazification tribunals at Stuttgart may be interpreted as showing that the tribunals' work is striking home.

Most Military Government officers are hopeful that the Germans will find the will to make the denazification law effective in time. Few believe that General Clay will find it necessary to carry out his threat.

**GERMANS CONTROL
CAMP IN U.S. ZONE**

**Put in Charge of 11,000 Nazis
Awaiting Trial—Expect a
Troubled Winter**

BY DANA ADAMS SCHMIDT
Special to THE NEW YORK TIMES.
DARMSTADT, Germany, Nov. 11—German authorities of the new government of the Land of Greater Hesse are preparing for winter at the largest internment camp of the American zone, a tent city surrounded by barbed wire on the outskirts of this city.

They replaced Americans ten days ago as the custodians of 11,000 internees, a considerable portion of the best talent of the Nazi regime. Since maintaining internment camps—that is, confining people who have not been tried—is at best an awkward business for a democracy and especially for one that is new and uncertain, the German officials were less pleased to receive their new charges than the Americans were to get rid of them. Their concern was to liquidate the camp as soon as possible, by trials and releases, and meanwhile to run it as humanely as possible.

Accompanied by James R. Newman, director of military government for Greater Hesse, I visited the camp to see how the German authorities were getting on. The ultimate responsibility remains with the military government as long as there is no sovereign government in Germany.

"This is no concentration camp—nothing like what the Nazis ran," declared the German camp director, Jakob Weyand, who represents the Greater Hesse Ministry of Denazification. Having been imprisoned several years as a

Social-Democratic leader in Nazi concentration camps, he is qualified to make comparisons and also to see into the prisoners' minds.

Denazification Courts Busy

As one of the changes undertaken by the German administration, he pointed out a crowd of women and children, some crying, some laughing, coming from a long shack just inside the entrance. Here every day fifty women, each accompanied by one child, may now meet their husbands, whom they probably have not seen in more than a year.

Another change has been to permit some men to leave the camp—on their honor to return—for six-to-fourteen-day visits to their families where there has been serious illness or death. The first few thus privileged have come back.

Ten denazification tribunals have begun operation. They have classified and sentenced 184 cases—twelve in Class 1, eighty-eight in Class 2, seventy-five in Class 3, nine in Class 4 and none in Class 5. Since Classes 1 and 2 involve sentences to labor camps and Class 3 usually means a heavy fine and limitation on employment, inmates bitterly criticize the severity of the decisions, Herr Weyand said, yet they are relieved that some disposition of their cases is at last being made.

He thought this the most positive effect of the switch to German administration, while on the other hand the inmates there were filled with fear that the new regime would not be able to feed them and heat their tents. A month ago, while the Americans were still in charge, there was a near riot when prisoners began tearing down the interior fence for firewood. Thereafter the Third Army shipped in a two-month supply of wood.

Thus far the Germans have maintained the 1,700-calorie ration standard set by the Americans. The internees looked better fed than their guards, who live on 1,550 calories plus unrationed supplements outside. Herr Weyand, however, anticipated a troubled winter. To help head off trouble, he has Paul Dietz, the "Oberbuergermeister" elected by the inmates, who relays complaints. Dietz, a six-foot-eight-inch giant, was a Nazi Ortsgruppenleiter near Dusseldorf.

Most of the prisoners were members of the Elite Guard and the party, business and professional men. While a few seemed markedly low and brutal types, the dominant impression was of men well above the average in intelligence and physique. One wondered whether these men, as they gradually regained freedom, could long be prevented from regaining leading positions in German life and to what ends they would use their talents.

November 12, 1946
Dear Mother:
This is going to be a short letter because I must get some sleep before I get up very early in the morning to drive to Nuremberg. I have a date there at noon to meet some men who know all about the documents to be used in the trial of the industrialists. It seems a long way to go for one story but I promised, so there it is.

When I get back I'll have only a few days before I leave for Paris. How fine that will be. Hope dear Lincoln Zephyr stands the test.

This afternoon Dick Clark and I went for a drive in the country to visit some farmers. Everybody talks about the farm problem but nobody ever talks to the farmers. We found the two we visited quite worked up about the danger of raiders coming out from the towns this winter to steal food from their barns. I must do a general "winter is coming" piece in the next few days. I've already had one on the Jewish deepees and the civilian internees. I wrote the civilian internee piece tonight; it cost me a lot of sweat and anguish; difficult subject. Newman the MG chief for Greater Hesse invited me to visit it with him a long time ago and I finally made him come across.

I've written weekenders for Markel now five or six weeks in a row. Quite a record for me. If I can't think of anything to suggest, he usually does. There might be one this week again since Clark is going away to Milan on Tuesday. He is going to fetch a supermultilingual Hungarian gal he thinks he needs as a secretary. Judging by the trouble he's taking she must be pretty good.

Airmail is obviously on the blink in this weather and no letter from you has come through this week, nor for that matter any other mail except magazines.

Mother, this winter in Germany is going to be really ghastly. I do not like to see people suffer. It was bad enough during the war when there was good reason for it, but now it stands out alone in all its grimness. People aren't starving but they're awfully low. It doesn't impress Americans much as long as it's generalized.

But when you get to know a few people in their homes it hurts, it makes me angry to find Americans so fat, smug and self-satisfied by contrast.

I bought another Nay watercolor on the way home today and plan to send it to Dorothy as a Christmas present. It's a glowing yellow and red impression of a reclining woman. Most people see red and yellow but that's about as far as they get. Nay seemed to be doing all right except that he couldn't use his studio because it is so cold most of the time and he can't get paints.

All my love now,
and Bon Nuit.

MILCH, GOERING'S EX-DEPUTY, FACES TRIAL ON SLAVE LABOR, INHUMAN MEDICAL TESTS

BY DANA ADAMS SCHMIDT
Special to THE NEW YORK TIMES.
NUREMBERG, Germany, Nov. 13—Air Field Marshal Erhard Milch, once Hermann Goering's deputy, was charged in an indictment today with crimes involving slave labor and medical experiments inflicted upon both foreign and German nationals.

The case probably will come to trial about Dec. 15 and run simultaneously with the trials of twenty-three Nazi physicians.

The first of the three counts in the indictment against Milch charged that he took part in war crimes, including the deportation of slave labor from Austria, Czechoslovakia, Italy, Hungary and other occupied countries, and that he authorized the use and mistreatment of prisoners in work connected with war operations.

The second count charged that Milch had been personally connected with medical experiments on helpless human beings, particularly high altitude and freezing tests of interest to the Luftwaffe.

The third count recapitulated the first two as "crimes against humanity" in which crimes against German nationals were specifically included.

One of the most significant aspects of the series of trials under the jurisdiction of the United States Military Government due to begin Dec. 5, court officials pointed out today, is the inclusion in the indictments of crimes against German nationals.

This, they held, would obviate the necessity of having any of the persons tried now brought to trial later by German courts on criminal charges, although in the United States zone they still might have to appear before denazification tribunals on political charges.

In contrast, the International Military Tribunal concerned itself only with crimes committed in the preparation of or during a war of aggression.

However, it was not obliged to make this limitation, either under its charter as originally drawn up in London or under Allied Control Council Law No. 10.

The limitation, officials disclosed, was decided by members of the Tribunal during the trial last Dec. 8 and was effected by substituting a comma for a semicolon in Article 6C of the charter. Thereby persecution on racial, religious and political grounds, instead of standing as an independent charge, was linked up with the words "before or during the war."

The change itself and the reasons for it never were explained during the trial. It may only be assumed that prosecution for this type of act against a country's own nationals was considered embarrassing to countries that indulged in similar acts in their own countries or dependencies. The Americans, now conducting trials exclusively, are freed from such international considerations.

GERMAN FORESEES 50% POPULATION CUT

Frankfort Professor Predicts Halving by 1996 Through Nation's War Losses

BY DANA ADAMS SCHMIDT
Special to THE NEW YORK TIMES.

FRANKFORT ON THE MAIN, Germany, Nov. 16—Fifty years from now there will be only half as many Germans as there were in 1939— 35,000,000 instead of 70,000,000. Germany by then will have become even more of an "old people's home," according to calculations made by Prof. Heinz Sauermann of Frankfort University.

This probability is based on the effects of war, which have aggravated prewar trends, he said. He suggested in an interview that Germany's population might be considered by the Big Four Foreign Ministers in weighing peace terms for Germany and the possible menace of Germany to other countries in the future.

While the population trends and war effects in other countries were similar, he held that they would prove most marked in Germany for the following reasons:

1. German war losses in manpower were proportionately higher than those of the other major countries.

2. More than 3,000,000 Germans in the best productive age groups are still prisoners of war, at least 2,000,000 of them in Russia.

3. While other countries are recovering economically from the war, German conditions are still deteriorating.

The postwar surge in birthrate observed in other countries is limited in Germany by the economic obstacles to marriage, while at the same time mortality, and especially infant mortality, is increased.

The professor's estimates included only the German population before Hitler's annexations of Austria and the Sudetenland. The influx of 10,000,000 to 14,000,000 expelled persons from the east, he pointed out, would increase the absolute number of population, but would, if anything, aggravate the trend toward contraction because the persons expelled, having suffered the same war losses as other Germans, have been obliged to leave behind many able-bodied males.

According to Professor Sauermann's figures, Germany's losses in manpower during the war totaled about 10 per cent, or 7,700,000—4,000,000 soldiers killed in combat, 1,000,000 civilians killed by bombing and during the fighting and 2,700,000 disabled to the point where they will require medical attention for the rest of their lives.

The figures were computed, he explained, from foreign estimates and figures supplied by a German Staff Officer who had had access to the German

High Command's statistics before they were burned. Taking into consideration the greater intensiveness and length of this war, the figure for fighting casualties was also in proportion to that of World War I.

Before the war, Professor Sauermann recalled, it had already been calculated that the German population would drop 43,000,000 by the year 2000, with a steadily increasing proportion of old persons over 65. The present ratio of 100 productive persons to seventy-five non-productive dependent ones, he believed, would continue to become less favorable unless there were a considerable and unexpected increase in the birth rate.

WORSE WINTER DUE FOR WORN GERMANS

All Vital Articles Scarce—AMG Uncertain on Food Imports— Refugees Add to Crowding

BY DANA ADAMS SCHMIDT
Special to THE NEW YORK TIMES.
FRANKFORT ON THE MAIN, GERMANY, NOV. 17—The first sharp frosts announce a shivering and portentous winter in the skeleton cities of Germany.

In every respect, it promises to be worse than the last one. The reserves of food and clothing have been used up, machinery has worn out, transport has broken down, spare parts and raw materials have been exhausted and nothing has been replenished.

Ten million persons expelled from the East spread among the four zones have painfully increased the crowding—Kassel probably has the record, with four to five persons a room.

Food, regardless of the announced ration scales, is scarcer. Fuel is as hard to get as ever. And more important, the physical resistance of the people, whittled down by the combination of hardships, is less than it was a year ago.

The Military Government of the United States zone is worried. It is not sure it is going to get the imports needed for the 1500-calorie ration it has planned for the winter; hence the frequent denunciations of hoarding by farmers and the assignment of American Army trucks to help distribute German farm produce.

Almost Meatless a Month

For example, Greater Hesse, whose density of population but not of resources now equals that of Belgium, has gone almost meatless for a month for lack of transportation to bring the meat in. The 120 pounds of firewood and 180 pounds of potatoes the citizens of Frankfort were to get as a winter reserve have been distributed only in part. The one point of notable improvement is the supply of sugar, which was almost nonexistent last winter.

Driven by the gnawing shortages, the putty faced townspeople of Frankfort, as of every German town, fare forth endlessly into the countryside. They would rather miss their pay for a day's work on a city job than give up the quest for extra food and fuel.

In the frosted fields, many now glean sugar beets where a little earlier they gleaned potatoes and wheat—men, women and children on their hands and knees, patiently searching out whatever the peasants have left behind. In the forests they gather firewood and find beach nuts—twelve pounds can be exchanged for a liter of oil.

What can be found for nothing is limited, however, and most of them bring along something to trade with the peasants. Unless ration coupons are supplied, such trading is illegal, but that scarcely interferes with the flow of shoes, overcoats, clocks, typewriters, cigarettes, coffee and jewelry from town to country. One Frankfort man argued with ration officials for six months to get a pair of shoes and then traded them for potatoes. Another made the same sort of trade with a new suit received from relatives in the United States.

Peasants Now Fearful

The peasants are getting rich and they also are becoming afraid. They know that after the gleaning and the trading comes stealing.

"On moonlight nights," one peasant complained, "the townspeople cut down my wheat and dug my potatoes. Now they will be raiding my barns. My dogs are forever driving off prowlers. If only the Military Government would let me have a shotgun."

The picture is a labyrinthine chaos of industrial areas of the British zone, and the neglected French zone is, if anything, more grim. Even the Russian zone, with all its farmland, appears to be faring no better.

As a matter of course, the city families move for the winter into a single room, whichever can be best heated. Central heating is out of the question, except in American-occupied houses. The Germans huddle around carefully tended stoves, nurturing the bitter thoughts and stratagems that will find their political reflections in the years to come.

Charity Only A Partial Aid

To be sure, there is relief CARLOG, the Committee of American Relief Organizations, provides hundreds of thousands of school children with hot lunches. Packages of "10 in 1" rations from CARE—the Cooperative for American Remittances for Europe—cheer hundreds of thousands of homes. The Swiss, Swedish, Irish and International Red Cross contribute. But charity is no solution. And more bitter than the physical hardship is the general hopelessness, the consciousness that while the rest of Europe is beginning to revive, Germany still is going down, with the collapse of the old scales of values, cynicism and nihilism.

The Germans, however, are not alone in their despair. In their midst this winter are some of Germany's victims now crowded in Wehrmacht barracks—a round million of former Polish, Baltic and Balkan slave laborers and concentration camp inmates, including 200,000 Jews who do not know how they ever are going to get out of Germany.

ELIZABETH SCHMIDT CRAHAN

PARIS, FRANCE
Nov. 24, 1946
Dear Mother:

After seven days in Paris I'm on my way back. What a delight it has been. I love Paris more than ever. It was good to see my old friends here again.

I called on the Williamses and had cocktails one day and dinner and theatre with them another day. They are pleasant company but the daughter doesn't interest beyond that. You would not be impressed either, I'm sure. She is annoyingly tied to her mama's apron strings. Extremely naïve, self conscious and rather tiresome. On the other hand, to be sure, she has a certain "petite" but very frail charm, likes music, theatre and other things I like, and is keen about writing. Well there is no use laboring the subject further.

I also called on Ida but found her out—twice. I left a note each time so she could call me at the hotel but didn't hear from her.

She has a quite modest but attractive apartment with her husband on the left bank. A number of mementos of her South Sea Islands days scattered about.

I had lunch with Gerald Norman and his wife and Joe Grigg. Saw Andre La Guerre who now represents Time *and* Life. *Dined with Jean Luc, and Sandhal, two French newspapermen with whom I covered the French army.*

I ate snails and steak and drank a lot of red wine. I went to the theater almost every night, except night before last when Sam Brewer arrived on his way to Spain. He used to represent the Chicago Tribune *in Turkey etc, and joined the* Times *a few months after I did.*

All my love,
Dana

December 8, 1946
Dear Mother:

The mails are so slow now that maybe I'd better start this off with a MERRY CHRISTMAS. It is too bad that as on so many Christmasses I cannot be at home, but we can look forward to my next vacation. It looks as though I would be spending the day in Frankfurt and I will try to telephone you. If it isn't possible that day I'll try to make it as near to Christmas as possible.

I'll be writing individual letters to the rest of the family and hope they arrive on time. In any case, Merry Christmas to all!

Just now I'm preparing to go to Nuremberg where we are having another set of trials. I'll stay only a few days.

The first Christmas parcel has arrived, full of delightful and delicious things. In particular I might mention the polish for Lincoln-Zephyr and the various fine cloths to go with it. Dates, Melba toast, Triscuits, chocolate, coffee, sandwich spreads and marshmallows make it a most valuable parcel that will brighten my own and my friends' holidays.

The New York Times *has sent a fruitcake to each staffer as it did last year.*

Down at Stuttgart the last few days I've been busy visiting some toy factories and think I'll get a fair Christmas piece out of them.

While I'm on the typewriter I must ask for something that is not exactly a Christmas present. Under the new policy cutting out living allowances I'll have to start receiving some of my salary over here. Now I can have the Times *send me part of it direct or I can continue to have it all sent to you as in the past and have you relay what I need. Would the latter arrangement be much trouble to you? I could just as well do it the other way, the only possible disadvantage being that the business office would always know how much I'm saving. Let me know what you think.*

Initially, however, before we decide how to handle the matter, you'd better send me a money order for $250. After that, beginning in January or February, I think I might need $100 a month, or most of what I am receiving as salary over a hundred dollars a week. It is not unreasonable. If I can save $100 a week I guess I shouldn't complain. Be sure to send a money order, not a check, as checks are difficult to cash here.

Ida Treat wrote me a charming letter from Paris saying she had tried desperately to get me on the phone after my calls but that the hotel phone was always "occupe". I don't doubt I'll get to Paris again and will make a special effort to see her that time.

Kathleen McLaughlin has left by boat, via Rotterdam, and is scheduled to be back here in February. You suggested I might do something nice for her and I thought it over very seriously. I'd like to have given her a little present, but just at that moment it would have looked as though I didn't expect her to come back, which may be the case. So I merely phoned and said goodbye.

I like the idea of doing something for the painter, too, but don't know him well enough as yet. Maybe after my next call. Even if I didn't feel the personal relationship justified a gift he might like to give me some paintings in exchange for paints from the US. I don't know whether that would be legal or not I'm sure but it would be reasonable.

All my love now. It is not very cold and doesn't feel much like Xmas around here. Dana

Munich
December 17, 1946
Dear Mother:
If the airmail flies you'll get this in time to make it a Christmas letter, so I'll say "Merry Christmas" once again.

Rather unexpectedly I'm down in Munich looking into the political situation, which is rather smelly. Apart from that Munich is quite agreeable. Pleasant little presscamp and a lot of agreeable people. Just a couple of days ago it suddenly turned bitter cold and there are a couple of inches of snow on the ground. Everything is turned to a sort of fairy land. I wouldn't mind spending the balance of the winter around here.

That Christmas box certainly zipped through in a hurry. I was worried that it wouldn't get there by Christmas! The little things I sent don't represent much in dollar value but the china and candle at least have personal stories attached to them and none of the stuff is black market or loot.

I'm looking forward to the Philco radio ever so much. That will be an ideal present.

Yesterday at the Bavarian Landtag meeting I ran into Oscar Reschke who was one of the U.P. combination office boy-teletype operators before the war. Now he is manager of the DANA news agency bureau here (the name, thank God, is going to be changed to DENA). He is a lively good natured tough little cuss much liked by all the UP. One of these days he will probably go back to them but he is holding out because they haven't made him a good enough offer yet.

I asked him over to the presscamp and we had a few drinks and then I went over to his house and spent the better part of the night with him, his wife and two of their friends killing a bottle of whiskey. That doesn't happen to me very often. This morning when I woke up my watch had stopped so I thought it must be late. I jumped out of bed and got dressed and then discovered it was only eight a.m. Altogether I didn't get much sleep.

Oscar is quite an "operator" and has all the local politicians eating out of his hand. Not bad for our former office boy. When he gets tight, incidentally, he lapses into Berlin dialect and becomes only half intelligible but his English never lets him down. He is a useful fellow to know.

I wonder what you and all the family will be doing for Xmas. I will phone if I can.

All my love now,
Dana

Please give my Christmas and New Years greetings to all our friends, Doctor and Mrs. Lowman, Dean Mary, the Sterlings and Murph. Eloise and Tom Landon too. And don't forget Tuckie. Give him an extra bone to bury, from me.

1947

The new year of 1947 that Dana celebrated in Berlin on January 1 was not the beginning of the Cold War. It had no formal beginning, but its roots lay in the fundamental philosophies in the organization of government—between the authoritarian, totalitarian regimes in the Soviet Union and the democratic governments of the Allies—Great Britain, the United States and France. These differences had been ignored during the War but became evident during the administrations of the zones of occupation of Germany following the War. It was hard to understand how fast the cooperation between the members of the Allies—Great Britain, the United States and the Soviet Union, could dissolve after their splendid cooperation against the Nazis. Another war, many people thought, was prevented by the mutual fear of the atomic bomb.

1947 was an important year politically, but for the people of northern Europe, it was a bitter ordeal. It began with a historically cold winter with inadequate coal, little food and rationing of clothing and other goods—like the years of the War. In early 1947, Truman announced his plan for extensive military and economic assistance for Greece and Turkey, which Britain could no longer afford. In June, Secretary of State George Marshall announced an extensive plan for the recovery and reconstruction of Europe, known as the Marshall Plan.

Berlin, January 2, 1947
Dear Mother:
With all the excitement of Christmas and New Years I've delayed writing till I got up here to Berlin.

ELIZABETH SCHMIDT CRAHAN

Really I have done pretty well this Christmas. The radio is simply indescribably wonderful. I could kick myself for not bringing it along up to Berlin, but it seemed such a little marvel that I hesitated moving it about for fear of damaging it, even though it is a portable. I won't do that again.

When I first tried it out it wouldn't work, so I took it down to the Presswireless office where people are supposed to know something about radios. They informed me that what it lacked was very simply, namely, tubes. Great was my distress until I recalled some rolls of cotton inside the cabinet which I had removed and tossed onto a top cupboard shelf. Sure enough, the tubes where there, intact, in the rolls. Good thing my miserly instincts prevented me from tossing the cotton in the wastebasket.

A few minutes after this discovery it was playing as clear as a bell and pulling in half a dozen stations. It has excellent tone. I am told by the technicians that I can use the current at our hotel even though it is 125 volts and the directions call for 115 but have hesitated thus far to try it. It would be tragic to burn something out.

Furthermore, I am now wearing the beautiful tan 70 percent wool, 30 percent fur, sleeveless sweater. Mrs. Justy, Delbert Clark's bride to be, keeps raving about it and wanting to feel it. (I trust it is the sweater she's interested in.)

Then there is all the candy and cookies and marshmallows and sandwich spread and magazines in the Xmas boxes. I've had a good taste myself and given most of it away to various families whose Xmas was considerably brightened thereby. Everything arrived before Christmas except the slippers to which I am still looking forward.

What a wonderful experience it was talking to you on the phone. Maybe you would like me to do it again from time to time. You and everybody sounded just the same. It gave me the feeling of being very near. Too bad Grandma had left.

Christmas as I told you I visited the families to whom we have sent Care packages. There are so many extra children around belonging to sundry relations that I was glad to be so well supplied with candy, etc to distribute.

Now I must tell you something sad. I went around to Niedstrasse 31 to deliver another Xmas parcel to Frau Sandrock and learned that she died on December 8. It seems that she had a heart attack after learning that some of her belongings stored in the country had been stolen. She was a dear old person and now of course I am sorry I did not do more for her while I could. So you may stop the Care packages for her. There is a young man, a nephew, who has the name of Leonard Sandrock, who is winding up her affairs. He seems quite able to look after himself and I do not want to pursue the acquaintance. Beyond that I know of no other Sandrock relations.

I will be in Berlin for some two weeks while Clark and Jack Raymond tour the zone. I am glad of the opportunity to learn more about the Berlin territory. You had better continue to write to me in Frankfurt. Incidentally, if you ever cable me I suggest that you do not use the APO address as that is not necessary anymore. Send it to Dana Schmidt, New York Times *correspondent, Park Hotel, Frankfurt. If the cable office is stupid about it you can insert care USFET Public Relations too.*

My phone conversation with Dorothy was splendid. She seemed very excited. Incidentally between the holidays I also drove down to Mannheim and spent an afternoon and evening with a girl who is lot of fun named Jinx Heffelfinger. She acts in a show organized by the CATS, which is initials for one of the army's theatrical groups. Her mother is in the Minnesota legislature, of all things.

I got to Berlin by car in time for the New Year's party at the press club here. The Berlin crowd is very "social" and seems to have all the best of everything.

All my love and best wishes for the New Year.

Dana

In all my numerous Xmas greetings it occurs to me for some reason I forgot to mention Eloise and Tom Landon. So please give them an extra New Years greeting from me.

Berlin
January 10, 1947
Dear Mother:
What with running this bureau single handed in a most literal manner all week my letter is rather late.

I find myself running around most of the day attending to administrative matters and have to struggle to find time to dig up some news. Whereas Clark would normally have another staffer or more here with him, plus his fiance Mrs. Giusti, the secretary Mrs. Stinksy, and the chauffeur, I am here all alone with the maid. Mrs. Giusti and the chauffeur are with Clark and Mrs. Stinksy chose this week to get sick.

However, I guess I've been making out all right. I managed to find an evening to go out and visit a German night club—the well known Femina—with four or five friends, and another to give a dinner party for six guests.

Clark will be back on Monday, having cut his trip a little short in order to get in an application for a Russian visa. Cyrus Sulzberger has told him to be ready in case he can be sent to the Moscow conference in March. I wouldn't mind going myself, but his absence may give me another whack at Berlin.

Three letters of yours including one full of clippings have been forwarded to me from Frankfurt, so I feel in touch. There was also a card from Pete Woodruff confirming your report that he is no longer with the Las Vegas Tribune. He worked with an engraving shop for a while and is now, I believe it is, with a clothing store. Doesn't sound too good to me. He said the paper changed hands and he and the managing editor got out.

My last weekender, on denazification, has appeared here in the Overseas Weekly, but this week there were no requests for anything from Germany. I too am not too impressed by the Daniell management, although of course ultimate control remains in the hands of Markel.

The young Leonard Sandrock insisted that I take a half dozen paintings and etchings from his uncle's collection, also a painting by an unknown artist which he believes to be of my grandfather Schmidt. Sandrock's paintings seem to me to be good, although I am no judge. Shall I send them all to 1132? Would you like to have them or not?

We've had a heavy snowfall here which, I hope, has broken the back of the cold. Heating in these parts is not excessive. It is a very cruel winter for the Germans and a lot of other people.

Berlin is a most fascinating city though hardly a pleasant one at present. I hope to have a little time to look around when Clark gets back and before I return to the zone. I expect I'll be going back to Munich very soon.

I haven't told you much yet about Mrs. Giusti. She is an Italian woman of rather la de da international background with whom Clark fell in love while he was in the army in Italy. I haven't quite figured out whether either of them have got their divorces from their first, yet or not. They may make out all right but I'm not too sure. She has already started a feud with Jack Raymond's wife and flaunts violent and oversimplified opinions such as "All Germans are Nazis." She serves as Clark's interpreter and inevitably influences him a great deal. He must have gone to a great deal of trouble to get her up here from Italy.

But withal she has a lot of charm and seems to like me and I don't mind her, so I won't worry about her.

All my love, as always,
Dana

PS: I do not think that your idea of coming to Switzerland or France is unfeasible. The main difficulty would be your medical attention. Help would certainly be cheaper in either country and the climate at say Montreux or on the Riviera should be good for you. Next time I see one of the airlines men here I'll talk to him about that ban on people who can't walk. Sounds silly to me.

Frankfurt
January 17, 1947
Dear Mother:

Here I am in my room in the Park Hotel, Frankfurt, listening to the soft strains of my Christmas radio, wearing my Christmas slippers and breathing the aroma of two enormous Christmas apples.

On my return here I found another big package from Los Angeles and also the airmail package containing gloves. Really I have had quite a Christmas this year. The slippers and gloves are truly beautiful and just the thing for this grim winter. I suspect that the gorgeous apples come from Oregon; they certainly keep their smell. The candy and cigarettes as you know are always welcome. And I enjoyed looking through the magazines. World Report I have decided contains much interesting material but tries to oversimplify. Harpers and Atlantic await my attention on my night table.

ELIZABETH SCHMIDT CRAHAN

My little Philco, by count of a few minutes ago, will receive forty three stations at eleven p.m. I'd say that was pretty good. I can hear England, France, Italy, Czechoslovakia, in addition to stations in Germany. I have just heard the BBC *home service news, which is a welcome change from the* American Forces Network.

I also have a pile of clippings from you to look through. I'll check them to see whether there are any unsigned items from the hands of Schmidt. As a matter of fact there should be a good many during my two weeks in Berlin as I filed a lot of "shorts," in addition to those which the desk "shortened." We are, oh woe, having a hold down drive. That sort of thing happens even on the Times. *But obviously they have been getting a little more than they can digest from Germany. We must all try to concentrate our stuff more.*

The time in Berlin was most enjoyable though busy. We had James Martin, head of the decartelization branch, and his wife to dinner before I left. They are the couple I met on the Autobahn when I had the leak in my gas tank some months ago.

You wrote on the eighth that I had no bylines yet in January, but I suppose you had not yet received the piece dated the forth on possibilities or a German signing the peace treaty or the Clay press conference two days later, both of which were signed. I have several pieces stored up that should be good for signers and will be going to Nuremberg for Papen's and Fritsche's denazification trials on the 24th, which should be interesting. Thereafter I may drop down to Munich again. And next month I will probably visit the French zone, at last.

Speaking of travel…my tires have at last reached Bremen. Now I have to wait until American Express *there receives the bill of lading I have sent them and figure out a way to get them transported up here. But at least I know they are within reach.*

I had to have the front springs of the Lincoln (Delbert has christened it Abraham) repaired in Berlin. The bad roads play hob with a good car. But the engine is perfect. It hasn't been touched since I got it and I've covered about 13,000 miles.

Which reminds me: I owe Dick Clark an inner tube, for a sixteen inch tire, diameter size 650. Could you buy me one and send it to me parcel post, charging my bank account. This paragraph should serve as a request for the post office.

Dick has just returned from thirty days in the USA. He paid his way both ways by air but says it was worth it. In the meantime, incidentally, his car, which has been stolen, was recovered by German police at Cologne. Pretty good work. It is a rather ancient but powerful Hudson cabriolet without a roof. The lock was broken and he unwisely left it out in front of the hotel all one night. At four a.m. someone saw it; it five it was gone.

About my expenses. The way I have worked things out with Delbert Clark, so as to have the whole staff on the same basis, I am now back on practically the same standard as before. The only change is that I pay for my meals when in Frankfurt. I was willing to pay my hotel too but he thought since the rest of the staff is getting its hotel bills paid I'd better too. So the money problem won't be too great. However, you'd better send me another $250, in money orders. That should hold me financially for quite a long time, and I won't be requiring monthly amounts. I must apologize right now, furthermore, for not having confirmed receipt of the first $250 sooner.

It is possible that I will give up my room in the Park soon and move my headquarters to Munich. There is not much reason to stay here now that the command of OMGUS and USFET are concentrated under Clay in Berlin.

All my love, and hope that stiff neck is better.
Dana
PS: Had a nice letter from Grandma for which I thank her very much. Also two from Dorothy.

February 3, 1947
Dear Mother:
This is just a note on the fly because I am leaving immediately for Heidelberg and then for Stuttgart and know it will be several days till I can get around to a letter again.

Your letter of the 25th just came in. I hasten to confirm receipt of the $100. You had better send the remaining $150 to me at the Frankfurt address. We the correspondents, have just taken over this hotel to run as a club and I have to cough up not only a $25 membership fee but also a $75 loan, although I expect to be going on to Munich.

Thanks for buying the inner tube for Dick Clark. He will be surprised to get it back.

The tires are at last on my car. Would you believe it, however, they sent me only two instead of the four I asked for. I almost sent off a snotty message about it but then decided that I could get by with the two and had best take no notice.

The list of my dividends is quite impressive. I guess Mr. Sterling knows his business.

It seems to me that the Lincoln should last another year, considering the initial investment. Its engine is still in perfect shape although there are some rattles which should be removed. Without going to a lot of special trouble, please, and when you happen to have an occasion, would you inquire whether it would be possible to buy a set of four shock absorbers for a Lincoln Zephyr '42 club coupe and whether they could be sent through the APO to me. Mine are in poor shape, with all these bad roads. If they should be easily obtainable this paragraph would serve as a request.

Yes, Raymond has been complaining bitterly about the clamp down on his by-lines. I don't understand it as a lot of his pieces seem to be merit signers in my opinion. He got Clark to write a letter to James about it. Raymond is a hysterically hard worker.

All my love now, Dana

February 12, 1947
Dear Mother:
With all the snow and ice the mails have slowed down and nothing has come through from you this week, which doesn't happen very often I must say.— I mean the mail is usually pretty regular.

Since I got back to Frankfurt I've been up to my ears in an accumulation of little matters and stories that pile up when I'm traveling. In every way I do find it an annoying town. The extreme destruction and crowding of both Germans and Americans seems to make everybody a little overwrought.

I don't believe I've told you that last Saturday I went skiing on the Feldberg in the Taunus mountains. I was most surprised to find that the American army had set up a most acceptable resort there and was renting out first class skis, boots, socks etc., providing food and truck transportation to the top of the mountain. Everything is free except the food. I really had a delightful afternoon with the American magazine correspondent whose name stupidly escapes me at the moment and Helen Kirkpatrick, friend of Chicago Daily News—their foreign staff was practically dissolved.

The two of them were here mainly because on that particular evening there was to be a terrific, but really, party at the Park hotel marking the opening of the Frankfurt Press Club. Even McNarney was here but did not stay long, having imbibed too many Martinis too early in the evening. There was fruit from Italy, champagne from France, lobsters etc. The women were in evening gowns and a few of the men in dinner jackets and tails. Perhaps I should see about getting a dinner jacket when I am home; social life is gradually getting back to normal.

A fellow named John M. Payne wrote me the other day asking me to help him get a job. He is a Pomona graduate, one of Dr. Salt's old students, and sounds like a nice earnest fellow. I'll relay his letter to Cyrus Sulzberger and will tell him in my reply that he may call on you in Los Angeles some day if he likes. I don't know what you can do for him except perhaps give him a cup of tea and some advice based on my experience and your own.

This is a depressing season of the year, like four a.m. in the morning as somebody said today. Unless one can spend one's time in the mountains the weather is fit for neither man nor beast, freezing thawing blowing raining.

There doesn't seem to be a great deal more to report so I'll say goodbye and

All my love to you all, Dana

I am so thankful our Tuckie escaped serious damage in his collision with a car. He has certainly turned into a beautiful fellow. Did I thank you for the picture?

Please, incidentally, thank Eliza for the splendid pictures of her two offspring. Uncle is delighted.

ELIZABETH SCHMIDT CRAHAN

February 16, 1947
Dear Mother:
I have replied to your cable about the beach lot saying "okay, sounds splendid." And that it does. I'd love to have a little parcel by the Pacific. I'm looking forward to further description by letter from you.

What can we do with my lot? Don't want to let it lie fallow do we? Maybe Eliza can devise a structure for it in her spare time. What about that? And you could use it, you and Steinie, rent free, whenever I wasn't there, and when I was there too. That would be my present to you. Yes, I think that would be a good idea, but I'll wait till I hear what you have in mind by letter.

Now here is real news: Delbert Clark agrees that I should take my annual holiday beginning about April 15, thirty days in the States at least, excluding traveling time. If no one higher up objects and the Moscow conference doesn't interfere it looks like that would be it. I am quite excited and looking forward particularly to seeing Dorothy. I'll want to spend some time in New York but maybe I could persuade Dorothy to come to California. She did some newspaper work before the war and is working for the Public Relations office of the Girl Scouts of America right now. She is a very superior gal. Her father as far as I know has some kind of automobile agency, but I've never met him or her mother. They were away on a trip when I was last in New York. The father of whom I speak is however her mother's second husband. His name is Lane. That is rather confusing. Let's leave it at that now, Mother, and I'll tell you more in time.

And here is more news: I spoke to Mr. Parsons who is Traffic Manager in Europe for American Overseas Airlines *about the possibilities of your flying overseas. He assured me that the rules of which you spoke could be waved and promised to look into the matter and let me know. His understanding was that the rule was not a safety precaution but designed for the convenience of other passengers since a persons who could not move freely might have difficulty using the toilet. I explained you would be traveling with a nurse in any case and would definitely not inconvenience anybody.*

I have been skiing again, this morning. There were scads of people out but it was most enjoyable. It does me a lot of good to get out in the air. Dick Clark, who can't ski at all, and Ed Hartrich of the Herald Tribune, *who is fairly good, went with me.*

Well I think that's enough good news for one letter.

All my love, to Grandma, Steinie, Eliza too.

Dana

Mother you had better send out some more CARE *packages for me to all the people you have been supplying. My German families, Klein & Ofenloch are really in desperate difficulties. I mean hungry. Roger sent me a note too via the Paris office thanking for the packages, so I guess he and his mother are pretty grateful. You will have to use your own judgment about the relations in the British zone as I don't know them. Don't forget the Pave family in Paris.*

In addition, please send packages to the following. I am merely asking you to do these as a convenience to me as I will charge them on my expense account.

Dr. Walter Becher
Ausschuss fuer Fluechtlinge
Waagemuellerstr 23, Munich

Oscar Reschke, Bureau Manager
DENA News agency
Ismaningerstr 67, Munich
Both these people have been of aid to me on the news side.

CARE *may be out of ten in one packages by now, but send their new kind if they are.*

Frankfurt, February 23, 1947
Dear Mother:

About that income tax slip. Delbert Clark tells me that it is customary NYT *procedure to send them out to employees. He also tells me that the auditor made a special inquiry at the Bureau of Internal Revenue shortly before he, Clark, left the States and was told that he would not, <u>definitely not,</u> be subject to income tax while working and living abroad as a foreign correspondent.*

In Clark's opinion it was not even a good idea to file a return. However, since my money is paid out care of you in Los Angeles I dare say that it is just as well to explain that situation. You can stick to that point in any case, that the money I earned as foreign correspondent in 1946 is not subject to income tax. None of the correspondents who are permanently stationed abroad and not residents of the U.S., like myself, pay income tax.

How fine that you managed to find the shock absorbers so speedily. I'm sure they will improve my driving comfort. If you should have difficulty mailing them perhaps you had better just hold on to them till I get home and I can arrange to ship them on my return to Europe. Since the last tires took more than five months to reach me I haven't asked the office to ship me any more before I go home on vacation. When I'm in New York I'll ask to have more shipped by a more expeditious route.

Winter is truly endless around here, which would be all right if I spent my time skiing. However I must leave sometime today for Nuremberg to cover von Papen's sentencing in the denazification trial. I don't have to go but I want to. It may well be a front page story.

This weekend I was planning to drive up to Marburg to visit the replacement depot where all American troops arrive. But I was tipped off not to leave town as there would be a good story breaking here Sunday morning. It turned out to be the announcement of another raid on underground Nazi movements.

I am listening to my Philco as I write. It is very pleasant to have it. I might add that my Xmas slippers and gloves are proving most comforting in this weather.

The buzzer downstairs has just buzzed twice, indicating important news. I presume that it is the announcement of names of some of those arrested in last night's raid. So I'll go see.

All my love now, to you all, Dana

March 2, 1947
Dear Mother:
I'm leaving for Munich very shortly and wanted to get this in the mail before I left.

Let me acknowledge receipt of the $150 money orders before I forget, as I usually do.

My news this week is positive but financially not too hot. For one, I have reserved a seat aboard a plane April 30. Delbert wanted me to postpone my departure until then. But Cy cables that I'm not entitled to a roundtrip-paid vacation this year, although I can take it at my own expense. So that's what I'll do. Cy only is going to Moscow.

The plane will cost $1009 round trip to Los Angeles and back. It will be best for me to buy it here since I avoid the 15 percent transport tax on tickets bought in the U.S.

......

I'm afraid there's been a slight interruption while I travelled to Munich, but I find this letter still in my typewriter at this end, at the Munich Press camp.

In addition I have loaned $200 to a friend here and don't expect to get it back for a long time. That makes quite a lot of money I'll be wanting. I have $300 on hand from the office so I won't be needing very much for current expenses. Altogether I think you had better send me $1500 in money orders. I must consider that I'll want money in New York.

I am enclosing that Hospital Insurance policy. I received it some months ago, pushed it in a drawer and forgot about it. There is a cardboard slip that goes with it which I am supposed to keep to show when and if I need to make a claim.

Yes, by all means invite Gladwin Hill to tea, or for a drink, which is more his style. I think you would enjoy him. He is the happy extrovert type. I am not sure but I think his family lives in California too. Last time I saw Gladwin was in the New York office when he was about to take off for a holiday in Cuba.

It gives me great satisfaction to think that I own, or practically own a beach lot. That and my travel money are going to keep my account down to rock bottom for some months I presume. I agree that it would probably be wasteful to build right now, but I think we should as soon as the experts advise that building costs are as low as they are likely to get. We can work that out while I'm home. The plan you outline sounds excellent, with your quarters downstairs and mine upstairs.

Now one more financial item I have your letter of February 8 telling about a possible course at the Institute for Crippled and Disabled in New York. If you can possibly get in I think you should not pass up the opportunity, and I would like to pay for it or at least share in the expense. Let me know if it would do any good for me to go see those people in New York when I am there.

So now I have finally transferred myself, books, papers, clothes, radio and all to Munich. I won't be here very long right now as I'm planning to go up to Nuremburg on Wednesday and then to visit several points in the northern part of the zone. The important thing, however, is that I have at last made the change of base. My moving around has diminished my output of late but I think there'll be a renaissance down here.

It is still freezing and there is a lot of snow on the ground, but the sun is out and some people think spring may come. Spring, you know, is the best time for skiing, in my opinion. A story on Garmisch seems called for.

My much belated birthday greetings to Steinie. My love to Grandma and Eliza and an extra pat on the head for Tuckie.

Lots of Love, Dana (note my new address, which you had better switch to.)

March 23, 1947
Frankfurt
Dear Mother:
I have received the shock absorbers. They certainly were quite a load and I'm sure they will greatly improve the rising comfort of my car when they are installed. I was told by the mechanics here that the ones I had were worn out and could not be repaired or replaced here.

You asked in one of your last whether I wouldn't like to send one of these blanket parcels. Yes, it might be quite a good idea, although food is probably even more appreciated. I do not believe that I have received confirmation from you that you sent off the last CARE *packages I asked for just before my last trip to Munich. There was one for Oscar Reschke and one for another man in Munich in addition to the usual recipients, in Frankfurt and elsewhere. Did you send these packages? Also have you sent the $1500, and to what address?*

I have finally got a crate made and will send off those pictures by Herr Sandrock in the next few days.

So much for business. Business as distinguished from work, that is. My efforts the past week have been of the long term variety and haven't paid off in any bylineable stories to speak of. But I don't think that should be cause for worry as long as what I have been doing has ultimate value.

I spent two days at Marburg visiting the Replacement depot, and since I've been back I've been interviewing some very interesting people who aren't exactly news but know what they're talking about. One was Eugen Kogon, a truly brilliant Christian Socialist writer who spent seven years in Buchenwald concentration camp and has written a remarkable book called, "Der SS—Staat." Another may turn out to be something of a story. Hanna Reitsch, the aviatrix, who is out of the klink and very active among the "Youth."

This evening I'm going down to the Main station to continue my soldier interviews. Still for that troublesome piece about GI's. I am enclosing some clippings, most of which are from among those you sent me. They are pieces by Schmidt, but unsigned. It has been raining cats dogs and small calves for days but I suspect that spring is at hand.

All my love now, to you all, Dana

Munich, April 7, 1947
Dear Mother:
Here it is Easter Monday and I am in Munich and thinking that I will be home ere long.

This week's letter I must admit is really last week's because the tour into the French zone I've just performed interfered with my usual schedule.

Here I found one of your letters enclosing money orders, for $400. The others had been forwarded to me in Frankfurt and will shortly be returned to me here. So I'll be able to pay for my air passage. It isn't cheap, is it? But it is worth it.

The French zone tour was rather unexpected. A fellow named Trevor-Roper turned up in Frankfurt for the Sunday paper. Since I was about to go South and he had no transport we decided to travel together. He is known as the British Intelligence officer who compiled the record of Hitler's last days, established that he was dead, found his will, and performed a number of other interesting feats.

By profession he is an Oxford Don, or is it don. Anyway, he is delightful company. I learned more from him in a few days than I had learned for many many months. His specialty is history and he knows how to relate it to current *affairs.* He told me I could easily study at Oxford, with my BA, MS degrees, an intriguing thought. Lots of people my age are there he said, making up for time lost during the war.

We called on Professor Jaspers, the most noted prof at Heidelberg, tracked down the brother of the Graf von Stauffenberg who tried to blow up Hitler, visited the editor of the best newspaper now being published in Western Germany, drank our share of the French officers' wine, and had a most stimulating time.

On the way out of the French zone we went to a place called Ottobeuren to see an astonishing Baroque church. Unfortunately I don't know much about architecture, but it was a thing of great beauty and heroic dimensions tucked away in a tiny town which I, for one, had never heard of.

The inhabitants of the French zone have very little to eat and the French mismanage the place and exploit it alarmingly. Gasoline is so short that we had to take a three days' supply; there are scarcely any vehicles on the roads in the zone. But I am still very fond of the French.

I was sorry to hear in your last that you have been unwell and trust that you are feeling better now. I expect to come home to a healthy mother! It will be fun to examine my lot and plan the house.

My thought at the moment, Mother, is to stop only a day or so in New York on the way home, then spend two weeks at home and finally return to New York to see Dorothy the rest of the time. I will try to persuade her to come out to California, although that is obviously a difficult decision for her to make. On the other hand I might decide after seeing her in New York not to return there for so long. I'm afraid that such matters are unpredictable.

It is a shame I can't plan to be in L.A. longer. Maybe I will. We will see how it works out. For the year that follows we must plan seriously on your making a trip to Europe. After all, it is not difficult, living conditions are getting quite civilized for those who can pay in Suisse and Francs, and I think I can afford it. Maybe Grandma would like to come too, which would be nice. For the vacation that follows this one I gather I am entitled to a round trip home paid by the office.

I am quite comfortably installed here in Munich and wouldn't mind staying. But this will be Kathleen's realm. Mine, in the west and in the French zone will be more productive of news, if less comfortable.

From here I must go up to Stuttgart to cover Schacht's trial and then to Nuremberg. I don't like trials, but I'm sure going to get them the next few days.

All my love to you all, Dana

Oscar Reschke and my other friends haven't got their Care packages yet. I imagine you have already confirmed sending them.

Enclosed some more items of mine for the clipping volumes. I'm looking forward to looking them over.

Munich
April 8, 1947
Dear Mother:
Several notes and letters came from you all in a bunch and enclosing the money orders for my trip home. So, in addition to confirming receipt by cable, I'll get off this note.

In your last note you say something about having sent part of the money from your account. I did not want you to do that, but if you have I am very grateful.

You should not worry about my spending a large chunk of money to come home. As you saw I did not feel upset particularly because Cy did not feel the Times *should pay for the trip this year. Next year I will be entitled to a free round trip.*

If I were to get married it would be worth a great deal to me, and I certainly am not likely to get married unless I come home. So the necessity of liquidating some of my stocks, even at a loss, for the purpose does not alarm me. On the whole I spend little money most of the year so that I can have a lot for the few important things, such as car, or trip home.

You say I have had less in The Times *in the last six months. I explained that that would be the case when we expanded our staff here. It was quite proper. I had too much on my hands before. As for change of assignment, I don't see how*

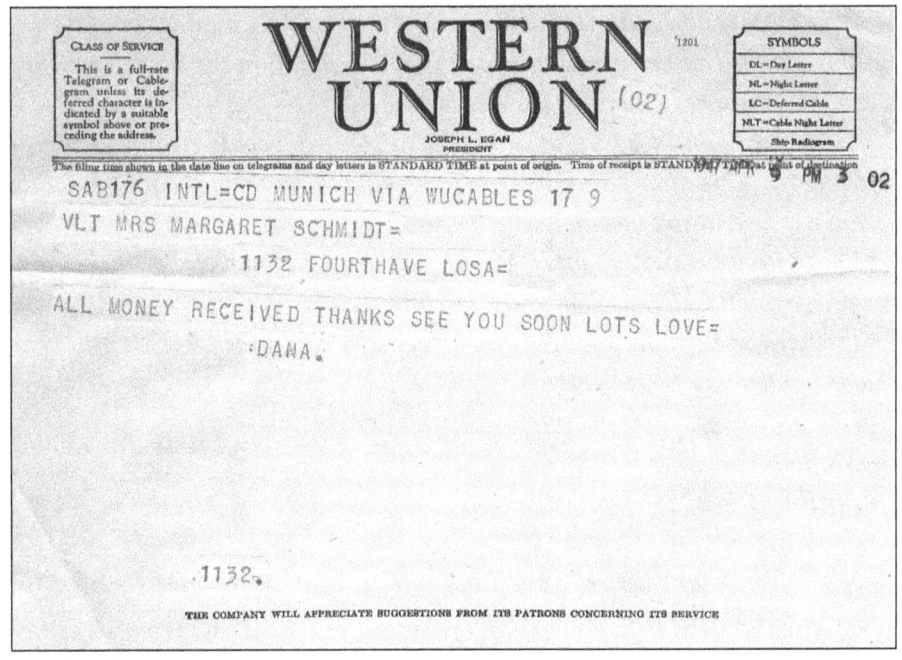

I can get out of another year in Germany. I still have in mind a book and so am not unwilling to take the additional year here. My trip home will enable me to keep in touch with the people who would determine any change of scene in the future.

You shouldn't have any regrets at all about the beach lot. I certainly haven't. I'll have made up the expense again ere long. Your planning has been splendid and I couldn't ask for a better business manager.

Finally, the international situation. I don't know what the Southern California hysteria-mongers have been putting about but in my humble opinion war is extremely unlikely for some time to come, for reasons I have discussed before. At any rate my reasons are as good as those that can be presented for the opposite argument, and there's no use worrying about things over which we have no control.

This note has turned out to sound something like a TASS "dementi". I'll write more fully at the end of the week.

All my love, to you all, Dana

PS: you may as well continue to use the Frankfurt address as I will return there soon before my departure.

A splendid package has arrived here for me including Dad's car's tire tubes and lots of wonderful cookies and candy! I certainly do have a wonderful family to look after me—
Love Dana

Munich
April 14, 1947
Dear Mother:
This will be one of my last letters before I see you, I suppose. It seems too good to be true.

The last weeks are jammed full of things to be done and stories to be written. As I wrote Grandma I have been dragged into the Publisher's efforts to prevent the home of a friend of his from being requisitioned. Now I must see about finding a pair of suspenders to go with his green Bavarian shorts. I am going to try to find some fancy pairs and present them to him when I get to New York. I hope he doesn't take to coming to the office in his Bavarian costume.

I see that Del Clark has been writing some extremely tendentious stuff about the German scene. I do not hold his judgment in high esteem in these matters. He is just back from the Russian tour. Dick Clark went for the U.P.

Tonight or tomorrow early I must drive to Stuttgart for the Laenderrat meeting. In a year's time I have missed only one if its meetings. It is always worth it just for General Clay's press conference.

I agree with you about wishing that I could get out of the German assignment, but not just yet. After another year. I'll speak to the Publisher about it.

Thanks for sending the Care packages. They are very slow just now, apparently. I heard of one sent in November that hadn't been delivered yet.

I am enjoying my newly acquired wealth of candy, cookies, marshmallows and other good things. The radio too is a god send. The room I have here is suitable for entertaining and I have had a number of people in for drinks. I have the Nay painting, a splendid Turkish pipe and a porcelain "Munchner Kindl" given me by the Mayor of Munich on exhibition.

I was quite startled this afternoon to find that half the people of Munich seemed to be out by the river sunning themselves in various stages of nudity. A welcome change of temperature.

The car is still functioning splendidly, but I'm thinking of putting it up in the AES garage at Stuttgart during my absence for a general overhaul. That is the best garage I've run into.

All my love Mother,
Dana

Munich
April 22, 1947
Dear Mother:
Question is whether you see this letter or me first, but I'll write anyway.

I have my ticket in hand. The cost rather less than expected—only some $970. They must have altered the fares since my earlier inquiry.

It is my intention to spend the last few days before my departure shuttling between Munich and Nuremberg where the Flick trial is in progress. Then I'll drive to Stuttgart, park my car in the excellent AES garage there for some overhauling and proceed to Frankfurt by train to catch my plane.

We are having such gorgeous weather that I find the mountains and lakes of Bavaria most distracting. Sunday I drove out to the Tegernsee with friends and spent some delightful hours in the sun.

In a few days I'll see if I can be of any help with that booklet. I'm no expert, however. You probably know more about that kind of thing than I.

If Mrs. Malcolm is on hand while I'm home that'll be fine. I agree that having Ida too would be quite a handful, but I knew you are quite capable of rising to any social occasion.

The clippings as always were interesting. I think you will have noticed a lot of my stuff last week, although this week is shaping up quietly.

I feel almost as though I ought to pop this in the envelope and run to the mail box, but I suppose that wouldn't do any good. Dorothy writes that she is waiting eagerly to see me in New York.

All my love, Dana

LETTERS HOME: 80 YEARS LATER

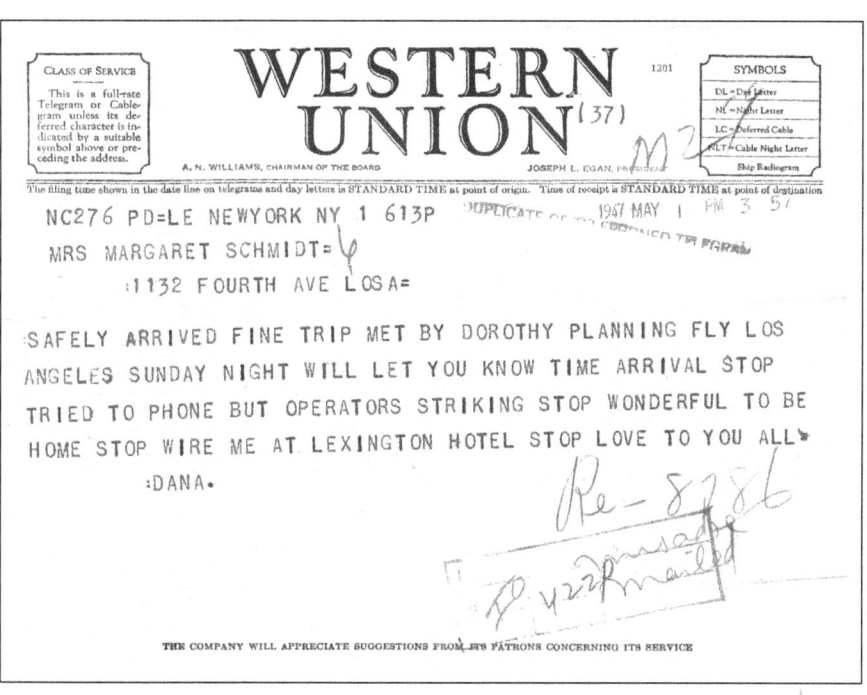

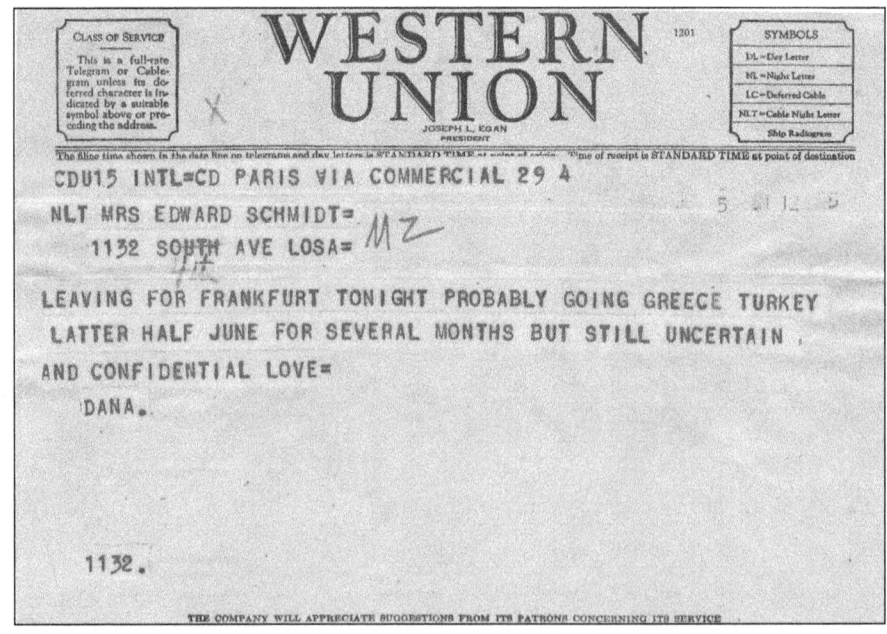

Frankfurt
June 7, 1947
Dear Mother:

It is after one a.m. and I have to catch a plane at nine tomorrow and pack my stuff together in the meantime, so this isn't going to be the letter I intended to write you on my return.

Anyway it is to tell you I am back and back at work. I must phone Cy in Paris on the eleventh to find out the final verdict on the Greece Turkey deal.

Here I went to some trouble today to re-orient myself on what goes on and turned out a little story on Frankfurt, the capital. In the evening Markel and Ray Daniel and Tania showed up in their twenty-five dollar a day army sedan and I went out to victory Guest house after dinner for a long chin about "Germany". Couldn't make it for dinner because of writing a story. I found Ray and Markel weren't quite as unreasonable in the approach to the German problem as I had suspected, especially Ray. Markel seemed mainly confused. Brilliant editors, of which he is doubtless one, do not of course have to be themselves brilliant political analysts.

Cy told me not to discuss it with anyone but Delbert Clark appears to be entirely au courant about my going to Greece though he thinks it's only for one month. It will obviously be longer if at all but I am pretty sure I'll be back.

Cyrus made it clear that he expected me to serve out two years in Germany before I got a permanent change of scene. He also confirmed that I would be due sixty days leave at the end of the year now beginning and was receptive to my idea of taking a few months leave of absence at that time to write a book. Asked me to give him a memo on it when the time came.

I also got Cy to get the office to pay for the shock absorbers auto tires and the new set of front and rear springs I bought in New York. The shock absorbers are of course the ones you bought for me.

Now let me tell you a bit about the trip. It was strictly routine as far as Shannon in Ireland where I perceived a TWA *plane bound for Paris and tried to be transferred aboard. They said it was too late, but I was allowed to wait for an* Air France *plane a couple of hours later which took me to Paris direct.*

That saved me the trip via London I would otherwise have had to take I should have explained that I had been unable to book a passage direct to Paris on the day I wanted it.

The office had reserved me a room at the old hotel Mont Thabor where I have stayed several times before quite comfortably. Had a chat with Callender, who remains self-centered as ever and lunch with Cy and his wife Marina, who remain as charming as ever. Would like to have spent more time with Lansing Warren who is always delightful, kind, interested and gentle. He begins to look quite old I'm sorry to say. Still lives half in the Ritz, at great expense, and half in his apartment, because his wife is such an elderly sissy.

There wasn't opportunity for much else except to see a few French friends and drop in at the Scribe to shake hands with the waiters and porters who all remember me. For my bad temper if nothing else. They always ask about Archambault who was their favorite. He was the sort of person for whom the head waiter would produce a glass of the best cognac at the same time he was telling Colonels and Generals in the same dining room that there wasn't any.

The affair of the office robbery remains unsolved. Apparently Roger was questioned without result. A couple of portable typewriters were stolen.

Come time to leave I couldn't get a sleeper to Frankfurt on the regular train. But Cy's secretary Mme. Kougoucheff managed to get me one on a French train that went as far as Mainz. That turned out all right although I had to wait three hours at Mainz for a local German train to Frankfurt.

Now I must really close.

Give my love to Grandma and Eliza and Ken and Steinie and please excuse the typing errors on this borrowed machine.

Oh, must tell you, I managed to collect PX rations for the entire time of my absence! Six cartons of cigarettes!

I am anxiously awaiting word about that nerve in your foot. Seems like the sort of thing that should clear up without too much trouble. And I do want to add that it will make me very happy if you will accept my suggestion that I pay for the lessons and take three hundred dollars off my account for the purpose. You don't need to take it all off at once.

Speaking of money, the American Automobile Association wrote that they never got the check for 26.80 I sent them from Los Angeles. Remember you gave me the check? They suggested they may have lost it in handling and asked me to stop payment on it. Would you look it up and stop payment? I will send them another from the account I opened with the Corn Exchange Bank Trust Co. in New York.

I had to open this new account, incidentally, because the East River outfit doesn't handle checking accounts. I over hastily closed my East River account when I discovered this and then, remembering that certain dividends were paid out to me there, I had to reopen it, with ten dollars. The bank made arrangements to see that anything sent to the old account number goes on my account all right. I will enclose the bank book so you can take care of it as before. Also some passport pix I had taken. The square one was taken by our photo dept in Paris and the other one by a commercial photog in NY.

Now, this is really the end. All my love,
Dana
I'm too tired to "copy read" this tonight, but you will be able to make it out.

June 18, 1947
Dear Mother:
Between my last letter and this one I have been to Munich and Stuttgart and recovered my car from the AES garage.

Munich was highly enjoyable as always. We have converted the press camp's lily pond into a swimming pool, but it was too chilly most of my time there to use it. The car had been worked on, but only a little. I'll put it in another garage, in Stuttgart this time, during my absence in Greece, and hope for the best. I want all the scratches and blemishes cleaned up and may possibly have it rebored.

I drove up from Stuttgart this morning in time to catch Clay's press conference (about ten seconds to spare). Tomorrow Arthur Hays Sulzberger will be here. He is driving from Minden in the British zone, will see General Huebner Friday morning and then drive to Nuremberg and thence to Munich. He obviously takes an exceptionally great interest in Germany. I am to see him for some special instructions on my work in Greece and Turkey. It is all quite intriguing.

Your letter of June 6 has come, but no other as yet. I am relieved to learn that you only pulled a muscle doing those exercises. Injury to a nerve, which I had previously thought it was, somehow seems more serious. A pulled muscle will be all right if given time according to my experience. Lots of people pull muscles when they start something strenuous after a long layoff, like football.

I knew you must have enjoyed the beach. Having Nell there too must have made it doubly pleasurable. In another year I should think we will have a little place of our own! Then Tuckie can enjoy it too.

I have gathered material for a "literary letter" and a Magaziner since my return and the next few days I'll be quite busy writing. It has been impossible for me to get a reservation on the plane to Athens this coming Sunday, when I was supposed to leave, and I am relieved to have the extra time. It will probably be Wednesday the 25th now.

From now on please send me everything you can on Greece and Turkey, as I see you have already begun. Not only from the Times, however, but from magazines of all kinds. You might even see if there are any books on the current scene or recent past that would be helpful. Greece is of course the main interest. You'd better send them to me care of the American Embassy, Athens. Be sure to mention NY Times on the envelope and you might add the words, please hold.

All my love now, Mother, also to Grandma, Steinie, Eliza.
Dana

Frankfurt, June 22, 1947
Dear Mother:
This is my last letter to you from Frankfurt for a while. I'll be leaving by Swedish airlines for Athens day after tomorrow. Meanwhile I am naturally in the midst of a great upheaval trying to do all the things that should be done before I go.

Most important are the various things I've been working on at Shep Stone's suggestion. Magaziner, literary letter, drama piece, and editorial on the War Department's requirement of ten years' citizenship for renewal of contracts.

Meanwhile I've tried to turn out a little news for the daily, and that's time consuming.

A lot of my friends have terminated their jobs here just recently so that it seems normal that I'm going. Dick Clark of the U.P. has been sent to Prague. Sam Wahrhaftig, a friend and a brilliant fellow in Military Government has been "kicked upstairs" to Berlin following a row. Peter Blake, another friend at Army HQ is gone; I saw him and wife in New York. Eleanor Fate in the Displaced Persons branch, a primary news source, has finished her contract. So when I get back here I'll have to make a few new beginnings.

Bill Freese our photo and business man here is going to take care of my car in my absence and see that the various parts that haven't arrived yet are put on in my absence. He is also going to receive all packages and mail for me and take care of them. He is a much more reliable person than was Gus Beck, his predecessor. I don't think I ever told you that Gus had something of a nervous breakdown and asked to be recalled. He apparently got a fixation that his job was too big for him, that he couldn't handle it, and worked himself into a collapse. For the last couple of months he looked a wreck and was a trying person to have around because he moaned about his troubles incessantly.

The Publisher has been here and gone again, to Nuremberg and Munich. He invited Freese and me out to the so-called VIP (Very Important Persons) House for dinner and we guided him out of town the next day. He's been traveling in a $25 a day War Department sedan with his son, a colored driver and an army Major as escort. His son is the one I once gave skiing lessons at an early age, known as Punch, now aged 21.

I wrote American Automobile Association about the check and assume the matter will be straightened out.

It was splendid that Nell Malcolm could make that visit with you. I'll collect the $20 some day when I'm in London.

In Athens I think you may as well stick to the care American Embassy address for a while. Shan Sedgwick's address is 15, Carneado Street, but I don't think I'll use it and will probably stay at the hotel Grande Bretagne.

I don't think you should re-subscribe to the magazines for the time being until I have returned to Germany or have another permanent post.

The letter you sent me to the New York office only just caught up with me. It must have reached NY too late, or they omitted to give it to me. It was a very fine letter.

All my love now, to you all. Next stop Athens.
Dana
P.S. I do hope your leg is better.

Athens
Hotel Grande Bretagne
June 28, 1947
Dear Mother:

I have arrived, at last, in beautiful, fascinating Athens and am in charge, effective today. Shan Sedgwick and his wife have gone to the airport—I think they preferred to make their adieus privately—and the baby is mine. Mrs. Sedgwick, however, remains here. She has had an invitation to lecture in the States, so I wonder what the future holds for them and for me.

The trip down here was a thing of extraordinary beauty. In Geneva, over Lake Geneva, which looked very familiar, then to Niece, where again I recognized the mouth of the river we crossed to liberate Niece. Everything quite peaceful, the air a caressing warm breeze. Rome wasn't quite so attractive, the way we hit it, at midnight; a couple of Roman scribes took two hours transcribing the data in our passports and took exception to my not having acquired a transit visa, which put me at the end of the procession. At last we were driven in to a clean place called hotel Diana. We were hustled to the airport without time for a proper breakfast and then had to wait till two p.m. while the plane's radio was fixed. But there was a pleasant crowd on board, the sort of people one traditionally meets on ships, and we had a lot of fun. There was a third secretary from the Ankara US. Embassy who energetically tried to climb a Roman fountain, two Arabs from

Saudi Arabia who sat on the ground at the slightest provocation, a pretty blond Dutch cabaret singer on her way to a job in Istanbul, and American engineer going to install machinery in Turkey, and me, among others.

At Athens Shan had left a note at the airport saying he couldn't wait to meet me as he had an important engagement. Rockwell, the third secy, gave me a lift into town in an Embassy car and I have seen him several times since. He is an old friend of Shan's and of the press generally apparently. Pretty well all the embassyites in Turkey I used to know have departed from what he tells me, although I believe Bob Kelly, once counselor of Embassy, now a businessman, is around. And of course the Turks are still there, including some I knew.

I was plunged immediately into the Greek maelstrom, first at a dinner Shan gave for me, to meet some of his friends, then in the course of visits to the American Embassy and the Greek foreign office. I was very kindly received by the Ambassador here, MacVeigh. We talked more than an hour, and after that I talked to one of the secretaries of Embassy for several more hours, absorbing background. I have accumulated a stack of books and pamphlets to read.

A couple called Butler (he British she Greek) have asked me to go sailing this weekend and I'll take along a book or two, although I know one rarely gets a chance to read on such outings. I hesitated about going off sailing before I've had half a chance to look around, but Shan insisted nothing ever happens here on the weekend and that they were a couple worth knowing. The thought is that I might use Mrs. Butler as an interpreter. I would frankly prefer someone whom I hadn't met socially but on a strictly business basis, and I would prefer a man. But not knowing my way around I think I'll have to use her.

The sun is terrifically hot here. Everything folds up between 1:30 and 5:00. In fact a lot of the Greeks don't work in the afternoon at all. They do get a fairly early start, however, at 8:30 or 9:00.

Probably I'll be going to Turkey at the end of July. It seems that our string correspondent there has got himself in a jam with the Turkish government and his case will come to a head at that time. In any event I would suggest that you continue to write me care of the American Embassy here in Athens. I think they are more reliable than the hotel.

I got all the projected stuff off to the Sunday paper before I left, which removed quite a load from my chest but didn't help me get much sleep those last days.

All my love now to you all, Grandma, Eliza, Ken, Steinie and a woof woof to Tuckie. I'm sure Tuckie is glad to have you home from the beach again. I trust your leg is better,

Dana

July 9, 1947
Athens
Dear Mother:

Today we have a really hot story on our hands, with 1400 Communists having been arrested last night. The weather is also suitably hot. The breeze wafting in my window feels as though it came straight out of Death Valley.

I see I was on the front page this morning, so my morale is quite good, in spite of the heat. Markel wants a long weekender and I've had two requests for special memoranda.

The opportunities for pleasant living around here are such that it seems incongruous that people should work, let alone make trouble. But trouble there is.

The sea trip I was about to undertake when I wrote last week was delightful. We went by motorboat to the island of Salamis and slept out in the open. The Greeks are keen on overnight camping trips. Masses of people go trekking off to the country with blankets and food every weekend.

This last Sunday the A.P. correspondent kindly invited me to a nearby beach. I am already several shades darker, thanks to the sun, than when I left Germany.

Everywhere I encounter evidence of the deep bias to which Sedgwick had allowed himself to become committed in his handling of the news from here. It made him popular with the incumbent government, but scarcely raised him in the esteem of his colleagues. Mrs. Sedgwick, while a charming hostess and all that, is a ferocious "right winger".

Such Greeks as I have met to date I find pleasing. They have tremendous charm in fact. So different from the Turks! If possible, incidentally, I'll be going to Turkey before the end of the month.

Your first letter has arrived, with some interesting clips including especially Churchill's article. I'm afraid there is no longer any APO in Athens. The L.A. post office is out of date with its information. Possibly one will be reorganized after the Griswold mission gets here, but for the time being you'll have to pay the full civilian freight. There is excellent civilian airmail service, incidentally. TWA flies direct from the U.S. here and KLM, the Dutch lines, will be doing so soon.

Sister Kenny is due here shortly, on a European tour.

Here I'm strictly in civilian clothes, although I brought a uniform along. I must say I much prefer being in civies. Correspondents don't belong in uniforms.

Glad your leg is better and trust you'll resume the lessons soon.

All my love to you all, Dana

P.S. My interpreter, an attractive but married Greek girl, bought these absurd envelopes.

Dana Adams Schmidt
The New York Times
Hotel Grande Bretagne, Athens, Greece
July 14, 1947
Dear Mother:

The news around here did not abate even for Saturday and Sunday and I am writing this before getting into the daily swirl on Monday. We are expecting Mr. Griswold today and probably a lot of military news. Seems as though I were doomed to be a "war correspondent" forever.

At a press conference the other day I unexpectedly met two old friends. One, Jean Roi, a young Frenchman I interviewed in Algiers after he had made a remarkable trip into Germany in the guise of a collaborationist journalist but actually for the Gaullist intelligence. He has since been to the States, is on his way to becoming a US citizen and will do some work for Look *magazine here.*

The other was Sherif Bey, a correspondent of the Anatolian Agency now stationed in Athens. He and his attractive wife had me out to Sunday dinner yesterday.

Did I tell you I was working with an interpreter here? Actually she doesn't do much interpreting, but her intimate social connections with all the political upper crust are useful. I must say, however, I'd still rather have a professional newspaper man, or woman, if one were available. I think I'll have to take on the tipster very shortly.

The shockingly hot weather has broken slightly. It is extraordinary what quantities of liquid one can consume in such temperatures. I have Sedgwick's jeep and have used it quite often to run down to the beach.

I've been gratified to see I was on the front page three times this past week. In addition the Sunday department came through with no less than six different requests for memoranda, for a weekender and for a magaziner. I delivered them all except the magaziner which isn't due for a while yet.

There was a fire in the British headquarters next door as result of which our telephone lines were burned out in the hotel. It is consequently almost impossible to phone to or from the hotel. Just one emergency line has been installed. A fine place for newspaper men to live.

I have vague memories of the money in Austria when we lived there. Hundreds of thousands of everything. It is the same here. My hotel bill for last week was slightly more than half a million Drachmas.

All my love now to you all. Please tell Grandma and Eliza that I promise myself to write them very soon.

Dana

July 21, 1947
Dear Mother:
I've been writing so much about what goes on here for the paper that a letter seems almost superfluous. The Sunday dept is still running wild with requests, but, barring a new "invasion" things should be quieter this coming week.

A lot of people in this hotel have dogs and sometimes their squalling is quite upsetting. There is one down the hall right now setting up an awful howl, because *it is locked in I suppose. I keep my door open all the time so as to get the benefit of the draft; otherwise the heat would be unbearable. I have a room and bath on the sixth floor, which is good as regards getting the breeze but not too good as regards avoiding the sun.*

The past week I spent two days at Jannina, capital of Epirus, where the United Nations subcommission was investigating the latest guerilla frontier violation. It was a chance for me to see something of the interior. I liked Jannina, a rather Turkecized place, but a lot cleaner than I expected. Frank McCaskie of the London Times *and I were at the third best hotel, since the others were full. It was run by one of the innumerable Greeks who've been to America and was clean as a whistle. UNRRA with its DDT powder has practically exterminated the bug population in this country and almost wiped out malaria too. Most houses have painted on them something like "DDT 6/7 46," indicating when they were last sprayed.*

I have my Greek interpreter, Mrs. Butler, to thank for the trip, I suppose. Her mother was a friend of the Minister of Air, and it was through this connection that we arranged for Frank and me to see the minister and make the trip in an airforce plane. Everything works that way here. If you don't know the right people you're out of luck. The Greeks wouldn't understand what was meant by "first come first served."

In the evening at Jannina Frank and I walked down to the lake where there are half a dozen restaurants each playing phonograph records of wailing local dance music over loudspeakers—very much like Turkish music and related to the Arabic. The cacophony we can hear billowing out onto the lake if you listen from the end a jetty is astonishing. To this music Greek males do their traditional dances, sometimes alone sometimes in pairs. The women don't dance in these parts. Greek families sit around watching in the open air restaurants until midnight or later, sipping Turkish coffee. All very much like Turkey.

If things should be quiet enough I'm planning to go to Turkey for a few days at the end of this month. Our correspondent there has got himself in Dutch with the authorities and I must try to prevent him from losing his professional license. He is a Turk who apparently doesn't think much of his government and consequently gets a rough time.

Life here is dramatically expensive. I'm glad I can charge the office for most everything. It costs about half a million Drachmae or $500 per week for me to live in the Hotel Grande Bretagne.

By the time you get this you should be on your way to the beach with Nini Barry. I look back on my brief visit to Yucca Loma with a lot of pleasure.

Cyrus Sulzberger and his wife, Marina, were in the States on vacation and I am writing them today to give them your address. I hope they get a chance to look you up.

All my love now, to you all, Dana

July 26, 1947
Athens
Dear Mother:

I will be leaving tomorrow morning for Turkey so I thought I'd better get this note to you off now.

First of all I want you to send a check for $1000 to Miltiadis Kyrtsis, Gotham Hotel, Fifth Avenue and 55th Street, New York City.

Secondly I want you to deposit another $1000 in my checking account with the Corn Exchange Bank Trust Company, 42nd Street Branch, 303 West 42nd Street, New York City.

This will take a hefty hunk out of my bank account, probably more than I have accumulated since my vacation, but it will be made good again in the next couple of months as the Times pays me my expenses.

This week has been a little quieter, but I've been working hard. Got off the magaziner and a "profile" of Nicos Zachariades, the top communist in these parts. Also sending a wad of cartoons, all of which will be paid for.

Hope nothing drastic happens here so I can stay in Turkey long enough to get my bearings and turn out a few stories. I'm looking forward to the trip like anything.

Last night Griswold gave a dinner for the American correspondents and I was an hour late—writing a story. But nobody seemed to mind and I had a long chin with Griswold after dinner. He is a likeable man but why, why is it necessary to send out people who are completely and utterly green about affairs in *this part of the world to guide our affairs here? To be sure he has the advantage of objectivity and that is a lot in this part of the world. In these respects he and the Ambassador are opposites, the Ambassador having been here, or with the exile government, for thirteen years.*

The Embassy too has been very nice and helpful to me. In fact everybody has and I have nothing at all to complain about except lack of time to reciprocate courtesies.

I have found a good friend in Frank McCaskie (or some such spelling) the London Times *correspondent. He is counted one of the heroes of the Greek resistance movement and travelled in and out of the country repeatedly during the occupation, was caught by the Italians, sentenced to death, but, as you see, not executed. A very interesting and likeable fellow.*

I'll try to write you something from Turkey and will cut this off short. Your letters are coming through very quickly.

All my love to all, Dana

August 10, 1947
Dear Mother:
The distraction of my trip to Turkey has caused me to miss last week's letter. But I dare say you're at the beach just now and won't mind so much. Mrs. Lowman certainly pulled a fast one, doubling the rent. All the more reason for us to build our beach place.

Your suggestions about the construction of our beach house sound good to me. If Eliza and Ken are delayed in starting theirs perhaps it would be more economical to build the two at the same time, next spring. With two houses to build contractors might be more interested.

Getting back to Turkey was quite a pleasure. I found some old local friends in Turkey and Ankara, but almost all the Americans had changed. Among them was Nezhi Manyas who used to work for Radio Ankara *and help Angronsky and me. He now works for the Turkish press department and is about to leave for the U.S. to help set up a publicity bureau for the Turkish government. I gave him your address and phone number in case he gets as far as Los Angeles. He is a pleasant fellow with a slight stutter. Partly educated in England.*

I accomplished my mission in Turkey about 50 pc. That is, I was unable to get Aslan Humbaradji's press credentials restored but I made arrangements for him to continue work without credentials. I believe I told you he had fallen into the bad graces of the govt. Aslan certainly showed poor judgment in some of his stories, but the Turkish government also showed itself anything but "democratic" in its efforts to silence him.

The Embassy did its best to help, but couldn't do much about a Turkish citizen. Anyway, they entertained me very nicely. Mr. Wilson the Ambassador sent his launch to take me across the Bosphorus to the Asiatic side where he was vacationing. He remembered me from Algiers. He is one of those extraordinarily kind and honest people who always expects kindness and honesty from others. It comes natural to him to believe in the Turks' protestations of "democratic" intentions, as it came natural to him to believe in de Gaulle in Algiers. In the case of de Gaulle I think he was right, on balance (and the State Department wrong); in the case of the Turks I'm not so sure.

I was intrigued to find how much Ankara has developed. There were buildings going up all over the place…128 building projects. A hundred million Turkish pounds is going into the new National Assembly building, thirty millions into the monument to Ataturk, three millions into the "provisional" Opera house. Such extravagance naturally offers the opposition a lot of ammunition. The park and lake in the middle of town which was just started when I left is just being finished now. American busses with electric trolleys have been installed in Ataturk blvd. And my old apartment is still occupied by Americans. I had lunch there. A fuzzy white little dog which Bob Brown acquired shortly before I left still lives there. I told you Bob Brown is air attache in Syria and Lebanon now, didn't I? He is a Lt. Col.

The newspaper "La Republique", a French translation of the Turkish "Cumhuriyet", was still arriving daily at the apartment, addressed to M. S-cedilla-chmit (Turkish idea of phonetic spelling of Schmidt). The telephone is in Agronsky's name and the landlord is still making a nuisance of himself and trying to get rid of his American tenants.

The Bus. Director Nedim Bey and I smoked the peace pipe extensively and he had the USIS *(U.S. Information Service) director and me to a lunch* that lasted from 1:30 to 4:00 p.m. All the waiters at Carpich and the porters and concierge at the Ankara Palace hotel remembered me. It is always nice to be remembered, although their recollections must be largely of me cussing them vigorously.

Back in Athens I find it hotter than any part of Turkey I hit. This afternoon I'm going to the beach with some people from Griswold's staff.

A few days ago I visited the excavations of the ancient Agora and will do a piece on them next Thursday when they wind up their work for the season. I sent some pictures ahead. I like that kind of story as a change from the blood and thunder of the present. An interesting fellow named Homer Thompson runs the digging. If I get time I hope to see more of him.

Sometime next week I'll probably be going on a trip to the provinces to see how the guerrilla fighting is getting on. Zervas invited me to come along on one of his tours and it seems a good opportunity.

You can rest assured that I'll not be needing to draw further on my bank account for a while. Anyway the last withdrawals do not represent spending but transfers.

My little portable radio is with me and is putting forth some enthusiastic Greek opera just now.

It will be nice for Grandma to go East for a change. Please give her my love. Hope you are keeping in good shape.

All my love,
Dana

I sympathise with you in your publishing and cinematic worries. I have to deliver a lecture on foreign correspondents for USIS in a few weeks.

"Facts" is a nice looking job I think. Very "modern". The back page with the Frau & baby are most impressive.

August 22, 1947
Dear Mother:
I hasten to write for I fear you will be feeling neglected. I've been up to Salonika and around northern Greece and so found a lot of things piled up when I got back.

ELIZABETH SCHMIDT CRAHAN

One of the things awaiting me here was the necessity of delivering a lecture for the United States Information Service. *I did it night before last without any disastrous results. My title was "How the American press gathers the news of the world." There were about a hundred and fifty people, Greeks and a handful of Americans. Afterwards the* USIS *people entertained me to cocktails and dinner. And this morning I have had a visit from two young men and two girls desirous of asking some questions about my lecture. All most extraordinary, and, I suppose, good practice.*

My trip to the north was worthwhile, but more from the point of view of background than news. I spent about four days in Salonika and got acquainted with a lot of the resident Americans who really know the place—the people at the American Farm School, at Anatolia College, and the Consulate. I shouldn't forget the Near East Foundation people, who were very good to me. They sent me out in one of their jeeps with one of their English-speaking Greeks all one Sunday to interview refugees. The next day I rode in one of their jeeps to Verria, about three hours away.

All these old American institutions have been hard hit of late by a falling off of charitable contributions from the States. It seems that when the Truman Doctrine was proclaimed a lot of people thought that the "Government will take care of Greece" and gave their money to someone else.

The Farm school has been going since the early part of the century, 1904 I believe. It tries to teach Greek farm boys more modern farming methods and at the same time give them a general education and some insight into American life. It has been very successful; its graduates tend to become the leaders in their villages. One of the big attractions out there, incidentally, is the milk. The school is the only place in this part of the world I know of where you can get real Grade A fresh milk. Under normal circumstance I think the school would be worth a magazine article, but at present I can only hope to work in a few references to it, at best.

Shep Stone, who is replacing Markel during the vacation season, has asked for a magaziner on "life at the frontier." I spent a day at Florina after leaving Salonika but it isn't quite enough for a magaziner. I'll have to go up there again and stay awhile.

You may have seen my piece on Florina. It is an extraordinary place. Surrounded by guerrillas.

Transmission is so slow that lately I've had a little trouble getting my stories to New York in time for the first edition. Do you get the first edition or what? If so I suggest that you write to the Circulation Dept and ask if you could have it changed to the last edition. I think they call it the "late city edition." If there is any difficulty I will write them. You will be more certain to get my stories in that edition.

I sent some pictures of the Agora excavations to Mr. Rae to go with a story and got a letter back thanking me and saying $10 would be placed on my account in due course. Much to my surprise.

The heat has abated somewhat and I have decided to hang on to my top floor room. In the autumn it will be very nice. And it looks to me as though I'd be here to Xmas at least. Sedgwick sends his cables to his wife to our local cable address which (in case you ever want to use it) is NYKTIMES ATHENS. As result they always pass through my hands and I am kept posted. He has told his wife that he isn't quite sure what the Times *wants him to do but that he doesn't think he'll be back in Athens before Christmas. I suppose that means I stay here, although no one has breathed a word about the future to me since I was assigned here. I have been thinking that if I am left with responsibility for Greece and Turkey for any considerable time I ought to be getting a raise.*

Mr. Chromie, first secretary of our Embassy, and Frank MacCaskie of the London Times *are coming to lunch with me today. I am going to ask Chromie about joining the local tennis club. I still have my racket with me although I haven't used it for years. Frank has just returned from Ikaria, the prison island. I would like to have tried going there myself but thought I'd been away long enough with my other trip as it was. He knows a lot of people in key places since he was in Greece as member of the Intelligence Service during the occupation. It helps him get privileges others cannot get and he was the first person to get to the island. First correspondent, that is.*

You will be back from the beach by now and Grandma will be getting ready to go East. All my love to you all, including Tuckie,

Dana

Athens
August 28, 1947
Dear Mother:

Another scorcher of a day is creeping round and I'll get off this letter before my sense of initiative wilts in the heat. Actually, it isn't so bad, and I'm inclined to think I prefer heat to cold. Heat is awfully debilitating though.

I'm ever so glad to find you bright and cheery after your holiday at the beach. Tough on Tuckie, I must say. Never heard of a dog living on cottage cheese. Everything happens in California.

This week we are having a governmental crisis. That is to say the government collapsed and nobody has been able to prop it up again. Maybe we will have a new government today.

I have at last begun to do something about joining the local tennis club and even have a date to play next Saturday. I'm sure it will do me good.

On Sunday I went out for a drive in the Times *jeep and wound up with the brightest reddest sunburn you ever saw. It doesn't seem to be peeling, however. Maybe my skin has toughened with age.*

So Eliza and Ken are actually going to build. That will be quite exciting. As you say, you and I will have to save our pennies, but I see no reason why I shouldn't have enough in hand by next spring. The Times *won't be paying off the $1000 all at once, but gradually.*

Mrs. Sedgwick is preparing to go to the U.S. on a lecture tour, to last from October until December. That's one more indication that I will be here until winter at least. My what a fierce creature she is. I pity old Sedgwick. No wonder he lost his objectivity. Now she has hooked onto the London Times *man and influences him profoundly. She is a rabid monarchist and right winger. I keep clear of her as much as possible, but have to keep civil. She is coming to have a drink with me before lunch, (with MacCaskie of the* Times *trailing along behind, of course).*

My excellent tipster, George Androulidakis, has been on the phone, trying to galvanize me into action. He is not entirely disinterested, of course, since he hopes I'll get some information from American sources which he can use in his paper.

I heard last night that a Greek government press officer in New York had cabled Athens evaluating the various correspondents. He found me "objective, but tending to sympathise with Sophoulis." Isn't that nice?

All my love, now to you all,
Dana

September 6, 1947
Dear Mother:
I guess you've seen a lot of me in the paper this past week. I've certainly been spending a lot of the Times' *money on cable tolls.*

Now I want to tie up a few loose ends of the political situation and then get out into the field again. I may take a trip with a correspondent named Potter, of the Baltimore Sun. *He is an amazingly indefatigable creature. His paper does not expect him to cover any of the spot news so that he is left freer than I am to concentrate on interviews, features, background etc.*

It is curious how things pile up sometimes. Tonight I have some four appointments, all at once. I have been invited to attend a beer party, a reception for Greek labor leaders, I have an appointment with the legal expert of the American mission and an appointment with Sophoulis, all between six and seven p.m. I'm keeping the date with Sophoulis, and maybe I can look in on the others later.

On Saturday I played tennis at the tennis club for the first time. It is a very nice club and I think I'm going to find it worthwhile. The advantageous thing for me is that it is just a few minutes away from the hotel. There is a swimming pool attached, also a restaurant where one can eat outside in the evening. This morning I played again, with the professional. I found my game picked up very quickly with the pro, but I got a blister on my hand which will make me pause for a day or so. That shows how much manual labor I've been doing in recent years!

One of the Counsellors of Embassy, named Minor, has also joined. Apparently very few Americans belong to this club and we are pioneers. The first week the club offers a free "transit" membership. Then for a month they have a "temporary membership." After that one may or may not become a permanent member. It is all very cagey, allowing the club and the visitor to look each other over carefully.

I am working on a "profile" of Griswold and have been interviewing some of his old associates. I think he is growing in stature the longer he is here. At first the Greeks were inclined to snicker at rough and ready "Nebraskan." He is certainly very different from the Greeks in mentality—straightforward, simple, emphatic where they are devious complicated and uncertain.

This afternoon I have succumbed to the "siesta" habit and have just got up from an hour and a half's nap. Maybe the Greeks know best after all how to live in this climate.

All my love to Steinie. Love, Dana

September 10, 1947
Dear Mother:
How nice it was to get your birthday cable. I had almost forgotten it was my birthday. Your cable was the only thing to mark the day, apart from the news being unusually heavy. And also I should mention that my friend Dick Clark of the U.P. got married to a girl name Heffelfinger that day, in Frankfurt. I cabled them best wishes.

Finally the government crisis is over and I am planning to go north to Salonika and the frontier region on Saturday next. I have got the Griswold profile out of the way and must start worrying about "Life at the Frontier." That should make a good piece if I get hold of the right material. But I'm not going to manufacture it out of my imagination.

Tonight I am having several people in to dinner, including Mrs. Sedgwick. The main purpose is to have a talk with Colonel Stathatos, the Greek liaison officer at the general staff. He should be useful in making arrangements for my trip north. I'm going to travel part of the time with Potter of the Baltimore Sun, although he is going ahead, tomorrow, aboard a Mission plane.

Last night I went out to dinner with the editor and publisher of Embros, a local daily which the press reviews sometimes describe as "Populist-militarist." He turned out, not entirely unexpectedly, to be an unenlightened and dull host. But he took his party to a very nice restaurant about fifteen miles out of

Athens. It was supposed to have particularly good "Rezina," and did. "Rezina" is local wine with resin mixed in it. At first it seems obnoxious, but most people get to like it. It is said the Greeks never get stomach ulcers, because they drink Rezina.

The weather has turned cool at last and everybody feels better. I have gotten my jacket out of the closet after scarcely wearing it for a month.

The depressing food news from western Europe reminds me that I would like you to send some Care packages for me. Please send a regular Care food package plus one four dollar "fats" package and one four dollar "flour" package to each of my two Frankfurt addresses and to Oscar Reschke in Munich. Reschke's address I believe you have, care of the DENA *news agency. My Paris address, the Pave family, has moved to a farm, so there's no use sending them food.*

Before my own dinner party tonight I must go to a cocktail party at which George Polk, the CBS *correspondent will announce his engagement to a Greek girl. Goodness knows when I'm going to write a story.*

I have been enjoying the clippings you send me. Keep it up. How are you making out with your film enterprise for the hospital? And the lessons?

All my love, to you all,
Dana

Here's the negative of a picture the AP *photo, took of me talking to the Prefect of Florina on the Florina airfield.*

Did you realize that the story on the AbiRA [sic] was just lifted from mine— in case you missed it I include both mine & the Times *clip for the scrap book. I sent in the picture too.*

Here's what a story of mine looks like in Greek. They have me down as <u>Miss</u> *Dana Schmidt, the well-known etc.—it is my last weekend with the all-Populist joint.*

Between Komotini and Drama, September 20, 1947
Dear Mother:
Since I have been traveling in some of the remoter parts of Greece for the past week I haven't had a chance to write you and am now balancing my typewriter rather precariously on my knees in the train.

ELIZABETH SCHMIDT CRAHAN

This trip has been of extraordinary value to me as I have gained a new appreciation of Greek reality. Also I have got a new appreciation of the Greeks. They are a splendid people, and I like them as much as I disliked the Turks. Unpretentious, friendly, sincere, lively. That is true of these simpler people of the provinces, not, I fear, of the high and mighty in Athens.

It is quite cool and sunny just now. The best time of the year, I suppose, and the best for a trip. I have been traveling with Morley Cassidy of the Philadelphia Bulletin. *Potter of the* Baltimore Sun *proved an unreliable companion and I got thoroughly fed up with him. One could never count on him to keep an appointment or to carry through a plan. A headstrong egotistical fellow given to terrific generalizations. He is a man of remarkable vigor and doubtless a good reporter, but I do not care for his personality or, for that matter, for his politics. He is inclined to place too much credence in the Russian view of things in this part of the world and has taken a contemptipis dos;ole fpr tje Freeks wjidj T didome qiote ipsettomf (the last line was typed in a tunnel and didn't work out very well) It was supposed to read . . . taken a contemptuous dislike for the Greeks which I find quite upsetting.*

Potter, Cassidy and I travelled as far as Drama together and there parted company. Potter remained in that part of the woods and Cassidy, a quiet studious sort of fellow, and I went on to Komotini. We had heard that Komotini was the most guerrilla-torn part of Thrace and we weren't far wrong. There was a real battle around the town night before last with machineguns, tracer bullets, flares, artillery and everything. I thought I was a war correspondent again.

The burned villages around Komotini we visited were as pathetic as anything I've experienced. That such poor, innocent people should lose so much. With just barely enough to keep themselves alive they are deprived of that little, their poor mud and plaster houses, a barnful of hay, a couple of oxen and a few sheep perhaps. Yet they do not take their disaster with loud wailing wringing of hands such as you might get among plenty of western peoples but instead with a quiet, sad dignity. It is a pleasant virtue I suppose.

The Greek army commander at Komotini was the soul of hospitality as was everyone else we encountered during the trip. The commander sent a mine detector detachment out at dawn one morning so that we could travel the road to his most advanced company near the Bulgarian frontier in safety at noon. We had a mess kit lunch and spent half the afternoon with the company. They took us through the underground fort half destroyed by the Bulgarians, sang for us, picked flowers for us, cut sticks for us to use as canes. It was most touching. After we have been in town forty-eight hours it was as though we were old friends with everyone from the commander down to the privates recognizing and greeting us.

Except in Athens foreigners have a very extraordinary position among Greeks. In the language of people, I am told, foreigners are referred to as "lords." They are treated not merely with hospitality but with great deference and as though their visit were the most delightful experience their hosts could imagine. In Komotini the army, the local officials, the local newspaper, etc. really were glad to see us I think for "nobody ever goes to Komotini." It is hard to get to and has few attractions except its troubles, which attracted us.

Newspapermen who have written about the difficulties of travel in Greece were judging strictly from experiences in Athens I am sure. My experience is that as soon as Greek officials in the provinces know you are a foreigner they dispense with all formalities, don't bother to look at your papers at all, and go out of their way to be helpful.

This is not a matter of obsequiousness. It is true that Greeks are normally ensnarled in bureaucratic red tape, but officials never publicly browbeat people the way they do in Germany; courtesy is universal. For all the extraordinary violence and cruelty of the guerrilla fighting they are a gentle people by nature.

My plan is to spend a few days in Salonika getting caught up on the general news and then go with Cassidy to Florina for a few days. When I've finished that I think I'll be in a good position to write the "Life on the Frontier" piece. In fact I think it should be a humdinger.

Cassidy and I both filed from Komotini. Ours were apparently the longest telegrams the post office had ever had to handle and they upset the telegraphic system of the whole of Thrace. Each town is supposed to have a certain allotted time to use the single line to Salonika, transmitting by hand signals. Our file used up the time of I don't know how many towns. We were lucky, for the guerrillas cut the line quite often.

You wanted an answer about bathtub or shower in our beach cottage. I think I would like a combination. Bathtub with shower attached. Certainly, in any case, I want the bathtub. I like to lie down when washing.

Aren't we due for a "recession" pretty soon? Then the price of the house will go down. At any rate I don't see how prices can keep going up without some kind of a break. But I agree that it is a mistake to put off such things as building a beach cottage out of considerations of price. The value to us will be far greater than the highest cost.

I gather from Eliza that Grandma is thinking of having a share in the cottage, with a suite of her own. That seems like a good idea to me. I am very pleased. By the way, what share of the cost are we paying Eliza and Ken for their work in designing it? I seem to recollect that architects normally collect quite a substantial percentage of the total cost.

The plan you enclosed in your last letter and the detailed plans in Eliza's look very fine to me, although I am not very good at figuring that sort of thing out. My only distinct notions are that there should be plenty of view fore and aft and that there should be nothing cheap about the place. I don't think we want to skimp on quantity and quality. It isn't a case of our being determined to get more house for less money.

Don't worry if the Times *is slow about paying out my expense money. They'll come across eventually. Afraid there's nothing you can do about the Gotham hotel gent. If he doesn't want to cash the check I guess we can't make him. Did I ever tell you I got a refund on my payment to the American Automobile Association? They found the record of the payment I originally made with your checks and returned your cancelled checks and my check.*

I haven't had a bath for a week or more and am probably getting rather ripe. Fortunately most of the people around me haven't either, so nobody minds. The hotel "Macedonia" where we stayed once had wash basins but they were removed by the Bulgarians during the war.

Just before I left Athens a letter from Grandma arrived. It was nice to hear from her and I hope she enjoys her trip East.

My love to you all, Dana

September 30, 1947
Dear Mother:
This one is going to be real short. It is two in the morning and I have that Magaziner hanging over my head not to mention a whole pile of office correspondence that has accumulated during my absence.

I enjoyed my tour in the north so much that I am sorry to be back. It was a most pleasant time, in addition to being instructive.

I want to tell you that the swap of lots you propose sounds okay to me. That other lot will certainly be more satisfactory from a number of points of view and if Grandma would like some space and wants to chip in so much the better.

It occurred to me that possibly Eliza and Ken would like to have the upper lot, if we are going to give it up. It would mean redesigning their house I suppose, but the upper lot has a better view. If they do, that's all right with me too.

My Greek assistant is away on vacation and I feel a little lost. He'll be back in a day or two.

The Turkish director of press is acting up threatening to upset the arrangements I made for Aslan during my trip to Turkey. A terrible nuisance.

The auditor has been questioning my retaining my room here while away traveling and also questioning my charging the office full expenses while in Greece, but I think I've given him good enough arguments to settle that. Let me know when he comes across with my expense money. He will, of course, eventually.

Mrs. Sedgwick has departed for the U.S.A.
All my love to you all,
Dana

October 8, 1947
Dear Mother:
Your letter enclosing an excellent picture of yourself at the homecoming party has arrived. Really, it is a very good picture. I'm glad you liked the one I sent of myself. I thought I explained that it was taken on the airfield at Florina.

I was supposed to be pointing to the mountains where the guerillas are. The gent with me is in the Nomach (prefect) of Florina province.

I was interested in your comments on the work of my colleagues in Germany. I have had notes from Kathleen McLaughlin, who finds the strain of covering the whole zone considerable, and from the Delbert Clarks, whom I had written a note of good wishes after getting your clipping on their marriage. Delbert said Murrow and Raymond were swapping places, that is, Raymond replacing Murrow in the British zone for a while. I never see the Times *in toto here; only my own clips and what you send me.*

Now that you have received the first installment returning some of the money I have put out for expenses you can expect them to continue more or less regularly. Financing myself has the disadvantage of putting me in the hole initially, but it is more convenient in the long run. Next week I'll be asking you to make another transfer of a thousand dollars. That may be inconvenient at times but you understand that all or most of it comes back, so that you need not consider it as an expenditure. I hope it doesn't interfere with payments for the lot, or lots. If it can be swung I'm all in favor of holding both lots. It may keep us on thin ice for a while but it seems like the best kind of investment at present. One of our visiting Congressmen said that Jesse Jones had told him he was putting all his money into building, regardless of cost because, "this year we have the 50 cent dollar, next year we'll have the 25 cent dollar and maybe the year after that we'll have the 12 1/2 cent dollar." (Of course that may or may not be an accurate quote, and may or may not be right, so don't take it too seriously).

About the Care packages. There is no harm in sending one to Roger, but I'd wait till around Xmas, and make sure it's from you. As for the others, I believe I told you to send some fats and flour packages. But I have just learned from the Athens CARE *representative that the fats and flour packages have been discontinued. So they may return your check. If so, please send the approximate equivalent in additional regular $10 food packages to be delivered a month after the ones already ordered.*

It seems too warm to be thinking about Christmas. It is so uncertain whether I am going to be here or in Germany that I think you'd better hold the Christmas box. Maybe we can make it an Easter box later. In the meantime, if you want to send me an Xmas present, or if somebody does, I'm tired of running downstairs to borrow the hotel pen and ink and would accept with pleasure a fountain pen, preferably one of the new streamlined affairs with a gold colored top and a nib that comes in a kind of sheath. Beyond that I would like some new ties of both moderate and immoderate hue, preferably the non wrinkling variety. I can also use socks and handkerchiefs.

Writing a book about Greece is not such a bad idea. Maybe I can write one here and one in Germany later. Perhaps I could borrow time to do one here when and if Sedgwick returns. As you say, I've been gathering plenty of background materials.

Those pamphlets are certainly keeping you on the jump. I'm sure you know a great deal more about those things than I do, now that you've been on the job, but I used to fancy myself as a modest sort of expert on type faces. That was when I was at college and did a term paper for Mr. Davis about type faces. I had about the same trouble with my last magaziner as you had with the Alumni news. I worked all one night to get it aboard a BEA, *British European Airlines, aircraft at eight in the morning. It was supposed to be received in London that night. But the plane was delayed in Rome, and then in London the envelope got lost in the Customs and wasn't found for three days. Usually all my stuff is cabled, but the rates are so dreadfully high from here that lately the Sunday department has been asking for its magazine stuff of "air freight."*

How splendid that you are making progress with the lessons. Good, please let me pay for the next month's fees. I can't think of anything I'd rather spend money on.

After forgetting for a long time, I am going to enclose the cancelled check you used to pay the American Automobile Assoc. last May. As I told you, they admitted their error and returned my check.

Also there is a paper from the Equitable Life Assurance saying that I am insured for $700. This, received from the NYT *appears to be one of their several insurance schemes.*

That was a clever rhyme about the Philco Portable. The only trouble with it in these parts is that there are too few middle and long wave stations. In Germany I could hear far more.

The piece on Trevor-Roper by Rosemary Benet is pretty good. I hope to look him up in England some day. He is a most likeable fellow but, like so many Englishmen, rubs most Americans the wrong way by seeming supercilious.

It is fairly quiet here for the moment and I suppose I seem to have dropped out of the paper. But it won't be long.

All my love to you all,
Dana

October 15, 1947
Dear Mother:
Before I forget. Will you please send a thousand dollars to Miltiades Kyrtsis, the Devon, 70 West 55th street, New York City. You see he has changed address.

Things have perked up around here a little but I can't see Greece on the front page much for the rest of this year unless the guerrillas should stage the much-rumored big offensive just before winter. The Mission tells me my Griswold profile was published but I haven't seen a clipping of it yet. They had it more than a month before they used it. So I suppose there is always hope for my frontier piece.

Autumn is upon us, with the first drizzles of the season. It hasn't really rained since February, I hear. But today is beautiful and in a few minutes I'm going out to lunch with Tanya, a white-Russian girl from Istanbul, and the Steven Barbers. Tanya is a girl I knew in Istanbul way back in 1940 when I first went to Turkey; she is visiting Athens for a while. The Barbers are the young couple I've probably mentioned who have fixed up the washrooms on the roof of an apartment house into a penthouse. They call it "Pooh Corner"— for Winnie the Pooh. I have bought them an electric toaster which I will present them forthwith.

I am glad you are going ahead with plans for the beach house. The new lot is obviously better than the old one. It is, as you say, nice to feel you are at the water's edge. I seem to be getting off easy on buying the new lot, paying less than half. Of course there are plenty of expenses to come.

It is just about time I put a new ribbon in my typewriter, don't you think? This machine has done a lot of mileage since Cornelius Murphy found it for us and hasn't given a bit of trouble except once in Frankfurt when some kind of a spring broke. I haven't heard you mention Cornelius lately. How is he?

I have put your excellent photograph up in my mirror. Everybody admires it.

The other day a woman who works for the Near East Foundation told me about her work at a training school for physiotherapy here. Her name is Mrs. Cooper. Before she was married, maiden name Miss Wilder, she worked for a Dr. W. B. Carrell at Dallas and met Dr. Lowman in the course of her work. She supposes Dr. Lowman would have forgotten her, but she remembers him.

The horoscope on my birthday you sent me was certainly written to order for me. "Writing should be pushed," it says. You're telling me! And I wonder where you [...] the clipping from the New York Paris Herald. Mme Plaisance, I suppose. I had a postcard from Mrs. Williams' daughter, from Prague, where she had been attending a youth conference.

All my love to you all, Dana

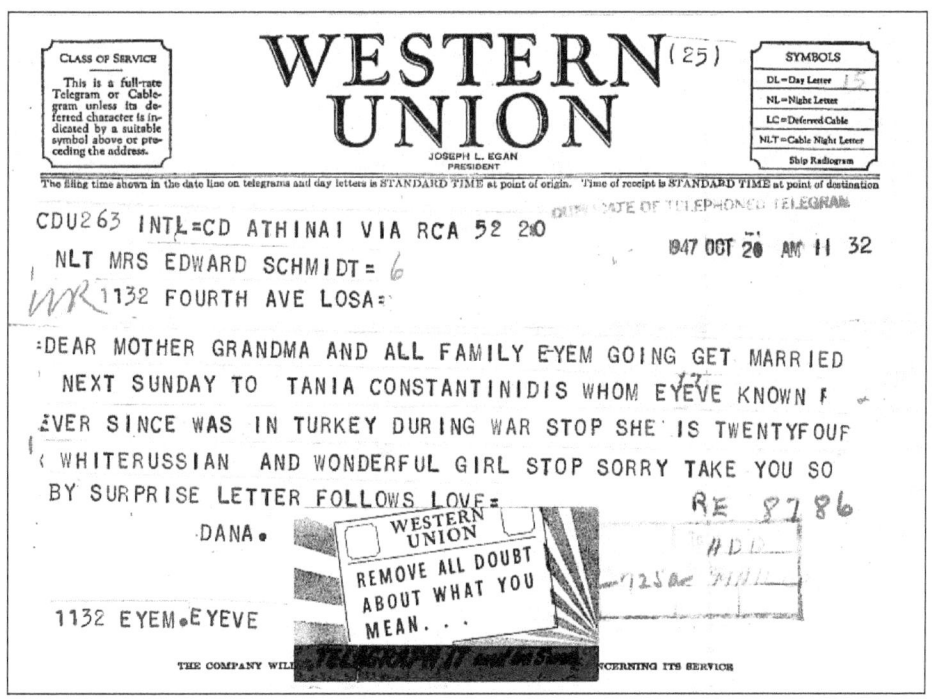

October 20, 1947
Dear Mother:

This is perhaps the letter you have been waiting for. I only wish I could have given you more notice, but matters came to a head rapidly, and it didn't seem right or sensible to wait.

I am going to be married to a girl named Tania at the Russian church here next Sunday. The name is Tatiana Constantinidis. It sounds Greek, but it isn't. Tania is all Russian, White Russian, that is. She is 24 and was a tiny baby when her family escaped from the Bolshies in Odessa.

I met Tania back in December 1940 when I first went to Turkey and I saw her quite often during my time there. Then I went back to Turkey a few months ago and met her again. You see what happened. Tania flew to Athens a week ago, and, after brief hesitation, this is it.

Tania's father was a Russian officer. Now he is a real estate broker in Istanbul. His real name is Ivan Constantinov, but, to get out of Russia, he acquired a Greek passport and the name Jean Constantinidis. Her mother is named Alexandra, and is a very fine woman indeed. Her grandmother is also living, with the father and mother. Their address is Mete Caddessi 18, Ayaspasa, Istanbul.

The family went first to Bulgaria and then to Turkey. Tania has also been taken on trips to Vienna. At one time, I gather, the family was quite well off, but hasn't been doing very well in recent years, although they have a nice apartment.

Tania can speak English or rather American perfectly and is always being taken for an American girl. She also speaks French, German, Russian, Greek, Turkish, and a bit of Bulgarian. She went to a convent school, worked for a time as a secretary, plays the piano and accordion, can sail a boat, swims well, rides horseback, and in general is a mighty fine girl. Sometimes she is a bit shy, but she'll get over that in time.

At the moment she is staying at the Minerva hotel, behind my hotel, but after the wedding we'll both live in the Grande Bretagne. If I stay here long enough we may get an apartment. There is a possibility of our getting a place of the penthouse variety by the month. Most landlords want to be paid a year in advance.

We are going to be married at the Russian church. We were there making arrangements today. Tania thought she'd like it that way, and I didn't mind one way or another, so it will be a Russian Orthodox ceremony, with a choir (they have no other kind of music) and maybe fifty or sixty guests. Afterwards there will be a reception at Dalli's restaurant. George Polk of CBS who was married recently had his reception there and it worked out very well. The wedding will start at 4:00 p.m. and the reception at 5:00. Everything will be quite simple, but, I think, quite nice. I'll get a photographer to take some pictures.

You can see by the pictures enclosed with this what a pretty girl Tania is.

One aspect of the matter will interest you particularly I'm sure. I am going to shave off my moustache for the wedding. Tania didn't object to it, the moustache, violently, but we agreed to see what it was like without.

I have been thinking of the lovely ring Grandma promised. I think it is too risky to send it here now. I suggest that we wait till I come home with Tania next year, much as I want her to have it as soon as possible. For the moment I have given Tania my ring, the one with the Cats Eye you gave me when I went away to College. It will have to be made a little smaller, but she is wearing it already. Then we will have to get some plain gold wedding rings. That seems to be the custom.

It has been quite a day, making arrangements for the wedding and not entirely abandoning my work. I sent Cyrus Sulzberger a cable and a letter. I'll let this be enough for today and write Grandma about the next stage of our progress tomorrow, and, if I can keep it up, Elizabeth the day after.

I am very happy, though a bit nervous about this new responsibility. Tania and I are very much in love.

All my love to you all,
Dana

Dear Mrs. Schmidt:
Though we have never met, through our children we became relatives. Please accept my sincere congratulation on the occasion of their wedding and I do hope their marriage will establish most friendly relations between us.

Their marriage didn't happen suddenly. My daughter knew your son for six years; all these years her heart belonged to him only. Unexpected arrival of your son in Istanbul has decided their fate. Their marriage is a result of nothing but mutual love. I trust she will be always true to him both as wife and companion. You dear son was here in Istanbul not long ago, we liked and loved him from the first day, as if our own son. Dana often told us about you and your mother. On this happy day we offered a toast to your health. Please give my regards to your mother and the best wishes for many happy years.

Permit me to tell you a little about myself. I and my relatives are from St. Petersburg. Father died in my youth, my mother lives with us. My husband, formerly colonel, is in business. We live in Istanbul for the last 20 years. Life is rather monotonous, a few friends, a movie and that's about all. The main part of life is struggle to make a living. My personal life is secluded and considers of house chores, the family and books. Istanbul is a cosmopolitan city, much like Odessa, its life is away from homes and in cards. Being from the north I couldn't and can't get used to their views and habits. And at present, as my daughter is married, I am filled with happiness. I don't wish anything better. The reason for my life is my dear children May God bless them with health, fullness of happiness and joy of life.

My heart, soul and thoughts are with them. I am waiting impatiently their arrival. Hope that is not too distant future my daughter will have good fortune of embracing her dear mother and grandmother whom she learned to love before meeting with them.

With best wishes and regards to you and your mother I am most devotedly yours

A Constantinidis

My address: Alexandra Constantinidis

Ayaz Pasa Mete cad. 10/10

Istanbul, Turquie.

P.S. If possible write to me in French. My mother and husband send you their greetings.

October 23, 1947
Dear Elizabeth and Kenneth:

As you no doubt have heard, Dana is getting married, and very happy about it. I have written a letter to Mother and to Grandma about it and here's another with more details for the forthcoming glorious event.

The number of things to be done the week before a wedding is apparently infinite. I think at last we have all the invitations out, but I'll probably think of several more who should have been included as we're walking down the aisle.

This afternoon Tania and I got away to go out to the aircraft carrier Leyte, whither we had been invited by Zenas Andrews. Remember? I met him at the entrance to the Grande Bretagne hotel the other day. Each of us thought the other seemed familiar, and so we were. He had dinner with us last night and we exchanged war reminiscences and had a very pleasant evening. He is a lieutenant commander, "damage officer" he calls himself

Tomorrow we must go out to call on Mrs. Ladas, the mother of Cyrus Sulzberger's wife. I should have done so ages ago; now the advent of a bride has brought matters to a head. I must hustle about and get the lady organized for a trip to Paris.

I don't think I've mentioned yet that my best man is going to be Steven Barber, correspondent of the London News Chronicle. He and Tania are the two persons in Athens who've known me longest. Steven was one jump ahead of office boy on the U.P. staff in Cairo when I first knew him in 1941 or 2.

Now, since it's your turn for a letter you get the big news. I got a cable from Cyrus Sulzberger congratulating me heartily on the coming wedding and informing me that Shan Sedgwick was returning to Athens at the end of November, that my assignment in Germany was terminated and that I would be transferred to the Middle East. No nearer specification, so I don't know what part of the Middle East yet. Sam Brewer, he said, will be working with me. It looks as though we were having a general turn about. Cliff Daniel and Gene Currivan who're in the Middle East now must be going elsewhere.

Cyrus wanted to know whether I wanted to sell my car in Germany and buy a new one or whether I would ship it to the Middle East. I think I'll sell it.

ELIZABETH SCHMIDT CRAHAN

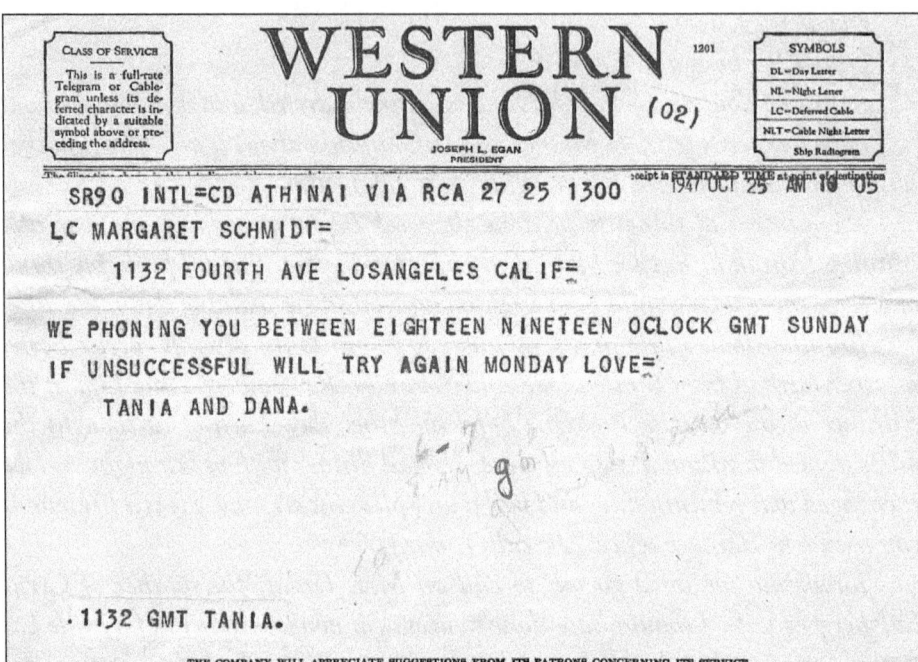

Telegrams of congratulation have been coming in from all sides, including a particularly nice one from you. I've also received one from Mother, one from the Publisher and one from James suggesting that I do a little story on the wedding. Shall do.

I must thank you both for the work sketching my house to be. It is too bad in a way that our houses won't be together but there is no doubt the other lot is better. I'll count on you to do a super duper plan for the new location, including room for a wife and ten children.

All my love,
Dana

P.S. Note the shocking overprint in our mistakes.

October 25
Dear Mother:
Tania & I are sending along these twenty announcements in case you want to mail some out to friends of the family I haven't thought of.

I have sent announcements to Mrs. Malcolm, Mme. Plaisance, Ida Treat, Mrs. Williams & Hume, & Mrs. Glandis & Mary.

Love,
Dana

Blowed if I can find George Martin's address anywhere, so I enclose one for him & his wife.

October 29, 1947
Dear Mother:
There is so much to tell you I scarcely know where to begin. The main point of course is that Tania and I are married. That's about all I managed to tell you on the phone. Too bad it was such a poor connection.

We have had messages of congratulation from you, Grandma and Eliza and Ken, and from practically all sections of the newspaper. From the publisher, Mr. James, Bernstein, Markel, Stone, Matthews and the London office, Tania Daniel, Delbert Clark and the German Staff, Bill Freese (our business and photo man) and the Frankfurt press club. I forgot to mention Cyrus who now advises us that Shan will be back about December 2 and that I should plan to remain here four or five days thereafter and then proceed to "whatever part of the Middle East Sam Brewer and you (meaning me) decide on." I'll try to get in touch with Brewer, though I'm not sure whether he's still in Spain or not.

Before I forget, I have had the more essential "shots" at last: typhoid, small pox, and cholera. When possible I'll add typhus and tetanus. I had all these just before the wedding, which was rather stupid, but anyway I had them. Tania is going to get some shots too now. Having married an American she'll be able to get them at the Mission.

Now for the wedding. I'll enclose some pictures if I can get them from the photog this morning; otherwise later. It was a very fine wedding as everyone agrees. *The Russian Orthodox ceremony is most colorful though rather lengthy . . . three quarters of an hour. Needless to say I couldn't understand the Russian, but managed to do the right thing until just the end when the priest told me to kiss the bride. This I did not understand, until he had told me four or five times and Tania had translated. Slight merriment was caused among our sixty wedding guests, especially because, when I finally understood, I responded with some violence. You will be able to judge by the picture.*

Tania's lovely wedding dress was borrowed from Mrs. Stephen Barber who is almost exactly the same size. Originally we had planned to have the wedding in ordinary clothes, Tania wearing the dress the pictures show her wearing at the reception. But Mrs. Barber came forward with her dress, which she had used a year and a half ago. She and Stephen were respectively matron of honor and best man. They were supposed to hold the crowns customary in Russian and Greek Orthodox ceremonies. But at the church it transpired that Stephen was too small to hold the crown over my head. So Dan Brewster, our consular witness, had to take on the job and Stephen held the one over Tania. The Consulate issues a certificate on the basis of Dan's witnessing statement.

As it was, both men were exhausted by the crowns. I could feel mine sinking lower and lower over my head, trembling and being hoisted back up again. They had to hold them throughout almost the entire ceremony, while the priest and his assistant chanted endlessly about Dana Adams y Tatiana, made us kiss the bible, exchanged our rings three times, blessed us and led us round the altar three times.

Among the more distinguished guests were Mr. and Mrs. Keeley, the charge d'affairs and his wife (the Ambassador being absent), Mrs. Griswold and Mr. and Mrs. Cochran. Mr. Griswold was out meeting one of the numberless groups of congressmen; Cochran is his deputy.

I was all for going to the wedding in the New York Times *jeep. But my friends insisted on taxies. I arrived about ten minutes before Tania and signed some things in the priests office. After the ceremony we departed together in a specially chartered and beautiful taxi which took us to Stephen and Mary's house where Tania changed. Then to the reception at Dalli's. We remained a respectable time and then left the multitude and made for* the Grande Bretagne, by circuitous routes. Now we are installed in room 623 amidst seven or eight enormous bouquets of flowers and some very nice wedding presents.

George Androulidakis gave Tania a really lovely mirror of wrought silver, from Jannina; the Keeley's gave us a silver ashtray; the press section of the Mission a set of five handsome wrought silver spoons; Griswold and several members of his staff a small vase; a man named Caramonas a Coty compact; Stephen and Mary a native water jug from Rhodes, a bottle of champagne, and one of three silver ashtrays. The other two ashtrays, which came in plush case and with the names of the donors inscribed on each, came from Keith and Bessie Butler (Bessie my former secretary and interpreter), and from Frank MacCaskie and Jasper Blunt (Frank the London Times man and Blunt an old acquaintance who was assistant British military attache in Ankara when I was there).

The flowers came from our more unimaginative friends. Since the next day was Tania's birthday, her 25th, I promised her a watch. Haven't bought it yet, however, since I haven't the necessary money in hand.

Now that I'm married I'll have to make some new financial arrangements, taking some of my salary over here. We'll continue saving a large part of it, however. We are anxious to carry on with the beach house. I won't make the decisions just yet, but will let you know in a week or so when I can see the shape of the future more clearly.

I forgot to mention that the day of the wedding our friends kept Tania and me carefully separated. Apparently bride and groom are not supposed to see each other the last day, or the night before. Stephen and some half dozen other males took me out on the traditional stag party the night before (ending in the A.P. correspondent and a British Colonel wrestling in the street and falling through a plate glass window; they gave their names as Zachariades). Sunday noon Stephen had me up to his place at noon for drinks. At 1:30 Tania was invited. When she arrived I was hustled into the kitchen and out the back door. So we actually didn't see each other till we got to church.

Tania has just been out buying an album in which to put the pictures and other souvenirs of the wedding. Also some typewriting paper, note paper on which to write Thank You notes, and a skirt. You see we are already an operating menage. I wish I didn't have to go to Turkey early in November. Will be gone about a week. Again, mainly in order to get the affairs of our correspondent Aslan straightened out.

We are a little crowded, with only bedroom and bath, but it will do until I reach my next assignment. Then I'll really try to get an apartment, or even a small house.

On Friday before the wedding Tania and I and Frank MacCaskie and his two sisters went out to call on Marina Sulzberger's mother and grandmother. The grandmother had a lot of people in to tea and Tania had to stand inspection. She did very well and became good friends with the grandmother and a Russian countess, both of whom came to the wedding. The mother and a Mrs. Vanderpool live in a big house surrounded by a huge garden. They are rather "boheme," keep very irregular hours and definitely prefer drinks to tea. Their maid, or rather one of them, is a Russian D.P. whom no one can understand. Tania had to function as interpreter. I think we'll be seeing more of them all.

It seems rather late, but Markel has asked me to revise my "frontier" piece along rather different lines. Terrible nuisance which will tie me up for most of the next two days.

Well, I think that will do for today, although I'm sure there's lots more to be said about the wedding and Tania. I'm sure you will love Tania. She already thinks you are wonderful, from your pictures and what I've told her about you.

All my love to you all, Dana

November 7, 1947
Dear Mother:
Here is my petition for issuance of immigration visa for Tania. It is complete except for the part on my financial status. In addition to the Statement from the Corn Exchange Bank which I have attached I need some kind of document from Bank of America indicating what my balance is, and Mr. Sterling should attach a statement of my other holdings.

Actually the bank account is sufficient, according to the Consulate, but I think we might as well attach the information on securities and war bonds for good measure. It is also possible that my account is down just now.

When that is done you or Mr. Sterling should send all the papers to The Commissioner of Immigration and Naturalization, Philadelphia 2, Pa. He will notify the Consulate here and send me confirmation when the visa is granted. It usually takes about three months. By then I'll be in the Middle East, but the Consulate and the hotel here will forward the papers to me.

Please give Mr. Sterling, his wife, son and daughter-in-law my best regards. Also, in anticipation of meeting, regards from Tania.

Dan Brewster helped us get the papers ready in double quick time this morning. I may have got father's naturalization date wrong, but it doesn't matter. Doug Werner, who was one of my witnesses, was a U.P. man in Germany when I first knew him. Harry Peel was with Stars and Stripes. Peel and his wife are at the moment touring round Europe in a Volkswagen. They have been from Frankfurt to Paris, through Spain, back to Paris, to Italy, to Yugoslavia, from which they were expelled, back to Italy, by sailing vessel from Bari to Patras in Greece. From here they are going to Salonika and then, they hope by road, through Thrace to Istanbul, and from there south into the Middle East. The little Volkswagen is going strong. They haven't had a major repair yet, although they broke a shock absorber after their first couple of miles on Greek roads.

Night before last I was up till four in the morning finishing the revision of my last magaziner requested by Markel. A fine way to act after ten days of marriage! Saturday Brewster, the Peels, Tania and I are going to a Greek theater. Most of us won't be able to understand very much but this particular show contains a lot of pantomime and political jokes which are said to be intelligible to all. Then on Sunday I'll be off to Istanbul for a week.

Tania was thrilled about the diamond pin you want to give her. She is not the sort of girl who wears a lot of jewelry, but she likes to have a few good things. Like Grandma's diamond solitaire, I think it best if you keep the pin in Los Angeles until we get there next summer.

You will have received our wedding announcements by now. They are, I see, just about in the form you recommended, but not engraved. I've noticed that engraved cards are very rare in this part of the world these days. If you haven't enough let me know and I will send more, or have more printed if they're all gone.

I don't think it would be wise to try to send us much in the way of gifts to Athens. It would be better to wait until we are established somewhere in the Middle East.

Married life is agreeing with me very well. We are very happy, Mother, and I'm sure you will be too when you get to know Tania.

We will definitely want to go ahead with our share of the beach cottage. As for the insurance, I think I should continue to make you beneficiary of part of it. Perhaps you would ask Mr. Sterling to work the whole thing out, make the transfers in so far as he, or you, can, and let me know what I have to do. I don't know any of the addresses of the Insurance Companies and am rather vague about for what and for how much I am insured. Let Mr. Sterling tell us how much he thinks I should have in Life Insurance, considering age and income, and we will increase the policy accordingly, when I get home.

Tania has had her first "shots" today. Now that she's married she can get them at the Navy dispensary. She started on typhoid and will get the rest while I'm away. She hadn't had any since she was a baby. I believe I told you I finally got around to getting mine, including cholera. Had to have the cholera shots to get a Turkish visa. Tania isn't feeling very well and has decided to take a siesta.

All my love to you all, Dana

Mr. and Mrs. Schmidt were delighted to get the joint letter from you and the Wielands and Steinie and Tuckie. Mrs. Wieland's was Tania's first letter in Russian since she was married. Russian is her mother tongue, although she speaks and writes French just about as well. English comes just a shade behind French.

Pera Palace Hotel
Istanbul
November 11, 1947
Dear Mother:
It's tough to have to go off on a trip without one's wife when one has been married such a short time, but it had to be done. Tania couldn't get her Cholera shots in time and so I couldn't take her along. But I have been writing her every day and sending her a wire every day too. I never did that before, did I? Must be love.

Of course I've been meeting the in-laws. And I have quite fallen in love with Tania's mother. She is a fine, delicate-looking lady, of a Petersburg merchant family. Apparently quite wealthy in those days. She took singing lessons secretly, because her family thought that ill-becoming to a lady, and might have made a career of it if she hadn't had an accident riding in which a horse stepped on her chest.

I've been to their apartment each evening since I got here on the ninth and have absorbed a lot of family lore. Mrs. Constantinidis told me how she met her husband, a Lt. Col. at 26!, while she was nursing wounded officers. When the revolution broke out she hid him in her house. Then they got away to Odessa where the revolution didn't strike until later.

Her husband was away on a mission in Istanbul when the Bolshies took over. She was arrested, but friends of her husband got her out and hid her. Then the White army drove out the Bolshies briefly and she and her husband got away to Bulgaria aboard a ship, with most of the possessions. Tania was born three months before they left, in 1923.

Mr. Constantinidis was a dashing young officer and has been a bit on the dashing side ever since. He and his wife are practically separated although they apparently remain civil and live in the same house. His outside interests are no secret. He is, or looks, quite a bit younger than she, which explains a lot. While she is frail and elderly and doesn't like to go out he is bursting with energy and wants always to be on the move. She is the kind who is always closing windows and he the kind who is always opening them.

He had some kind of shipping business in Odessa and later Varna, in Bulgaria. Now he is apparently doing very well as a real estate agent. Anyway he made several references to how prosperous the last few years had been. He has bought a couple of apartments in Tania's name and a lot of the household furniture is hers too. Apparently we are free to take the furniture, at least, whenever we have a menage of our own. But I think we'll be wanting our own things.

I am to take a lot of clothes, and a batch of home-baked biscuits, to Tania. Sunday night when I arrived I met a number of the family's Russian friends and tomorrow night I am going to meet some more at dinner.

ELIZABETH SCHMIDT CRAHAN

Apart from these family affairs I have been concerned with getting Aslan straightened out. This time I think I'll really pull it off. The Prime Minister has asked Huseyin Cahid Yalcin, the dean of the Turkish press corps, to make recommendations as to what should be done to improve the present arrangements for the press. The Prime Minister and everybody else is dissatisfied with Nedim Veysel Ilkin, the press director who has made so much trouble for Aslan. And Yalcin has undertaken to take Aslan's matter in hand and see that he gets his press card back. (I can't remember whether I explained the troubles of Aslan, our local representative, before.)

Friday I'll be going to Ankara and on Sunday, or early next week, I'll be returning to Tania.

All my love to you, now, and to Steinie too.
Dana

November 19, 1947
Dear Mother:
I am happily back from Turkey and back with Tania. We have been thrilled to receive your post-wedding letters and ever so glad that you got the announcements and pictures all right. Tania said she thought you must be a wonderful person after reading your letter.

The time is now too short, I fear, for you to send us anything to Athens. If however you can give something to Dorothy Day's mother-in-law, to be sent to us by pouch from Madrid later, when our new address is known, okay. But I really wouldn't advise sending the ring, even by pouch. I know the Embassy people are usually very strict about what goes into the pouch these days and it might lead to complications if we try to send a valuable piece of jewelry that way. However, I'll speak to some Embassy friends about it. Sam Brewer is already in Cairo and I have just cabled Cyrus for his cable and mail addresses so that I can begin talking over the precise location of my future headquarters.

Tania immediately put on the nylons you sent, to wear to a cocktail party we were going to. They are the most fashionable shade, it seems. Today, unfortunately, she is in bed with a bad cold. But as soon as she is about she will figure out her

American sizes with some of the American girls here and let you know. There is nothing she would like better than clothes from the States.

I was relieved to learn in your latest letter that you are feeling better and may not need the cystoscopic. I'll be eager to see what progress you've made with your young teacher.

I'd like ever so much to make our honeymoon in Switzerland, but I think it's too far and expensive. We can go there some time later. For the moment Tania will be just as happy with some place nearer my future assignment. I think we'll have to spend a couple of days in Istanbul with Tania's parents, which will have to come out of the ten days honeymoon time. Then I thought we might try to get some sunshine farther south. If it turns out that we are to go to Egypt first I thought we might try Luxor (Luksor?), on the Upper Nile. I've heard it is a wonderful place for a holiday and that the climate is fine in December.

Tania still has a few more shots to go, but I have decided to fill out my "Navy immunization card" by getting the typhus shots. It is all done at the Navy dispensary attached to the American Mission.

If anyone wants to give Tania some wedding presents I am sure the regular household variety will be welcomed. We fully intend to have an apartment or small house in the Middle East. We haven't got a cocktail shaker, or an electric toaster, for example, which even a portable household can use. Of course I have no idea what Tania may receive when we get across to Turkey together.

As I see it my expenses here haven't been so heavy as would seem at first glance. You still have more than $800 coming from the NYT which I have charged them for expenses. The $1000 transferred to the Corn Exchange are still there. Counting the $800 already returned that means I've consumed about $400 for personal expenses since I got here. Of course there've been other expenses for which you have had to lay out money in Los Angeles.

Leaving aside other income my salary for the months of July August September October should be about $2,000.

Now the expenses of the wedding—church, reception, announcements, invitations, rings, license fees, medical exams, and what not, have been considerable. Anyway, around $700. Also, Tania's birthday was the day after the wedding and I promised her a watch which I haven't bought yet. So I am making another transfer of $1,000 to Mr. Miltiadis Kyrtsis, "The Devon Hotel," 70 West 55th Street, New York City. Will you see that the check is sent out in due course. There is no rush.

I quite agree with you about holding down the overhead. Here it has fortunately been possible for Tania to move into the room I was already using and there has been no increase in rent, except for the room she occupied at the Minerva before we were married.

Will you please let me know what my balance is after you've made this last transfer? I can't tell from here what the cost would be but the speculative house on my lot sounds very interesting. I would appreciate knowing exactly what it would involve. If it can be built in a relatively short time, that is, before next spring, I don't see how one could lose. Let Mr. Sterling be the judge. He might turn in one of my investments in exchange for the speculative house costs. Of course I would not want to do this if it entailed risking my ability to share in the beach cottage which we are actually going to use. As I believe I said, Tania loves the beach and swims like a fish.

Yes, a good deal of the time Tania functions as secretary and interpreter. She has a lot to learn about such things, but has all the basic knowledge and ability, including typing, and a great desire to be helpful.

Being married is making an enormous difference. I suddenly find myself being quite sociable. Life seems definitely much more enjoyable.

Tania and I both send love to you, and Steinie too.

Dana

Got letter from Mme. Plaisance, with clipping from the L.A. Times *announcement*.

November 23, 1947
Dear Mother:

Tania and I have had a fairly quiet Sunday because she has been in bed with a bad cold. It went first to her head and then her chest. We called in a doctor from the Mission and he gave her sulfanilamide which seems to be clearing the *thing up. Tonight she feels much better and it took all my husbandly authority to keep Tania in the room.*

I went out to a cocktail party given for the members of the new United Nations Balkan Committee and Tania had a couple of friends up in the room for drinks. When I got back we all had supper, in the room, after I had written my story.

Good evidence that Tania is back to normal is that at this moment she is washing out the stockings you sent her. She has been wearing them ever since they arrived, apparently. In a few minutes we will make an outline of her feet on pieces of typewriting paper and tomorrow Tania is going to meet an American girl and get her measurements made in inches. I'll enclose the results.

Airmail has been rather slow the last few weeks as you may have noticed largely because TWA stopped flying here after the Greeks cut communications with Egypt. TWA thought Egypt more important to them than Greece, cholera or no cholera. Now TWA has resumed.

Tania says to tell you that she looks awful, with a red nose which isn't improved by continuous applications of cold cream.

The story I did on Griswold's threat to resign has caused a lot of repercussions. The State Department is mad at me, again. I'm afraid it isn't possible for a correspondent to do a conscientious job these days without making the State Dept. mad sooner or later. But the important thing is to gain a reputation for being courageous and enterprising.

Since we have been married invitations are coming in from all sides. As you suggested in your letter, social life develops considerably after the wedding and we must take care to entertain in return.

Not only must I start preparing our departure, visas etc., but I have to try to get Cyrus' mother-in-law off to Paris. He keeps bombarding me with cables about it. Sometimes he is a terrible worry-wart. He certainly wastes a lot of money on cables.

Yesterday Tania and I were delighted to receive a letter from Margaret Acker. Please tell Margaret we were very pleased and will be writing an answer soon.

Lots of love, Dana

George Androulidakis, my friend and Greek assistant left Athens for London yesterday. Eventually he will go on to the U.S. and has promised to phone you from New York, REVERSING The CHARGES. I am very fond of George. Apart from being a thoroughly honest, balanced and well-informed newspaperman he is a very likeable person. I hope someday you can entertain him.

Love Dana

P.S. Your letter of Nov 6 came today.

I have written twice and even 3 times a week to you Grandma or Elizabeth since just before the wedding so that it astonishes me to hear that you haven't heard from me lately.

The unsigned pieces from Istanbul were by Aslan, product of his tour of Eastern Turkey.

We are looking forward eagerly to the nylons, socks and neckties. Steinie, that was very sweet of you.

No Tania doesn't know much about cooking. A little though, enough to cook out of cans. But she's interested in learning when she gets a chance.

We still don't know whether we are going to Jerusalem or Cairo. I have written to Brewer with whom to decide "what is best" according to Cyrus.

Wonderful progress Mother, to think that you can sit down in a chair from the crutches! I think the lessons must be having a wonderful effect.

Love,
Dana

December 2, 1947
Dear Mother:

Tania and I are expecting word almost any day now about Shan Sedgwick's arrival. He should be in London already, but I have had no word. We have all our visas ready but haven't made plane reservations yet. It certainly looks as though we were going to have a busy time in the Middle East.

Just got word from Markel that my magaziner will be printed next Sunday, which is gratifying. Also have a weekender due for Sunday, so my windup in Greece will definitely be in print.

We have been making out nicely in our hotel room at the Grande Bretagne, but I am looking forward to the day when we will have a place of our own. The real trouble with hotel life from our point of view is that it doesn't leave much for Tania to do. You just press the button and things are done for you. Helping me is not a full time job. If Tania has a little home to look after it will give her a lot of satisfaction I am sure, and me too. Then she would also have time to start some of the things she likes and is good at; maybe music—she plays piano and several other instruments, maybe drawing, maybe riding. With our time here so limited we haven't got that sort of thing organized. In due course, of course, there will no doubt be children, and that will be a full time job and then some.

When I find out where we are going to make our headquarters we will certainly want to begin gathering things like nice linen and silver. I'll try to find out when we pass through Istanbul what the prospects are from Tania's family. We are both very much touched at your offer to give us the flat silver we most definitely will want. Perhaps we can work that out when we come home to California next summer.

Thanks for the clippings from Palestine. I have added them to the collection Tania has started and will be using them to bone up on Middle East background when we start our move.

You must be tremendously busy with translation for Doctor Lowman added to your work on the booklets. They must be about ready now. When I get to Los Angeles I'll probably be able to offer my not so expert advice on a new batch.

Zenas Andrew description of Tania was pretty good. Yes, Tania's eyes are definitely blue. Her eyes in fact are one of the most attractive things about her. She looks very young, younger than her 25 years, and people meeting her for the first time are sometimes startled to learn she is married. She has a rather large mole under her chin which probably could be removed if she ever wanted it done, but I have never even mentioned it.

Just at this moment Tania is out visiting a Turkish girl named Burhan who is visiting in Athens. Burhan used to run a sheet called the "Tourists weekly" in

Istanbul and now considers herself a foreign correspondent, for the Cumhuriyet *of Istanbul.*

Thanks for making the corrections on the immigration papers. I always seem to get those things wrong.

Tania was overjoyed with Nini Barry's case of lipsticks; seems she had been wanting just such a thing. She'll write a note to Mrs. Barry. I think that when we reach the Middle East you can send the sweater by air, or, if they still won't accept it, there will be time for ordinary mail.

I am sending some little Xmas presents from us both to the family by air freight. Been some delay as I had to get exit permits! I have discovered incidentally, that the tie you sent me is of the non-wrinkling kind of best English wool, and a real prize. After some hesitation on my part Tania persuaded me to go out with Steinie's gorgeous symphony of color, and now it's my favorite.

I believe I told you I would sell my car in Germany and probably buy a new one. Cyrus has now offered to buy it for the New York Times. *I have left it up to my friend Bill Freese in Frankfurt, who has been looking after it and has all the papers, to set the price, so I don't know yet how much I'll get.*

How exciting that you are learning to JUMP between the crutches. Your young teacher must have been doing wonderful work.

Just so we don't get crossed up I suggest that you send your next letter care of American Embassy, Istanbul, with a carbon in care of American Legation, Beyrouth, marked "please hold;" then the letter after that to the Beyrouth address with a carbon to American consulate, Jerusalem. From Jerusalem I'll send you a cable, if not before.

All my love, now, to you all,
Dana

Athens
December 8, 1947
Dear Mother:
This is our last night in Athens and Tania and I are just about worn to a frazzle. As always there were a thousand and one things to be attended to, tickets

and reservations and visas and goodbyes and packing. Now there remain only my accounts and I have half decided to take them along to Istanbul with us.

Went round to the Embassy and picked up your last letter, of November 27, giving a breakdown of my income and outgo of the past four months. Yes, the outgo has indeed been quite heavy and I will have to settle down to a more systematic system of financing my overseas expenses. I think I should set aside a certain amount of each week's salary for our living expenses and for savings. That way you would know more precisely what you could count on having in my account, for investments, the house, etc., and I would be able to make my plans here more easily. I'll determine the amounts when we get to the Middle East.

In the immediate future you'll be getting a fair sum from the sale of my car. It is not certain that I will buy another right away; Sam Brewer tells me he has not done so and that prices are very high. On the other hand possession of a car is a great professional advantage. We'll see what we can get. There'll also be a hundred more from my magaziner and my last weekender.

I am extremely anxious to pay for your third month's walking lessons, as planned when I was home. Let's count that as certain. I would also like to pay for the new wheel chair and braces, as my Christmas present to you. Life is too short and precious for me to be sitting there with a lot of securities when you are really needing something like that, which amounts to only a little more than a week's salary. I know you guard my funds zealously and want me to avoid unnecessary expenses, but these are necessary and they are things I very much want to do. Now is that understood, Mother? The lessons I will pay for as previously arranged and the wheel chair and braces are my Christmas present.

About the insurance. Go ahead and make the change in the accident policy now if it can be done in my absence. We'll take care of the life insurance when I'm home.

I'm attracted by the speculative house project and would like to do it unless Mr. Sterling vetoes.

I don't think you need worry about my not being in the news in the Middle East, with this Palestine partition blowing up. I'll be interested in any clips and also any books you run across on the Middle East. Clippings, that is, by my colleague on the Times *and from other newspapers, magazines, etc. The ones you have sent in the past have been very helpful.*

I don't know just what Tania will get out of the property in her name. I'm not counting on anything from her Pa. Anything that did materialize would be sheer windfall. He hasn't mentioned anything about wedding expenses and I certainly won't. Incidentally, these customs vary a bit, I gather. According to English custom my best man should have paid for the post-wedding reception, but since he just didn't have the money the questions did not arise.— Steven and his wife Mary are coming out to the airport with us at 7:30 tomorrow morning! They'll drive the jeep back to town and turn it over to Sedgwick. We are taking the Turkish plane.

We'll be seeing Tania's family tomorrow. The plane leaves at nine a.m., so we'll be there for lunch. Her mother wants us to stay at their apartment, but Tania doesn't want to. I'm neutral, although I would be inclined to stay with her mother if that will make her any happier, even if it were not particularly comfortable or convenient. We'll have to cut our visit in Istanbul as short as possible as it is not a holiday and I don't want it to count as our honeymoon time.

Tania says I'd better make this a Christmas letter, as the next one might be late. So I'll say Merry Christmas to you, and to Steinie, Elizabeth and Ken, Grandma, Eloise, Dean Mary, Murph and all our friends! Maybe we'll go to Bethlehem for Christmas!

We have sent a box airfreight containing some little things for Christmas.
All my love,
Dana

I wish you would keep a special copy of last Sunday's (yesterday's) paper. It was a banner day for me, with a magaziner, a weekender and a story on the front page. My swan song from Athens.

Sedgwick has arrived. I don't think he learned a thing during his stay in the U.S. same old rabid Royalist reactionary. But perhaps he'll be more careful. His wife is still lecturing but will be here in a few days. I turned over my file and a lot of other papers and correspondence to Sedgwick, which is rather more than he did for me, when I arrived.

Incidentally, I managed to get Cy's mother-in-law's passport and visa. Something of a local triumph. She would have been months over it if left to her own devices. Of course being the representative of the Times *makes that sort of thing easy. She is going to Paris for three months, regardless of the troubles.*

Hotel Saint Georges
Beyrouth
December 16, 1947
Dear Mother:
We have a new home where the Mediterranean splashes round the rocks off Beyrouth. It is warm, wonderfully, unbelievably warm, and we have been swimming in the sunshine. One can swim from the rocks on which this hotel is built but we went out with my old friend Bob Brown and his wife yesterday to a vast sandy beach outside town.

Soon there will be skiing in the mountains above Beyrouth and Tripoli. This is a real California. I am delighted, for Tania's sake even more than mine, that the news has taken us here.

It begins to look as though Beyrouth and Damascus would become headquarters for the Arabs in the Palestine conflict, and I will for the time being cover their end of the show. Unfortunately it is a lot harder to get information out of Arabs than Greeks.

We got here night before last and as yet I haven't felt justified in writing a story. Don't feel I know what's going on yet. It was a hectic journey from Athens to Beyrouth. We got to Istanbul by air early Tuesday, were met at the airport by Tania's parents, and left by Taurus Express Thursday morning. Three nights and four days on the train to get here. The "express" part ended at Aleppo where we were three hours late and had to wait 24 hours for a locomotive. The main part of the train, with locomotive, left us there for the run to Bagdad. Then from Tripoli down to Beyrouth the train deteriorated into a kind of tramcar, stopping at every hamlet.

However, it was fun, even though exhausting and rather dirty. We had the day in Aleppo and took in the "soukhs," or bazaar, the old fort and such standard attractions. Bought some camel's hair to make Tania a camel's hair coat and a brocade which now hangs on our wall.

My efforts to get Aslan's credentials restored have borne fruit. He got them a week or so ago.

In Istanbul Tania spent most of the time with her parents, or rather, mainly with her mother, while I scrambled round and got her a new passport containing her married name, tickets etc. Unfortunately there wasn't time for much else. We would have had to wait nearly a week for the next train, and I didn't think the office would have been very pleased about that. I had already asked approval of the detour via Istanbul so Tania could pick up her steamer trunk and other belongings.

For your private information Tania's father said nothing about wedding expenses, so we'll consider that matter closed. Her mother gave her a very lovely diamond broach, a valuable sapphire ring and some other jewelry. And of course she was able to take along a lot of clothes, not to mention useful things like an electric water heater.

If it hadn't been so hectic the trip would have been something of a honeymoon. But fortunately we still have that to look forward to. We will, if the news doesn't interfere too much, take the time off around Christmas and New Years.

After talking it over by telephone with Sam Brewer in Jerusalem I think I'll be working Syria and Lebanon for some weeks to come. So please write to me here until further notice. I would suggest you use the Legation as address, although the Hotel will be all right. There is only the possibility of our moving to another hotel. If you have already sent something to Jerusalem don't worry. I'll be going there from time to time as soon as I get a Lebanese re-entry visa.

It was a good break to find Bob Brown, who is Air Attache, here. He was able to break the ice a little for us both. He has been married only six months himself. You'll remember he was one of those who shared our apartment at Ankara. You met his mother once. I believe she lives in some remote part of Los Angeles.

Your little Philco is playing merrily on the dresser. I had had a transformer installed in Athens so that I could use it on the local 210 volt current. Here

I've had a gadget installed to permit me to switch it from 210 to 110 which is voltage in Beyrouth and the one for which the radio was built.

It is also time I was getting to bed.

All my love to you all, Dana

Hotel Saint George
Beyrouth
December 23, 1947
Dear Mother:

We have just one hour and a half before the car leaves for Haifa, and I want to get this word to you off. The system in these parts is that you take a couple of seats in one of the big sedans used to maintain communications between the large towns. I had originally planned to leave tomorrow, but since they may be finding cholera in Lebanon any minute and close the frontiers I think we'd better move while we can.

Yesterday we had planned to go to Damascus, but couldn't because of cholera regulations. Instead we took a trip out to visit the Near East Foundation representative at Chtaura. He and his wife turned out to be most interesting and pleasant people, in fact the nicest we've run into around here. We have decided to take our honeymoon at Chtaura where there is a nice hotel, good food, horses (mainly for Tania), mountains. The place is located between the Lebanon and anti-Lebanon mountain ranges at an altitude of about 3000 feet.

The schedule is: we will spend the 24th, 25, 26, 27th in Palestine, then proceed to Chtaura on the 28th, and stay there till after New Years, about the third or fourth. It will be interesting to be in Jerusalem on Christmas, and we will have our honeymoon after that.

Before we go I'll run by the Legation and see if there is any mail. Am eager for a letter from you. Perhaps there'll be one at Jerusalem.

The weather has been brilliant and balmy most of the time. Seems too good to be true. If it weren't for a certain feeling of isolation I get here this would be an ideal news spot. Considering that half of the Palestine conflict is being run from here it seems to me that the U.S. press gives Beyrouth & Damascus mighty little attention.

Sunday we went to the races and lost a moderate amount of money. George Bitar, the local U.P. stringer, is a great racing fan but doesn't seem to give very good advice.

I must close now.

Love to you all,

Dana

Continue to write to us here. We'll be back.

WESTERN UNION
1947 DECEMBER 24 AM 7:30
P.CDY66 INTL= CD BEYROUTH VIA RCA 21 24.
NLT MARGARET SCHMIDT =
1132 FOURTH AVE LOS A=
MERRY CHRISTMAS MOTHER GRANDMA ELIZABETH KEN STEINIE TUCKIE LOVE FROM LEBANESE HONEYMOON=
TANIA DANA

Hotel Massabki, Chtaura
December 31, 1947
Dear Mother:

Tania and I have almost finished our little honeymoon. It has been a rest which both of us needed. I am glad we could include the hectic holidays, although tomorrow we will go back down to Beyrouth in time to attend an open house held by the military attache.

Contrary to what I said I was going to do in my last letter, we took our honeymoon time before I went down to Jerusalem and visited Damascus. The reason therefore was that the new cholera restrictions made it impossible for us to move immediately.

Now, when we get back to Beyrouth I will get on my way to Jerusalem immediately and have my consultation with Sam Brewer. After that I'll have a better idea what we'll be doing in the Middle East. I won't take Tania with me on this trip, as it seems unnecessary to expose her to the risks of travel in Palestine if we are not to stay there. If however it turns out that I shall work in Palestine *for a longer period of course she'll come with me. The danger is not so much in living there, since she can choose a quiet place, as in travelling on the highways.*

Here at Chtaura we have been riding horseback, walking in the hills and eating and sleeping. One day we spent around the ruins of Baalbek. And we have spent a lot of time with Frank Anthony of the Near East Foundation and his wife. They live here in a little stone house almost opposite the hotel, running an experimental agricultural station, trying to help Arabs raise their pitiful standard of living and, very keenly, observing the life around them. Very good company.

Christmas eve Tania and I exchanged some Xmas surprises and celebrated in a very modest way. She presented me with a Parker fountain pen and a new shaving brush, and I her with four intriguing brown teddy bears and a mouth organ—she would prefer a piano, but that will have to wait—and three filters for her Contax camera. Mostly nonsense but it gave us a lot of fun. Incidentally, don't mention the fountain pen to Eliza if she has sent me one, as I believe you said in a letter a while back.

I have been busy wearing my Christmas neckties and socks amidst general admiration. Did I tell you I bought Tania three meters of Camels hair material for a coat which is now being made up. Also some French material which is being lined with the fur of a fur coat which Tania had hitherto shunned. For some reason Tania doesn't like fur coats, unless the fur is inside.

We got your Christmas cable. It was phoned up to us from the hotel and added greatly to our Christmas cheer. But I didn't answer your inquiry about how long we would be here since there was nothing definite I could say that I hadn't said before. Perhaps it will turn out to be most intelligent for me to make a headquarters here, where Tania can live, and to circulate out through the Middle East from here. I have been playing with the idea of acquiring a jeep station wagon for travel. After I've found out the relative prices in Palestine I'll make a proposition to the Times. *I haven't been paid yet for my car in Germany and will not be until a notarized statement confirming the transfer has been received from me in Germany.*

Tania is about to tell my fortune with cards. She does it very well. Tells me very good fortunes. She is also trying to toast some of her mother's cookies on our wood stove. We have still not managed to consume all the cookies and cakes and jam her mother gave us to take along.

This morning a lawyer from Beyrouth who is also staying here drove us to Ksara where the Jesuits have a tremendous winery (is there such a word?). Anyhow they have vineyards and make wine, cognac, liqueurs, a kind of champagne etc. It is the best made in the Middle East, I am told, and about one fifth the price one pays for it at a hotel like the Saint George. We bought about $10 worth.

I've been fascinated the last few days watching developments in Greece. Looks as though the predictions I made in my magazine article were coming true. I'll be interested very much indeed in your comments on how Shan Sedgwick is handling things. Would appreciate some of his clippings if they are of interest.

By the time we get back to Beyrouth there should be some letters from you. I've been missing them of late.

Now here's wishing you and Grandma and all the family a very Happy New Year.

Love,
Dana

P.S. I trust you aren't worrying about cholera. There really isn't a thing to worry about. No Europeans have got it, only "felahin," the Arab peasants. The worst thing about it all is the taking of shots (which doctors say are not very effective anyway in the case of cholera).

P.P.S. Please transfer $500 to my Corn Exchange Bank Account in New York.

LETTERS HOME: 80 YEARS LATER

1948

Shepheards hotel
Cairo
January 5, 1948
Dear Mother:
What with Christmas and New Years my letter this week is most disgracefully late.

We were terribly disappointed on Christmas day not to be able to be through to L.A. I was not able to ascertain for sure why we did not get the connection but thought it best to cancel the call.

We thought of you all waiting and waiting for the call to come through and hope it didn't spoil your Xmas part at 1132. We went out to Tom Stauffer's apartment for Christmas dinner and ate a noble Turkey with a few people from the Embassy, then went around to call on the Ambassador, and that's about all. He was here briefly between trips for the refugees.

Xmas eve we went to the home of Mrs. Bible, white Russian wife of an Englishman and had some quiet celebrations around the local version of a Christmas tree... a kind of fir. And finally, New Years eve we decided to stick to the hotel where quite a party had been lined up, with the New Year in the shape of a pretty young gal chasing the bearded and limping old year off the stage at midnight.

I gave Tania a bolt of Beirut brocades and a special wire brush for the dog (it fits on the hand like a glove and was originally designed for horses) and she gave me four pairs of socks and a special gadget for cleaning and stomping my pipe.

Those were our festivities. We really had quite a modest time. The important thing, our next move, hung over everything. Still we don't know for sure whether it is to be Vienna or home leave first. I know the confidential reason for the delay in decision. It has nothing to do with us and depends on something in Vienna.

Albion Ross has arrived and I am busy taking him around and getting him started. He has never been in these parts before which is both advantage and disadvantage. He is a nice, intelligent, middle-aged but rather dull fellow. We like him. Last night he wrote his first story, but I will carry on the main burden until just before we leave.

I think there has been enough news here lately to satisfy even you and me. But I hold to my belief that this will be a pretty quiet corner during the balance of the year. Albion has been telling us a lot about Vienna and Prague and Budapest and we are filled with enthusiasm. Living conditions in Vienna are apparently pretty good, especially for Americans, and quite cheap, and there is ample news, though not always front page.

This is all too brief and sketchy for such a delayed letter but I really am madly busy with Ross. Tania and I both send all our love to you all, and hope we'll be in that beach house soon. Dana

>
> *Hotel Saint Georges*
> *Beyrouth, Lebanon*
> *January 8, 1948*

Dear Mother:

Since I last wrote lots has happened. For one thing a letter of yours has arrived and I suspect there's another waiting at the Legation for me now.

For another, I've been to Jerusalem and for yet another, directly connected with my trip, we have acquired a dog, a Boxer, aged six weeks, whom we have named Cleopatra, or Cleo for short. (Needless to say she is female.)

Tania wanted an Alsatian, but there just weren't any to be had in Jerusalem, although it is the best place to get Alsatians and dogs of all kinds in the Middle East. I must have called up half the owners of pedigreed Alsatians in town. It wasn't the season for young ones. But Boxers are in fashion at present and at last I tracked down a litter. We wanted a male, but the litter was all female, so that ended that.

Fortunately the Saint Georges has stone floors, so no one minds the messes too much. Tania is delighted. She wanted a dog very much. I hope and pray we will raise this one all right. Cleo is so terribly young and helpless. Her eyes were still blue and half blind when I got her, but in the last forty-eight hours they have begun to turn brown and she isn't bumping into things so much. She has only just learned to walk properly and still loses her balance sometimes.

She loves to play. Doesn't hesitate a minute to wake us up in the middle of the night to indicate she'd like to play. Now she pulls gently at things like coat sleeves and shoe laces; when she is four times as large she'll be a terror. Donovan of NBC has a huge Boxer in Jerusalem who constantly spreads havoc and disorder in the pressroom and adjoining bar. Ed Curtis of the A.P. has one too, but keeps it at home.

We bought a basket for Cleo but have decided it is too small, so now she sleeps on a pile of the hotel's blankets. Also bought a dish to eat out of and a bowl to drink out of and a collar and lead. I took her to the veterinary this morning to have her ears clipped (Tania didn't want to witness the act) but was told that she was still too young. Have to wait another two weeks.

Well, so much for Cleo. After our honeymoon I absorbed another cholera shot and took off for Jerusalem in a taxi. Travelling on the inland road through Nablus, mainly in Arab territory, I had no trouble at all. Day before yesterday I came out the same way, accompanied by Clay Gowran of the Chicago Tribune.

The result of my trip was that it is now fairly definite that I will spend a few more days here, then go to Damascus for a few weeks. After that we will have to decide, that is Cyrus will have to, whether I go on to Bagdad and Teheran or go to Tel Aviv to cover the United Nations Commission and the new Jewish capital. Of course no one knows when the U.N. will move in. Also it is uncertain whether a new crisis is brewing in Teheran or not. So Hotel Saint Georges or U.S. Legation remains the address.

The visit to Palestine was really an eye opener. I did not fully realize how serious things are there. Not even during the war have I often felt so insecure. Everyone is, as the British say, "windy." Sniping and bomb throwing are so unpredictable. Both sides mean business, are confident of success, and underestimate the strength and determination of the other. You may, I hope, have got something of the atmosphere from the one story I wrote.

Sam Brewer does not like it and will take the first opportunity to go off on a tour of some other points of interest. Then either Gene Currivan or I will take over in Jerusalem. I will certainly not take Tania if I go there. If I go to Tel Aviv I might, but it is by no means certain. I would go ahead and look it over. The Jews say it is the safest place in Palestine. But if the U.N. sets up there it may change.

I saw lots of old friends in Jerusalem. All the old Turkey and Middle East crowd. It is rather a different crowd from the German or French ones. John Wallis who used to be Reuters in Turkey and now does Daily Telegraph paid me back $100 I loaned him in Algiers in 1944! Farnie Fowle of CBS was there, living in Gershon Agronsky's house. That's Martin Agronsky's uncle, editor of the Palestine Post. Carl Gossett, our NY Times photographer from Frankfurt, was there for a brief spell. And lots of other old acquaintances whose names you wouldn't recognize.

I have saved the real news for the end. Tania is going to have a baby. That's what the doctor said three days ago, and they aren't often wrong. We haven't told anybody here just yet, for no reason except that we enjoy keeping the secret. Tania has all sorts of instructions about what she can and should eat. The doctor told her it would be all right to have a drink now and then but advised her not to smoke. That sounds unusual, but he is the chief obstetrician at the American University's American hospital and is supposed to be a renowned expert. Also told her to take a short nap after lunch, to eat fresh foods and drink milk. She'll have to drink milk boiled or out of cans, because there is no pasteurization plant here.

Apparently the baby is due in about eight months. It is astonishing, isn't it? I am tremendously happy, although somewhat startled. We certainly didn't waste any time. Now the thing to do is to time the coming of the baby with my long leave in the U.S.

I want the baby to be born in the U.S., and the leave will make it possible. What date do you think we should shoot at? Assuming the baby is due about

September 5. Should we plan to come in July and leave in September, or come and leave a month later? Or do you think I should send Tania ahead, or leave her in L.A. a while after I leave? I want your advice on this. In any case it is evident that my home leave should be some months later than we had planned. That will, incidentally, give us a better chance to get the house built at the beach before we arrive.

There is one more news item. I have written to Mr. James changing the system by which my salary is paid. For a while beginning February first we will try having $45 weekly sent to you and the rest including money from the Sunday Times, *paid into my Corn Exchange Account. That will give Tania and me $80 a week to live on. I don't think we need that much, but we'll try it. If I find money accumulating I will transfer it to you for my savings account or investment, or for the house, or we'll revise the system.*

You will know exactly how much money you will be receiving in future. I won't be calling on you suddenly for sudden transfers of large sums. That'll simplify your planning.

Having money paid into the checking account will be advantageous in the Middle East since I find it possible to cash checks here, a thing that was never possible during the war. That is obviously more convenient than having to write you for a transfer of funds.

Let me know whether you think this is a wise move. We can always change it.

Tania and I have spent a lot of money getting married and since. We've bought a number of things. But we will live more economically from now until the babe is born. Then we'll have another big spate of expenses. So we must save.

I enclosed some pictures. We'll send one of Cleo as soon as we have one.

All my love. I know Grandma will be especially interested to hear about the baby.

Dana

Additionally, Beyrouth is in Lebanon not Syria. They are supposed to be separate Republics.

P.S. Cleo sends love to Tuckie!

ELIZABETH SCHMIDT CRAHAN

9-1-1948
Beirut
Dear mother:
I received your letter yesterday and the day before I've sent you one. You say that you haven't heard from me since a long time. But I did write you lately. I wrote you two letters without any answer.

I am very sorry to hear that you were ill. I hope that you are well now. I wish I was there to look after you.

I'll send Dana the clippings and the paper. You even can write to each other more often because there is a journalist who lives in Amman now so I can send Dana letters through him. So if you can't write him because I don't think the mail goes to Palestine, you can send me the letters and I'll send it through Amman.

The weather here was very hot till this morning and today is Sunday and it's raining but maybe it will change in the afternoon.

Something happened to my pen so I better stop.
Good bye dear mother I wish you a good health.
Yours
Tania.

January 13, 1948
Hotel Saint Georges
Beyrouth, Lebanon
Dear Mother:
Tomorrow I am leaving for Damascus and expect to stay there for some time. As soon as this is certain and I have a good place for Tania to live lined up I'll bring her up from Beyrouth. It is not a very long journey but is at the moment complicated by cholera regulations. In a few days these will lapse, if they have not already lapsed in practice.

Cyrus has asked me to carry on in Lebanon and Damascus for the time being, using my own judgment as to where to work, and obtaining visas for Irak, Iran, Persia and Palestine. Cy will then decide which of us goes where.

You are right in thinking this is not the best news spot in the world, but it has improved in the last few days. There is not much spot news, and what there is is highly unreliable, but there are things of great interest and importance going on, if only one can put one's finger on them.

Cleo is thriving, growing almost visibly from day to day. Tania has half decided not to have her ears clipped, having read in a magazine that it is the fashion in England at the moment not to do so. Personally I think she would be better looking with unclipped ears; I'd agree to the operation only in deference to custom . . . Sorry the pictures of her aren't ready yet.

You would scarcely believe what beautiful weather we have here. Day after day of flawless sunshine. Tania has got quite brown sitting out on the terrace overlooking the sea with Cleo. Just like Calif., only no smog.

Tania hasn't had any letters from her mother since we arrived here and is getting very worried. She telegraphed the other day and got a reply back in Turkish saying the letters hadn't been going through. It was most peculiar that the telegram was in Turkish, since her mother scarcely speaks Turkish and would never communicate with her daughter in that language. So Tania is more worried than ever. I have telegraphed to our man Aslan to go and see her and find out just what the trouble may be. I told you that Mr. and Mrs. Constantinidis were not getting on well; that is, he had taken up some outside interests and was spending a lot of money on them. I fear that this may be the root of the trouble.

Last night we had Bob Brown and his wife to dinner at one of the best, and at the same time smallest, restaurants in town, named Maxim's, run by a German refugee Jew. He, the Jew, is now faced with expulsion from Lebanon, as result of the uproar over Palestine. What a lot of trouble human beings make for each other.

Bob and his wife had been up to the Cedars for a weekend of skiing. I would like to do that but don't feel like taking the time just now. Also would like to introduce Tania to real skiing under the most favorable circumstances, when it is really warm in March or April.

All my love to you all now, Dana

16-1-1948
Beirouth
Dear mother,
I was very glad to hear that you have received the Xmas presents, and I am glad that you liked the scarf, isn't it cute.

Dana left for Damascus yesterday afternoon at two, when he will decide whether to stay there or not, he will come here and we'll both go there.

He just called me up from there and says that he will be back on Sunday and pick me up. He thinks we will stay there for several weeks.

Two days ago I had a terrible hemorrhage, with terrible pain, I don't know why, tomorrow I'll go and see the doctor. I was so happy that I was going to have a baby and now that stupid thing happened.

Dear mother good bye now
Love Tania.

Shepheards hotel
Cairo
January 17, 1948
Dear Mother:
On Friday of this week we are off, so this will be my last letter from Cairo. Just about everything is lined up, but as always the last days are crowded with last minute things. As usual there are a couple of stories I think I simply must write before we go. One about the pyramids another about the development of the Nile. Both requiring a good deal of study.

Ross has about taken over. I've introduced him to nearly all my news sources and friends. Surely no newspaperman was ever introduced into a new milieu with such care.

We will fly to Rome with the Egyptian airlines SAIDE *which is about twenty-five or more percent cheaper than* TWA. *This is worth doing since we will be flying with all our very considerable imepedimenta, including dog and two steamer trunks. This line will take the excess baggage as freight, and on the same plane, but even so the baggage will cost almost as much as the tickets. But considering the complications of train to Alexandria, getting aboard, getting off* at Naples, on another train to Rome and changing in Rome, I think it is worth burdening the NY Times *with this extra expense.*

Your letter is overdue this week. Hope something comes before we get away.

In Vienna you can write to us c/o New York Times, *Bezirk 1, Loewelstrasse 8, until I give you a more precise address.*

Yesterday I went out to Sakkara and was taken into the bowels of one of the pyramids, the northern Dashur pyramid which is being explored completely for the first time. The archaeologist thinks he is going to find the King's burial chamber. If he does it will be a find equal or greater than that of Tut Ankh Amen, and 1,500 years older. All quite thrilling. He gave me a piece of rope made of papyrus that was presumably left there by thieves some three thousand years ago.

Had a Christmas card from Martin A. in Washington including pictures of his three little girls and a note that he still hasn't built his $30,000 house. Did I tell you of the project? Do you ever hear him on the radio?

Since we had Cleo wormed and started putting calcium in her food she has developed so much pep we don't know what to do with her. Now I must go to the Embassy to get some pictures and return some books, and take Tania to the house of a friend who is making a splendid pastel of her.

All my love to you all, Dana

Hotel Orient Palace
Damascus, Syria
January 22, 1948
Dear Mother:
After looking over Damascus for a day or two I went down to Beyrouth to pick up Tania and move with all our baggage plus dog to Damascus. It is a distinctly more interesting spot than Beyrouth, especially since the expectation that the Mufti would set up shop there did not materialize.

While in Beyrouth I picked up a couple of letters from you. I can understand that you feel Beyrouth is not a major news center. I had not thought of it as a long-term center of operation, unless it became the political headquarters for Arab efforts in Palestine, as Damascus has become the military headquarters.

Covering Arab countries at any time, and especially at this time, is slow and hard business. The Arabs have no experience with public information as we know it, they are suspicious, and when they do come across with something they are highly unreliable.

But what the Arabs are up to is important news. By sending me to look over the Arab countries just now the Times *is proving its objectivity in the Palestine matter. The news available inside Palestine, incidentally, is mainly of the police beat and handout variety. In the Arab countries, whose actions will probably determine the outcome of the Palestine conflict, a more complex kind of reporting is required.*

Last Sunday Markel asked for a 1500 word weekender. There was some delay about getting press filing privileges, so I don't know whether it was used or not. Markel has also asked for a magaziner, which he describes as a possible "big lay out" on the "Arab leaders, Arab peoples, what goes on in mind of average Arab, how much he cares about Palestine thing, what they respond to, what they read, etc." It's a pretty tall order and I told him it would take three weeks.

I have got my Transjordian visa and hope to have the Irakian shortly so I may take some side trips from here. Probably will leave Tania here as living conditions elsewhere are uncertain to say the least.

The Orient Palace has a pretty bad reputation for food and service, but we have found that it isn't as bad as people say. I found a nice corner room with balcony which gets the sun most of the day. That's important as the heating is sketchy. The balcony is fine for Cleo, who is growing by the hour. And we eat outside at a restaurant called "Oasis" a good deal of the time.

This is the real "Orient," a much more satisfactory place than Beyrouth, which is or pretends to be half European. I find the American colony much more friendly and helpful too than at Beyrouth. We have been entertained almost every night since we arrived and are dated up for three days in advance now. Next Sunday or Monday we will take a brief run down to Beyrouth, however, to keep a dinner date with the military attache. It is only two and a half hours by car.

I have written a note to the Istanbul consulate asking them to forward the Insurance papers of which you speak. So I'll receive them here in due course.

We got a note from Steinie thanking for her birthday bracelet. I'm always pleased when I hear from Steinie.

Still no word from Cyrus on payment for my car, but there's no use pressing. I cabled a day or so asking whether he would like to buy a jeep station wagon for me to use. No answer yet. I would have a chauffeur if I used it in the Middle East, so it would be neither more nor less safe than taxies, and a lot cheaper and more convenient. I'll grant you driving in Palestine is none too safe, but you need not worry about us while we are in the surrounding countries.

I am happy to know that the lessons have done you a lot of good. Steinie mentioned it too. I hope you'll keep it up.

You will have had my cable asking you to transfer $1000 to my checking account. This will enable me to continue financing myself until the end of the month or more. At the end of the month I'll be doing my accounts for a six week period and will then be able to have the office reimburse me. It takes quite a long time, as you know from Greece, but it makes a great deal of difference in the long run whether I finance myself or have the office send me money. In this part of the world the difference is about one quarter of the total expenditure, so it is worth the inconvenience and delay in the long run.

All our love, now, from Tania and me,
Dana
Better switch to American Legation, Damascus, as address, although things will be forwarded from Beyrouth.

Shepheards hotel
Cairo
January 23, 1948
Dear Mother:
This is our last day in Cairo and my last letter to you from here. We leave at 7:00 Monday morning. I had to postpone leaving from Friday because my exit permit was not issued in time.
Yesterday I got your letter of January 12 marked "please forward." Albion Ross will take care of any that come later.

Tania and I are disgusted to hear that the contractor has been dragging out completion of the beach house. In any event it will be in working order when we get there, thanks to yours and Steinie's efforts. We are happy to hear about the lamps for the bedroom which are your present to us for Xmas. It will be a happy day when we can settle down to making use of them for a while.

Glad you liked the brocades. Curious that both lots arrived within a few days of each other since the dates of their mailing were far separated. In my opinion you and Steinie got the best pieces. I think the white and black and gold are the most gorgeous.

We have been reading about your California snow. Sounds nice for the Ski Mountaineers, but probably for very few other people. I'm glad that we will have missed most of the Austrian winter. Cy wanted me to spend "most of January" with Albion, in order to break him in, and I have done just that.

Before we go I have to finish a mailer on pyramid excavations. It has been fun working it up, although also tedious at times. That sort of thing is ten times as much trouble as a political story.

Tania is busy packing. What a relief not to have to do that. Then I must get everything over to the airline office to be weighed. Also have to go to the ministry of Interior to get some papers that are being censored. Also am supposed to go to the mouskey to buy a copper tray. And lunch guests. And people to say good bye. I think I'd better get busy.

All my love, mother, to you and all the family, Dana
P. S. I lost my fountain pen, for the hundredth time in my life.

Hotel Orient Palace
Damascus
January 29, 1948
Dear Mother:

We are back from another brief trip to Beyrouth and I have some very disappointing news. Tania has had a miscarriage. It is fortunate that it happened so soon, and not after several months. The doctor says she will suffer no ill effects, and it will not affect her having a baby later. We are terribly disappointed, of course, but thankful that no harm was done. It will be a lesson to us to be more careful next time.

I trust Elizabeth is getting along all right. It's too bad she and Tania couldn't be going through this business together. But I think we will stick to our original plan, of taking my vacation at the end of the summer or in the autumn. That should permit me to see through the most critical part of the Palestine affair.

You will have seen a little more of my stuff in print just lately. I do wish you would not fret about my assignment. The assignment I have now is not particularly rewarding in headlines but it is a particularly responsible one, as I have already explained. No correspondent can expect to be covering front page aspects of the news all the time. While I was getting plenty printed from Germany and Greece Sam was vegetating in Spain.

This week I have another weekender order, and as you know I'm working on a magaziner.

I can guess that you were disturbed by my cable asking you to transfer $1000. But you can be sure to get it refunded, or at least most of it. It will not interfere with the cottage. Tania is already getting much intrigued by the idea of a cottage on the beach of the Pacific. (Tania adds that Cleo is intrigued too. Cleo is getting enormous.)

The Times *does not pay the expense of a wife except when the correspondent makes a major move. Thus they paid Tania's travel expenses from Athens to Beyrouth. They will pay them when we go home on "home leave." Her living expenses, food and rent, are not covered by the office at any time. Actually only food is involved, since the office pays for a double room with bath for me anyway.*

The office, that is, Cy Sulzberger, has agreed to buy me a car for use out here. He okayed my buying a nearly-new jeep station wagon that was available, but unfortunately the cable arrived a day after it was sold. Now I have proposed either a new jeep station wagon, cost $2,950 in Beyrouth, or a used DeSoto, cost $2,100.

My love to you all, especially to Elizabeth,
Dana
P.S. Tania wrote the thank you note to Mrs. Nye.

Incidentally, it would be nice if you would write Tania a note some time telling her how lovely our Christmas presents were. She put a lot of love and care into helping me pick them out and in packing them. I wish you'd also mention the many pictures we have sent from Athens and here. Tania took most of them, with her camera, which is a fine Contax. Some of them were taken with a gadget that permits you to set the camera, then run around and get in the picture before it clicks.

Dana

February 2, 1948
My dear dear Mother:

Your last letters to me, about our expecting the baby and losing it, and your letter to Tania, were so wonderfully good and such a comfort. I was so overjoyed at the prospect and terribly broken up at what happened. I suppose it is the price we pay for the kind of life we have to live just at this stage of my career. I pray that we may in the not too distant future be able to live where Tania can have a home and some peace. She is such a dear girl, and I love her so very much. She is not very practical as you will see and is most sensitive, although she doesn't always show it. Please do remember when we come home to make infinite allowance for any shortcomings you may find in her, and you undoubtedly will find them. She tries very hard and makes me a splendid wife, if it were only for the fact that I am always happy to be with her.

Your advice is not at all resented. I am tremendously grateful, and we will try to follow it. I only hope Elizabeth will be all right.

I have just sent off my expense account for the past six weeks which calls for the Times *to pay me $862.03. This money will eventually be paid into my checking account according to my new instructions, along with $80 of my salary. As soon as possible I will send you a check for a thousand dollars which will make up for the transfer you effected. This may not be for several months.*

Tania has gone down to Beyrouth just for a day with the Peels, a couple I knew in Germany who are touring a large part of the globe in a Volkswagen. I believe I mentioned them in Greece. Since then they've driven across Turkey to Damascus and are next going on to Bagdad. If they delay long enough we may accompany them. While Tania is in Beyrouth she will have the pup vaccinated against distemper.

Tonight, when, I trust Tania will be back, we are going out to have dinner with a North African Prince. He claims to be the rightful spiritual and temporal ruler of Algeria. The French kicked out his Grandfather.

I must run now to get up to the Legation before it closes. All my love to Grandma and Elizabeth and Steinie.

Love,
Dana

Hotel Orient Palace
Damascus
February 9, 1948
Dear Mother:

I am at last enclosing the Lloyd's Accident Proposal Form. I suppose that is what you sent to Istanbul. Is it not? I did not completely fill out question six, about accident insurance, as I was not sure what particulars to give. Would you complete that for me?

I've been quite busy trying to finish that magaziner and also explaining to the local authorities that I have nothing but the best journalistic intentions. Some eager beaver in the Syrian Surete appears to have reported that I was a suspicious person associating with suspicious persons and gathering information on military movements. But a little explaining and remonstrance to the right persons by myself and the Legation seem to have set things right.

I now have visas for Teheran and Amman and am expecting one for Bagdad soon. Here's hoping Cyrus okays the purchase of that car before we start on the move again. That car being a '42 DeSoto coupe belonging to the assistant military attache in Beyrouth.

Today we are having lunch with Bob Brown (Lt Col.) and his wife and a gal named Miss Hearn, in a native restaurant in the old city. Miss Hearn is the retired American lawyer from the middle west who is spending the winter living with a native family in the Christian quarter of the old city. Sounds quite mad, but she isn't. Just wanted to try something different after a lifetime of being a lawyer. She spent some four months in Cairo before, and is going on to Bagdad and Afghanistan later.

Tania is in fine shape, as is Cleo. Tania is running around in my big warm fluff-lined slippers and giving Cleo a dose of cod liver oil, which she loves.

This Hotel Orient Palace is supposed to be one of the worst in the world, but we are not suffering particularly, having fixed up our room quite nicely. We put a sort of tapestry affair we bought on the wall, a bright little rug from Greece over a chair, a cloth on the table, some flowers in the vases we received as wedding presents, and the place is quite livable.

We are now living quite economically and will stay that way. I definitely do NOT want to back out of the beach house project. There will be funds reimbursed from the Times coming from me, and the money for my car in Germany, and perhaps money from my other piece of land, and if you have to sell a few shares of something in addition it will be worth it.

Hope you are keeping on with those walking lessons and doing well.
All my love to you all,
Dana

13-II-948
Damas
Dear mother,

Dana and I were very sad that I had lost the baby, but as you say, we have planty of time to have another one, I am sure of that.

Dana got a cable from his office yesterday, and I think we will be going to Jerusalem sometimes after the twentieth. Dana thinks I should rather stay in Amman which is the capital of Transjordan and is very near to Jerusalem, then he will be able to come for week ends or more often. It is the place where all the british officers keep their wives and children. It is a very small village nothing interesting there, but of course I'll be nearer to Dana there.

Yes Dana told me about Tuckie in Athens, I know all about him. Our Cleo is wonderful too, she is quite a problem already. She has beaten all my hands, and now she starts on the furnitures. She loves apples and oranges. We took *some pictures of her the other day, I ordered some copies which will be ready by tomorrow, Dana will send you in his letter.*

I am very glad when I get a letter from you.
With love
Tania

Hotel Orient Palace, Damascus
February 15, 1948
Dear Mother:

Just a short letter to let you know what I'm going to be up to in the immediate future. Cyrus wants me to go to Amman, capital of Transjordan, for a few days and then go to Jerusalem to relieve Sam Brewer. Sam will go to Teheran for an indefinite period. When he comes back I will go on to some point in the Middle East not yet determined, or will work together with Sam in Palestine. My hunch is that the time is fast coming when we will need two men there all the time.

So tomorrow morning, Monday, we are flying over to Beyrouth with Bob Brown to take care of a few odds and ends, some shopping and some stories to check, and returning to Damascus by taxi the same day.

I have finally convinced the local authorities that neither I nor the Times *is dangerous to them, and they have extended our residence permits, so I feel free to move on. Didn't want to leave until they had gone through the formalities of giving us the extension.*

It has been raining off and on, mainly on, for more than a week. Rather trying for us city dwellers, but the Syrians are busy happily figuring out what it will mean to them in wheat and dollars.

I'm enclosing some pictures of our Cleo. She is a darling dog. Grows while you watch. I never knew a pup with quite such sharp teeth. She bit Tania's hands all to pieces, playing, and loves to ruin stockings.

I should have added that when I go to Jerusalem I will leave Tania and Cleo in Amman. A lot of Britishers have their wives there, so she will not be without company. Otherwise, I gather the town is not much to look at or brag about. Little more than a village in the desert. But it is near to Jerusalem, as you can see on the map, and the road from Jerusalem to Amman is supposed to be quite safe. So I will be able to get over to see Tania from time to time.

The advice in your last letter meant a lot to me, Mother. Marriage brings plenty of new problems, doesn't it.

Beginning now you'd better start writing to me care of American Consulate, Jerusalem (there is no Legation). I think I'll get there between the 25th and the end of the month. Hardly worth trying to write to me at Amman, although you might try care of the British Legation (there is no American representation there).

All my love to you all,
Dana
P.S. I got off my Magaziner the other day
P.P.S. Tania maintains I MUST have a new pair of pyjamas, but I balk at buying any. She says I should ask you to send me some to Jerusalem!

The Philadelphia Hotel
Amman, Transjordan
February 23, 1948
Dear Mother:

This is one town I never expected to be writing to you from. Looks like I'll be here a week before moving to Jerusalem, and Tania will stay here at the "Philadelphia". Unless things should change, or Tania really wants to come, I think it's best for her to stay out of Palestine.

Just at the moment Sam Brewer plans to be away in Iran three weeks. But there is no telling how things will work out.

The "Philadelphia," believe it or not, turns out to be quite a nice little hotel. We have a room and bath, but, to Cleo's regret, no balcony. The food is far better than what we had to eat in Damascus, and there is a cheerful, comfortable lounge and bar. There's a good many wives and families in the hotel, evacuees from Palestine.

Right opposite the hotel is a huge ancient amphitheater. Since we only got here last night I haven't had time to find out what it's all about, but it's impressive.

All of Transjordan has a population of only some 400,000 (some say twice as many, but it doesn't matter) and the capital is basically a village. But it is full of shops selling every American product on earth at quite decent prices. The reason therefore is that customs charges are far lower than in other Middle Eastern countries. This raises the possibility of buying a car here at a reasonable price, if I can get Cyrus interested. He unfortunately decided against all the other prospects I lined up.

I've started lining up interviews with Prime Minister, Foreign Minister and King. Should make some good pieces.

I've written to Bill Freese asking for the lowdown on payment for my car. I had put all arrangements in his hands, so he should know. Also have written Cy Sulzberger on the subject of the high cost of living in the Middle East. I didn't ask for a raise, but it may give him the idea.

Tania and I got very nice letters from Grandma, Steinie and Elizabeth before we left Damascus. Tania has already written to Grandma. I, as always, intend to. Tell Elizabeth that we'd be tickled to see some plans of the beach cottage.

I don't always mention them, Mother, but the clippings you send me are invaluable. I pick up information that way that would otherwise have escaped me entirely, and I keep many of them.

All my love to you all. I enclose a postcard of this hotel and the amphitheater.
Dana
Dr. Lowman may be interested in the Transjordan stamps.

Public Information Office, Jerusalem
March 5, 1948
Dear Mother:
This is the only paper I can find just now, but it will do for a very belated letter. The effort of getting into Palestine has kept me pretty preoccupied this week. You will have seen the story I sent about it yesterday.

Just after I arrived I managed to get through to Tania on the phone, but since then the phones have been out of order and I feel very cut off. But I have written and will telegraph tomorrow if the phone service doesn't reopen.

I can see that this is going to be a very busy period. Today I got off a very long insert, about 1500 words, for the Magaziner I did on the Arabs. I hope it is printed soon. Also called on the Jewish Agency. Tomorrow I'll see the Arab Higher Committee. Covering two sides of a war at once, as we must here, is a pretty tricky business. We are all wondering how we will manage it when the British leave.

I tried to see the man who sold me Cleo today, but found his shop had been bombed. So I left a message for him at another shop. I hope to get the pedigree he promised to send.

After I got here a message from London informed me that my interview with King Abdullah took seven days, no less, to reach London from Amman. I could have got it there faster by mail. I don't know whether they tried to use it in spite of the time lag or not. Funny thing is that I had in the meantime written a piece from Beyrouth commenting on what the King had told me.

Also, among mail forwarded from Athens, was the fountain pen Elizabeth and Ken sent me for Christmas. It is a lovely pen. I am going to give it to Tania who gave me a very similar one for Christmas. I'm sure Elizabeth and Ken won't mind. Tania only has a very old and leaky one.

Last night Sam Brewer had Bill Porter, second in command at the American consulate, to dinner. He was a very interesting fellow. Was in Washington, handling the Palestine desk of the State Department for a long time and well informed about all the political skullduggery that was used to put across partition. Soon he is to open our first consulate in Cyprus.

Generally social life here is at a low ebb. It is too hard to get around at night. I was going to send Tania a telegram tonight but was told that the post office accepts personal telegrams only until two p.m. and that anyway no one would go near the post office at this time of night.

Of course you understand (I don't know why you really should) that we live most of the time inside the zones surrounded by barbed wire and guarded by British troops. The Arab friend I mentioned in my story, about my trip up here, incidentally, works in the office that administers the zones. Zones are pretty safe.

I am living at a place called the Saint Julian hotel but will move into the Pantiles as soon as Sam Brewer leaves and I can get into his room. The Pantiles is much in demand among newspapermen as it is only about a hundred yards from this office, a great advantage after dark.

All my love to you all. I am going to dinner at the Pantiles. Dana

Public Information Office
Jerusalem
March 14, 1948
Dear Mother:
I'm sure you won't mind this paper, which is the only kind at hand, for a very belated letter.

I am back on the job here after a quick trip out to Beyrouth to see Tania. It looked as though it would be my last opportunity for some weeks, as Sam Brewer is leaving for Teheran on Monday or Tuesday. I am taking over from him entirely beginning tonight.

There'll probably be a weekender in this Sunday's (today's) paper which I wrote while in Beyrouth. And there'll be another in next Sunday's according to a cable just in from Markel. He will use a long roundup of Arab and Jewish strengths which I offered the daily with a note that they should turn it over to Markel if it wasn't suitable for their purposes. Markel called it an "excellent job" (I'm still a sucker for flattery).

It was wonderful to be with Tania for two days after being separated for a while. She is all right in Beyrouth, but I am worried that I may have to leave her alone longer this time. I took the occasion to apply for a Turkish visa for her in case we decide that she should go to Istanbul to stay with her parents for a while. Apparently there has been a great reconciliation between her mother and father, so it mightn't be so bad. Still I hope it can be avoided. If I could only find a corner for her I'd bring her to Palestine, but quiet corners seem to be nonexistent. Another solution which you suggested is that she go to Los Angeles and stay with you. I'd really prefer that, although I had hoped to introduce her to the USA myself.

Any move to the US will in any case have to wait until I have Tania's visa. There should be word from the Athens consulate waiting for me at the consulate here, but I haven't had time to go there yet.

It is extraordinarily cold here. In striking contrast to Beyrouth, where it is balmy and sunny, as Tania told me on the phone this morning. While I was in Beyrouth we went to Saint Simon beach with Cleo. It was Cleo's first encounter with a beach and she loved it. She was very suspicious of the water, however, and wouldn't go near it until, during one of her wild gallops, she forgot where the beach ended and dashed right into the water. Up over her head. She was so surprised she just stood there, underwater, emitting bubbles, until we hauled her out. It was about as funny a sight as I have seen.

I feel I have neglected you by not writing the past week and should tell you more, but I am very tired and had better get to bed. I find fatigue is one's greatest enemy on a job like this. Once one lets oneself get worn down it is hard to catch up again.

On my trip to Beyrouth, incidentally, I traveled by Arab taxi through Transjordan and Syria. It is long—about nine hours including customs and passport inspections—but perfectly safe. The main difficulty is getting a Transjordian visa.

Hope Eliza is getting on all right.

Tania and I are looking forward to the things you've mailed.

All my love, and goodnight, Dana

Public Information Office
Jerusalem
March 21, 1948
My dear Mother:

This past week you must have seen enough of my by-lines to satisfy even a mother. It is satisfying to know I am getting into print again, although the pace is pretty hard.

For the past week the phone lines to Beyrouth have been out of order and I haven't been able to get through to Tania at the Saint George. Today I sent her a telegram and told her to send me one. I write every day. Curiously enough there is airmail from Beyrouth to Jerusalem but none from Jerusalem to Beyrouth.

The other day I moved over to the Pantiles which is much more convenient. Gossett in a double room at the YMCA is holding a bed for me there. He has

LETTERS HOME: 80 YEARS LATER

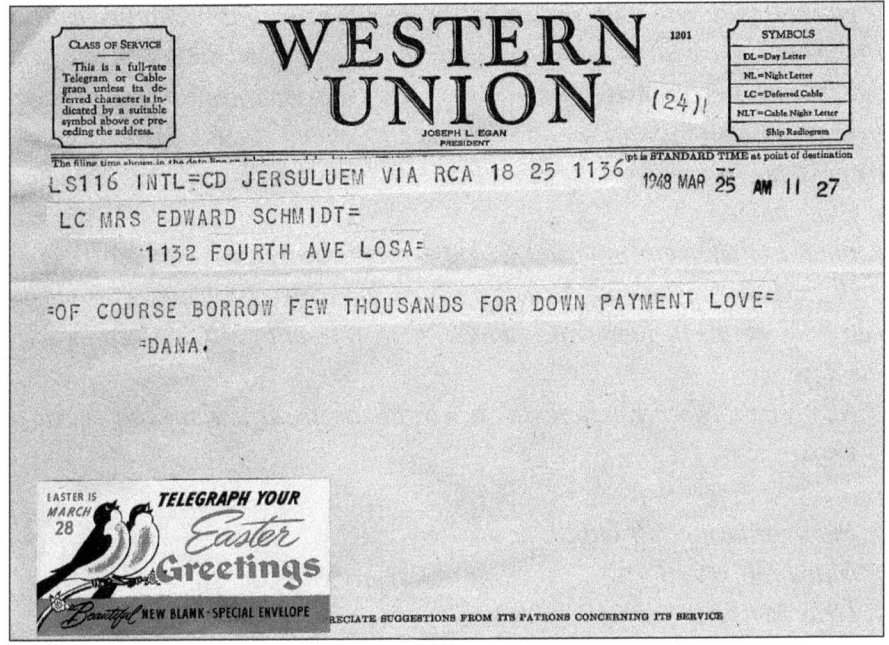

persuaded the photo department to let him buy a British M.G. car. He really needs one more than the reporters do. It is a curious vehicle, built like a racing car, with only two seats. Very fast and tricky to handle. But they are all the fashion among the correspondents, partly because they are quite cheap.

A letter forwarded from Damascus reached me today, but none direct from you this week. It may be that discontinuance of TWA service to Lydda will slow down the mail.

I have made a lot of acquaintances on both the Jewish and Arab sides and think there'll be a lot of good stories for me. It is ever so much easier, however, to get information from the Jews than from the Arabs. Consequently it is hard to present an objective picture. For instance the only regular sources of information on the daily incidents are the British police and the Jews. The Arabs come along days later, if at all, with "interpretative" accounts which are usually useless or out of date. They are simply not organized for information.

It is gratifying to know that you are all well and that Elizabeth and her baby are making out all right.

Have I told you that Brewster, the vice-consul who was our "consular witness" at the wedding wrote me that Tania's approved immigration papers came through in record time, only 17 days. He has forwarded them to Damascus where some more formalities must be gone through. The visa, when issued, is only good for four months, so we will not actually take it until I know when I am going home.

Had a letter from my good friend George Androulidakis in Athens. He is still expecting to become his paper's New York correspondent, but has been given assignments in Rome and London first. You will probably see him one of these days.

All my love, Mother, to you all, Steinie, Elizabeth, Grandma and Tuckie too.
Dana

Public Information Office, Jerusalem
March 30, 1948
Dear Mother:
There seems to be a slight lag in the usual rush today and I hasten to write my letter to you.

You will be able to judge by my stories what I've been doing. I had the dubious pleasure of witnessing the end of the fight and the surrender of the Jews in the Kfar Etzion convoy. Next weekend I hope to take a trip down to Tel Aviv with Carl Gossett. We will go in his little M.G. The beauty of those peculiar little vehicles is that almost nobody in Palestine has one except journalists.

A letter from Tania finally came through, apart from those she has sent me by hand. It took just fifteen days. But now that the first one has arrived I can count on a steady flow. We haven't been able to talk to each other on the phone since two or three days after I arrived, and I dare say it will be many many months till the lines are restored now.

She enclosed a passport picture of herself which we had taken while I was in Beyrouth, for her Turkish visa application.

It has suddenly turned cold again. The "hamsin," the wind from the desert is sweeping in a cold rain. In summer it is hot and dry, but at this time of year just the opposite. I am wearing the thick sweater with the cable stitch you made for me a couple of years ago.

This is one place where there is practically nothing to do but work (or stand in the bar or play poker). And I have done a good deal so far. Three weekenders since I got here and a feature for the magazine. Another magaziner on the stocks. The piece I did for the magazine in Damascus seems to have been shelved. I haven't been able to get any reply to two or three inquiries as to its fate, and now it is out of date. But when I leave here I'll bring it up to date and try again.

I'm not quite clear from your letters whether you sent off a package via Air France *or not. I will check with them, but you might clear up the point in your next letter. I'm afraid I don't know any of the Consular people here well enough yet to ask them to violate their rules on the use of the diplomatic pouch. Of course they will, on occasion, but only for someone they know very well.*

I suppose you got my cable saying you should go ahead and borrow a few thousands for the down payment on a new house. From what you say it sounds like a wise move.

All my love to you all, including Tuckie.
Dana

Public Information Office
Jerusalem
April 7, 1948
Dear Mother:
Your wandering son has returned to Jerusalem, safe and sound. I've had four most instructive days on the coast, as you know from my stories. I sent a last one off under a coastal dateline tonight and wrote the day's news from Jerusalem in addition.

The most important thing about this letter is that I am enclosing a check for $1000 for the expenses of our beach house. The office has finally paid up for my car. $2000 minus $275 required to send spare parts from the U.S. I do not dare send more for the house right now, as I do not know how much money I'll be needing for Tania if and when she goes home to Turkey for a while.

Tel Aviv is an extraordinary place. Everything brand new, built in the last 30 years, and most of it in the last fifteen. All in the modernist functional style, some excellent, but a great deal on the cheap and shoddy side. The plaster and cement peels and gets streaked with brown very quickly. New houses now have to be covered with stucco in front.

It would be a balmy peaceful place if it weren't for Jaffa next door. Things were quiet while I was there, but occasional snipers' bullets still go singing through the air. The whole thing was quite fascinating and provided me with background that will be invaluable in the immediate future.

Tomorrow I must get off a weekender on the battle for Jerusalem, especially the threat to the holy places. Then I have a request for a short piece on the reactions of children, Arab and Jewish, to the fighting. And another longer magaziner for which I am now ripe. I'm afraid the Arab magaziner is lost in the files. Guess it wasn't what they wanted, although I was asked for a long cabled insert.

Tomorrow I'll go along to the Consulate where, I'm sure, there will be a letter waiting for me. Your letters mean ever so much to me, Mother. Don't ease up on the clippings. I read them all and find much valuable information in them.

I'll be eager to hear what you did about the house, or houses. I wonder if Elizabeth could send some drawings of the beach house as it will eventually look to Tania. I know she would love it.

What of your walking lessons? You haven't mentioned them lately. It made me happy to think you had made so much progress. I hope your ear is better; such things can make one terribly miserable.

My love to you all. To Grandma especially today. I know she understands my letters to you are meant for her too, and that the scarcity of my letters doesn't mean I've forgotten her. Dana

Public Information Office, Jerusalem
April 13, 1948
Dear Mother:
Another heavy week lies behind me, with tons of words written and more tons waiting to be written. The story has been on the front page the past three

days, I've another weekender request and the magaziner hanging heavy on my hands.

Sam Brewer has wired that he plans to stay in Teheran till the seventeenth, spend two weeks in Bagdad and visit Damascus. That means he won't be back here for a month. Meanwhile Gene Currivan is due here the end of this week, to take on the Tel Aviv assignment. I am going to try to have him take over here for a few days while I slip away to Beyrouth, but I'm not sure it can be arranged. Poor Tania must be very lonely and I'd like to get over there and cheer her up and start her on her way to Istanbul, if that seems wise at the time.

If Sam gets back here the middle of May, and Currivan is in Tel Aviv, we will have no one covering the Arab countries. I don't know how it will work out but it seems quite possible that I'll take that on for a spell till Sam is worn out and we switch around again.

I am still at the Pantiles, the little Christian Arab hotel around the corner from the P.I.O. But as May 15 approaches it may close down, and I'll move into the YMCA. The transmission facilities now in the P.I.O. will also move to the YMCA. It is a huge modern edifice built with a million and a half dollars of American money. Its normal inhabitants are rapidly drifting away, leaving plenty of room for the press, consular officials and others who must stay here. I'll send you a postcard of it when I get hold of one.

It is now pleasantly warm and sunny here, after a delayed and extremely raw winter season. I think the winter was almost as uncomfortable here as it was in Germany, mainly because there are no adequate heating arrangements in this part of the world.

I am looking forward to my home leave in late summer or autumn with the utmost pleasure and delight. It will be such fun to introduce Tania to America and so nice to be home. Maybe I'll be able to get back to Europe after that, but there's no guarantee.

I must get on with the job now.

All my love to you all,

Dana

P.S. If you want to send some things to Tania you can airmail them right to the Hotel Saint George, Beyrouth. Airmail to Beyrouth works quite well.

ELIZABETH SCHMIDT CRAHAN

c/o American Consulate, Jerusalem
April 19, 1948
Dear Mother:
There doesn't seem to be much I can tell you this week except that I seem to be doing a lot of work. Your letters still come through regularly, I am happy to say, but I wonder how much longer it will continue.

There is a lot of talk of a truce in the wind. Both sides are getting interested. At the critical moment people are beginning to bobble at the prospect of complete chaos. It would be wonderful if there were a truce. Then Tania could come here without risk.

I have collected the visas I would need if I can arrange a trip to Beyrouth. Currivan has arrived, and I am awaiting Cy's okay on my taking a quick run out while he takes over, preliminary to proceeding to Tel Aviv.

Don't think much of that fellow, so far. Seems to be tight and tied up with his girl friend most of the time. I've scarcely seen him since he came yesterday noon. As somebody said, when I mentioned that he was coming: "Well, he's always good for a laugh, anyway."

Had a long talk with our new Consul, Mr. Tom Wasson, this afternoon. He is an outstanding man, far above the standard of most consuls, as befits the situation. The State Department is running him ragged just as the Times *is running me ragged. It is apparently impossible to satisfy the appetite for information on what is going on here.*

Yesterday I went to see an interesting Jewish woman who runs a children's home. About my piece on the reactions of children to the fighting. I have always found the keen, lively intelligence one finds in some Jews most attractive. Her feeling is that here the Jew can be his natural self, develop according to his own culture and inclination, whereas in other countries he is always imitating, aping the people among whom he lives. She put forward a lot of moral arguments for establishing a Jewish State, all of them valid. But the Jews can't get around the moral and historic argument that this happens to be an Arab country which the Jews are, to all intents and purposes, invading. It WAS a Jewish country, or part of it was, 2000 years ago, but that doesn't establish any indisputable right now.

You asked me whether I thought there was going to be another war. Yes, surely there will be. But I don't think just yet. It will take five or ten years, maybe more, till the Russians are ready.

I've been on the run a good deal and must get some sleep. Good night, and love to you all,
Dana

c/o American Consulate
Jerusalem
April 27, 1948
Dear Mother:
Since airmail has stopped I am sending this out to London with a friend who will mail it there.

Airmail stopped a bit sooner than we expected. Everything is collapsing more quickly than we expected.

Tomorrow the Pantiles Hotel is closing. Fortunately I had not already moved to the YMCA, for that is being taken over by the International Red Cross *as part of a neutral "refugee zone."* Those of us who are still in the Pantiles and several others have decided to take the place over and run it ourselves in the absence of the regular management. The management is Arab and they are afraid this place will be overrun by the Jews. But we have lined up a cook who is willing to take a chance and will have to make our beds ourselves. I suppose the place will go uncleaned, and we will have to do without hot water.

Our calculation is that this is the one place where we can hope to maintain our neutrality and maintain contact with both sides. How long it will last I couldn't say.

In any event I feel that the worst of the fighting will soon be over. The Jews have turned out to be far stronger than anyone, including the British, realized. Unless the Arabs bring in their regular armies in a serious way the Jews will have things their own way.

You don't need to worry about me. If anyone in Jerusalem is safe it is the correspondents.

In a way I'm glad I didn't get a car. Carl Gossett has had his stolen in Tel Aviv. Henshaw, a Paramount *movie man had his stolen the day before he left. One of the Jewish correspondents had his stolen from in front of the P.I.O. And tonight Camenada, the* London Times *correspondent had his stolen.*

I was offered a "hot" 1947 Ford for 150 Pounds the other day, but didn't take it. I couldn't saddle the Times *with a stolen car and wouldn't want it myself.*

I was planning very seriously to get out to see Tania this week. But the Embassy plane came suddenly and unexpectedly, and was away before I could be notified. Now I'm glad I didn't go, for I would have had a devil of a time getting back, Lydda airfield having ceased operations. It is a shame for Tania, and I am terribly sorry. But now it is best that I should see the show through before we are reunited. I know you will write to her, and I send out letters by hand whenever I can, and that should help. She has made friends with a young American couple with children, which pleases me very much.

My love to you all. What fun it will be when I get to L.A. with Tania and we are building, or living in our beach house! Give Steinie my best especially today.

Dana

c/o American Consulate
May 5, 1948
Jerusalem
Dear Mother:

This Letter will go out via Amman, which seems to be the only mail route left. Of course I haven't had anything from you since the mails closed down here, but you will have got the message I sent through the office for you to write me care of Tania.

Today I am feeling quite optimistic. It looks as though we were working towards some sort of truce. Peace may not be as far off as most people thought it would be at this date.

A telegram from Sam Brewer says he is in Bagdad and planning to move on to Damascus and thence to Amman. That's the route to Jerusalem, so I may soon be able to get out of the country a while.

Yesterday Stewart Rockwell, one of the secretaries of the Ankara Embassy, arrived to work at the Consulate here. I stayed at his house in Ankara when I went there from Athens. He is a good fellow. It is pleasant to know a lot of people in the diplomatic service and run into them wherever you go.

I am curious to know what the status of our beach house is. Did you get the check I mailed you? And have you been feeling well again? And Grandma? And how is Elizabeth getting on towards the new baby? And what of Steinie? When I don't hear from you I begin to wonder about everything.

It was generous of Grandma to help so much with Elizabeth's and Ken's house. Married life, as I have discovered, is expensive and doesn't leave much margin for saving. Apart from wanting to be together again I will be glad when Tania and I can share the same rent bill. It is shockingly expensive to have her paying a hotel bill in Beyrouth, which I can't put on the expense account, and me running another one here.

Just at this moment I am not paying any rent at all, however. I believe I told you the Arab management of the Pantiles cleared out and left everything in the hands of the resident correspondents. We are doing all right, too. We have a house keeper, an Armenian girl, a cook and a houseboy. The place is getting a little dirty, but we are eating very well. Better than when the regular management was there.

Dan Deluce is in town. He has left his wife at Amman, which is a dreadful place swarming with refugees just now. Civilians always seem to get the worst of wars. Most of the other correspondents have sent their wives to Cyprus. There is quite a colony of them there. If I find I can't have Tania with me and she doesn't go to Istanbul I might send her to Cyprus. It would be a lot cheaper.

How are you making out with your work these days. You always take on so much. I hope Doctor Lowman thought of paying you for the work you are doing for him.

It is getting hot here, quite suddenly. All my love, to you all, Dana

6-V-1948, Beirut.
Dear mother
I received a letter from my mother in which she says that I have package from you. They will take it from the customs next week, and either send it to me or

keep it till I get there, which is more possible. I'll probably have my visa by the 15th of May, but I'll have to travel by train because of Cleo, they wouldn't accept her on the plane. She looks just exactly like the picture of the boxer you send, the same splash on the neck, the same black face, and I'm sure she will be just as big.

I always get news from Dana through people who come and go to Palestine. They bring me letters from him, and the same way take mine there. There is always someone coming from there or going there, so we are more or less in contact with Dana.

Dear mother I want to thank you for the things you've send me I can hardly wait till I see them.

I have Tuckie's picture on the table, I'm sure he and Cleo will fight when they meet.

Good bye mother give my regards to Steinie.

Yours, Tania.

[handwritten letter] c/o US Consulate,
Jerusalem
May 12, 1948
Dear Mother:
I am writing this at the Consulate so it can be taken out to Beyrouth by Bob Brown.

Bob has been flying in and out lately with all sorts of new personnel. All the married people, except the military attache, have been taken out.

We also have a band of young guards, as do most of the other Consulates.

Our famous "cease fire" blew up with a bang last night, but I persist in my belief that peace is not far off—at least in Jerusalem. I wouldn't be so hopeful about Palestine and the Middle East in general.

I really can't report and [...] hard work. As always I have so many assignments from the Sunday dept that I don't have enough time to do any real reporting.

Anyway, the paper must be full of Schmidt.

Sam should be getting to Damascus today. I wired him to get in touch with Tania in Beyrouth. He can at least phone from there and tell her when he is going to relieve me for a while.

LETTERS HOME: 80 YEARS LATER

> c/o US Consulate
> Jerusalem
> May 12, 1948
>
> Dear Mother:
>
> I am writing this at the Consulate so it can be taken out to Beyrouth by Bob Brown.
>
> Bob has been flying in and out lately with all sorts of new personnel. All the married people, except the military attaché, have been taken out.
>
> We also have a bunch of young guards, as do most of the other Consulates.
>
> Our famous "cease fire" blew up with a bang last night, but I persist in my belief that peace is not far off — at least in Jerusalem. I wouldn't be so hopeful about Palestine & the Middle East in general.
>
> I really can't report much activity except hard work. As always I have so many assignments from the Sunday dept

First page of Dana's handwritten letter May 12, 1948

I have to go and dig up some information on Glubb Pasha and Abdullah war.

My love to you all, Dana

Hotel Pantiles
Jerusalem
May 26, 1948
Dear Mother, Grandma, Elizabeth Ken and Steinie (and Tuckie too):
I have just finished a letter to Tania and will write one to you all to be taken out tomorrow morning by a group of correspondents who are leaving with the assistance of the International Red Cross.

Wish I could go with them. But this is my assignment, and I'll have to see it through, unpleasant as it is. I wouldn't mind so much if it weren't for poor Tania. I have now written her that if she hasn't got her Turkish visa yet she should go to Cyprus, where she can stay with a whole group of correspondents' wives and will be much safer. My mind would be much easier if she were there, if she can't rejoin her folks in Turkey.

I suppose the siege of Jerusalem sounds pretty grim when read in the papers. And it is not very funny. Still, things are never as bad as they seem in the newspapers. I am perfectly well and safe. I'm still getting my meals regularly (I've started taking vitamin pills for the first time, just in case).

Thus far I've held out at the Pantiles, which was very quickly overrun by the Jews the day the British pulled out. The advantage of the place is that it has a well. As long as the electricity works, and with it our pump, we are all right. There is also an electric heater. But we have about used up our food stocks and eat most of our meals in town. We pay about a pound, or four dollars for lunch or dinner. It is quite good stuff. But we lack fresh things. That's where the vitamin pills come in.

There has been a lot of shooting at times. Most of our windows have bullet holes. But we sleep with our mattresses on the floor, usually in the hall or one of the back rooms.

It has been extremely hot. We are getting the Hamsin, or desert wind, which adds to the general discomfort.

Since there is no way of getting anything washed in town, since there is not enough water for laundries, I have taken to washing my own. Washed seven shirts the other day. Getting them ironed is not so difficult. Wonder how clean the collars will be!

I know you are all writing to Tania every now and then. I have also told her to try to get her immigration visa now so that she will be ready to leave for the States. If I should really be caught here indefinitely she might go ahead.

All my love to you all. Wish I was there! Dana

Beyrouth
June 22, 1948
Dear Mother:
After a long time, at last I can write to you again. Tania and I are reunited happily and will soon be off to Egypt.

It is too bad, too too bad, that Tania couldn't get her visa to go to Turkey during this very long time, but now I have received telegrams from Ambassador Wilson and from the secretary of the foreign minister saying that orders have been given to issue the visa. I will get it for her and it will be on hand should it be desirable for her to go to Istanbul later.

It has been very hard for Tania to be alone. Don't think I underestimated that. But there was nothing I could do apparently, to get the visa. It is simply a matter of Tania being one of the Turkish "minorities", and being treated accordingly. Just a little example close to home of something akin to "racial discrimination."

But she has pulled through all right and we are happy indeed.

Tania sent the last of your letters off with a friend to Cyprus, and I missed them. I spoke to Bob Brown on the phone to Damascus and he said he had tried to send me some papers from you, including a power of attorney. But I didn't get that either.

So you'd better duplicate anything that is important to me care of American Consulate, Cairo. We will probably be at Shepheards for a while, but then I will try to get an apartment. I asked Cy whether I could count on home leave in the next four months and he said that in view of the unsettled conditions

Beyrouth
June 22, 1948

Dear Mother:

After a long time, at last I can write to you again. Tania and I are reunited happily and will soon be off to Egypt.

It is too bad, too too bad, that Tania couldn't get her visa to go to Turkey during this very long time, but now I have received telegrams from Ambassador Wilson and from the secretary of the foreign minister saying that orders have been given to issue the visa. I will get it for her and it will be on hand should it be desirable for her to go to Istanbul later.

It has been very hard for Tania to be alone. Don't think I underestimated that. But there was nothing I could do, apparently, to get the visa. It is simply a matter of Tania being one of the Turkish "minorities", and being treated accordingly. Just a little example close to home of something akin to "racial discrimination."

But she has pulled through all right and we are happy indeed.

Tania sent the last of your letters off with a friend to Cyprus, and I missed them. I spoke to Bob Brown on the phone to Damascus and he said he had tried to send me some papers from you, including a power of attorney. But I didn't get that either.

So you'd better duplicate anything that is important to me care of American Consulate, Cairo. We will probably be at Shepheards for a while, but then I will try to get an apartment. I asked Cy whether I could count on home leave in the next four months and he said that in view of the unsettled conditions here I could not, although, of course, he hopes it will be possible. So it will be worth while probably for us to try to have an apartment in Cairo. Most years people move down to Alexandria for the summer but this year the government officials at least have not moved very much, I hear.

It is a shame that we won't be home sooner. Especially since I see by your letters to Tania that work on the beach cottage has begun. I wonder whether you got it for the original price or not.

Mother I never got a letter confirming that you had received a check for $1000 for the beach cottage. I sent it just before the end of postal services and it is possible that it didn't get out. Please let me know. Since then I have twice asked you to make transfers amounting to a total of $1000. After I get to Egypt and have myself financially sorted out I plan to make this good so as not to upset your calculations. At the time the only way I could handle transactions was by cabling you.

It is murderously hot now and of course I don't like it very much. There seem to be a lot of things in life you just have to put up with. For instance, having Tania living here alone was a most expensive, I might say ruinous affair. I don't think I did any saving those three months. In fact I know I spent more than I earned. But there was no other way. Together we will be able to be more economical. Tania did her best, but living separately cannot help but be expensive.

This ribbon seems a bit messy. Tania just put it in for me.

First page of Dana's June 22, 1948 letter

here I could not, although, of course, he hopes it will be possible. So it will be worthwhile probably for us to try to have an apartment in Cairo. Most years people move down to Alexandria for the summer but this year the government officials at least have not moved very much, I hear.

It is a shame that we won't be home sooner. Especially since I see by your letters to Tania that work on the beach cottage has begun. I wonder whether you got it for the original price or not.

Mother I never got a letter confirming that you had received a check for $1000 for the beach cottage. I sent it just before the end of postal services and it is possible that it didn't get out. Please let me know... Since then I have twice asked you to make transfers amounting to a total of $1000. After I get to Egypt and have myself financially sorted out I plan to make this good so as not to upset your calculations. At the time the only way I could handle transactions was by cabling you.

It is murderously <u>hot</u> now and of course I don't like it very much. There seem to be a lot of things in life you just have to put up with. For instance, having Tania living here alone was a most expensive, I might say ruinous affair. I don't think I did any saving those three months. In fact I know I spent more than I earned. But there was no other way. Together, we will be able to be more economical. Tania did her best, but living separately cannot help but be expensive.

This ribbon seems a bit messy. Tania just put it in for me.

Tania has received a letter from her mother that the things you sent to Istanbul will be brought here by some friends. She is delighted but chagrined that we will probably leave before the things arrive. I will try to arrange to get them on to Cairo. It seems that Tania's mother paid a packet of duty, but of course she was glad to do it, and Tania is thrilled to have presents from her American family.

Our dog Cleo is now enormous, but quite well behaved. Tania has trained her a good deal. Thank God for Cleo. Without the dog she would have been too lonely for words.

I flew from Amman to Beyrouth, but we'll probably take a boat from here to Alexandria.

Mother there are lots and lots of things for me to tell you. I am sorry I couldn't write for so long, but you will understand and there'll be that much more to tell when I am home.

Please give my love to Grandma and Eliza and Ken, and to Steinie.
All my love,
Dana

July 7, 1948
Cairo
Shepheard's hotel
Dear Mother:
I don't know quite how this paper came into my possession, but I might as well let you have the benefit of it.

As you will have seen by the paper I've been fairly busy here. It is not too easy, under the circumstances. I wish they could have sent me to Europe. But here we are and might as well make the best of it.

Cyrus, of all people, has decided to come here for a visit. Due on Sunday next. I'll have plenty to tell him. Of course he wants to see all the big names and I will be tied up the next few days trying to make appointments for him. That won't be too easy either.

We have found an apartment into which we will move on the 18th! It is not the one I mentioned before but it is nice and suitable for our purposes. Telephone, refrig, radio, fan, complete with servants, linens, silvers. So we won't have to pay anything but the rent, which is thirty pounds monthly, and the servants and electricity and gas.

We can have it for three months. Thereafter, if still here, we'll have to see what can be had elsewhere. It will be our first "home" outside of hotels. Belongs to an elderly British newspaperman, the Dean, in fact, of the local press corps, aged 76. He is going to England on leave.

We are getting quite a lot of invitations from local Americans and others. There are a great many here. Of course such a large "American colony" lacks the intimacy one gets in smaller places. Tomorrow night we are dining with Jefferson Patterson and wife and the night after with Evans, the press attache.

It is so hot most afternoons that it is best to take a siesta. I was never in Cairo at this time of year before. This afternoon, however, Tania has gone out swimming with a girl friend she once knew in Turkey. There is a very nice pool at a place called the "Auberge des Pyramides". We will also soon belong to the Gezira club. It is just around the corner from our apartment.

No letters from home yet, but I'm sure there will be some soon.

All my love to you all. Dana

July 21, 1948
118 Fuad el Awal
Cairo
Dear Mother:

I'm a bit late in writing to you this week. It has been hectic, with our moving from the hotel to this apartment, and the various local events on top.

Perhaps you have been worrying about us. Well, we were worried too for a few days, but things have quieted down now.

I am thankful that I made the decision to move out of the hotel to an apartment. It makes a world of difference. We are going to be very happy here I believe. There are advantages from the working side, too, as it is a good place to entertain news sources.

We have this apartment for thirty pounds a month, which is about the minimum around here. It belongs to Philip Taylor, an English journalist who has been out here more than fifty years. A couple of years ago the local press corps gave him a dinner and a present of fifteen hundred pounds! Quite a tidy sum. Apparently he has nothing to retire on and is still working. Right now he and his wife are vacationing in England. Due back in three months. I haven't yet started to think what we'll do then.

Cyrus was here, and what a rat race that was. Occupied my full time for nearly a week. Also completely discombobulated me financially, as I had to pay all his expenses, which were enormous. Suite with bath at Shepheards, entertainment, etc.

I managed to get him appointments with most of the people he wanted to see. He had reason to be satisfied. Also thrashed out a lot of my personal problems with him. As a result I learn that I along with most of the staff am getting a ten percent raise. Cy agreed that apart from the ten percent my salary was too low and undertook to get it increased.

He couldn't tell me exactly how long I'd be stationed here since he couldn't tell what was going to happen in Palestine. But it seems very likely that it will extend until autumn. I don't think it is going to be a terrific news center. But one of our crew has got to cover it, and it is a break, from the point of view of personal life, that it is me for a few months.

I tried to pin Cy down to a promise that I'd be transferred to Europe after this tour of duty, but couldn't. Still, he didn't exclude it. Nobody seems to want to work in this part of the world. The romance of the East fades rather rapidly for those who've been out here a while. Except in the case of a few incorrigibles.

Cy also half committed himself to pay for the car I acquired from Clay Gowran. Cost $1400, plus license registration etc. Even if he doesn't put that one across with the New York office I can sell the car for that much or more at any time. There is a ready second hand car market here as it is difficult to get new American cars into the country. It is a Ford Tudor, 1946, slightly battered about the fenders but otherwise in fine shape. The price seems high by American standard but is not excessive here. New cars sell for about <u>twice</u> their U.S.A. price.

One of the good aspects about this apartment is that it is a completely going concern. There are two servants (two of them cost about forty dollars a month) one of whom has been in the house 15 years. There is a radio an electric fan and a refrigerator (rare out here in spite of the heat). The place is 100 percent equipped with everything.

It is really a bit big for us and it would be nice if we found a suitable person to occupy one of the bedrooms. But we don't want that right at the beginning. It is such a blessing to have a place all our own, and a little space to move about in after nearly nine months of hotel rooms.

The place is cool. And let me tell you that counts in Cairo in summer. In the hotel there simply weren't any cool rooms, although we had one of the least hot ones; from noon till midnight the room was sweltering. But here we are on the fifth floor and get a breeze from the north most of the time.

The layout of the apartment is as follows. You enter into a combination vestibule and living room. Rather dark, as its two windows both open onto the courtyards, but cool and airy. There is a fireplace there (for other seasons) four comfortable chairs, bookcases, radio, fan, etc. At the other end of this vestibule you turn left to three bedrooms and the bathroom, go straight ahead into the dining room, or turn right to the kitchen and salon. The salon is large and comfortable, but we don't use it much as it doesn't get much breeze. We had guests last night and sat there for the first time.

The cook and "sufragi" are not very bright but very well meaning. They were quite excited about our having five people to a buffet supper last night. Delighted to do the extra work, apparently. It seems the Taylors never entertained except to cocktails.

Elizabeth would get a big laugh out of the furniture. It is style 1890. Pictures of friends and relations and everything else all over the walls.

I see that Stone is in charge of the Sunday department while Markel is touring Europe. Always a good thing for me. Had weekender requests the past three weeks. Last week's wasn't printed however as Stone, as he cabled me, was afraid my predictions would go wrong (But I was right).

Now I must get to work. Tania is fine, on the whole, although she has a cold right now and is just recovering from an operation on her knee. There was a small piece of cartilage that had been knocked loose when she bumped her knee in a slight car accident in Beyrouth. It had to be removed. We went to a Dr. Honey, South African, whom the Americans here regard as the best in town. Now Dr. Honey and his wife (Greek) have become good friends of ours. They were among our guests last night. The others were an Egyptian Prince and his girl friend and Mr. McCabe a British member of Bernadotte's staff.

Your news of the beach cottage is exciting. Yes, the expense is heavy. We will be able to live more cheaply in this apartment. We definitely want to contribute our share and look forward to moving into our Los Angeles beach "home" even if it is only for a few months of home leave.

All my love to you all, Grandma, Eliza and Steinie.

Dana

P.S. I enclose the Power of Attorney

ELIZABETH SCHMIDT CRAHAN

Cairo 118 Fuad el Awal
July 26, 1948
Dear Mother:

It is nice to be writing you from my own desk in our own apartment instead of from the eternal hotel bedroom table. Needless to say the apartment involves many difficult and unforeseen problems, but it is worth all the trouble.

I have arranged for a temporary membership in the Gezira club, which is just around the corner, and we are going there this afternoon. The place is so crowded that it is difficult to get even a temporary membership.

Walter Collins and an Egyptian editor are coming to lunch. Tania is out doing the shopping. So you see we are a going menage.

But don't think I spend all my time at the apartment. As soon as I leave here, in a few minutes, I will go to an interview with the Prime Minister.

There hasn't been a great deal of news from here as the Arab League has been working out of Beyrouth. It will come back here, however. Generally this is the political headquarters of the Middle East.

It is still pretty hot but we haven't been worrying about it very much since we got out of the hotel. It is much cooler here, away from the center of town. A South African Doctor, named Honey and his wife have a villa on the edge of the Nile nearby. I believe we will be able to let the dog run in their garden sometimes. We can also let her run in parts of the Gezira club, on the polo grounds I believe.

The A.P. has been on the front page with Cairo dateline stories twice lately, much to my annoyance. The first story was not really a Cairo story, but one obviously cooked up in New York or London from information out of Beirut and Tel Aviv. The second was simply erroneous—about a state of emergency having been declared in Cairo. I pointed out the latter matter to our New York desk.

All sorts of old friends have been turning up here, and it has been nice to be able to invite them out here for a drink or a meal. A South African aviator we knew in Damascus is here just now, and I have helped him get his exit visa, and a correspondent of Swedish and Swiss papers whom I knew in Ankara in days of yore has just gone through.

We have become quite friendly with a fellow named McCabe, an Englishman of the U.N. staff. His wife is in New York. They were married only three or four months ago, although he must be 40. Now they have been separated just as Tania and I were.

All my love to you all,
Dana

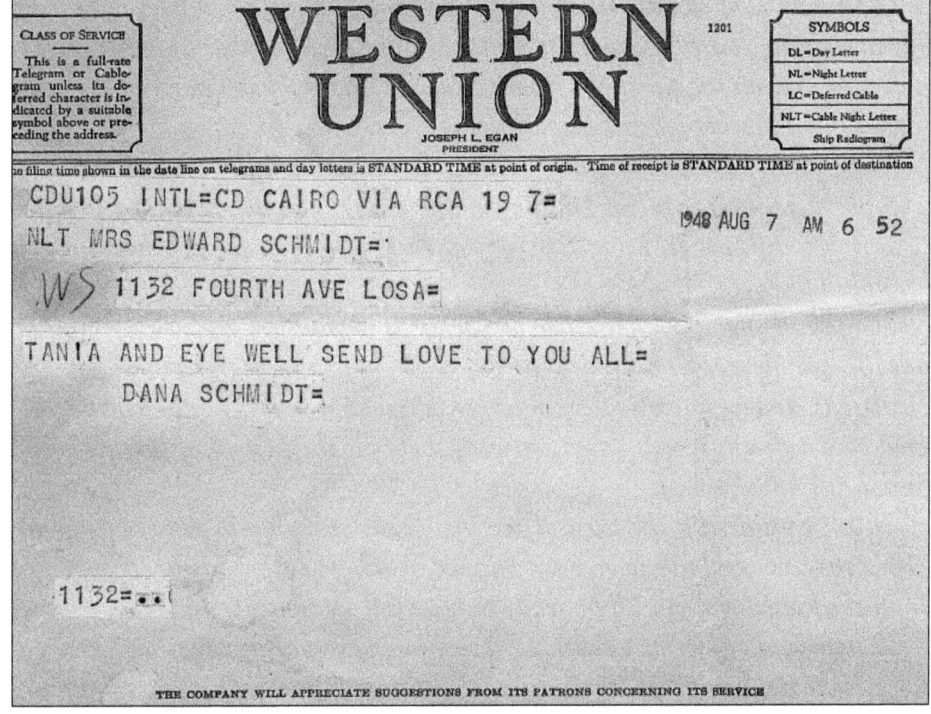

118 Fuad el Awal
August 11, 1948
Dear Mother:
My face is very red and I am returning the Power of Attorney properly signed. In a way I don't think it was my fault. I took it to the Embassy and asked the

proper people what to do with it, and did everything they told me. I don't profess to understand such documents. Pretty feeble excuse, though.

Perhaps, as you say, this apartment is a little expensive and large for us. But it isn't any more than other correspondents of my standing have. Anyway, it was the one thing that offered itself at the time. It seemed to me above all important that I get Tania established in something of a home. This serves that purpose quite well. We have it only for three months, and I don't think it will break me.

The car has of course knocked my New York account for a loop, and I am operating very close to the margin. But the Times *pays for the running expenses and may take on the car itself. If not, I can get about what I paid for it on the second hand market when I leave.*

This place has not been very rewarding journalistically, and if it doesn't improve I see little point in hanging on very long. I suppose you can imagine some of my difficulties. I am doing my darnedest to improve matters, but it is an uphill fight.

Gradually our personal circle of friends is expanding and we are finding our life here agreeable. Yesterday evening we went to a cocktail party at Jefferson Patterson's, and we knew a whole crowd of the guests. I couldn't help remembering how very different it was when we went there for the Fourth of July reception and didn't know a soul.

I am considering the idea of having Tania go home to visit her parents about the time we have to give up this flat. My hope is that about the time she is finished visiting them I'll be ready to head for the States.

I have had orders for weekenders every week except this one since I arrived. Shep Stone has been running the Sunday dept while Markel was away, and you know he is a good friend of mine. I have however only got two of them printed, because of the difficulties I've mentioned.

We are leading a quiet life and keeping out of harm's way, so don't worry too much. Soon we will be in California and enjoying the beach cottage with you. I wonder whether you could live there, since you find our neighborhood so obnoxious now. A bit far from the hospital, I fear. If you were thinking of giving up work at the hospital and returning to freelancing, maybe that wouldn't be so bad.

Glad to hear Grandma is keeping well. I am not surprised to hear that Steinie, as always, is proving herself invaluable and indispensable and loveable.

All my love to you all. Tania sends love too. Dana

August 18, 1948
Cairo
Dear Mother:

I was glad to hear that my letters have been getting through and that you are not feeling cut off. There are bound to be exceptional delays these days.

I am hopeful that I will be able to resume my interpretative Sunday pieces next week. I think that the difficulties of which I have spoken have about been ironed out.

Gradually our circle of friends here has widened, which makes life much pleasant from a social and more profitable from a newspaper point of view.

The heat here has not been so bad as it usually is. This is said to be a "cool" summer. If everything goes according to plan I think we will go down to Alexandria the first week of September for a meeting of the Arab League.

I'm still waiting for more definite word from Cyrus, but I am thinking that at the end of the three month period for which we have rented this apartment Tania might go home to visit her parents for about a month. My hope is that after that I could pick her up and we could go on to the States for that much over-due home leave. Sam Brewer is on vacation right now, in Rome. He isn't due for home leave. But Gene Currivan is. He has been out in this part of the world for about three years.

Tania has learned a lot running this apartment. It has made a world of difference. It would truly be too much to ask a girl to spend all of her first year of married life in hotel rooms. It was essential that we have something of a home.

It is too bad there hasn't been very much news in Cairo. You seem to have an idea that the amount of output and the amount that is printed by any one correspondent depends on how much work he does. That is true only in a most relative sense. It depends much more on where he is and when. No matter how much I turned out from here the Times *would only want to print an amount in proportion to the importance of Cairo as a news center. I'm not ignoring the importance of initiative and enterprise; I just didn't want you to think that the relative scarcity of my stories from here was due to idleness.*

The clothes you sent to Turkey were received joyfully, and Tania's mother has been trying to find a way to send them to her ever since. We thought it had been arranged once in Beyrouth, but then we had to leave to come here. You understand that duties on things like that are enormous in this part of the world. What is wanted is a friend who can adopt the clothes as part of her own baggage.

I must go to work now.

All our love to you all, Dana

Cairo
September 2, 1948
Dear Mother:

Pretty soon it will be my birthday. How very fast the years go by. Probably we will be in Alexandria on the sixth. I must go there for the meeting of the Arab League Political Committee. At least I think I must.

There has been no confirmation in your letters that you have received that Power of Attorney. I suppose you must have it by now. Tania had to have a very similar one made out so that her father could handle an apartment which is in her name in Istanbul.

I have made reservations at a hotel called the "Summer Palace" in Alexandria and will probably drive down with Woodford, a British newspaperman, and with Adil Sabit, an Arab League official. It takes about three hours, I'm told. There is a dead straight road right through the desert.

Tania and the wife of the foreign office press officer are going out to Mena house to swim today. Oddly enough this girl is also a White Russian and Tania knew her in Istanbul. She and her husband will soon be leaving for Paris where he will be on the Egyptian delegation.

I enclose some pictures taken on our balcony and at the Gezira club. You have to watch your step about where you take pictures these days.

It has been a blessing to be so near to Gezira during the hot Egyptian summer. As usual I am intending to get in some tennis.

I must make this letter fairly short as I must be going down town and want to take this with me.

My love to you all, Grandma and Eliza and Steinie and you,
Dana

Hotel Summer Palace
Alexandria
September 8, 1948
Dear Mother:

I've been spending a few days down here during Bernadotte's visit and the sessions of the Arab League Political Committee. Tania didn't come with me. She felt it wasn't worth putting up with the discomfort of living in a hotel with the dog for just a couple of days at the sea, and rightly, she feared I would be busy most of the day and not be able to go to the beach with her. She was also nervous about the trip down here in the car; there are so many exaggerated stories going around, and women have a way of picking them up.

Nonetheless I have been in the water twice and have a fair burn. I'm going back to Cairo Friday morning and may, perhaps, pick Tania up and bring her down here for the week-end. I think the change would do her good. The events here about which you have read in the papers seem to have upset her a good deal. We are planning that she should go home to visit her mother about the middle of October when we are due to give up the apartment.

Tonight I am having an interview with Azzam Pasha. He is quite an admirable fellow; tops among the politicians around here. There have been a number of stories here and I trust that you have seen a little more of the Schmidt by-line.

I don't think I ever told you that I had a letter from Cyrus in which, among a lot of other things, he said he would try to get me a new assignment, that it would "take time," but that when it came it would be a "good one." I had told him how I felt about my present assignment and pointed out to him that in Paris, Germany and Greece I have had responsibilities of bureau manager for prolonged periods without ever acquiring that dignity or being paid as such. I feel that France and Germany are my terrain, the part of the world I know most about and am most interested in.

No letter from you this week as my mail is being held in Cairo, but I'm sure there'll be one when I get back. Elizabeth's baby should have arrived by now. I must write to her. With three kids on her hands she will be really a busy girl. I wonder whether their beach cottage will be finished sufficiently so she can take it easy for a while at the beach. And how is ours getting along? We are still looking forward to some photos indicating progress! I'm sure it would all have been impossible without Steinie. We should really erect some sort of monument to Steinie in the garden of our beach house.

All my love to you all,
Dana
P.S. I drove down here on my birthday and we omitted all observances.

118 Fuad el Awal, Cairo
September 16, 1948
Dear Mother:
Still no letter from you and I am beginning to worry. If one doesn't come soon I will send a cable, although I am sure that I would get a cable from you if there is anything to prevent you from writing. Of course what has probably happened is that one letter has been delayed, leaving a long gap.

We have only about a week more in our apartment. The Taylors wrote they were coming back a bit earlier than expected, and we have no alternative but to depart. Actually it upsets us by only one week. We were counting on Tania catching a ship on October 7 and on going down to Alexandria for the week before the ship leaves.

Tania has really not been very well lately, although she is feeling better the last few days. Not that she's been sick, but the situation around here makes her sleepless and nervous, for which I must say I don't blame her. A great many of the Embassy people have now sent their families home.

Sam Souki, one of the boys I knew here during the war, is back from Rhodes, where he has been covering for U.P. He tells me Sam Brewer will go to Paris during the General Assembly, the idea being that his work covering the

Mediator's activities puts him in a specially good position to "expert" developments in Paris. Sam is determined to go too, even if he has to do it at his own expense. We are having him out to lunch today, along with the BBC man John Nixon and his wife.

It has cooled off here to a point where the heat is really no problem anymore. But it is still damp, oddly enough, because of the Nile flood.

Yesterday we bought Cleo a ball with which she played happily all evening. During the night she lost the ball. We've searched under and behind every conceivable object. Must have dropped it over the edge of the balcony. What a dog.

The other day Tania and I were looking over a plan of the beach house you sent me a long time ago. She thought it was wonderful, as do I. We are so eager to see it and live in it. I have a hunch that will be possible when the Paris conference is over. By that time Currivan will have finished his vacation, and Brewer has just had one in Italy.

Now I must go down town and see if there is any news. The Ford is still operating admirably. No trouble at all.

All my love to you all, Dana

c/o American Embassy
Cairo
September 20, 1948
Dear Mother:

It now appears that the best boat for Tania to take to Istanbul leaves on the 28th, and so she will leave then if I can get all the formalities of Egyptian exit, Turkish visa and her American visa finished by then. Actually everything is done except the American visa which I have left purposely till the last minute so there will not be any danger of its four months validity expiring before she actually heads for the States.

We are pleased you liked the pictures. Also, I'm glad you got the power of attorney at last.

It was good to have your long letter about financial matters. It is reassuring to know that there is a steady well-intentioned mind in the family to keep a check on these things and it means the world to me. That is why I have left my affairs to such a large extent in your hands.

Now about some of the specific points you mention. It is no use our thinking too much about what Tania's family <u>should</u> have done or should do in the future for us, regarding wedding expenses, trousseau and such. It would indeed have been a big help to have these things, but it is most unlikely that they will be forthcoming. It is true, of course, that Tania's family hasn't had much opportunity, since we were married in Athens and spent only a few days in Istanbul and it is very difficult to send things in this part of the world.

It is best that we should not count on <u>anything</u> from that quarter. And above all I beg of you not to mention or imply anything in that connection in writing or talking to Tania. It would only hurt her and not do a particle of good. She is as aware of the failings on her side of the family as I am. Don't forget that there is a bad situation between her father and mother which is only spasmodically patched up. He has the money; she has nothing. Tania loves her mother very much; she definitely dislikes her father. I am of course most cordial to both, although I certainly prefer the mother. I have written them both several times, always together, and have had very nice answers.

Incidentally, Tania's mother says she wrote to you several times but the letters apparently did not get through.

Now while I think of it, I noticed a long time back that you mentioned a contribution for Tania's and my Blue Cross Insurance. I have a "Hospital Service Identification Card, associated Hospital Service of New York, 370 Lexington Avenue, New York 17." I suppose that is it. But I have none for Tania. Can you get one for her. Send it to me and I will see she gets it.

You say every woman you know "feels she must add to her husband's income—by actual money, by her own labor; or in the home. Drones are very definitely out of style."

Now Tania is anything but a drone, and I trust you will never say anything to her that would give her that impression. She positively <u>loves</u> to work and has never been so happy as in the past few months when she could do a lot of work in the house. She has made something of a home for me, and believe me, leading *the kind of life I have, that is what I wanted and the greatest service she can possibly give.*

Although we could not fire servants which came with the apartment about a month ago she sent the cook away on "holiday." For one thing he was stealing a lot of food and for another Tania wanted very much to do the cooking. That she has done ever since, including the times we entertain. It turns out she is much handier at household tasks than she herself suspected. In addition she keeps the second servant out of the house most of the time and does the cleaning, washing up, etc. because she <u>likes</u> to do it. Our cost of living has come down sharply since we got rid of the cook.

But it is unlikely that Tania will be able to <u>earn</u> money. She would like to and has often spoken of a job. But how to find something for her when we are so much on the move? When the time comes that we have a permanent, long term post maybe we can work out something. But please do not press her or give her the idea she isn't pulling her weight. She is, and longing to do more.

In general we have to bear in mind that Tania like anyone else is limited by her past environment. American as she is in many ways, she grew up in Istanbul. And the ideal of work has been far more cultivated in the U.S. than in most other countries. Tania is young and eager but also sensitive, and sensitivity need not be confused with selfishness. She will grow and change in many ways and I want to be the one who influences her growth and change.

Don't think that I am in any way rejecting your advice, Mother. If you don't "rake up old coals" for me who will? But it just seemed to me that I should point these things out.

The other day I weighed myself and found that I have gained nearly twenty pounds in Cairo. I'm back up around 165, which is where I was before. That period in Palestine really took it out of me. Tania has been feeding me frantically and is delighted.

I have just had a letter from Elizabeth telling about the baby. Please tell her I was very happy that young Steve arrived in such size and good health. Now she really will have her hands full.

It delights both Tania and me to hear that the Beach house is getting along. It cannot fail to be a good investment, I'm sure.

ELIZABETH SCHMIDT CRAHAN

I believe you will find I have had two, if not three weekenders from Cairo. The last one appeared on August 29th according to a clipping I saw at the embassy. And didn't you see my Palestine magaziner? I happen to have a copy of the magazine it was in and will clip and enclose it for you in case you missed it.

Isn't the cost of a nurse for Elizabeth fantastic? Seems incredible. Maybe we'd better think twice about having our baby in the States, when the time comes (I'm only kidding).

I think I must have missed a letter of yours because yours of September 11 was the first news I'd had of Elizabeth's baby. Probably you have missed some of mine.

There is an outside chance that we might get to the States for Christmas. I'm waiting for word from Cy.

All my love to you all, now. A letter to Grandma is long over-due. Do tell her I haven't forgotten, not by any means.

Dana

Please be sure to confirm you got this letter

118 Fuad el Awal
Cairo
September 30, 1948
Dear Mother:
Tania has gone and I am feeling very much alone and sorry for myself. I drove her down to Alexandria and saw her off on the Turkish ship Kadesh.

We decided on this boat because the next one didn't leave until the end of October, and the Taylors will be back October 1.

Tania took Cleo along, of course, and our plan is that she should leave the beast with her mother when I pick her up to go to the States. Hope that will work out; Cleo is so very strong and difficult to manage that I'm not sure how Tania's mother will make out.

Before she left I got Tania's U.S. immigration visa. So she is all set to go to the States. Hope we can swing it within four months. If not, the visa can be renewed, but it would be a nuisance.

I believe you have Tania's Istanbul address. It is c/o Mrs. Alexandra Konstantinidis, 18 Mete cadessi, Ayaspasha, Istanbul. (You can spell that name with a C or a K, as you please, in Turkey. Normally they would use a K in Turkish and a C in French and other languages).

There is a lot going on here in the political sphere but not a great deal I can write. It is a thoroughly unsatisfactory news center.

Of course you have heard about Dave Woodford of the London Daily Telegraph *and John Nixon of the* BBC? *They were both stationed here, went off on a tour of the Middle East, and were killed when their plane was shot down by a Jewish fighter between Beyrouth and Amman. A most tragic affair. Nixon and his wife had been at our house for lunch only a few days before he was killed, and Woodford had become a good friend. Mrs. Nixon had a baby and was expecting another. Of course Tania and I immediately offered to do anything we could for Mrs. Nixon. But at such times there is nothing that can be done that would really help; the little superficial things were being taken care of by friends with whom they were more intimate than with us.*

I was thrilled to read all the details about the house furnishings and I will relay them to Tania. Incidentally, I would be happy if you would write her a nice letter to Istanbul. She is planning to write you too as soon as she has seen the clothes you sent from the States. There are only two items about houses that occur to me. One is that I hope you will arrange a rather wide double bed for us. We don't like twin beds. The other is that it might be wise, if it is possible, to arrange for a fence around that house high enough so that any dogs present could be suitably confined.

I get the impression that you have been at least partly won to the "modern" school of architecture and interior decorating. That's all right with me, although I like old stuff too.

I am sorry to hear that Grandma has not been well. Please give her my love.

All my love to you all,

Dana

P.S. Happy birthday to Eliza! I hope you'll send us some new pictures of the whole brood soon!

ELIZABETH SCHMIDT CRAHAN

Shepheard's Hotel
Cairo
October 6, 1948
Dear Mother:

I am now safely installed in Shepheards in a quite attractive single room overlooking the garden. A telegram has come from Istanbul from Tania announcing that she has arrived safely. Now I'm waiting for her first letter. It is unquestionably a wise thing for her to go home to her mother for a little while; it was the first time in her life she had been away from her mother for any length of time.

There has been a flurry of local news, but I suppose that with all the big stuff in Paris we are buried far in the back of the paper, if they bother to bury the stuff at all.

Yesterday I was pleased to catch sight of Sherif, a Turkish newspaperman I knew in Ankara and Athens, and his wife. They were here on a vacation trip and I took them out to lunch. It seems that things have changed very little in Athens, except for the departure of Griswold.

I don't think I ever told you I finally got around to having a game of tennis a while back. Now, however, my temporary membership in the Gezira club has expired and I must wait till the membership committee has passed on my application for a permanent membership. Tania and I were extremely fortunate to find an apartment fully equipped and obtain a temporary membership in the club for the time she was here. Apartments are hard to get and the club is supposed to have discontinued all temporary memberships.

Today is Elizabeth's birthday, so I will once more convey my wishes to her for a Happy birthday, and all my love. Incidentally, I just got your letter announcing the birth of Steven Edward Acker. It had been somewhat delayed. Elizabeth certainly did well to keep working up to the end and start up again right afterwards. I'm proud of her too.

Ever hear anything of George Martin? I shall have to make up for lost time in performing my duties as godfather when I get back.

I had quite a struggle to get a decent room in Shepheards. At first they offered me one on an inside court of the air cooling system which makes a buzzing noise. I declined it and left all my stuff in my car. They still had nothing else that evening and I slept in an extra bed in the room of an Australian newspaperman. It wasn't till the evening of the next day that they finally came across with this room.

Now I must go along to the Embassy. I am having lunch with our Egyptian "press analyst" who is quite a mine of information.

My love to you all, Dana

Shepheards hotel
October 14, 1948
Dear Mother:

I just got your excellent and absolutely delightful photographs of our beach house. I revel in them. They are marvelous, or rather the house is marvelous. It looks good and it sounds good. My congratulations to Elizabeth and to you. And isn't it fine not to have a great highway between us and the sea. I can't wait till I'm there. Remember when we first discussed the project of a beach house and looked at an old ruin that might have been fixed up and made some tentative phone calls. How things grow.

Tomorrow morning early I'll be flying with the Ambassador to Beirut, and thence to Damascus and maybe farther. It should be interesting, and I'll be pleased to see some of the people I know there, especially in Damascus. The Minister there, Mr. Keeley, was Charge d'Affaires in Athens and attended our wedding.

We are having the Kurban Bayram, which is a sort of Moslem Christmas, and there isn't much doing. But I did a piece on cotton today, and see the local papers have cabled back a piece I did three days ago on the incidents in the Negev.

I am enclosing a wad of clippings the paper has sent me. You said you hadn't seen anything of mine for weeks and I thought you must have missed some things.

You will have seen in the paper that Sam Brewer got married in Paris. His second, I understand. I like him quite well, though he is of a rather dour disposition. He had been drinking a good deal too much in the Middle East, but perhaps marriage will change him.

While we speak of marriage, Mother . . . I did not want to arouse bitter feelings in you in bringing up, as I did, some of Tania's failings. I have wanted you to know more about Tania so that you would meet her with a constructive understanding. It is not that I fear that "people" will criticize her; I already know something of the problems of marriage to a non-American and am quite prepared for that sort of thing. What I feared was your criticism in the form of the destructive innuendos of which you are sometimes capable; I did not want to add unnecessarily to our problems. I am sorry you were offended by her notes; I know well that she meant them kindly and lovingly. It is a shame she should have mentioned vodka in writing to Grandma; but how should she have divined Grandma's sensibilities, since they would never occur to her own grandmother and vodka is a very ordinary and respectable thing in most Russian families. As for "moulding" . . . well, perhaps that's not the right word. But we all grow and change throughout our lives. Incidentally, Tania will be 26 on October 27. Our wedding anniversary is the day before.

I have been moderately active in a social way, with some cocktail parties, lunches and dinners. Tonight Tom Stauffer, our labor attache, and I were invited to dinner by a man named John Ross, a TWA navigator. The main guest however was a man named Ludwig Keimer, a most brilliant Egyptologist and a delight to talk to. He is a man of a hundred specialties, from special studies of the various species of rhinoceros, to studies of the uses to which the ancients put the camel's tail, to the use of giraffes in Egyptian hieroglyphics. You see he has a special penchant for animal studies. But that is just a sideline to amuse himself.

He lectures at various universities and makes a living by functioning as ultimate and infallible expert for Cairo antiquarians. His apartment, which we visited at the end of the evening, is lined from floor to ceiling, literally, with books. And there is quite a section for the books he wrote himself.

It seems that when he was a boy, in Germany, his father would not finance a trip to Egypt for him. So he went through school and a whole series of universities studying Egypt from every possible angle. He got a law degree with a thesis on ancient Egyptian law, for instance.

When he finally got to Egypt he submerged himself in the country, crisscrossing it north and south, east and west, examining the villages and every excavation, becoming an authority on the modern as well as the ancient religions and politics of the land. Truly a fascinating guy. He urged me to come and see him and talk politics—which is about the only subject on which I could hold my own with him.

Well, that will be enough for tonight.
All my love to you all, as always, Dana

c/o American Embassy
Cairo
October 19, 1948
Dear Mother:
Don't worry about the beds or the garden of our beach house. I'm sure the beds will be dandy, and we haven't been planning to bring the dog. As regards fences for restraining dogs, I was thinking really in terms of the distant future.

I am back from the Ambassadorial tour of Lebanon and Syria. It was most interesting from many points of view. Apart from learning something about the refugee problem I had a chance to refresh my impressions of political situations up there, and of getting to know the Ambassador. It is too bad that he probably won't be with us after the elections, being a Truman appointee. He is a most exceptionally outstanding gent.

I saw Bob and Sally Brown in Damascus. They are due to return to the States soon, having rounded out two years in the Levant. Also many others whose names you are not so familiar with, including the new Minister in Damascus, Keeley, who is a peach. So is his wife. I first got acquainted with that family by helping to get Mrs. Keeley a ride on a plane from Salonika to Athens (which she didn't use). Then they both came to our wedding and sent us a silver ash tray with a nice inscription as wedding present.

(I suppose this typing is waking up the people trying to take a siesta on both sides of me. Do them good, although Napoleon and Churchill both testify to the virtues of the siesta and I sometimes take one myself.)

In Beirut I bought a certain something for Christmas presents. I sent it to 1132 by mail. With any luck you won't have to pay customs. In that case the proper thing is, "Do not open before Christmas." That means you and Grandma.

I'm glad you are already enjoying the house and that you will send some pictures to Tania. I was going to send her some of the ones you sent me, but will not. Between the house and your work you must be mighty busy. I am thankful that you are feeling well again.

In my absence the character I described in my last letter, Dr. Keimer called and left his card. So I really must go and return the call now.

Yes, it is too bad to be in an unsatisfactory news center. But such situations are not always all bad. It is usually in the times of slack news that I learn most— learn the things that contribute to output of real value later. I have, incidentally, just completed a very exhaustive memorandum on religious questions for Cy Sulzberger. Of course I get no public credit out of that, as he will use his by-line, but working on it got me into some interesting circles that I could not otherwise have penetrated.

All my love to you all, Mother, Dana

c/o American Embassy
Cairo
October 28, 1948
Dear Mother:

The weeks slip by and it is a month since Tania left. She is now beginning to think eagerly about coming back, and that seems the best thing for her to do.

I have been in touch with Cyrus by letter and cable about my next move. At first he said I would definitely have to stick to this post until the end of next April, then he suggested I might take leave after January 1 and then be assigned to Vienna. The matter is still in the air.

Unfortunately the one certainty that has now emerged is that I will not be able to be home by Christmas. I had hoped we would make it this year. It would have been a nice time to bring Tania home. But there it is, and we will have to hope for the future.

Last night I went to a movie called Captain of Castile, or something like that, shown by the U.S. Navy on the occasion of Navy Day. I wished Tania could have been along. Although rather on the corny side I enjoyed it. Hadn't been to a movie since we went to one in Athens last year. There was one private showing

Tania and I went to here, on a spacious terrace belonging to an American Embassy couple. Towards the end we were suddenly pelted by raw eggs and some rather liquid cheese. One of the eggs landed on my head. The show stopped and we went in search of the pelters, to no avail. The projectors were turned on again, and the pelting resumed. This time with garbage. We were never able to figure out who was responsible and why, whether someone objected to the noise or to the fact that we were Americans. I overlooked telling you that story when it happened a month or so ago.

Not being sure what our future movements will be I am going right ahead with the formalities towards our becoming members of the Gezira club. We had temporary memberships which have now expired. It is a fabulous club. I'm sure you've heard of it. Near the center of town, complete with club houses, tennis, swimming pool, squash courts, golf courts, polo fields, places for children to play, places for old men to play bowls, croquet lawns. There is little they haven't got, and the attraction is so great that a good section of the Anglo-American colony lives nearby. Nowadays, of course, there is great pressure from Egyptians to join, and little by little the club is being Egyptianized.

Lately I have almost given up smoking. Those things go in waves with me.

I was pleased with the additional picture of the beach house enclosed in your last letter. Yes, I see we have built pretty much up to the edge of our land. Hope nobody builds another house smack against us.

I read a book called "Kaputt" by Curzio Malaparte the other day. Extremely good in a rather florid way. He was an Italian war correspondent in Poland Russia and Finland.

Glad you are all keeping well. All my love, Dana

c/o American Embassy, Cairo
November 3, 1948
Dear Mother:
Not much new around here except the election. Weren't you surprised? I certainly was.

They are both such mediocre men that I find it difficult to be very partial one way or the other. On foreign policy there was little to choose between them; on domestic policy I preferred Truman's slant on civil rights, price control and the Taft Hartley act. I suspect that you and Grandma preferred Dewey. Certainly Grandma did. (So did the New York Times, although at one time one of our editorialists wrote that Dewey could never be President because he was simply not a big enough man.)

I have had a succession of cocktail parties lately. Tonight there is one at the home of the British press attache. I won't stay long, as I was sick the day before yesterday and am still a little under the weather. Must have been a dysentery bug I picked up. But Dr. Honey (a South African), put me on sulphaguanedine, and that seems to have killed the bug in short order.

Nothing positive on my assignment yet. Cy cabled that "it takes time to arrange all these switches."

If we get to Los Angeles soon after New Years the beach house should be just about finished. It won't be exactly the season for the beach, but we'll enjoy it, nonetheless.

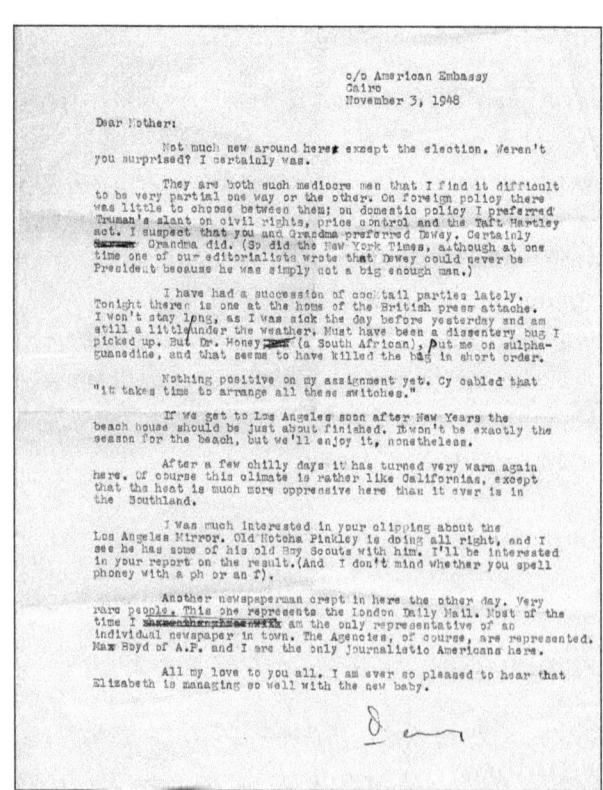

After a few chilly days it has turned very warm again here. Of course this climate is rather like California's, except that the heat is much more oppressive here than it ever is in the Southland.

I was much interested in your clipping about the Los Angeles Mirror. Old Hotcha Pinkley is doing all right, and I see he has some of his old Boy Scouts with him. I'll *be interested in your report on the result. (And I don't mind whether you spell phoney with a ph or an f).*

Another newspaperman crept in here the other day. Very rare people. This one represents the London Daily Mail. *Most of the time I am the only representative of an individual newspaper in town. The Agencies, of course, are represented. Max Boyd of A.P. and I are the only journalistic Americans here.*

All my love to you all.

I am ever so pleased to hear that Elizabeth is managing so well with the new baby.

Dana

c/o American Embassy, Cairo
November 9, 1948
Dear Mother:
This has been a busy week, but unfortunately the conditions of work here are such that a lot of the time one feels one is on a treadmill. I am lonely without Tania. Wish the office would hurry up and make up its mind where it is going to send me and when.

Sam Brewer cabled me he is returning to Beirut on the 15th, so I won't be going there for the UNESCO *conference. That being the case I'm going to go to Khartoum for a few days to cover the first Sudanese legislative elections and have a look at darkest Africa. I've been seeing a number of people about the Sudan, reading some pamphlets, and believe I can turn up some rather readable pieces. The Sudan and its election are of course of the essence in Britain's differences with Egypt. Allan Humphreys, a* London Daily Mail *correspondent from India, is probably going with me, or may precede me by a day or two.*

There is plenty of news around here, although you have read little of it. Last night there was a particularly good yarn, of which I had an eyewitness account, but you'll have to wait till I get home to hear about it. At the time I was at the home of Quilliam, the London Times *correspondent and his wife who have just returned from a holiday in the States. He has been out here for thirty years and of course knows everyone and everything. During the war he was one of the Colonels in Intelligence who gave the press a weekly lecture on what was going* on at the front. The London Times *has a number of men like that. Another was Frank MacCaskey in Athens who worked with the Greek Resistance during the war, was arrested by the Italians, condemned to death, escaped, and became a minor national hero in Greece.*

I believe I told you I played tennis the other day. But I haven't been able to play regularly since I'm not yet a member of the Gezira Sporting Club. Previously we had temporary memberships which have lapsed. I felt I'd better go ahead with our applications for this club even though we probably won't be here. You never can tell. It is not a very expensive membership.

By now I dare say our beach house is in working order. It should be a great satisfaction to you, Steinie and Grandma. I hope you can get in and out without too much difficulty. The interesting picture you enclosed recently showed Steinie and Elizabeth (or is that someone else?—I see "Helen Corle" written on the back) tugging hard.

Now I must go and see if I can find some news that is publishable.

All my love to you all.

Dana

Shepheards hotel
Cairo
November 21, 1948
Dear Mother:

This time I've really missed a whole week in writing to you, although I sent a little note to Steinie from Khartoum. It was because of that trip that I didn't get around to writing as usual.

The trip was most fascinating, but the Times *was apparently not overpowered with interest. I filed four stories during the five days I was away, and when I got back, found a cable from New York saying that they had all been so delayed, apparently by the censors here, that none had been used. So I wrote a rather lengthy roundup and am hoping it got printed.*

In any case I feel the trip was worthwhile to anyone who wants an understanding of issues affecting the Middle East. Also it gave me my first look at what is really Africa. I spent most of my time in Khartoum talking to British officials and Sudanese politicians and others, but the last day I arranged a trip out to the great irrigation works known as the "Gezira," between the White and the Blue Niles. The British Public Relations officer provided a car and I was accompanied by a fellow from the British Embassy in Cairo.

The British engineer who supervises a section of the project showed us around and gave us lunch, and then I asked to be taken to a Sudanese village. It was a tiny place of three hundred people with square mud huts, one room each, and faced with donkey dung. My British friends spoke Arabic and through them I asked what they thought about the elections (which was very little indeed), how they made their living, etc. They finally persuaded us to enter one of the huts, which was what I wanted to do, and we sat on their beds and continued the chatting. The windows were just holes cut in the wall, one on each of two sides. The floor was earth. There were no facilities of any kind for heating. The only furniture was three beds, and a table in the middle of the room covered by a ragged cloth.

Strangely enough everything was clean—incredible to anyone who knows villages elsewhere in the Middle East. The Sudanese are in fact a remarkably clean people. Instead of the filthy nightgowns one gets accustomed to around here they wear white shorts and shirts down to about knee length that are almost always spotless.

To get back to the village. There were no sanitary installations at all. That is, they just go out behind a bush somewhere. Yet the place did not smell. Probably thanks to the liberal ration of sunshine in that part of the world.

The peasants offered us coffee and we declined. They offered us sweetened water and we declined again. At last we accepted cigarettes. No matter how poor, peasants everywhere seem to feel they <u>must</u> offer visitors something. More was to come. As we were making for our car a boy dragged up a sheep by the hind leg. I was given to understand that it was for me, a gift to the man, whose name they did not even know, who had come from so far away to visit them. I could not refuse; that would have been a disaster. For a moment I thought I had better give them something in return, and for lack of anything else at all was fingering my fountain pen. But the Britishers advised me that return gifts were not expected until some time later.

So the sheep went into the front seat of our car and back to Khartoum. I made a gift of the poor creature to the British Public Relations Officer, who offered to provide me with sheep's kidneys, or some other revolting dish, for breakfast. I told him I thought that would be too hard on the sheep and suggested tentatively that the sheep could be kept for trimming the lawn. But I fear that by now it has been eaten.

The British live very nicely in these tropical parts. Spacious houses and gardens. They work till 1:30 or 2:00, then take the rest of the day off. Dress for dinner, of course. The climate does not seem to be hard on them as far as health goes; the women say it is bad for their complexions. November is of course a good time of year; warm by day and cool by night. The cool wind blows steadily across the savanna, the great plains, not quite desert but too dry to cultivate without irrigation, that lie between the desert and the equatorial jungles.

You drive over tracks across the savanna. There are no roads outside the towns. Every few hundred yards there is a low thorny bush. Occasionally a struggling tree. On the horizon are mirages; the same bushes and struggling trees with reflections in nonexistent pools of water. My British friend explained to me exactly why a mirage is what it is, but I wouldn't undertake to repeat.

As you pass the native villages a huge black mammy squatting in front of a doorway may draw a shawl over her naked breasts, or a stark naked boy will duck out of sight. They haven't all reconciled themselves to wearing clothes all the time, but they've learned to be self conscious when a European is in sight. Of course these Arabic-speaking, Moslem natives in the northern two thirds of the country are relatively advanced. In the southern third they are pagan and really "just out of the trees."

You'd think I might have written some of such descriptive stuff for the Times, *but here just didn't seem to be an opportunity, specially since my day to day stuff didn't get printed. And I had to hasten to pick up the Cairo news when I returned.*

Tania is due to take a ship that leaves on the 23rd. So she'll be here by the 26th. Unfortunately I still have no definite word from the office as to how long I'll be here and so haven't been able to take an apartment. We'll probably stay here or at Hotel Semiramis.

Your letter of November 10 has just reached me. Yes, I can well understand that the beach house is a big financial burden, but I think it will prove to be worth every cent of it. I was especially interested in the analyses of the elections you enclosed, by "Scotty" Reston and "Tomorrow's" Newsgram.

I've been invited to a performance of Hamlet tonight and must hasten now to check up on the news situation. We have been having a bit lately.

All my love to you, Mother, and to Grandma Elizabeth Steinie and Ken. Keep well. Dana

P.S. Tania is very eager to get back as the family difficulties I've told you about have meant that her time in Istanbul has not really been very happy. That is why she probably hasn't written you.

Shepheards hotel
Cairo
November 28, 1948
Dear Mother:
I had hoped Tania would be back by now, but it was not possible for her to get her visa in time for the last boat. Now she will try for next Friday's plane.

My goodness, you and Elizabeth and all the rest of you have certainly been busy these last few months. Well, I've not been laggard around here either, but it must be difficult for you to imagine how much slower is the pace of life out here. Time counts for very little. Standards are different in many respects, and Europeans are affected in spite of whatever standards they bring with them.

There seem to be parties of one kind or another every day here; that's another characteristic of the place, or of a certain social strata. It is, I suppose the general inactivity of the women that leads to excessive social life.

The other day a notice to all correspondents came in from the Publisher stating that in future correspondents abroad will be entitled to three months home leave, including travel, every three years, and that the Times *will pay for travel of correspondents, wife and children to New York and back. That is good news for us, as I'd been figuring on having to pay Tania's fare both ways. As it is we will have only fares for the two of us from New York to LA and back, which is enough to be sure.*

Dr. Pablo Azcarate and his wife had me to their room this evening for a drink. He is a Spanish Republican political figure who somehow became the UN representative in Cairo. He is a most intelligent man and a pleasure to talk to. He married a large middle-aged woman here recently and lives in rooms just above me.

Did I tell you that my good friend Tom Stauffer, the Embassy's Labor attache has been seriously ill with amoebic dysentery and all sorts of complications for weeks? I go to see him frequently. He is by far the most intellectually stimulating person I've met in Cairo and should go far in government service or politics. We fell in together first because of our mutual interest in Germany where he was dealing with military government labor problems until recently. As a sideline he has made himself an expert on Chinese art, oriental carpets, etc. A product of progressive education and, more particularly, of Chicago University. So lacking in inhibitions he gets on some people's nerves; yet he stutters.

This isn't very good letter paper but it saves weight. My love to you all.
Dana

Shepheards hotel
Cairo
December 8, 1948
Dear Mother:

I have your letter of November 28 and am delighted to hear all about the progress of the beach house. Murph certainly is good to put in all that work. If he has no financial share he certainly will have a moral share in the house.

I don't think you need to worry about my proposing to sell any stock just now as I think we will have enough money, accumulated from the part of my salary that comes to me, to pay for the expenses of our home leave, when it comes. The only possibility of my wanting to dip into capital would be if we decide that we should buy a car in the States to take back to Europe. (It won't be another Lincoln, you can bet.)

We have had very bad luck on Tania's return trip from Istanbul. She has been waiting for a plane to take off since last Friday, but the weather has been so bad that none has been able to leave. I'm hoping it will get away by the coming

Friday. If not I think it might be sensible for her to come by boat at the end of the month, which is slightly cheaper.

On my advice Tania didn't try to mail me the pictures of the house you sent her as there is a <u>strong</u> possibility of their being removed from the mail between here and Istanbul. For some entirely illogical reason mail within the Middle East seems to be more strictly supervised than mail to and from overseas. As a rule pictures are simply removed as a matter of routine.

However when Tania gets here, probably within a very few days, I will see them.

We have been in the news from here as you will have seen. Something of a change.

Today I went with Mr. and Mrs. Brian Dyer to visit a 300 year-old house in the old city of Cairo. He is one of the Rockefeller foundation representatives and had arranged for us to be accompanied by the chief of police of that part of town. The house was moderately interesting. I was more particularly interested to meet the chief of police there. Mrs. Dyer is white Russian and a great friend of Tania's.

I have moved from a very small room in Shepheards to one with bath and telephone in anticipation of Tania's return. Have also lined up a small ground-floor flat with garden in case we stay here long enough to make it worthwhile. Wish Cy would make up his mind; he says the decision is up to the Publisher, who is on vacation.

We are now getting into the season of many parties. Tonight there is one given by Dr. Azcarate, the U.N. representative.

I have a very nice letter from Grandma to Tania and me and will, I promise, answer it very soon.

All my love to you all, Dana

Shepheards hotel, Cairo
December 23, 1948
Dear Mother:
A warm sun is streaming in the window and I would find it hard to remember that it is nearly Christmas if it weren't for various Christmas parties,

ELIZABETH SCHMIDT CRAHAN

Christmas cards and telegrams of good wishes from the New York office. However, I suppose it's just as warm in L.A.

I will be sending you a telegram to remind you that we are telephoning on Christmas day, but I dare say you have our letter.

Today Tom Stauffer, a girlfriend of his and Tania and I went down to the mouskey (bazaar) to look at pharaonic antiquities, modern craft work and other attractions. It was Tania's first trip to that part of town and she thoroughly enjoyed it. We acquired a camel's bell, a pair of slippers and a single dice taken from one of the excavations. The latter is a pretty thing, quite transparent when held up to the light, which we will give to Tom for Christmas. We are having Christmas dinner at his house.

Unfortunately the fighting has started up again in the Engeve and I must keep a watch over that over the holidays.

The office came through with a Christmas plum pudding and fruit cake this morning. Somewhat to my surprise I received it without difficulties in return for ten piasters customs. You will probably have to pay more than that on the brocades we have sent the family. Still, they are worth it, for they are infinitely more valuable in the States than they are out here.

One thing Tania and I want to buy if we have enough money and if we wish to go directly to Vienna from here is a large copper tray, with or without silver inlay. They make a magnificent cover for a coffee table. The Persian ones are usually considered best, but fine ones are also made here and in Damascus.

We will be thinking of you and Grandma, Steinie Ken and Elizabeth at the beach house or houses on Christmas. Hope you got your electricity in time, although I suspect the most pleasurable time is while the sun is out.

All our love once again to you all, and Happy New Year,
Dana

LETTERS HOME: 80 YEARS LATER

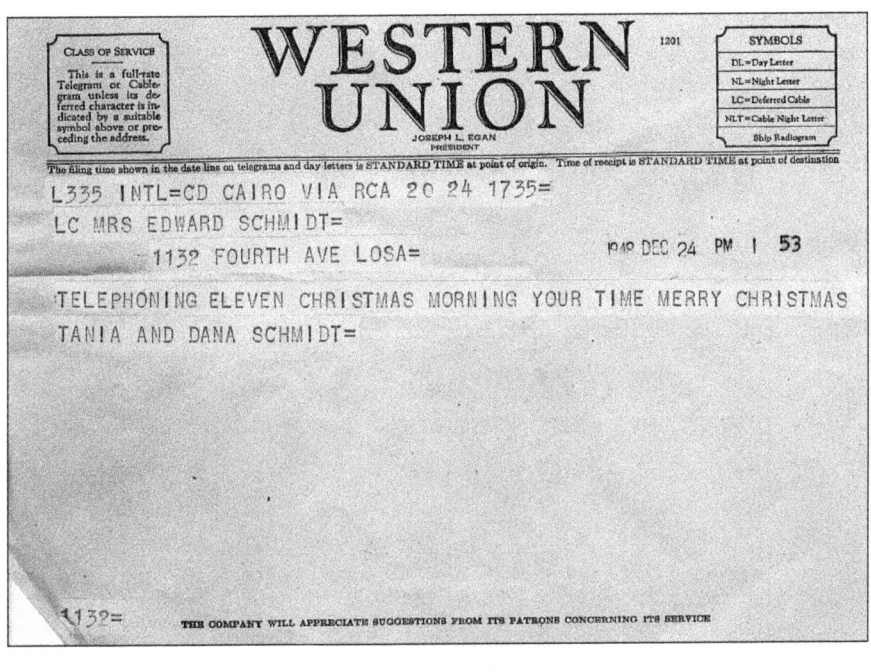

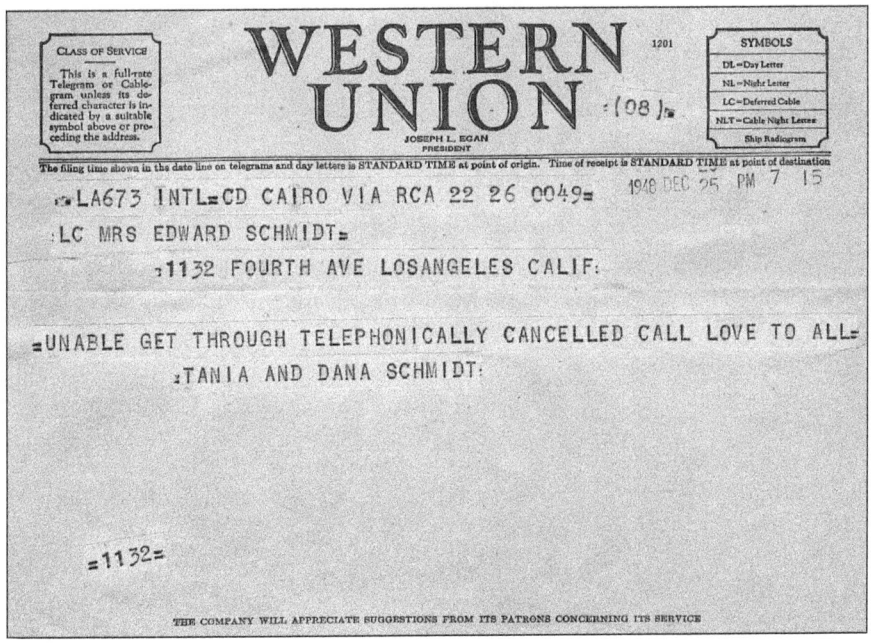

"... I got a job with *United Press* from a triumvirate consisting of Webb Miller, Harry Flory and Virgil Pinkley."
—Dana Adams Schmidt

Epilogue

[Editor's Note:] From 1949 until 1994 at the age of 78, when he died, Dana's life was just as extraordinary as it had been throughout the war years. What follows here are Dana's own words summarizing his illustrious career:

5618 Massachusetts Avenue, Bethesda, Maryland 20016
February 25, 1981

The following is an account of my career, beginning with my graduation from college and leading up to the present. I will, of course, be glad to supply any additional information required about my family, childhood and personal life.

LOS ANGELES: I received my B.A. from Pomona College, Claremont, California, and spent several months of the summer of 1937 getting my first practical newspaper experience working for the *LOS ANGELES CITY NEWS SERVICE*. Then in the fall I departed for New York, for a year at the Graduate School of Journalism of Columbia University.

From Columbia, I received a Pulitzer Travelling Fellowship at the end of the school year.

That summer I travelled as a wiper aboard a Union Oil tanker from Los Angeles through the Panama Canal to Baltimore. From there I made it aboard a freighter to London where I got a job with United Press from a triumvirate consisting of Webb Miller, Harry Flory and Virgil Pinkley. Because I could speak German they sent me to Berlin. (I had learned German as a child while we lived for several years in Vienna and Hamburg.)

WITH UNITED PRESS:

BERLIN: The next two years, with *U.P.* Berlin might justify a book. I was the junior man in the bureau, but I got good assignments. Apart from taking in calls from all of Europe I was sent into Sudetenland to monitor the German invasion. And up to Sweden to check the German invasion of Norway. And into France and the Lowlands where the Nazis were trying to convince the world that they were irresistible. We saw Stuka dive-bombing demonstrations and interviewed the top Generals.

In Berlin I was assigned to keep track of the Jewish persecution. I kept in touch with the "Juedische Gemeinderat". And generally I became the Jewish expert of the office.

In November, 1940, I was in Sofia, where we expected the Nazis to strike next. And then our correspondent in Istanbul was expelled and we exchanged posts. Thereby I got clear of the German sphere, in December, 1940.

ISTANBUL: Turkey for two years, a treasure to remember. The Bosporus sparkling in summer, the world of diplomacy and intrigue all year round. We covered the Germans in the Balkans and Greece, the Germans in Russia, and the British in Syria. German Ambassador Franz von Papen was nearly blown up a block from my house. American airmen who had bombed Ploesti came down in Turkey like rain, and were interned. We were briefed by British Ambassador Sir Hugh Knatchbull Hugessen, whose valet later sold his secret files to the Germans.

From time to time, *U.P.* asked me to help out in Cairo, British headquarters for the desert war. And on the way I got acquainted with Palestine, especially with Agrons, the founder of the Palestine Post. In Palestine I began to sense the full meaning of what I had learned as "Jewish expert" in Berlin.

AND THEN THE WAR: I served as war correspondent with the U.S. and British and French armies, navies and air forces. I did bombing tours with the Americans in Tunisia and with the British in Sicily. And I spent a lot of time with British destroyers around Italy and British motor torpedo boats looking for U-Boats. And because I could speak French it fell to me to cover the French army in Italy and during the liberation of France. I landed with the French in southern France and in Corsica.

My friend of the *London Times* and I "liberated" a French Ford and managed to go ahead of the U.S. forces into areas controlled by the French guerrillas. Because we were the first persons in allied uniforms (war correspondents) to arrive in Vichy some of the French believed we had been parachuted in. It was a moving experience. In every village the peasants rushed out to welcome us with fruit and milk.

WITH THE NEW YORK TIMES: In Paris towards the end of the war I switched allegiance from *U.P.* to the *New York Times*. Harold Callender was my boss. Liberated France was grand, and for a time I dreamed of becoming a French specialist. But soon I was transferred to Frankfurt, Germany.

FRANKFURT: There was a time in 1945 when our Sunday Review editor said I was writing the best copy out of Germany. I had the advantage of knowing Germany before the war, of speaking German, and of having studied Germany seriously in college.

I covered the Nuremberg trials. I was there when Goering was NOT executed. And my flash was first to say he had committed suicide, "cyanide-wise."

Next came Greece. I will always love Greece and the Greeks. I got up north into the areas where the Communist guerrillas and the royalist army were struggling. Hospitality of the villagers was beautiful.

In Athens I married Tania, a White Russian girl I had met in Istanbul seven years earlier. Our honeymoon turned out to be a transfer to Beirut and then to Damascus, and then to Amman and then to Jerusalem and then to Cairo.

MIDDLE EAST: From Damascus I was expelled as a spy, which is a funny story, and later reprieved thanks to the intervention of the U.S. Chargé and the Syrian President himself. We moved on to Amman by taxi, with Tania's steamer trunk sticking out the back. And we interviewed King Abdullah together (Tania interpreting in Turkish).

It came time for me to go to Jerusalem and Tania had to wait in Beirut. Too much shooting in Jerusalem. I got acquainted with the Israelis in the first days of the state. But then the *Times* asked me to move to Cairo. I managed to cross the front line during a truce, which is another hilarious story.

In Cairo we viewed King Farouk cavorting at the Semiramis roof garden. We had mock bombings and riots. But there was the Gezireh athletic club for relaxation. And we had our first apartment.

PRAGUE: In 1949, before the Palestine war was quite over I was sent to Vienna with instructions to try to get into Prague or Budapest. I got a visa to Prague and for the next year, April 1949 to May 1950, spent most of our time in Czechoslovakia. This was an experience bordering on the traumatic. The Czech people were loveable, foolishly open in friendship. The Communists were systematically destroying the middle class. The upshot of it all was a book, *ANATOMY OF A SATELLITE*, my first, published by *Atlantic Monthly Press*.

I wrote most of the book while on a NIEMAN FELLOWSHIP at Harvard. That year almost won me to the academic life. But the *New York Times* as usual lost no time whisking me away, this time to Israel.

Two years in Israel, or more, in 1950, '51 and '52. Years when Israel was a fledgling [state] and the Jewish refugees were still in temporary camps, and food was rationed. In Israel we met people who loved their life and their work. We made some friends.

I think the *Times* liked my Israel coverage, because my next assignment was Washington.

WASHINGTON: Seven years in Washington, as diplomatic and State Department correspondent. Golden years. My son was born. We had a great house on Wyoming Avenue. We entertained. We frequented the embassies.

In 1959 I managed a tour during which I interviewed Nasser, Kassem, the Shah, and Ben Gurion. Throughout my time in Washington I remained the Middle East specialist although I was also responsible for the general run of news.

This continued until April, 1961, when we were sent back to the Middle East, headquarters in Beirut.

MIDDLE EAST AGAIN: I cannot begin to recount the stories and the things we did in and out of Beirut. Coups in Syria and Baghdad, and a number of small wars.

In July, 1962, I went to Kurdistan, secretly, by subterfuge, in disguise. By mule and on foot I crossed the north of Iraq, through the mountains, to Mulla Mustafa Barzani. I wrote my second book about that, JOURNEY AMONG BRAVE MEN, again with *Atlantic Monthly Press*. And ever since I have kept in touch with Kurds.

For the stories about Kurds I received the George Polk Memorial Prize from the Overseas Press Club of New York. Another prize from Long Island University. *The Times* put my pieces up for a Pulitzer, but I didn't make it.

Dana with the Kurds

LONDON: In 1965 the *Times* sent us to London. This was fortuitous because, just before our departure from Beirut, I had a jeep accident in the desert of north Yemen and broke my neck. The Yemenis, republican and royalist, provided me with the materials for my third book, YEMEN, THE UNKNOWN WAR, this time published by *Holt, Rinehart and Winston*. I found London a fine place to live and work. But I yearned for the Middle East. And in 1968 the *Times* sent me back.

MIDDLE EAST A THIRD TIME: Second time round in Beirut my adventures were with the Palestinians. More difficult than Kurds or Yemenis. Suspicious. But I got some good pieces on training camps when they were new, and the first interview with Arafat. And of course I did all the other things, in the Gulf and Saudi Arabia, in Iran and Turkey. Even a bit in Greece. We departed before the deluge in terms of anti-foreigner riots. I found time to begin my fourth book, *ARMAGEDDON IN THE MIDDLE EAST,* again with *Holt, Rinehart and Winston.*

WASHINGTON: In August, 1970, the *Times* moved me to Washington again. I worked at the State Department and the Pentagon, and I did a lot of special stories on the drugs epidemic.

In October, 1972, I took early retirement from the *Times* to take a job as senior writer with the *Christian Science Monitor.* For the *Monitor* I flew to the Middle East with Nixon and with Kissinger, and to Moscow with Nixon. And I covered the State Department and the Pentagon.

In October, 1977, I decided to try free-lance work, and to concentrate on writing my fifth book, on the Persian Gulf. Twice I made extensive tours of the Persian Gulf and especially Iran. I interviewed the Shah for the fourth time. That was just a few months before he was overthrown. In June, 1980, I joined the *Voice of America*. This is a stimulating job on the Middle East Desk and writing special articles.

SPECIAL HONORS:
1934: Won $1,500 Bank of America contest for an essay on *The World 30 Years from Now.*
1938: Pulitzer Travelling Fellowship.
1966: Doctor of Letters, honorary, from Pomona College.

BOOKS:
ANATOMY OF A SATELLITE (about Czechoslovakia)
JOURNEY AMONG BRAVE MEN (about the Kurds)
ARMAGEDDON IN THE MIDDLE EAST (about Arabs and Israelis)

LETTERS HOME: 80 YEARS LATER

YEMEN, THE UNKNOWN WAR (about Yemen's civil war)
Still to come: book on the Persian Gulf.

In Dana's final years, he continued working for the *Christian Science Monitor*. He battled medical issues, including a successful surgery on a pituitary tumor that, however, diminished his working life considerably.

The health of his son Dana Junior, struggling with a lifetime of schizophrenia, consumed much of his time and money.

At the time of Dana Adams Schmidt's death, the *New York Times* published an obituary.

Dana with King Faisal of Saudi Arabia

ELIZABETH SCHMIDT CRAHAN

Dana's mother: Margaret Adams Schmidt

Appendix

Ftn. 8, Page 23
At the beginning of World War II, just before the attack on Pearl Harbor, Saburo Kurusu was sent as a special envoy to Washington to negotiate for peace terms with Secretary of State, Cordell Hull. Some people said that Kurusu's mission was to distract our leadership while Japan prepared for the attack on Pearl Harbor. People who knew him well did not believe that he had been told of the Japanese plan. Nevertheless, he was interned from December 1941, until June 1942.[1]

Dana had not seen the Kurusus since we lived in Vienna, but our mothers had kept in touch.

Ftn. 13, Page 34
Dana couldn't have been more pleased that Ed Beattie was one of the guests at his first breakfast at the Longs. He admired Beattie very much. Here are some comments by other correspondents that describe him:

William Shirer in *Berlin Diary* (1941), page 55:
". . . a moon-faced Churchillian countenance behind which is a nimble wit and a great store of funny stories and songs."

Quentin Reynolds on a dust jacket advertisement for *Freely to Pass:* ". . . one of the great reporters of this war. After all, he is head of the London

---

[1] Kaga, Otohiko. *Riding the East Wind*. Tokyo, New York: Kodansha, 1999. This dramatic novel is based on the life of the Kurusus during World War II. The names have been changed, but historical details have been preserved.

U.P. Bureau and the U.P. is not putting Boy Scouts in spots like that. We were together during the Battle of Britain and no more vivid reporting or brilliant writing has emerged from the war than the chapters on the Blitz in his magnificent book *Freely to Pass*—a title I like so much that if he hadn't used it I was going to steal it from him for a book of mine."

Wallace R. Deuel in the *New York Herald Tribune Books*:

"He is a red-haired giant with a consuming curiosity about life, a contempt for cant, and a hatred of inhumanity, and yet also with a robust humor . . . . Secret agents, princesses, poets, peasants, priests, policemen, chorus girls, diplomats, sailors, hotel porters, generals and correspondents throng the pages of *Freely to Pass*. No better reporter's account of this war has yet appeared."

Ed Beattie was captured by the Germans near Chaumont. Hence, he could not be considered for the position of manager of the U.P. Bureau in 1944.

Ftn. 15, Page 37
'Hostile World'
Warned at
German's Bier

Nazis Hurl Sharp Warning to World
Hitler Silent at Bier of Envoy
As Aide Accepts 'Challenge';
U.S. Issues Second Berlin Recall
By DANA ADAMS SCHMIDT

DUSSELDORF, Germany, Nov. 17—(U.P.)—Sharp warning to the world that Germany "takes up the challenge" of the assassination of Ernst vom Rath today echoed through the huge Rheinhalle where the 29-year-old nazi diplomat, slain in Paris by a Jewish youth, was given a martyr's funeral.

Joachim von Ribbentrop, German foreign minister, stood before the swastika draped catafalque and berated a "hostile world that believes it will be able to hold up the evolution of a new idea by blind hatred" as fuehrer Adolf Hitler sat with folded arms a few feet away, gazing sternly ahead.

The reichsfuehrer, who journeyed here by special train to lead tens of thousands of Nazis in tribute to Rath, did not speak at the ceremonies and hurried back to Berlin without going to the Dusseldorf cemetery where Rath was buried beneath a motto "Love never ends."

Both Ribbentrop and Ernst Bohle, head of the organization of Germans abroad, used their eulogies for biting attacks upon the Jews who have suffered a wave of nazi terrorism as result of the slaying of Rath by Herschel Grynszpan, 17, Polish Jew.

"Lies, slander, blood and terrorism are instruments of international Jewry and other destructive elements," Ribbentrop said.

"The latest victim was murdered by a cowardly paid assassin.

"Dear comrade! You, from year to year, witnessed Germany's rise under Der Fuehrer. This is more than most humans obtain from providence. You may sleep in peace. The old world is sinking.

"No terror, no hatred will again be able to enslave Germany. A nation will never perish whose sons are ready to give their lives for it. Great nations had martyrs. They are nowhere as numerous as in Germany.

"Any new wave of hatred in the world and any new attempt to slander us will find the German nation filled with deep indignation and determined to follow Der Fuehrer in ever closer union.

"I repeat Hitler's words: 'We understand the challenge and we take it up.' So we march united into Germany's future."

He referred to Hitler's eulogy and warning at the funeral of Wilhelm Gustloff, nazi leader in Switzerland, who as slain February 4, 1936, by a young Yugoslav Jew.

At the conclusion of Ribbentrop's speech the orchestra played the old German army song "Good Comrade."

Bohle, who spoke first at the catafalque as rain clouds cast gloom upon this town of 500,000 persons, said "The entire German nation is standing deeply embittered in mourning at the bier of this young German who lost his life only because he was German and hence national socialist.

"Rath's memory will remind all Germans abroad that every German abroad, whatever his vocation, is in the first place a national socialist."

Thousands lined the streets between the railroad station where Hitler arrived from Berlin and the hall as he rode slowly between lines of rigid stormtroopers.

Entering the hall, Hitler stood in his simple brown nazi garb in a moment's silence before the catafalque. Torches blazed at each corner of the bier.

The services opened to the strains of the funeral march from Beethoven's "Eroica" symphony at noon. When the service was over, 38 minutes later, Hitler clasped hands with Rath's parents and brothers, saluted and strode out of the hall.

[Caption for photo accompanying article: DEATH of Ernst vom Rath (above), young German diplomat who was fatally shot by a 17-year-old Polish Jew in Paris, is given as the cause of continued persecution of Jews in Germany by nazi spokesmen. The youth who fired the shot that is causing international complications is Herschel Grynszpan.]

Ftn. 22, Page 50

Nikolaus Horthy de Nagybana (1868-1959) commanded the Austro-Hungarian fleet in World War I. He was elected Regent of Hungary in 1920. He blocked two attempts of former Emperor Charles I to regain his throne and found himself Regent of a kingless kingdom. He guided Hungary through the years between the two World Wars. Hungary entered World War II as an ally of Germany, and despite Horthy's opposition, Germany occupied Hungary in March 1944. In October 1944, when Russian troops entered Hungary, Horthy surrendered, but the Germans forced him to revoke the surrender and resign instead. He was taken to Bavaria and later freed by the Americans. He appeared as a witness in the Nuremberg war crimes trials.

Ftn. 32, Page 100

Dana was, indeed, introduced by an expert. Robert Van Nice and William Emerson, both architects, were each carrying out their own projects in studying Hagia Sophia's structural aspects and conducting an architectural survey of the building, occasionally collaborating with the Byzantine Institute staff and Thomas Whittemore (1871-1950).

One of the largest churches in the world, Hagia Sofia, was built between 532 and 537 in the reign of Emperor Justinian. The extraordinary mosaics illustrating Christian themes were part of the original church. In 1453, Constantinople was conquered by the Turks, and Sultan Mehmet ordered that Hagia Sophia become a mosque. Minarets were added at this time, and the figural mosaics were covered with plaster and paint.

Hagia Sofia

In 1847, Sultan Abdul Medjed commissioned the Fossatis, architects and brothers of Switzerland to clean and restore the mosque. The Byzantine figural mosaics were discovered by accident during work on the revetments and plaster in 1848. A newly uncovered mosaic was shown to the Sultan, and he was so impressed by the golden cubes he saw that he ordered the mosaics cleared of plaster. The Fossatis understood the significance of the mosaics and prepared drawings and watercolors of them. But further work was not done. Because of the Islamic prohibition of representation of the human figure, the figural panels were re-covered with plaster and painted.

Thomas Whittemore claimed that the mosaics survived largely due to the work of the Fossatis. In 1931, Kemal Atatürk, President of Turkey, opened the mosque as a museum. Under his auspices, restoration of the mosque was again begun. The leader and promoter of the restoration was Thomas Whittemore, one of the Founders of the Byzantine Institute, whose purpose was to promote the study of Byzantine art, history and architecture. The Institute gave priority to uncovering and consolidating the mosaics of the Hagia Sophia in one of the largest conservation projects of the 20th century. The project took eighteen years. The Byzantine Institute is under the auspices of Harvard University, with headquarters at Dumbarton Oaks outside of Washington, D.C.

This information is from Teteriatnikov, Natalia B. *Mosaics of Hagia Sophia, Istanbul: the Fossati Restoration* and the Work of the Byzantine Institute. Washington, D.C. Dumbarton Oaks, Trustees for Harvard University, 1998; and from Yenen, Şerif, *Turkish Odyssey: a Cultural Guide to Turkey*, 3rd ed. Istanbul, 2001.

Ftn. 34, Page 114

In 1941, Iran conducted substantial trade with Germany, and many Germans lived in Iran. They valued the Germans as business partners and for their technical ability. After Germany invaded the Soviet Union in June of 1941, the expansionist aims of Hitler became clear. The Allies were concerned about the possibility of another attack on the Soviet Union through Iran. They demanded that Iran deport the German colony so close to the border with the Soviets. The Shah, Reza Pahlavi, refused, and on August 25, the British and Soviets invaded Iran. They encountered little resistance, and on September 17, the Iranians surrendered. The Shah was forced to resign and was sent to Africa. His son, Mohammad, who was friendly to the Allies, was installed as Shah.

The Allies had other reasons for the invasion. They wanted to protect their source of oil and the Anglo-Iranian oil company, as well as the Persian corridor and the Trans-Iranian Railway.

Ftn. 37, Page 118

The attitude of Turks concerning dogs is based on the Hadiths, which along with the Koran, formed much of Islamic ideology. According to Jonah Goldberg in the *National Review* of December 2, 2002, the Koran makes reference to dogs only a few times and then, not negatively. The Hadiths contain some 400-500 references to dogs, all derogatory. The Hadiths are collections of purported sayings of Muhammad, supposedly by his contemporaries. Following are a few concerning dogs:

1. Money from the sale of a dog is as dirty as money from the earnings of a prostitute.

2. Angels will not enter a house if it contains a dog or a picture of a living creature.

3. Dogs are unclean. If a dog has licked a dish, you must purify it by washing it eight times—seven times with water and once with earth.

4. Muhammad ordered all dogs killed, except dogs used for hunting, guarding herds or protecting cultivated lands, and protection of houses. The Anatolian sheepdog, well known for guarding sheep, would therefore be welcomed.

Ftn. 43, Page 152

Our mother was, indeed, an accomplished writer. She valued clear writing and good literature, read us the children's classics, and encouraged our writing simple thank you notes as soon as we could form letters. She was aware of her own ability to write, honed at Pelham Manor, preparatory boarding school, and Western Reserve University. A summer session at Columbia's Graduate School of Journalism encouraged her to write for publication.

When we lived in Europe, she published a steady stream of articles in the *Chicago Tribune* and *The Christian Science Monitor*. She wrote for magazines, including *Spur, Business Week* and *Travel*. Her topics were many and diverse: the harbor in Hamburg, Germany, business and high tariffs, exports and imports, and even, the swans on the Alster, the central lake in Hamburg. She wrote about horse derbies and shows and dog shows, as well as tennis tournaments and the new babies at the Hagenbeck Zoo.

Her stories for children were published in magazines such as John Martin's Book, *Girls' Companion, Boys World* and *Storyland*. These were usually based on Dana's and my adventures as we were growing up, living in Europe, going to school in foreign lands, vacationing at the seashore or skiing in the Alps, learning to ride horseback, learning to play tennis and to swim. The topics were manifold.

Mother's long editorship of the *Alumni News*, which became the *Orthopaedic Hospital News*, in Los Angeles, was a major achievement. She served as editor from the inception of the *Alumni News* in 1935 until her death in 1978. The publication was highly prized by the staff of the hospital and its supporters. Besides its value for attracting financial support and building morale among patients, it served as a history of the hospital.

Ftn. 51, Page 159

Kenneth Acker was my first husband. We met as students at the School of Architecture at the University of Southern California and were married in June of 1938. Ken went on to take the State Board Exam and practiced architecture. He had an interesting interlude working with the renowned designer and industrial artist Charles Eames and worked on his famous house in the Pacific

Palisades (on the coast in Santa Monica, California.) Ken was very helpful with the steel frame and structural aspects of the Eames home. During the War, Ken worked for the US Navy.

Ftn. 53, Page 160

Towards the end of World War Two, many city planners and architects (including Ken and me) were envisioning an ideal postwar world in which planning of all aspects of the environment for living would be intelligently carried out, and shortcomings of the past would be remedied with new creative thinking.

A group of Los Angeles area professionals: city planners, architects, furniture designers, landscape architects, transportation experts, and a few social workers formed an organization called "Telesis." The name was derived from Greek *telein,* to complete, and *telos,* end. It was interpreted to mean "progress intelligently planned and directed." [*Webster's Third International Dictionary of the English Language*, Unabridged, 1993]

The group was interested in developing new plans for housing, including landscape design and community resources, city planning and transportation, hospitals, schools, recreation and athletic facilities, swimming pools and athletic fields, and shopping centers.

Models of ideal communities were made. The new freeways were shown connecting residential areas to each other and to the metropolitan centers of finance and industry. (We thought freeways were magic solutions for getting around sprawling cities.)

We put our ideas together, the models and suitable text, in an exhibition offered at the Museum of Science and Industry. We were pleased when the *Los Angeles Times* featured the show in a special section.

Our thinking was, of course, influenced by the great designers and architects of the period. To name a few, I remember—Eero Saarinen, Frank Lloyd Wright, Le Corbusier, Charles and Ray Eames, Isamu Noguchi, Alexander Calder, Alvar Aalto, Norman Bel Geddes, and Lewis Mumford.

Ftn. 54, Page 160

Ida Treat (1884-1978) was one of the most interesting and inspiring people I have known, and I am sure Dana would agree. She was Mother's friend from college days; they both went to Western Reserve University in Cleveland and to the Sorbonne in Paris.

Ida stayed in France after earning a Doctorate of Letters at the Sorbonne. She married André Bergeret, a captain in the French Merchant Marine. Dana and I met Ida when we were teenagers and spent several summers with her and our mother on a little island off the rocky coast of Brittany where Ida had bought a typical Breton stone house. Dana and I were introduced to French intellectual life through the many artists and writers who came to visit.

Ida had traveled widely in Europe and also in China, the South Seas and Africa. I remember her talking about romantic-sounding places like Mozambique. Nobody we knew had ever been there.

When World War II broke out, Ida was in France. In *The Anchored Heart,* she describes France during the occupation from her home in Brittany, the same stone house where we had spent summers with her. Dana went to see her at the end of the war in Paris.

As children, we were fascinated by Ida's tales of visits to her mother-in-law in the little village of Fiacre in the French Pyrenees. We were excited to hear of her exploration of caves with prehistoric drawings of bison, horses and reindeer.

Ida taught English at Vassar from 1948 to 1954. Her several books and voluminous correspondence with authors and artists are in the Vassar archives.

Ftn. 71, page 202

It is unlikely that many of the men knew that the first organized school of medicine was established here at Salerno in the early 11th century. It attracted students from all over Europe, Asia and Africa and was one of the places where Arabic medicine and the teaching of advanced thinkers, like Avicenna, were introduced to Europe. Some of the men may have been able to go ashore here and see some of the ruins, but British and American troops could not spend time thinking of history. The war was too important and commanded most of their thinking and energy.

Ftn. 73, Page 208

Elaine Meekins was a good friend I met at Wellesley College. We lived in the same dormitory in an old house in the Village when we were both freshmen and spent many nights together writing papers and having long discussions. I remember we ate lots of delicious litchi nuts (fruit of a Chinese tree). Elaine graduated from Wellesley in 1935. My family moved to Los Angeles, and I transferred to the School of Architecture at the University of Southern California. The summer we spent at La Jolla, Elaine lived with her mother at nearby Laguna Beach. She was doing freelance writing, which was being published. I was impressed. She married Gordon Fowler, a naval officer, and lived in Italy for many years. I had lost track of her, but according to the Wellesley Alumni Directory, she is living in Fairfax, Virginia.

Ftn. 74, page 213

La Maddalena and Corsica became vital for fuel and military supplies in the invasion of Italy and later in the invasion of southern France.

At Maddalena, 59,000 barrels existed for bulk storage of oil. The Allies constructed an additional 111,000 for bulk storage on the island.

They constructed a small, artificial port at Porto Vecchio on the southeast coast of Corsica, not far from La Maddalena, and connected it with a pipeline to Bastia (on the northeastern coast). This pipeline had a capacity of 45,000 barrels daily and could be operated in either direction. In addition, 100,000 barrels in tankers were kept as floating storage at Maddalena.

On Corsica, 14 airfields were constructed, which maintained supplies needed to maintain 40 U.S., British and French squadrons, vital for the success of the Allies' landings on the coast of southern France in August of 1944.

Capri, at the southern entrance to the Bay of Naples and loved by tourists for its rugged coastline with the blue grotto and handsome villas and gardens, is a small but strategically located island. It was a resort loved by Roman emperors. On September 12, the Allies took Capri without firing a shot.

Ftn. 82, Page 230

General Theodore Roosevelt, Jr. (son of President Theodore Roosevelt) won a Congressional Medal of Honor for his gallantry and intrepidity at the risk of his life above and beyond the call of duty. The citation read in part:

"After two verbal requests to accompany the leading assault elements in the Normandy invasion had been denied, Brig. Gen. Roosevelt's written request for this mission was approved, and he landed with the first wave of the forces assaulting the enemy-held beaches. He repeatedly led groups from the beach over the seawall and established them inland. His valor, courage, and presence in the very front of the attack and his complete unconcern at being under heavy fire inspired the troops to heights of enthusiasm and self-sacrifice. Although the enemy had the beach under constant direct fire, Brig. Gen. Roosevelt moved from one locality to another, rallying men around him, directed and personally led them against the enemy. Under his seasoned, precise, calm, and unfaltering leadership, assault troops reduced beach strong points and rapidly moved inland with minimum casualties. He thus contributed substantially to the successful establishment of the beachhead in France."

Ftn. 83, Page 230

|: John Brown's body lies a-mouldering in the grave, :|
John Brown's body lies a-mouldering in the grave,
But his soul goes marching on.
Chorus:
|: Glory, glory, hallelujah, :|
Glory, glory, hallelujah,
His soul goes marching on.
|: He's gone to be a soldier in the Army of the Lord, :|
He's gone to be a soldier in the Army of the Lord,
His soul goes marching on.
Chorus
|: John Brown's knapsack is strapped upon his back, :|
John Brown's knapsack is strapped upon his back,
His soul goes marching on.

Chorus
|: John Brown died that the slaves might be free, :|
John Brown died that the slaves might be free,
His soul goes marching on.
Chorus
|: The stars above in Heaven now are looking kindly down, :|
The stars above in Heaven now are looking kindly down,
His soul goes marching on.
Chorus

Ftn. 94, Page 258
Their plans culminated on July 20 at Hitler's headquarters at Rastenburg, East Prussia. Count von Stauffenberg placed a bomb in a briefcase under or near Hitler's desk. Unfortunately, someone moved the briefcase to see more clearly the map Hitler was studying, and Hitler was injured but not killed. Other officers who were nearby were killed.

Had the bomb succeeded, it was agreed that in the future, the army must not dominate the new government. Western allies would be persuaded that German militarism was not to be perpetuated. *World War Two.* American edition London, New York: Dorling Kindersley, Ltd., 2001 p. 544.

Ftn. 100, Page 339
Maurice Thorez was born in 1900 into a poor family. At age twelve, he worked in the coal mines. He joined the Socialist and then the Communist Party in 1920 and was imprisoned several times for agitation. In 1930, he became secretary-general of the party. In 1934, he was called to Moscow for talks. He switched the party to collaboration with the Communists, Socialists, and Radical Socialists. They won the election of 1936 and enacted long -neglected social legislation.

The Daladier government banned the Communist Party for its opposition to the War. Thorez was tried in absentia and stripped of his French citizenship, leaving Jacques Duclos to be leader of the underground. He went to the USSR in 1943.

In 1944, after France was liberated, de Gaulle exonerated and restored his citizenship. Thorez was elected to the Chamber of deputies and became minister of state in 1946 and 1947.

In 1958, with de Gaulle in power again, the Communist party had only ten seats in the Chamber, but Thorez retained his seat.

Ftn. 106, page 361
Article by Dana: **CHANNEL ISLANDS FACE CASH INQUIRY**
See newspaper clipping page 845.

Ftn. 107, page 372
Article by Dana: **EISENHOWER GETS TOP FRENCH HONOR**
See newspaper clipping page 847.

Ftn. 108, page 377
Article by Dana: **FRENCH CHALLENGE BRITAIN ON LEVANT**
See newspaper clipping page 850.

Ftn. 109, 110 page 378
RUSSIANS DEMAND VOICE ON TANGIER
Anglo-American-French Parley Set for Today Postponed Because of Request
By DANA ADAMS SCHMIDT
By Wireless to THE NEW YORK TIMES

PARIS, July 2—A conference to determine the provisional international status of Tangier to replace Spain's administration, which was to have begun among French, British and American representatives here tomorrow, was postponed today after the Russian Government had notified the French Foreign Ministry that it desired to participate.

Russia, which has just emphasized her interest in access to the Mediterranean by demanding bases in the Bosporus and the Dardanelles, thereby put on record her interest also in the western exit from the Mediterranean. Some diplomatic quarters expressed the opinion that a general conference with

Russian participation would eventually be necessary to settle the manifold interrelated problems of the entire Mediterranean.

French officials said that the immediate question of Russian participation in the Tangier conference would have to be discussed with Britain and the United States through diplomatic channels. They suggested that the representatives already on hand, however, might carry on as a gathering of experts to draft a joint note to Madrid laying down the steps by which the Spanish authorities should evacuate the international zone.

The American delegation here is composed of Henry Villard, chief of the African division of the State Department; J. Rives Childs, the former American chargé d'affaires in Tangier, and Ernest J. Dempsey of the American Legation there. The head of the British delegation is Charles Peake, British Consul General in Tangier, and the chief French delegate is Jacques Meyrier, administrative director of the Foreign Ministry.

The Russian communication to the French Foreign Ministry stated that the Russian Government had been officially informed by the French only last Saturday that the conference would take place and that the Russians "would be kept informed." The Russian request for participation raises a new complication in that Russia has no diplomatic relations with Spain. It had been tentatively proposed to bring Spaniards into the Tangier discussions later in view of the evident Spanish interest in the area situated within Spanish Morocco.

Neither Russia nor the United States is a signatory of the Tangier Convention of 1923. The American view has been that an entirely new international regime should be set up. This is understood to be also the Russian view.

The French position, however, has hitherto been that the old convention should be declared to be again in force and that the United States and other interested parties should be brought into the regime by special arrangement. This would have insured the maintenance of all former French rights and of the rights of the Sultan of Morocco, who is also Sultan of Tangier. The British, taking a middle ground, have favored the modification of the old convention.

Ftn. 111, page 379
Article by Dana: **DE GUALLE TRIUMPH IS ANTICIPATED IN FIGHT FOR A 2-HOUSE PARLIAMENT**
See newspaper clipping page 851.

Ftn. 112, page 380
Article by Dana: **FRANCE AND RUSSIA SIGN ACCORD TO RETURN 500,000 FRENCHMEN**
See newspaper clipping page 853.

Ftn. 113, page 380
Article by Dana: **FRENCH ASSEMBLY DEBATES ALGERIA**
See newspaper clipping page 855.

Ftn. 114, page 381
Articles by Dana: **LAVAL LODGED IN PARIS CELL; BRITISH CALL HIM WAR PLOTTER** & **LAVAL IS LODGED IN CELL IN PARIS**
See newspaper clippings pages 856–858.

Ftn. 115, page 382
Article by Dana entitled: **THOREZ CRITICIZES DE GAULLE REGIME**
See newspaper clipping page 858.

Ftn. 116, Page 390
Yalta Conference (February 4-11).
This was Roosevelt's last meeting with Churchill and Stalin.
Following are some of the postwar concerns discussed and agreed upon:
Germany was to be divided into four zones of occupation to be administered by the United States, Britain, France and the Soviet Union.
Germany was to be demilitarized. War criminals were to be tried by an international court (Nürnberg).

In the liberated countries of eastern Europe and accepted by Stalin, interim governments representative of all democratic elements of the population were to be included, and early free elections were to be held.

Poland's frontiers were discussed but not determined.

A secret agreement was reached with the Soviet Union providing that, in return for its entering the war against Japan in two to three months after Germany's surrender, the Soviet Union would regain territory lost to Japan in the Russo-Japanese War of 1904-05. The Soviets were assured that the status quo would be maintained in Outer Mongolia. Stalin agreed to sign a pact of friendship with China. Roosevelt and Churchill trusted Stalin, and also they thought that Russian assistance might be needed in the war against Japan.

Dumbarton Oaks (August-October, 1944)

Plans were made for dividing Germany into four zones of occupation: U.S., British, French, and Soviet. Similarly, Berlin was divided into four zones.

Plans were laid for the formation of the United Nations and to invite France and China to a founding conference to be held in San Francisco. Stalin succeeded in getting agreement to admit Ukraine and Belorussia (Belarus) to the United Nations. The Yalta Conference had confirmed the policy of demanding Germany's unconditional surrender.

Yalta Conference (2006) in Encyclopedia Britannica. Retrieve August 13, 2006, from Encyclopedia Britannica Premium Service: http://www.Britannica.com/eb/article 9077748.

Ftn. 117, page 396
Articles by Dana: **FRENCH TELL U.S. OF POST-WAR NEED & FRANCE TO SHARE IN THE SURRENDER**
See newspaper clippings page 861 & 863.

Ftn. 118, page 412
Numan Menemencioglu, born in Baghdad in 1893, was the product of two prominent intellectual families. His father and his grandfather were both in the Turkish diplomatic service, and his mother came from a leading Swiss family. One of her relatives was the well-known poetess Nafik Kemal. Menemencioglu

was sent to schools where French was the language of lessons—very important in the world of diplomacy. He also learned some German before studying law at the University of Lausanne.

Menemencioglu's father's great grandfather was said to have been a farmer in Sussex. When farming was poor in England, he emigrated to Turkey, where he married a Turkish woman. There was an international atmosphere in this family. It was not surprising that Numan became a prominent minister of foreign affairs. One of his outstanding achievements was to intervene when the Vichy government attempted to send Turkish Jews to concentration camps. He insisted to the Vichy authorities that Turkish Jews were Turks and could not be deported. There would be grave consequences, he warned. He saved many Jews.

Ftn. 127, Page 460
Ernst Wilhelm Nay was born in Berlin in 1902 and studied with Karl Hofer at the Berlin Art Academy from 1925-1928. Karl Hofer, a German artist, spent many years in France and Italy during the war. His style, with harsh, brilliant colors, perhaps expressed his bitterness with the war. Nay was inspired by the work of a number of other artists, especially Ernst Ludwig Kirchner, Henri Matisse and Nicolas Poussin. Kirchner was the leader of a group of Expressionist artists called 'die Brueke' (the bridge). In 1937, the Nazis confiscated many of his works as 'degenerate.' His work was characterized by erotic themes, vibrant colors, and often angular forms. He committed suicide in 1938. The well-known French painter Matisse was already well established when Nay was a student, and his work, as well as that of other Impressionists, influenced Nay. Nicolas Poussin, the famous French Baroque artist of the 17th century, was also said to have influenced Nay. In 1931, while studying at the Villa Massimo in Rome, Nay began to produce abstract and surrealist paintings. He received a grant from the expressionist Norwegian artist Edvard Munch, which enabled Nay to spend time on the Lofoten Islands in Norway, where he achieved his first noteworthy work. Two of his works were displayed in the notorious exhibition of 'Degenerate Art,' and Nay was forbidden by the Nazis to exhibit any longer. Nay's work is exhibited in many American and European galleries. *Cambridge Biographical Dictionary, 1990.*

The water-color which Dana bought of 'a man returning home' is reproduced in black and white on page 460 of this book. It was, of course, a universal theme in 1946.

Page 463
Article by Dana: **GERMAN CITY VOTE CLOSE IN BIG POLL**
CHRISTIAN SOCIAL UNION LEADS FOR WHOLE U.S. ZONE, WITH SOCIAL DEMOCRATS STRONG
COMMUNIST TALLY LAGS
CATHOLIC PARTY MAINTAINS HOLD IN BAVARIA BUT FALLS BELOW ITS EXPECTED STRENGTH
See newspaper clipping page 865.

CHANNEL ISLANDS
FACE CASH INQUIRY

**Confiscation of Black-Market
Profits Is Being Considered
by British Authorities**

By DANA ADAMS SCHMIDT
By Wireless to THE NEW YORK TIMES

ST. PETER PORT, Guernsey, May 20—The possible confiscation of black-market profits made during the German occupation and the horrors of a Gestapo concentration camp on Alderney Island were the main topics of conversation among Channel Islanders tonight, a fortnight after their liberation.

Home Office and local officials, it was understood, are studying the possibilities of clamping a tight exchange control around the islands and checking bank accounts and hoarded currency. This would be facilitated on Guernsey by the fact that the island has its own special currency—£45,000 of it—almost all of which disappeared from circulation during the occupation.

If all this old money, as well as the currency issued in exchange for German occupation money, should be called in, a census of illicit fortunes would be well on its way. Most of the black marketing concerned French manufactured goods, wines, flour and coal bought or smuggled from the Continent.

It seemed unlikely that the full truth would ever be known about the Alderney concentration camp, where about 1,000 Jews and Russians are believed to have been murdered by starvation and beatings. British officers are examining mass graves and two Russian prisoners who were confined in a separate punishment camp on the island confirmed the local inhabitants' stories that at least 800 persons died.

The entire camp has been carefully destroyed by the Germans and all the troops involved are gone. The people of Guernsey and Jersey, cut off from all inter-island communication, knew nothing about the horrors until reporters had visited Alderney.

One hundred thirty-one Russian and 194 French North African prisoners are still on Guernsey. Of the 27,500 Germans on all the islands, 3,300 are being kept here to help clear 250,000 land mines and to rehabilitate the houses that they occupied. They are being kept in reservations in the center of each island.

Meanwhile the islanders are returning to their normal affairs—the cultivation of tomatoes and potatoes, keeping cows and preparing to receive tourists. Seen from the air, the islands still sparkle in the sunlight with a myriad glass houses from which Britain's earliest vegetables come, but much of the glass was broken in a score of bombing and strafing raids or used to replace the towns' broken windows. The Germans made repeated efforts to exploit the industry but rarely succeeded in transporting tomatoes to the Continent before they rotted.

Tourists are unlikely to be welcome until next year because of the food problem. But cows are more numerous than before because the Germans, surprisingly, requisitioned only a few and were contented with a large proportion of milk. The stock's fame has been slightly polluted by the importation of continental bulls, but in Guernsey farmers succeeded in diverting the foreign bulls to slaughter houses.

There is no doubt that the Germans, at vast expense, dug themselves in for a long stay. No one knows what the Germans would have imposed if they had conquered all Britain, but on the Channel islands there was no attempt to organize the Nazi party or recruit for the Elite Guard troops. Prayers for the King were permitted to continue in the churches and Germans tried to convince the islanders that they—good Nordics like themselves, notwithstanding the predominant French normal element—had only the eastern Bolshevik hordes to fear and should never have gone to war with Germany. The front pages of newspapers were monopolized by communiqués and Lord Haw Haw's broadcasts.

EISENHOWER GETS TOP FRENCH HONOR

Paris Acclaims General Wildly as de Gaulle Presents Cross of Liberation

By DANA ADAMS SCHMIDT
By Wireless to THE NEW YORK TIMES

PARIS, June 14—Gen. Dwight D. Eisenhower spent today, his last full day before his triumphal return to the United States, as a guest of the first country liberated by his armies, and he received from Gen. Charles de Gaulle the highest honors that France can bestow.

The roar of welcome that he received from hundreds of thousands of Parisians as he drove down the Champs-Elysees—five years to the day after German troops had done the same—standing, saluting and grinning in an open car after having received the Cross of Liberation from General de Gaulle at the Arc de Triomphe, was meant for the man who more than any other in the French mind personifies liberation and victory. Tonight General Eisenhower sat at General de Gaulle's right at a ceremonial dinner in General de Gaulle's offices

EISENHOWER GETS TOP FRENCH HONOR

Paris Acclaims General Wildly as de Gaulle Presents Cross of Liberation

By DANA ADAMS SCHMIDT
By Wireless to THE NEW YORK TIMES

PARIS, June 14—Gen. Dwight D. Eisenhower spent today, his last full day before his triumphal return to the United States, as a guest of the first country liberated by his armies, and he received from Gen. Charles de Gaulle the highest honors that France can bestow.

The roar of welcome that he received from hundreds of thousands of Parisians as he drove down the Champs-Elysées—five years to the day after German troops had done the same—standing, saluting and grinning in an open car after having received the Cross of Liberation from General de Gaulle at the Arc de Triomphe, was meant for the man who more than any other in the French mind personifies liberation and victory. Tonight General Eisenhower sat at General de Gaulle's right at a ceremonial dinner in General de Gaulle's offices in the Rue St. Dominique and received from him a gold-hilted sword that had belonged to Napoléon Bonaparte as First Consul, as well as a gold cigarette case with five small sapphire stars set in a circle.

General Bedell Smith, General Eisenhower's Chief of Staff; Air Chief Marshal Sir Arthur William Tedder, his deputy for air; Lieut. Gen. Sir Frederick B. Morgan, General Smith's deputy; members of the French Cabinet and Allied diplomats were present. The American Ambassador, Jefferson Caffery, sat at General de Gaulle's left.

Praised by de Gaulle

Toasting General Eisenhower, General de Gaulle declared that he had brought the United Nations "to a victory beyond imagination in this gigantic and strange war of coalition." He praised particularly "his manner of doing it * * * his aptitude for grasping problems by their human as well as their technical angles." General de Gaulle said:

"Among the facts that this war has brought out and that will henceforth incalculably influence events is the fact that the United States is now a very great power. When such development is reached by a nation, it confers great power, which brings great responsibilities."

Replying, General Eisenhower said:

"You have criticized me, but I have been criticized by experts. Your criticism was that I was too friendly an American to be in Europe. But in one way or another America owes a debt of sentiment or some other kind of debt to every nation in Europe. There is the blood of every nation of Europe in America. There may have been differences—you and I have had some. But let us bring our troubles to each other frankly and face them together. * * *

"I hope that America will be friendly with every nation in Europe. If ever I have to be hanged, I hope that it will be for being too friendly."

Workers Cheer Loudest

On his triumphal tour through Paris, General Eisenhower stopped at the Invalides, looked down at Napoleon's sarcophagus and stood for a moment before Marshal Foch's monument. The loudest cheers of all came as he drove through the workers quarters around the Place de la Bastille on his way to the Hôtel de Ville for a reception by the President of the Municipal Council, André Le Troquer, whom he knew well as a French Commissioner in Algiers.

Several hundred of France's and the Allies' great and near-great crowded in the reception halls of the Hôtel de Ville heard General Eisenhower say that, while men would always argue what had been the turning-point of the war, he for one thought that it was the moment when the Germans discovered that France, like other occupied countries, could not successfully be enslaved. "Hitler found that the resistance made France a drag on him instead of an asset," he said. He traced the activities of the French Forces of the Interior in blowing up bridges, cutting lines of communications and of even overpowering garrisons.

"One thing I can tell you which will make you glad," he declared amidst applause, "if, like many Americans, you have a trace of vengeance in your hearts. Berlin is destroyed."

"Three million Americans will now carry back to America affection and admiration for France."

All the way in from the Orly airfield on the outskirts of Paris, Parisians lined the streets, stood on rooftops and hung from trees, lamp posts and flag-draped windows to see the hero. Among the generals, admirals and diplomats at the Arc de Triomphe he found an old friend from French North Africa, General Henri - Honoré Giraud. General Eisenhower paused for several minutes in earnest conversation with him as he waited for General de Gaulle.

General de Gaulle had invited General Giraud to attend the ceremonies, The Associated Press reported.

in the Rue St. Dominique and received from him a gold-hilted sword that had belonged to Napoléon Bonaparte as First Consul, as well as a gold cigarette case with five small sapphire stars set in a circle.

Lieut. Gen. Walter Bedell Smith, General Eisenhower's Chief of Staff; Air Chief Marshal Sir Arthur William Tedder, his deputy for air; Lieut. Gen. Sir Frederick B. Morgan, General Smith's deputy; members of the French Cabinet and Allied diplomats were present. The American Ambassador, Jefferson Caffery, sat at General de Gaulle's left.

Praised by de Gaulle

Toasting General Eisenhower, General de Gaulle declared that he had brought the United Nations "to a victory beyond imagination in this gigantic and strange war of coalition." He praised particularly "his manner of doing it * * * his aptitude for grasping problems by their human as well as their technical angles." General de Gaulle said:

"Among the facts that this war has brought out and that will henceforth incalculably influence events is the fact that the United States is now a very great power. When such development is reached by a nation, it confers great power, which brings great responsibilities."

Replying, General Eisenhower said:

"You have criticized me, but I have been criticized by experts. Your criticism was that I was too friendly an American to be in Europe. But in one way or another America owes a debt of sentiment or some other kind of debt to every nation in Europe. There is the blood of every nation of Europe in America. There may have been differences—you and I have had some. But let us bring our troubles to each other frankly and face them together. * * *

"I hope that America will be friendly with every nation in Europe. If ever I have to be hanged, I hope that it will before being too friendly."

Workers Cheer Loudest

On his triumphal tour through Paris, General Eisenhower stopped at the Invalides, looked down at Napoléon's sarcophagus and stood for a moment before Marshal Foch's monument. The loudest cheers of all came as he drove through the workers' quarters around the Place de la Bastille on his way to the Hôtel de Ville for a reception by the President of the Municipal Council, André Le Troquer, whom he knew well as a French Commissioner in Algiers.

Several hundred of France's and the Allies' great and near-great crowded in the reception halls of the Hôtel de Ville heard General Eisenhower say that, while men would always argue what had been the turning-point of the war, he for one thought that it was the moment when the Germans discovered that France, like other occupied countries, could not successfully be enslaved. "Hitler found that the resistance made France a drag on him instead of an asset," he said. He traced the activities of the French Forces of the Interior in blowing up bridges, cutting lines of communications and even overpowering garrisons.

"One thing I can tell you which will make you glad," he declared amidst applause, "if, like many Americans, you have a trace of vengeance in your hearts. Berlin is destroyed.

"Three million Americans will now carry back to America affection and admiration for France."

All the way in from the Orly airfield on the outskirts of Paris, Parisians lined the streets, stood on rooftops and hung from trees, lamp posts and flag-draped windows to see the hero. Among the generals, admirals and diplomats at the Arc de Triomphe he found an old friend from French North Africa, General Henri-Honoré Giraud. General Eisenhower paused for several minutes in earnest conversation with him as he waited for General de Gaulle.

General de Gaulle had invited General Giraud to attend the ceremonies, The Associated Press reported.

FRENCH CHALLENGE BRITAIN ON LEVANT

Again Charge London Broke 1941 Agreement on Control of Syria and Lebanon

By DANA ADAMS SCHMIDT
By Wireless to THE NEW YORK TIMES

PARIS, June 23—Replying to the British rejection of the French suggestion for a five-power conference to mediate the Lebanese dispute, the French Government sent a note to the British Foreign Office tonight charging that the British even now were preparing to intervene in Lebanon and that their intervention in Syria had violated the Lyttelton-de Gaulle agreement.

The terms of the note were incorporated in an inspired commentary issued by the semi-official French News Agency on yesterday's British Government statement threatening British military intervention against whoever might be guilty of fomenting disorder in the Levant states.

This statement, according to the agency, implied a "prelude to new measures of eviction" directed against the French in other regions.

The British statement, according to the agency, indicated the following points:

That the British Government admitted it had violated the Lyttelton-de Gaulle agreement of July 23, 1941, which delegated the responsibility for the maintenance of order to the French. The statement said that the British had assumed this function and intended to continue to exercise it.

That the necessity of evacuating French forces and civilians, which the British claim to have undertaken to protect their lives, showed that the British were unequal to the self-imposed tasks of maintaining order.

That the British intention of handing over the responsibility for the maintenance of order to the Syrian and Lebanese Governments had no legal basis, since the British already had formally recognized French responsibility for order in the Levant, and that the British intention would place the maintenance or order in the hands of those who provoked the disorder, thanks to which the British carried out their intervention.

These considerations, the agency observed, determine the "weight that should be attached to the British declaration that the intervention of British troops does not imply any British intention to evict France from Syria and Lebanon."

De Gaulle Triumph Is Anticipated In Fight for a 2-House Parliament

By DANA ADAMS SCHMIDT
By Wireless to THE NEW YORK TIMES

PARIS, July 6—Although the special meeting of the French Cabinet tomorrow to decide what kind of body shall be elected to write a new French Constitution next autumn, is expected to be stormy, all indication tonight were that Gen. Charles de Gaulle would get his way without precipitating a Governmental crisis.

He is expected to insist on the election of a two-house Parliament—a Chamber of Deputies and a Senate—in the manner of the Constitution of 1875, despite the opposition of all Left Wing and Resistance groups, who demand a single-chamber Assembly. Even the most pro-de Gaulle political group of all, the Catholic Popular republican movement, which counts three Cabinet Ministers as members, has argued against the two-chamber project, and only the Radical socialist and Right Wing groups have supported General de Gaulle.

Communists Deny Rumor

The belief that General de Gaulle would be the winner in this trial of strength was supported by a statement issued by the Communist party saying that, contrary to rumor, the two Communist members of the Cabinet would not resign even if the Government imposed a two-chamber body. The statement was issued after consultations between Communists Maurice Thorez and Jacques Duclos and a group of Socialists who favored the joint Communist-Socialist threat of resignation if General de Gaulle proved adamant.

The socialists tonight still were divided on whether or not to resign, but such a move was thought unlikely. One socialist remarked bitterly that the Communists, after leading the campaign for a single-chamber Constitutional Assembly, had left their allies out on a limb.

This situation led some quarters to believe that "the States General of the French Renaissance," a vast gathering of representative of Committees of National Liberation from all parts of France scheduled July 10 to 14, may prove something of a political dud.

Paris Papers Bitter

The Communist, who had taken the most active part in organizing it, had intended it to be a great demonstration of working class unity and to formulate a demand for a single-chamber Assembly to which the Government would be responsible. But by the time it meets, the Government's decision already will have fallen, even if, as some observers believe, it is not officially made public until General de Gaulle speaks during Bastille Day ceremonies July 14.

Commenting bitterly on this, today's Humanité wrote: "It is astonishing that deliberations of this most qualified of bodies could not be awaited before decisions of highest political importance are taken."

The Combat, after reflecting that France could not afford to risk provoking General de Gaulle into resigning, concluded: "It is grave and regrettable that he should have imposed himself on the opposition in this manner. For the parties it is grave to have to bow in this manner, but almost impossible to refuse."

**France and Russia Sign Accord
To Return 500,000 French**

DANA ADAMS SCHMIDT
By Wireless to THE NEW YORK TIMES

PARIS, June 30 (Delayed)—The signature of a Russian-French agreement in Moscow yesterday regulating the repatriation of 500,000 to 600,000 French prisoners and deportees still in Russian territory "does not resolve all the difficulties that until now delayed their return, but it will eliminate a certain number of them," the semi-official French news agency said tonight.

The announcement closely followed complaints in the French press that repatriation from the Russian zone had been unnecessarily slow, that many prisoners had been stripped of their personal belongings and that only two members of the official French repatriation mission had been allowed to enter Russian territory. Almost all the 1,500,000 French captives in the American and British-occupied zones have now been repatriated, while about 90,000 have been sent home by the Russians. The Minister of Prisoners, Henri Frenay, has announced that several thousand sick Frenchmen remaining in American and British hands are being moved to Baden, in the French zone of occupation, from where they are being flown to Paris.

ELIZABETH SCHMIDT CRAHAN

> ## France and Russia Sign Accord To Return 500,000 Frenchmen
>
> **DANA ADAMS SCHMIDT**
> By Wireless to THE NEW YORK TIMES.
>
> PARIS, June 30 (Delayed)—The signature of a Russian-French agreement in Moscow yesterday regulating the repatriation of 500,000 to 600,000 French prisoners and deportees still in Russian territory "does not resolve all the difficulties that until now delayed their return, but it will eliminate a certain number of them," the semi-official French news agency said tonight.
>
> The announcement closely followed complaints in the French press that repatriation from the Russian zone had been unnecessarily slow, that many prisoners had been stripped of their personal belongings and that only two members of the official French repatriation mission had been allowed to enter Russian territory. Almost all the 1,500,000 French captives in the American and British-occupied zones have now been repatriated, while about 90,000 have been sent home by the Russians. The Minister of Prisoners, Henri Frenay, has announced that several thousand sick Frenchmen remaining in American and British hands are being moved to Baden, in the French zone of occupation, from where they are being flown to Paris.
>
> Under the title of "Silence in the East," François Mitterand, vice president of the Prisoners' Federation, declared in a newspaper article that political and security considerations should not be allowed to weigh in the balance with the accumulated anguish of thousands of prisoners. "Excessive precautions hardly favor sincere and ever so necessary friendship," he said.
>
> Philippe Viannay, in another article, recalled the cries of indignation in the French press when the repatriation from the American and British zones seemed slow. He added: "Very few voices, by comparison, are raised in alarm about the frightening mystery of our nationals east of the Oder. Yet it would be honest to do so, for the very silence about them is tragic. We have scarcely any news and no letters come at all.
>
> "That among those who have returned many complain that their watches and wedding rings have been stolen does not disturb me. I am far more disturbed that no mission has reached them and that, far from speeding up, the returns are slowing down. We know that the Russians have an immense fear of espionage and that it is for that reason that they do not want to receive missions. We hope that that is not why they do not repatriate our men."

Under the title of "Silence in the East," François Mitterand, vice president of the Prisoners' Federation, declared in a newspaper article that political and security consideration should not be allowed to weigh in the balance with the accumulated anguish of thousands of prisoners. "Excessive precautions hardly favor sincere and ever so necessary friendship," he said.

Philippe Viannay, in another article, recalled the cries of indignation in the French press when the repatriation from the American and British zones seemed slow. He added: "Very few voices, by comparison, are raised in alarm about the frightening mystery of our nationals east of the Oder. Yet it would be honest to do so, for the very silence about them is tragic. We have scarcely any news and no letters come at all.

"That among those who have returned many complain that their watches and wedding rings have been stolen does not disturb me. I am far more disturbed that no mission has reached them and that, far from speeding up, the returns are slowing down. We know that the Russians have an immense fear of espionage and that it is for that reason that they do not want to receive missions. We hope that that is not why they do not repatriate our men."

FRENCH ASSEMBLY DEBATES ALGERIA

Assimilation Favored—Delegates Unable to Agree on Roots or Cures of Troubles

By DANA ADAMS SCHMIDT
By Wireless to THE NEW YORK TIMES

PARIS, July 11—The progressive assimilation of Algeria, making it more and more a part of France itself, was the long-term solution envisage by Consultative Assembly delegates during the first two days of debate on the problems of this region, where more than 100 Europeans were killed in riots and some thousands of Moslem natives were slain in reprisals last May.

But no two delegates could agree on the immediate causes or remedies for the trouble, which, it was felt, was linked with the similarly strained situation in the adjoining territories of Morocco and Tunisia and with France's difficulties in Moslem Syria. The Minster of the Interior, Anrdré Tixier, who has just completed a tour of Algeria, hinted that some of the wealthy estate-owning colonists hoped to take advantage of the situation to prevent the realization of the political reforms promised by Gen. Charles de Gaulle in March, 1944, which would give some 80,000 educated natives French citizenship and the right to vote. He declared that the reforms would nonetheless be carried out and he intimated that the municipal elections scheduled for July 23 would take place.

Pierre Bloch, a Socialist, speaking for the Assembly's Commission on Moslem Affairs, remarked that, whenever serious political and economic reforms in the interests of the natives had been proposed, reactionary Algerian economic interests appeared to have fomented disorders causing their postponement and that the Algerian "elite" that once favored assimilation had been repeatedly disappointed and driven toward nationalism.

Paul Cuttoli of Constantine defended the wealthy colonists and declared categorically: "There has been a veritable revolt against French sovereignty prepared with care and directed with method." Pascal Muselli of Oran, in a similar vein, disclosed that on May 19, a week after the riots at Sétif and Guelma, near Constantine, another revolt had been nipped in the bud near Oran, where "a plot with ramifications throughout Algeria was discovered" after telephone lines had been cut and mysterious fires had been discovered. Raymond Blanc, also of Oran, declared, on the contrary, that talk of a general conspiracy was poppycock and that only a handful of intellectuals had been involved.

Etienne Fajon, for the Communists, maintained that the entire affair was a "fascist plot" fomented by agents of Vichy and Hitler. Curiously, he also ascribed the ferocious reprisals to unpurged Vichyites. March Rucart, a Radical Socialist, suggested that "our Allies who look on Algeria with covetous eyes" might be responsible for the trouble.

Laval Lodged in Paris Cell; British Call Him War Plotter

By DANA ADAMS SCHMIDT
By Wireless to THE NEW YORK TIMES

PARIS, Aug. 1—Pierre Laval, haggard beneath a deep suntan, arrive from Austria at Le Bourget tonight in a small French transport plane and was whisked to the Fresnes prison to await trial for treason. The Court of Justice, busy trying Marshal Henri-Philippe Pétain, said that Laval would be tried in about two months and that his arrival would cause no interruption of Pétain's trial.

Laval wore the white tie of old and carried a cane. He kept his hat well down over his eyes and had a gray overcoat buttoned to his chin. His wife, pale and apparently ill, had to be helped from the plane.

About 300 persons, most of them policemen in and out of uniform, were on hand to welcome him. Some with unprofessional emotion raised cries of "Salaud!" and "Down with Laval!"

Greeted by Magistrate

The first man to speak to Laval at Le Bourget was an examining magistrate, Pierre Beteille, who stepped forward and said: "In the name of the law I arrest you." Laval, as if he had not heard, turned and embraced his wife.

Three automobiles had driven up beside the plane. Mme. Laval was helped into the first. Laval, with M. Beteille and a French army captain who had accompanied him from Austria, got into the second. Laval's baggage—one large suitcase and several small ones—was put in the third and all headed at sixty miles an hour for Fresnes.

As he leaned back against the cushions, Laval, usually a chain smoker, refused a cigarette offered by M. Beteille but appeared to be beginning a lively conversation. He held a small black brief-case on his knees.

In Fresnes, Laval will enjoy no special privileges. A cell separated from the rest of the prison by wooden planking has been ready for him for several weeks. In it are a metal bed with one blanket, a stool nailed to the floor and a desk that folds out from the wall.

A Court of Justice official said that Laval would be brought to court for interrogations before trial. He will be confronted with Pétain during the examination.

Although Mme. Laval went to Fresnes with him tonight, she will not be allowed to remain with him, since there is no charge against her, and Laval is to be treated like any other prisoner.

The French News Agency carried a dispatch from Madrid quoting Laval as saying before he left Spain that he was returning to France "to defend myself and to accuse." According to the dispatch, he told a Spaniard who was not identified: "Pétain knew very well, when the Germans arrested Blum, Daladier and Reynaud that they intended to shoot them. Pétain raised no objection and it was I alone who persuaded the Germans not to shoot them. I am tired of always being accused. I intend to assume responsibilities. But I want to defend myself, and I will defend myself."

**THOREZ CRITICIZES
DE GAULLE REGIME**

**Attacks Foreign and Domestic
Policies as Communists
Open 4-Day Convention**

**By DANA ADAMS SCHMIDT
By Wireless to THE NEW YORK TIMES**

PARIS, June 26—Opening the first national congress of the French Communist party since 1937 with a five-hour speech today, Maurice Thorez criticized the Government's policy of "prestige," its tendencies to reaction and its secret police, but he envisaged expanding Communist participation in coalition governments "of national unity."

Two thousand delegates heard M. Thorez methodically review the past eight years, justifying the Russian-German pact and the Communists' role during the "phony war" period and the occupation, and mapping the future. Among those on the platform with him were Marcel Cachin, presiding; Jacques Duclos, the party's secretary, who hid out on a farm near Paris during the occupation; André Marty, who led the Odessa mutiny of the French fleet after the First World War and went to Algiers from Moscow in 1943, and Dolores Ibarruri, La Pasionaria of the Spanish civil war, who arrived from Moscow two months ago.

"Comrades," M. Thorez cried, "the patriotism of the masses has thwarted the treason of the trusts. France is among the victors. But our country suffered terribly. We must not forget that, to drive out the Germans, we needed the help of our Allies. Weakened as we are, we shall still need the assistance of our friends and Allies. And that should incite modesty and prudence rather than vain prattling about the greatness of France.

"One must not be deceived: the greatness of France must be recreated. * * * Today it is the quantity and quality of our material production and our position in the world market that measure the greatness of France. * * * The people know that an entente among Britain, the Soviet Union and the United States remains necessary to assure a solid, durable peace."

M. Thorez criticized "the not very democratic character of the institutions that now rule us." He continued:

"I shall be told that it is provisional. But it is proverbial that nothing lasts like the provisional. It is so true that some persons now propose to limit the role of the next National Assembly elected by the people to the elaboration of the Constitution. They would maintain the provisional Government and the no less provisional Consultative Assembly even after the elections, and doubtless also a certain police whose provisional quality has already lasted all too long."

M. Thorez alleged that certain industrialists had sabotaged French industrial recovery, "first by cutting in half the quantity of machine tools to be delivered from the United States and second by delaying the arrival of those that we deign to accept." The industrialists, he maintained, are bent on keeping obsolete French machine tools whose average age is 25 years.

To show that "there was never any Russian-German collusion or Russian betrayal" involved in the Russian-German pact of 1939, M. Thorez quoted Marshal Klementi Voroshiloff's explanation that Russia had signed with the Germans only after conversations with the British and French had reached an insurmountable impasse on the question of the Russians' right to military transit through Poland. Without that right, he contended, an alliance was worthless to the Russians.

He maintained that the Communists had supported the war effort and begun resistance even before Germany attacked Russia.

Reviewing the party's position, M. Thorez announced that it had issued 906,729 membership cards up to the present "and we are on our way to 1,000,000." At the time of the last previous congress there were only 340,000 members.

FRENCH TELL U.S. OF POST-WAR NEED

De Gaulle Said to Have Brought Report on Reconstruction Requirements to Truman

By DANA ADAMS SCHMIDT
By Wireless to THE NEW YORK TIMES

PARIS, Aug. 25—How little had been accomplished toward reconstruction in France because of the lack of means and how urgent was the need for American help were set forth in a report on the work to date and future plans that Gen. Charles de Gaulle took to Washington to show President Truman, French officials disclosed today.

Of 1,361,000 damaged buildings, for example, only 191,000 so far have been permanently repaired, the report said.

Officials understood that the Reparations Commission had agreed or would shortly agree to the allocation of 1,750,000 German prisoners of war to France by July of next year. The French plan to use 1,000,000 of these men, plus 500,000 French workmen, in the reconstruction program. The Germans would work for France for three years at a cost of 100 francs a man a day and the total would be deducted from France's share of German reparations.

Hear U.S. Will Give Share

Just what France's share of the reparations will be was still not known today, but rumors circulated in governmental quarters today said that the United States might turn over 50 per cent of its share of reparations to France as a result of General de Gaulle's conversations.

The report on reconstruction, compiled by the Ministry of Reconstruction, showed that out of 100,000,000 explosive mines on French soil only 6,000,000 had been removed up to the end of July. Demining, the report said, is the first step in reconstruction. The number of men engaged in this work, mostly

German prisoners, rose from 200 in March to 20,000 in July and is expected to rise to 200,000 by the end of next winter. By the summer of 1947 French soil should be clear of mines, the report declared.

Slightly more than half the task of clearing away rubble in preparation for reconstruction had been completed in devastated areas up to the end of July, according to the report. The work will be finished early next year, the report added.

Only 500,000 out of about 4,000,000 persons who lost their homes in France as the result of the war have received new quarters to date, the report declares. It is hoped that all will receive some kind of shelter before the winter.

Building Program Cited

About 1,000,000 square meters of timber in barracks, one third of it supplied by the United States, will be available by October while another 1,000,000 square meters are on order in Germany. Prefabricated houses have been ordered in the United States, Britain and Switzerland and a few have arrived.

By the end of 1947 the Ministry of Reconstruction plans to have rebuilt 150,000 dwellings, more than one-third of those destroyed, and 40,000 industrial buildings, or more than 50 per cent of those destroyed. At the same time it plans to have repaired 600,000 buildings of all kinds and to have built 60,000 entirely new dwellings.

The new dwellings will be constructed under a ten-year plan on which the Ministry is working for the construction of 1,500,000 new dwellings.

FRANCE TO SHARE IN THE SURRENDER

Allies Formally Invite Her and China Hopes She Will Send Troops to Indo-China

By DANA ADAMS SCHMIDT
By Wireless to THE NEW YORK TIMES

PARIS, Aug. 20—Just before his departure for Washington to visit President Truman, Gen. Charles de Gaulle learned that the United States had invited France to take part in the signature of the Japanese surrender and Britain and China had agreed to French participation in local surrenders in French Indo-China.

[France has accepted the invitation, The Associated Press reported.]

Quarters close to General de Gaulle said that he and the Cabinet, which heard the news at a special meeting today, "were extremely gratified" that the most important and immediate French claims in the Far East had thereby been recognized. They added that the general's conversations in Washington could consequently take place under the most favorable auspices. Up to the last minute the French had feared that they might be excluded from the surrender and their claims in Indo-China might be disregarded.

Maj. Gen. Jacques-Philippe Leclerc de Hauteloque left by special plane today for Manila to take part "in conferences concerning the Japanese capitulation and in signature of the articles of surrender," in accordance with the terms of the note that the American Ambassador, Jefferson Caffery, handed to Foreign Minister Georges Bidault last night. General Leclerc commands the expeditionary forces that the French desired to send into the Far Eastern campaign and that they still want to send to reoccupy Indo-China. Although there was no mention of the return of French troops to Indo-China in the American or British communications, the Chinese note expressed the hope that French troops would return to Indo-China "as soon as possible."

FRANCE TO SHARE IN THE SURRENDER

Allies Formally Invite Her and China Hopes She Will Send Troops to Indo-China

By DANA ADAMS SCHMIDT
By Wireless to THE NEW YORK TIMES.

PARIS, Aug. 20—Just before his departure for Washington to visit President Truman, Gen. Charles de Gaulle learned that the United States had invited France to take part in the signature of the Japanese surrender and Britain and China had agreed to French participation in local surrenders in French Indo-China.

[France has accepted the invitation, The Associated Press reported.]

Quarters close to General de Gaulle said that he and the Cabinet, which heard the news at a special meeting today, "were extremely gratified" that the most important and immediate French claims in the Far East had thereby been recognized. They added that the general's conversations in Washington could consequently take place under the most favorable auspices. Up to the last minute the French had feared that they might be excluded from the surrender and their claims in Indo-China might be disregarded.

Maj. Gen. Jacques-Philippe Leclerc de Hauteloque left by special plane today for Manila to take part "in conferences concerning the Japanese capitulation and in the signature of the articles of surrender," in accordance with the terms of the note that the American Ambassador, Jefferson Caffery, handed to Foreign Minister Georges Bidault last night. General Leclerc commands the expeditionary forces that the French desired to send into the Far Eastern campaign and that they still want to send to reoccupy Indo-China. Although there was no mention of the return of French troops to Indo-China in the American or British communications, the Chinese note expressed the hope that French troops would return to Indo-China "as soon as possible."

This Chinese gesture had the appearance of a recognition of the French move last Saturday in returning to China the French mandate port of Kwangchowwan, although a Foreign Office spokesman denied any connection. He declared that, in returning the port, strategically situated north of Indo-China, which was obtained on a ninety-nine-year lease in 1898, France sought merely "to show a spirit of conciliation and a desire not to profit by advantages obtained at a moment of China's weakness."

The French view, foreign observers thought, might be received with interest in London, where concern has lately been expressed over the future of similar British-leased territory on the mainland opposite Hong Kong.

The first French troops to re-enter Indo-China, if the Americans and British agree with the Chinese, would be 5,000 to 6,000 French colonials from Indo-China who have taken refuge and been re-equipped in southern China, the Foreign Office spokesman thought. He added that the "zones of surrender" for the Allies' various forces had not yet been decided, although French representatives would in all cases be present.

The French Government accepted the American and British invitations to take part in the control commission that will supervise the Greek plebiscite and elections in accordance with the agreement signed on Feb. 12 by the Greek Government and the Eam. At the same time, a French note to the American, British, Greek and Russian Governments expressed regret that Russia had declined to participate. France promised to keep the Russian Government informed of all developments.

This Chinese gesture had the appearance of a recognition of the French move last Saturday in returning to China the French mandate port of Kwangchowwan, although a Foreign Office spokesman denied any connection. He declared that, in returning the port, strategically situated north of Indo-China, which was obtained on a ninety-nine-year lease in 1898, France sought merely "to show a spirit of conciliation and a desire not to profit by advantages obtained at a moment of China's weakness."

The French view, foreign observers thought, might be received with interest in London, where concern has lately been expressed over the future of similar British-leased territory on the mainland opposite Hong Kong.

The first French troops to re-enter Indo-China, if the Americans and British agree with the Chinese, would be 5,000 to 6,000 French colonials from Indo-China who have taken refuge and been re-equipped in southern China, the Foreign Office spokesman thought. He added that the "zones of surrender" for the Allies' various forces had not yet been decided, although French representatives would in all cases be present.

The French Government accepted the American and British invitations to take part in the control commission that will supervise the Greek plebiscite and elections in accordance with the agreement signed on Feb. 12 by the Greek Government and the Eam. At the same time, a French note to the American, British, Greek and Russian Governments expressed regret that Russia had declined to participate. France promised to keep the Russian Government informed of all developments.

GERMAN CITY VOTE CLOSE IN BIG POLL

Christian Social Union Leads for Whole U.S. Zone, With Social Democrats Strong

COMMUNIST TALLY LAGS

Catholic Party Maintains Hold in Bavaria but Falls Below Its Expected Strength

By DANA ADAMS SCHMIDT
By Wireless to THE NEW YORK TIMES

FRANKFORT ON THE MAIN, Germany, Monday, May 27—Nearly complete returns from yesterday's municipal elections in the thirty-eight larger towns of the American zone showed the Christian Social Union probably still the dominant party in the zone as a whole. The latest count gave the Christian Social Union a slight lead over the Social Democrats, who had earlier today been ahead. The Communists lagged; and any hopes that the city dwellers would swing decisively to the left seem to have been disappointed.

[Returns at 5 A. M., German time, reported by The United Press, showed: Christian Social Union, 677,984; Social Democrats, 610,697; Communists, 142,406; Liberal Democrats, 70,333; others, 86,679; invalid, 37,795.]

The Christian Social Union, which considers Bavaria its particular bailiwick, got a scare in Munich, where it won only twenty seats to the Social Democrats' seventeen, the Communists' two and one each for two smaller groups.

At Nuremberg the Social Democrats with nineteen seats topped the Christina Social Union, which go fifteen, followed by the Communists with four and others with three.

Rain Fails to Cut Balloting

The Christian Social Union, which is Catholic-supported, had won in the two earlier elections in the American zone this spring in rural and smaller communities. The Communists, while gaining yesterday over their previous showing still polled only about 10 per cent of the votes cast.

The voting was heavy, in spite of intermittent rain, exceeding 80 per cent almost everywhere. The Social Democrats and the Christian Social Union in Munich and Frankfort sent sound trucks through the streets calling voters to the polls.

Complete results for Greater Hesse gave the Christian Democratic Union the designation on the ballots of the Christian Social Union 160,762 votes and 139 City Council seats; the Social Democratic party, 191,652 votes and 165 seats; the Communists 53,845 and six seats, the Liberal Democrats 45,446 and eleven seats and others 15,918 and five seats.

In Frankfort the Christian Democratic party got 66,577 votes and twenty-eight seats, and the Social Democrats, 77,738 votes and thirty-two seats. The Communists got 23,000 votes and the Liberal Democrats 22,356, with no seats for either group.

In Baden the poll was: Christian Democrats, 85,389 votes and thirty-eight seats; Social Democrats, 86,610 and thirty-six seats; Communist, 29,679 and ten seats; German People's party, which is the same as the Liberal Democratic party, 2,487 and twelve seats.

Four of the Communists seats in Baden were won in Mannheim and two each in Pforzheim, Karlsruhe and Heidelberg.

Partial Returns in Bavaria

In Wuerttemberg the results had not yet been tabulated, because of delays caused by a complicated write-in system. The Social Democrats were ahead in Stuttgart.

In Bavaria, 722 out of 1,284 districts gave the Christian Social Union 212,000 votes, the Social Democrats 190,000, Communists 30,000 and the Economic Reconstruction party 15,000.

Except for the monolithic Communist poll, it was difficult to evaluate the significance of the party votes since the parties contain a great diversity of elements still struggling for domination.

While the Liberal Democrats are widely considered farthest to the right in Greater Hesse, in Wuerttemberg and Baden they or the equivalent German People's party stand to the left of the Christian Social Union.

In Bavaria the Christian Social Union is strongly right-wing and includes many Nazi sympathizers, but in Greater Hesse it contains strong "Christian Socialist" elements. The social Democrats, like the Socialists everywhere, range from those who believe in "authoritarian" socialism and would merge with the Communists to those—in the majority—who stand for evolutionary socialism.

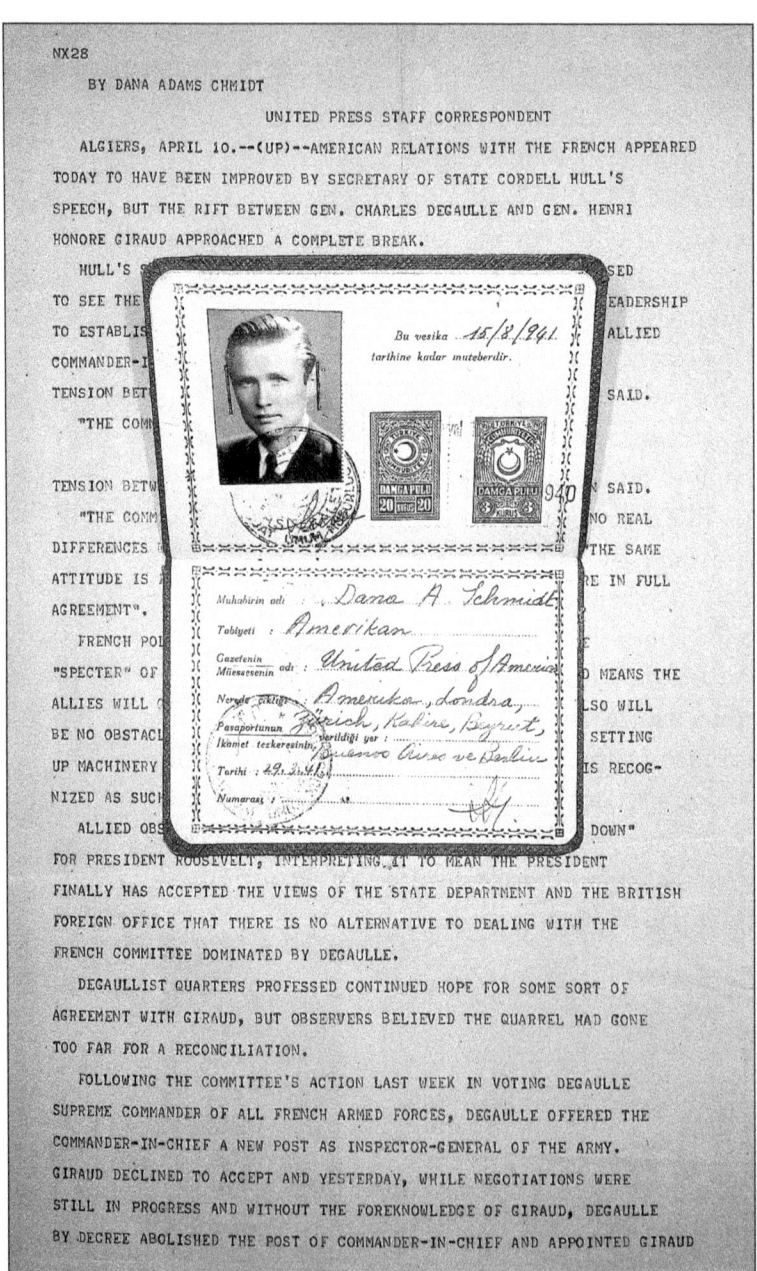

Dana's passbook and an original UP dispatch

THE RESERVE RECORD
September 12, 1939

**Dana Schmidt
1933 Grad Tells of Work
With United Press in Berlin**

"Is Dana Schmidt still in Berlin? If he is, I wonder what's happening to him these days." That is the query that Dana's classmates are putting to themselves and to each other now that war has broken out.

Dana, member of the class of 1933, went to Berlin last fall on a Pulitzer Fellowship from the Columbia University School of Journalism to serve with the United Press staff there. He may have left the country, for a letter from him dated last May 23 remarked, "Looks at the moment as though the only way I can hope to get transferred is to get expelled or wait for a war."

Dana expressed himself as not very well pleased with living conditions and other elements of the situation in Germany but requested that his words be kept from publication because of the delicacy of his position.

Dana arrived in Berlin just in time to help cover the Munich crisis. Describing his work, he wrote, "There were weeks during the march into Czechoslovakia and Memel when we all worked 15 hours a day seven days a week. Once I didn't have a day off in five weeks.

"It's not just a matter of covering Germany. We are the funnel, or relay bureau, through which all the Central European countries from Sofia to Tallinn file. We have to transcribe and edit and instruct and curse and soothe them all and try to keep queries from London and New York and Buenos Aires at bay.

"For three months our chief German telephone listener-to, Dictaphone transcriber, and teletype puncher was away for military service, and I, as junior member of our bureau of 12, had to do a large part of his work, in addition to keeping my usual place on the desk and covering my specialty, the wretched Jews."

During his vacation beginning June 4 Dana was planning to fly to Warsaw, to Budapest, to Vienna, to Rome, to Paris, to London, and back "to have no end of thrill and to see the men and methods at the various U.P. bureaus en route."

Reserve Record

September 12, 1939

Dana Schmidt
1933 Grad Tells of Work With United Press in Berlin

"Is Dana Schmidt still in Berlin? If he is, I wonder what's happening to him these days." That is the query that Dana's classmates are putting to themselves and to each other now that war has broken out.

Dana, member of the class of 1933, went to Berlin last fall on a Pulitzer Fellowship from the Columbia University School of Journalism to serve with the United Press staff there. He may have left the country, for a letter from him dated last May 23 remarked, "Looks at the moment as though the only way I can hope to get transferred is to get expelled or wait for a war."

Dana expressed himself as not very well pleased with living conditions and other elements of the situation in Germany but requested that his words be kept from publication because of the delicacy of his position.

Dana arrived in Berlin just in time to help cover the Munich crisis. Describing his work, he wrote, "There were weeks during the march into Czechoslovakia and Memel when we all worked 15 hours a day seven days a week. Once I didn't have a day off in five weeks.

"It's not just a matter of covering Germany. We are the funnel, or relay bureau, through which all the Central European countries from Sofia to Tallinn file. We have to transcribe and edit and instruct and curse and soothe them all and try to keep queries from London and New York and Buenos Aires at bay.

"For three months our chief German telephone listener-to, dictaphone transcriber, and teletype puncher was away for military service, and I, as junior member of our bureau of 12, had to do a large part of his work, in addition to keeping my usual place on the desk and covering my specialty, the wretched Jews."

During his vacation beginning June 4 Dana was planning to fly to Warsaw, to Budapest, to Vienna, to Rome, to Paris, to London, and back "to have no end of thrill and to see the men and methods at the various U. P. bureaus en route."

Used by permission of Western Reserve Academy

400 West Adams,
Los Angeles.

THE WORLD THIRTY YEARS FROM NOW

"It is no longer the problem of man's capacity to create wealth, but that of his will to control it, which bars his way to Utopia," says J. M. Keynes, the British economist. And in this problem of control lies the challenge to my generation, which 30 years from now, will be in its prime as leaders of the world of thought and action. The physical sciences have progressed so rapidly during the last 100 years or more, that man finds himself suddenly introduced to a new world, totally changed in physical aspect, capable of producing more than enough for all; he finds himself faced with an economy of abundance. He discovers that changes in social and political structures have not kept up with physical changes, that they are

(I) "The Quest for Economic Utopia" by Harold Callender, New York Times Magazine, April 8, 1934.

Dana's prize-winning article: *The World Thirty Years From Now* hopelessly out of gear, and that he himself is equipped with an outworn set of rules to guide him in human relationships.

During the next 30 years the scientific attitude -- permitting no prejudice or rationalization, insisting on fact as basis for every conclusion -- must be applied to man as well as matter, until balance between the two is restored.

Of course, physical science will continue to develop with increasing swiftness. In addition to vastly increased producing capacity in every industry that supplies human needs, 1964 will surely see such developments as these: safe mobile airplanes, perhaps a form of autogyro, will combine with the automobile to provide transportation for individuals. Dirigibles will combine with phenomenally swift, streamlined trains for heavy transportation work. Television, flashing and photographing printed words on an apparatus in every home will transform the newspaper with which we are now acquainted, and will bring movies and the theater into the home. Medicine may well have come near eliminating disease as a menace to mankind. Telescopes with lenses of 500 inches or more will pierce ever farther into the universe about us, perhaps giving a clue as to the presence or lack of life on other planets. Those of us who do not live in huge apartment houses, built in the sleek, graceful style of modern utilitarian architecture, will no doubt pick a steel and glass home from a catalogue as though it were an automobile. And so the changes will go on, till

1964 differs more from 1934 than 1934 does from 1904.

But if all these things took place, and nothing else, there would be only change, not progress. Their importance is that they will make it easier for science to inject itself into the realm of human relationships. The world will be infinitely more closely drawn together; centralized control of production and distribution by a non-profit-seeking government will be practicable, for the first time. As security for the individual increases - and this must involve unemployment, health and old-age insurance - the importance of acquisitiveness as a motivating force in life will be reduced; energies will be devoted to more stimulating enterprises. The fine arts will evolve from their present too subjective, extreme forms, to one truly representative of the times. Our concept of the family will change as the state assumes greater and greater responsibility for the education of the child. And here, in education, we are going to have a development with extraordinarily far-reaching results, a development which is already under way. Education will play the most important part in setting up the new social balance. The possibilities of training an infant systematically from birth on, are already being investigated. Such education may be expected to have its bearing on the solution of crime, sex and marriage problems. Reformatories will surely take the place of prisons for adult criminals. Sterilization of the physically, mentally or morally totally unfit will be considered a natural protection of society.

A change, which, though it will not affect the general trends I have discussed, will be of profound importance during the next 30 years, will be that the white race is likely to lose its present dominant position in the world, if only for the reason that its birth rate tends downwards, while the yellow races' steadily increases. In addition, it is losing its economic dominance as fast as the yellow races equip themselves with the arms of industry which the white man first introduced into the orient.

I have here given a long range view of possible developments during the next 30 years. For the present, nationalism ensnarls the world, war seems imminent; and until either the fear of war and the barriers of tariffs, embargoes and national prejudice are removed, or until the conflict is over, logic an be only half-heartedly applied to the world's problems.

But for all the dangers of war, and nationalism, (which is interested not in the development of the individual, but in making the state an efficient machine) and, I might add, those of dictatorship, I believe my generation can face the future with more confidence of fulfilling man's ageless dream of Utopia than any before it could; for it posesses a new power which none before it have known, that of producing in abundance.

About the Author

ELIZABETH ADAMS SCHMIDT CRAHAN was born on October 6, 1913, in Cleveland, Ohio, to Margaret Adams and Edward Schmidt.

In her early years, she and her younger brother, Dana, the subject of this book, attended primary school in Cleveland, and in 1921 they both attended school in Vienna, Austria, before going to live in Hamburg, Germany, from 1924-28. Crahan graduated from Kreusler Schule with the Abitur before attending an English boarding school at Châtelard at Chamby sur Montreux, Switzerland, in 1928; she received Oxford and Cambridge exemptions. In 1931, she returned to the United States to attend Wellesley College and then transferred to the University of Southern California's School of Architecture in Los Angeles, where she completed her bachelor's degree in architecture in 1937. There, she met her first husband, Kenneth Acker; they went on to have four children together.

From 1937 to 1943, she worked for renowned California architect Sumner Spaulding and belonged to Telesis, a city planning group of architects, landscape architects and urban planners from the Bay Area of San Francisco. Then, between 1944 and 1948, Crahan worked for Douglas Aircraft and *Mademoiselle Magazine.*

Crahan spent the latter half of her career as a medical librarian. She joined the Los Angeles County Medical Association Library the year before obtaining a master's degree in library science from the University of Southern California in 1961, becoming director in 1978, and retiring in 1990.

She became president of the Special Libraries Association and co-founded the Medical Library Scholarship Foundation in 1969. She was a member of the University of Southern California School of Library Science Alumni

ELIZABETH SCHMIDT CRAHAN

Association, Libraris Sodalitas, the Zamorano Club (Southern California's oldest organization of bibliophiles and manuscript collectors, founded in 1928), the Medical Library Group of Southern California and Arizona, the California Book Club, Stanford Associates, and Friends of the Huntington Library. She shared a keen interest in collecting rare books with her second husband, Marcus Crahan, MD.

At 87 years of age, she had her dream home built on the ocean blufftops near Elk, California, overlooking the Pacific. She there devoted much of her time to writing a biography about her brother, Dana Adams Schmidt, who was a newspaper foreign correspondent during World War II for the *United Press* and later *The New York Times*. Her book tells his story through the 1000 letters he wrote home while away on assignment. She died at the age of 100 before she could see this book published.

Elizabeth Adams Schmidt Crahan

www.ingramcontent.com/pod-product-compliance
Lightning Source LLC
Chambersburg PA
CBHW082002150426
42814CB00005BA/195